Studies in Women and Religion/
Études sur les femmes et la religion : 3

Studies in Women and Religion /
Études sur les femmes et la religion

Studies in Women and Religion is a series designed to serve the needs of established scholars in this new area, whose scholarship may not conform to the parameters of more traditional series with respect to content, perspective and/or methodology. The series will also endeavour to promote scholarship on women and religion by assisting new scholars in developing publishable manuscripts. Studies published in this series will reflect the wide range of disciplines in which the subject of women and religion is currently being studied, as well as the diversity of theoretical and methodological approaches that characterize contemporary women's studies. Books in English are published by Wilfrid Laurier University Press.

Inquiries should be directed to the series coordinator, Pamela Dickey Young, Queen's Theological College, Queen's University, Kingston, ON K7L 3N6.

COORDINATOR: *Pamela Dickey Young*
Queen's University

COORDINATRICE: *Monique Dumais*
Université du Québec à Rimouski

ADVISORY BOARD /
COMITÉ DE DIRECTION: *Eva Neumaier-Dargyay*
University of Alberta
Monique Dumais
Université du Québec à Rimouski
Pamela J. Milne
University of Windsor
Marie-Andrée Roy
Université du Québec à Montréal
Randi Warne
University of Wisconsin Oshkosh
Pamela Dickey Young
Queen's University

STUDIES IN WOMEN AND RELIGION/
ÉTUDES SUR LES FEMMES ET LA RELIGION

Volume 3

Profiles of Anabaptist Women
Sixteenth-Century Reforming Pioneers

C. Arnold Snyder and
Linda A. Huebert Hecht, Editors

Published for the Canadian Corporation for Studies in Religion/Corporation Canadienne des Sciences Religieuses by Wilfrid Laurier University Press

1996

This book has been published with the help of a grant from the Humanities and Social Sciences Federation of Canada, using funds provided by the Social Sciences and Humanities Research Council of Canada. We acknowledge the financial support of the Government of Canada through the Book Publishing Industry Development Program for our publishing activities.

Library and Archives Canada Cataloguing in Publication

Main entry under title:
    Profiles of Anabaptist women : sixteenth-century reforming pioneers

(Studies in women and religion = Études sur les femmes et la religion ; v. 3)
Includes bibliographical references.
ISBN 978-0-88920-277-1 (pbk).—ISBN 978-0-88920-603-8 (PDF).—
ISBN 978-1-55458-790-2 (epub)

1. Anabaptists – Europe – Biography. 2. Christian women – Europe – Biography. I. Snyder, C. Arnold. II. Hecht, Linda A. Huebert (Linda Agnes Huebert), 1946- III. Canadian Corporation for Studies in Religion. IV. Series: Studies in women and religion (Waterloo, Ont.) ; v. 3.

BX4940.P76 1996   284'.3'09224   C96-932001-9

© 1996 Canadian Corporation for Studies in Religion / Corporation Canadienne des Sciences Religieuses
Second impression 1997, third impression 1998, fourth impression 1998, fifth impression 1999, sixth impression 2002, seventh impression 2008.

Cover design by Leslie Macredie, using an illustration that depicts the arrest of Catherine Müller from the Knonau district, near Zurich, in the year 1637. Müller is not profiled in this book, but she belongs to the Swiss Anabaptist tradition. Etching by Jan Luyken, in Tielman Jansz van Braght, *Het bloedig tooneel, of martelaers spiegel* [*Martyrs' Mirror*], vol. 2, 2d ed. (Amsterdam, 1685). Used with permission of Conrad Grebel College Library and Archives, Waterloo, ON.

The author and publisher have made every reasonable effort to obtain permission to reproduce the secondary material in this book. Any corrections or omissions brought to the attention of the Press will be incorporated in subsequent printings.

Profiles of Anabaptist Women: Sixteenth-Century Reforming Pioneers has been produced from a manuscript supplied in camera-ready form by the editors.

All rights reserved. No part of this work covered by the copyrights hereon may be reproduced or used in any form or by any means—graphic, electronic or mechanical—without the prior written permission of the publisher. Any request for photocopying, recording, taping or reproducing in information storage and retrieval systems of any part of this book shall be directed in writing to the Canadian Reprography Collective, 214 King Street West, Suite 312, Toronto, Ontario M5H 3S6.

Dedicated to our Mothers

Doris Darlene [Swartzentruber] Stephenson
Tena [Kroeker] Huebert (1917-1994)

our Daughters

Carrie Anne Snyder
Edna Kate Snyder
Melinda Hecht-Enns

and our Sisters

Margaret Anne [Snyder] Schipani
Ruth Katherine [Huebert] Loewen

TABLE OF CONTENTS

Acknowledgments	ix
Abbreviations	xi
Illustrations	xiii
Introduction	1

I. SWISS ANABAPTIST WOMEN

The Swiss Anabaptist Context	19
Agnes Zender of Aarau	25
Agnes Linck from Biel	32
Adelheit Schwartz of Watt	38
Margret Hottinger of Zollikon	43
Elsbeth Theiller of Horgen	54
Anna Scharnschlager of Hopfgarten, Tirol	58
Margaret Hellwart of Beutelsbach	64

II. SOUTH GERMAN/AUSTRIAN ANABAPTIST WOMEN

The South German/Austrian Anabaptist Context	71
Anabaptist Women Leaders in Augsburg	82
Sabina Bader of Augsburg	106
Magdalena, Walpurga, and Sophia Marschalk von Pappenheim	111
Helena von Freyberg of Münichau	124
Anna Gasser of Lüsen	140
Anabaptist Women in Tirol who Recanted	156
Elisabeth von Wolkenstein of Uttenheim	164

Katharina Purst Hutter of Sterzing 178

Wives, Female Leaders, and Two Female Martyrs from Hall 187

Ursula Hellrigel of the Ötz Valley and Annelein of Freiburg 195

Women in the *Chronicle of the Hutterian Brethren* 202

Women in the Hutterite Song Book
(*Die Lieder der Hutterischen Brüder*) 222

III. NORTH GERMAN/DUTCH ANABAPTIST WOMEN

The North German/Dutch Anabaptist Context 247

Margarethe Prüss of Strasbourg 258

Ursula Jost and Barbara Rebstock of Strasbourg 273

Hille Feicken of Sneek 288

Divara of Haarlem 298

Fenneke van Geelen of Deventer 305

Women Supporters of David Joris 316

Anna Jansz of Rotterdam 336

Maria and Ursula van Beckum 352

Elisabeth and Hadewijk of Friesland 359

Soetken van den Houte of Oudenaarde 365

Anna Hendriks of Amsterdam 378

Soetjen Gerrits of Rotterdam and Vrou Gerrits of Medemblik 384

Appendix: Review of the Literature on Women in the
    Reformation and Radical Reformation 406

Index 416

Contributors to *Profiles of Anabaptist Women* 436

ACKNOWLEDGMENTS

The publication of *Profiles of Anabaptist Women* is the culmination of a dream and an idea that began to take definite shape in 1992. From April 30 to May 2 of that year Conrad Grebel College hosted a conference titled "In a Mennonite Voice: Women Doing Theology."[1] In her contribution to that conference, Lois Y. Barrett mentioned that some years before, she and a few other Mennonite women had been approached concerning the possibility of publishing biographies of sixteenth century Anabaptist women. The general consensus at that time was that given the current state of research, such a volume was not feasible. The idea was dropped.[2]

Lois Barrett's comment proved to be a significant catalyst for the current editors. We were convinced that the stories of Anabaptist women needed to be told, that the state of research had changed significantly in the past decade, and that a biographical project should be undertaken. As this volume will demonstrate, we do indeed know enough about Anabaptist women to be able to publish a substantial volume of biographical sketches, or "profiles," of these sixteenth century reforming pioneers. With the support of research funds from the Social Sciences and Humanities Research Council, the project got underway shortly following the "Women Doing Theology" conference.

The book was conceived initially as a modest collection of biographical sketches, built around a core of original research carried out by the editors. Soon it assumed less than modest proportions. We sent out an early call to other Anabaptist scholars in North America and Europe, inviting collaboration on the project. The response was impressive: in the end seventeen scholars, not counting the editors, contributed to this volume. Readers should know that different chapters in this monograph were written by one or more of these contributing scholars. A special thank you goes out to: Lois Y. Barrett, Marlene Epp, Cornelius J. Dyck, Brad Gregory, Pamela Klassen, Walter Klaassen, Marion Kobelt-Groch, Elfriede Lichdi, Helen Martens, Cheryl Nafziger-Leis, John Oyer, Werner Packull, Bonny Rademaker-Helfferich, H. Julia Roberts, Matthias Schmelzer, Piet Visser, and Gary Waite. Their personal expertise and generous contributions made this book possible. Readers citing from this book should identify the author(s) of chosen material by referring to the list of contributors at the conclusion of this book.

Special thanks must be given to Sandra Woolfrey and to Wilfrid Laurier University Press for their support of this project: may their faith and hope be amply rewarded. Carroll Klein's expert copy editing, and the comments and corrections of two anonymous readers, saved us from many potential errors of commission and omission. Thanks also to Clifford Snyder who prepared all of the maps for this book. Those maps, along with some introductory material drawn from C. Arnold Snyder, *Anabaptist History and Theology: An Introduction* (Kitchener: Pandora Press, 1995), are used with permission of Pandora Press. Conrad Grebel College provided further research funds in support of this project, enabling the preparation of the final manuscript. Christine Matsuda worked assiduously to prepare the manuscript for the press, amidst unsettled conditions and trying circumstances. She deserves special thanks.

Grateful acknowledgment is here given to the Mennonite Historical Library for permission to use illustrations from their archives, and to the Westfälisches Landesmuseum für Kunst und Kulturgeschichte, Münster, for permission to reproduce the portrait of Queen Divara of Münster. Likewise, we gratefully acknowledge that this book has been published with the help of a grant from the Humanities and Social Sciences Federation of Canada, using funds provided by the Social Sciences and Humanities Research Council of Canada.

Finally, the editors would like to thank their respective spouses, Linda L. King and Alfred Hecht, for their unfailing support and encouragement.

C. Arnold Snyder
Linda A. Huebert Hecht

Notes

1 Papers presented at the conference are published in *The Conrad Grebel Review* 10 (Winter, 1992).
2 Ibid., 1.

ABBREVIATIONS

ARG = *Archiv für Reformationsgeschichte*

CGR = *The Conrad Grebel Review.*

LHBr = *Lieder der Hutterischen Brüder* (Cayley, Alberta, 1962).

Martyrs' Mirror = Thieleman J. van Braght, *The Bloody Theater or Martyrs' Mirror of the Defenseless Christians Who Baptized Only Upon Confession of Faith, and Who Suffered and Died for the Testimony of Jesus, Their Savior, from the Time of Christ to the Year A.D. 1660*, trans. Joseph F. Sohm (Scottdale, PA: Herald Press, 1950)

ME = *The Mennonite Encyclopedia* (Scottdale, PA: Herald Press, 1955).

MQR = *The Mennonite Quarterly Review.*

QGTS, vol. 1 = L. von Muralt and W. Schmid, eds., *Quellen zur Geschichte der Täufer in der Schweiz*, 1. Band, Zürich (Zürich: Theologischer Verlag, 1952).

QGTS, vol. 2 = Heinold Fast, ed., *Quellen zur Geschichte der Täufer in der Schweiz*, 2. Band, Ostschweiz (Zürich: Theologischer Verlag, 1973).

QGTS, vol. 3 = [Unpublished. Ms. used with permission of Dr. Martin Haas.] Martin Haas, ed., *Quellen zur Geschichte der Täufer in der Schweiz*, 3. Band. (Aarau, Bern, Solothurn).

QGTS, vol. 4 = Martin Haas, ed., *Quellen zur Geschichte der Täufer in der Schweiz*, 4. Band, Drei Täufergespräche in Bern und im Aargau (Zürich: Theologischer Verlag, 1974).

TA, *Baden und Pfalz* = Manfred Krebs, ed., *Quellen zur Geschichte der Täufer: Baden und Pfalz* (Gütersloh: Bertelsmann Verlag, 1951).

TA, *Brandenburg* = Karl Schornbaum, ed., *Quellen zur Geschichte der Wiedertäufer, II, Markgraftum Brandenburg* (Leipzig: M. Heinsius Nachfolger, 1934)

TA, *Hesse* = Günther Franz, ed., *Urkundliche Quellen zur hessischen Reformationsgeschichte* (Marburg: N. G. Elwert'sche Velagsbuchhandlung, 1951).

TA, *Elsass*, I = Manfred Krebs and Hans Georg Rott, eds., *Quellen zur Geschichte der Täufer, VII. Band, Elsaß, I. Teil: Stadt Straßburg 1522-1532* (Gütersloh: Gerd Mohn, 1959).

TA, *Elsass*, II = Manfred Krebs and Hans Georg Rott, eds., *Quellen zur Geschichte der Täufer, VIII. Band, Elsaß, II. Teil: Stadt Straßburg 1533-1535* (Gütersloh: Gerd Mohn, 1960).

TA, *Elsass*, III = Marc Lienhard, Stephen F. Nelson, and Hans Georg Rott, eds., *Quellen zur Geschichte der Täufer, XV. Band, Elsass, III. Teil, Stadt Straßburg 1536-1542* (Gütersloh: Gerd Mohn, 1986)

TA, *Elsass*, IV = Marc Lienhard, Stephen F. Nelson, and Hans Georg Rott, eds., *Quellen zur Geschichte der Täufer, XVI. Band, Elsass, IV. Teil, Stadt Straßburg, 1543-1552* (Gütersloh: Gerd Mohn, 1988)

TA, Ost.I = Grete Mecenseffy, ed., *Quellen zur Geschichte der Täufer, Österreich, I. Teil*, (Gütersloh: Gerd Mohn, 1964),

TA, Ost.II = Grete Mecenseffy, ed., *Quellen zur Geschichte der Täufer, Österreich, II. Teil* (Gütersloh: Gerd Mohn, 1972).

TA, Ost.III = Grete Mecenseffy, ed., assisted by Matthias Schmelzer, *Quellen zur Geschichte der Täufer, Österreich III Teil* (Gütersloh: Gerd Mohn, 1983)

TA, *Württemberg* = Gustav Bossert, ed., *Quellen zur Geschichte der Wiedertäufer, I, Herzogtum Württemberg* (Leipzig: M. Heinsius Nachfolger, 1930)

Plate 1. The castle of Münichau, former residence of Helena von Freyberg (see p. 124). Built in the fifteenth century and destroyed by fire in 1912, it has been restored and is used today as a *Schloss* hotel. Photo by Linda Huebert Hecht.

Plate 2. The castle of Branzoll above Klausen, where Katharina Hutter was in prison in 1535 (see pp. 181-82). Photo by Elfriede Lichdi.

Plate 3. The castle of Gufidaun near Klausen, where Katharina Hutter was in prison in 1536 (see p. 183). Photo by Elfriede Lichdi.

Plate 4. The residence of Plankenstein in the village of Uttenheim in Tirol, the former home of Elisabeth von Wolkenstein (see p. 164). Photo by Matthias Schmelzer.

Plate 5. Maria van Beckum is chained to the stake just before her execution by fire; Ursula van Beckum is led away, to be burned at the stake later the same day, 13 November 1544 (see pp. 352-54). Etching by Jan Luyken, in Tielman Jansz van Braght, *Het bloedig tooneel, of martelaers spiegel* [*Martyrs' Mirror*], vol. 2, 2d ed. (Amsterdam, 1685). Used with permission of the Mennonite Historical Library, Goshen College, Goshen, IN.

Plate 6. Anna Jansz of Rotterdam on the way to her execution, offering her son Isaiah to a local baker, who promised to raise the child (see p. 341). Etching by Jan Luyken, in Tielman Jansz van Braght, *Het bloedig tooneel, of martelaers spiegel* [*Martyrs' Mirror*], vol. 2, 2d ed. (Amsterdam, 1685). Used with permission of the Mennonite Historical Library, Goshen College, Goshen, IN.

Plate 7. Ursula of Essen is flogged in an effort to have her reveal the names of fellow church members. She refused, and was burned to death in a hut of straw at Maastricht, 1570. Etching by Jan Luyken, in Tielman Jansz van Braght, *Het bloedig tooneel, of martelaers spiegel* [*Martyrs' Mirror*], vol. 2, 2d ed. (Amsterdam, 1685). Used with permission of the Mennonite Historical Library, Goshen College, Goshen, IN.

Plate 8. Queen Divara of Münster. Although the woodcut is titled "Gertrude from Utrecht, the Anabaptist Queen of Münster," general consensus has it that the portrait must be of Divara. Woodcut by Heinrich Aldegrever (ca. 1535). Used with permission of the Westfälisches Landesmuseum für Kunst und Kulturgeschichte, Münster.

Plate 9. An Anabaptist congregation is discovered and arrested in the Netherlands, 1558. Etching by Jan Luyken, in Tielman Jansz van Braght, *Het bloedig tooneel, of martelaers spiegel* [*Martyrs' Mirror*], vol. 2, 2d ed. (Amsterdam, 1685). Used with permission of Conrad Grebel College Library and Archives, Waterloo, ON.

Plate 10. Maria of Monjou, moments before being drowned for her faith, 1552. Etching by Jan Luyken, in Tielman Jansz van Braght, *Het bloedig tooneel, of martelaers spiegel* [*Martyrs' Mirror*], vol. 2, 2d ed. (Amsterdam, 1685). Used with permission of Conrad Grebel College Library and Archives, Waterloo, ON.

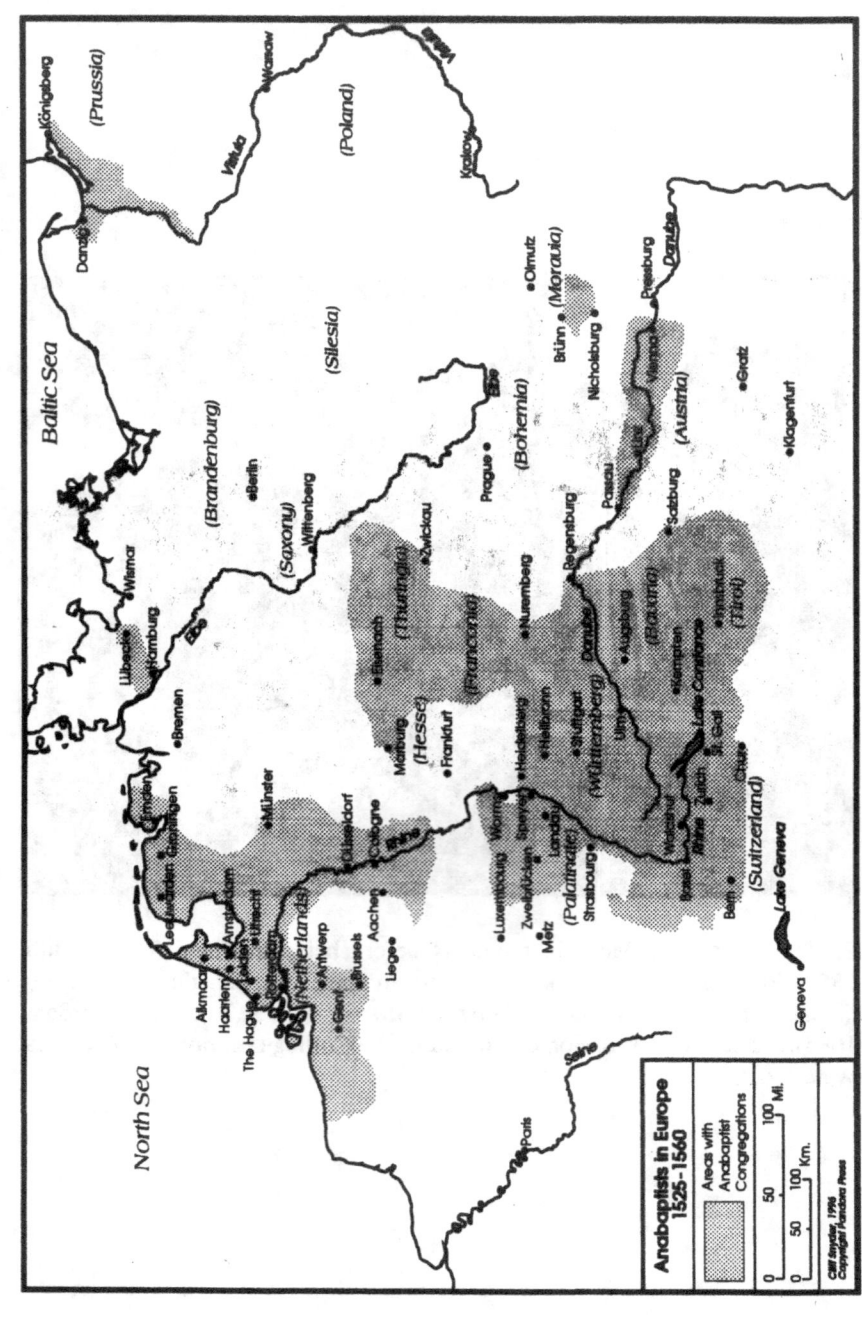

INTRODUCTION

The story of Anabaptist women of the sixteenth century is just now beginning to be told. The scarcity of references to women in historical accounts undoubtedly has been due, at least in part, to the general orientation of historians. One proposed definition of the discipline of history calls it "systematic narration and critical interpretation of events worthy of memory in human society"; the historian, then, is someone who decides what is worthy of memory for society at large.[1] In recent years social and cultural historians in particular have begun revising their views about what is worthy of memory, and have begun to include the experiences of the so-called "little people"–in particular the poor and women from all stations of society–in their rewriting of history.

The challenge of making women from the past visible also has been taken up by Anabaptist scholars and historians. These women deserve to be remembered as reforming pioneers in their own right, even though they may not always be considered role models in the confessional traditions that claim Anabaptist roots. More broadly speaking, these women deserve a place in the collective memory of human society. Making visible the lives of women from the past benefits us all by bringing needed balance to the historical memory of humanity.[2] The purpose and focus of this book is to contribute to the process of bringing more visibility to the women of history; to that end this volume brings to light some hitherto neglected stories of Anabaptist women.[3]

Anabaptism: A Radical Reforming Movement
Anabaptism was a church reform movement that emerged in 1525, eight years after Martin Luther publicized his ninety-five theses; it saw itself as part of the general reform movement that was identified with Martin Luther and Ulrich Zwingli. But Anabaptism soon was outlawed in the Holy Roman Empire, and virtually all western European states and territories followed suit. Anabaptism emerged as a distinct church reforming movement when its adherents insisted upon adult baptism following individual confession of faith. Opponents attached the label of "Anabaptists" [in German, *Wiedertäufer*] to adherents of the baptizing movement. The label literally meant "rebaptizers," since those who practised adult baptism already had been baptized once, as infants, into the Catholic communion; but the word also carried connotations of fanaticism, heresy, civil disobedience, and sedition.

Of course, the rebaptizers rejected the label; they insisted that the "infant bath" they had received as "unknowing children" was no baptism at all. They were not rebaptizers, they said, but believed in only one, true baptism–their freely chosen adult baptism. In spite of these disclaimers, the reproachful name Anabaptist stuck; it remains the best historical term to describe a widespread, diverse reform movement that managed to survive in spite of systematic persecution. Direct descendants of the Anabaptists are present-day Mennonites, Hutterites, Amish, and some groups of Brethren, such as the Mennonite Brethren, the Church of the Brethren and the Brethren in Christ; the present-day Baptist denominations also can claim significant roots in the Anabaptist movement of the sixteenth century.

Modern historical studies of Anabaptism have identified a diversity of historical origins, teachings, and practices among Anabaptist groups. The most widely accepted historical description of sixteenth-century Anabaptism now speaks of the polygenetic origins of Anabaptism. The origins of three primary Anabaptist groups have been identified and described in some detail: Swiss Anabaptism, South German/Austrian Anabaptism, and North German/Dutch Anabaptism.[4] The organization of the profiles in this book follows the organizational pattern delineated by the polygenesis historians: one major section will be devoted to the stories of Anabaptist women of the Swiss, South German/Austrian, and North German/Dutch movements, respectively. Each of these major sections will be prefaced by an introduction that outlines the particular ideological and geographical contexts out of which these various expressions of Anabaptism emerged. In terms of its origins and its early forms of expression, the movement was characterized by diversity.

In spite of undeniable diversity within the Anabaptist movement, there was at the same time a fundamental core of doctrine and church practice that was shared by all Anabaptists, and that marked the movement in all regions.[5] This shared core of beliefs took as its point of departure the reform principles outlined first by Martin Luther, whose basic teachings soon came to circulate as theological slogans, accepted by many but increasingly interpreted in a variety of contradictory ways. The authority of scripture alone and the principle of salvation by faith through grace were accepted as bedrock truths in the Anabaptist movement. These reforming emphases often were expressed negatively in anticlericalism, anti-sacramentalism, and iconoclasm. "Radical" (or "impatient") reform emerged with these last points in particular: if priests, sacraments, and holy images were not commanded in Scripture, and therefore human inventions, they were to be abolished forthwith. In place of the medieval Catholic practices and structures, the radical stream of reform took another page from Luther's early writings, and proposed establishing a church on the basis of the priesthood of all believers.

When Luther returned to Wittenberg in 1522 from his exile at the Wartburg, he made clear to Andreas Karlstadt and to everyone else that his idea of reform had nothing to do with unruly, egalitarian, grass roots reform. Luther's aim was to proceed in a measured, orderly fashion, under the direction of theologians working in concert with the political authorities. The radical stream of reform that emerged in 1522 emphasized (as Luther did not) the importance of the independent activity of the Holy Spirit in the interpretation of scripture.

The identification of this radical "spiritual" emphasis is crucial to the telling of the story of Anabaptist women. Appealing to the Holy Spirit as the central interpretive agent meant that a spirit-filled, illiterate, or semi-literate woman or man would be a truer exegete of Scripture than would a learned professor lacking the Spirit.[6] This spiritual and egalitarian approach to scripture, which emerged in Luther and Zwingli's own movements, opened the door to the participation of women and uneducated commoners in radical and Anabaptist reform.

In the same way that "Scripture alone" was reinterpreted in light of the direct activity of the Holy Spirit, radical reformers also were critical of Luther's understanding that salvation came by "faith alone,"and not by works. Salvation, said the radical reformers, is by faith through grace, but God's grace brings about a spiritual rebirth within, and empowers a new and reformed life, which is characterized by works. Faith without works is dead.[7] Luther's emphasis on faith also led naturally to a rethinking of the nature of the sacraments, in particular baptism and the Lord's Supper. If human beings are saved by faith, and not by the sacramental waters of baptism, what then could be the rationale for infant baptism? Although neither Karlstadt nor Müntzer insisted on baptizing adults on confession of faith (and so were not Anabaptists), nevertheless their questioning of the validity of infant baptism prepared the way for the emergence of a baptizing movement that reserved baptism for adults, following a mature and fully conscious profession of faith.[8] The same emphasis on faith raised questions about the Lord's Supper: if Christ's body is not made present in the elements of bread and wine by the words of a priest, then how is the "communion with Christ" in the Supper to be understood? In all these ways the groundwork was prepared for a more spiritual, egalitarian church of those regenerated by the Spirit—one that did not rely on a specially consecrated or politically legitimated priesthood. The Anabaptists, following the lead of Karlstadt and Müntzer, set out to establish churches in which the priesthood of all believers would be put into practice. Luther and Zwingli, on the other hand, soon backed away from this radically egalitarian way of defining "church."

The broadly populist reforming stream had its heyday in 1525 and 1526 with the Peasants' War–an upheaval that involved around 300,000 people in central and southern Germany, Alsace, and the Tirol. This attempt by the common people to put into practice the principle of "Scripture alone"–with non-learned interpreters turning to the Bible in search of a blueprint for the structuring of society–resulted in a critique of the social, political, religious, and economic order of the day.[9] But the peasants and commoners were defeated on various fields of battle, and the Reformation after 1525 came to be directed by leading theologians and firmly controlled by princes and city councils.[10] Anabaptism was the most visible continuation of the earlier populist reforming movement. It was more than coincidental that the first adult baptisms took place in Zurich around the same time that the Peasants' War emerged; the same radical appropriation of evangelical reforming principles stood behind both movements. But whereas the programmes that emerged from the Peasants' War focussed on the reform of society, the Anabaptist critique focussed much more (although not exclusively) on the reform of the church and the calling of individual women and men "out of the world" into the "true church."

The Core of Anabaptist Theology and Church Practices
In spite of regional differences of emphasis, there was a common core of theological beliefs and church practices that bound together all Anabaptists as sisters and brothers of a related movement. These same emphases also distinguished Anabaptist reform from other branches of reform.

Anabaptist Doctrinal Emphases
Holy Spirit. The strong emphasis on the activity of the Holy Spirit affirmed, the living nature of the Spirit that led individuals to repentance, faith, regeneration, water baptism, and a new life. This beginning point was crucial for the participation of women in the movement, for the living Spirit directly called individual women and men alike to a living faith.

Spirit and Letter. Just as there could be no true faith without the inner work of the living Spirit of God, neither could there be a true reading of the letter of Scripture without that same Spirit. At different times in different parts of the Anabaptist movement, this strong spiritual emphasis led to extra-biblical revelations, dreams, and visions, granted alike to women and men.

Salvation. Anabaptism insisted that the only faith that saves will be a living faith that expresses itself in action in the world. True faith will obey the commands of Scripture—especially the command to teach and then baptize those who have believed (i.e., adults). Furthermore, true faith will "obey God rather than man"—an injunction that led some women to leave husbands and families. Discipleship (living a new life, based upon regeneration by the Spirit of God) was expected of women and men alike; the "obedience of faith" sometimes led Anabaptist women and men to radical social action, as well as martyrdom.

Freedom of the Will. At the heart of Anabaptism was freedom of choice and personal responsibility for that choice, for both women and men. A common way of expressing that choice was to speak of the need for yieldedness or surrender [*Gelassenheit*] to God and to the Body of Christ on earth (the church). This yielding meant allowing the Spirit to work directly in one's life (and many times resulted in a spiritual "calling" and in prophetic activity); but yielding also meant accepting water baptism and the admonition of the community of saints (which could and did result in the suppression of prophecy). Both the freeing and restrictive tendencies are evident in the development of the roles taken on by Anabaptist women.

Anabaptist Church Practices

The distinctive Anabaptist doctrines described above were given visible expression in four common church practices that were performed and interpreted in an Anabaptist manner: the baptism of believers, church discipline (the Ban), the Lord's Supper, and economic sharing.

Baptism of Believers. As already noted, the baptism of those who had come to a mature faith and then chose to be baptized, was the most visible identifying mark of the movement.[11] It was matched by an intense opposition to infant baptism. One Anabaptist noted with some humour that in the pope's church "one mumbled to the child in Latin, and even though one now does it in German, [the infants] understand the German as well as they did the Latin."[12] In spite of their insistence on adult baptism, the Anabaptists still maintained that "the water is just water." It was the inner baptism of the Spirit that was primary and essential. The water baptism was simply an outer sign of the true baptism, which was spiritual and inward. At another level, however, baptism in water was seen as a crucial seal or commitment to the rest of the Body of Christ and a response of obedience to scriptural command that was not to be ignored or set aside. Both baptisms fell to individual women and men alike, and called for their obedience to Scripture and the community, regardless of the consequences.

Discipline. Anabaptists believed that baptism in the Spirit and in water bound believers to the Ban, or church discipline by the collective members of the Body of Christ. A true faith had to bear fruit in deed; deed had to correspond to creed. The personal commitment to fraternal admonition rested on the inward baptism (or regeneration and rebirth) of the Spirit: those truly regenerated by the Spirit were expected to live new lives, in community. The practice of the Ban also had a clear scriptural referent in Matthew 18:15-18. Fraternal admonition, like baptism, applied to women and men alike.

The Lord's Supper. Anabaptists understood the Supper to be a memorial or remembrance of Christ's death and sacrifice, a feeding by faith in Christ. In this practice the Anabaptists in Switzerland, Germany, Austria, and the Low Countries followed the path marked out by the sacramentarians in the Netherlands and the reformers Andreas Karlstadt and Ulrich Zwingli. For Anabaptists everywhere, the Lord's Supper was also a closed Supper, open only to those who had accepted baptism and had thus committed themselves to church discipline.[13]

Economic Sharing. One of the central deeds expected of all Anabaptist believers was radical economic sharing, the visible sign of one's commitment to the community, the Body of Christ on earth. Sometimes, as in several communities in Moravia in the 1520s and 1530s and later with the

Hutterites, this emphasis took the form of an organized community of goods. But in all cases it meant caring for the poor, the widows, and the orphans, and generally living as "members of one body." The economic support of such a community was crucial for the well-being of single mothers and their children. The radical economic sharing espoused by the Anabaptists had been one of the strongest common desires of the peasants in 1525; it lived on in underground fashion in the Anabaptist conventicles.

Sixteenth-Century Communication and Anabaptism[14]

It is undeniable that the Reformation was made possible by the widespread use of Gutenberg's invention–the first application of modern mass communication. But all the same, older and more traditional oral/aural forms of communication were at least as crucial as was print in the communication of the original reform message to the masses of people, the great majority of whom could not read the newly printed pamphlets, broadsheets, and vernacular Bibles. In the sixteenth century, ideas were spread primarily in non-literate ways, even if writing and print were crucial intermediate steps in the rapid diffusion of new ideas.[15] The masses of people still were stirred by popular preachers, excited by the "news" read aloud from broadsheets at the market, informed and entertained by "news songs" (and slanderous ditties) sung in taverns, and introduced to new ideas by radical craftsmen in their places of work. And, rather than being read in silence, early Reformation texts (and vernacular Bibles) also were most commonly read aloud to listeners who could not themselves read; there is evidence that many Reformation pamphlets were deliberately composed with such oral performances in mind.[16] In other words, as Robert Scribner has noted, in the sixteenth century "even the printed word was most often mediated by the spoken word."[17] The oral/aural medium, furthermore, was radically egalitarian: women and men of all social stations could and did communicate new ideas primarily in conversation with one another.

Social conflict was sharpened by the principle of Scripture alone. This undermined the interpretive privileges of the old guard, and also sharpened social and political conflict as the masses began hearing and interpreting the Bible in the vernacular. The appeal to Scripture alone was further sharpened by the notion of a priesthood of all believers. From this affirmation one could deduce the right–even the duty–to interpret Scripture for oneself.

Particularly crucial in bringing together the ideas of Scripture alone and the priesthood of all believers for the illiterate majority were the women and men who had learned to read a vernacular language, but who were not theologically learned. Clerical and upper-class literacy in the sixteenth century remained the preserve of those who had had access to Latin school and university educations; such people were to be found in important pulpits and council chambers in the cities. But the commoners who had attained some measure of literacy in a vernacular tongue quite naturally related to the oral/aural world of the lower classes, and exercised their literacy in that social context–among the craftspeople in the cities and villages and the peasants in the countryside. Thanks to print, vernacular reforming texts and Bibles could be bought and read aloud, and in this process the literate lay commoners played a crucial mediating role in bringing new ideas to, and promoting radical dissent among, the people at the grass roots. Once these reforming ideas were in circulation in the oral/aural communication network, they took on a life of their own.

Another phase in this Reformation communication process emerged, however, when key reformers made alliances with the politically powerful, and began to gain control of the official communications channels–the church pulpits and the local presses. Anabaptists quickly found themselves on the margins of power, limited for the most part to the informal, oral/aural channels of communication. What developed in some territories was a virtual propaganda war to win the hearts and minds of the people. Even as reformers and governments won the battles for the pulpits and the presses in the cities, they constantly worried that they might lose the war because underground, alternative, and hostile communication was undermining them at the grass roots and in the countryside.[18]

By 1530–and in most territories well before this date–Anabaptist communication and evangelization took place of necessity in a clandestine, informal, oral/aural mode. On the one hand this posed difficulties, for Anabaptists were forced to live and travel in secret; they had little access to printing presses and even less to pulpits. All the same, the majority of Anabaptist members and leaders after 1527 were drawn from the working classes, and communication among the lower social orders in the sixteenth century was still operating in the predominantly medieval, communal, and oral/aural mode, drawing upon the communication ability of women and men alike.[19] The fact that the Anabaptists often were mobile craftspeople and were operating in their own social milieu gave them an advantage over the learned and politically powerful preachers who often were viewed with suspicion by those in the lower social orders.

The following profiles of Anabaptist women must be read against the backdrop of late medieval/early modern communication patterns among the common people. In such a setting, the oral/aural communication of ideas by women played a much larger role than historians (who generally rely on written and printed evidence) usually assume. In fact, the role of Anabaptist women in the communication of reforming ideas can be made relatively more "visible" only because their imprisonment and recorded testimonies have left us a substantial written legacy–although written by their enemies. Anabaptist women and men worked very hard to conceal their activities from the authorities (and so successfully concealed many of their activities from us). Conversations around the spinning wheel or the table of an inn do not survive as historical records—unless something goes wrong. The profiles presented here can be retold, in large measure, because "something went wrong": women were arrested, questioned, and their testimonies recorded by court scribes. These stories thus represent the tip of the proverbial iceberg; for every story that can be retold, even in fragmentary fashion, there are thousands of stories that cannot be told at all.

While we cannot reconstruct conversations around the distaff or the loom from the surviving records, nevertheless many thousands of records do exist which open important windows through which we may catch glimpses of womens' reforming activity at the grass roots. Along with the evidence provided by court records, Anabaptist women also left a legacy of martyr testimonials, they wrote letters, and they composed hymns. Readers of these profiles will know that Anabaptist women were no less involved in the preservation and communication of Anabaptist ideas than were the men; that they exercised their freedom of religious choice no less than did the men; that being more "invisible" than were the men, they many times provided the essential leadership, strength and continuity that enabled the underground movement to survive.

The Role of Women in the Anabaptist Movement
The "calling of the Spirit" which provided the foundation for the Anabaptist movement was radically egalitarian and personal, even though it led individuals into a commitment to a community. No man or legal guardian was ever expected to be "called by the Spirit" on behalf of someone else. Within the Anabaptist movement, women were understood to be individuals who needed to receive the same spiritual "call" as did men; Anabaptist women were called to repent, accept God's will and water baptism as their "highest commitment." Anabaptist women were persons called and empowered by the Spirit to a "new life" of discipleship. Some Anabaptist women were called to leave an unbelieving marriage partner as a result of their "higher commitment" to God. Anabaptist women were individuals called to ultimate faithfulness when they were imprisoned, tortured, and threatened with death. Some Anabaptist women were called by the same Spirit of God to leadership roles. However, we must ask whether there were practical limits to the leadership activity of Anabaptist women, and if so, why this was the case.

One might suppose, on the basis of the spiritualistic and individualistic principles that lay at the heart of the movement, that Anabaptist communities were radically egalitarian in practice, offering full religious equality to women and men as well as to peasants and aristocrats.[20] Some historians have drawn this conclusion, extrapolating from Anabaptist principles. Roland Bainton and George Williams, among others, claimed that a "radical equality" prevailed between Anabaptist women and men.[21] Harold Bender wrote that "The Anabaptist emphasis upon voluntary membership, adult baptism, and personal commitment inevitably opened up new perspectives for women."[22] Wolfgang Schäufele stated even more emphatically that "The woman in Anabaptism emerges as a fully emancipated person in religious matters and as the independent bearer of Christian convictions."[23]

Such conclusions have not gone unchallenged. Social historians, more interested in what actually was the practice in Anabaptist communities, have revised the earlier idealized picture by pointing to the restrictions placed upon Anabaptist women. Claus-Peter Clasen's groundbreaking work in the Swiss and South German Anabaptist sources led him to conclude that "Revolutionary as Anabaptism was in some respects, the sect showed no inclination to grant women a greater role than they customarily had in sixteenth century society."[24] Likewise, Joyce Irwin claimed to have found no evidence for religious equality in Anabaptism, nor did she find evidence of women preaching, missionizing, or taking leadership roles in Anabaptist congregations.[25]

In fact there are good documentary reasons for tempering both poles of opinion. Even some of the more recent detailed studies have tended to rely on narrow selections of sources–for example the readily accessible martyrologies[26] and the writings of male Anabaptist leaders–to the exclusion of court records and testimonies. Other studies have relied on a narrow spectrum of court records, from one locale or historical period, and have then extrapolated conclusions about Anabaptist women from that document base. It may safely be said that a reliable and comprehensive account of the role of women in the Anabaptist movement has yet to be written. In order for such a task to be accomplished, much more intensive analysis of the Anabaptist court records (Täuferakten) is needed, for the full nature and extent of the involvement of Anabaptist women is most clearly seen there. The immensity of this task should not be minimized, but serious efforts in this direction have already begun.[27] Preliminary results of these meticulous, gender-specific studies fall somewhere between the two positions noted above: While Anabaptist women usually were not "equal" to men in terms of the "official leadership roles" within the movement,[28] they did experience far more freedom of choice than was the social norm, especially in the earlier more pneumatic stages of Anabaptist development.[29]

In citing evidence purporting to shed light on the roles played by Anabaptist women within the movement, particular attention must be paid to the developmental stage from which the sources are drawn. Harold Bender recognized a significant change when he noted that "after the creative period of Anabaptism was past, the settled communities and congregations reverted more to the typical patriarchal attitude of European culture."[30] Linda

Huebert Hecht has examined this same point using Max Weber's analysis of the "religion of the disprivileged classes," which in its early stages of development tends to "allot equality to women," particularly in allowing them prophetic roles. In later stages of development, "as routinization and regimentation of community relationships set in, a reaction takes place against pneumatic manifestations among women."[31]

These latter observations are particularly relevant to a study of the roles played by Anabaptist women, for Anabaptism moved steadily away from "spiritual" manifestation and legitimation. As Harold Bender noted, and as preliminary work in the Täuferakten confirms, the openness of the early Anabaptist movement to manifestations of "the spirit" allowed wider roles to women than would be the case in the later, more settled communities. The profiles that follow are drawn from all the developmental stages of the movement. The introductions to the individual sections below will outline the developmental contexts from which the individual profiles emerge. Readers will have occasion to note the particular roles assumed, or not assumed, by Anabaptist women in church leadership (proselytizing, preaching, prophecying, baptizing) and the roles assumed by women in congregational life generally.

Conclusion

In spite of the incomplete nature of the scholarship, we may nevertheless draw some general conclusions concerning the role and the status of women in the Anabaptist community of saints. Certainly it is true that "at no time was the ideal of full equality achieved" in the Anabaptist movement.[32] At the same time several factors worked together to give women wider individual choice and greater opportunities for participation in the Anabaptist movement than was possible for them in society at large. Among these factors must be noted: the egalitarian and spiritualistic base of Anabaptist faith and practice; the emphasis on individual adult choice, commitment, and responsibility; the decentralized and lay nature of the early Anabaptist movement; and the practical egalitarian dimensions (such as economic sharing) that took shape within the unsettled social, economic, and political conditions of the sixteenth century.[33]

In its broadest outlines a fundamental tension can be seen within Anabaptism because of the crucial role played by the Holy Spirit in "calling" men and women alike to lives of costly discipleship. The initial call of the Spirit never was considered to be gender-specific; furthermore, the Spirit was to accompany believers throughout their walk on the narrow way "in this world," right up to the moment of death. But even in the earlier, more spiritualist period there were clear restrictions on the activity of women. There may have been very isolated cases of women baptizing, for example, but such an event would have been an extraordinary exception to the general rule. There were gender limits from the very start. It thus would be a mistake to characterize early Anabaptism as a "golden age" of pure spiritual equality that opened up the same leadership possibilities for men and women alike, for such was not the case. Anabaptist beginnings were relatively, but not absolutely egalitarian, as "Spirit-elected" leaders assumed a variety of roles within their communities.

From the relatively egalitarian beginnings, however, there was also a further steady movement away from spiritual legitimation, to increasing reliance on literal Scripture as providing the "rule of life" for the Body of Christ on earth. Although the pouring out of the Spirit upon all of humankind has scriptural backing, turning to Scripture in search of concrete rules of church behaviour appealed to very different texts. In the more "literal" context, Paul's injunctions concerning the "proper" role of women in the congregation came increasingly to the fore, as did the biblical tradition ascribing to Eve the lion's share of the blame for the Fall.[34] Without a doubt prevailing societal assumptions about "proper" leadership roles for men and women also had an effect on the way in which gender relationships were understood within Anabaptism. In the end, these societal assumptions lent the weight of cultural legitimacy to the establishment of a "biblical" patriarchal church order.

All surviving Anabaptist groups arrived eventually at very similar paternalistic leadership structures. The Swiss maintained the highest degree of authority for its rank and file members of both sexes; Swiss Brethren ministers remained accountable to the members to a significant degree. The Hutterite and Dutch communities, on the other hand, were led by restricted groups of male elders. Nevertheless, a crucial part of the Anabaptist story lies in the movement on the way to that eventual church structure, when the tensions between inner renewal/outer behaviour and spirit/letter were being worked out. It is evident that the early phase of Anabaptist development opened up many more possibilities of direct participation and leadership for women than was the social norm in the sixteenth century, or than would become the norm in later Anabaptism.

As individuals called to faith and discipleship, women needed to respond personally to that call; no husband or guardian could take that step.[35] If their faith commitment was threatened by an "unbelieving" spouse, women were free to leave that relationship. Women exercised remarkable "informal" leadership in proselytization, Bible reading (in some cases), in "unofficial" teaching and preaching, in hymn-writing, and (in the early movement) in prophetic utterance. Future studies need to focus much more on the area of the "informal" leadership of Anabaptist women. It is only by sifting carefully the individual stories of Anabaptist women, as they emerge in the court records and other sources, that we will gain an adequate picture of how women actually functioned in the emerging Anabaptist communities. Concentrating only on the later stages, or access of women to the "official" leadership offices–while it is a pressing question currently– misses a crucial and dynamic dimension in the story of Anabaptist women.

Finally, women chose of their own volition to suffer imprisonment, torture, and death for their faith. From available figures, a third or more of all Anabaptist martyrs were women; in some regions the figure rose to 40 percent during certain periods of intense persecution. In all of these ways Anabaptist women were empowered to choose for themselves, contravening common societal restrictions on their gender. It was to the extent that Anabaptism widened the horizons of personal choice that it can be considered "radical" in the sixteenth century social and religious context.

Notes

1 Adriana Valerio, "Women in Church History," in Elizabeth Schüssler Fiorenza and Mary Collins, eds., *Concilium, Women, Invisible in Church and Theology*, (Edinburgh, Scotland: T. & T. Clark, 1985), 63. As Valerio has noted, "History, traditionally read from a masculine and elitist standpoint, has generally emphasized political events, great personages, the victors of the moment, authorities, institutions, leaving out of account aspects of daily life and the experiences of the "common" people, the little people, and women." Ibid.

2 "Once we look at history for an understanding of women's situation, we are, of course, already assuming that women's situation is a social matter. But history, as we first come to it, did not seem to confirm this awareness . . . . The moment this is done–the moment that one assumes that women are part of humanity in the fullest sense–the period or set of events with which we deal takes on a wholly different character or meaning from the normally accepted one." Kelly-Gadol, "The Social Relations of the Sexes: Methodological Implications of Women's History," in *Signs*, 1, 4 (1976): 810.

3 Merry E. Wiesner explains that it is not just a matter of "add women and stir," but that "We have to use our new information to completely rethink categories of analysis and ways of asking questions in order to integrate the new material and come up with a better understanding of the period." "Beyond Women and the Family: Towards a Gender Analysis of the Reformation," in *The Sixteenth Century Journal*, 18 (Fall 1987): 317. The stories of Anabaptist women presented here, while not always directed methodologically by a "gender-analysis" approach, nevertheless bring forward some needed historical data with which gender analysis may proceed.

4 The seminal delineation of this view is by James Stayer, Werner Packull and Klaus Deppermann, "From Monogenesis to Polygenesis: The Historical Discussion of Anabaptist Origins," MQR 49 (April 1975).

5 The following is drawn from C. Arnold Snyder, *Anabaptist History and Theology: An Introduction*, (Kitchener, ON: Pandora Press, 1995), chapters 1, 2, 6, 8, and 18.

6 Müntzer would say "If a man in his whole life had neither heard nor seen the Bible, he could none the less have an undeceivable Christian Faith through the teaching of the Spirit–like those who wrote the Scripture without any books." Cited in Gordon Rupp, *Patterns of Reformation* (London: Epworth, 1969), 216. For graphic examples from Müntzer, see his "On Counterfeit Faith," in Peter Matheson, *The Collected Works of Thomas Müntzer* (Edinburgh: T & T Clark, 1988), 214-24, esp. the concluding paragraph on 224. On the pneumatic aspects of Karlstadt's appeal to scripture, see Ronald J. Sider,

Andreas Bodenstein von Karlstadt: The Development of His Thought, 1517-1525 (Leiden: Brill, 1974), 120-22; 277. See also the summary account in Ronald J. Sider, "Andreas Bodenstein von Karlstadt: Between Liberal and Radical," in Hans-Jürgen Goertz, ed., *Profiles of Radical Reformers* (Scottdale, PA: Herald Press, 1982), 45-53. On Zwingli's early egalitarian approach to scripture, see Arnold Snyder, "Word and Power in Reformation Zürich," *ARG*, (1990), 263-85.

7 Karlstadt said: "Christ lives in the new-born man. Therefore, he has a Christ-like life. The supernatural birth results in an obedient life of conformity to Christ." Sider, *Karlstadt*, 224. On Müntzer, see especially his "Protestation or Proposition" and "On Counterfeit Faith," both published in 1524, in Matheson, *Works*.

8 Karlstadt held that "Since regeneration is the prerequisite for baptism, infant baptism is not permissible." Sider, *Karlstadt*, 292-93. The following is illustrative of Müntzer's critique: "I would be obliged if any of our learned men of letters could show me a single instance from the holy letters [scripture] where an immature little child was baptised by CHRIST or his apostles, or if they could prove that we are commanded to have our children baptised in the way it is done today." "Protestation or Proposition," in Matheson, *Works*, 191.

9 See the excellent collection of documents from the Peasants' War, edited and translated by Tom Scott and Bob Scribner, *The German Peasants' War: A History in Documents* (London: Humanities Press, 1991).

10 See James Stayer, *The German Peasants' War and Anabaptist Community of Goods* (Montreal and Kingston: McGill-Queen's University Press, 1991).

11 A fundamental Anabaptist argument for the practice of adult baptism was an appeal to the "great commission" as found in Matthew 28:18ff and Mark 16:15ff. What was significant to the Anabaptists was the *order* that they read in those verses: first go forth and teach all peoples, then baptize them, then teach them "to observe everything that I have commanded you." This appeal to simple scripture concerning baptism and a life of obedience (discipleship) would be repeated in thousands of court testimonies throughout the sixteenth century of which the examples in the profiles that follow are a small sample.

12 Balthasar Hubmaier, "Dialogue with Zwingli's Baptism Book," in H. Wayne Pipkin and John H. Yoder, *Balthasar Hubmaier, Theologian of Anabaptism* (Scottdale, PA: Herald Press, 1989), 196.

13 An anonymous Swiss Anabaptist writing that dates from around 1580 noted, concerning the Supper that the "popish mob" practised many things that went counter to what Christ had commanded, and paid little attention to the meaning of His commands; the Lutherans "made no distinction concerning the figurative speech of the Lord" (i.e., they took the words of institution "this is my body" literally, rather than figuratively); while the Zwinglians, although they made the proper distinction concerning the Lord's "figurative speech," nevertheless misused the Supper "since they have no Ban and make no distinction between the godless and the pious." The Anabaptist Lord's Supper was a sacramentarian or "memorial" Supper, but it differed from the Zwinglian Supper in that it was open only to those who had committed themselves to the discipline of the community through water baptism. *"Ein kurtze einfaltige erkanntnuß uff die dryzehen artickell so verlouffens 1572 (sic) Jars zu Franckenthal in der Pfaltz disputiert worden, allen der warheitt begierigen Gottsgeliepten / on fleysch partheyischen hertzen ze erwegen und urtheyllen heimgestellt . . ."* (Ms. in the Berner Bürgerbibliothek, dated 1590; microfilm copy #203 in the Mennonite Historical Library, Goshen College, Goshen, IN), 345-46.

14 This section summarizes work previously published elsewhere. See Arnold Snyder, "Konrad Winckler: An Early Swiss Anabaptist Missionary, Pastor and Martyr," MQR (Oct. 1990); "Word and Power in Reformation Zürich," ARG (1990); "Biblical Text and Social Context: Anabaptist Anticlericalism in Reformation Zürich," MQR (April 1991); "Orality, Literacy and the Study of Anabaptism," MQR (Oct. 1991); "Communication and the People: The Case of Reformation St. Gall," MQR (April 1993); and *Anabaptist History and Theology: An Introduction*, chapter 7.

15 Elizabeth L. Eisenstein, *The Printing Press as an Agent of Change*, 2 vols. (Cambridge: Cambridge University Press, 1979). A condensed version of this basic work is *The Printing Revolution in Early Modern Europe* (Cambridge: Cambridge University Press, 1983). Although Eisenstein urges that due attention be paid to the impact of print in making the Reformation possible, she also recognizes the key role played by oral transmission: "It is because the printed page amplified the spoken word and not because it silenced it that Luther regarded Gutenberg's invention as God's 'highest act of grace'. To set press against pulpit is to go against the spirit of the Lutheran Reformation." Eisenstein, *The Printing Press as an Agent of Change*, 374. See also Robert Scribner, *For the Sake of the Simple Folk* (Cambridge: Cambridge University Press, 1981), and the observations of William Graham, *Beyond the Written Word: Oral Aspects of Scripture in the History of Religion* (Cambridge: Cambridge University Press, 1987), especially chapter 12, "Hearing and Seeing: The Rhetoric of Martin Luther," 141-54.

16 Robert W. Scribner, "Oral Culture and the Diffusion of Reformation Ideas," in Robert W. Scribner, *Popular Culture and Popular Movements in Reformation Germany* (London: Hambledon Press, 1987), 50-51; 54 ff. See the detailed study of Johann Eberlin von Günzburg's oral techniques in Monika Rössing-Hager, "Wie stark findet der nichtlesekundige Rezipient Berücksichtigung in den Flugschriften?" in Robert Scribner and Hans-Joachim Köhler, eds., *Flugschriften als Massenmedium der Reformationszeit* (Stuttgart: Ernst Klett Verlag, 1981), 77-137. Also Werner Kelber, *The Oral and the Written Gospel*, (Philadelphia: Fortress Press, 1983), 17.

17 Scribner, "Oral Culture," 50-51; Graham, *Beyond the Written Word*, 39-41.

18 Robert Scribner notes that the urban population numbered only 10 percent of the total at the time of the Reformation in Germany, and that the importance of the countryside has been underestimated. "It was rural, rather than urban support which turned the reform movement into a mass movement . . ." Robert Scribner, *The German Reformation* (Atlantic Highlands, NJ: Humanities Press, 1986), 30.

19 The parallels in the communication strategies of medieval heretical groups and those of Anabaptist groups in the sixteenth century are striking indeed. See Sophia Menache, *The Vox Dei: Communication in the Middle Ages* (New York: Oxford University Press, 1990), chapters 10 and 11.

20 For a fuller survey of the literature concerning Anabaptist women, see the Appendix to this book.

21 See Roland Bainton, *Women of the Reformation in Germany and Italy* (Minneapolis: Augsburg, 1971); George H. Williams, *The Radical Reformation* (Philadelphia: Westminster, 1962), 506-07.

22 "Women, Status of," in ME, IV, 972.

23 Wolfgang Schäufele, "The Missionary Vision and Activity of the Anabaptist Laity," MQR 36 (April 1962), 108. Similar positive assessments were made by Sherrin Marshall Wyntjes, "Women in the Reformation Era," in Renate Bridenthal and Claudia Koonz, eds., *Becoming Visible: Women in European History*, (Boston: Houghton Mifflin, 1977), 165-91; and Elise Boulding, *The Underside of History: A View of Women through Time* (Colorado, 1976), esp. 548. After noting that in Lutheranism, patriarchy, hierarchy, and

misogyny remained the rule, Robert Scribner noted cautiously, "Perhaps only Anabaptism, with its strong emphasis on the fellowship of all Christians, male and female, managed to break out of this mould." Scribner, *The German Reformation*, 59.

24 Claus-Peter Clasen, *Anabaptism: A Social History, 1525-1618* (Ithaca: Cornell University Press, 1972), 207.
25 Joyce L. Irwin, *Womanhood in Radical Protestantism, 1525-1675* (New York: Edwin Mellen, 1979). See Linda Huebert Hecht, "Faith and Action: The Role of Women in the Anabaptist Movement of Tirol, 1527-1529" (unpublished cognate essay, Master of Arts, History, University of Waterloo, 1990), 11. Keith L. Sprunger, "God's Powerful Army of the Weak: Anabaptist Women of the Radical Reformation," in Richard L. Greaves, ed., *Triumph Over Silence: Women in Protestant History* (Westport, CT: Greenwood Press, 1985), 45-74, also concludes that Anabaptist women were not active in preaching or leadership roles. A. Jelsma concludes that leadership positions were "seldom" open to women, even in the Radical Reformation. A. Jelsma, "De positie van de vrouw in de Radicale Reformatie," *Doopsgezinde Bijdragen*, nieuwe reeks 15(1989): 25-36. "Ook in de radicale reformatie waren zulke posities zelden voor vrouwen weggelegd." Ibid., 29.
26 See Jenifer Hiett Umble, "Women and Choice: An Examination of the Martyrs' Mirror," MQR 64(April 1990), 135-145; Sprunger, "God's Powerful Army"; Wayne Plenert, "The Martyrs' Mirror and Anabaptist Women," *Mennonite Life* 30 (June 1975), 13-18.
27 The work of Linda Huebert Hecht has already been mentioned. Her intensive work in the Tirolean court records spanning just three years has yielded impressive results. Marion Kobelt-Groch's work also has been based on intensive work in the Täuferakten. See her "Aufsässige Töchter Gottes: Frauen im 'Bauernkrieg' und in den Bewegungen der Täufer," (Ph.D. dissertation, Hamburg University, 1990).
28 Lois Barrett notes that "One cannot really ask about Anabaptist 'feminism'. Feminism is an anachronism when applied to 16th-century Europe. . . . The question which Europeans in the 16th century asked was whether the Spirit of God could so fill a woman or give her such an extraordinary vocation that she would be authorized to prophecy and preach." Lois Barrett, "Women's History/Women's Theology: Theological and Methodological Issues in the Writing of the History of Anabaptist-Mennonite Women," CGR 10 (Winter 1992), 12-13, passim. Cf. Lois Barrett, "Wreath of glory: Ursula's prophetic visions in the context of Reformation and revolt in southwestern Germany, 1524-1530," unpublished Ph.D. dissertation, The Union Institute, 1992, 114.
29 See Marion Kobelt-Groch's conclusion in "Why Did Petronella Leave Her Husband? Reflections on Marital Avoidance Among the Halberstadt Anabaptists," MQR 62 (January 1988), 40. On page 40, note 57, Kobelt-Groch cites corroborating work that also "raises substantial doubts about Clasen's sweeping conclusion . . . ."
30 ME, IV, 972.
31 Max Weber, *The Sociology of Religion* (Boston: Beacon, 1922), 104; cited in Hecht, "Faith and Action," 82, note 50; cf. her discussion on 22-23.
32 Hecht, "Faith and Action," 11.
33 Ibid., 2.
34 Keith Sprunger's conclusion is essentially correct: "Anabaptism was both legalistic and spiritualistic. Where legalistic doctrines prevailed, Anabaptist women were the quiet sisters; but in communities where the Spirit broke forth abundantly, women grasped many opportunities. Following the heroic Reformation era, the 'Mennonite sister' (Menniste zusje) settled into an unprominent place in church and home." "God's Army of the Weak," 69.
35 There was no ecclesiological "cuius regio, eius religio" in Anabaptism; the husband or father was not the "ruler" of a woman's conscience or faith.

I.

SWISS ANABAPTIST WOMEN

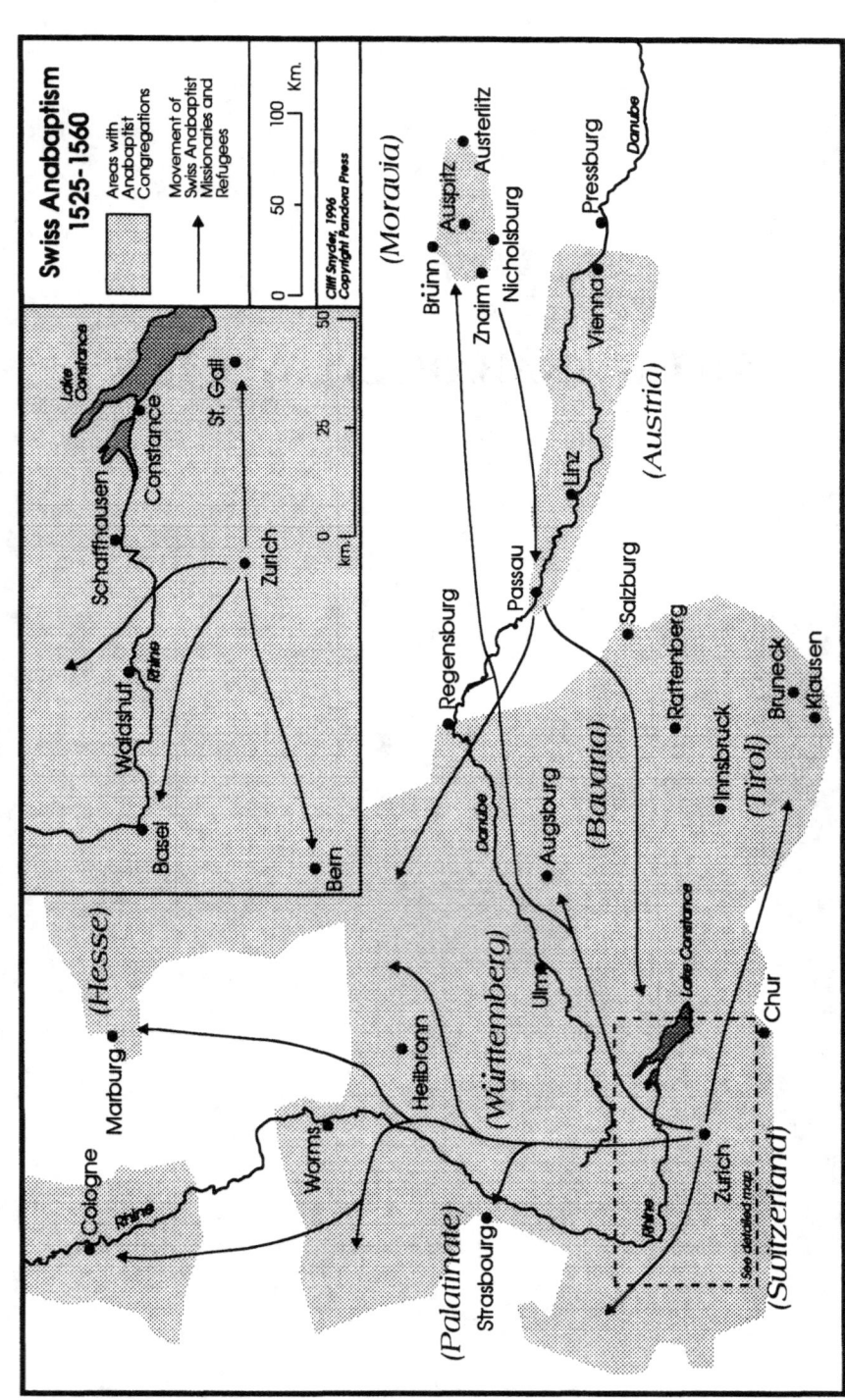

THE SWISS ANABAPTIST CONTEXT

The first known cases of adult baptism in the sixteenth century occurred in Zurich, Switzerland, in January 1525.[1] Involved in that first rebaptism were former followers of Ulrich Zwingli and early supporters of his reforms–most notably Conrad Grebel and Felix Mantz–who had become dissatisfied with the pace of reform in Zurich. In particular they were not satisfied that the rite of Christian baptism continued to be administered to infants rather than being linked to an adult faith in Christ. Adult baptism was a reforming idea that had some popular appeal, as events were soon to prove. The first baptisms in Zurich took place in the home of Felix Mantz's mother, where as many as fifteen people may have been present. The only surviving accounts of these baptisms in Zurich do not say whether women were present or baptized at that time,[2] but within days women were involved in the establishment of the first Anabaptist congregation in the neighbouring village of Zollikon (see the profile of Margret Hottinger); they remained a mainstay of the movement thereafter.[3]

In spite of the early leadership of individuals such as Conrad Grebel, Felix Mantz, Balthasar Hubmaier, and Michael Sattler, the early Swiss Anabaptist movement initially took on the characteristics of a popular protest and reforming movement "from below." Beyond some fundamental principles–such as the insistence upon adult baptism as a confirmation of inner faith, and as evidence of the intention to live a new life–early Swiss Anabaptism lacked cohesion and definition, and incorporated a wide variety of ideas and practices. The call by Grebel and Hubmaier for an adult baptism following profession of faith was based, they believed, on "the plain words of scripture," but early Swiss Anabaptist women and men often were "called by the Spirit of God" to preach repentance, baptism, and a new life. The early Swiss movement could sometimes be very biblicistic, and at other times downright spiritualistic. As the movement spread out from Zurich to other cities and villages in 1525 and 1526, Anabaptism sometimes took on the appearance of a charismatic revival movement: many people wept, confessed their sins, and accepted baptism. There were some cases of ecstatic spiritual utterance and outlandish behaviour: the most notorious took place in Appenzell, near St. Gall, where a group of Anabaptists literally "became as little children," babbling and playing in the dirt.[4]

Nevertheless the early Swiss baptizing movement was not all Bible, repentance, and Spirit; from the start it also had been intertwined with the social, political, and economic grievances of the peasants in Switzerland, Swabia, and the Black Forest.[5] Conrad Grebel and Balthasar Hubmaier seem to have hoped for a full-scale territorial Anabaptist church, to rival Zwingli's church in Zurich. For a time during the abortive 1525 peasants' uprising, such a church existed in the city of Waldshut, led by Balthasar Hubmaier in alliance with the peasant troops of the Black Forest.

By 1526 the peasant revolt had been crushed by the armies of the Swabian league, and one possible Anabaptist church expression came to an end with the fall of the city of Waldshut. In fact, in spite of its sporadic links to movements of social unrest, the Swiss baptizing movement proved to be most fundamentally a movement of religious renewal, rather than a movement for social revolution. As a religious reform it continued to spread to the Aargau, Bern, and Basel to the west; it also reached the city of Strasbourg and began to travel down the Rhine. Swiss Anabaptists had first gone to the north of Zurich, to Hallau, Waldshut, and Schaffhausen, but the movement soon extended well beyond the Rhine into the Black Forest, Württemberg, and Swabia. Swiss Anabaptism spread to Constance in the northeast and reached the south German cities of Ulm, Nuremberg, and Augsburg; and it moved to Chur in the southeast and beyond, to penetrate the Tirol. By the summer of 1526, after the fall of Waldshut, Balthasar Hubmaier found refuge even further east, in the city of Nicholsburg, Moravia, where he managed for a time to establish another Anabaptist state-church, with the help of the Lords of Liechtenstein. The religious toleration of the von Liechtenstein family and other Moravian lords meant that the Moravian territories would become a crucial destination for Swiss Anabaptist refugees for the rest of the sixteenth century–even though the city of Nicholsburg itself faded in importance as an Anabaptist centre as the century wore on.

Judging from the surviving historical records, the participation of women in Swiss Anabaptism was of a different order before 1527 than it came to be after 1527. The Swiss movement cannot be characterized as mystical, but in the first two years of its existence it certainly had its share of spiritualism: there was a consistent appeal to the power of the Holy Spirit. In some specific cases this spiritualism freed Anabaptist women for missionizing, prophetic, and leadership roles: their authority came directly from God, and not from men. Two of the Swiss Anabaptist women profiled in this book–Agnes Linck from Biel and Margret Hottinger of Zollikon–appear to have received their calling in this way and to have exercised a charismatic leadership in the early Swiss movement. This early spiritualistic phase of Swiss Anabaptism was not destined to last much beyond 1527.

Of all the Anabaptist groups, the Swiss Anabaptists were the first to establish firm community guidelines. The Brotherly Union of Schleitheim (or the seven Schleitheim Articles of 1527) played a central role in this process.[6] The first three articles of Schleitheim describe adult baptism, church discipline (the Ban), and the celebration of a memorial Lord's Supper in ways that were common to Anabaptists everywhere, but articles four through seven were distinctively Swiss. They describe a church made up of baptized believers who through their baptisms necessarily became separate from the world: they were to be radical followers of Christ who would not resort to weapons of war or swear oaths. Furthermore, the members of these congregations would be responsible for electing and commissioning ministers and for disciplining their ministers, if such were necessary. In addition to what would quickly become the Swiss distinctives of separateness, nonresistance, and the non-swearing of oaths (all of which were maintained by the rigorous exercise of the Ban), the Swiss Anabaptists also insisted upon economic mutuality within their group.[7] They also came to be known for the strict enforcement of outward norms of behaviour by means of the Ban; one South German Anabaptist in 1527, for example, spoke about Swiss Anabaptist legislation enforcing simple dress–a practice with which he did not agree.

The drawing of stricter community boundaries among the Swiss Anabaptists was, in part, an understandable reaction to the varied views and events that had manifested themselves in the first two years of the movement in Switzerland. However, such strict and external boundary formation also dampened the spiritualist stream among the Swiss Anabaptists. In what probably was a repudiation of events such as had occurred in St. Gall, the Schleitheim Articles rejected some "false brothers among us" who had thought that they were practising "freedom of the Spirit."[8] Such people said Schleitheim, "have fallen short of the truth." The call of the Spirit which initially had empowered some women, increasingly was replaced in the Swiss Anabaptist movement by the calling of male pastors *by the community.* Likewise the written word (and its interpretation by a male leadership) came to be emphasized over the direct activity of the Spirit in Swiss Anabaptism after 1527.

These developments did not, of course, mean the end of involvement by Swiss Anabaptist women. Although no place was made for women in the official positions of church leadership (as pastors or bishops authorized to baptize and lead in the Lord's Supper), nevertheless Swiss Anabaptist women retained a high degree of participation in church governance. According to the Schleitheim Articles, the congregation was to have the final say over the pastor: if a shepherd did something worthy of reprimand that was confirmed by two or three witnesses, he was to be disciplined. Women were not excluded from exercising this disciplinary function. Furthermore, there is evidence that in some Swiss Anabaptist communities the traditional social norm that considered women to be subject to the corporal discipline of their husbands was broken; wife beating became classified as a sin and an offense for which Swiss Anabaptist men could be banned from the fellowship.[9]

There were individual cases of informal female leadership that continued among the Swiss Brethren, particularly instances of active proselytization. In one spectacular example of such activity, Margaret Hellwart was so active in persuading other women to join the movement that frustrated local authorities chained her to the floor of her house. Finally, there was banishment, imprisonment, torture, and martyrdom for Anabaptist men and women alike–the ultimate tests of an individual's commitment to Christ. The final choice of sacrificing one's life was a decision in which women and men were equally free.

Swiss Anabaptist women continued to be the mainstay of the underground church. The unspectacular case of Anna Scharnschlager demonstrates the kind of steady support that enabled the movement to survive. The call of the Spirit to repentance, baptism, and a new life continued to be heard by women and men. That call was considered to be higher than human commitments. There are several instances of Swiss Anabaptist women leaving their lower call to husbands and families because they were not being allowed to practise their faith at home; the case of Adelheit Schwarz of Watt is one such example. There were numerous cases of heroism and steadfastness by persecuted and imprisoned Swiss Anabaptist women; Agnes Zender of Aarau, Elsbeth Theiller of Horgen, Adelheit Schwarz of Watt and her imprisoned circle of friends, and Margret Hottinger–who also suffered martyrdom–all provide examples.

By 1530 the number of Swiss Anabaptists actually living in Switzerland had dwindled: persecution in Swiss territories was fierce, and effectively checked the popular spread of the movement. For those who wished to stand by their Anabaptist convictions, only two options remained: either continue to practise in secret (usually in the more remote, rural Swiss areas), or flee from Switzerland to areas where more toleration was evident. Any numbers are speculative, but many hundreds, if not thousands, of Anabaptists fled Switzerland in the sixteenth century. The case of Margret Hottinger, who met her death while fleeing to Moravia, is a typical story of danger while on the road to the promised land of religious freedom.

In their places of refuge the Swiss met Anabaptist refugees from other regions; some differences in doctrine and practice soon became apparent, in spite of agreement on general principles. It was in such refugee settings, some time around 1530, that other Anabaptists first identified the followers of the Schleitheim Articles as "Swiss Brethren." By mid-century, the number of Swiss Brethren living outside Switzerland well outnumbered those living inside the Confederacy. By the end of the century there would be Anabaptists identifying themselves as Swiss Brethren living as far north as Hesse; these were people who had never set foot in Switzerland, and likely never would. In the end, the designation Swiss Brethren indicated a particular way of being Anabaptist, rather than a geographical location. By the end of the sixteenth century, the few Swiss Brethren left in Switzerland were hanging on in remote areas in the cantons of Zurich and Bern. The larger concentrations of Swiss Brethren were refugee communities to be found primarily in Moravia, Alsace, and the Palatinate; there were smaller groups of Swiss Brethren in Württemberg and Hesse, as well.

Although only a few surviving sources provide details about the informal leadership of women among the exiled Swiss Anabaptist communities throughout the sixteenth century, we catch enough glimpses in the surviving documents to be able to say with confidence that the underground communication of the Anabaptist message routinely was carried forward by women, within their circles of family, friendship, and acquaintance. Furthermore, the actual functioning of the Swiss underground church communities depended in large measure upon the planning, hospitality, and communication provided by Anabaptist women. As persecution became increasingly fierce in Zurich and Bern, Anabaptist women were jailed in large numbers, some subjected to torture and martyred, sometimes in complete anonymity.[10]

The few profiles and stories offered in this book are some of the more complete narratives from literally hundreds of appearances of Anabaptist women in surviving sixteenth-century court records and in other sources. These profiles present a limited but accurate cross section of the kind of testimony that has survived to document the convictions and activities of these women. In one aspect, however, the profiles presented here paint a misleading demographic picture. We could not include even one profile of the many refugee Swiss Anabaptist women living in Moravia—where there were large concentrations of Swiss Anabaptists—because of a complete lack of documentation. While we may regret this fact as historians, we can be thankful for the people whose stories did not leave a paper trail: the absence of judicial records indicates the absence of persecution.

Notes

1 The following is drawn from C. Arnold Snyder, *Anabaptist History and Theology: An Introduction* (Kitchener, ON: Pandora Press, 1995), chapter 4.
2 Beyond Grebel, Mantz, and George Blaurock, no other names are given in the surviving records. See Leland Harder, ed., *The Sources of Swiss Anabaptism* (Scottdale, PA: Herald Press, 1985), 338-342. Felix Mantz was the first Anabaptist martyr in Switzerland. He was drowned in the Limmat river, January 5, 1527.
3 The story of the first Anabaptist congregation in Zollikon is told by Fritz Blanke, original edition *Brüder in Christo* (Zürich: Zwingli Press, 1955); English translation, *Brothers in Christ*, trans. Joseph Nordenhang (Scottdale, PA: Herald Press, 1961).
4 QGTS, vol. 2, 615-16.
5 See James Stayer, *Anabaptists and the Sword* (Lawrence, KS: Coronado Press, 1976).
6 Translation of the Schleitheim Articles in John H. Yoder, *The Legacy of Michael Sattler* (Scottdale, PA: Herald Press, 1973), 34-43.
7 The evidence is reviewed in James Stayer, *The German Peasants' War and Anabaptist Community of Goods* (Montreal and Kingston: McGill-Queen's University Press, 1991).
8 Johannes Kessler of St. Gall wrote in his chronicle the *Sabbata* that "Some [of the Anabaptists] maintained that Christ said 'If the Son has made you free, you are free indeed', and therefore they should have been able to use their freedom as their hearts

desired." QGTS, vol. 2, 629.

9 In testimony given in Augsburg in 1550, Jörg Maler testified that he did not agree with the Swiss Brethren in Appenzell who were of the opinion "that no one was to punish or strike one's wife, no matter how grave the fault, but rather one should put up with it." Maler clarified his own understanding as follows: "Since Paul wrote that the woman is subordinate to the man, and that the man is the head of the woman and ought to be her lord, therefore it is right that in cases of need a man should chastize and punish his wife as a father does a child; and that a brother who does such a thing should not be punished for this, nor has he sinned in doing such a thing." It is apparent that some Swiss Brethren had moved beyond the societal norm–unfortunately we are not given the reasons that supported their rejection of corporal punishment of wives. Maler, on the other hand, was voicing the common sixteenth-century opinion. QGTS, vol. 2, 239.

10 See, for example, the stories of the women and men imprisoned in Zurich from 1635 to 1645 in "Ein Wahrhaftiger Bericht . . . ," printed as an appendix to the Swiss Brethren hymnal, the *Ausbund, das ist Etliche schöne Christliche Lieder* . . . (numerous editions; I have used: Elkhart, IN: Mennonitischen Verlagshandlung, 1880). See also the numerous accounts of the imprisonment of women in Bern in the latter part of the sixteenth century, in Isaac Zürcher, *Die Täufer um Bern, Sonderdruck aus "Informationsblätter"* 9 (1986), Schweizerischen Vereins für Täufergeschichte.

AGNES ZENDER OF AARAU

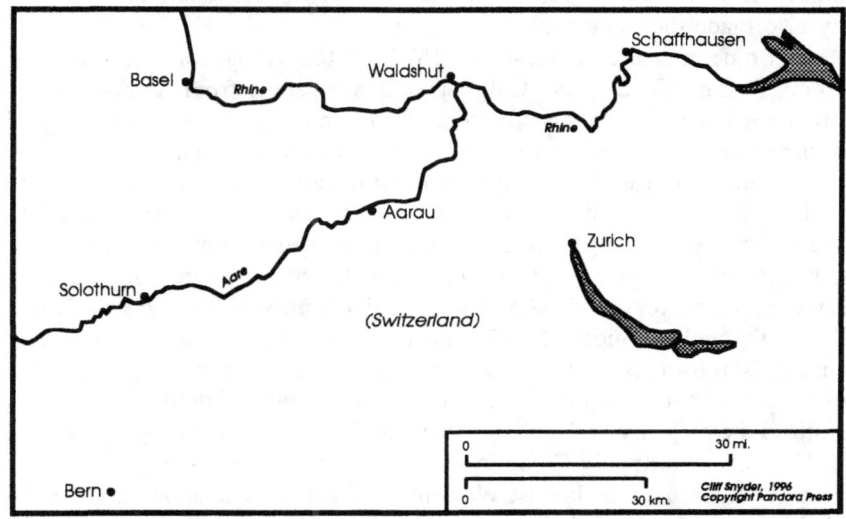

The story of Agnes Zender of Aarau, like that of so many Anabaptist women, can be told only in a fragmented way. She appears in the historical record only briefly, and then disappears again, leaving too many questions unanswered. But even from the brief glimpse we get into her life, we gain a better understanding of the kind of commitment Anabaptism demanded of both men and women in the sixteenth century.

The region of Aargau, with its small capital city of Aarau, lies in a rural region of northwestern Switzerland surrounded by larger urban centres.[1] To the east of Aarau lies Zurich, to the north, across the Rhine, Waldshut; to the northwest, Basel; to the south, Lucerne; and to the southwest, Bern, which, in the sixteenth century, was the political and legal overlord of the city and region. Although Bern remained the court of final appeal in legal cases, Aarau had retained a good measure of legal autonomy and self-government.

Given its location as a crossroad between larger urban centres, sixteenth-century Aargau, and the city of Aarau in particular, were places where various currents of church reform won adherents among the local population. Early reforming events in Aarau reflect the kinds of disturbances that were happening elsewhere in the region: in April 1523, a peasant in neighbouring Zofingen burned a holy picture; in November of that year, the priest in Aarau spoke against the Mass; in June 1524, Bern took legal action against Hans Pfistermeyer (later an Anabaptist leader in the region) for "reading" in public places; in October of that year, some people in Aarau violated an official church fast by eating meat; in 1525 there were instances of refusal to pay the tithe (an ecclesiastical tax) in the region.[2] In due course, all of the anticlerical, iconoclastic, and antisacramental issues of the day also made their appearance in Aarau.

Sometime after August 19, 1525, in the village of Zollikon near Zurich, Niklaus Guldi of St. Gall baptized two people from Aarau–the first notice we have of Anabaptist activity in the city. The two who accepted baptism were Hans Pfistermeyer of Aarau, and an unnamed hatmaker (either Heini Seiler or Heini Steffan, both hatmakers from Aarau, and both Anabaptists).[3] It is probable that Agnes Zender was first introduced to Anabaptist ideas through some of these local leaders, but the sources say nothing about this possibility. Instead they describe the direct influence of a stranger to the region: the Anabaptist furrier from Waldshut, Jakob Gross.

Throughout most of 1525, nearby Waldshut was a live source of Anabaptist reform, for at Easter of that year, Balthasar Hubmaier, a Waldshut reformer, accepted baptism from Wilhelm Reublin.[4] Hubmaier, in turn, baptized the majority of the city council and hundreds of citizens, in defiance of Waldshut's militantly Catholic Austrian overlords. It was the time of the Peasants' War, and Anabaptist Waldshut had a cordial relationship with the rebellious commoners. It provided volunteers for peasant armies in the region; they, in turn, provided Waldshut with a measure of military protection–at least as long as the Peasants' War was going in favour of the peasants. By the fall of 1525, however, the peasants were being defeated militarily on all sides, and Waldshut fell again to the Austrians in early December of that year. There was great concern by authorities in the region about Anabaptist refugees from the city. In early January of 1526, Bern sent a special warning to the overseers of its subject territories to be on the lookout for such refugees, and not to tolerate their presence in Bernese territories.[5]

Jakob Gross, however, had come to the Aargau well before the fall of Waldshut. He was not a typical Waldshut Anabaptist, and had been expelled from the city (most likely in late summer of 1525) for refusing to kill another human being in the case of an attack on the city.[6] He would stand watch, and even carry weapons, but he refused to use the weapons. After his banishment from Waldshut, Gross appeared in Grüningen, where he is said to have baptized thirty-five people in a single day. He was arrested and sentenced to banishment from that district (September 20, 1525), but he refused to take the required oath, saying that his yes meant yes, and his no meant no (Matt 5:37).[7] The Grüningen authorities finally expelled him without benefit of an oath, and he appeared next in the Aargau.

On December 18, 1525, there is notice of a judgement against Hans Senger of Aarau. He was in some ways no ordinary citizen, since he was the son of Rudolf Senger, the city secretary [*Stadtschreiber*] of Aarau. Nevertheless, he was to be fined "because of the meeting that he held in his house." The others present at this meeting also were to be fined, namely,

Hans Kallenberg and Agnes Zender. If this were to happen again, the culprits would be imprisoned and fined again.[8] This meeting in Hans Senger's household would not be the last in which these three people were involved, as becomes clearer when we follow the document trail over the next few months.

About one month later, the court in Aarau–responding to an appeal by a member of the Zender family–overturned the sale of a garden plot by Agnes Zender to one Barblen Imhoff, and returned the garden to Agnes or to the Zender family.[9] We discover from this notice that Agnes Zender was a property owner who had tried to exercise her legal right to sell some of that property. How did Agnes come to be a landowner, and why was she trying to sell some of her property in Aarau?

Some answer to these questions comes in a later document: on February 19, 1526, the authorities in Aarau banned Rudolf Senger's wife and his son Hans, along with Hans Kallenberg and Agnes Zender, from Bernese territory for the crime of having taken part in an unauthorized celebration of the Lord's Supper.[10] Here more details are clarified about another meeting, this time in the Rudolf Senger household. We discover that the city secretary's unnamed wife, who was also the mother of Hans, was actively involved in this meeting, and was also to be punished with exile. What it would have meant to the Senger household to have husband and wife separated in this way can easily be imagined. Furthermore, we discover why Agnes Zender was attempting to turn her property into cash: she was preparing to move away from Aarau, probably knowing full well that she was likely to be banished from Bernese territory.

Rudolf Senger, the city secretary, did not simply accept the judgement of the Aarau authorities that his wife, son, and neighbours were to be banned from the territory; he availed himself of every legal recourse, and asked for a review of the case by the higher authorities in Bern.[11] This hearing was set for March 5, 1526, in Bern. In preparation for the appeal, Rudolf Senger sent a detailed letter of explanation to Bern in which he pleaded his case and that of his neighbours. From this letter we learn even more about the meeting in his house in late fall of 1525, and we also get a glimpse of how reforming ideas spread among the people of Aarau.[12]

In his letter Rudolf Senger described three separate episodes, and although it is not entirely clear how they were related to each other, they paint a picture of growing reforming radicalism and conflict with the authorities. First, Senger described how some people, among them his son Hans, were asking to be instructed from Scripture. Their question was how God could be coerced from His heavenly throne to take up residence in the host, in flesh and blood. For this his son was imprisoned and fined five pounds, and Senger complained that the Aarau authorities were taking too much from poor people. Second, Senger described how a "good, pious man from Waldshut" (Jakob Gross) had come to Senger's cousin's house, seeking work. He did find work, not with Senger's cousin, but with Hans Kallenberg. It then happened, said Senger, that a group of men and women were working together, spinning and weaving, in a large room in Langeweile. Thereupon the city constable arrived, arrested Gross, and accused everyone there of having an illegal religious meeting. But it was no such a thing, argued Senger, "since there was no reading or singing, either by the men or the women." The ensuing fines imposed on all those present, said Senger, were a real hardship, but in spite of the protests that the fines were unjust (since there was no illegal meeting), no notice was taken by the authorities in Aarau.

Rudolf Senger was particularly good at special pleading, choosing not to mention inconvenient details, and glossing over incriminating evidence. The working scene he described in his letter was surely depicted too innocently. From this little notice we get a glimpse into what was a typical Anabaptist schoolroom: the common working rooms of the people involved in the crafts. Undoubtedly these people in the Aargau *were* working together, that is, spinning and weaving, but also without a doubt they were discussing religious topics, such as the Lord's Supper, with the "good and pious man from Waldshut," the furrier Jakob Gross. Was Agnes Zender found among them? The sources do not say, but it is possible. Furthermore, from what Senger claimed *did not* take place, namely singing and reading by men or women, we get a glimpse of what he considered to be a meeting–and what undoubtedly had taken place on other occasions, most likely in his own house.

The third episode Senger justified in his letter (but likely the second event chronologically) was the most incriminating of all. His wife had been very ill, he said, and had been bedridden for several days. She had been so ill that they had sent for the priest, and he had given her last rites. Later that same night a group of people had gathered in his house, namely his wife's sister and her husband from Bremgarten, "a pious neighbour" Agnes Zender, his good neighbour Hans Kallenberg, his son Hans, and Jakob Gross. Jakob Gross was there because he had asked Hans Senger for lodging, claiming to have a letter from the authorities saying that this was allowed. At some point in the evening his ailing wife had said to her friends, "I beg of you that you eat the Supper with me, just as Christ did with his disciples, commanding them that as often as they did this, they should eat in remembrance of his bitter suffering and death; we should also eat in this way, because you don't know how long I will be with you." And so they ate, but only in this simple and good sense of remembering Jesus' suffering, and only at home, and not publicly. They were not trying to recreate the sacrament of the altar, said Senger, but only eating simply, in remembrance. And although it was true, concluded Senger, that his son Hans had read Scripture, he had done this at home, and not in violation of Bern's mandates. In short, the ban imposed by the Aarau authorities was far too harsh, for the members of the fledgling Anabaptist community were all Bernese by birth, and wished to remain so.

Senger's appeal received a favourable hearing in Bern, and in a judgement delivered March 5, 1526, those who had been banned (including Agnes) were allowed to stay, with appropriate warnings concerning further misbehaviour.[13] But the reprieve was only temporary for Agnes Zender, because in the meantime Jakob Gross had been imprisoned (apparently arrested at his workplace in Langeweile), and was being questioned closely. His testimony shed a slightly different light on events in the Senger household when the Supper had been celebrated "as a simple remembrance." According to Gross, Rudolf Senger's ill wife had asked him "to instruct them on how they should live so that they might achieve eternal salvation. And so he had spoken and taught God's Word and after that had given them the Lord's Supper, together with Hans Kallenberg, the priest Wolfgang of Heilbronn, and also Agnes Zender. Gross stated that he had only baptized the widow Agnes Zender, and none of the others, and had simply given them all the Supper as Christ had established it, and had used the words of Paul written in the first epistle to the Corinthians (1 Cor. 11: 23-26). With this incriminating evidence in hand, the Bernese authorities now proclaimed that Agnes Zender must be expelled from the territory, after swearing an oath never to return.[14]

With Jakob Gross's testimony, several more pieces of the Agnes Zender puzzle fall into place. In the first place, as a widow she had certain legal rights over family property. However, her attempt to sell some of that property, namely a garden plot, was met with a legal challenge by Marquart Zender, perhaps related to Agnes's deceased husband, acting in the interests of the Zender family. The court in Aarau had decided that Agnes could not sell the property, but must retain possession of it herself or offer it back to the Zender family, to whom it had originally belonged. Converting this real estate into liquid assets would not be possible for Agnes. In the second place, from Jakob Gross's testimony we discover that Agnes had accepted rebaptism—something none of the other defendants involved with her had done. Without a doubt her preparations to leave were related to the realization that her "crime" would probably come to light. And it is clear that she was prepared to accept the consequences of her decision.

On March 19, 1526, Gabriel Meyer (the new city secretary of Aarau) noted that all of Agnes's goods and assets were to be frozen, since she had fled "on account of the rebaptism which she had received from Jakob the furrier from Waldshut."[15] Two days later, the court in Aarau noted that the sale of the garden plot to Barblen Imhoff had been blocked, but since Barblen had already invested time and work on that land, she should be allowed to keep it for one year, in return for a reasonable rent.[16]

There is no notice concerning Agnes in the Aarau record for three months. Then on July 26, 1526, the Bernese authorities wrote to the city officials at Aarau that if Agnes Zender had paid the original fine of ten pounds that she owed for having partaken in the Lord's Supper, she should be expelled officially from Bernese territory on the strength of her word only, without the accustomed oath. Two days later, the authorities in Aarau reported that Agnes had appeared before them carrying a letter from Bern, and that she was to be banned from the territory "after which her goods may be allowed to follow her."[17] Just what Agnes's goods amounted to is not specified in the record, but it is clear that Agnes had decided to abide by her baptism and to leave Bernese territory permanently. Thus she had made the legal arrangements necessary to have at least some of her personal property released from Aarau. What the value was of the immovable goods she had to leave behind, we do not know, but it is clear that Agnes Zender was a woman of some means.

With this notice, unfortunately, the records of Aarau fall silent concerning Agnes Zender. We can assume that between the time of her flight, and her return to Aarau for the settlement of her legal affairs and her official banishment, she had found a suitable haven in some other community, and that after her banishment she returned there to live with such earthly goods as she was able to take along. She chose to abide by her choice in accepting baptism, leaving the security of property behind.

This writer does not know of any other mention of Agnes Zender in the historical record dealing with Anabaptists, but such a mention may well turn up. Until such time, we cannot say any more about her. We do know, however, that by March 12, 1527, Agnes's neighbour and good friend, the unnamed ill wife of the old *Stadtschreiber* Rudolf Senger, had died. Although she does not appear to have accepted rebaptism, Rudolf Senger's wife remained religiously independent until the end, for this time she suffered through her final illness without benefit of last rites. Although we do not know where or how Agnes Zender spent her remaining days, her friend was punished in death by being buried in unsanctified ground, "in the field by the little hay barn."[18] One suspects that neither she nor Agnes would have found this too high a price to pay for their religious convictions.

Notes

1 A summary of Anabaptist events and persons is found in ME, I, 4-6.
2 QGTS, vol 3, documents 2, 3, 4, 5, 6, 7, 8.
3 QGTS, vol. 1, 119, pp. 117-20. On the early notices concerning Pfistermeyer and the hatmakers, see QGTS, vol. 3, documents 9, 10, 11, 12, 13, 14, 17.
4 For a concise overview, see Christof Windhorst, "Balthasar Hubmaier: Professor, Preacher, Politician," in Hans Jüergen Goertz, ed., *Profiles of Radical Reformers* (Scottdale, PA: Herald Press, 1982), 144-57.

5 TA, Baden und Pfalz, documents 370, 371, pp. 389-90; also QGTS, vol. 3, documents 19a, 19b, 20.
6 On Jakob Gross, see ME, II, 598-99. On his wife Veronika, see ibid., 599, and the profile of Anabaptist women in Augsburg, in this book. Information on his expulsion from Waldshut in QGTS, vol. 1, document 107, pp. 108-9.
7 QGTS, vol. 1, document 238, pp. 261-62. Further information on Gross is found in documentation dating after his arrest in Augsburg in 1527. See the letter from Zurich to Augsburg (Sept. 28, 1527) in ibid., document 239, pp. 262-63 and the letter from Brugg to Zurich (Sept. 26, 1527) in QGTS, vol. 3, document 57 (original found in the STAZ, signature E I, numbers 1 to 1B).
8 QGTS, vol. 3, document 17. On this and later events, see the summary account in J. Heiz, "Täufer im Aargau," in *Taschenbuch der historischen Gesellschaft des Kantons Aargau* (Aarau: Sauerländer, 1902), 114-15.
9 QGTS, vol. 3, document 21.
10 Ibid., document 23.
11 Ibid., document 25.
12 The details that follow are found in Senger's lengthy letter to the Bernese authorities, in ibid., document 26.
13 Ibid., document 27.
14 Ibid., docments 30, 31.
15 Ibid., document 33.
16 Ibid., document 34.
17 Ibid., documents 42, 43.
18 Ibid., document 48.

AGNES LINCK FROM BIEL

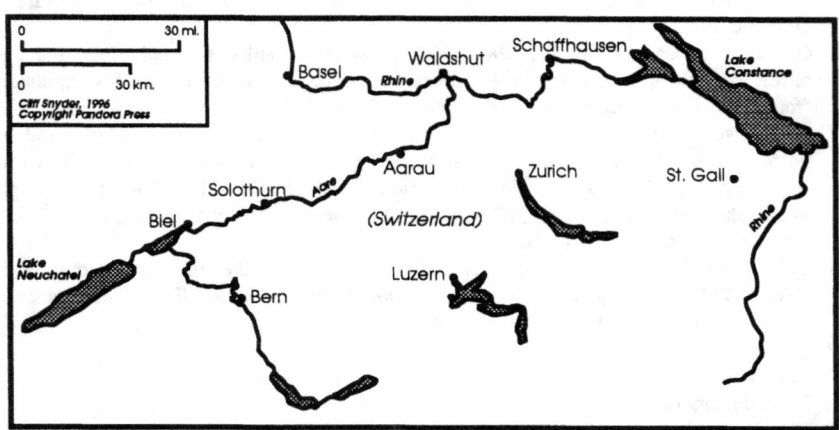

There are people who, in spite of only brief mention in the historical sources, nevertheless leave the unmistakable mark of their personalities etched there. Agnes Linck was one such person.

On April 16, 1528, Agnes Linck, from the small Swiss city of Biel, was questioned in Solothurn, on suspicion of heresy. Her statement, as recorded by the court scribe, reads as follows:

> What she said earlier concerning the institution of the sacrament [i.e., the Lord's Supper], publicly before milords in the meeting at the school, is true. She hopes to stand by that and not fall away from it, with the help of God the almighty, her one and only Lord. She sets her faith upon no earthly thing at all; and furthermore, she places as much value on the new Lord's Supper, as it is practised now in Zurich and in Bern, as she did on the Supper practised in the Old Faith (Catholicism): both are useless. For it is all done on account of money. And she still cannot partake of the Lord's Supper now; not until she has been further freed from sin and received more of God's grace.
>
> Concerning baptism and the Anabaptists, she said that she had been rebaptized by no person. But six years earlier she had been baptized in spirit and in truth, and she desired and hoped to remain with that baptism. No Anabaptist or any other person had taught her such a faith; rather she had been instructed by Christ her Lord; and she continued saying such things with many words.[1]

Agnes Linck was not one to shy away from controversy, or to fail to speak her mind. She was quite willing to share her biting analysis of the Protestant celebration of the Supper in a public meeting, in the presence of officials and others, and then equally willing to repeat her critique for the court scribe after her public comments had led her to prison. The Protestants, she said, had simply made an economic arrangement; it was no true Supper they were celebrating.

Agnes also was quick to reveal the foundation for her self-confidence: her Lord was higher than any earthly lords. Not only that, but she had received a baptism in "spirit and truth" straight from her Lord, who had taught her directly. She owed neither her faith nor her baptism, she said, to any man; she owed everything to Christ her Lord. And so she continued, apparently, to argue with her questioners. Unfortunately, the scribe did not deem her "many words" worthy of legal record; a fuller account from this confident and articulate woman would have been welcome indeed.

The following day, April 17, the court record noted that Agnes Linck of Biel to be banned on oath, but April 18 found her still in prison. Agnes, with characteristic conviction, refused to swear an oath, and so finally the Solothurn authorities banned her without benefit of an oath, and advised her that if she were ever to return to Solothurn, she would be punished appropriately.[2]

After her expulsion from Solothurn, Agnes disappeared from the historical record for two and a half years, only to be arrested in late September 1530, in Basel. Judging from her unrepentant and self-confident testimony in Solothurn, and from the testimony she was about to give in Basel, we can safely assume that Agnes Linck spent those years actively telling others about her faith–and also telling all who would listen her negative assessment of the government-sponsored church reforms.

At some point in the four to five weeks of her imprisonment in Basel, Agnes gave her testimony, duly recorded by the court scribe.[3] The first line of that testimony states that Agnes Linck of Biel has confessed to being an Anabaptist, and to having been baptized by a man in Biel. Apparently Agnes had not been completely frank with the authorities in Solothurn two and a half years previous–there had been some human Anabaptist involved in her baptism after all. However, the defense that one had been taught "by no man," but rather directly by God or God's Word, was one commonly used by Anabaptists, although usually with inauspicious legal results. The argument that one had been baptized directly by God (and not by man) also was known elsewhere in the Anabaptist movement, and up to a point was theologically defensible: the Anabaptists held, after all, that the water was of no essential account, and that the real baptism was God's baptism of the Spirit.[4] It appears that Agnes successfully equivocated on these points at her first arrest in Solothurn; the Basel authorities were not so easily convinced.

The questioning in the Basel prison continued: What had she said in the bookshop located "at the Key"? Agnes answered that she had only asked if the bookshop sold a New Testament that had no introduction (that is, a New Testament without the Reformed preface) and no pictures of saints; and she had explained herself to a person who had asked about it. Concerning the "little letter" [*briefflin*], she had with her at the bookstore, she denied that it said anything extreme; it said, she claimed, only that whoever proclaimed the word of God, and then did not live according to it,[5] had acted wrongly. From the fact that Agnes was interested in purchasing a New Testament, as well as the fact that she had in her possession a "little letter" we may conclude with some certainty that Agnes was one of a select few women of the lower social order who had learned to read, and that she had put her literacy to reforming use. Knowing what the word of God said, and proclaiming that word, however, was not an end in itself: the point was to live according to one's knowledge of the word. We hear in this sentence not only an anticlerical judgement commonly pronounced by the Anabaptists against the "lack of fruit" of Reformed preaching, but also the demand that a life of discipleship must follow a profession of faith.

Agnes testified further that she had been in Basel for some five weeks; Margaret Pfeffer had lived with her, but Agnes denied having instructed her. She had, however, taught two children; she had never once gone to the Protestant church to hear a sermon. Agnes confessed further that earlier she had been imprisoned in Solothurn for five days "because she had insulted their idols and St. Urs [the patron saint of Solothurn] by calling them chimney sweeps." It was for this reason that they had exiled her from the city and the territory.[6] This bit of testimony confirms one's initial suspicions: that Agnes was accustomed to instructing others–something her personality and her literacy would have equipped her to do; that she had long since been alienated from the state church reform; and that in addition to her criticism of the Lord's Supper, as is documented in the Solothurn documents, she also was strongly and vocally iconoclastic. Contrary to the impression left by the Solothurn court record, Agnes recalled having been expelled because of her insults to the saints.

In addition to Agnes's own testimony, the court collected the testimony of two eyewitnesses to the events in the bookstore. Thomas Girfalck, preacher at the Augustinian monastery and deacon at the cathedral, testified that on a Monday, approximately four weeks before, he had been in the bookstore "at the Key" when a woman from Biel had come in and asked for a New Testament "that had no idols inside or the heretical preface." When she was asked to clarify what she meant concerning such a New Testament, she answered that she had "chopped out the idols from her New Testament, or blotted them out with ink, for she had the Spirit of God, and what was against Christ was also against her."[7] While the preacher undoubtedly parodied Agnes's actual words, her testimony in Solothurn confirms that she commonly did appeal to the direct authority of the Spirit of God in her life. That she appealed in some way to God's Spirit also in the bookshop in Basel is entirely consistent with that earlier testimony.

Also consistent was the anticlericalism she expressed in the bookshop in Basel, but the generality of the earlier criticism was now tinged with socio-economic protest as well. According to pastor Thomas, Agnes said that earlier she had heard from her own preacher, Herr Jacob, that one should not pay the tithe; but now the same man was preaching that one should pay the tithe. Opposition to the payment of the tithe was shared by the peasant insurrectionists in 1525 and by the early Anabaptists, and pastor Thomas had no trouble identifying Agnes's leanings. The pastor testified that once he had understood what her mistaken opinion was–that is, that she was an Anabaptist–he proceeded to instruct her concerning baptism with passages of scripture; he said that he had asked her specific questions, but that she was not able to answer him. Agnes's only reply was that the preachers had "taught falsely, and whoever did not wish to be misled should stay away from the preachers and not listen to them." Rudolph the bookbinder corroborated the preacher's testimony, except that he claimed to have heard nothing concerning heresy.

A third witness, an unnamed schoolteacher, contributed hearsay evidence that reveals some of the breadth and spread of Agnes's viewpoints in the oral network of communication. The schoolteacher testified that he had heard from his wife that the woman from Biel was supposed to have said that she would rather be put to death than go to hear the preaching in the state church. He also had heard that she was supposed to have said publicly in the street that the preachers were going around telling lies, but he also had heard from Magdalena Pfeiffer that Agnes had not been speaking about the preachers in Basel, but rather about the preachers in Biel. The schoolteacher testified further (he seemed to know this first-hand) that Agnes had "instructed" the son of the hatmaker who lived by the Eschamertor, and also had taught a young woman. He said that he had scolded Magdalena Pfeiffer and had told her that she shouldn't have anything to do with Agnes Linck, but Magdalena answered him that she was quite capable of making up her own mind.[8] Agnes's independence of spirit appears to have been contagious.

On October 31, 1530, the court entry reads that the Anabaptist woman, Agnes Linck from Biel, had been a member of the accursed Anabaptist sect for a long time, and had persisted in it, to the point that no instruction could shake her from it. Nevertheless, reads the entry, through the industrious efforts of milords, Agnes had now "freely" recanted her errors. Therefore she had been released from prison on the last day of October on the strength of an oath, in which she swore to stay out of the city and territory of Basel; if she did not keep her oath, she was to be drowned.[9] A financial record dated November 5 notes that Agnes Linck had paid 4 pounds, 19 shillings, and 6 pennies to cover the costs of her imprisonment–a fine that corresponds to a period of imprisonment of four to five weeks.[10]

With this last expulsion the historical record concerning Agnes Linck falls silent. Did Agnes herself also fall silent? Did she continue to participate in Anabaptist communities elsewhere, perhaps in Moravia? The patterns of Anabaptist behaviour from elsewhere would suggest that a cursory oath and expulsion such as she offered in Basel would not have silenced as convinced an Anabaptist as Agnes Linck. But, in the absence of further evidence, this is pure conjecture. Nevertheless, the bits of evidence that Agnes left for us in the historical record are invaluable, because they provide a rare and important window through which we may catch a glimpse of the convictions and the active reforming activity of a remarkable individual from the "common people."

Agnes Linck is a prime example of a self-appointed lay Anabaptist leader, called and convinced by the Spirit. But Agnes was not simply a visionary or a dreamer of dreams. In addition to the conviction that she had been called by the Spirit of God, Agnes also exercised the very concrete skill of literacy, which placed her in a position of being able to instruct others in a biblical faith. It is not surprising that Agnes ran afoul of the law, for her understanding of biblical truth, interpretive authority, church reform, and the Christian life all ran counter to the state-run movements of reform. Agnes could not, and did not, remain silent, to which fact we owe what little we know about her. That someone with her strength of personality, with her profound convictions and gift of expression, also spoke freely and with great influence in her own social circle is beyond question. In a predominantly oral/aural culture, a woman of Agnes's abilities had the capacity to shape popular, lay opinion to an extent that we can only dimly appreciate. However, beyond such an assertion we are not permitted to go: the questions of where she lived and worked, whom she may have persuaded, and what exactly were the results of her activities of instruction are sadly not matters of historical record.

Notes

1 QGTS, vol. 3, document 844.
2 Ibid., documents 845, 846.
3 The three documents pertaining to this imprisonment are published in Durr and Roth, eds., *Aktensammlung zur Geschichte der Basler Reformation in den Jahren 1519 bis Anfang 1534, V. Band, October 1530 bis Ende 1531* (Basel: Verlag der historischen und antiquarischen Gesellschaft Universitätsbibiothek Basel, 1945), documents 39, a-c, pp. 39-40.
4 The contention that one had been taught "by no man" appears with some frequency. See as one example the testimony of Hanns Hottinger, in QGTS, vol. 1, document 54, p. 61. Heinrich Aberli argued in 1526 that the reason he had denied baptizing anyone in reply to questioning (when in fact he had baptized someone with water) was that "he had not baptized anyone, but rather God the Heavenly Father did the baptizing, and the water

was not the baptism." Ibid., p. 161.
5 "dem nit nachvolge"
6 Durr and Roth, *Aktensammlung*, V, p. 39.
7 Ibid., document 39, c, pp. 39-40.
8 Ibid., p. 40.
9 Ibid., document 39, a, p. 39.
10 Ibid., document 48, p. 44. The estimate of 4-5 weeks is made by Martin Haas, in QGTS, vol. 3, document 350, d, note 19.

ADELHEIT SCHWARZ OF WATT

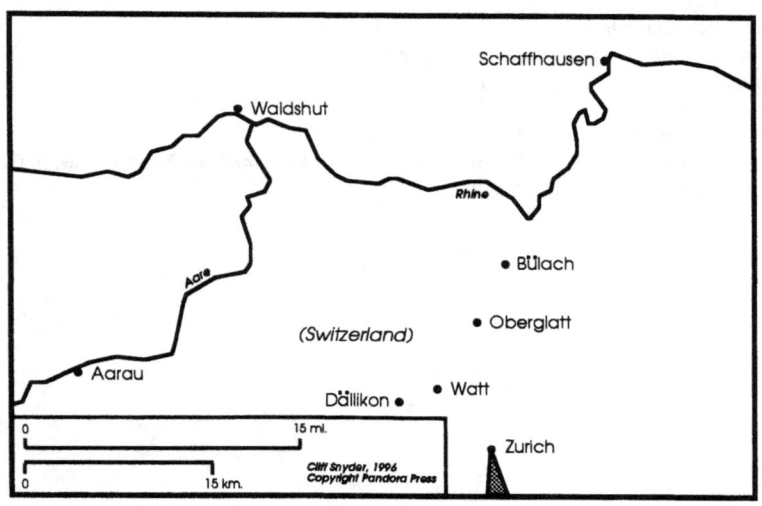

We first meet Adelheit Schwarz in spring of the year 1529. In testimony reported to the authorities in Zurich, Bartli Hug of Dällikon said that several women from Watt had come to Dällikon, and had gone into Elsa Spilmann's house where they had had a discussion. They included Jakob Fry's wife and Konrad Fry's wife. Furthermore, Wilhelm Reublin had read and preached at the inn in Weiningen, and present there had been Hans Grossman, Elsa Spilmann, her daughter Barbara, Balthasar Spilmann's wife, Adelheit Spilmann and Felix Fry's wife from Watt. Since all citizens had been admonished to oppose strangers who tried to preach, Bartli Hug continued, he himself had gone and tried to stop the proceedings. "For this they locked me out, and told me I would not be saved," he reported.[1]

Adelheit Spilmann, Balthasar Spilmann's wife, was also known by her maiden name of Schwarz; she came from the village of Watt, although she lived with her husband and their family in the village of Dällikon. In this, her first appearance in the historical record, we note a pattern that will continue throughout. Adelheit Schwarz was attracted to Anabaptism; also, as a rule, she was in the company of other women who shared her religious interests; and finally, the women with whom she kept company were women who were not afraid to speak their minds or to act boldly on their convictions.

The usual result of reports like that of Bartli Hug was that the Zurich authorities would make arrests. This appears to have happened to Adelheit, for in late April of 1529 a court record notes that on one previous occasion Adelheit Spilmann had been in prison on account of the "Anabaptist business."[2] Another witness testified around this same time that Adelheit was not attending the official state church very regularly (which she was obliged to do by law), and that he had never seen her at the celebration of the Lord's Supper in the local church.³ Adelheit was changing religious allegiances.

The Zurich authorities were anxious to suppress Anabaptism, and it was especially vexing to have Anabaptists meeting just a few kilometres from the city some four years after the official outlawing of the movement. There was a concentration of Anabaptist activity in the region of Bülach, just north of Zurich. Anabaptism in Bülach proved stubborn indeed, as time would prove, but in the space of one week, in December of 1529, the Zurich authorities made a concerted effort to stop the movement. They arrested at least twenty-eight people from the area, of whom six or seven proved not to have accepted rebaptism. Almost half of those arrested–twelve, in fact–were women, and we find Adelheit Schwarz among them, arrested now for the second time.[4]

The initial questioning and testimony of these women is particularly interesting because of the creative (and disruptive) strategy of passive resistance that they carried out. Adelheit's questioning comes first in the document, and the scribe noted that she simply wouldn't give a straight answer to the questions. "And no matter how long or often one asks, if it is this or the other, and one wishes to know her opinion about which baptism she holds to be the true one, she says that she holds that baptism to be correct which God has commanded. But which one God commanded or to which one she holds, no one can make out." Appollonia Schnider gave essentially this same answer. Margaret Wiener of Bülach admitted that she had been baptized about one year previously, but she refused to say who had baptized her, nor would she say anything about their practice, no matter how long she was questioned. Her mother, Annli Wiener of Bülach, was next on the list, and the scribe simply noted that "one can get less out of her than out of a stone," since she answers now with a "no," then with a "yes," and half-swallows her words. In similar fashion Annli Sidler confessed that she held to the baptism that God commanded, namely that those who believe and are baptized are saved. Other than that, she resisted answering.[5]

It is obvious that these women had planned their joint strategy with some care, and although they were powerless in the conventional sense, they had devised a clever way of throwing sand into the gears of official machinery.

Two more women were included in this first round of questioning, but they recanted and were released. The subsequent document, however, includes the names of three more women (apparently arrested later in the same week), plus the names of those who had persisted in the first round of questioning. But now a frustrated officialdom responded to these stubborn women with the weapon of physical torture. Regula Kernn was first questioned kindly, reported the scribe, concerning "who had brought her into this error and had baptized her," but she said little that was useful to her questioners. She was then beaten with rods, but the scribe noted that they got absolutely nothing further from her despite the beating. Annli Sidler simply refused to say who had baptized her, since she would not inflict more suffering on him. Appollonia Schnider, obviously responding to torture with thumbscrews, said outright that her jailers could "pressure her finger as long and as hard as they wished, but she would not say who had baptized her; for she would not be guilty of his blood."[6]

Precise dating in these cases is often difficult, but we know that these three women endured at least ten months more of prison before they recanted and were released. When they did recant, they also named the man who had baptized them: it was Konrad Winckler of Wasserberg, who had been arrested at the same time as they had, and subsequently had been executed by drowning by the authorities.[7] In spite of jail and torture, their testimony had formed no part of the judgement against Winckler.

Adelheit also was questioned in this second round, and it now came to light that she could have spared herself considerable trouble and pain, had she wished. She now admitted that she had not yet been rebaptized. Nevertheless, concerning the question of baptism, she answered as she had before, that she wished to hold to the baptism that God had commanded. But in her conscience, she said, she did not know which baptism was correct.[8]

It is a remarkable fact, but all the evidence points to the conclusion that, although she had not accepted rebaptism, Adelheit had chosen to remain in prison with her Anabaptist friends. This is made clear one month later, sometime in the second week of January 1530, when she again appears in the court records along with eleven other women from the region. This document lists multiple recantations–Regula Kernn, Appollonia Schnider, Annli Sidler, and Adelheit are among them. They had been in prison since the first arrest in the spring of 1529. Concerning Adelheit, the report in January of 1530 simply says that she had not been rebaptized. Since this was so, no official recantation was demanded of her nor was she fined, although she did have to pay the costs of her year-long imprisonment. In the end, however, she agreed, in the words of the scribe, "to consider good what Milords hold and consider good, and to conform to Milords."[9]

Adelheit clearly was a person of unusually strong character, for since she was not rebaptized, she could have left prison at any time with little apparent concession on her part. But she could not, she said, burden her conscience in this way. Although in the end she consented to the official wording concerning baptism, she would soon change her mind about that as well as her obedience to Milords.

A little more than one year later, on March 13, 1531, Balthasar Spilmann of Dällikon appeared in "marriage court" in Zurich and asked for a divorce from Adelheit Schwarz of Watt. She was, he said, an Anabaptist who had twice been arrested. She had borne him seven children, but one night she had packed some things and left, and he did not know where she was. He wished to divorce her, he said, because he had to care for his thirteen children, and he needed a wife. He had suffered much with Adelheit, but to no avail. The court told him to be patient, but gave him a letter setting forth the facts in the case. He was to find his wife and ask her to appear before the court, with safe conduct, so that the court could hear both sides in the case.[10]

On April 27, Balthasar Spilmann was back before the court. He said that he had made inquiries and had located Adelheit, and had then sent a daughter to fetch her. Adelheit had come back with the girl, and had stayed overnight, but had left again immediately. And although he had shown her the letter from the court, and had asked her to appear with him before the judges, she had said insulting things and would not agree. She said, furthermore, that "she wished to be obedient to God, and not to the earthly authorities."

Two days later the court granted Balthasar a divorce from Adelheit.[11] In its letter to the city council the court rehearsed the facts in the case: Adelheit had been arrested twice because of her connection with Anabaptism; she had been earnestly warned to distance herself from the movement, and had sworn an oath that she would, but now she had gone back again to the "Anabaptist gang," to which she wished to belong. "And she left her husband and seven of their children without reason, undeservedly." Since Adelheit would not respect the authorities, or esteem his or the children's love, Balthasar had asked for a divorce. This problem, noted the court, was a growing one; there were several more cases like it. As a corrective measure the court recommended "strong punishment on such unfaithful, deserting persons by means of searches, writings, proclamations and proscriptions."[12]

Is this a story of willful abandonment or one of escape and liberation from a life of drudgery and servitude? Is it a story of coming to consciousness of personal worth or one of devotion to God over husband and family? The documents might suggest any of these interpretations. But what exactly this all meant to Adelheit, where she went, what further contact she had with her children, and how she lived thereafter remains a closed book. Nevertheless, a chance comment in a later document gives us some further information about Adelheit. We know that she persisted in her Anabaptist faith for a long time after she left her husband and family, that she met with other Anabaptists for worship in woods and forests quite near Bülach, and that she may have influenced a daughter and granddaughter to join her in that faith.

In the year 1548, some seventeen years after the events recounted above, a man named Hans Fisher was arrested for Anabaptism by the Zurich authorities. Following repeated questioning, he finally gave a full recantation, including the names of people with whom he had worshipped. He had been baptized nine years before, in a forest near Kaiserstuhl by the Rhine. He also confessed where the Anabaptists had held their meetings, namely in forests and woods in the Swiss district of Baden, near Kaiserstuhl, near Glattfelden, and in the woods near Bülach. Among the people he named explicitly as fellow worshippers were "Adelheit Spilmann and her mother," as well as Adelheit Spilmann from Dällikon.[13]

Again, the sources say far less than we might wish. Adelheit Spilmann from Dällikon, of course, is none other than Adelheit Schwarz of Watt, for Spilmann was her married name, and she had once lived with her husband and family in Dällikon. But who is the younger Adelheit Spilmann, and who is her mother? What relationship, if any, do these women have to Adelheit Schwarz? We know that Adelheit Schwarz would have been an older woman by 1548, most likely in her early fifties, given the number of children she had already borne in her early Anabaptist days. Might the younger Adelheit Spilmann mentioned in 1548 be a granddaughter of Adelheit Schwarz? Unfortunately the sources do not help us answer this question, but given the fact that Adelheit Schwarz continued to meet other Anabaptists for worship in the geographical area of Bülach, the possibility remains that in the intervening seventeen years Adelheit Schwarz did maintain contact with her family, and may have exerted a religious influence on at least one daughter and a granddaughter.

Notes

1 QGTS, vol. 1, document 281, p. 296.
2 Ibid., document 285, p. 300.
3 Ibid., document 287, p. 303.
4 The arrests are recorded in ibid., document 293, pp. 307-10; Adelheit appears on p. 310.
5 Ibid., p. 310.
6 Ibid., document 294, pp. 310-11.
7 Ibid., p. 311, n. 2. On Winckler, see Arnold Snyder, "Konrad Winckler: An Early Swiss Anabaptist Missionary, Pastor and Martyr," MQR (Oct. 1990): 352-61.
8 QGTS, vol. 1, document 294, p. 311.
9 Ibid., document 302, pp. 320-21; document 304, pp. 324, 325.
10 Ibid., document 330, pp. 352-53.
11 Ibid., p. 353.
12 Ibid., document 338, pp. 357-58.
13 Confession of Hans Fischer, found in the STAZ, signature EI 7.2, document 94.

MARGRET HOTTINGER OF ZOLLIKON

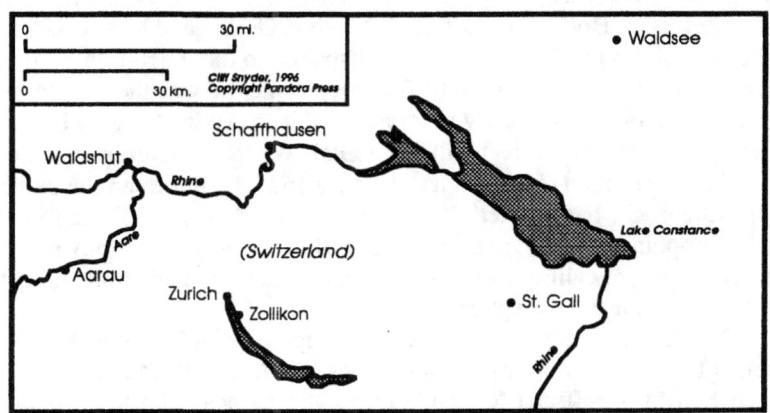

That we know anything at all about Margret Hottinger is remarkable, for people of her economic and social station have rarely left a mark in the historical records. In Margret's case, we owe the existence of historical records to the fact that she was born into a family for whom questions of faith and religious reform were considered of utmost importance. These interests led to religious radicalism, arrests, questioning, and thus historical records. Margret's father, Jakob Hottinger the elder, was a peasant farmer in Zollikon. He belonged not to the wealthier, higher class of peasants in the village, but rather to the lower-middle economic class. The Hottinger clan in and around the village of Zollikon was extensive, and Jakob Hottinger's family also was large. It is impossible to unravel all the Hottinger family connections through the mists of time: the historical records are not complete enough to allow such precision. However, we can piece together the facts that Margret Hottinger had a brother Jakob, named after their father, that she had a younger brother named Felix, that she had several more brothers and sisters who remain unnamed in the record, and that her paternal uncle Klaus Hottinger shared an interest in religious matters and an uncommon zeal for reform. In addition, there was an extended clan of Hottingers in and around Zollikon and Zurich, many of whom became involved in one way or another in the Anabaptist movement. The index to the Anabaptist court records for Zurich identify thirty-one different Hottinger individuals, with several more named but impossible to identify precisely. Whether some or all of these were directly related to the Jakob Hottinger clan, it is no longer possible to know.

The first Anabaptist congregation was established in the village of Zollikon, just three kilometres from Zurich, shortly after the first baptisms had taken place in Zurich in the home of Felix Mantz's mother, near the cathedral.[1] While all of those involved in the first stage of the Zollikon congregation were men, very soon women joined the movement in large numbers. Margret Hottinger testified that "when Grebel and Mantz had come to them in Zollikon and read to them and spoken to them about these things, no one had yet been baptized, until Blaurock came; he was the first to begin baptizing."[2] George Blaurock was a charismatic, fiery leader who based his baptizing ministry on a direct call from God. When he interrupted a public sermon in the Zollikon church in late January 1525, he informed the preacher that he, Blaurock, had properly been sent to preach [by God], and not the preacher appointed by Zurich.[3] In the early phases of the movement in Switzerland, direct calling from God and individual proclamation and action were the rule, not the exception.

The Zurich authorities initially attempted to defuse the Anabaptist movement by means of arrests and fines. In April of 1525, the Zurich authorities sent an official to Zollikon to collect fines from those who had been rebaptized. He reported that he had encountered a group of very angry and stubborn women. The wife of the local overseer had been rebaptized, but she refused to pay her fine, saying that she would wait until the others had paid. While she was refusing to pay, an older woman standing nearby joined the discussion: "If I," she said, "were involved in this thing like the others, then we women would stick together and we would see if we had to pay the fine or not." She continued for some time to give the official a tongue-lashing "with many nasty words," as he said. The wives of Wishans Hottinger and Jacob Unholtz "spoke evil and shameful words" to the official, "as if milords were doing them an injustice; they also refused to answer whether they intended to pay their fines or not." After some resistance, Regula Lochman finally did give something as security on her fine, but Elsy Lochman refused to pay. So did Elsy Boumgartner, who was noted to add a common peasant reproach that "God created the earth for her as much as for milords."[4]

Although many women were actively involved in the early Anabaptism of Zollikon, there is no evidence that these women took on official leadership roles within the congregation. Leadership in baptizing, and in presiding over the Lord's Supper was exercised by men in all the recorded testimonies. Nevertheless, it is safe to say that the Anabaptist women of Zollikon were actively involved in informal proselytization for the movement; they were not reticent in expressing their views.

Margret Hottinger stood out among the Anabaptist women of Zollikon because of her zeal and determination; she appears to have exercised some prophetic gifts as well.[5] She came by her reforming sentiments honestly enough; in her family, reforming ideas could not be avoided. On June 23, 1523, we first encounter her father, Jakob Hottinger the elder, in the historical record. Doctor Lorenz, preacher at the Gross Münster (the cathedral) in Zurich, came to the parish church in Zollikon and preached a sermon concerning Christ's passion. After the sermon an old man with a full beard came up to the good doctor of theology and with "sharp, hard and intolerable words" (as the court record says) maintained that Lorenz had lied to the congregation. The old bearded man–who was in fact Jakob Hottinger–clarified what he meant. Lorenz (maintaining Roman Catholic eucharistic doctrine) had preached that the sacrament of the altar, in the form of the bread, is the true God, the humanity, blood, and flesh. At this time, communicants in the Roman Catholic church were given only the host, and not the wine, on the understanding that the full body and blood of Christ were contained in the bread alone. "This," said Jakob, "is not true; and you should no longer lie from the chancel. We want you to tell the truth from the chancel." When Doctor Lorenz tried to prove that Christ's body was contained in the host (probably by explaining the doctrine of transubstantiation), Jakob answered, "We don't want philosophical proofs; you should demonstrate with the Gospel; for Christ took the bread, gave it to his disciples and said: take this, this is my body; after which he took the cup and said: take this, this is my blood." Jakob concluded by telling the priest that he had not received the sacrament that morning, and did not intend to do so until he found someone who would give him both the bread and the wine, as the biblical account stated. When Doctor Lorenz confessed that he was unsure on the point, Jakob answered "If you will not do it, then let me do it."[6] Evidently, Jakob Hottinger the elder did not stand in awe of the clergy.

This bit of surviving testimony gives us valuable information about the familial atmosphere in which Margret grew up. Although her father was a simple peasant, we know from later evidence that Jakob was literate, for he functioned as a reader of scripture in Anabaptist meetings in Zollikon, and wrote twice to the Zurich authorities in a very clear and distinctive hand.[7] Thus, although the record does not tell us when, where, or with whom Jakob began studying scripture, his ability to read German put the vernacular New Testament within his reach. Jakob Hottinger's readiness in 1523 to argue with a doctor of theology concerning the Lord's Supper was not simply the cheekiness of an upstart peasant, but was a demonstration of biblical literacy. Jakob, like his brother Klaus, was putting into practice the Reformation principles of scripture alone and the priesthood of all believers. His ability to read the "clear Word of God" had placed him on an equal footing with the learned doctors, who now were called to account before the bar of scripture.

From this one little window in the historical record, we get a glimpse of the Hottinger household in the early 1520s, at the height of the general reforming enthusiasm. The atmosphere in the Hottinger home during these years must have been electric, with Bible reading and discussion forming the energetic centre around which daily life and labour continued. Furthermore, a strong anticlerical current is palpable, along with a corresponding conviction that before God and the truth of God's Word, social and economic rank are of no account.

Margret's father, as we might expect, was soon in trouble again. It seems that Jakob had a peasant's sense of humour, for he is credited with telling an earthy anticlerical joke which (judging from the number of people who reported it to the authorities) quickly made the rounds in the parish. For those who may be scandalized by Jakob's humour, we must remember that Jakob was a peasant living in a time when natural biological functions were not delicately hidden away. In any case, one Sunday morning, a few months after he had been called before the Zurich authorities, Jakob waited until the local preacher had finished the mass, and then he stood in the church and asked his neighbours to wait because he had something to say to them. When his neighbours had gathered around him, Jakob said that a woman had come to him and recounted a rumour that Jakob had said he would rather see a cow defecate than take the mass. Had he said that? Jakob clarified that in fact he had not (he testified later that his brother Klaus had said it), but that he would say it now–and he proceeded to repeat the entire thing in the church. His point was, he said, that "up to now people have been defecated upon and deceived with the mass." He said he could prove this with scripture, but he said that the pastors were the ones who ought to be preaching the Gospel.[8]

This was not the only earthy, anticlerical statement that witnesses reported hearing from Jakob and Klaus–all their remarks were visually striking, and highly insulting to the clergy–but there is no need to go into further detail here.[9] Suffice it to say that the authorities in Zurich were not amused: Jakob was thrown into prison and was released only after he had sworn an oath of obedience and paid a hefty fine of one hundred gulden. These events occurred in October of 1523, but Zurich's legal action was not enough to restrain Jakob; in February of the next year, the court record tells us, he had to be given a rebuke and received another fine for repeating one of his witticisms concerning the mass and the priests who administered it.[10]

Margret's uncle, Klaus Hottinger, lived in Zurich and practised the trade of salt seller; later he appears to have joined the shoemakers' guild.[11] He was an early partisan supporter of Zwingli's reforms, and a close friend and confederate of Conrad Grebel. After being banished from Zurich in November 1523 for destroying a public crucifix, he was arrested and martyred in March 1524, in Catholic Lucerne. Heinrich Bullinger lauded Klaus Hottinger as the first martyr of the evangelical faith in Switzerland.[12]

Klaus's brother Jakob, Margret's father, also was involved in the early days of reforming agitation, with at least two documented cases of public argumentation with clergy.[13] Jakob was also close to Conrad Grebel, and it was no surprise when he was in the first group to be arrested for Anabaptism in Zollikon. Jakob functioned as one of the leaders of the

Zollikon Anabaptist group; two of his sons were baptized before February 1525 and Margret received baptism shortly after, as well.[14]

In November 1525, Margret Hottinger was arrested for Anabaptism as part of a further crackdown by the Zurich authorities. The list of prisoners sentenced on November 18 reads like an early Anabaptist "who's who": Conrad Grebel, Felix Mantz, George Blaurock, Michael Sattler, Ulrich Teck, Martin Linck, and Margret Hottinger. The official records note the following remark concerning Margret specifically: "it is our decision that she be spoken to, and asked whether or not she will persist in rebaptism and the teaching of Grebel, Mantz, etc. And if she persists, she should be placed in the Wellenberg."[15]

Michael Sattler and Martin Linck, later both notable Anabaptist leaders, demonstrated at this time much less determination than did Margret: they swore oaths that they would desist from rebaptism, and were released from prison. Margret, on the other hand, refused to recant and was imprisoned in the tower along with the rest of the "stubborn ones." Her testimony before the court was recorded as follows:

> Margret Hottinger has said that she holds infant baptism to be incorrect and rebaptism to be right. Likewise she asked milords that they prove infant baptism to her; if they can prove to her that infant baptism is correct, then she will desist. On the matter of her not attending church [she said that the reason was] that she had been slandered from the chancel; also that Kienast and her father were not responsible for her not going to church.[16]

Margret was still in prison in March of the next year; when questioned and urged to recant, her testimony was even stronger. The court scribe wrote that "Margret Hottinger . . . will stay with her baptism, which she holds to be right and good; whoever is baptised will be saved, and whoever does not believe in it and opposes it, such a one is a child of the devil."[17]

The following day the court pronounced sentence on a large group of recalcitrant Anabaptists. The women sentenced were Margret Hottinger, Elsbeth Hottinger of the neighbouring village of Hirslanden (probably a relative of Margret's), and Winbrat Fanwiler of St. Gall. In her testimony, it is noted, Winbrat argued that "What God, her heavenly Father, has not planted must be rooted out and burned in the eternal fire. And since one can find no word in the scriptures that one ought to baptize infants, therefore infant baptism is not right and the baptism she accepted is right, for God used [adult baptism] and ordered it to be used."[18] The court wanted a different answer from the prisoners. The collective sentence against them specified that the prisoners were

> to be placed together in the New Tower and are to be given nothing more than bread and water to eat, and straw to lay upon. And the guard who watches them must swear an oath not to allow anyone in or out. Thus let them die in the tower. Let it be so until one is willing to desist from opinion and error and be obedient. . . . The women and daughters are to be treated in the same way, and placed together, and in all things to be treated as stated above.[19]

While Margret and others wasted away in prison, the Zurich authorities continued their arrests and questioning. The testimonies of four more women are recorded: Anna Mantz, Anna Widerker, Dorothea "the furrier's wife," and Regula Gletzli. In reply to questioning about Anabaptist activities, Anna Mantz's testimony illustrates why women had relatively more freedom to proselytize than did the men. The authorities wanted to know about the male leaders, but Anna denied that any male Anabaptist leaders had been in her house. The only "strangers" who had been with her were "just some women."[20] The authorities evidently did not follow this up, not being interested in "just some women." It was their mistake. From evidence elsewhere we know that these apparently innocent women's gatherings were actually subversive conventicles, and formed the hidden backbone of the movement (see the collective profile of Anabaptist women in Augsburg found in this volume, for example).

Finally, after six months of harsh imprisonment, Margret, along with a group of other Anabaptists, agreed to a recantation written by a court official. It read:

> Margret Hottinger confesses that she erred; she holds infant baptism to be correct and rebaptism to be useless and incorrect. She asks milords that they be merciful to her and do the best; she wishes to be obedient to them from now on. The judgement was read to her, and she accepted it. Done this first day of May, 1526.[21]

In spite of this recantation, Margret Hottinger was not yet done with rebaptism, nor did she display much obedience to the authorities in her subsequent activity.

Sometime later in 1526, Margret travelled to the nearby city of St. Gall, in the company of her brother Jakob Hottinger the younger. Johannes Kessler of St. Gall described Margret in a remarkable, if hostile, vignette in his chronicle, the *Sabbata*.

There arose wild and arrogant error through the women of the Anabaptists, particularly one young woman from Zollikon in the canton of Zurich named Margret Hottinger . . . who lived a disciplined way of life, so that she was deeply loved and respected by the Anabaptists. She went so far as to claim that she was God. And many other Anabaptists believed this and defended it against opponents, protecting and sustaining it with the words of Christ, 'Have you not read in the law, you are gods, etc.' [John 10:34]. And also: 'Whoever keeps my commandments abides in me and I in him, etc.' [John 15:10]. Moreover, this Margret forgave and absolved the sins of those praying and would say nothing about it nor give further judgment, but abide by the words. Following that she undertook to speak of things that nobody could understand, as if she were so deeply raised up in God that nobody could comprehend her speech, and then began to say, 'Is it not written, cursed is he who is hung upon a cross?' [Galatians 3:13]. But still [she] would say nothing further to anyone. She lived an austere life and overcame many obstacles, so that many of her followers declared that whoever speaks the most or can do the unusual which nobody can comprehend or evaluate, those were held to be the most devout and most immersed in God.[22]

One must allow for undeniable hostility and exaggeration on Kessler's part (it is highly doubtful, for example, that Margret claimed to be God), but the picture emerges of a charismatic and prophetic young woman who exercised considerable influence among the early Swiss Anabaptists. Kessler reported further on other prophetic activities and pneumatic manifestations on the part of Anabaptist women in St. Gall in 1526, which he linked to Margret Hottinger. Unfortunately our only source for these stories is Kessler, so we cannot be entirely certain of the details.[23] Magdalena Müller of St. Gall, Kessler claimed, said that she was Christ, and she drew in two other women, namely Barbara Mürglen and Frena Buman (also identified as Frena Guldin). Frena Buman, said Kessler, claimed to have heard a heavenly voice that penetrated her heart. She was convicted of sin, and called on the others to repent and leave aside useless things "so that we not grieve the Holy Spirit."[24] At this point Winbrat Fanwiler of St. Gall, who had shared a prison cell with Margret in Zurich in 1525, changed her name to "Martha" and joined the other women. They preached publicly that those who wished to follow the Lord should come, and Kessler reports that a weaver named Lienhardt Wirt was convinced by their words, left his work, and accompanied them.[25] Kessler says that they gathered in a house in the village of Buch.

Those assembled in the house at Buch proceeded to confess their sins to one another, but subsequent events, if we may judge from Kessler and the official records of arrest and exile, degenerated quickly from charismatic calls for repentance to bizarre forms of behaviour. Frena, who seems to have been the prophetic leader, may well have lost touch with reality. Kessler claims that she said things such as "I must give birth to the Antichrist," and he also reports that Frena did some prophesying in the nude; charges of sexual impropriety reported by Kessler are substantiated in the official records of the city.[26] Without a doubt Frena's prophetic activity took the group around her well beyond repentance for sin, adult baptism, and a "new life." Under the influence of her ecstatic utterance, it appears that normal rules of conduct were suspended.

The story of the charismatic women prophets of St. Gall is not one that can be called an edifying example; they stepped beyond the bounds of the normal under what they considered to be the guidance of the Holy Spirit, and entered fearlessly into a realm where only "spiritually revealed" rules of conduct applied. Other men and women in the Anabaptist movement would also follow the prophetic path subsequently, although not necessarily with such scandalous results. The story of these inspired, charismatic Swiss Anabaptist women is important, however, for it makes clear that in the first two years of the Anabaptist movement in Switzerland, appeals to the Holy Spirit as the basis for teaching authority, as well as pneumatic manifestations among Anabaptist women, were not uncommon.[27] Such anointed women as Margret Hottinger, Winbrat Fanwiler, Magdalena Müller, Barbara Mürglen, and Frena Buman did not wait to be appointed prophets by a church community or a male authority: they had been called directly by God, and they acted with uncharacteristic freedom as a result.

The Schleitheim Articles of 1527 mark a turning point in Swiss Anabaptism. The preface notes that "A very great offence has been introduced by some false brothers among us, whereby several have turned away from the faith, thinking to practice and observe the freedom of the Spirit and of Christ."[28] In light of events in St. Gall in 1526, these words probably were directed in part against pneumatic manifestations of the kind Kessler described. Among other things, the Schleitheim Articles now prescribed how leadership among the Swiss congregations was to be structured: the "shepherd" of the church must be a morally upright person (1 Timothy 3:7); the shepherd will preside in the congregation in reading, exhortation, teaching, warning, admonishing, in prayer and the Lord's Supper.

Clearly there was no thought of electing a woman to such a position: "He shall be supported . . . by the congregation which has chosen him," say the Schleitheim Articles.[29] There is further evidence that corroborates this early exclusion of women from official leadership posts in the Swiss congregations following Schleitheim. At his trial in December 1529, Konrad

Winckler (who had baptized a large number of women into the movement) testified that "it was forbidden for women to teach and to baptize."[30] And of course, there is no mention of "prophecy" nor any place given in the Schleitheim Articles to ecstatic utterance. It appears that, by 1527, the charismatic leadership of women such as Margret Hottinger was marginalized, if not negated completely, in Swiss Anabaptism.

Although the movement from pneumatic enthusiasm to the congregational election of male leaders took place among the Swiss in only two years (1525-27), the same general pattern would be repeated over a longer span of time elsewhere in the Anabaptist movement, for the same basic reasons: direct spiritual revelations and pneumatic manifestations came under suspicion, and were replaced by the revelation of written scripture, interpreted by a male leadership. And as Anabaptist groups moved steadily away from spiritualism toward biblicism, the words of Paul came ever more into play. The diminished leadership role of women in Anabaptist congregations was thus roughly proportional to the victory of letter over spirit in Anabaptism.

Nevertheless, it would be a mistake to overstate the inequality of the patriarchal congregational polity outlined at Schleitheim. In spite of the exclusively male leadership delineated by the Schleitheim Articles, women were granted considerable disciplinary authority as members of the congregation. According to Schleitheim, the congregation was to have the final say over the pastor. Pastors were subject to discipline by the congregation, and women participated in that process. There are, as well, numerous individual cases of informal female "leadership" that continue among the Swiss Brethren, particularly instances of active proselytization. A few of these cases will be noted in subsequent profiles. And finally, there was banishment, imprisonment, torture, and martyrdom for Anabaptist men and women alike–the ultimate tests of an individual's commitment to Christ. The final choice of sacrificing one's life was one in which women and men were equally free.

Unfortunately there is no documentation that records Margret Hottinger's activities for the years 1527 to 1530. The Zurich authorities had succeeded in repressing the Anabaptist movement in her home village of Zollikon by 1527, and much the same had happened in St. Gall. The Zollikon Anabaptists who retained their Anabaptist convictions did so secretly. That several did manage to hide their Anabaptist beliefs successfully we know from later events; Margret, her father Jakob, and her brother Felix were three who did so. In the year 1530, Jakob Hottinger the elder, Margret, Felix, and a group of other Anabaptists decided to flee to Moravia, where there was religious freedom as well as flourishing Anabaptist congregations. Unfortunately they were arrested on the way, just north of Ravensburg. Margret Hottinger and her father paid with their lives for their convictions:

Margret was drowned as an Anabaptist; her father, Jakob, was beheaded.[31] According to one account

> She was graciously pulled out of the water and asked again to recant, but in no way did she wish to do that. Rather she said: "Why did you pull me out? The flesh was almost defeated." With that the judgement was carried out [i.e., she was drowned].[32]

The call of the Spirit was heard by Swiss Anabaptist men and women alike and led them individually to commit their lives to Christ and the "Body of Christ on earth." This individual call of the Spirit may have been dampened, but it was not extinguished by the emergence of Swiss Anabaptist congregational polity.

Notes

1. The best account is found in Fritz Blanke, original edition, *Brüder in Christo* (Zurich: Zwingli Press, 1955); English translation, *Brothers in Christ*, trans. Joseph Nordenhang (Scottdale, PA: Herald Press, 1961).
2. QGTS, vol. 1, document 124, p. 126.
3. QGTS, vol. 1, document 29, p. 39.
4. QGTS, vol. 1, document 69, pp. 76-77.
5. A. Nüesch and H. Bruppacher, *Das alte Zollikon* (Zurich, 1899), 72, correctly identify Margret as the daughter of Jakob Hottinger the elder of Zollikon; Klaus Hottinger of Zurich was therefore her uncle. In 1526 she travelled to St. Gall with her brother, Jakob Hottinger the younger, of Zollikon. Leland Harder, ed., *The Sources of Swiss Anabaptism* (Scottdale, PA: Herald Press, 1985), 548, confuses Jakob Hottinger the elder with Jakob the younger, coming to the mistaken conclusion that Margret Hottinger was the sister of Jakob Hottinger the elder and of Klaus Hottinger.
6. Emil Egli, *Actensammulng zur Geschichte der Zürcher Reformation in den Jahren 1519-1533* (Zurich, 1879; reprint Nieuwkoop: B. de Graaf, 1973), document 369, pp. 133-34.
7. Hans Bichter identified the primary "readers" in Zollikon as Jakob Hottinger the elder, Rutsch Hottinger, the tailor *Ockenfuss*, and "all who knew how to read." QGTS, vol. 1, document 56, (Mar. 16-25, 1525), pp. 64, 66. Jakob Hottinger's two extant letters are found in STAZ, EI, 7.2, nrs. 44 and 45; printed in QGTS, vol. 1, documents 103, 113.
8. Egli, *Actemsammlung*, document 438, p. 176. Other witnesses say that Hottinger was even more impolite, saying to Niklaus: "Hey you, preacher! When is it enough of this rascal life and dissolute work and idolatry?" Ibid.
9. One of Jakob's graphic sayings was "when a priest goes up to the altar to pray (in the Mass), it means as much to me as when a peasant goes behind the bushes to relieve himself." Egli, *Actensammlung*, document 438, p. 176.
10. Ibid., document 495, p. 216 (February 6, 1524).
11. Thomas Schärli, "Die bewegten letzten zwei Jahre im Leben des Niklaus Hottinger, Schuhmacher, von Zollikon, enthauptet zu Luzern 1524," in Emil Walder, et al., eds., *Zolliker Jahrheft 1984*, (Zollikon: Baumann, 1984), 28. Bullinger called Klaus a "shoemaker," and praised him as a "wolbeläßner und der religion wol berichter redlicher man." J.J. Hottinger and H.H. Vögeli, eds., *Heinrich Bullingers Reformationsgeschichte*,

3 vols. (Frauenfeld: Ch. Bepel, 1838-1840), vol. I, 127.
12 See Bullinger, *Reformationsgeschichte*, I, 149-51.
13 In June 1523, Jakob confronted Dr. Lorenz in the Zollikon parish church, as has been noted. On Jakob's public dispute with Kaspar Grossmann in January 1525, see QGTS, vol. 1, document 23, p. 33; translation in Harder, *Sources*, 331-32.
14 See QGTS, vol. 1, documents 30, 31, pp. 39-41.
15 QGTS, vol. 1, document 133, p. 136.
16 QGTS, vol. 1, document 134, p. 137.
17 QGTS, vol. 1, document 170, p. 177. Testimony of March 5, 1526.
18 Ibid.
19 QGTS, vol. 1, document 170a, p. 178.
20 QGTS, vol. 1, document 170b, p. 179.
21 QGTS, vol. 1, document 173, p. 183.
22 See selection of Kessler's *Sabbata* in QGTS, vol. 2, p. 618. Translation from Harder, *Sources*, 548, with minor changes.
23 See QGTS, vol. 2, pp. 618-22. Kessler's apologetic intent and hostility is clear in his *Sabbata*; it is a source that must be used with care. Nevertheless, he cannot on that account be discredited completely as a historical source, as John Horsch attempted to do. See "An Inquiry into the Truth of Accusations of Fanaticism and Crime Against the Early Swiss Brethren," MQR 8 (Jan. 1934): 18-31.
24 See QGTS, vol. 2, pp. 618-19.
25 Lienhardt later married Frena Buman. QGTS, vol. 2, p. 619, n. 135.
26 One Bartlomee Schömpperlin was exiled from St. Gall for a year and a day for "unseemly and unchristian actions" he took with Frena Guldin on April 10, 1526. QGTS, vol. 2, document 499, p. 419. See ibid., documents 492, 493, 498, 500 for more documentation from the official city records.
27 Cf. the case of Agnes Linck of Biel, above.
28 John H. Yoder, *The Legacy of Michael Sattler* (Scottdale, PA: Herald Press, 1973), 35.
29 Yoder, *Legacy*, 38-39.
30 "es sige och den wybern zu leren und zu touffen verbotten." QGTS, vol. 1, p. 313. See Arnold Snyder, "Konrad Winckler: An Early Swiss Anabaptist Missionary, Pastor and Martyr," MQR 64 (Oct. 1990).
31 In QGTS, vol. 2, pp. 578-80, Johannes Rütiner reports on a conversation (in 1537) with Felix Hottinger, in which Felix describes the death of his father (Jakob) and sister (Margret). In QGTS, vol. 2, pp. 586-87, Fridolin Sicher recounts the execution at Waldsee in 1530.
32 QGTS, vol. 2, p. 587.

ELSBETH THEILLER OF HORGEN

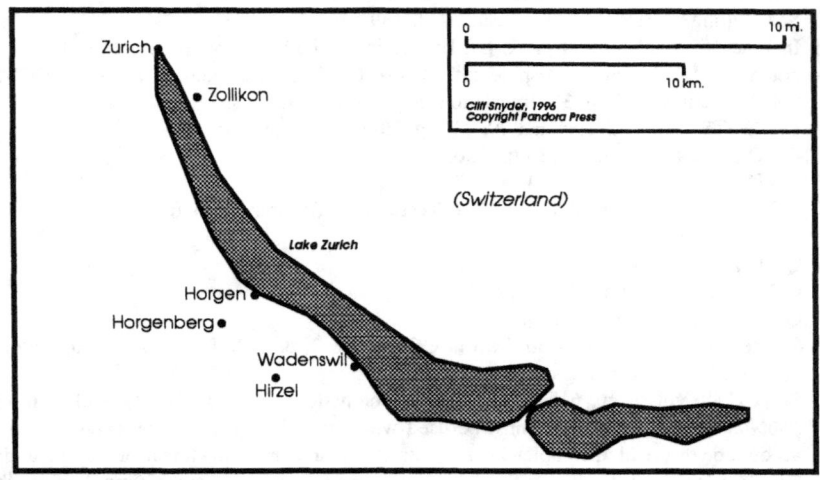

It is a well-known and often-repeated fact that the Zurich authorities were successful in suppressing the Anabaptist movement by the 1530s. A prime example is the village of Zollikon, where Anabaptism had flourished in 1525 as a mass movement among the common people, but had vanished, leaving barely a trace, by 1535. It is less often observed that Anabaptism managed to survive in stubborn pockets of resistance, sometimes in places geographically very near to Zurich, for more than a century after the first baptisms. The fact was that after the suppression of public Anabaptism and the defeat of Reformed forces at the second Kappel war, Zurich's attention was directed more to matters of external politics than to internal questions. Furthermore, Zurich's jurisdiction and power of enforcement was not uniform, and in places where the population was scattered on isolated farms, the local bailiffs appointed by Zurich had limited policing power. Often these local bailiffs had little desire to antagonize the peasant population, who generally were more sympathetically disposed towards their Anabaptist neighbours than to the Zurich authorities. The truly systematic elimination of Anabaptism in Zurich's territories was completed only after the end of the Thirty Years' War, in the late 1630s and 1640s.[1]

Because Anabaptism was illegal, its activities were carried out in underground fashion–sometimes literally so. Near Baretswil in the canton of Zurich one may still visit a large cave in which Anabaptists met for clandestine worship. As a result of this hidden existence, the sources documenting Swiss Anabaptism in this period are rather sparse. We only receive notice of Anabaptist activity when a local bailiff was urged to action by written complaints from the local pastor to the Zurich authorities. These bailiffs would then gather evidence and make some arrests, but with few exceptions the letter of the law was overlooked as a matter of course.

One pocket of resistance to Zurich's religious policies was the town of Horgen, on the western shore of Lake Zurich, along with the neighbouring villages of Horgenberg and Hirzel, located on the mountain slopes above Horgen. As late as the 1640s, the Zurich authorities were still arresting Anabaptists in this area and confiscating their property, as the appendix in the Swiss Brethren hymnal, the *Ausbund*, relates.[2] There is continuing but sporadic documentation of Anabaptist activity in the Horgen/Horgenberg/Hirzel area throughout the sixteenth century. Around 1555, Hanns Slecker of Stendiswil was arrested; he eventually identified some Anabaptists from Horgenberg.[3] We know little more about Anabaptists in that area, but we know that the movement continued from the record of a later arrest, dated tentatively around 1570. It is this document that tells of the arrest of Elsbeth Theiller, and preserves her testimony.[4]

The document informs us that Elsbeth Theiller of Horgen was an Anabaptist, married to Hans Suter of Horgenberg. She was arrested and questioned by the authorities, and gave her testimony in response. At the end of this initial questioning she refused to recant or to give the names of others in the Anabaptist fellowship. As a result, she was to be placed in the Kratz Turm [Kratz tower] "until she gives a more satisfactory answer."

The record does not say how long she remained in prison. But at some later date (for this second notice appears written in another hand, on another sheet of paper), she offered her recantation and also named some Anabaptist co-participants.

Her recantation needs to be put into perspective. First, Elsbeth's initial refusal to name names undoubtedly bought time for those whom she would name eventually, and allowed them to flee until the situation had calmed down. Second, the cases are too numerous to mention of Anabaptists "going back" on coerced oaths of obedience and agreements to attend the state church. Time and again we read testimony from rearrested Anabaptists that God had called them back again to their communities, and therefore (in obedience to God) they had to go against their coerced oaths. Therefore it is not fair to assume that Elsbeth ended all contact with the Anabaptists upon her release. In fact, one would suspect just the opposite. Finally, prison conditions in the sixteenth century would qualify today as cruel and inhumane. Prison cells typically were cramped, dark, unheated holes, often only with some straw on which to lie and only bread and water for nourishment. That people recanted rather than live out their days in such conditions is not surprising; more surprising is the fact that so many withstood such conditions at all, let alone for years at a time.

Unfortunately, we know no more about the life of Elsbeth Theiller of Horgen beyond what has been sketched above. Nevertheless, because of her arrest, her initial refusal to recant, and her willingness to suffer further imprisonment, Elsbeth did leave us the legacy of her testimony. We translate that testimony here, and allow it to speak for itself. It is typical of very many court records documenting the participation of women in Anabaptism in that it offers a glimpse, however brief, of the reasons behind her commitment to the movement. One would wish to know more about these witnesses, but knowing this much, at least, allows us to glimpse something of their lives and beliefs. The testimony is written in the third person, from the point of view of the hostile scribe; we retain that form in the translation.

Testimony of Elsbetha Theiller, the Anabaptist, wife of Hans Suter of Horgenberg.[5]

[The authorities] asked Elsbeth to give her reasons for refusing to attend church and the Christian [Reformed Church] meetings, and tried to bring her back again to the true way and obedience through many and repeated proofs from Holy Scripture. But indeed she persisted throughout in her false opinion, and she refused to name names.

Some years ago, after she had zealously attended [the Reformed] church, God had spoken to her heart, [and said] that if she did not accept another way of being and living, and she did not better herself, she would never be able to come to true holiness and salvation. There were very many attending the [Reformed] church in Horgen who were not repentant at all, but rather followed every kind of madness. And since it could be seen that they persisted in their sinful lives in spite of all warning, punishment and admonition, for these reasons she justly left this church and assembly. She went to a few persons who lived blameless and God-pleasing lives, and from whom she saw nothing but all virtue and honour. Nevertheless she was instructed by no one to leave the [Reformed] church, nor did she persuade anyone to leave it, and she was willing to be obedient to the authorities in all those things which were not contrary to God's will. She asked Milords that they treat her mercifully.

And although she was earnestly entreated to give the names of the leaders, preachers and also the meeting places of her sect, nevertheless she answered that she was not able to do that at this time. It pained her to know that such [named] persons would also be arrested, and because of her would have to expect the same cross that she herself was experiencing.

[Written on the back]: She is to be placed in the Kratz Tower until she gives a more satisfactory answer.

[On another sheet of paper, in another hand]: Elsbeth Theiller of Horgen will go to church at Horgen or at Hirzel, where the [Reformed] preachers preach, and will no longer go to those places around here where the Anabaptists preach, and will no longer follow or belong to the Anabaptists, but rather will entirely renounce the Anabaptist sect.

Item, Rudolf Üsöllring, called Herzog Kramer, is one who preaches [in the Anabaptist meetings]. Caspar Landertz's two sons also belong to the Anabaptists. Item, Klachtharen is also a pious man who belongs to them. Merni Hess of Wädiswil, the son, also belongs to the Anabaptist sect. There are many more who go to them and are Anabaptists, but she did not know them, nor what their names were. She asks Milords for grace and release from prison.

[On the back; different ink]: This Theiller woman has promised to go to preaching and to be obedient in all things. She is to be released from prison after paying the costs [of her imprisonment].

Notes

1 See Cornelius Bergman, *Die Täuferbewegung im Kanton Zurich bis 1660* (Leipzig: H. Nachfolger, 1916), passim.
2 The *Wahrhaftiger Bericht von den Brüdern im Schweitzerland* ["True Report from the Brothers in Switzerland"] is found in the *Ausbund, Das ist: Etliche schöne Christliche Lieder* . . . , (Many editions since 1583. I used an edition published in Elkhart, IN: Mennonitischen Verlagshandlung, 1880), 1-52 of the second appendix.
3 In this testimony, Hanns Slecker names eight persons involved in Anabaptism in and around Horgen, of whom two were women. STAZ, signature EI 7.2, document 97.
4 STAZ, signature EI 7.2, document 119.
5 Ibid.

ANNA SCHARNSCHLAGER
OF HOPFGARTEN, TIROL

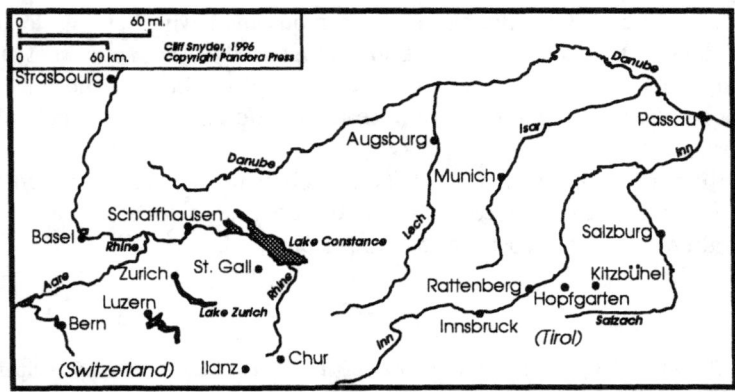

The year was 1530. It was a situation made for panic and would have paralysed a weaker person. But not Anna Scharnschlager. She dealt with it deliberately and with an eye to the future.

She and her husband Leupold were forced to leave the home where they had lived for over twenty years, and the beautiful town of Hopfgarten near Kitzbühel in Tirol, where she had lived even longer.[1] The future was entirely uncertain.

It was a new and strange experience for Anna Scharnschlager. She was by then at least forty years old, an aging woman according to the life expectancy of the time. Until now it had been a good, comfortable, and secure life. Her parents, Konrad Honigler and Margaret Rieper, had been well-to-do citizens of Hall, near Innsbruck. Johannes Rieper, her maternal uncle, was Dean and Provost of the cathedral in Brixen (Bressanone).[2] What would the Dean, that traditional churchman, think of their sudden departure? And what about her brother and sisters. Would her parents ever have dreamed that such a thing could happen to their daughter? Perhaps it was just as well that they were dead and did not have to experience what might for them have been a great shame and sorrow. Anna loved and was loved by her family.[3] The grief of having to leave was tempered by that secure love and so she was able to do calmly and carefully what now had to be done. Ursula, already twenty years old but still at home, helped her mother pack.[4]

The Scharnschlagers were leaving their sumptuous home and secure life because they had become Anabaptists.[5] Anna's husband, Leupold, had come from Rattenberg, a small town on the Inn River about twenty-five kilometres west of Hopfgarten. The new teaching, considered by the church authorities to be dangerously subversive, had come to Rattenberg two years earlier. Its most famous convert was Pilgram Marpeck, a prominent citizen, civil servant, and mining engineer. Perhaps it was Marpeck who had persuaded Leupold Scharnschlager to join the fledgling movement that was committed to a thorough reform of the church in living as well as in theology. That Anna also decided to join may be regarded as certain, for she was much too self-confident and independent a person to have simply followed her husband into such a dangerous and insecure future. But she was a private person; her few letters reveal nothing about her personal convictions. They left their home, she explained to her brother in a letter five years later, because her husband was threatened with persecution, torture, and coercion in his faith.[6] His choices were staying and becoming untrue to his conscience, the prospect of death for his faith (between 1528 and 1542, 139 Anabaptists were executed in Rattenberg and Kitzbühel), or exile. They chose exile, and there can be little doubt that it was a joint decision.

Sometime before their departure they had paid a visit to Anna's sister and her husband, Veronica and Hans Steger, in Kitzbühel. Hans Steger was a lawyer, and the purpose of the visit was to dispose of the Scharnschlager estate. Steger himself bought it, and the documents of the sale were drawn up and notarized.[7] Anna made the sale.[8] The proceeds were to sustain the Scharnschlagers through sixteen years of refugee existence. Anna also committed to Veronica a trunk of personal belongings. There was some jewellry, several heirlooms, and a number of items of clothing with a total value of seventy-seven guilders, a considerable sum in those days when a carpenter's annual income was under two hundred guilders. She specified that some of the items were to be sold. Included also were gifts for Veronica and her daughter Regina. It was agreed that Veronica would keep the trunk and its contents until Anna should need them.[9]

That having been arranged, the Scharnschlagers left for the distant city of Strasbourg, perhaps by invitation of their friend Pilgram Marpeck, who had gone there a year earlier. They found a house in the *Stadelgasse* and Anna set about to restore what normalcy was possible. Although they had financial resources, Leupold took up soap-making to provide for the family.[10] It quickly became evident that their residence in Strasbourg could also be temporary. Early in 1532 Marpeck was compelled by the city government to leave Strasbourg, even though the city could scarce afford the loss of its civil engineer. But he had become too dangerous an opponent to the public policy of the Reformer, Martin Bucer. Anna's husband took over responsibility as leader and teacher of the Marpeck group of Anabaptists in the Strasbourg area. Early in 1531 whatever remained of the Scharnschlager estate in Hopfgarten, mostly furniture and other movables, was confiscated by the authorities. The earlier sale of the estate by Anna was confirmed as legal and could not be touched.[11]

Despite expulsions of people like Marpeck, there was always a measure of religious toleration in Strasbourg and so, for the time being, Anna was able to breathe more easily. Her concern for Ursula's future was allayed in part when a young man named Hans Felix, a member of the Anabaptist fellowship in Strasbourg, asked for her hand. They were married in 1533. Hans was a clockmaker and locksmith, and so was also known as Uhrmacher. He was able to provide for a family. The next year Ursula and her husband left for Moravia, where they settled.[12] They kept in regular contact with Anna and Leupold by letter.

A year later Anna and her husband were expelled from Strasbourg as well.[13] Before they left in June 1534, Leupold made a moving and eloquent plea for religious toleration to the City Council.[14] It is not known where they went, but they may have sought the company of Marpeck who was at that time in St. Gall, where he was employed as an engineer. By this time Anna was becoming concerned about the property she had given her sister for safekeeping. She had written to her brother-in-law Hans Steger several times but had received no reply. She turned to her brother for help, requesting him to go and see Steger and ask him to keep her things until she needed them.[15] Any message from Steger was to be delivered to Pilgram Marpeck who would forward it to her. At least one reason for the silence was that in the meantime her sister Veronica had died and Steger had remarried. Moreover, it was a difficult time for reliable communications because the Scharnschlagers moved around a lot. It may also be that the earlier good relationships with this side of the family had not been able to surmount the religious divisions.

In October 1538 they received a letter from their son-in-law, Hans.[16] It brought news of the family, of extended, near-fatal illness as well as of a period of unemployment, and the promise of an early visit. The heartiness and warmth of the letter, and especially the loving reference to Anna herself, testifies to the strength and health of family relationships for which Anna must be given a good share of the credit.

Doubtless it was in response to a family health crisis that Anna copied out five medicinal recipes to reduce swelling. It is worth including them here as an illustration of how women dealt with bodily ailments.

    1. Leaves of elderberry boiled in salt water will relieve swelling in feet caused by infection. Relief instantaneous.

    2. Pigeon droppings and barley flour boiled in vinegar dispels all swelling. Apply as plaster hot or cold.

    3. Flax seed boiled in vinegar and put on the swelling as a plaster will reduce it.

    4. Elderberry juice, oil of balsam, and dog fat, mixed and applied often will totally reduce swelling.

    5. Chop pine cones finely and boil in wine. Spread on the swelling and keep moist. Will eliminate swelling.[17]

By 1546 the Scharnschlagers were settled in the town of Ilanz, in what is today the eastern part of Switzerland. Leupold had been appointed schoolmaster.[18] From then until their deaths they lived a quiet life there, free of persecution, with Leupold as head of the Anabaptist congregation. By this time he had become an elder and had responsibilities for far-flung and scattered Anabaptist congregations.

The family visit promised in 1538 seems to have occurred sometime after the Scharnschlagers had settled in Ilanz. On that occasion Hans repaired the village clock.[19] It must have been a joyful occasion for Anna who was probably often alone. She had not seen her daughter for at least twelve years and had never met her four grandchildren, two girls and two boys.

Apparently it was the return of stability, but perhaps also approaching old age with its concern for financial security, that prompted Anna to try once more to regain her property in Kitzbühel. In March 1546 she addressed a letter to her niece Regina, Veronica's daughter, whom she had located in Salzburg. She itemized in detail what she had left with Veronica, and stated that now she needed her things and desired to have them sent to her. That done, she wrote, she would send Regina a receipt so that everyone, including Ursula and her children, would know that the matter was settled. She also inquired about money owed her by Regina's father. At least thirty years earlier she had sold him a barrel of wine for sixty guilders. He had given her fifty, and she had, until that day, withheld a receipt until the other ten guilders were paid. She also asked whether her uncle, Johannes Rieper, was still alive or whether he had died. If he had died, she wanted to know whether his will included anything for her. Finally, she sent Leupold's greetings to Regina.[20]

The reply came quickly with the news that Regina knew nothing of the matter nor could she find out, now that both her parents were dead. But she assured Anna that a legal settlement of the debt would be made.[21] Presumably it was, since there is no further reference to it. As to the will of the deceased Dean of Brixen, Anna was informed that she would have to make inquiries at Brixen. Given the attitude toward Anabaptists in Brixen, Anna may not have pursued the matter any further.

Twenty years later, in 1563, she was still at it. She had attempted to recover a loan from a tanner in Chur. He replied that he hoped for patience since a shipment of his leather had gone down in Lake Zurich. He promised to come to Ilanz to settle the matter.[22]

It appears from this story that Anna conducted the financial affairs of the family, from the sale of their home in Hopfgarten to the collection of debts, with shrewd competence. The continuing concern about property may have been partly stimulated by real, if intermittent, need. It was a concern shared by her husband. About 1540 he drew up an order for the life of an Anabaptist congregation in which he pleaded that ministers in the churches should be financially supported by the congregation so that they would be free to do their work as God required them.[23] It is clear that Anna's assumption of responsibility for the family's business set Leupold free to do his work as an elder. All the evidence indicates that she was his faithful co-worker throughout their life together.

Leupold died in the spring of 1563. By this time Anna was well over seventy years of age and no longer in good health. In the two remaining years before her own death, she twice wrote to Ursula to come to Ilanz to look after her until her death. But sometime during those two years Ursula herself died; Anna never saw her daughter again. She died alone, with no family near her, early in 1565.

The momentum of Anna's business energy and ability seemed to carry on beyond her death. A local man went to court to get the Scharnschlager inheritance for his wife who, he claimed, was Anna's cousin. He turned out to be an imposter.[24] At considerable expense, local officials in Ilanz located the remaining members of the family, Anna's two grandsons, in Moravia. They eventually inherited what Anna had so carefully protected.[25]

Although there is not a single trace of evidence regarding Anna's own faith, we do know that she was a woman who made decisions about the direction of her life. The story strongly supports the view that by her own decision she took upon herself the tribulation of Christ that was the lot of those who, in the sixteenth century, dissented from the official religious orthodoxies.

Notes

1 Anna's story could well be included alongside those of other Tirolean Anabaptist women. We have chosen to include her story with those of Swiss Anabaptist women because she spent the final twenty years of her life living in Ilanz, Switzerland.
2 QGTS, vol. 2, p. 528.
3 This is evident from a letter she wrote to her brother. QGTS, vol. 2, pp. 511-13.
4 Ibid., p. 520.
5 Ibid., p. 511.
6 Ibid.
7 TA, Ost. II, p. 461.
8 QGTS, vol. 2, p. 523.
9 Ibid., pp. 518-20.
10 TA, Elsass, II, p. 343.
11 TA, Ost.II, p. 461.
12 QGTS, vol. 2, p. 512, especially note 11.
13 Ibid., p. 511, note 6.
14 See TA, Elsass II, pp. 346-53 for the text of this important statement. An English translation is found in William Klassen, "Leupold Scharnschlager's Farewell to the Strasbourg Council," MQR 42 (1968): 213-18.
15 QGTS, vol. 2, pp. 511-13.
16 Ibid., pp. 513-14.
17 Ibid., p. 523.

18 Ibid., p. 541.
19 Ibid.
20 Ibid., pp. 518-21.
21 Ibid., pp. 521-23.
22 Ibid., p. 528.
23 For an English translation see Donald F. Durnbaugh, ed., *Every Need Supplied* (Philadephia: Temple University Press, 1974), 48-52.
24 Ibid., pp. 530-32.
25 Ibid., pp. 532-41.

MARGARET HELLWART OF BEUTELSBACH

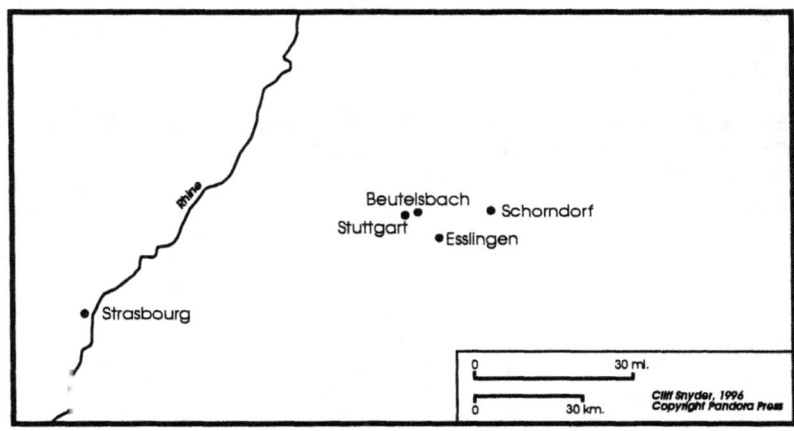

Margaret Hellwart was born about 1568 and lived a few kilometres east of Stuttgart, in the village of Beutelsbach, one of a number of villages whose administrative centre was Schorndorf. Her husband was Georg Hellwart. He was not an Anabaptist, but seems to have supported his wife. There is no record of children.

Margaret's story begins for us in the spring of 1608, when she was forty years old. The first entry about her, which appears in a report made by the Lutheran General Superintendent to the Synod, reveals that previously she had been warned numerous times to attend church and the Lord's Supper at the parish church, but that the warning was unsuccessful.[1]

Anabaptists had been in Beutelsbach and area in considerable numbers since at least 1555. In the 1560s the group in Beutelsbach was large enough to have its own leader [*Vorsteher*].[2] People were normally identified as Anabaptists if they did not attend Sunday worship or the Lord's Supper at the Lutheran village church. The Anabaptists repeatedly said over the years that there was no church discipline amongst the Lutherans, and that they could not take the bread and wine with unregenerate people. Some would, under pressure, attend the regular preaching services, but drew the line at the Lord's Supper. Anabaptists met for worship wherever they could. A wood near Esslingen, not far from Beutelsbach, was a common meeting place in 1602.[3]

Sometime before 1575 Swiss Brethren missionaries passed through, and a number of people must have been baptized, for there were considerable numbers of Anabaptists in the area.[4] It was perhaps this Anabaptist activity that prompted the Lutheran church authorities in Stuttgart to renew an ordinance from 1571 that provided for measures by which to control Anabaptism.[5] A significant section of this ordinance dealt with what to do with Anabaptist women.[6] It refers to a number of very energetic Anabaptist women, most of whose husbands were not Anabaptists. They had tried exiling the women, but that had caused much hardship for the families and involved a lot of public expense in looking after them. The authorities then devised the method of chaining the women to their houses. Thus they could prepare food and look after their children, but could not leave the house. The ongoing records suggest that the growth of the movement in the area around Beutelsbach was mainly the work of these women.

Margaret Hellwart was perhaps the most prominent of the Anabaptist women. In the spring of 1608 she was summoned to appear before the Consistory, a church court, to answer for her refusal to conform to Lutheran faith and practice.[7] Nothing was accomplished because she would not yield. A year later she was again interrogated, with the same negative result. Now the church authorities had become impatient, and had decided that, like many Anabaptist women in the area, she was to be chained, but that the pastor and a special visitor should continue attempts to convert her.[8]

The sentence was carried out and she was chained to the floor of her house. In fact this chaining was carried out no fewer than twenty-one times between the spring of 1610 and 1621. She seems to have been the original escape artist, because no sooner had the chain been put on her ankle and fastened to the floor, but she was free again.[9] The authorities suspected that her husband or others helped her, but they could never be sure who her accomplices were.[10] Once when she was supposedly chained, the church superintendent and the mayor called unannounced to check on her. Margaret did not immediately open the door, they reported later, but they could hear her put her chain back on.[11] She disregarded the order to receive no visitors in her house.[12] Apparently she was free most of the time, going about her work, visiting others in Beutelsbach and neighbouring villages, and attending Anabaptist meetings.[13] There she would report that she had been released from her confinement as Peter had in Acts chapter 12.[14] The authorities were especially worried that this determined woman would make more converts for Anabaptism. Sometime before spring 1616, she won over a neighbour, the widow Maria Niessmüller.[15] After that the two supported each other. Maria was also chained. Much to the frustration of the church authorities, these two women claimed in public that they could not be defeated because they had right on their side.[16] Margaret felt very sure of herself, because it was reported that during an interrogation in 1616 she listened, but had a mocking smile on her face. The authorities concluded that they could do nothing, and that the matter ought simply to be left to God.[17] Again and again other women came to Beutelsbach and the neighbouring villages to see Margaret Hellwart.[18] Some of them became Anabaptists.

Margaret Hellwart appears to have been unusually gifted with self-confidence. Perhaps it was part of her personality, but it was mainly her faith that enabled her to endure this long struggle to hold to and practise her confession. The church interrogators tried to correct her; she laughed at them. She did not, like many other Anabaptists in the area, leave for Moravia to escape the constant harassment. She stayed to face down her persecutors year after year. When once more she was summoned to appear before the church court in 1618, she said that she was now over fifty years old and past learning anything new. In any case, she said, she knew the true way that God had taught her and she desired to obey God rather than human authorities. She wanted to do good and avoid evil. There was no point in trying to convert her because she intended to remain an Anabaptist until the end of her life.[19] Three years later she finally asked them just to leave her alone. She would not, she said, live long in any case, so what was the problem?[20]

The Anabaptists of Beutelsbach were helped in their struggle by the Swiss Anabaptists, but especially by Menno Simons's *Foundation of Christian Doctrine*.[21] While there is no specific statement of beliefs from Margaret Hellwart, the confessions of others from the area reveal what she believed and had committed herself to. God had commanded that people should love one another. Anyone who lived as a Christian was by that fact alone a member of the church, said another woman when questioned. Maria Niessmüller said that the true church was in her heart and that she could hear the Word of God at home by having someone read it to her.[22] Gertrude Klein, who had been baptized by a Swiss Brethren leader, confessed that a Christian could not be a magistrate and punish with the sword. She rejected oaths and military service as unchristian. She could not accept infant baptism because only those who repent, have been taught, and believe should be baptized. She refused to attend the Lutheran church because there was no church discipline. She said that she would receive the bread and wine with other Anabaptists, but not with those who had no faith in Christ.[23]

Margaret Hellwart seems to have been a good instructor in whom other women had confidence. In 1618 Katharina Koch testified that she did not need to go to church because Margaret Hellwart taught her all she needed to know.[24] Maria Niessmüller, her nearest neighbour and sister in the faith of Christ, testified that Margaret had helped her and that she had heard nothing but good about her.[25]

After January 19, 1621, the records on Margaret Hellwart fall silent. She was then fifty-three years of age and, by the standards of the time, old. There seems no doubt that she got her wish to die as an Anabaptist.

Margaret, in all likelihood, lies somewhere in her village of Beutelsbach in unconsecrated ground, awaiting the Great Resurrection.

Notes

1. Gustav Bossert, ed., *Quellen zur Geschichte der Wiedertäufer I. Bd. Herzogtum Württemberg* (New York and London: Johnson Reprint Corp., 1971), 800. Since all of the references are from this one work, only page numbers will be cited from now on.
2. 247, 526.
3. 763.
4. 440.
5. 295-334; 569-78.
6. 577-78.
7. 800.
8. 814.
9. 821, 828, 830, 844, 846, 848, 862, 867, 871, 879, 884, 887, 889, 891, 893.
10. 846.
11. 879.
12. 844.
13. 848, 887.
14. 828.
15. 871.
16. 890.
17. 875.
18. 888, 902.
19. 887.
20. 902.
21. 802, 1128; see *The Complete Writings of Menno Simons*, L. Verduin, trans., (Scottdale, PA: Herald Press, 1956), 103-226.
22. 884.
23. 1125-26.
24. 888.
25. 871.

II.

SOUTH GERMAN/AUSTRIAN ANABAPTIST WOMEN

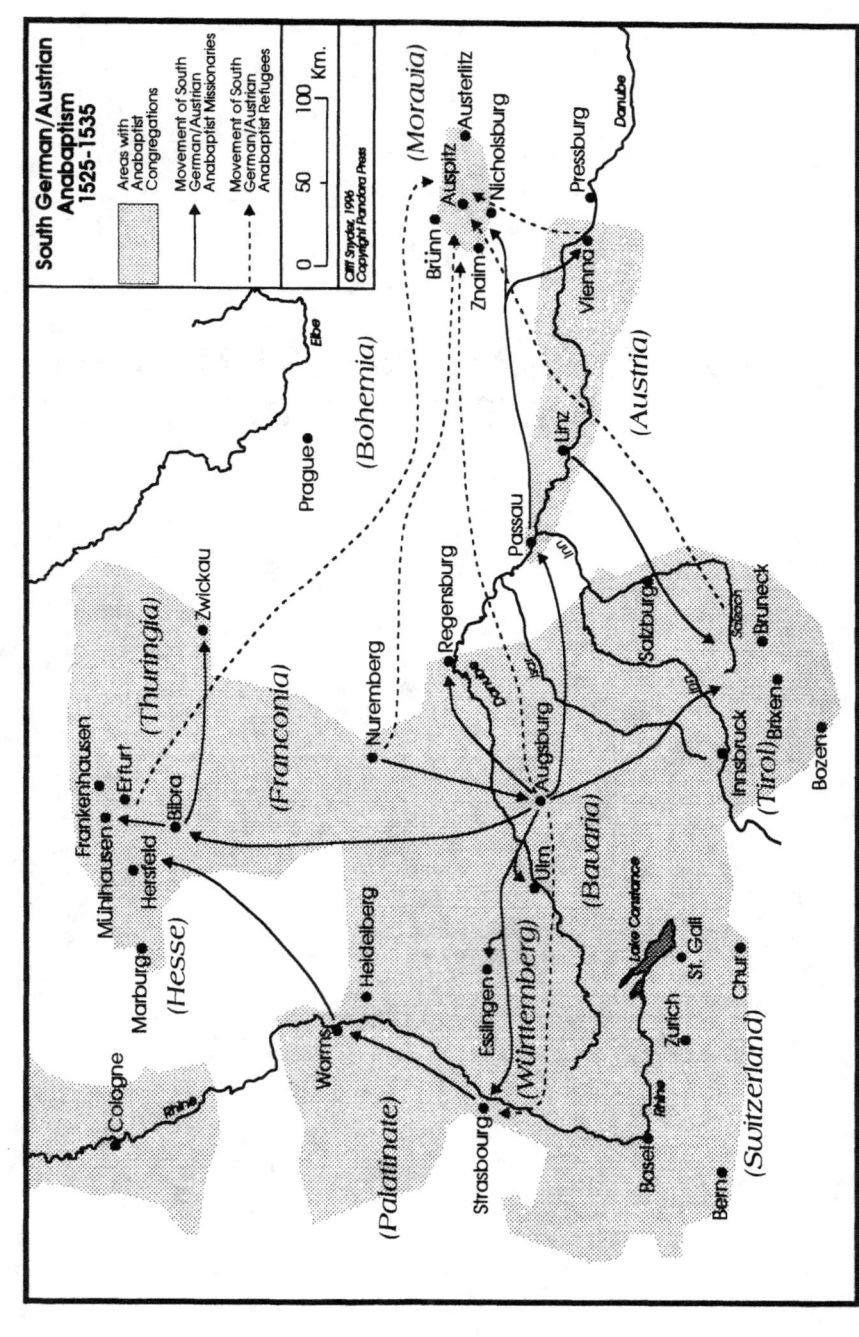

THE SOUTH GERMAN/AUSTRIAN ANABAPTIST CONTEXT

South German/Austrian Anabaptist Origins
The theological tap root of South German/Austrian Anabaptism ran to the same source from which Swiss Anabaptism drew: the evangelical critiques brought into focus by Martin Luther.[1] Equally important, a second theological root ran back from both Anabaptist movements to the radical stream of evangelical protest represented by Andreas Karlstadt and Thomas Müntzer. It is perhaps for these reasons that there was such a similarity in theological form and core doctrines between the Swiss and South German Anabaptist movements: the road to adult baptism and the uniquely Anabaptist understanding of salvation had been prepared in both cases by radical evangelical critiques of Luther's teachings. Nevertheless, the unique geographical and theological point of origin gave the South German/Austrian Anabaptist movement a distinctive character.

There are no obvious historical connections that associate the origins of South German Anabaptism to the earlier Swiss baptizing movement, although the close links that quickly developed among Anabaptist refugees from both the Swiss and South German groups argues for there having been more early contact than the historical records can confirm.[2] The Augsburg congregation, for example, relied on a network of committed women and men from both the Swiss and South German streams, as will be seen in the following group profile of Anabaptist women in Augsburg.

The historical and theological origins of South German/Austrian Anabaptism are found in the ashes of the Peasants' War of 1525 and in the theologies of Thomas Müntzer, Hans Denck, and Hans Hut.[3] The story of South German Anabaptism must begin with Thomas Müntzer, even though Müntzer was not an Anabaptist, never having instituted adult baptism.[4] Müntzer's evangelical reform was inspired not only by Luther, but also by his reading of mystical writers such as John Tauler, and by Müntzer's growing conviction that he was witnessing the events of the Last Days.[5] In part because of Müntzer's own influence on later Anabaptist leaders, mysticism and apocalypticism became identifying features of the early Anabaptist movement in South German and Austrian lands.[6]

Thomas Müntzer's apocalyptic convictions eventually led him to the disastrous battle of Frankenhausen, where some ten thousand peasants lost their lives, and which led to his own arrest and eventual execution. Also at Frankenhausen were two followers of Müntzer who would soon play leading roles in Central and South German Anabaptism: Melchior Rinck, who participated as a combatant, and Hans Hut, who was arrested at Frankenhausen while (as he claimed) he was selling books. Also significant in the establishment of South German Anabaptism was the mystically inclined Nuremberg schoolteacher Hans Denck, who may have had some direct contact with Müntzer. Hans Hut, while an active member of Müntzer's circle, came to Nuremberg on at least two occasions to have some of Müntzer's writings printed; he testified later that he had stayed with Denck at least once in 1524.[7]

By January of 1525 Hans Denck had been expelled from Nuremberg as a religious dissident.[8] By September of 1525, he was in the South German city of Augsburg, where he would remain for thirteen months. At some point–whether in Augsburg or at some point prior to his arrival there is no longer clear–Denck accepted baptism, and became an active Anabaptist leader. On May 3, 1526, in a watershed event for the history of South German Anabaptism, Hans Denck baptized Hans Hut into the Anabaptist movement.[9] Augsburg thus became the hub from which would spread the earliest South German Anabaptists, even though most of the leaders from Augsburg were actually immigrants and refugees from other parts of Germany, Austria, and even Switzerland. The group profile of Anabaptist women leaders in Augsburg illustrates how South German Anabaptism functioned in this pivotal urban centre in its first years (1527-28), and the crucial role played by Anabaptist women in the running of an outlawed, underground urban church.

Central to Hans Denck's understanding of reform was the importance of the "inner word" over that of the "outer word." The inner, mystical emphasis in his thought would remain a constant for Denck throughout all his travels and changes; this same emphasis is reflected in aspects of the Anabaptism descended from Denck.

Hans Hut was a bookbinder and a bookseller who also filled the office of sexton for four years in the town of Bibra in Central Germany. His bookselling activity took him to Würzburg, Bamberg, Nuremberg, Passau, and into Austria, as well as to Wittenberg, where he showed a preference for Karlstadt's and Müntzer's views.[10] When Thomas Müntzer had to flee Mühlhausen in September 1524, he spent a night and a day at Hut's house, and entrusted Hut with the task of having his *Manifest Exposé of False Faith* printed in Nuremberg, where Hut had also come to know Hans Denck. By the end of 1524, Hut refused to have his child baptized in Bibra and, given the choice of having his child baptized or being exiled, he chose exile.

Following the defeat of the peasants at Frankenhausen and his acceptance of baptism at the hands of Hans Denck, Hut set out on an amazing itinerant ministry. Even a partial list of the places where Hut founded Anabaptist congregations is impressive: Haina, Coburg, Königsberg (Franconia), Ostheim, Bamberg, Erlangen, Nuremberg, Uttenreuth, Augsburg, Passau, Nicholsburg, Vienna, Melk, Steyr, Freistadt, Linz, Laufen, and Salzburg. There were in addition very many smaller villages and rural locations where Hut baptized.

The sources say next to nothing about Hut's wife. It appears that she did not accompany Hut on his mission trips, but in 1527 she was reported to have found refuge with a peasant in the town of Staffelstein, where there was a concentration of Anabaptists. One witness described her as "middle-aged, accompanied by a son," and maintained that she had moved on and he did not know where she was.[11] The evidence, fragmentary as it is, suggests that she too had accepted Anabaptism and was thus forced to live on the run.

Hut communicated his urgent "End Times" Anabaptist message to his converts and they, in turn, set out on their own missionary journeys. Hut and his followers baptized adults by making a mark with water on the foreheads of those receiving baptism, and so marked them as members of the 144,000 elect of the Last Days. One story out of many illustrates the way in which South German Anabaptism spread.

Anstadt Kemmerer of Halle in Thuringia was baptized by some of Hut's followers, after a chance encounter at an inn where he was eating breakfast with a friend. After a brief conversation with a "little man" who was making the rounds speaking with patrons, Anstadt was convinced that time was short and that Jesus was about to return. He decided to be included among the 144,000 elect by water baptism. Someone brought a "little mustard pot" of pure water, and in the presence of three or more men and the same number of women (people Anstadt did not know), they read from books that they carried, they prayed, and then asked him to kneel. Anstadt did, and recited the Creed out loud, after which they poured water on him and made the sign of the cross on his forehead. Then they admonished him to be faithful, to treat others in the fellowship kindly, and not to be involved with usury. They told him further that the Lord would return in eleven months, and that there were some sixteen thousand already in the company of the elect, including "great and honourable people, margraves and others."[12]

Hut's Anabaptism was adult baptism in an urgent, hurried, apocalyptic mode. Constantly on the move, Hans Hut was responsible for the rapid spread of South German Anabaptism into the cities of South Germany, Austria, and the countryside of the Tirol, as well as into Franconia, Hesse, and Thuringia–Hut's home territory. Most of the Anabaptist women profiled in this section trace their introduction to the movement indirectly to Hans Hut, having been baptized directly by one of Hans Hut's followers. Hans Hut accomplished all of his missionizing in less than a year and a half of Anabaptist activity. He was arrested in Augsburg in September 1527. After suffering horrible tortures (he was racked severely and repeatedly), he died in prison under mysterious circumstances, asphyxiated as the result of a fire in his cell. In the absence of a living Hans Hut, the court publicly condemned his lifeless body to death and burned it at the stake.

The following distinctive features of this early South German/Austrian Anabaptism may be noted. The tradition of *German mysticism*, as appropriated by Müntzer and Denck and passed on to Hut, gave to much of

South German and Austrian Anabaptism a strongly spiritualist cast that distinguished it from the more biblicistic Swiss: there was a consistent emphasis on the inner work of the Holy Spirit in believers, and here and there an openness to direct revelations of the Spirit to prophets.[13] There was also a marked stress on *suffering* as a way of conforming to the way of Christ, initially in the painful coming to faith, but also in the later Christian walk. There was, in the third place, a strong leaning toward *community of goods* in Hut's Anabaptism and among his followers–although such a tendency was not unique to the South German movement. Fourth, there was a strong identification with the social upheaval of the *Peasants' War* in the beginnings of this Anabaptist movement. And finally, the strong *apocalypticism,* so visible in Müntzer and Hut, had an intense (but surprisingly short) life span in South German Anabaptism. By 1527 Hut had died, and the following year saw the failure of his prediction that Christ would return by 1528.

In spite of the true generalization that at its origins it was a more mystical, spiritualistic, and apocalyptic Anabaptism, the South German movement showed little uniformity in its development after 1527. Four primary groups emerged from the Hut-Denck beginnings.

1. A few Anabaptists developed Hut's militant apocalypticism some steps further. Augustin Bader was one such person. His hopes for the millennium and the rule of his own son as the Messiah ended with his arrest and execution in March 1530.[14] Sabina Bader, his resourceful wife, is profiled in this text.

There was an openness by Hut and some of his followers to direct visions, revelations, and prophecies, such as those that inspired Augustin Bader. In spite of the demise of Bader, and the relatively small number of persons involved in his movement, individual yieldedness "prophets" in the Hut tradition remained active. Some migrated to Strasbourg, where they played important roles in Melchiorite Anabaptism after 1530. However, the prophetic, apocalyptic strand of Anabaptism very quickly moved to the margins of the South German movement; after 1530 it played an insignificant role.

2. There were some direct heirs of Hans Denck's mystical and spiritualist tendencies, men such as Hans Bünderlin, Christian Entfelder, and Jakob Kautz. We have no profiles of spiritualist Anabaptist women in this collection, but the spiritualist position is represented here by Helena Streicher, who defended Caspar Schwenckfeld's views against the Anabaptism of Magdalena von Pappenheim and Pilgram Marpeck.

3. The Anabaptism that emerged in the Tirol was a synthesis of mysticism, apocalypticism, and separated congregationalism mediated by persons like Leonard Schiemer, Hans Schlaffer, and others baptized by Hut. An earlier Swiss Anabaptist missionizing presence in the southern Tirol, in

the person of George Blaurock, may have coloured Tirolean Anabaptism as well. The Anabaptist women of this region are richly represented in this collection: Anna Gasser, Dorothea Maler, Ursula Ochsentreiber, the group of Tirolean women who chose to recant, Elizabeth von Wolkenstein, and Helena von Freyberg, all profiled here, represent early Tirolean Anabaptism. Pilgram Marpeck, who also emerged from this Tirolean setting, carried his Anabaptism to Moravia, Switzerland (St. Gall), Strasbourg, and the South German cities of Augsburg and Ulm. Helena von Freyberg and Magdalena, Walpurga, and Sophia von Pappenheim, whose lives are chronicled in this text, were members of Marpeck's communities in South Germany.

4. The numerically most significant continuation of the South German/Austrian Anabaptism of Hut and Denck was the communitarian Hutterite movement that emerged in Moravia. The Hutterite communities were built exclusively of refugees from other territories. The Tirol, Silesia, Switzerland, and Central Germany were crucial areas, providing members for the Hutterite communities in Moravia. The profile of Katharina Hutter, wife of Jakob Hutter, tells part of the story of the trials of the Hutterite community around 1535; the group profile of women whose stories were recorded in the *Hutterite Chronicle* offers a window from the later history of the Hutterite communities; the study of the portrayal of women in the Hutterite song book offers yet another angle of vision on the experience of Hutterite women.

Women in Tirolean and Moravian Anabaptism
The appeal to a direct and spiritual call from God as the basis for preaching, teaching, and action was stronger in Hans Hut's circle than it was among the Swiss.[15] This might be expected to lead to more overt prophetic activity among South German Anabaptist women than among Swiss Anabaptist women. It is not yet evident that this was in fact the case, since systematic examination of the role of women in the larger South German/Austrian movement has only just begun. It should be noted that the high proportion of Tirolean profiles in this collection, and the absence of profiles from, for example, Thuringia, is more a comment on the current state of research than it is an accurate reflection of the state of the sources. Much more research remains to be done on the role of women in the South German/Austrian movement as a whole. But it may be the case that the documentation available for South German/Austrian Anabaptism will not allow a fuller picture to emerge.[16]

Linda Huebert Hecht's detailed study of one volume of published court records for the Tirol has revealed a high percentage of female participation in the early Anabaptist movement from 1527 to 1529. Out of 455 Anabaptist members who appeared in the court records for these years in Tirol, 210 of those arrested (or 46 percent) were women.[17] In this earliest period of Anabaptist growth in Tirol, Huebert Hecht counted more than fifteen lay leaders and missioners, and forty-nine martyrs, from among the 210 Anabaptist women identified.[18]

There is good evidence for the proselytizing activity of Anabaptist women in the Tirol in this earliest period, but very little evidence that sheds light on their spiritual calling. This probably is due to the nature of the surviving evidence, rather than to fundamental differences in Anabaptist regional movements.[19] Ursula Binder and her husband had been baptized by Hans Hut, who then sent them to missionize in Salzburg; the court record suggests that she was as active in this as was her husband, but gives no further relevant details.[20] One would like to know more about the woman who, it was reported, said that she had "made six new Christians in a short time."[21] Kinship, friendship and leadership networks clearly were important in the spread of Anabaptism in the Tirol, with women participating actively in proselytization within those networks and beyond, as the profile of Anna Gasser will demonstrate. In several cases the court records name women along with men as "principal baptizers and seducers."[22]

In spite of much leadership activity of an informal kind, there is no compelling evidence that women in the Tirol were involved in the actual baptizing of believers into the movement.[23] Thus the profile of involvement by Anabaptist women for this early phase of the Anabaptist movement in Tirol matches closely what can be noted for the Swiss Anabaptists around Zurich: although women do not appear to have performed the formal rites of baptizing believers and leading in the Lord's Supper, they made up almost half the documented Anabaptist membership (that is, members who were arrested) in the earliest phase of the movement and were extremely active in missionizing and proselytizing, particularly through their networks of family and friends. As such they were actively sought out for arrest by the Austrian authorities and were all too often tortured and martyred along with the men.[24] The Tirolean records are silent concerning explicitly prophetic activity on the part of women–whether because there was no such activity, or because the record is deficient, we cannot say.

As persecution increased in the Tirol, and life for Anabaptists became untenable in that land, more and more fled to Moravia, joining the communal groups that had emerged there in 1528. Jakob Hutter was instrumental in leading Tirolean Anabaptist refugees to the safety of those communities in Moravia, beginning in 1529.[25] The Tirolean refugees encountered a very different social ethos when they entered the Moravian communities. The strong emphasis on a biblical "rule of life" necessary to sustain a communal endeavour soon restricted the potential scope of public activity for women.

The implicit contradiction between a democratic, theological ideal of spiritual equality before God and a hierarchical and patriarchal ordering of the community was nowhere more in evidence than in the Hutterite communities.²⁶ Spiritual equality was even more strongly stressed by the communal Anabaptists (following in Hut's footsteps), given the emphasis on individual [*Gelassenheit*] which was expressed concretely in a renunciation of private property and a shared communal life. Paradoxically, this spiritual equality of yieldedness resulted in a highly structured community life ordered by strict external rules [*Ordnungen*] governing all of life.²⁷

In establishing the "God-ordained" order for their communities, the Hutterites appealed to familiar biblical examples. In this way "spiritual equality before God" became a practical inequality within the Hutterite communities. Writing in 1545, the great Hutterite leader Peter Riedemann stated that men, as those "in whom something of God's glory is seen" were to have compassion on the "weaker vessel" even as men "went before" and exercised spiritual and physical leadership and authority;²⁸ women, for their part, were to be humble, submissive, and obedient. The patriarchal frame of mind was pervasive in Hutterite community organization, and extended even to the most basic participation in decision-making processes: the men alone exercised voting power within the congregation, and excluded women from such votes. Thus, in spite of the levelling appearance of communities that held all things in common, the Hutterites were even less egalitarian in church polity than were the Swiss.²⁹

The one area in which women had exercised considerable initiative and leadership in the early Tirolean period, that is as lay leaders, missioners, and proselytizers, appears to have closed for them once they joined a Hutterite community and submitted to its rule–if the extant documentation tells anything like the full story. The Hutterites were the most active missionaries of all the Anabaptist groups after 1540, but their systematic and extensive activities were to be undertaken by men, duly selected and commissioned by Hutterite leaders, not by spiritually anointed and self-appointed leaders.³⁰ Occasionally the "duly appointed men" would be accompanied by their wives on missionary journeys, but the work of proselytization does not appear to have been shared equally by men and women.³¹ In short, leadership within the Hutterite church and community was in exclusively male hands; the context of individual choice for women remained in the initial commitment to baptism and the community, in the freedom to leave unbelieving spouses, and in the testimony of their faithfulness in the face of a wide variety of challenges, including martyrdom.

Anabaptist Women in Pilgram Marpeck's Communities

The South German communities led by the Anabaptist leader and refugee from the Tirol, Pilgram Marpeck, were notable for the active roles taken by several remarkable women, among them Anna Marpeck, Helena von Freyberg, Magdalena Marschalk von Pappenheim, Walpurga von Pappenheim, Kunigunda Schneider, and Anna Schmidt. Marpeck never spoke explicitly concerning the "proper" role of women in his congregations, but the evidence leads to the conclusion that certain women in his circle exercised leadership and teaching skills.[32] This is particularly true of two noblewomen who were part of that circle: Magdalena von Pappenheim and Helena von Freyberg, both of whom are profiled in this book.[33]

Although there are no typical instances of women's participation in Anabaptism, the cases of Magdalena von Pappenheim and Helena von Freyberg are especially unusual because of the sustained leadership they undertook, even if that leadership was at the informal level. Their aristocratic status undoubtedly gave them more political space than was granted to commoners–the political authorities proceeded more carefully with the nobility. Their noble standing–unusual within the movement as a whole–also may have had something to do with their readiness to assume leadership within the movement. Within the Anabaptist family of "communities of saints," noble birth seems to have lent a stronger voice to women. The written confession of Helena von Freyberg, translated later in this text, gives a sense of the context in which her own leadership was exercised.

Conclusion

The South German/Austrian Anabaptist movement defies easy classification. Its unique mystical, spiritualist, and apocalyptic beginnings were not simply a direct continuation of Swiss Anabaptist emphases, but added elements not seen in the earlier movement. At the same time, Swiss and South German "baptizers" recognized each other from the start as members of the same general movement, even though some disagreements surfaced almost immediately in their shared places of refuge. In a movement that parallels developments in Swiss Anabaptism, an earlier, more chaotic spiritualist period soon gave way in South German Anabaptism to the establishment of settled communities, particularly after 1528. The later communal settlements in Moravia, under the leadership of Jakob Hutter, came to represent the majoritarian South German Anabaptist tradition; the scattered groups of followers of Pilgram Marpeck in South German territories represent a second important strand; the few who remained convinced of Hut's apocalyptic message were perhaps the smallest surviving group, but these Hutian "prophets" exerted a direct influence on the emerging North German/Dutch Anabaptist movement in Strasbourg, as will be seen. The profiles that follow are drawn from both the earlier and later periods in the South German/Austrian area; the stories of Hutian-influenced women prophets in Strasbourg will be taken up in the selections from the North German/Dutch Anabaptist stream.

Notes

1 Drawn from C. Arnold Snyder, *Anabaptist History and Theology: An Introduction* (Kitchener, ON: Pandora Press, 1995), chapters 2, 3, 5, and 18.
2 There is a remote possibility that Hans Denck was baptized by Balthasar Hubmaier in Augsburg in 1526, but the evidence is not strong. In any case, if such a baptism did take place, it did not succeed in giving a "Swiss" cast to Denck's understanding of Anabaptism. See Werner Packull, "Denck's Alleged Baptism by Hubmaier. Its Significance for the Origin of South German-Austrian Anabaptism," MQR 47 (Oct. 1973): 327-38.
3 See here especially the work of Werner Packull, *Mysticism and the Early South German-Austrian Anabaptist Movement, 1525-1531* (Scottdale, PA: Herald Press, 1977); Gottfried Seebass, "Müntzers Erbe: Werk, Leben und Theologie des Hans Hut (1527)," Habilitationsschrift der Theologischen Fakultät der Friedrich-Alexander Universität zu Erlangen-Nürnberg (1972); and James Stayer, *Anabaptists and the Sword* (Lawrence, KS: Coronado Press, 1972).
4 On Thomas Müntzer, see Gordon Rupp, *Patterns of Reformation* (London: Epworth Press, 1969); Hans-Jürgen Goertz, "Thomas Müntzer," in Hans-Jürgen Goertz, ed., *Profiles of Radical Reformers* (Scottdale, PA: Herald Press, 1982), 29-44; Hans-Jürgen Goertz, *Thomas Müntzer: Apocalyptic, Mystic and Revolutionary*, trans. by Jocelyn Jaquiery, ed. Peter Matheson (Edinburgh: T & T Clark, 1993).
5 See Abraham Friesen, *Thomas Muentzer, a Destroyer of the Godless* (Berkeley and Los Angeles: University of California Press, 1990).
6 Walter Klaassen, *Living at the End of the Ages* (Lanham, MD: University Press of America, 1992).
7 Packull, *Mysticism*, 37-9.
8 Ibid., 39.
9 Ibid., 64. By the summer of 1527 Denck had withdrawn to Basel, disillusioned by Anabaptist divisions. He died in Basel in mid-November of 1527, a victim of the plague. Translation of Denck's major works, with accompanying German text, in Clarence Bauman, trans. and ed., *The Spiritual Legacy of Hans Denck* (Leiden: E.J. Brill, 1991).
10 Hans Guderian, *Die Täufer in Augsburg* (Pfaffenhofen: Ludwig Verlag, 1984), 63. Hut came to be a signed member of Thomas Müntzer's secret "Eternal Covenant."
11 Paul Wappler, ed., *Die Täuferbewegung in Thüringen von 1526-1584* (Jena: Fischer, 1913), number 2, 242: "sei mittelmessiger jare und hab ein knaben bei ir . . ."; see also number 1, 235. Thanks to Werner Packull for this reference. Staffelstein is a village some 60 kilometres due north of Nuremberg, between Bamberg and Coburg.
12 Wappler, *Täuferbewegung in Thüringen*, number 12, 259.
13 Werner Packull noted that these Anabaptists "took their theological starting point not from the Reformers but from a popularized medieval mystical tradition." James Stayer, Werner Packull, and Klaus Deppermann, "From Monogenesis to Polygenesis," MQR 49 (April 1975): 110.
14 On some of the variant expressions of Hut's Anabaptism, and especially good details on Bader, see Packull, *Mysticism*, 118-38; also Klaassen, *Living at the End of the Ages*, 42-44.
15 As noted by Hans-Jürgen Goertz, *Die Täufer: Geschichte und Deutung* (München: Beck, 1980), 51.
16 The authorities in Thuringia, for example, were much more interested in arresting Anabaptist men than women, especially in the early years of the movement. The early court records present an almost exclusively male list of detainees. This simply means

that the activity of women remains hidden from view. The broader picture emerges on occasion in the male testimonies, such as when the arrested Hans Weischenfelder (baptized by Hans Hut) provided a list of others who were present at his baptism: six women were there, along with three men. Wappler, *Täuferbewegung in Thüringen*, number 22, 279. See Marion Kobelt-Groch, "Why Did Petronella Leave Her Husband? Reflections on Marital Avoidance Among the Halberstadt Anabaptists," MQR 62 (Jan. 1988): 26-41.

17 Linda Huebert Hecht, "Faith and Action: The Role of Women in the Anabaptist Movement of the Tirol, 1527-1529" (unpublished cognate essay, Master of Arts, History, University of Waterloo, 1990), 33-34. Hecht is working with Claus-Peter Clasen's figures, as well as her own. Figures from Augsburg from 1526 to 1529 show that 43 percent of documented Anabaptists were women. This dropped to 29 percent after 1532 (noted on 33). Hecht's evidence is drawn from TA, Ost.II.

18 Hecht, "Faith and Action," Table 1, 33a.

19 The colourful information provided by chroniclers in St. Gall is not replicated in the Tirol; the result is a fairly one-dimensional portrait of Tirolean Anabaptist women, based almost exclusively on official court documents.

20 The evidence is suggestive, but not overwhelming. Cf. Hecht, "Faith and Action," 53.

21 TA, Ost.II, document 330, p. 229. Cf. Hecht, "Faith and Action," 56.

22 Hecht, "Faith and Action," 62ff. In the Austrian county of Steyr, next to the Tirol, three women were reported as preaching actively in houses in 1528. Ibid., 65, n. 253; original sources in TA, Ost.I, pp. 154-55. See also Marion Kobelt-Groch, *Aufsässige Töchter Gottes: Frauen im 'Bauernkrieg' und in den Bewegungen der Täufer* (Frankfurt and New York: Campus Verlag, 1993), chapter 5, 147-63, esp. 150 where an Anabaptist woman from Central Germany is said to have conducted a service.

23 "Compelling" evidence would be the testimony of an imprisoned Anabaptist who would identify a woman as the person baptizing. Such evidence has yet to come to light.

24 Women comprised 40 percent of Anabaptists put to death in the Tirol between 1527 and 1529. Linda Huebert Hecht, "Women and religious change: The significance of Anabaptist women in the Tirol, 1527-29," *Studies in Religion* 21(1992): 61.

25 ME, II, 851ff.

26 Claus-Peter Clasen, *Anabaptism: A Social History, 1525-1618* (Ithaca: Cornell University Press, 1972), 255. Clasen's lack of gender analysis is critiqued by Julia Roberts, "Hutterite Women in the Sixteenth Century: The Ideal and Aspects of the Reality" (unpublished paper, University of Waterloo, 1990), 2. Also helpful is Marlene Epp, "Women and Men in the 16th Century Hutterite Community" (unpublished paper, University of Toronto, 1991).

27 The Hutterite *Chronicle* notes: "So there has to be an order in all areas, for the matters of life can be properly maintained and furthered only where order reigns . . ." *The Chronicle of the Hutterian Brethren*, vol. 1 (Rifton, NY: Plough Publishing House, 1987), 406-7.

28 A man is to "go before his wife and guide her to blessedness." Peter Riedeman, *Account of Our Religion, Doctrine and Faith* (London: Hodder and Stoughton, 1950), 101.

29 "None of the leadership positions were open to women nor did they have a voice in filling them as women were not allowed to vote or speak at community meetings." Marlene Epp, "Women and Men," 7, with reference to Mary Ault Harada, "Family Values and Child Care During the Reformation Era: A Comparative Study of Hutterites and Some Other German Protestants," (PhD dissertation, Boston University, 1986), 130. The practice among modern Hutterites reflects sixteenth-century practice: male members nominate potential preachers (all male) who are then chosen by lot. Elders are elected

directly by "the voting body," which consists of "the male members of the church." John Horsch, *The Hutterian Brethren, 1528-1931* (Cayley, AB: Macmillan Colony, 1985), 148.
30 This applied to both women and men. Riedeman is most explicit: "It is not for all and sundry to take upon themselves such an office, namely that of teaching and baptizing . . . none must take upon himself or accept such power, unless he be chosen properly and rightly by God in his Church and community . . ." Riedeman, *Account*, 80.
31 See Clasen, *Social History*, 215-16. Marlene Epp notes some possible exceptions in "Women and Men," 10-12. Some informal proselytizing may have occurred when women accompanied their husbands on missionary journeys, as in the case of Apollonia, Leonhard Lanzenstiel's wife, who was arrested and drowned in 1539. Ibid., 11. Nevertheless, such cases (which are, unfortunately, poorly documented) would have been exceptions, rather than fitting the usual Hutterite pattern.
32 Stephen B. Boyd, *Pilgram Marpeck: His Life and Social Theology* (Durham, NC: Duke University Press, 1992), 96, n. 132; see 7, 52, 139, 146 for further references. Marpeck's only explicit remark is equivocal: it reflects the prevailing view of women as "weak members," but notes the positive role they played in proclaiming the good news. In spite of their weakness, says Marpeck in arguing against the spiritualists, Christ chose them to announce the resurrection, and the apostles believed them. Pilgram Marpeck, "A Clear and Useful Instruction," in William Klassen and Walter Klaassen, trans. and eds. *The Writings of Pilgram Marpeck* (Scottdale, PA: Herald Press, 1978), 91-92.
33 On Helena von Freyberg, see also Linda Huebert Hecht, "An Extraordinary Lay Leader: The Life and Work of Helene of Freyberg, Sixteenth Century Noblewoman from the Tirol," MQR 66 (July 1992): 312-41.

ANABAPTIST WOMEN LEADERS IN AUGSBURG
August 1527 to April 1528

This chapter will explore religious leadership roles among Augsburg Anabaptist women in the dynamic period from August 1527 to April 1528. Except for Dutch Anabaptist women captives, court interrogators usually asked very little of Anabaptist women, frustrating the researcher who wishes to know more about their lives and thoughts.[1] The Augsburg hearings, however, provide enough information to make Anabaptist women something more than merely names or ciphers.[2] Augsburg records permit one to write brief biographical sketches, even though all but a handful of these women disappeared completely from the historical record after they were sentenced.[3]

Related to the question of leadership is the matter of how Anabaptists operated an underground church. A few decades ago, scholars were carried away by the sudden discovery of records concerning Anabaptists who had heroically demanded that they be heard in crucial places, including regular Protestant church services. In point of fact, only a few Anabaptists had insisted on public hearings or demanded the right to declare themselves, and only for relatively short periods of time. In most of those regions where Anabaptists began their religious life together, they scrupulously avoided any public notice for the best of all possible reasons: it was dangerous. They quickly learned how to remain undercover, something late medieval heretical groups had long understood.

Anabaptists in Augsburg
The broader outline of Anabaptist developments in Augsburg are generally well known; here only a short account will be necessary. Ludwig Hätzer, an early opponent of infant baptism who did not quite join the Anabaptists, began to meet with a small circle of religious dissenters early in 1525 when he was working for Augsburg printer Silvan Othmar. In autumn the group was joined by Hans Denck, who had been expelled from Nuremberg shortly after Hätzer was expelled from Augsburg. Balthasar Hubmaier came to Augsburg late in spring 1526, and may have baptized Hans Denck. In May 1526 Denck baptized Hans Hut, that intrepid apostle who travelled all over southern Germanic regions preaching and baptizing hundreds of people, including many in Augsburg.

It was Hut who gathered a congregation in Augsburg. In February 1527, under Hut's leadership, Sigmund Salminger was selected as leader and Jakob Dachser as his assistant. They founded a distinct pattern for caring for the poor among them. Eitelhans Langenmantel, from a venerable family of Augsburg patricians, was converted early in 1527, and wrote venomous pamphlets against Lutheranism probably in response to the Lutheran preacher Urbanus Rhegius, who attacked the Anabaptists vigorously and urged the

City Council to act against them. The Council, however, was not ready to act, one suspects largely because it could not decide which religion to favour: Catholic, Lutheran, or Zwinglian. Because of that indecision, the Anabaptists apparently felt they had the unique opportunity to live out a fourth religious option. Their congregation grew rapidly during the course of the spring and summer of 1527.

In August 1527, approximately sixty Anabaptists met in Augsburg to decide a number of issues, principally that of assigning "apostles" to evangelize selected geographical areas in southern Germanic regions. This meeting, together with the continued growth of the group, alarmed city officials and opened their ears to the complaints of the Protestant preachers against the Anabaptists. On September 6, Rhegius issued his new pamphlet, *Against the New Baptism Order, A Necessary Warning*.[4] Late in August the city seized a number of leaders and examined them under torture, seeking the names and residences of their fellow worshippers in the city. They arrested a group gathered for worship on September 15, and the search continued. Throughout that month and into early October they captured more, and then imprisoned the principal leaders–Salminger, Dachser, Jakob Gross, and Hut. They gathered others and compelled them to swear (1) not to sell their goods and leave the city without permission from the government; (2) not to attend Anabaptist meetings; and (3) to obey the government in all matters. A further sweep of Anabaptists, and sympathizers who had not yet joined, led to a public oath from these folk that they (1) would not meet; (2) would not be rebaptized; and (3) would obey the government's summons to appear. On October 11 in a public forum at the city hall square, these Anabaptists and friends were commanded to baptize infants, not to rebaptize anyone, not to lodge itinerant Anabaptist ministers, and not to attend Anabaptist meetings.

Some Anabaptists refused to swear oaths in response to any of these government demands, and were consequently exiled with the threat of further punishment if they returned; death was hinted. But reasonable Anabaptists protested these heavy strictures, especially the one forbidding any kind of assembly for religious reasons. Surely, they begged, a few people could meet to read the Bible and discuss it. The government relented, granting permission to meet two or three at a time to read and discuss. The Anabaptists parlayed this concession into the convening of many meetings of small groups, larger than two or three, usually at least six or eight, sometimes as many as fifteen or eighteen. Despite the danger of more severe punishment, they continued baptizing new converts and convened meetings of even larger numbers, culminating in a gathering of almost two hundred[5] on Easter Sunday, April 12, 1528. Clasen has estimated that they convened as many as sixty meetings from January to mid-April 1528.[6]

Augsburg Anabaptists were served by a large number of resident and itinerant ministers and baptizers. At least twenty persons baptized others in

Augsburg from 1526 through April 1528; another eleven preached but did not baptize, and their names were only vaguely known by auditors in the city.[7] The variety of preachers produced a variety of religious opinion, an aspect of Augsburg Anabaptism to which little attention has been given. One could assess that variety as one expression of religious vitality. But the continued vitality of the congregation took other forms, including the orderly commissioning on April 11, 1528, of two ministers who were to be sent elsewhere. Indeed, there are many marks of an extraordinary religious vigour in this congregation.

April 12, 1528, marked the beginning of the end. Several hundred Anabaptists gathered before sunrise at the house of Susanna Doucher,[8] to be led in worship by regular ministers Jörg Nespitzer and Hans Leupold. Within an hour word came that a police raid was imminent; Leupold gave the alarm and invited those present to leave. Quite a few did. The remaining eighty-eight were captured, led off in irons to prison, and interrogated carefully over the next few weeks.[9] Humanist Konrad Peutinger, who had been employed by the city in the autumn of 1527 to interrogate Anabaptist prisoners, again undertook that task. He kept his own protocol of responses, written much more legibly than most early sixteenth-century writers. His principal purpose was suppression of the movement. Therefore he set about to learn the names of other Anabaptists and sympathizers, their meeting places, the names of leaders resident and itinerant, and other relevant information that would enable the city to eliminate this religious threat.[10] He routinely applied the rack to the men and the thumbscrew to the women, and he threatened additional torture to those of sluggish tongue. Schooled in law, especially Roman jurisprudence, and then drawn to humanism by Italians such as Pico della Mirandola, Peutinger retained a strict adherence to rigorous legal measures and embraced none of the religious tolerance of Erasmus, the leading humanist north of the Alps. His interrogations always carried a hard edge.[11]

Augsburg eliminated the threat of Anabaptist growth by these strenuous measures. The movement subsided, and late in the summer of 1528 the Anabaptists decided not to meet, even in outlying regions of the city.[12] One finds some continuation of a congregation until late in that century; its greatest vigour was probably under the leadership of Pilgram Marpeck, but he was strangely quiescent in the city itself and the government seems to have virtually ignored him.[13]

Anabaptist Women in Augsburg
Augsburg's Anabaptist women helped hold the congregation together after its first setback late in the summer of 1527. The severity of punishment meted out to those women caught in the police sweep of April 12, 1528, points out the degree of their complicity, and indirectly indicates some of

their leadership roles.

Some of the women offered their homes for meetings, overnight lodging of itinerant ministers, or longer-term housing for refugees; they also frequently provided meals. The executioner branded these women on both cheeks, an unmistakably permanent mark of criminality in the society of that time. And they were exiled for life, with the threat of physical punishment–death was intended[14]–if they returned to Augsburg. Under the threat of this punishment, steadfast Anabaptists who would not recant were tied on the pillory and then beaten out of town with rods as added incentive to vanish forever.

Some of Augsburg's Anabaptist women convened meetings, and they or others announced those meetings to small circles of initiates or potential converts. Other women distributed alms in some form, either to refugee or to poor Augsburg Anabaptists. The Augsburg authorities did not punish explicitly for these activities though they were assiduous in uncovering them.

The covert activities of a cluster of Augsburg Anabaptist women is the focus of this essay. Of course there were men who helped in each of these activities; we concentrate on the women because they have generally been less fully treated for the best of reasons, namely, that the primary sources are biased against them in both quantity and quality. One needs to read between the lines, acceptable for the reader of fiction, perilous for the historian. In the absence of richer sources, we hope to attribute neither too much nor too little to them.

Women Who Hosted Others
Susanna Doucher

Wife of prominent sculptor Hans Adolf Doucher, Susanna became an Anabaptist against her husband's wish, or at least against his better judgement. She was baptized by one Thomas, probably Thomas Waldhauser,[15] in November 1527, notably after the first restrictions against Anabaptists. She was baptized in the house of lacemaker Conrad Huber, in the absence of both Conrad and his wife Felicitas. Susanna's sister Maxentia Wisinger was baptized at the same time. Susanna knew none of the other people present, and she disclaimed further knowledge of itinerant baptizer Thomas.[16]

Peutinger dragged out of her more information about other Anabaptist meetings, generally of a handful of Anabaptists only half of whom she knew, at the homes of people she usually did know. One short report after another tumbled reluctantly from her memory, most of them relatively insignificant. She had fuller knowledge than some of an April 11 meeting at Gall Vischer's house, but she reported none of the special activities of that occasion. But there was one meeting two months earlier, in mid-February 1528, that attracted thirty Anabaptists. They met first in the woods by "St.

Ratha" (present-day Radegundis, a small hamlet at the edge of the Rauher Forst, two kilometres west of Göggingen), but that venue did not suit them well. Augustin Bader, Hans Leupold, and Jörg Nespitzer were the teaching ministers. Susanna reported that she spent one day there, leaving Augsburg in the morning and returning before the gates closed in the evening. Here was a more daring attempt to gather a small congregation in worship, significantly more than the normal six to ten people, but outside the city walls in a forest. Other Anabaptists known to be present managed to avoid reporting this meeting.

Like all of the captives, Susanna tried to disclaim involvement, up to the limit of her integrity. Yes, she had given some small sums of money, or of goods, to one indigent Anabaptist, widow Gertraut Heisses; and, yes, she had bought wine and bread to feed those who gathered at her house on April 12. But she had not given money regularly to Anabaptist brothers and sisters; nor had she housed them–except for two women overnight on April 11. She told Peutinger her husband would not have tolerated more charity; one suspects that she intended the comment as proof of her innocence, knowing that Peutinger knew Doucher was opposed. But the comment reveals her own courage and conviction, in the light of her husband's opposition.

Peutinger got little from her about the April 12 events, perhaps because he asked little. She knew nothing of attempts to mark her house with chalk to designate the place of meeting, until she learned of markings from fellow captives in prison. She knew of no special messenger who announced the venue to others; she thought news of place and time had been spread by word of mouth. She reported lamely that Hans Leupold and Jörg Nespitzer preached. They spoke "from the word of God."[17]

Susanna's deviant activity–housing and feeding refugees and using her house for an Anabaptist meeting–called for the severe penalty of branding on both cheeks followed by exile. Since she was pregnant, the city omitted the branding and merely led her out of the city bound in irons, a humiliating indignity. She was exiled for life, and we do not hear about her again–where she went or what became of her.[18] One suspects that she was permitted to return to Augsburg after some time, because of the prominence of her husband.[19]

Dorothea Frölich

Dorothea belonged to the small circle of Augsburg Anabaptist women who permitted meetings in their houses, housed and fed Anabaptists, and therefore suffered the punishment of branding on both cheeks and exile. Her story is more quickly told because there is less information about her. Other Anabaptists made frequent reference to her–present in meetings, charitable to others, etc. But these become repetitious and give us no fresh data about her. She sponsored at least two meetings in her house, both during Lent 1528, for one of which at least eighteen people were present. She was bolder than many.[20]

She bore several nicknames: *Dull Zieglerin, die Frölichin*, sometimes *Schadenfroin*. The first name might indicate that her husband had been a tile or brick maker; she was reported to be a widow. Perhaps the second nickname was a reference to her disposition, presumably joyful. Here I follow interrogator/recorder Peutinger who insisted on Frölich as her name, unlike historian Friedrich Roth who always named her Dorothea Zieglerin.

She had been baptized late in September 1527 by an itinerant Anabaptist, Hans Greuel, about whom she said she knew nothing. He lived in Augsburg for a time, baptized at least two others there and three who later came to Augsburg, and left without a trace in the summer of 1528, long after the April 12 arrests and subsequent police sweeps in the city.[21] He comes to us as one Anabaptist minister who succeeded, at least for a limited period of time, in evading capture in Augsburg.

Under the usual threat of torture, applied routinely at the end of her testimony to determine that she verifiably knew no more, she revealed that she had visited meetings; we can count eight of them. She declared she did not know how many she attended, that she went whenever she heard one was taking place. From her own court testimony and that of others, it appears that she was one of the most faithful participants in Anabaptist meetings, an Anabaptist who had her ear attuned most keenly to any word of meetings, and earnestly followed them up.

She knew several ministers–Hans Leupold, Claus Schleiffer, Jörg Nespitzer, Augustin Bader, and Georg Schachner. She seems to have had a sense of the Augsburg government's intention and advised some of these ministers to flee the region the week before that fatal meeting on April 12. She also tells us more clearly than anyone who the properly selected deacons were: Simprecht Wiedenmann, Laux Kreler, and then later Gall Vischer. She did not give the names of women in this instance, though she had to have known that some did, indeed, distribute alms. Despite her prominence in Anabaptist circles, she remains elusive for us because Peutinger did not press her for more information.

Scolastica Stierpaur

Scolastica was the wife, and by April 1528 the widow, of diplomat Crispin Stierpaur, who apparently served the city as a minor travelling emissary.[22] They joined the Anabaptists, she first in September 1527, he some time later. Jakob Gross baptized her. She often attended Anabaptist meetings, but it is not clear in what time period. She insisted that since early January 1528 she had not attended any meetings, until the larger one on April 12. She and her husband were absent from the city, presumably on official business, for periods of time, certainly from early January 1528 until shortly before Lent. Still, it is clear that she frequented Anabaptist meetings, harboured Anabaptist refugees, especially ministers, permitted baptisms in her house, and finally perjured her oath of October 1527 to obey the government's strictures against Anabaptist activity. These activities brought her the severest censure from the government.

Three ministers stayed overnight at her house: Leonhard Dorfbrunner, an unnamed and unidentified "Swiss" brother,[23] and the "Furrier from Salzburg."[24] She did offer overnight lodging to refugee Anabaptists, including Veronica Gross, wife of Jakob, probably after he was imprisoned in 1527. She reported that the Anabaptists held meetings in her house three times, but only after her husband joined; before that, he had refused to allow it, which suggests that she had urged him to. But she did not tell Peutinger when those three meetings were held. Els Hegenmiller told Peutinger that she had been baptized in Scolastica's house,[25] but that is the only meeting in her house that we learn about from other testimonies. Scolastica reported that only three people were baptized in her house: her husband, Veit Westermair, and a grocer-woman whom we know through the records though Scolastica claimed not to know—Els Hegenmiller. These admissions were pried out of her, undoubtedly by threat of torture; at the end of her second hearing, the thumbscrew was routinely applied, but by that time she had told all she had to tell.

She did sew in the house of Kicklinger, who has to have been a seamstress but remains unidentified;[26] she also visited Dorothea Frölich in her house. Here one senses a circle of like-minded women or women of the same social class—at least these three were together. She did not associate with Els, who was poor; that encounter seems to have been almost accidental, though Susanna Doucher was friendly enough to Els. Scolastica Stierpaur dropped from the records after her branding and exile.

Women who Distributed Alms
Katharina Wiedenmann

Katharina and her husband Simprecht were baptized by Jakob Gross in the summer of 1527. The Wiedenmanns kept a house almost constantly open to Anabaptist visitors, including leaders.[27] Simprecht's trade as a cobbler made an open house possible. Probably there was no Augsburg Anabaptist couple who talked with coreligionists as frequently as they did. In her answers to Peutinger's probes, Katharina tried to appear as innocent of Anabaptist contacts as possible, both in and out of Augsburg. Reluctantly, she reported that she had visited Agnes Vogel (who only just happened to be an Anabaptist), that she had brought one person eggs, another lard, another baked goods, and then drank around the table with still others. These visits were not quite as innocent as she tried to maintain, at least in the eyes of her Anabaptist friends. And as Peutinger pressed her for more information about other meetings in their house, out tumbled more information—about ministers such as Leupold and Nespitzer, or refugee Bavarian agriculturists, or a circle of regular Anabaptist friends who included Laux Miller, Laux

Hafner, Hans Lauterwein, Maxentia Wisinger, and Susanna Doucher. Still, she was careful to deny that another member of that circle, the wife of Laux Kreler, had ever heard the word read in the Wiedenmann house; Kreler's wife had come only one time, to have two shoes cobbled, and she still owed the Wiedenmanns for that work. The Wiedenmann household emerges as a veritable centre of clandestine Anabaptist activity, much beyond the innocent business activities of any cobbler.

Her husband, Simprecht, was less careful to obey the Council's decrees of September and October 1527. He seems to have freely visited many Anabaptist meetings. But their own house was used constantly by visitors—especially those who came to have their shoes repaired, but also those women who came together to sew, who assembled around the distaff as the record quaintly puts it. Both husband and wife tried to make it sound as if Anabaptist meetings happened only spontaneously in connection with these other legitimate business reasons for coming to the Wiedenmann house. Both of them were trying to make it appear that they had, indeed, obeyed the Council's orders not to assemble or to harbour ministers.

From this house, always wide open to Anabaptists of all persuasions, alms were distributed. Indeed, the congregation's choice of Simprecht as one of several deacons surely had to have been dictated in part by that traffic, as well as by the perceived steadfastness of the Wiedenmann couple.

Simprecht Wiedenmann, Laux Kreler, Hans Lauterwein, and Spitzendrat had been elected to the office of purse-keepers, though no record tells us precisely what that meant.[28] Later commentators add Gall Vischer. Wiedenmann, Kreler, and Vischer did distribute some money and material goods, according to the testimony of Anabaptist captives.[29] But so did the wives of Wiedenmann and Kreler. Indeed, the records mention Katharina Wiedenmann and the unnamed wife of Laux Kreler more frequently than they do their husbands, as distributors of Anabaptist largesse. The two deacon families came from different social classes and had different standards of living. Perhaps the congregation in its particular wisdom wanted it that way, in order to find easy contacts with Anabaptist recipients of different social classes and economic means. It is clear that Katharina gave gifts to others. Although Peutinger set about to uncover any evidence of community of goods and material aid, he did not question Katharina about her role as deaconess.[30]

Katharina served as a messenger for Anabaptist news. The records tell us of one instance in which she helped to circulate a pastoral letter, sent to the women of Augsburg by Balthas Berchtold late in 1527, after he had been exiled. She, with other women, carried it from one Anabaptist family to another, though she was not literate and could not read it herself. The contents, she reported, were entirely devoted to godly affairs.[31]

Their home was open to all. Still, over time, Katharina and her husband learned that they did not always mingle easily with some of the wealthier Anabaptists, such as the Krelers, the Laux Millers, and the Lauterweins. Simprecht Wiedenmann was one of two poorer Anabaptists who complained to the Augsburg authorities that they, the poor, were haled into court while the wealthier among them, of a higher social class, were ignored; or that these poorer Anabaptist captives were tortured while the wealthier were (merely slapped lightly on the wrist.)[32]

Katharina was led out of town and exiled, and her husband was beaten out with rods. Neither seems to have been able to return; the wealthier Anabaptists could return if they retracted.

Wife of Laux Kreler

Laux Kreler was a goldsmith, a profession that made him wealthier than most Augsburg citizens. The Krelers housed Anabaptists, but more important, they handed out money and goods to some. Laux had visited Anabaptist meetings in 1527, but had not been baptized by September 19, 1527, when he was compelled to promise on oath not to attend Anabaptist meetings. Yet he was baptized in the spring of 1528 by Jörg Nespitzer (though Augustin Bader reported later that he had baptized Kreler[33]). As soon as the arrests of Anabaptists widened after the Easter meeting of April 12, 1528, Kreler, and presumably also his wife, fled Augsburg. Such was the privilege of the socially more important Anabaptists; they somehow learned of prospective moves against them and fled. One suspects that highly ranked Anabaptists had ready sympathizers within the city government.[34]

Laux's wife remains elusive in the available records. Despite the couple's higher social standing, even in the extant archival records her first name is not given; she is referred to only as Kreler's wife.[35] Simprecht Wiedenmann reported to the interrogator that when Jörg Nespitzer told him that Wiedenmann, Laux Kreler, Hans Lauterwein, and an unnamed weaver whom we know as Spitzendrat had been chosen deacons to look to the needs of the poor, he did not want to collect money for that purpose.[36] His report to Peutinger was more negative than his behaviour. It is clear that Kreler did give him money for that purpose, without indicating its origin. This seems a sound pattern for alms collection and distribution: the richer couple tapping wealthier resources for funds, with the distribution in the hands of that couple most constantly in touch with needy folk among the Anabaptists.

But Kreler's wife distributed money to the poor and sick: to Jakob Rotenstein when his wife and child were sick;[37] to Els Knöll, a widow who housed two poor Anabaptist refugees;[38] probably to others who did not report the gifts in court. And she and her husband housed Anabaptists, including Hans Leupold, Leonhard Dorfbrunner, and other leaders immediately after the all-night meeting in the cellar of Barbara Schleiffer's house, on the night of April 2-3, when they elected two new leaders, Claus Schleiffer and Peter Ringmacher.[39] The records tell us they also housed

Anna Haller Salminger, wife of preacher Sigmund after he was jailed in September 1527.⁴⁰

These and the Kreler's 1528 baptisms were activities bound to bring down the swift wrath of the city; had they been caught, they should have been branded and exiled. Perhaps their higher social status would have earned them something less severe. As it was, they fled untouched and reappeared in Strasbourg.⁴¹

Women Who Ministered to Anabaptists in Other Ways
Barbara Schleiffer

Barbara Schleiffer, a grocer by trade, commanded a dynamic centre of Anabaptist life in Augsburg. Her unnamed husband and one son, Jörg, did not join, but Jörg helped the group. Another son, Gall, and two daughters–Anna who married Simprecht Mair and Ursula who married Sebald Penthelin–did join and vigorously promoted the Anabaptist cause. Barbara used their house for meetings, sometimes when her husband was absent. One of the most important meetings took place in the cellar of her house on April 11, 1528, where the decision was made to gather a larger group of Anabaptists on Easter Sunday. Non-Augsburgers, presumably refugee Anabaptists, were constantly coming and going through her house; indeed, Anabaptist traffic through her house was so heavy that in a fit of exaggeration one Anabaptist called it "daily."⁴² One woman reported that the Lord's Supper was celebrated in Barbara's house.⁴³ In the testimony of other Anabaptists captured on April 12, her name was given at least forty-two times, more than that of any other Anabaptist except a few of the ministers. After the autumn 1527 city strictures against the Anabaptists, her steadfastness was a major factor in keeping the Anabaptist movement alive. She had been beaten out of town on January 20, 1528;⁴⁴ obviously she returned, and the city authorities apparently winked at the fact. After the late April 1528 roundup of stray Anabaptists, beyond those captured at the Easter Sunday raid, she disappeared. Probably she fled, never to return.

She never led the Anabaptists in any formal or official manner. She did lead in the form of inviting them constantly into her home, and obviously encouraging them.

Elisabeth Hegenmiller

Els was a relatively minor Anabaptist. She had a loose tongue; and Peutinger, seeing his advantage in gathering data on others, plied his craft more vigorously and increased the threats of torture–which he eventually applied near the end of his interrogation. His principal intent was to discover who the Anabaptists were and the locations of their meeting places for his larger juridical purpose of demolishing the movement by catching and punishing all of them. Unwittingly, she gives us bits of information on how the Augsburg Anabaptists ran their church.

Els managed a small grocery shop with her husband in the "Lutz Corner House," beside small shops with other goods. They handled staples such as salt, flour, lard, and candles. They lived in the Fuggerei, that early Western-world model settlement designed to provide decent housing for low-income families.[45] Residence in the Fuggerei tells us that they were people of only modest means; nonetheless, their charitable energies were considerable.[46]

She joined the Anabaptists in December 1527, after the city forbade further meetings and baptisms; she was induced by the preaching of Leonhard Dorfbrunner, who baptized her. Dorfbrunner was one of more than thirty Anabaptist preacher/teachers in Augsburg, most of them itinerant like him. Els was also probably influenced by other Anabaptist grocers; indeed, the guild of Augsburg grocers was extraordinarily active in the Anabaptist cause. Led by Anabaptist Andreas Widholz until his forced exile on October 17, 1527, it numbered at least six known Anabaptists and three sympathizers who met with the Anabaptists and helped them but did not join; in addition there were at least seven grocer-spouses who were Anabaptists. Two of these Anabaptist grocers harboured meetings in their houses—Widholz and Barbara Schleiffer. Here was a guild evangelizing first its own members, then reaching out to others. While Els did not tell Peutinger who had persuaded her to join, her daily contacts with other grocers would surely have influenced her decisively.

Perhaps her kinsfolk influenced her to join the Anabaptists. Certainly her sister Regina Weisshaupt joined, though Els disclaimed knowledge of when Regina joined or who baptized her.[47] Her husband, however, never joined though he seems not to have opposed her religious conversion; on the contrary, he helped her distribute groceries to needy Anabaptists, even initiating the activity in one remarkable case of a Bavarian Anabaptist refugee woman named Zelestin.[48] His complicity was not serious enough to warrant government intervention or recorded inquiry. He was not called to his wife's hearings.[49]

Els's testimony gives us insights into other aspects of Anabaptist underground church life.

a. *Convening of Secret Meetings*

She learned of one meeting of Anabaptists from two sources whom Peutinger compelled her to name. The unnamed servant of Stainmair the glassmaker, then Martin Wegman,[50] told her; one suspects that these people were customers in her shop. They told her the meeting would be held in the house of Scolastica Stierpaur; she went and found it to be so. We learn of other meetings she attended through the ungentle prodding of Peutinger. At that first assembly, Els had met Susanna Doucher, whom she asked to inform her if there was to be another meeting. Consequently, Susanna sent a Bavarian refugee sister to inform Els of the big gathering at the Doucher house on Easter Sunday. Els had known that sculptor Hans would be absent at that time because she had asked him; the convenience of her grocery shop, located in a well-frequented part of the city, gave her unusual access to people. Els's own daughter had also learned of the meeting time and place and relayed it to her mother.[51] Clearly, there was a network of informants, usually scrupulously careful about revealing information to potential opponents. Some major parts of that network were laid bare for modern researchers by Peutinger's unkindly persistence.

b. *Nature of Meetings*

At subsequent hearings Peutinger prodded Els to reveal the nature and venue of other meetings, which she did reluctantly. We learn that they gathered around a table, or two of them if the group's size required it; that at some of the meetings they served small breads together with wine, beyond their needs for the Lord's Supper; that the meetings were attended by six or eight people, substantially larger groups than the two or three persons permitted by the authorities in October 1527. There was always a teacher or preacher present, but she claimed not to know the names of some of them. She seems genuinely not to have known as many as half the Anabaptists, or candidates for membership, who met on these occasions.[52] Here were all the markings of an underground church, operating with success until the Anabaptist leaders too boldly planned a meeting of several hundred and came to rue their audacity.

c. *Religious Content of the Meetings*

Els related those things that would not harm any Anabaptist—reading the Bible and teaching from it, someone having another book which was read, etc. From her first meeting she carried away a burning recollection of the preacher admonishing them all to charitable acts toward the poor. Peutinger seems not to have cared much for the religious ideas and practices of the Anabaptists; he was only interested in the names and meeting places of Augsburg citizens who violated their October 1527 oath or who were converted and baptized after that event, as Els was. He was interested in arrest and punishment, not in persuading Anabaptists to recant and return to the true faith.[53]

d. *Charitable Activities*

This Augsburg Anabaptist congregation had selected deacons to provide for its poor, but there were individual members like Els who donated to others. She gave food and other basic supplies to indigent and refugee brothers and sisters. For those acts she should have been punished specially, but Peutinger seemed not to care very much. In a state of some alarm, Augsburg authorities had instructed him to probe the Anabaptist practice of community of goods.

Peutinger used the threat of torture, and finally the thumbscrew itself, to satisfy himself that Els had told him everything of relevance. Like other prisoners, she gradually revealed more information of the kind he wanted; the shadow of the small thumbscrew hung over the interrogation of each Anabaptist woman.

Els was punished severely. The Augsburg authorities had her tongue cut out and then exiled her as soon as her tongue had healed, a savagery administered to her because she had blasphemed, in their opinion, the sacrament of the altar. She had barked out choice epithets at the maid of the couple who ran the butcher stall next to hers, calling the host that "slimy idol" or "bread idol" [*rotziger Herrgott* or *gotzenbrot*]–loudly enough for others to hear and tattle.[54] Her hearing reveals that Els could incline toward secrecy when she had to; otherwise she talked too freely.

Veronica (Albrecht) Gross

Veronica Gross and Anna Salminger were married to two Anabaptist leaders who were jailed in September 1527. These women held firm, encouraged, and supported others, and urged others to remain steadfast under government pressure.

Veronica Gross was cited nine times in the testimony of others, primarily women in Augsburg. A native of Waldshut, she had been baptized in the early days of the Anabaptist movement, in April 1525,[55] probably by Wilhelm Reublin. She reported coming to Augsburg with her husband, Jacob, and staying in the home of Eitelhans Langenmantel. After her husband was jailed, she stayed in Langenmantel's house in Göggingen, where she took up the trade of seamstress. She returned to Augsburg only on April 11, 1528. She supplied her interrogator with many Anabaptist names and venues, both in and outside the city. It is clear that she knew and was known by many Anabaptists, especially women.

How did she learn the time and place of a meeting? Anabaptists passed on the information, one to another; she knew of no special messenger, but she reported that sometimes "they" announced meetings to the sisters, who in turn spread the word to others. Here was a special role for women.[56] She defended meetings, however suppressed, as occasions for reading scripture and strengthening each other in the faith. She reported that she instructed some of the Anabaptist women[57] and that she stayed with this religion because "it was the right way, and [she] would not hold to the former way at all."[58]

She plied her trade, sometimes in the houses of Augsburg people, sometimes in outlying villages. So she earned her keep and required no charity–the interrogator prodded her on this point several times. She did report seeing money pass from hand to hand among Anabaptists, but thought little of it except that some needed it. She seemed pleased that she could earn her own bread, which she reported taking with her to meetings. She also made some small change by selling a few of her husband's books. Caught at the Easter gathering in April 1528, she would neither recant nor swear the oath to remain in exile; consequently she was beaten with rods and driven out of the city.

Her steadfastness in staying where her husband was imprisoned, visiting many Anabaptists in their homes, supporting herself financially, and maintaining a high level of courage had to have been a strong inspiration to others.

Anna (Haller) Salminger

Baptized by Hans Hut in Langenmantel's house on February 2, 1527, Anna was one of the earlier Augsburg women to join the Anabaptists there. She and her husband were caught in the early fall roundup of 1527; her husband was imprisoned, and since she refused to take the oath to remain in exile, she was led out of the city on September 17, 1527. Clearly she returned, but we are not told when. In the four or so months prior to the major arrests of April 12, 1528, she had moved among many Anabaptists in the city. She had stayed several weeks with Honester Krafter, some time with Laux Miller's family, and then with the Laux Kreler family. But she also lived for longer periods of time with Anabaptist friends in the villages and towns outside Augsburg. She finally sold her household goods for twelve guilders to gain the means to keep herself. She was also helped financially by others, even in the form of money received from Augsburg Anabaptists when she was living outside the city; when she asked about the donors, she was told it did not matter.

Caught at the Easter meeting, she would not recant nor promise to remain in exile; in consequence she was beaten out of the city as one who had violated the city's earlier 1527 injunction to remain in exile. Still, in 1530, when Sigmund, her broken, dying husband, finally recanted and was released from prison, she too recanted, and together they remained in Augsburg. Her steadfastness between September 1527 and April 1528 was helpful to many Anabaptist women.[59]

Concluding Observations

Differences Among the Nine Women.

These nine women constitute a cross section of Augsburg's Anabaptist population and reflect a wide variety of differences: in financial means, social class, trade or occupation, marital status, and other ways. They carried out their Anabaptist activities with or without their husbands' support: two were widows (Stierpaur and Frölich); the husbands of two were ministers, in prison at the time, and obviously supportive of their wives' activities (Gross and Salminger); the husbands of two were Anabaptist deacons who supported their wives' work and perhaps even mandated some of it (Kreler and Wiedenmann); the husband of one never joined, but sympathized (Hegenmiller); the husband of another never joined, and appears to have been indifferent (Schleiffer); finally, the husband of Susanna

Doucher opposed the Anabaptists, and had to have made the exercise of her faith difficult.

These nine women were baptized by seven different ministers. Two of the seven, Jakob Gross and Jörg Nespitzer, were resident in Augsburg until their capture, though they came from outside the city. One, Hans Hut, was semi-resident and died in prison there, though he came from Central Germany. Three—Leonhard Dorfbrunner, Hans Greuel, and Thomas Waldhauser—were itinerant ministers, though Dorfbrunner remained in Augsburg for several months. Finally, Wilhelm Reublin baptized Veronica Gross before she came to Augsburg. All told, some twenty-three different ministers baptized the forty-five native Augsburg Anabaptists caught at Susanna Doucher's house on April 12, 1528. Twenty were baptized within Augsburg itself.[60] Surely that plethora of baptizers, each with his own kind of religious appeal and perhaps theology, lent a considerable variety to Augsburg Anabaptist religious life; we can only conjecture on the shapes and forms of that variety, since the congregation dissolved so quickly.

Religious diversity was enlarged, then, by a large number of ministers who read the Word and instructed at meetings of Augsburg Anabaptists. Beyond the known twenty-three who baptized in addition to preaching, records can be found for at least eleven ministers who merely preached or taught. One suspects that there were more; most of the prisoners revealed as little as they could, and there were other itinerant Anabaptist ministers in regions around Augsburg.

Variety of that magnitude was hardly conducive to congregational unity. Some fissures between groups were beginning to develop in mid-1527. In an intercessionary statement laid before the Council for the Anabaptist minister Jakob Dachser, who had been baptized by Hut, reported that he had accepted only those Anabaptist teachings that he considered valid; "but when some among them had prophesied and held such opinions, he had opposed it and stirred up such displeasure among them that they wished to expell him."[61] Surely the Augsburgers brought at least some charges against Hut in the August "Martyrs' Synod." In court testimony after the 1528 Easter Sunday sweep, one Anabaptist reported that Jörg Nespitzer cautioned against the teachings of Hut,[62] even though Hut's recent death surely would have cast him in heroic mold to many. Further, in April 1528, minister Hans Leupold reported that when Hut had some nine months earlier, preached his time-specific end of the world, Leupold and "others" left Gall Vischer's house where the meeting was taking place.[63] With Leupold and Nespitzer in virtual command of the congregation for several months before Easter 1528, and plainly in charge of the Easter meeting, one wonders what the future of Hutian Anabaptism in Augsburg might have been if Hut had lived.[64]

The final dispositions of the nine women varied. Three (Stierpaur,

Frölich, Hegenmiller) were exiled after excessive physical punishment; we have no reason to believe they ever returned. Three (Schleiffer, Kreler, Wiedenmann) fled and very probably did not return to Augsburg. Gross and Salminger recanted two years later when their nearly dead husbands recanted as the price for release from prison. Doucher was exiled and we hear nothing more about her; I suspect she recanted, or returned later with some pardon–Augsburg tended to be lenient toward its prominent citizens.

Differences aside, what bound these women together was their common dedication to the religious cause. During this period of time, they were among those most fixed in purpose and tenacious in their religious conviction, despite a clear expectation of punishment.

Leadership Roles, a Summary

1. Some of these women hosted meetings in their houses, sometimes despite the opposition of their spouses, but always against the clear intention of the Augsburg civic ban that forbade meetings of more than two or three people at a time. They tended to keep the number of participants low, six to ten, occasionally fifteen or eighteen. But hosting the meetings required giving some notice, personally or through others. Some of these women also helped to spread word of meetings held elsewhere. One has to read between the lines, but surely their convening and advertising of Anabaptist meetings had to include some minimal degree of prior planning. Veronica Gross reported that word of pending meetings was given to the sisters, who spread it.[65] We are not told that these women were religious leaders, yet in this particular they did lead, privately.

At least one of the nine, Barbara Schleiffer,[66] hosted sewing circles, women with their needles and distaffs, either professional or private seamstresses or spinners of yarn. Other Augsburg women provided what seem to be regular sewing venues. One such meeting seems to have been nicknamed a *Gunkel* [distaff] meeting.[67] Anabaptist Felicitas Huber testified that she had "invited [Katharina Wiedenmann] with the distaff," as if she held it aloft or waved it about in the street to summon other Anabaptist women.[68] The sewing or spinning assembly proved ideal for the reading of scripture with commentary; at this task women had to have been the originators and organizers.

2. Several of the women distributed alms; two were the wives of men selected as deacons by the Anabaptist congregation for that purpose. They appear to have distributed as much as their husbands did. And some Augsburg Anabaptist women distributed alms privately, from their own supplies or those of others.

3. Augsburg Anabaptist women housed and fed itinerants, both ministers and simple refugees. A fuller study of the Augsburg records demonstrates that the pattern was widespread, certainly much beyond the activities of these nine women. Augsburg authorities moved sharply against

any hosting of visitors, because they considered it possible to suppress the harbouring of aliens through a closer watch on each of the gates and on individual homes within the city. The authorities knew that the Anabaptists were nourished by a stream of people from outside the city. They decided to divert that stream by sending part of it to a smaller centre, Göggingen, a few miles southwest of the city. It was relatively easy to put patrician Eitelhans Langenmantel under house arrest in his Göggingen house, with the expectation that itinerant Anabaptist leaders would contact him there and perhaps thereby give Augsburg itself a wider berth. With a merely reasonable exercise of caution, the movement could be arrested in its tracks, then completely suppressed. But they needed to exercise diligence in ferreting out any Augsburgers who proved too hospitable to strangers, then punishing them severely. Four of the nine women were vulnerable on this count. Their hospitality did indeed give significant support to the movement.

Some of the Augsburg Anabaptists gave work to refugee Anabaptists. Peutinger was unable to find what one suspects was a large amount of that kind of mutual aid. The city decided to release and exile all the foreigners captured on April 12, 1528, and the natives were coy and disingenuous when it came to providing information on this point.[69] This select nine were not involved in this kind of activity, but a comment is necessary to give a fuller view of Augsburg Anabaptist congregational life.

4. Some Augsburg Anabaptist women helped spread the good news of their particular faith quietly by word of mouth, especially to potential converts. For example, we have the account of Dorothea Ott, who attended the Easter Sunday meeting although she was unbaptized. She told Peutinger that the maid of Simprecht Wiedenmann had invited her as she, Dorothea, was on her way to worship at the Holy Cross church. The maid suggested she change course in order to "hear wonderful things." Dorothea left her prie-dieu at the Wiedenmann's house and went with the maid to Doucher's house. To Peutinger she denied any connection with the Anabaptists beyond a passing interest. But it was in this manner that the Anabaptist women invited potential converts.[70]

5. Finally, Augsburg Anabaptist women gave earnest and constant support to those who were under pressure to surrender the Anabaptist way. They were remarkably steadfast. As with the majority of Anabaptists, eventually some did give up and return to the prescribed religion. During the period of our study, when Anabaptism managed to expand despite severe restrictions, these women were faithful and supportive.

Why did these women lead, especially in convening meetings, distributing alms, and lending moral support to those who might give way under pressure? Surely in part because they were less conspicuous than men. They could advertise meetings while shopping at grocer stalls, or while carrying out normal household functions such as sewing in small groups.

Certainly the men were watched more closely. Nothing in the records tells us this directly, but the women's assumption of these roles speaks for itself. In sixteenth-century Europe, men could move more easily than women from one geographical location to another. Men could join the Anabaptists, considered heretical by governments and severely suppressed, more easily, and in larger numbers, than could their female counterparts.[71] But if men were freer than women to travel the longer distances, women were perhaps more mobile than men within cities such as Augsburg. They could move about less observed and communicate privately, unheard by authorities. Probably most Anabaptists recognized their covert condition and encouraged the women to exercise these functions. Augsburg's Anabaptist women carried through certain organizational functions under conditions requiring the utmost caution to avoid detection.

One more comment about alms and the sharing of material wealth among these Anabaptists: although the city fathers showed some alarm at the possibility of full-blown community of goods as they perceived it among the Anabaptists, Peutinger failed to pursue the topic in interrogations.[72] Their system of mutual aid ran competition with the city's, and Peutinger thought this activity to be revolutionary. Still, the Anabaptists were spared his pressure; we would have profited had he troubled to extract more information from them.

Whatever leadership roles Augsburg's women carried, they were not permitted access to the process of selecting ministers. Anna Salminger, wife of imprisoned minister Sigmund, reported explicitly that the women had no vote in selecting ministers or in determining where some might be sent as missioners.[73]

Some Rules for Operating an Underground Church.

In the earliest years of Anabaptism, at almost all geographical locations, the brothers and sisters learned to conduct their religious affairs in secret. Augsburg was no exception. The researcher learns to detect certain obvious patterns of behaviour designed to maintain a vital church underground (or at least partly so). Even after the events of September and October 1527, Anabaptists still hoped the Augsburg authorities would let them live out their religious option, despite the imprisonment of leaders Dachser, Salminger, Gross, and Hut (who died in prison in December). Here, in conclusion, are a few techniques these Augsburgers practised, without ascribing them to particular Anabaptists.

1. Do not ask or learn the name of your baptizer or of any travelling minister. Do not learn the name of the man or woman who provides free housing and food if you are a refugee. Then you will be unable to disclose their names if you are caught and taken into court and tortured.

2. Hide the leaders at different places; disguise them; have them remain anonymous or use pseudonyms. Move them out of town or village on

their itinerant ways when it becomes dangerous to keep them longer.

3. Meet secretly: in a forest, a gravel pit, some isolated building at the edge of a village where the group can sing hymns without being heard, within the city in the more isolated houses that have been hung with blankets, etc., on the inside to block spying eyes, or in very small groups in normal city houses where people gather anyway for routine social purposes.[74]

4. Greet each other simply so as to allay suspicion, but in some environments with an exchange that indicates to each party the Anabaptist inclination of the other. In this way strangers may recognize the Anabaptist in each other. One says, "God greet thee, sister in the Lord." The other answers, "God thank thee, sister in the Lord." Some greetings are less elaborate, but very particular. (Some Anabaptists denied there was any special greeting; others declared that there was. But special greeting was a common point of interrogation wherever Anabaptists were caught.)[75]

In these and other ways the Anabaptists sought to keep their religious life vital and to save their own lives. They were only partly successful in both undertakings.

Notes

1. See for example the Hearing of the Sorga Anabaptists, Central Germany, August 28, 1533, in TA, *Hesse*, 64-69. The Anabaptists were required to answer nine specific questions. The court heard ten husbands answer both for themselves and also for their wives; the court did not ask the women to speak. Obviously a researcher gains no understanding of those ten women.

2. There is a large literature on Anabaptists in Augsburg, some of which follows: Friedwart Uhland, *Täufertum und Obrigkeit in Augsburg im 16. Jahrhundert* (diss. Tübingen; Clausthal-Zellerfeld: Bönecke, 1972); Werner O. Packull, *Mysticism and the Early South German-Austrian Anabaptist Movement 1525-1531* (Scottdale, PA: Herald Press, 1977), an excellent treatment of Augsburg Anabaptists, especially on Hut, Denck, and Bader, but including many of the obscure leaders; Friedrich Roth, *Augsburgs Reformationsgeschichte*, 4 vols. (Munich: Theodor Ackermann, 1901-1911) (hereafter Roth, 1901-11), archivist in Augsburg, provides one excellent chapter on the Anabaptists; Claus-Peter Clasen, *Anabaptism: A Social History, 1525-1618* (Ithaca, NY: Cornell University Press, 1972), with excellent material on the Augsburg Anabaptists; Hans Guderian, *Die Täufer in Augsburg: Ihre Geschichte und ihr Erbe* (Pfaffenhofen: Ludwig Verlag, 1984); Hege, "Augsburg," ME, I, 182-85; Paul J. Schwab, "Augsburg and the Early Anabaptists," in *Reformation Studies: Essays in Honor of Roland H. Bainton*, ed. Franklin H. Littell (Richmond, VA: John Knox Press, 1962), 212-28; Stephen Blake Boyd, *Pilgram Marpeck: His Life and Social Theology* (Durham: Duke University Press, 1992), especially good for Anabaptism in later years, beyond Marpeck's time there.

3. Primary sources: Roth transcribed the hearings of Anabaptists after the April 12, 1528, capture, and published them in "Zur Geschichte der Wiedertäufer in Oberschwaben: III. Der Höhepunkt der wiedertäuferischen Bewegung in Augsburg und ihr Niedergang im Jahre 1528," *Zeitschrift des historischen Vereins f. Schwaben u. Neuburg*, 28 (1901): 1-154 (hereafter Roth 1901). He also transcribed hearings of Langenmantel and friends and

published them in "Zur Geschichte der Wiedertäufer in Oberschwaben. II. Zur Lebensgeschichte Eitelhans Langenmantels von Augsburg," *Zeitschrift des Historischen Vereins f. Schwaben u. Neuburg,* 27 (1900): 1-45. Earlier, Christian Meyer had transcribed Augsburg archival records about Hans Hut and published them in "Zur Geschichte der Wiedertäufer in Oberschwaben: I. Die Anfänge des Wiedertäufertums in Augsburg," *Zeitschrift des Historischen Vereins f. Schwaben u. Neuburg,* 1 (1874): 207-56. Chronicler Clemens Sender provides much interesting, albeit often erroneous, data about the Anabaptists, in *Die Chronik von Clemens Sender von den ältesten Zeiten der Stadt bis zum Jahre 1536,* Friedrich Roth, ed., *Die Chroniken der deutschen Städte von 14. bis ins 16. Jahrhundert,* 23 (Leipzig: S. Hirzel, 1894).

4 *Wider den Newen Taufforden, Nothwendige Warnung an alle Christgläubigen* (Augsburg: [Heinr. Steiner], 1527).
5 Sender, *Chronik,* 198, had a regrettable tendency to exaggerate. Packull, *Mysticism,* 126, uses a much more conservative figure, suggesting that only a few left the meeting before eighty-eight of them were captured.
6 Clasen, *Social History,* 64.
7 Clasen, ibid., 54, counts 15 leaders including itinerant "apostles," far too modest a figure. See below for a fuller discussion of number of leaders.
8 Sender, *Chronik,* 198, also reported that Susanna Doucher began preparing her house three days prior to the meeting on Easter Sunday; among other things, she hung rugs and blankets in the windows ostensibly to thwart curious eyes.
9 Roth 1901-11, 247-50, has the fullest collection of details of this meeting.
10 Uhland, *Täufertum,* 159, has reconstructed the questions Peutinger asked the forty-three non-Augsburgers; Augsburg records do not supply this information.
11 See Lewis Spitz, *The Religious Renaissance of the German Humanists* (Cambridge, MA: Harvard University Press, 1963), esp. 272-73. His biographers declare him an Erasmian. Perhaps they are right—on the issue of not "tearing the seamless robe of Christ," and others. But he showed no Erasmian interest in tolerance in matters of religion, nor was he compassionate toward anyone he considered a civic deviant. He had a three-year-old girl buried alive and a twelve-year-old boy beheaded, both for murder. See *Allgemeine Deutsche Biographie,* XXV, 561-68. He had a distinguished career as city secretary and syndic—keeping Augsburg's records, handling the city's correspondence, and carrying out many of its diplomatic missions, especially with successive emperors. Emperor Maximilian befriended him, and warmly supported Peutinger's forays into collecting antique Latin inscriptions, Roman coins, and valuable manuscripts, many of which Peutinger published. Although he had welcomed Luther early in the Reformer's career, he remained Roman Catholic to the end. In 1534, when the city finally decided to change its religious practices toward Protestantism, he remonstrated and was finally eased into retirement in 1538. See Uhland, *Täufertum,* 119, 287-89, for Peutinger's views on the Anabaptists, especially what he considered dangerous in their activities.
12 Hearing of Jacob Walch, Roth 1901, 125. About 20 Anabaptists met in a meadow outside the city, late in August, and made this decision. Augsburg had the largest congregation of Anabaptists in southern Germanic regions. Clasen counts 359 members between 1526 and 1528, around 1.5% of Augsburg's total population of approximately 25,000. See Clasen, *Social History* 27, 442 and n. 7. Figures like these make the movement appear miniscule, and one wonders why any city official was worried. Clasen never quite reckons the fact of growth of the movement, and official alarm at what that movement might become. Augsburg chronicler Sender, *Chronik,* 186, reported that 1100 people gathered for Anabaptist meetings. Did he merely reflect the alarm at the growth of Anabaptism and exaggerate in consequence, or was he privy to some respectable

estimate of heads based on size of gardens in which they met, etc.?

13 Perhaps scholars have given up too easily on the continuation of an Augsburg Anabaptist congregation. Granted, a congregation of 20 Anabaptists decided to suspend meetings, and the archival sources are not rich on Anabaptists after 1528; but there is some material that few have adequately examined. In his pursuit of Marpeck's trail, Stephen Boyd has done more work than anyone on that later period of Anabaptist life in Augsburg.

14 The government killed Augsburger Hans Leupold, the principal Anabaptist leader caught on April 12. Four leaders had languished in jail until they either recanted or died, as Hut had already. Otherwise the Augsburg punishments were milder than those administered by many other governments. To the Augsburg women, however, the threat of punishment by execution had to have been shockingly real.

15 Sometimes called Thomas of Grein, Waldhauser was a chaplain in Hapsburg lands; he became Lutheran, but dissatisfied, he turned toward the Anabaptists under the influence of Leonhard von Freisleben. He associated with Anabaptists in Styria, then took up an Anabaptist teaching ministry stretching from Bavaria to Moravia, where he was burned at the stake on April 10, 1528 (Brno). ME, IV, p. 876. He baptized at least one more person in Augsburg.

16 Most of the relevant information about Susanna Doucher's Anabaptism comes from her own hearings, April 13 and 16, 1528, Roth 1901, 51-53. Other Anabaptists testified to her presence at meetings, and about her making her house available for the Easter Sunday meeting of Anabaptists, April 12, 1528.

17 Hearing of Susanna Doucher, ibid., 52. I find her credible in reporting that she did not know of the chalk symbol on her house until someone told her when they met in prison. Ibid. Obviously someone else put it on her door. Clasen, *Social History*, 69, decided she put it there herself.

18 Hege has a brief article on her, "Doucher, Susanna," ME, II, 95, drawing entirely from the Roth 1901 transcriptions of Augsburg records.

19 See Roth 1901-11, I, 252, for accounts of some who were permitted to return. Augsburg's formal records call her absent husband Hans Adolf Doucher, but usually only Adolf. Historians of art name that Augsburg sculptor active in 1527-28 simply Hans Dauher. He was born around 1488 and died in 1538 in Augsburg. He was the son of an Adolf Dauher, and both of them were sculptors. Father Adolf had been born around 1465 in Ulm and died in Augsburg in 1523 or 1524. See *Der grosse Brockhaus* (Leipzig: Brockhaus, 1929), IV, 433. Adolf sculpted choirstalls for the Fugger chapel at St. Anne's in Augsburg. He was one of first artists to bring Rensaissance style sculpting into Germany, and his son continued that style. Hans sculpted several figures in Augsburg and other neighbouring cities including Munich. He lived in his own house "am hinteren Lech." In spring of 1528 he did indeed leave Augsburg to carry out an artistic commission in Vienna, then returned later. See *Neue deutsche Biographie* (Berlin, 1957), III, 526; see also Roth 1901-11, 268, n. 135.

20 The best information comes from her own hearings, Roth 1901, 48-49. Curiously, Roth suggests as her husband the husband of Magdalena Ziegler, who made gingerbread and lived by the Göggingen Gate. Roth is normally scrupulously accurate. Ibid., 153, 108, 109.

21 Roth 1901-11, I, 254. Anabaptists in the court hearings of April 1528ff. refer to him eight times. See also the scanty information in Neff, "Greuel, Hans," ME, II, 578.

22 She was nicknamed the Rispinin, derived from her husband's first name, Crispin. Peutinger himself was the principal emissary sent on the most important of Augsburg's diplomatic missions. Stierpaur had to have been a much lesser figure.

23 "Schweitzer." Swiss Brethren, or someone from Switzerland? Her report does not tell us plainly. Perhaps Gregorius of Chur, about whom we know little. Langenmantel's servant Herman Anwald reported Gregorius among the several Anabaptist ministers he had known. See hearing of Anwald, Friedrich Roth, "Zur Geschichte der Wiedertäufer in Oberschwaben. II. Zur Lebensgeschichte Eitelhans Langenmantels von Augsburg," *Zeitschrift des Historischen Vereins f. Schwaben u. Neuburg*, 27 (1900): 22.

24 Who is he? There was a certain minister, Hans of Salzburg, otherwise not identified, who visited Augsburg. See Scolastica's hearing, Roth 1901, 51 and the hearing of Veronica Gross, ibid., 67. Did she mean furrier Jakob Gross of Waldshut?–hardly mistakable for Salzburg. Is this an Anabaptist leader, unidentifiable because he escaped detection? Uhland, *Täufertum*, 185, lists him without identification.

25 Els Hegenmiller hearing, ibid., 53.

26 Hearing of Scolastica, ibid., 50. Susanna Doucher was born a Kicklinger.

27 Testimony from her own hearing must be supplemented by reading that of her husband, since he reported most of the groups that came as well as sundry comings and goings. Hearings of Simprecht Wiedenmann, ibid., 91-97; hearings of Katharina, ibid., 97-98.

28 In his section on leaders, Clasen, *Social History*, 51-62, does not discuss deacons–surely the task was too ill-defined. See ibid., 465, n. 78, for his discussion of Augsburg men who were selected to keep the purse. Clasen writes that they refused the task. I find that refusal valid for Lauterwein–as an innkeeper he surely was too exposed for such a dangerous task–but not for the other men. See hearing of Hans Lauterwein, Roth 1901, 99-100. When Wiedenmann was told by Nespitzer that he had been selected by the congregation, he replied that he did not want to receive money to distribute. Hearing of Simprecht Wiedenmann, ibid., 92-93. We have no word from Kreler and Spitzendrat because they managed to flee before capture. But Kreler and Wiedenmann did indeed distribute alms, and one suspects they felt some official calling for the task. Gall Vischer also did some deacon service.

29 Hearing of Dorothea Frölich, ibid., 49; hearing of Anna, daughter of Benedict Schneider, ibid., 44.

30 Hearing of Katharina Wiedenmann, ibid., 97-98.

31 Ibid. 98 and n. 10.

32 Hearing of Simprecht Wiedenmann, ibid., 97. But see also the hearing of Matheis Huber, ibid., 101-2, who complained that the authorities permitted the richer Anabaptists free run of the city while incarcerating the poorer ones, and reported that other Anabaptists thought the same.

33 TA, *Württemberg*, 963.

34 Augsburg City Archives, Ratsbuch, Vol. XIV, fol. 147b, for information about Kreler and his wife; on September 19, 1527, they swore to obey the Council and not to attend Anabaptist meetings. Obviously they were forsworn. Roth 1901, 92, n. 5; Roth 1901-11, I, 235. Many other citations in testimonies of other captive Anabaptists.

35 Augsburg City Archives, Ratsbuch, XIV, fol. 147b.

36 Hearing of Wiedenmann, Roth 1901, 92. See above, n. 28.

37 Hearing of Jacob Rotenstein, ibid., 134.

38 Hearing of Els Knöll, ibid., 86.

39 Hearing of Hans Leupold, ibid., 63.

40 Ibid., 64.

41 TA, *Württemberg*, 962, from testimony of Augustin Bader.

42 Hearing of Anna Butz, Roth 1901, 41.

43 Hearing of Elisabeth Schweizer, ibid., 32.

44 Roth 1901-11, I, 238.

45 *Der grosse Brockhaus*, II, 80, reports that Jakob Fugger established it in 1519 as low-cost housing, some fifty-three houses for renters of small means.
46 Hearing of Matheis Huber, Roth 1901.
47 Hearing of Els Hegenmiller, ibid., 54.
48 She could name Zelestin whom the authorities did not catch, leading us to believe she probably fled the city before the April 1528 sweep. Ibid., 55.
49 The Augsburg records do not give his name. In February 1529 Anabaptist Hans Nadler reported that Bartel Hegenmiller had been baptized at Alterlangen. See TA, *Brandenburg*, 153. Perhaps Bartel was the husband of Els, and perhaps they reestablished their life together in Alterlangen, some 150 kilometres north of Augsburg.
50 Who was beaten out of the city with rods as a perjurer of his Oct. 1527 oath, since he continued his Anabaptist activities. Augsburg City Archives, Ratsbuch, XIV, fol. 151a. See Roth 1901, 35, n. 1.
51 Hearing of Els Hegenmiller, Roth 1901, 53.
52 Ibid., 53-55.
53 In contrast to the city fathers who held Dachser, Salminger, and Gross captive until they recanted, limiting food and virtually starving the men until they did finally succumb. See Roth 1901-11, esp. 256f. Uhland, *Täufertum*, 204, scores the authorities' disinterest in probing Lord's Supper observations of the Anabaptists; the issue was too sensitive because of differences of opinion between Zwinglians and Lutherans.
54 She claimed that she got the terms from "Claus" [Schleiffer; of Vienna]. Roth 1901, 54, 55.
55 Hearing of Veronica Gross, ibid., 66.
56 Ibid., 67.
57 Ibid., 69.
58 Ibid.
59 Hearing of Anna Salminger, ibid., 69-72.
60 I have not yet been able to identify the baptizers of all of the forty-three refugee Anabaptists caught on April 12, 1528.
61 "da aber unter ihnen sich etliche herfür thäten, prophetisierten und hielten seltsame Opinionen, widerredet er das, dass er solche Ungunst bei ihnen erwarb, dass sie ihn wollten ausgeschlossen haben." Fürschrift, cited and quoted by Roth, 1900, I, 233, and n. 76.
62 Widow Els Knöll reported that Nespitzer warned his auditors against the imminent (that is, spring 1528) Judgement Day prediction of Hut; Nespitzer turned the specific-time prediction of Hut into a much more general warning of suffering for the faithful, for which everyone should prepare. Hearing of Elisabeth (Els) Knöll, ibid., 85.
63 Hearing of Hans Leupold, ibid., 65. Leupold was reporting on the exclusion of Anabaptists who were unfaithful to their calling–presumably excommunication and the ban. He seemed pleased that in his conduct of Augsburg Anabaptist affairs, circumstances had not required that he exclude members; it sufficed for him to preach repentance. But he reported that Hut had taught the necessity for exclusion of members who in some degree were unfaithful. Leupold was the disciple of Jakob Dachser who had opposed Hut's view of the end. See Packull, *Mysticism*, 94.
64 Ibid., 121-29. One of Packull's richest contributions is his discussion of religious emphases of several of the more prominent Augsburg Anabaptist ministers, often taking his information from sources away from Augsburg. In addition to Hut, his primary focus, he treats Dorfbrunner, Leupold, and Nespitzer, then lesser figures Philip Plener, Georg Schachner, Melchior of Salzburg, and Burkhart Braun. Uhland, *Täufertum*, 185-87, decided the Augsburg congregation itself brought order into this chaos in April 1528 by

designating Leupold as well as Nespitzer as their responsible leaders.
65 Hearing of Veronica Gross, Roth 1901, 67.
66 Anna Salminger and Veronica Gross sewed or spun several times in the house of Konrad Miller, according to his hearing, ibid., 79.
67 About the meeting at Barbara Schleiffer's house, hearing of Anna Butz, ibid., see 41.
68 "mit der gungel geladen." Hearing of Felicitas Huber, Roth, 1900, 110.
69 See, for instance, the testimony of another loose tongue, Anabaptist Anna Butz, about the peregrinations and work of refugee Anabaptists; hearing of Anna Butz, ibid., 40.
70 Hearing of Dorothea Ott, ibid., 37.
71 In my statistic-gathering research in southern Germanic regions, covering approximately 1200 Anabaptists to date, I find a ratio of 62.5 percent men to 37.5 percent women.
72 Odd, strange, in view of some alarm he had expressed about their private alms; it conflicted with the city's own system, and Peutinger considered that downright revolutionary. Uhland, *Täufertum*, 119.
73 Hearing of Anna Salminger, Roth 1901, 71.
74 One Augsburg example: Thomas Paur worshipped four times outside the city: two times in the forest by St. Radegundis, one time in a gravel pit by Göggingen, once in a meadow. Hearing of Thomas Paur, Roth 1901, 45. Veronica Gross had to have worshipped in neighbouring hamlets many more times than four.
75 Uhland, *Täufertum*, 194, for his observations. I make these points, drawing from the behaviour of both Augsburg Anabaptists and those from many places beyond that city. I expect to elaborate this topic in the near future. But see also Clasen, *Social History*, 147, for some greetings elsewhere.

SABINA BADER OF AUGSBURG

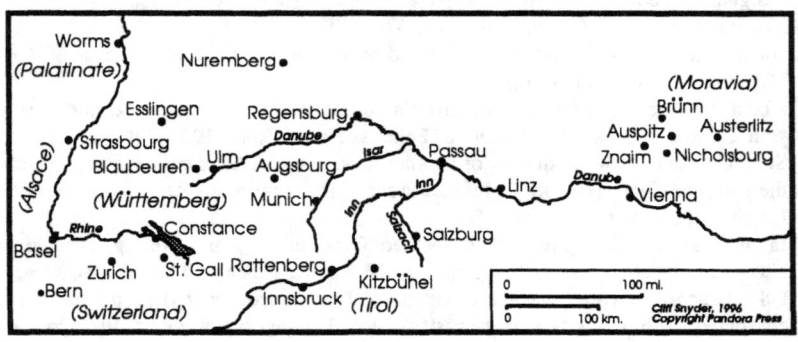

It is surprising that the origins of Sabina Bader are totally unknown. At one stage in her life she moved in the company of prominent people, and she was, by any measure, a remarkable woman herself. Thus she first stands before us in Augsburg in September 1527. She and her husband Augustin were surprised at an Anabaptist meeting by the Augsburg police and arrested on September 15.[1] A month earlier, an Anabaptist meeting referred to as The Martyrs' Synod had met there, and several who had participated in it, including Hans Hut and Jakob Gross, were taken prisoner with the Baders. Hans Hut had agreed at that conference that he would speak of his views on the endtime only to those who asked him: Sabina and her husband had asked.

Sabina, along with her husband, had been baptized by Jakob Gross.[2] Then, as now, baptism meant different things to different people. Just what it meant to Sabina is not at all clear. Many, among them, apparently, Sabina and her husband, believed fervently that they were living in the last days of human history. It was exciting because unusual, unprecedented events were about to take place according to the numerous books on the endtime that were in circulation. Sabina could read and thus had direct access to this literature. More immediately, the Baders knew Hans Hut, who had taught that baptism was the sign that one belonged to those who would survive the terrible tribulations that were coming, and who, as God's Elect, would reign on earth with Christ the Judge.[3] Baptism in order to be on the safe side could have been Sabina Bader's motivation. There is no other clue either in what she is reported to have said or in what she did.

Now she was in the custody of the Lutheran authorities of Augsburg. It was serious. The Baders had four children, the youngest only eight weeks old. Only if she renounced her baptism could she remain in the city. On September 19 she refused to do this and left Augsburg with her baby.[4] The other children were cared for either by relatives or by city welfare. Her husband remained in prison until, on October 19, he recanted and was released. Before long, however, Sabina's concern for her children drove her to write a letter to the authorities, begging for readmission so that she could look after her children. It was granted upon her recantation.[5]

Both she and her husband promptly returned to the Anabaptist fellowship, however, and became very active again. Augustin had now become an elder. But when, on the night of February 25, 1528, they heard the police enter their front door, the Baders were prepared. They had constructed a secret exit in the space under a stairway that led to a concealed closet for just this kind of emergency, and now they used it. They were not discovered. A day or two later Augustin walked out of the city undetected.[6]

Sabina apparently remained in Augsburg. The authorities were not so much after her as after her husband, now an Anabaptist leader. In March he secretly returned to Augsburg, but within a few days left again for Switzerland. Sabina remained to take care of the children.[7]

Near the end of September, Sabina again had a visit from her husband. He told her that he had travelled from Switzerland to Strasbourg, and then east to Nuremberg and as far as Moravia and back again to Strasbourg, everywhere meeting with Anabaptists. He had been driven, he said, by his need to get clarity about the endtime events and that, in consequence, he had had several visions. But because Anabaptists almost everywhere had repudiated his views and his claim to be a prophet, he had, in turn, repudiated Anabaptism. Then, just before he had come home, he had called a meeting in a town near Strasbourg to form a new group with whom he would share his prophetic knowledge. To the four who remained with him, he revealed the revelations he had received. The Turks would invade, the Habsburg monarchy would fall, all government would be abolished, and Christ's kingdom would be established on earth after all wickedness had been destroyed.[8] Another attempt to arrest him failed; when the police arrived at the house, he had already left again.

Until July 1529, Sabina lived with her children in Augsburg in the house they owned. Just before she left, she sold the house for 126 guilders cash. Then she joined her husband with her children in a hamlet near Ulm, where they lived with another couple and their children. Soon after their arrival, Sabina gave birth to a son. When after a while she was asked why she did not have the child baptized, she replied that God himself would baptize it.[9] In November 1529, they were joined by Bader's four devoted followers, and a community of goods was instituted.[10] Bader assured them that the final judgement on the world would commence at Easter in 1530; an invasion by the Turks would be the first act. After that a new divine order would be established on earth, with Bader's little son as the messiah and king. Until the boy grew up, he, Augustin, would be his regent.[11] Whether Sabina shared her husband's convictions is not clear; that she supported him is. The two seem to have resorted to sleight-of-hand tricks to convince their followers, for they agreed to spend a good deal of their common treasury to have a royal ring, a chain of office, a silver goblet, crown, and sceptre made, and to have a sword they owned gilded. A goldsmith was hired to make these items at a total cost of 111 guilders. Sabina, an accomplished seamstress, and others prepared the royal robes. The Baders were now honoured as royalty by their followers.[12]

The miller, in whose rented barn-converted-to-a-house all this took place, began to worry at all the comings and goings, and alerted the authorities. In the night from January 15 to 16, 1530, they surrounded the barn, arrested the whole group, and imprisoned them. That same night Sabina succeeded in escaping, taking with her the gold ring, the goblet, and the rest of the community treasury. She made her way to friends nearby to whom she explained that one of the guards had offered to release her husband in return for sexual favours, but that she had not consented, and so had to flee, leaving her children behind.[13] Before she left there, she wrote a letter to the authorities who held her husband, begging them to release the children to her, since they could be properly brought up only by their mother. She also requested the return of their clothing, their cow, and other property.[14] Then she made her way to Augsburg, paying for her transport with the gold ring. The children remained in the care of the authorities in Blaubeuren where her husband was imprisoned.

During the next few months, Augustin was interrogated repeatedly and tortured savagely in order to get an admission that they had conspired to overthrow the government.[15] He was executed on March 30, beheaded with his gilded sword.[16]

Sabina's relatives interceded for her with the city authorities of Augsburg, asking that she might be permitted to have her children again, but they refused and threatened legal sanctions if her relatives should proceed on their own.[17] The only thing on her mind seems to have been how to rescue her children and give them the care they needed.

She turns up next in St. Gall, Switzerland, where a tailor, who was an Anabaptist, gave her directions to get to Alsace. Because she was afraid of highwaymen, she left a sum of money with him to keep for her for the eventual support for her children.[18] She made her way to Strasbourg where she was hospitably received in the household of the reformer Wolfgang Capito.[19] Capito was, to use a modern term, a "soft touch" when it came to religious refugees. Sabina apparently told him exactly who she was and that her husband had been executed. Capito was very sympathetic to her story that she was a victim of Anabaptist leaders, and that her husband had been a good, though somewhat simple man.[20] Capito took up her cause; he helped her get her money from St. Gall. On October 7 the Strasbourg reformers sent her off to Augsburg with a letter interceding for her, reminding the Council that she should not be made responsible for her husband's misdeeds. They gave her a good character reference.[21] Martin

Bucer later described her as morally irreproachable, a good housekeeper, and an attractive, feminine woman. They suggested that she be allowed to make her living in Augsburg. She also hoped, they wrote on her behalf, for the Council's help in getting back her children.

One could conclude that Sabina was simply an accomplished con artist trying to strike it rich, and that judgement has been made about her. But it is equally plausible that her long journey to Strasbourg and specifically to the house of Wolfgang Capito was a bold stratagem designed to recover her children. Her story thus far has shown her to be extraordinarily resourceful and decisive. She knew that getting her children back from a Catholic jurisdiction called for the intervention of people with public influence.

She arrived back in Augsburg in late October, recanted her former "errors," and then requested the Council to help get her children released and back to her. The Council refused, citing as a reason that the Catholic authorities of Württemberg would not listen to the pleas of a Protestant city, and would certainly not return the children to the wife of Augustin Bader, the mendacious prophet, who had been executed for sedition.[22]

This might have been the end of Sabina's story had not Wolfgang Capito's wife died just then. Martin Bucer was concerned to get another wife for him, and then became aware that Capito was in love with Sabina and meant to have her for his wife. Bucer, however, reasoned that the marriage of a noted churchman with the "queen" of a discredited tragi-comic "king" could only expose the new Protestant movement to mockery and derision. So he quickly arranged for Capito to meet another, more suitable, mate, who then duly became Capito's second wife.[23]

There is no evidence that Sabina knew about Capito's plans for her since by then she was no longer in Strasbourg. The trail of her life is uncertain after this. She resumed her former links to the Anabaptist fellowship in Augsburg, where she continued to live.[24] She probably got her children back after Württemberg became Protestant in 1536, and public authorities would have been glad to be rid of them. She was poor now, and lived until at least 1547.[25]

Sabina Bader was a woman with a high level of self-confidence which she no doubt received in part from her upbringing in relatively well-to-do circumstances, and because she was literate and a skilled artisan. She was also adventurous, apparently hoping that, like so many other ordinary people in her time, she would share in the glorious new world promised by the visions of Hans Hut and others, which were to come into being within months. But primarily she was a mother, using whatever means she had at her disposal to be reunited with her children. Her oldest son became a weaver in Augsburg.

Notes

1. Gustav Bossert, "Augustin Bader von Augsburg, der Prophet und König und seine Genossen, nach den Prozessakten von 1530," ARG, 10 (1912): 124.
2. W. O. Packull, *Mysticism and the Early South German-Austrian Anabaptist Movement* (Scottdale, PA: Herald Press, 1977), 130.
3. Ibid., 131.
4. Bossert, "Bader," 124.
5. Ibid., 124-25.
6. Ibid., 126.
7. Ibid., 132.
8. Ibid., 147-49.
9. Ibid., 153-55.
10. Ibid., 157-58.
11. Ibid., 158.
12. Ibid., 159-65.
13. Ibid., 236-39.
14. Ibid., 239.
15. Ibid., 297-98.
16. Ibid., 324.
17. Ibid., 327.
18. Ibid., 328.
19. Ibid., 329.
20. Ibid., 329-30.
21. Ibid., 331. For the letter see TA, Elsass, I, pp. 347-48.
22. Ibid., 331-32
23. Ibid., 332-33
24. Ibid., 332.
25. Ibid., 334.

MAGDALENA, WALPURGA AND SOPHIA MARSCHALK VON PAPPENHEIM

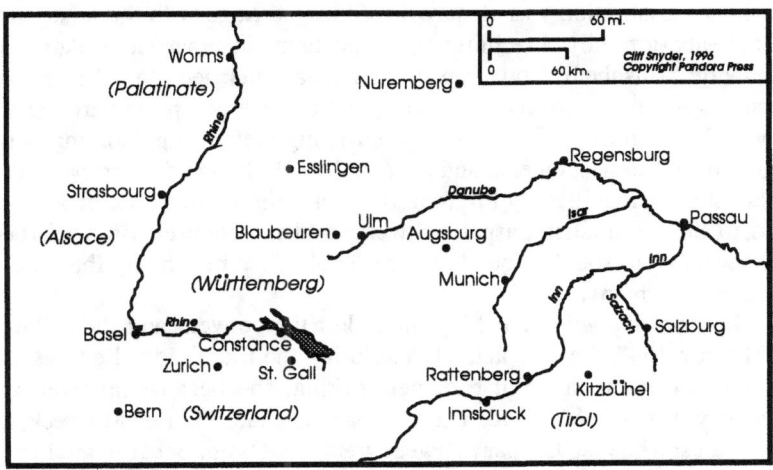

The stories of Magdalena Marschalk von Pappenheim, her niece Walpurga, and Sophia von Pappenheim are unique in the annals of Anabaptist history. The few appearances of these strong and remarkable personalities in the historical record have left an indelible imprint. They were born into a venerable south German family whose family seat was located near the city of Nuremberg. As manorial lords of Kalden, the Marschalk von Pappenheim family had occupied a respected place among the landed aristocracy of southern Germany since the twelfth century; one of their ancestors had been the imperial *Hofmarschall*.[1] Joachim von Pappenheim (d. 1536) appears to have been the first to have been drawn to Protestantism, and probably was the one who made initial contact with the Anabaptist leader Pilgram Marpeck. After Joachim's death, his sister Magdalena and his daughter Walpurga continued the close family relationship with Marpeck and the "Marpeck circle." Sophia Marschalk von Pappenheim also joined the Marpeck circle. Although she clearly was a member of the same family, given her family name, her exact familial relationship is not known; she may have been a sister to Walpurga, or perhaps a cousin.

Magdalena von Pappenheim and the "War of the Radical Ladies"

At the start of the Reformation, Magdalena Marschalk von Pappenheim (d. before 1571) was a nun in the Benedictine convent at Urspring in Swabia, near the city of Ulm–a natural choice for an aristocratic woman with strong religious interests.[2] The monastic records of the convent do not say when she professed vows, and there is some disagreement in the sources concerning her parents. The best sources indicate that her father was Wilhelm Marschalk von Pappenheim, and that she had at least one brother, Joachim, and one sister, Elisabeth.[3] The von Pappenheim family in Magdalena's generation was closely linked by marriage with the aristocratic von Laubenberg family: Joachim von Pappenheim was married to Anna von Laubenberg; Elisabeth von Pappenheim was married to Caspar von Laubenberg, who was Anna's cousin.[4] Within these complex marriage and family relationships swirled also conflicting reforming commitments. Joachim, his sister Magdalena, and his daughter Walpurga formed part of the Anabaptist movement led by Pilgram Marpeck; Elisabeth, on the other hand, looked to the spiritualist Caspar Schwenckfeld for counsel. Both Marpeck and Schwenckfeld sought, found, and fostered adherents among the nobility of southern Germany.

It is not known when Magdalena left the convent and the religious order, but by 1542 she was actively exploring the more radical expressions of Protestantism. In the course of her seeking, she became involved in a controversy that erupted between the Anabaptist leader Pilgram Marpeck, and the Silesian spiritualist, Caspar Schwenckfeld von Ossig. Because the literary battle between Marpeck and Schwenckfeld seems to have been initiated, in part, to secure the allegiance of influential radical Protestant women in the area–of whom Magdalena was one–and because the Marpeck-Schwenckfeld battle was carried out by means of letters and treatises written for these women and passed on by them, the struggle has been described by George H. Williams as the *Damenkrieg*, or the "war of the radical ladies."[5] Magdalena von Pappenheim emerged solidly on the Anabaptist side, and championed Marpeck's cause in correspondence with Schwenckfeld and his strong supporter, Helena Streicher.

By 1541 Magdalena had befriended Helena Streicher in the city of Ulm. Helena was the widow of a local shopkeeper and the mother of five daughters and one son. Differences in social rank do not appear to have impeded their friendship; later correspondence reveals that Magdalena and Helena had repeated conversations on spiritual questions; they shared a passionate interest in spiritual matters. Their emergence in the middle of a theological quarrel seems to have been occasioned in the first instance by their honest seeking for the truth, which led them to make inquiries in writing both to Schwenckfeld and to Marpeck. In the early debates, Helena Streicher, not Magdalena von Pappenheim, was the more self-assured in her convictions.

Helena Streicher had been won over by Schwenckfeld's spiritualist teachings; she participated in his conventicles and also frequently hosted Schwenckfeld in her home in Ulm. Her daughter Agathe and her son were physicians, and attended to Schwenckfeld's illnesses.[6] Helena pursued her religious convictions with some zeal, sending letters directly to Pilgram

Marpeck which, she hoped, would persuade him of the correctness of Schwenckfeld's views.

Although early details are missing, Magdalena clearly related in some way to the Anabaptist congregation that looked to Pilgram Marpeck for leadership. But it appears that she may have had some doubts, or at least peripheral interests: Magdalena wrote to Caspar Schwenckfeld and expressed a desire to meet and speak with him. According to Schwenckfeld's later reply (August 1542), Magdalena had once written to him wishing to converse specifically about the "Kingdom of God, the Lord Jesus Christ, and eternal salvation." Schwenckfeld does not say why the meeting never took place, although he suggests that he was awaiting another invitation when he received "a writing by Pilgram written under your (Magdalena's) name."[7]

In spite of her interest in meeting and speaking with Schwenckfeld, Magdalena grew closer to Marpeck and his circle as time progressed. She became the personal means by which Helena relayed two letters to Marpeck, and also the means by which Marpeck corresponded with Helena. In the spring or early summer of 1542, Pilgram Marpeck wrote a letter of reply to Helena Streicher, but he sent it directly to Magdalena, who was to pass it on to Helena. In all likelihood Marpeck was writing as much for Magdalena as for Helena, for he was concerned that Magdalena might be moved in a spiritualist direction. By the time of this letter of reply from Marpeck to Helena (or perhaps because of it), Magdalena became convinced of the truth of Marpeck's position. Before Magdalena passed on Marpeck's letter to Helena Streicher, she made a copy for herself and then composed and sent a letter of reply to Schwenckfeld, under her own name, in which she defended Marpeck's position and copied verbatim large parts of Marpeck's reply to Helena Streicher. Manuscript copies of this letter continued to circulate under Magdalena's name, long after the controversy itself had died down. The preface to one of the extant copies of this letter states: "The following epistle was written to Mrs. Helena Streicher at Ulm. When it reached Schwenckfeld, he became vehement, and wrote against the brother Billgram Marpeck and Miss Magdalena Marschalckin von Bappenhaim."[8]

Schwenckfeld received both Magdalena's letter and, through Helena Streicher, Marpeck's original letter to her; he cited parts of Magdalena's letter in subsequent correspondence. He had no difficulty discerning Marpeck's hand behind Magdalena's writing. Thus began a sharp literary exchange between the radical reformers, Marpeck and Schwenckfeld, with Magdalena and Helena at the centre of it all. The noblewoman and former Benedictine nun, Magdalena, would take the side of the patrician and Anabaptist Marpeck; the widow of a shopkeeper, Helena, would take the side of the aristocrat and spiritualist Schwenckfeld.

The spiritual and theological issues that Magdalena/Marpeck and Helena/Schwenckfeld were discussing, and that they resolved in opposed fashion, were central ones in radical Protestantism. All parties agreed, first of all, that the essential work of Christ in believers is an interior work of the Spirit; thus salvation cannot be tied to any external or earthly elements. This thoroughgoing rejection of the Roman Catholic sacramental understanding of salvation was a common thread running through radical Protestantism. But the antisacramental beginning point left some fundamental problems unresolved: what status is one to give, then, to the outward and earthly signs (formerly sacraments) by which the church had been recognized? In particular, what was to become of baptism by water and the celebration of the Lord's Supper with the elements of bread and wine? Should the earthly signs of water, bread, and wine continue to be used at all, and if so, what theological or biblical basis could be given for such a continuation? Furthermore, is the church of Christ to be recognized by means of these external signs, or is that church to be recognized only by its love and possession of the Spirit of Christ? Central to all of this were two opposed christological conceptions: Marpeck upheld the joint humanity and divinity of Christ, while Schwenckfeld denied that Christ had ever been a "creature."[9]

Helena/Schwenckfeld desired to take the logic of the antisacramental critique to a spiritualist conclusion: since the essential action for salvation is internal and spiritual, any requirement for external, earthly elements is misplaced. The true sacraments are internal; the true church is a spiritual community. In their letters of 1542 to Helena and Schwenckfeld, Magdalena/Marpeck rejected what they called the splitting apart of "spirit and life": "In Christ there is only one teaching, outer and inner, and not two." The essential saving action is internal, but the result is manifested externally, with a harmony between the inner and the outer: "Where the Holy Spirit moves and creates life, there, too, the same physical reality becomes Spirit and life through faith in Christ." The outer manifestations of church, namely the outward and earthly signs, are therefore to be used by believers: "Because of the participation of the Spirit, the believers do not separate the physical usage of either the water, or the bread and wine, from the spiritual reality."[10]

According to Pilgram Marpeck and Magdalena von Pappenheim, the church of Christ is a visible entity in which the inner work of the Spirit is manifested in the continuation of the external signs of that regeneration, especially in baptism with water and the celebration of the Supper with bread and wine. They concluded, "the inner and the outer have to be kept distinct, but to divide the one from the other, to use one and not the other, cannot be substantiated by any Scripture."[11]

By the summer of 1542, another aristocratic Anabaptist woman had joined the discussion. Helena von Freyberg (see her profile, in this volume), in exile from Tirol and living in Augsburg, sent Schwenckfeld a copy of another writing by Marpeck, his lengthy "Admonition" written earlier in 1542. Helena von Freyberg had close contacts with both sides: she was a member of Pilgram Marpeck's Anabaptist fellowship in Augsburg, but she also had familial contacts with Caspar Schwenckfeld: from 1540 to 1547 Schwenckfeld lived at Justingen, in the castle of Georg Ludwig von Freyberg, who was none other than Helena von Freyberg's brother-in-law. Michael von Freyberg, a younger relative of Helena (likely a nephew), also lived at Justingen and apparently was won over to Schwenckfeld's position: he is said to have carved a five-line summary of Schwenckfeld's understanding of the "Glorified Human Nature of Christ" into the mantle of the fireplace of the Justingen castle.[12] Helena disagreed with her relatives on this theological point, for Helena von Freyberg was and remained part of Pilgram Marpeck's community, and throughout the controversy stood solidly behind him and her aristocratic friend and fellow church-member, Magdalena von Pappenheim.

By August of 1542, Schwenckfeld had composed the *Judicium*, a detailed response and refutation of literature and correspondence he had received from the Marpeck circle. Schwenckfeld pointedly kept the aristocratic Anabaptist women at the centre of the debate: in a letter to Helena von Freyberg he reported that he had sent copies of his *Judicium* (or more likely a twelve-point summary) only to her and to Magdalena von Pappenheim, as well as to "a few others of our opinion." One would thus surmise that he also sent a copy to Helena Streicher, his supporter in the disagreement, but there is no documentation to that effect.[13]

Magdalena and Marpeck both responded, in separate letters, to Schwenckfeld. Although Magdalena's letter has been lost, part of what she said can be reconstructed from Schwenckfeld's reply to her. She had, first of all, admonished Schwenckfeld to read his New Testament with more care. Schwenckfeld thanked her for the admonition, and promised to read Scripture as carefully as possible, with Christ's help. Furthermore, Magdalena had asked Schwenckfeld how he could accuse Marpeck of incorrect doctrine, and at the same time speak of him as a pious person. Schwenckfeld answered that one can be god-fearing, yet mistaken. Pilgram Marpeck's central error, said Schwenckfeld, is revealed "in his letter written under your name," namely that he opposed Schwenckfeld's teaching concerning "the resurrected glory of our reigning Lord and King Christ, which God the Father graciously has revealed to us." After summarizing the twelve central points of contention between himself and Marpeck–which he had expounded at length in his *Judicium*–Schwenckfeld concluded by asking Magdalena to accept his writing in the best spirit, and to write back to him, or to Helena Streicher.[14]

With this, the direct exchange of letters came to an end. Pilgram Marpeck made a trip to Ulm in an attempt to meet with Schwenckfeld, but such a meeting never took place; we know of one more letter written by

Magdalena von Pappenheim to Helena Streicher, and thus indirectly to Schwenckfeld. But the growing distance between the parties is evident: when Schwenckfeld wrote yet a further "summary of articles" in May of 1543 for the benefit of Marpeck and Magdalena, he sent the writing to Helena von Freyberg saying that he did not know where to find either Marpeck or Magdalena; Helena von Freyberg presumably did know where and how to contact them.

By virtue of her aristocratic birth, education, and training as a Benedictine nun, Magdalena von Pappenheim seems to have entered naturally into the debate between Marpeck and Schwenckfeld, not hesitating to take up pen and paper in defense of the position that had convinced her of its truth. Helena von Freyberg, while she participated less actively in the debate itself, nevertheless closely followed the ebb and flow of the discussion, not hesitating to initiate correspondence with Schwenckfeld, or to pass on what she considered to be relevant theological literature. More surprising is the continued involvement of Helena Streicher, who did not share the aristocratic birth or educational advantages of Magdalena von Pappenheim or Helena von Freyberg. She must have been a strong and able woman indeed, to have entered into such a dialogue and sustained it in the face of what must have been the formidable opposition of two aristocratic and determined Anabaptist women.

Finally, it is significant that both Marpeck and Schwenckfeld continued to carry out their disagreement "through" the women concerned. The continued support of these women–and the family networks they represented–clearly was important to them. Thus, while Marpeck and Schwenckfeld sought to convince each other of the truth of their respective positions, their interchange took place in the larger context of the radical Protestant women who had joined the discussion and continued to participate in it.

The *Damenkrieg* came to an end with the cessation of direct communication between the opposed parties; nevertheless, the active involvement in Anabaptism by several women of the von Pappenheim family did not end here. Magdalena von Pappenheim continued to have literary contact with Pilgram Marpeck, and to look to him for spiritual guidance. From the subject matter of two further letters addressed to her from Marpeck, it appears that she had a real preoccupation with sin, the state of her soul, and the certainty of her salvation. In a letter that has since been lost, she wrote to Marpeck concerning her doubts about whether she truly had been raised up and was indeed alive in Christ. In his reply in 1545, Marpeck exegeted the "fine parable of the dead Lazarus," and then spoke directly to Magdalena: "Thus, my beloved, since you have been raised up in the call and act of Christ, and since Christ calls you to go forth with hearty joy from your mourning and suffering, from death and the grave-clothes, according to the command of Christ, we release you from the fear of death in which you were imprisoned."[15] Speaking for the church, Marpeck in effect "loosed" Magdalena from a spiritual bond which had been afflicting her.

A second letter addressed to Magdalena von Pappenheim from Pilgram Marpeck has survived, this one written in 1547. Unlike the first, it does not seem to have been occasioned by a direct inquiry from Magdalena, and its subject matter is general rather than personal, although related to that of the first letter. In this epistle, Marpeck also addresses the question of sin in those who have been set free through faith in Christ. He opposes the doctrine that "Christ established before God a grace and mercy which demands no repentance, no forsaking of sin." On the contrary, for Marpeck, "Those who have received grace are not sinners; they are the redeemed." These are the chosen of the Lord who are born through the word, cleansed from sin, and baptized into the communion of saints. Marpeck's emphasis in this letter is not on sinlessness, but rather on "true remorse and sorrow over sin." Following such true repentance, "one can receive grace upon grace" in order to resist sin.[16]

This letter is the last direct notice we have in the historical record concerning Magdalena von Pappenheim. The records we do have, however, testify to her earnest seeking after the truth, to her sensitive and penitent spirit, and to her intelligent and decisive nature. By the year 1571 she had passed to her final rest.

Walpurga Marschalk von Pappenheim

Pilgram Marpeck was not one to pass up an opportunity to express his views in writing. By January 1544, or even earlier, he had composed a lengthy reply to the first half of Caspar Schwenckfeld's lengthy *Judicium*. Marpeck's reply, called the *Verantwortung*, was circulated in manuscript copies; he promised to produce the second half in due course, and with the help of associates, in due course he did.[17] It is because of the survival of one particular manuscript version of Marpeck's writing that we learn a little more about Walpurga Marschalk von Pappenheim, niece of Magdalena von Pappenheim, and identified as composer of hymn 75 of the *Ausbund*, the Swiss Brethren hymnal.[18] One of the surviving manuscript copies of the *Verantwortung* is the copy that Walpurga herself owned, today preserved in the Stadtbibliothek in Zurich: the facing page reads "Walpurga Marschälkin 1571." Later in the manuscript she gave her place of residence as Bobhaim.[19] Thanks to some of the marginal comments she made in her own hand, we gain valuable information concerning Marpeck's writing and the course of the controversy with Schwenckfeld; we also gain some insight into Walpurga's own religious convictions.

Pilgram Marpeck had given Magdalena von Pappenheim a copy of his *Verantwortung*, probably shortly following its composition. Walpurga inherited this manuscript from her aunt, and in 1571 she utilized Magdalena's original copy to correct and improve her own manuscript version. Walpurga noted in her manuscript: "I have corrected the first part of this book in the year 1571, using the book of my deceased aunt Magdalena Marschälkin, which Pilgram, now deceased, had given her, so that now the first part of the book has been corrected." On the following page, Walpurga noted that although the corrections to the first part of the *Verantwortung* had not been numerous, the second part of her own manuscript contained many errors, such as the omission of individual words, parts of sentences and entire sections.

Walpurga, like her aunt Magdalena before her, was part of the Marpeck circle of Anabaptists, and she highly valued this particular writing by Marpeck and his associates. She noted in her own hand, "I, Walpurga Marschalk, had this 'Judgement' [the *Verantwortung*] copied for the sake of God's glory." In an extended comment, written again in her own hand, Walpurga speaks further about the controversy and the book she had just corrected.

> The elder brothers composed this testimony against the Schwenckfeldian errors and in the first part furnished an answer concerning the living body (of Christ). But we received no answer. Then Caspar Schwenckfeld von Ossig died; he had much vexed all true believers. Therefore the elder brothers took many pains, through grace, to rescue the truth in the community of God. It took many days and years until the brothers wrote and ordered everything according to God's law, [but] their lives were spared. Therefore one should truly preserve this book as a remembrance, for the entire world has gone over to the devil, sin, death and hell; but the Lord Christ has conquered all with his truth. To Him be praise, honour, and glory from eternity to eternity. Amen.
>
> The elder witnesses of God of the entire community and brotherhood, namely Pilgram Marpeck and Leupold Scharnschlager, Sigmund Bosch, Martin Blaichner, Valtin Werner, Annthoni Müller, Hans Jakob, together with other elder brothers and believers in all lands, judged and answered concerning this. And when it was thus determined that it would stand the test before God, it was to be allowed to go forth to whomever would wish to have it. But for me, God demands that this book should go only to those who have a true faith and a zeal for God. They should consider therein the salvation of their souls, and [the book] should not come into the world, for above all I would have it go to all the believers.[20]

Walpurga was not afraid to speak in the first person to her brothers and sisters in the faith; in her view, Marpeck's *Verantwortung* contained words of salvation that would benefit the true believers [*warglaubigen*], but which would be wasted "in the world." Walpurga looked steadfastly to the Anabaptist community of faith which, by 1571, was a small and persecuted remnant set apart from "the devil, sin, death and hell."

Later in the manuscript, after reviewing again the controversy between Marpeck and Schwenckfeld, Walpurga notes: "Thus did the truth come to light, and untruth had to yield. To God be given the glory eternally, who strengthens his weak people through his Holy Spirit and who will preserve them until the end of the world, Amen, against all the deceitfulness of the serpent."[21] Walpurga's vibrant spirituality of reliance on God's Spirit and providence is reflected in these words.

Although the few words reproduced above provide us with virtually all that we know of Walpurga, still we feel the imprint of her personality across the centuries. Her close personal identification with the Marpeck circle, as well as her commitment to the Anabaptist community of true believers is beyond question. In the midst of the controversy, which had erupted thirty years earlier, she saw the hand of God at work; her painstaking correction and annotation of Marpeck's voluminous *Verantwortung* testifies to its importance to her.

A few words should be said about the hymn "Oh pious heart, so glorify," which is translated below.[22] The hymn was first published in 1531 by Michael Weisse in the *Gesangbuch der Böhmischen Brüder* [Songbook of the Bohemian Brethren].[23] This has led some scholars to conclude that the hymn was simply taken into the *Ausbund* and attributed to Walpurga. Other scholars have noted that although Michael Weisse was responsible for composing the texts of most of the songs published in the 1531 *Gesangbuch*, some of the songs were, in fact, composed by others, although Weisse did not acknowledge the fact.[24] Thus the possibility remains that Walpurga von Pappenheim may have been the original composer of the hymn in question, and that the *Ausbund* contains the correct attribution. If this is true, Walpurga would have been a very young woman (as the *Ausbund* introduction notes) when she composed the hymn, probably no more than twenty years old. As was common practice in the sixteenth century, the text was written to be sung to the tune of a popular song, in this case to the tune of the popular Lutheran hymn, "Out of Deep Distress" [*Aus tieffer Not*].

Sophia von Bubenhofen, Born Marschalkin von Pappenheim

Sophia von Bubenhofen, born Sophia Marschalk von Pappenheim, obviously was a member of the same aristocratic family as were Magdalena and Walpurga. She formed part of Pilgram Marpeck's Anabaptist group. Beyond these bare facts, we know very little about Sophia, although more work in archival sources may turn up further information. We know of Sophia only because a letter addressed to her from Hans Bichel was preserved in the *Kunstbuch*, a collection of writings gathered by the Marpeck circle.[25]

Reading between the lines of that brief letter, which is translated below, it appears that Sophia had lost a child to death, and had been grieving at the loss. The letter is an attempt to strengthen her faith and her hope. It is not known what is meant by the "transgression" [*Übertretung*] to which the letter refers.

Letter to Sophia von Bubenhofen, born Marschalkin von Pappenheim

"This following writing was done by a brother to Sophia von Bubenhofen, born Marschalkin von Pappenheim, for her improvement.

Dearly beloved sister, in hope. Sophia, the congregation at Augsburg, above all Pilgram [Marpeck] and Hans Jakob, greet you heartily and also the others who are with you and who live in the Faith. Everything is going well, as usual, for the congregation at Augsburg, as far as I know. May the Lord again have mercy on you and also on us, and grant you true Love and Peace, and also take from you and remove the heavy burden and grave stone with which you have been tortured and weighed down (for a long time now, because of your transgression), even unto death. But God our Saviour did not leave the distressed woman comfortless, who grieved with tears and cries concerning her son who had died, as one reads (Luke, chapter 7). And God had mercy on the mother and spoke a command to the child to rise up, and he did, and the Lord Jesus gave him to his mother again, free and alive. This will also be your comfort of hope: God always will hear the requests of the mothers of the Church of Christ, and give them back their sons who have died [Margin: Luke 15]. Saved and blessed are those who have taken part in the first resurrection, that is, when they are resurrected through true repentance, into a new life (through trust in faith, that God forgives and is able to awaken one from death, no matter how great the transgression may be, for nothing is impossible for God), [Margin: John 11] to the praise and honour of God their creator, who can call into being what is not. The second death (that is: the eternal death) will have no power over such people [Margin: Romans 6], but this death will follow for all the unbelievers who do not unite with God in the time of Grace, while they are still on the way, etc. The almighty God wishes to grant you and us what we require, to our salvation and to his praise, through Jesus Christ our Saviour. Amen.

Receive a true and sincere greeting from me and all the women in my household, which we pass on to all those who are with you, who fear God.

Dated, Waiblingen, on Monday following Holy Three Kings' day, 1555.

By me, Hans Bichel, a fellow companion in the Faith of Christ."

Ausbund, Song 75

Another beautiful sacred song written by a young Noblewoman, Walpurga of Pappenheim.

To the tune of: "Out of Deep Distress"

1. Oh pious heart, so glorify,
   And give praises to your Lord,
   Be mindful He is your father
   Whom you should honour always,
   Without Him there is not one hour
   With all the worry in your mind
   That your life can be nourished.

2. He is the one who loves you from His heart,
   His blessing he shares with you,
   Forgiving you of your misdeeds,
   And healing you of your wounds,
   Arming you for the spiritual war,
   So Satan not overcome you,
   And disperse all of your treasures.

3. He is merciful and so good
   To the poor and destitute,
   Who turn from all their arrogance,
   And convert to his truth.
   He accepts them like a father,
   Seeing that they reach the end
   Of the true path to salvation.

4. How like a true father He bends,
   Doing good to His children,
   God has opened Himself to us
   Blessing us poor sinners.
   He has loved us and has graced us,
   Forgiving us our trespasses,
   Making us victorious.

5. And He gives us His good Spirit,
   Which renews all of our hearts,
   Through this we fulfill his commands,
   Although with the pain of love.
   He helps our need with grace and healing,
   Promising us a glorious share,
   Of the eternal treasures.

6. According to unrighteousness,
   He has not recompensed us,
   Instead He showed us compassion,
   When we should have been doomed.
   His mercy and His goodness
   Is readied for every one of us
   Who love Him from the heart.

7. What He has begun out of love,
   He also wants to finish.
   We offer ourselves to God's grace
   With loins that have been girded,
   With all we have, even our flesh,
   Hoping that, to His praise,
   He will change our every way.

8. Oh Father! Be gracious to us,
   While we are in wretchedness,
   May our actions be upright,
   And come to a blessed end.
   Light us all with your shining word,
   So that we can, in this dark place
   Be not beguiled by false light.

9. Lord God! Accept our praise and thanks,
   That we are humbly singing,
   Let your word sound in us freely,
   Let it penetrate our hearts.
   Help us that we, with Your power,
   Through true spiritual knighthood
   May achieve the crown of life.

   Amen.

Notes

1 On the von Pappenheim family, see ME, IV, "Pappenheim," 114-16; Gerhard Taddey, ed., *Lexikon der deutschen Geschichte* (Stuttgart: Kröner, 1977), "Pappenheim, Familie."
2 On Magdalena von Pappenheim, see Stephen B. Boyd, *Pilgram Marpeck* (Durham, NC: Duke University Press, 1992), 104-6; George H. Williams, *The Radical Reformation*, 3rd ed. (Kirksville, MO: Sixteenth Century Journal Publishers, 1992), 703-16.
3 Immo Eberl, *Geschichte des Benediktinerinnenklosters Urspring* (Stuttgart: Müller and Gräff, 1978), 251.
4 Elmer Ellsworth Schultz Johnson, ed., *Corpus Schwenckfeldianorum*, vol. 7 (Leipzig: Breitkopf and Härtel, 1926), 35-36.
5 Williams, *The Radical Reformation*, 1st. ed. (Philadelphia: Westminster, 1962), 466-72.
6 Williams, *Radical Reformation*, 3d ed., 707.
7 Caspar Schwenckfeld von Ossig, *Corpus Schwenckfeldianorum*, vol. 8, ed. C.D. Hartranft and J.E. Schultz (Leipzig: Breitkopf and Härtel, 1927), 217; also Johann Loserth, *Quellen und Forschungen zur Geschichte der oberdeutschen Taufgesinnten im 16. Jahrhundert* (Vienna: Fromme, 1929), 17-18.
8 Loserth, *Quellen*, 50-51.
9 On the Marpeck/Schwenckfeld debate, see Boyd, *Marpeck*, 115-25.
10 William Klassen and Walter Klaassen, trans. and eds., *The Writings of Pilgram Marpeck* (Scottdale, PA: Herald Press, 1978), 376-89, passim.
11 Ibid., p. 389.
12 Williams, *Radical Reformation*, 3d. ed., 709-10.
13 The letter is found in the *Corpus Schwenckfeldianorum*, vol. 8, 616-18.
14 Ibid., 280-85.
15 Klassen and Klaassen, *Writings*, 410.
16 Ibid., 464-83, passim.
17 Critical edition published by Loserth, *Quellen*.
18 On Walpurga von Pappenheim, see *Allgemeine Deutsche Biographie*, vol. 25 (Berlin: Duncker and Humblot, 1970), "Pappenheim, Walpurga."
19 Loserth, *Quellen*, 49.
20 Ibid., 49-50.
21 Ibid., 51.
22 Found in the *Ausbund, Das ist: Etliche schöne Christliche Lieder . . .* , hymn 75. (The 1583 edition has been reprinted numerous times to the present, with minor changes; the numbering of this hymn has not been changed since 1583. I used an edition published in Elkhart, IN: Mennonitischen Verlagshandlung, 1880.)
23 The author consulted Michael Weisse, *Gesangbuch der Böhmischen Brüder* (1531); Facsimile edition (Kassel: Bärenreiter, 1957). Only very minor differences exist between the texts of Weisse's "O Glawbig herz benedey" and the Ausbund's "Du glaubigs Herz, so benedey."
24 See Rudolf Wolkan, *Die Lieder der Wiedertäufer* (Berlin: Behr, 1903; reprint edition Nieuwkoop: B. de Graaf, 1965), 123-24; Philipp Wackernagel, *Das deutsche Kirchenlied*, III, (Leipzig: Teubner, 1870), 290-91. Page 290 of Wackernagel has the text from Weisse (number 333); page 291 has the Ausbund text (number 334).
25 Number 36, *Das Kunstbuch*. A critical edition of the *Kunstbuch* is being completed by Dr. Heinold Fast, Norden, Germany. The author's translation is based on the copy found on page 347 of the Geiser transcription of the *Kunstbuch*, located at the Mennonite Historical Library, Goshen College, Goshen, Indiana.

HELENA VON FREYBERG OF MÜNICHAU

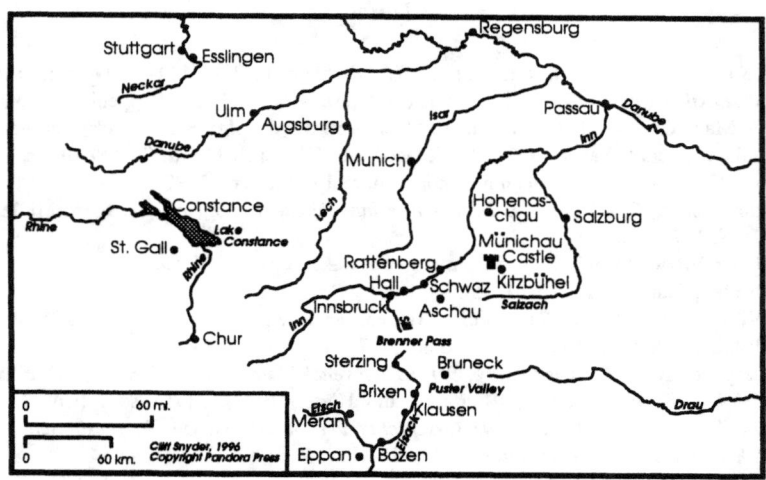

Of the 210 women who became members of the Anabaptist movement in the Austrian territory of Tirol, the story of Helena von Freyberg is one of the most intriguing.[1] That a person from the upper classes would even consider taking the risk of being baptized as an adult was already unusual. The mandates of Archduke Ferdinand I made it very clear that the government would arrest anyone taking such action. Even more unusual were the choices she made to leave her native Tirol and trade a comfortable life in her castle at Münichau for a life of exile.

Helena's parents, Gilg von Münichau and Magdalena von Hamerspach, belonged to the lower nobility of Tirol. Helena's maternal grandparents were Ulrich and Magdalena Sigwein. Her paternal grandfather, Hanns Gilg, lived at Münichau, three kilometres from Kitzbühel in western Tirol in a castle that had been built in the mid-fifteenth century. He had come to this region when the rulers of Bavaria expanded their territories southward. Perhaps, like Helena, he was an adventurous type of person, seeking out new places when the opportunity arose. Helena's father, Gilg (Egidius) von Münichau, graduated from university with a law degree in 1473 and carried on the family tradition of functioning as a professional and a civil servant in the position of crown administrator [*Pfleger*]. For a time he was also a chief justice. In 1491 he bought "mining and grazing rights" from Heinrich Marpeck, father of Pilgram Marpeck. Thus the family connection between the Marpecks and the Lords of Münichau had been well established one generation before Pilgram Marpeck and Helena von Freyberg became members of the same Anabaptist congregation.[2]

Pilgram Marpeck, later to become a prominent Anabaptist leader, was also a professional and began his career as a mining judge in the town of

Rattenberg on the Inn River due west of Kitzbühel. Rattenberg would later become the place where many Anabaptists were arrested and gave up their lives, since it was here they boarded vessels to continue their journey of escape to Moravia. However, after becoming an Anabaptist, Marpeck left Rattenberg for the safer environs of Strasbourg, before the persecution in Tirol became severe. The links between Pilgram Marpeck and Helena began, then, with their fathers, Gilg and Heinrich. As we shall see, Helena maintained the link to Pilgram throughout her life.

Helena von Freyberg, the only child of Gilg and Magdalena, grew up at Münichau. By the time her mother died in 1506, Helena was already married and probably around twenty years of age. Her father married twice more, first to the daughter of Hans Fieger, a wealthy mine owner in Rattenberg. When she and her young daughter both died in 1507, he married Elizabeth von Frauenberg, who bore four children. As a member of the upper class, Helena married a man of equal rank.[3] Onophrius von Freyberg was a nobleman or baron [*Freiherr*] of Swiss-Bavarian descent from Hohenaschau, southwest of Chiemsee in Bavaria. As far as we know, after their marriage they lived at Aschau, near Kitzbühel. They had four sons who were all knights. Pankratz, the eldest, was born in 1508 and later played an important role as leader of those sympathetic to the Reformation in Bavaria. He and Christoph Georg became the sole owners of Münichau after Hanns Sigmund died in the wars in southern France and Wilhelm was killed in Salzburg. When it became evident by 1538 that they were not spending much time at the castle, Pankratz and Christoph sold it for 7,500 rheinisch gulden.[4]

Legend has it that Martin Luther visited Onophrius von Freyberg in his castle at Hohenaschau in 1518.[5] We do not know if Helena was present at this meeting, if in actual fact it took place. If it did, it may have been her first exposure to Reformation ideas. References in the court records make it clear that the secular and religious authorities, determined to defend the established church, viewed both Lutheranism and Anabaptism as sects. But as the Anabaptist movement expanded its influence to include prominent members of the upper class, such as Helena, the Lutheran sect came to be viewed as less dangerous. Thus, in spite of his Lutheran leanings, Onophrius lived out his life in Tirol, while his wife was not able to do so.

In 1523, Elizabeth von Frauenberg, Helena's widowed stepmother, relinquished all her rights to the castle at Münichau in order to free herself of a debt of 5000 gulden. Onophrius was the official owner [*Lehenträger*] of the property, but Helena occupied the castle and soon made it a centre of Anabaptist activity, despite the fact that her husband chose to remain a Lutheran.[6]

The first mention of Helena in the Tirolean court records was in a report of March 7, 1528. It states that she and her whole household had been baptized. If this report proved to be correct, local officials had the right to confiscate her property and goods as was customary for persons accused of being Anabaptists. But, as we shall see, it would take almost two years before the proof needed to arrest her was obtained.[7]

In addition to this first notice that Helena and her whole household were "tainted" with Anabaptism, other incriminating evidence was reported that spring. It was said that a former clergyman named Paul Rassler had preached about rebaptism in Helena's castle and in other homes near Münichau. He and his student, Hanns Rat, had the full support of the noblewoman. It has been suggested that even Pilgram Marpeck attended these Anabaptist preaching meetings at Helena's castle but there is no evidence for it.[8] This house church, or more correctly, "castle church," flourished under Helena's patronage for more than two years, from the fall of 1527 to December of 1529. Here Anabaptists found refuge; Helena herself was head of the congregation.

A visit she made to a group of thrity-six Anabaptist prisoners in July 1528 indicates the fearlessness and confidence with which Helena went about her work. These prisoners were part of a larger group of 106 Anabaptists who had been arrested. The thirty-six had already recanted once and later rejoined the movement. It is possible that Helena was the one who brought the prisoners a letter from the Anabaptist preacher Jacob Partzner, another leader whom she aided and protected. Why Helena had been allowed to associate with these Anabaptists when she herself was under suspicion was the reprimanding question that Archduke Ferdinand's officials asked the local authorities.[9]

While her husband declared to the government in April 1529 that he was not an Anabaptist,[10] Helena chose to neglect reporting to the authorities. She continued her Anabaptist involvements in various ways, providing financial as well as moral support to various members. It was reported that she had sent one group of Anabaptists eleven gulden. This amount of money was approximately equal to one month's salary for a civil servant of that time.[11]

The government reports of the 1520s emphasize the work of male Anabaptist leaders like Paul Rassler, Hanns Rat, and Jacob Partzner. The strategy was to eliminate the leaders so that the Anabaptist movement would collapse. Since Anabaptism was entrenched in the grass roots, this of course did not happen. But the government miscalculated in another way. While they were obliged to use caution so as not to violate the rights of the nobility, they did not, in these early years, perceive Helena to be a leader among the Anabaptists.

Finally, late in 1529, the testimony of a recanting Anabaptist verified all of the earlier reports. Helena was indeed a baptized member. She had given lodging to Anabaptist leaders and allowed them to preach at Münichau.

This information was further verified in the testimony of an Anabaptist martyr, Peter Äschlberger. By this time, a total of sixty-six Anabaptists had been executed in the area of Kitzbühel alone. No further proof was needed than the word of a person willing to lay down his life for the Anabaptist cause. The order for Helena's arrest was issued.[12]

Helena did not react passively. She fled, first to Bavaria and her husband's residence. Then, as the authorities continued to pursue her, she went as far south and west as Eppan, near Bozen. Finally she realized there was no safety for her in Tirol and left her homeland completely. Archduke Ferdinand now ordered the confiscation of her properties in Tirol. But when Helena's sons and close friends of the family asked Ferdinand to reconsider, he did so, and her sons obtained possession of them.[13] In July 1530 these matters were finalized, and two years later Helena was granted a pardon by Ferdinand's government on the condition that she recant. Thus, there was a way open for her to return if she so chose.[14]

Early in 1530 Helena settled in Constance and soon was involved in activities similar to those for which she had been forced to leave Tirol. When the city officials became aware that Helena was sheltering Anabaptists, they issued a warning to her. However, she ignored it and for the next two years carried on as she had in Tirol. From the correspondence of Ambrosius Blaurer, the Zwinglian Reformer in Constance, we know that Helena had considerable influence in that city. On two occasions he wrote to his brother Thomas to forewarn him about the activities of the *Freybergerin*. It is obvious from his comments that Helena was allowing Anabaptists into her home and meeting with them. Moreover, Ambrosius considered Helena's friendship with the Anabaptist leader Pilgram Marpeck to be a threat, since Marpeck had already stirred up trouble for the authorities in Strasbourg with his writings. Thus, when the city council dispossessed Helena of the property she owned in Constance in 1532, Ambrosius was in full agreement with them. He wrote to his brother that the council had taken action to stop the "contagious Anabaptist evil." Clearly Helena's influence as an Anabaptist proselytizer and leader was not appreciated by the Protestants of Constance.[15]

After this second expulsion, or "civil death" as it has been called, Helena went to Augsburg for a short time and then, with the help of influential persons, returned to Tirol.[16] By December 1533 her case was being discussed again by the Innsbruck government. Now she intended to recant and return to her husband. The debate that ensued between the different levels of government informs us of several things. First of all, it shows that by this time the authorities were less naïve about Helena's role and influence in the Anabaptist movement. Repeatedly, the central government in Innsbruck, protector of the established church, admonished and informed local officials that Helena could not be excused from public recantation. They insisted that if she were to reject her Anabaptist faith, it had to be done publicly in the local parish church in front of as many people as possible. This would have been the church in which her father had dedicated a mass to her grandfather, Hanns Münichau, in 1506. Now Helena was to be reinstated in the church in this same place by recanting her sectarian faith. The communications from the central government to the local one stated clearly that she had been a primary cause for many people in that region joining this outlawed sect. As an example to the common people, she was to make her recantation publicly in the church and not just to secular officials in private.[17]

The authorities knew full well that the recantation of a prominent leader like Helena would weaken the movement considerably. As Grete Mecenseffy says regarding the recantation of Jacob Partzner in Kitzbühel, "Such conduct by a leader injured the Anabaptist cause more seriously than all the exertions of the government. . . ."[18] Since the Anabaptist movement was gaining strength, the recantation of this influential noblewoman would have to be used to good advantage by the government.

Helena von Freyberg continued to appeal against a public recantation. In July 1534 local officials were told again that no one should be excused from public recantation, especially not a person like the *Freybergerin* who had sinned more than anyone else in leading others astray. On the other hand, Helena was already making a compromise for her survival and sought to carry out the recantation in a manner that would harm as few people as possible.[19]

Helena's resistance to government demands had influenced other members of the nobility. When, in October 1534, Sigmund von Wolkenstein, son of Anton and Elizabeth Wolkenstein, similarly asked the government to excuse him from public recantation, his request was denied on the grounds that his mother had already recanted publicly and that Helena von Freyberg would soon be doing so.[20] But the government assumed too much. Later that month, Helena achieved her goal of giving her recantation in private. It was done in front of the viceroy, a lower-order government official at Innsbruck. The historian Johann Loserth tells us that "with words loud and clear" Helena declared that she would desist from her erring ways. Perhaps the government relented, thinking it better that Helena should recant in private than not at all.[21]

Having won at least part of her battle against the government, one would think Helena would now be able to live at ease in her homeland. Instead, she left Tirol again and, as far as we know, never returned. She spent the last eleven years of her life with Anabaptists in Augsburg. Her departure verifies that she had by no means relinquished her Anabaptist faith. Like so many other recanting Anabaptists, she had made a compromise to buy time and her life. Helena willingly conceded her castle property and the rights she had in her homeland for the sake of her Anabaptist beliefs. But her subsequent activities and the confession she wrote to fellow believers in Augsburg indicate that she was willing to sacrifice even more than she had in Tirol.

Events in other parts of Europe were a factor in what happened next. In 1535, the defeat of the Anabaptists who had taken over the North German city of Münster made all the governments of Europe suspicious of Anabaptists, even in more tolerant cities like Augsburg. The number of Anabaptist arrests increased sharply and Helena was included in the imprisonment. On the Sunday after Easter, April 4, 1535, a group of Anabaptists was arrested while meeting in a cave near Rosenau in the region of Augsburg. In the subsequent testimonies it was mentioned that Anabaptist meetings had taken place in Helena's home. She was required, therefore, to appear before the city council and give an account of her actions.

Helena von Freyberg's oral testimony, the only evidence we have of her own spoken words, is very informative. She related that her three sons were knights, and that she assumed that they were with their father. Unlike other Anabaptist refugees, Helena had financial support from her husband and sons. But she gave no reason for having left her family and come to Augsburg. She said the cause for her expulsion from Tirol and her reasons for coming to their city were known to the mayor, the city doctor, and two local preachers named Bonifacius Wolfart and Michael Keller. Helena was in frequent contact with these leading Protestant citizens of Augsburg, and had engaged them in theological discussions: her views were well known to them. But she emphasized that the gatherings in her house had not been large, that "Only two, three or four brothers came and went, and they talked about the Word of God."[22]

It was her admission to having been baptized that incriminated Helena most. But she had been an Anabaptist now for nearly eight years and remained true to her Anabaptist beliefs. Although she readily gave the names of the leading citizens who supported her, Helena would not comply with the demand to name other Anabaptists, stating that she knew of no brothers or sisters other than those who were imprisoned. She also stated that no one had been baptized in her house. Furthermore, Helena testified that she had not become intricately involved with anyone and that she did not think she had erred in any way, but if she had, she would gladly have it pointed out to her. Her attempts to downplay her involvements in the local Anabaptist congregation were not successful at this time. Her perseverance demanded that she be punished. She was laid in chains overnight and the next day expelled from the city of Augsburg.

One historian claims that Helena returned to Tirol after her exile from Augsburg, but to date we have no proof of this.[23] Her name disappears from the records until January 1539. Her husband died in 1538 and her two surviving older sons, Pankratz and Christoph Georg, wrote a letter from Aschau where they lived to the Augsburg city council, vouching for the Christian character of their widowed mother and asking that she be allowed to live in Augsburg. As a result Helena was able to return to Augsburg and as far as we know remained there until her death in 1545.

By no means did Helena interpret the permission for her return to mean that she should curtail her Anabaptist activities. In 1542 she instructed her tailor, Hans Jacob Schneider, in the fundamentals of the Anabaptist faith. She had continued to take advantage of everyday situations to teach others about Anabaptism. Later in her confession she would discuss her desire to teach the people in her church. Hans Jacob Schneider became the major Anabaptist leader in Augsburg in the late 1550s and early 1560s and was a close associate of Pilgram Marpeck. Helena's instructions thus contributed directly to the continuing survival of the Anabaptist movement.[24]

Helena also played the part of intermediary between Pilgram Marpeck and the Silesian nobleman Caspar Schwenckfeld, who was promoting a radical spiritualism. Pilgram Marpeck had written a book called *The Admonition*, outlining Anabaptist beliefs. Helena had sent Schwenckfeld a copy of Marpeck's book; she knew where to find Schwenckfeld, since he was staying with her brother-in-law, Baron Georg Ludwig von Freyberg, in the latter's castle at Justingen. Schwenckfeld sent Helena a letter on May 27, 1543, and asked her to pass on his own twelve-point summary and response to *The Admonition*. She was to send it directly to Marpeck, or to Magdalena Marschalk von Pappenheim (see her profile) who would then pass it on to Marpeck. Schwenckfeld had no other way of sending something to Marpeck than through these two women who were both members of the Anabaptist congregation in Augsburg. The spiritualist leader also wanted Helena to convince Marpeck to accept his summary willingly and to send any response from Marpeck to him at Justingen.[25]

Schwenckfeld's letter illustrates that Helena was still "closely identified with Pilgram Marpeck" in 1543.[26] Schwenckfeld knew that they were trusted Christian friends. The theological debate between Marpeck and Schwenckfeld was intense and impassioned. It was a battle to gain the support of influential women and has been called the "war of the radical ladies" [*Damenkrieg*].[27] But Helena's contacts with Schwenckfeld did not result in a change of heart or mind. She remained part of the Marpeck circle as she had been since choosing to emigrate westward to South Germany instead of eastward to Moravia as had so many Anabaptists from Tirol.

Thus far we have reconstructed the events of Helena von Freyberg's life from the evidence in the court records, correspondence of various Reformation leaders, and her own testimony to the city council of Augsburg. From her last years in Augsburg, we have a very personal composition, written by Helena herself, which could be called her spiritual autobiography.

It is unusual to have something written by an Anabaptist woman, since the majority of the sixteenth-century population could not read and write. At the same time, it is rare to gain insight into the spiritual life and process of development of an Anabaptist, especially a lay leader. The preservation of this confession in the *Kunstbuch*, a book of writings by various members of Marpeck's circle, makes it possible for us to learn more about Helena. The translation of Helena's confession follows this profile.[28]

While her beliefs concerning grace, love of the neighbour, and authority from God resembled those of other Anabaptist women in Augsburg, Helena's confession was given for a different reason. She was confessing a "sin" about which we have no further information. Helena's confession illustrates that discipline and admonition were still practised among Augsburg Anabaptists at this time. While Helena's baptism as an adult in 1527 represented her new commitment to God and the Anabaptist church, her written confession is a positive response to "communal admonition" and a recommitment to serve God and the congregation at Augsburg. She wrote from her heart to reveal a depth of commitment to her God and Lord, as well as to the Anabaptist congregation in which she practised her faith. Though she had debated theological issues with Protestant and radical reformers alike, hers was a faith based on a personal experience of God's grace and forgiveness. That Helena, a noblewoman by social status, presented this humbling confession to her fellow believers illustrates the levelling quality of Anabaptism, and Helena's acceptance of the authority of the congregation.[29]

The introductory lines of the confession illustrate her conviction that she was not approaching the congregation on her own authority, but through God's will. God's power was stronger than that of the devil who had deceived her. Thus, her opening words end with a prayerful affirmation of God's strength: "But God my Lord is even stronger and deprives him of his power and might through Jesus Christ, His beloved Son. To Him be honour and praise. Amen."

When Helena spoke of God breaking her will, and of her own resistance to allowing the Lord's will to happen in her life, her words are reminiscent of the medieval mystics who aspired to be united with God in their souls. Her attitude of self-denial, which involved the removal of self so that God could work in her, is the classic language of yieldedness and complete dependence on God used by her spiritual predecessors: she shared this language with many other Anabaptists.[30]

Helena also confessed her dependence on the work of the Holy Spirit who had created her awareness of personal sin. She was now conscious, she says, of an absence of the fruit of the Holy Spirit in her life, especially in her lack of patience in the face of God's discipline. The historian Merry Wiesner suggests that such dependence on the Holy Spirit allowed sixteenth-century women to take on public roles. This appears to have been true for Helena, but her dependence on the Holy Spirit also represented her aspiration for a deeper spiritual life which had been stunted through her "disobedience."[31]

Whatever her sin may have been, (the reference to civil authorities may indicate that it was her recantation)[32] Helena had failed to love God first and her congregation second. She used the passages from 1 Corinthians 13, the chapter on Christian love, and the verses in Matthew 7 about the beam and the twig to discuss her sin. She had wanted to teach others while not being willing to accept discipline herself.[33]

Because Helena chose to walk in the path of Christian love, she emerged from her struggle and inner turmoil feeling cleansed of her sin. She asked the forgiveness of her congregation, an action that Anabaptists believed was necessary to receive God's forgiveness. Moreover, she felt ready to grant forgiveness to those who had wronged her, as well. For Helena, yieldedness to God did not mean a loss of personal self, but rather empowerment through God's grace.

It has been said of women in the nineteenth-century Holiness movement that: ". . . people felt compelled to renounce their attachment to their possessions, their children, their spouses, in that ascending order, and sometimes to their own reputation or pride."[34] This sums up Helena of Freyberg's life very well. In 1529 she left her family and her Tirolean property behind to live in exile. When she was dispossessed in Constance she returned to her home, only to leave a second time in 1534. Her confession to fellow Anabaptists shows how, toward the end of her life, she dealt with her pride.

Helena was an Anabaptist woman who persevered in the Anabaptist faith for eighteen years. If she was around the age of twenty at her marriage, which took place before 1506, she was approximately forty years of age when she became an Anabaptist and thus died in her late fifties. Her story is one of courage, leadership, growth, and commitment.

Helena of Freiberg, Confession (as follows) on Account of Her Sin

Beloved in God, I ask you through God's will that you hear my accusation of myself, and the recognition of my guilt, in writing, since I truly cannot speak of it with my mouth, without turning red with shame, for flesh and blood have refused to confront it, sought escape where possible and remained silent when I have tried for a long time in the past (to deal with it).[35] And so flesh and blood must for this (and can no longer avoid it) be disgraced due to its malice (and trickery). The devil has covered me over many times, and distorted the light and made me white while I was black, and perverted the Holy Spirit into a spirit of the flesh. This is what [the devil] does in all spiritual things, he presents himself as if he were white as an angel (and very humble). But God my Lord is even stronger and deprives him of his power and might through Jesus Christ, His beloved Son. To Him be honour and praise. Amen.

First of all: I confess and from the bottom of my heart acknowledge my guilt before God and all His saints in Heaven and on earth, how I have sinned and incurred guilt in the matter which has now been revealed to me by God's grace through the goodness of the Holy Spirit through the mercy and goodness of God my Lord and Father. God does not neglect to discipline His wicked quarrelsome child; unfortunately I have rebelled against God and as a result I have lost the grace of the Holy Spirit.

The fruit of the [Holy Spirit], patience, righteousness, gentleness, humility, kindness, true love, faithfulness, peace, self-discipline, no longer can be seen, which mocks true faith and the Word of God. From the bottom of my heart I am guilty of great impatience before godly discipline and punishment, which has resulted in the bitterness of my heart, in many unfruitful, irresponsible words and behaviour. Also, [I confess] that I have carelessly sworn by the name of God and in disobedience to the Holy Gospel, have not followed its rule, the teachings of Christ my Lord (and Redeemer), where He says, learn of me, I am gentle, patient and humble from the bottom of my heart; He was patient and did not object when injustice was done to Him, and yet I do not want to suffer because of my guilt. This is far from the mind of Christ, which a Christian should also have; for children of the Heavenly Father should have His nature. Christ teaches us to leave ourselves and the life of self behind, not to seek ourselves, and to follow Him in power, in simplicity and uprightness, like a child without falseness or deceit.

I also confess that my prayer is not righteous, for I do not gladly allow the Lord's will to happen in me, in that I resist what goes against my will or wants to break it.

I am guilty from the bottom of my heart, of not being genuinely god-fearing, of not having God constantly in my sight, therefore I lack the godly wisdom that comes from the fear of God. I exhibit this in my walk; I barely grow or increase in the body of Christ, as an old woman in the faith [should], so that I feel worthless and shameful before God and His own. I am weak, miserable, lukewarm and tired in my watching and praying. Wherefore all my trouble has befallen me. In this I have only myself to blame and no one else.

I confess myself to be guilty and to have failed completely in loving God first and my brother, and have broken the command of God, wherein the whole law is contained, that is in forbearance and kindness. For love has no evil passion, and is neither contrary nor complaining, boastful or puffed up, is not undisciplined, bitter or ever angry. Love endures and forbears all things, and trusts that all will go well, has no evil suspicion, does everything for the best according to the prompting of the Holy Spirit, and also does not seek its own advantage.

In all this I have failed and broken [faith]. I wanted to teach and discipline my brother, but I was not teachable or amenable to discipline myself. I have sought the twig in him, and not seen the beam in my own eye. Also, I have been troublesome in the way I have acted towards my brother and foremostly in my great impatience, with which I caused anger and great impatience, from which regretfully no good thing followed and happened. Thus the fault is mine alone and falls on me and no one else.

Especially I have sinned and become guilty concerning those in civil authority, [*Hündt*][36] about which I was spoken to in the beginning; according to my understanding and intention it was not sinful according to the evangelical order. I have resisted at this point with impatience and tactlessness in word and deed. I forcefully wanted to retain the freedom which I thought I had, not wanting to be restricted or compelled, seeking my own good to the detriment of my neighbour, which caused my brother to stumble, resulting in his vexation. In this I did not take into consideration the love of or the good of my brother, and have loved the creature for its own sake. This I confess before God and His own. I have been completely uncooperative and impatient towards those who have resisted me in this. I have often wanted to separate myself from them. In all of this I confess that I have done wrong, above all with those in civil authority [*Hündt*] (having the improper attitude and excessive conduct). Unfortunately, I have not been able to understand it otherwise until now, but God has revealed it to me, through His Holy favourable (charitable) Spirit, to whom be praise eternally. Amen.

Thus, I am guilty from the bottom of my heart of committing a sin and becoming indebted to God and my brothers and neighbours, [both] knowingly and in ignorance as God my Lord knows best for me, inwardly and outwardly. Because of me the name of God has been blasphemed. Consequently, many evil, careless, unfruitful, and blasphemous words have been said before God.

I confess before God, that I well deserve every punishment because of my sin and guilt, yes probably even more than He has given me, and am worthy only of humiliation, disgrace and ridicule. Surely it would not have been a wonder, for all that I have deserved from God, if He had readily allowed me to perish. But God acts as a faithful father to His angry, quarrelsome child, and punishes me until I become aware of [my sin]. Due to the great love from God (through Christ) I have experienced grace and mercy (which will speak for me at the judgement); to God be given thanks eternally.

So I am in the same position as the lost son, I have made a useless mistake, with what my Lord and God the Father (in grace) has given me, yes have used it unfruitfully. I said, I am no longer worthy to be called His child, and I say along with public sinners, God be gracious and merciful, and forgive me (needy as I am) my sin and transgression and provide (for me the poor one) a perfect and appropriate repentance in all yieldedness [*Gelassenheit*], humility and self-denial through the holy blood of Jesus Christ. For I am sorry from the bottom of my heart, God knows what I have done. Therefore I also ask His holy congregation, especially here at Augsburg, whom I have offended greatly, in particular Pilgram [Marpeck] and Valtin [Werner?], to forgive and pardon what I have done against them, for which I am sorry from the bottom of my heart (as previously mentioned) and as God knows. And now however, the consolation and assurance in the shedding of the holy blood of Jesus Christ my God and Lord, promise sanctification and reconciliation. For He says that in the hour in which sinners sigh in their hearts over their sins, they are forgiven. To this I cling in faith, that my sins are forgiven through Jesus Christ, which prepares me for death. This I say in praise, honour and thanks for God's great grace and mercy, to whom be praise, honour and laud from eternity to eternity. Amen.

I ask and plead with God from the depths of my heart through Jesus Christ and through the intercession of the saints and children of God and His holy congregation (whom the Lord knows) whom I ask from the bottom of my heart (and it is also my wish) that they would pray on my behalf (to God) for help and strength, that in future I may withstand all that is opposed to God, end my life following God's will, to the honour and praise of His holy name. Amen.

Thus, I yield myself to the discipline and punishment of God my heavenly father, His holy congregation and Christian church as long and however much, as is pleasing to the Holy Spirit, and may the will of God be done in me according to His grace (along with all those who desire it and who are in need) Amen.

This is at present my will and final decision. May God the Lord require of me whatever He wills. I forgive (forget) and pardon from the bottom of my heart those whom I suppose to have done things against me. I ask God also to forgive and pardon them, yes that God would give them grace to help them recognize their sin (as I have done through God's grace). Amen.

Laus Deo

Notes

1 The court records in TA, Ost.II reveal that in Tirol over 200 women joined the movement between 1527 and 1529. See Linda Huebert Hecht, "Faith and Action: The Role of Women in the Anabaptist Movement of the Tirol, 1527-1529," (cognate essay, University of Waterloo, 1990). The role of Helena of Freyberg as a lay leader in the early Anabaptist movement of the Tirol is discussed there briefly, pp. 65-66. See also, Linda Huebert Hecht, "An Extraordinary Lay Leader: The Life and Work of Helene of Freyberg, Sixteenth Century Noblewoman and Anabaptist from the Tirol," *MQR*, 66 (July 1992): 312-41. Earlier information about Helena's life was published in: Robert Friedmann, "Helene von Freyberg," in ME, II, 397 and Wilhelm Wiswedel, "Freifrau Helene von Freyberg, eine adlige Täuferin," in *Zeitschrift für bayrische Kirchengeschichte*, 15 (1941): 46ff.

2 The information about Helena's family is taken from: Kaspar Schwarz, *Tirolische Schlösser, Heft I, Unterinntal, I Teil* (Innsbruck: Verlag der Wagner'schen Universitäts Buchhandlung, 1907), 66-68 and Klaus Kogler, *Stadtbuch Kitzbühel, Bd. III, Baugeschichte, Kunstgeschichte, Theatergeschichte, Schlösser* (Kitzbühel: E. der Stadt Kitzbühel, 1970), 355, Tafel III. Regarding Heinrich Marpeck, see Stephen B. Boyd, *Pilgram Marpeck, His Life and Social Theology* (Durham, NC: Duke University Press, 1992), 5, n. 3; 6, n. 4.

3 The inclusion of the prefix 'von' in both her given and her married names indicates Helena's membership in the landowning and lower nobility in the Austrian territory of Tirol. In the German language she is referred to as "Frau" which indicates her status in the nobility. "die Benennung Frau, . . . [war] blos für Weiber der Bürgers und Herrenleute geeignet, . . ." Johann Schmeller, *Bayerisches Wörterbuch*, (1961) vol. I, 802. In the English language one would say "Lady." In some references she is called *Schlossfrau*, meaning mistress of a castle and *Freifrau* a title she would have had as the wife of a *Freiherr*. See Wiswedel, "*Freifrau*," 47. The title *Freiherr* or Baron, indicates her husband's social status in the highest ranks of the lower nobility. Helene was thus a Baroness. Her social status gave her a certain authority in that society, and made her a natural leader, that is, one expected to lead others. "Neither the Protestant nor the Catholic reformers differentiated between noblewomen and commoners in their public advice to women; noblewomen, too, were to be 'chaste, silent, and obedient.' Privately, however, they recognized that such women often held a great deal of power and made special attempts to win them over. . . . Noblewomen, both married and unmarried, religious and lay, had the most opportunity to express their religious convictions, and the consequences of their actions were more far-reaching than those of most women." Merry E. Wiesner, "Nuns, Wives, and Mothers: Women and the Reformation in Germany," in Sherrin Marshall, ed., *Women in Reformation and Counter-Reformation Europe, Public and Private Worlds* (Bloomington: Indiana University Press, 1989), 21.

4 Kogler, *Stadtbuch Kitzbühel*, 355.

5 Friedrich Roth, *Augsburgs Reformationsgeschichte, 1531-1537 bezw. 1540, Bd.II* (Munich: Theodor Ackermann, 1904), 410; 422, n. 53.

6 Kogler, *Stadtbuch Kitzbühel*, 355; Schwarz, *Tirolische Schlösser*, 67.

7 TA, Ost.II, p. 95. In the original document the word *Hauszvolck* is used for those baptized at the same time as Helena. In her summary of this document, Mecenseffy uses the word *Gesinde* meaning servants. Eduard Widmoser emphasizes that her whole household was baptized with her. He gives several references to this event in the records while Mecenseffy gives only one. "Das Täufertum im Tiroler Unterland" (Dissertation, Leopold Franzens Universität, Innsbruck, 1948), 120. Ten days later local authorities

were reminded to inquire about Helena and her two sons. Likely these were her two younger sons, Wilhelm and Hanns Sigmund. TA, Ost.II, p. 96. A month later Helena and her husband, following procedures by which they could protect themselves, both submitted written statements to the authorities. TA, Ost.II, p. 108.

8 TA, Ost.II, p. 110. Widmoser gives the full name of this preacher as Paul Rassler. "Das Täufertum," 120. Marpeck may have been influenced by the missionaries Leonard Schiemer and Hans Schlaffer, ". . . although he had probably previously attended some Anabaptist meetings conducted by a certain Paul in nearby Kitzbühel and in the Münichau Castle, whose owner, Helena of Freiburg, favoured the movement (Marpeck later had connections with her). This could have been in November and December of 1527, since a report of such meetings was given to the authorities in Salzburg on December 9 of that year." See "Pilgram Marpeck," by Johann Loserth in ME, III, 492. It is clear then that there were mutual influences between the Baroness and Pilgram Marpeck. Johann Loserth tells us that the houses in which nocturnal meetings had been held and where communion had been taken were to be burned or dismantled as an example to the population. Münichau was on the list of such places. *Causa Domini II*, 206, 207, cited in "Der Anabaptismus in Tirol von seinen Anfängen bis zum Tode Jakob Huters (1526-1536), Aus den Hinterlassenen Papieren Des Hofrathes Dr. Josef R. von Beck," *Archiv für Osterreichische Geschichte*, 78 (1892): 466.

9 TA, Ost.II, p. 150. Partzner had worked in Kitzbühel, Rattenberg, and Kufstein. TA, Ost.II, p. 153. The fact that she had never yet reported or answered to the government for her actions ("noch nie verantwurt noch purgiert hat") is what incriminated her. The clergyman, Paul, here is called the main seducer ("den rechten und ersten verfuerer").

10 TA, Ost.II, p. 223.

11 TA, Ost.II, p. 258; p. 311. See also Widmoser, "Das Täufertum," 120-21; Jan J. Kiwiet, *Pilgram Marbeck, Ein Führer in der Täufer Bewegung der Reformationszeit* (Kassel: J. G. Oncken Verlag, 1957), 38.

12 TA, Ost.II, p. 312, ll.20-22; p. 338, ll.5-34. On January 2, 1530, the Sunday after New Year's, an armed guard came to Hohenaschau to arrest her. Roth, *Augsburg II*, 410-11. Friedmann thought that Helene came into contact with Anabaptism in 1528 and was baptized then. "Helene," ME, II, 397. Wiswedel assumed she was baptized at Münichau but gives no date. "Freifrau," 47. Later in Augsburg, Helena testified that she had been baptized in the region of Bavaria ("im land zu Bairen"). Roth, *Augsburg II*, 427. Although the actual location of her baptism is less clear, that it took place in 1527 is certain.

13 TA, Ost.II, document 520, pp. 354-56; p. 371; p. 401. Loserth tells us: "Freunde und Verwandte bewirkten indess, dass ihre Güter ihren Söhnen zurückgestellt wurden." "Anabaptismus in Tirol," 490.

14 Schwarz, *Tirolische Schlösser*, 68.

15 Christian Neff, "Constance," ME, I, 703. TA, *Baden und Pfalz*, p. 468; p. 469. Traugott Schiess, *Briefwechsel der Brüder Ambrosius und Thomas Blaurer, 1509-1548* (Freiburg i. Br.: Friedrich Ernst Fehsenfeld, 1908), 321, 379.

16 TA, *Baden und Pfalz*, 469. There is much correspondence in 1530 about Partzner, who was arrested at Augsburg but whom the council would not extradite to the territory of Tirol. Anabaptist were better off in Augsburg. Roth, *Augsburg II*, 411.

17 TA, Ost.III, p. 115; p. 194; p. 197. See also, Widmoser, *Täufertum*, 122 and Loserth, "Anabaptismus in Tirol," 586.

18 Grete Mecenseffy, "Anabaptists in Kitzbübel," MQR, 46 (April 1972): 107.

19 A communique from Innsbruck on January 21, 1534, made clear why the central government wanted Helena to recant publicly in front of as many people as possible in the region of Kitzbühel. It stated: "She has been so intensely involved in the Anabaptist sect, providing lodging for persons who have been rebaptized in the regions around Kitzbühel, some of whom have been executed, so that she has been the primary cause of so many people joining this movement. Therefore, we do not find it wise or advisable that she recant to us, but rather to the multitude in the church at Kitzbühel." TA, Ost.III, document 232; pp. 200-1; p. 260.
20 Ibid., p. 264.
21 Loserth, "Anabaptismus in Tirol," 490.
22 Her oral testimony of April 1535 was published in Roth, *Augsburg, II*, 426-27.
23 Friedmann, "Helene," ME, II, 397.
24 Statements made by the Anabaptist Jörg Maler provide information about Helena's house church and the people she influenced. "His testimony reveals two groups with whom he then had contact. One group centred in the house of Helena of Freyberg in Rosenau, just outside the city gate to the east. The members included Pauls Weckerlin (weaver), Philip Schlosser and Bernhart Schmidt (wool carder)." Boyd, *Pilgram Marpeck*, 133. Hans Jacob Schneider gave his testimony in Augsburg in 1562. See ibid., 134.
25 Wiswedel, "Freifrau," 48; Boyd, *Pilgram Marpeck*, 106; Elmer Ellsworth Schultz Johnson, ed., *Letters and Treatises of Caspar Schwenckfeld von Ossig*, vol. 8 (Leipzig: Breitkopf and Härtel, 1927), 161-64; 616, 618. (Hereafter, CSL.)
26 CSL, vol. 8, 616.
27 George H. Williams, *The Radical Reformation* (Philadelphia, PA: Westminster Press, 1962), 468.
28 "Helene von Freiberg, Confession (as follows) on account of her sin," in *Das Kunstbuch*, No. 28, fol.243r.-246r. The Geiser transcription of the *Kunstbuch* from the Mennonite Historical Library, Goshen, Indiana was used. (Hereafter the translated version will be referred to as *Confession*). For a discussion of the *Kunstbuch* and its contents, see Heinold Fast, "Pilgram Marbeck und das oberdeutsche Täufertum. Ein neuer Handschriftenfund," *Archiv für Reformationsgeschichte*, 47 (1956). There are hints that Helena wrote many letters to various leaders which are no longer extant. Hans Guderian says of her: "jahrelang mit Marbeck in brieflicher Verbindung stand. . . ." *Die Täufer in Augsburg, Ihre Geschichte und ihr Erbe, Ein Beitrag zur 2000-Jahr-Feier der Stadt Augsburg* (Pfaffenhofen: W. Ludwig Verlag, 1984), 102. However, Jörg Maler, editor of the *Kunstbuch* preserved only this personal confession by Helena. A number of factors suggest that Helena wrote this confession between 1539 when she returned to Augsburg and 1545 when she died. She spoke of herself as "an old woman in the faith" and of being prepared for death. Also, Marpeck was in Augsburg after 1544 and his name is mentioned in the confession. (Valtin, likely Valtin Werner, whom Helene also mentions, was a fellow Anabaptist in Augsburg and shared Marpeck's concerns.)
29 Helena struggled for a long time before writing this confession. Marpeck felt strongly that discipline or the ban was not to be used hastily. It was the final step in a process of discipline. Walter Klaassen, "Church Discipline and the Spirit in Pilgram Marpeck," in I.B. Horst, A.F. DeJong, and D. Visser, eds., *De Geest in het geding*, (Alphen aan den Rijn: H. D. Tjeenk Willink, 1978), 172.
30 Raymond Bernard Blakney, *Meister Eckhart, A Modern Translation* (New York: Harper and Row, 1941), 104, 105; Walter Klaassen, "*Gelassenheit* and Creation," CGR, 9 (Winter 1991).

31 Merry Wiesner, "Women's Defense of Their Public Role," in Mary Beth Rose, ed. *Women in the Middle Ages and the Renaissance, Literary and Historical Perspectives* (Syracuse: Syracuse University Press, 1986), 18. In Tirol, Anabaptists characteristically greeted one another with the words "Peace be with you!" to which the fellow Anabaptist would respond, "The Holy Ghost live in you!" TA, Ost.II, p. 89. "Marpeck gives much attention to a careful description of what the exercise of the ban under the guidance of the Spirit means. Walter Klaassen, "Church Discipline," 172.

32 In her confession she uses the word *Hündt* which is a reference to a person in civil authority at the local level. See Hans Fink in *Tiroler Wortschatz an Eisack, Rienz und Etsch* (Innsbruck: Universitätsverlag Wagner, 1972), 134. Perhaps Helena was referring to the *Statthalter* before whom she had recanted at Innsbruck in 1534.

33 Helena's attitude of teachability reminds us of Marpeck's views in the introduction to his book, *The Admonition*. See William Klassen, *Covenant and Community, The Life, Writings and Hermeneutics of Pilgram Marpeck* (Michigan: William B. Eerdmans Publishing Company, 1968), 79. As a member of Marpeck's circle, Helena's emphasis on Christian love was not surprising. For Marpeck it was imperative that children of God be ruled by love. He said: "Here there is no coercion, but rather a voluntary spirit in Christ Jesus our Lord." The guidance of the Holy Spirit would bring voluntary repentance. See Walter Klaassen and William Klassen, eds., *The Writings of Pilgram Marpeck* (Scottdale, PA: Herald Press, 1978), 112-13.

34 Nancy Hardesty, Lucille Sider Dayton, and Donald W. Dayton, "Women in the Holiness Movement: Feminism in the Evangelical Tradition," in Rosemary Ruether and Eleanor McLaughlin, eds., *Women of Spirit, Female Leadership in the Jewish and Christian Traditions* (New York: Simon and Schuster, 1979), 242.

35 Round brackets are words in the original text; square brackets are inserted words.

36 See n. 32 above.

ANNA GASSER OF LÜSEN

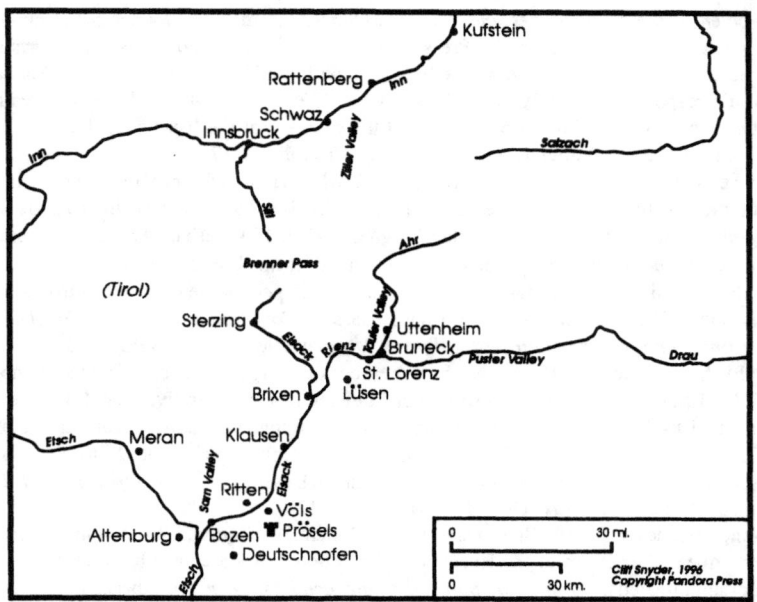

A study of the court records for the Austrian territory of Tirol reveals that each of the women discussed there had a somewhat different experience. This is particularly true for Anna Gasser. We know for certain that in 1525 she participated with her husband, Hans, in the Peasants' War. Either during that time or immediately following the failed revolt, both Hans and Anna became Anabaptists. For these outlawed activities, the Gassers were imprisoned several times; Hans ultimately paid with his life. Anna's punishment was at first only a public beating, for she was pregnant. However, by the time the government finally released her from prison after the death of her husband, she had miscarried. As we shall see, Anna remained undeterred by all these experiences, and eventually left her home and family for the sake of her faith.

Anna Mairhofer Gasser was probably born in Lüsen in South Tirol.[1] She had two brothers that we know of, one who preached and conducted Anabaptist meetings and another who lived in Gufidaun. She married Hans Gasser and moved to the region northwest of Bozen to live on the mountainside of the Ritten in the district of Wangen.[2] Like most women in early modern Europe, Anna married and remained close to the place of her birth.[3] Hans Gasser was a peasant farmer who belonged to that class of society called the "common people."[4] As the wife of a peasant farmer, Anna would have been active in the same occupational pursuits as her husband except that her focus would have been the domestic economy, child care, and work inside the home.⁵ During the time of Hans and Anna's involvements in the Peasants' War and Anabaptism several of their children were already grown. We know of a son Thomas who was an Anabaptist and a daughter Barbara who left home because she did not want to become an Anabaptist.⁶ The Gasser household included two maids, Lucia and Agatha, as well as several male servants, or *Dienstboten*. It was Anna's job to supervise the work of the maids; it is of note that Lucia and Agatha, both her maids, became Anabaptists. Another prominent Anabaptist family living on the Ritten, Margret and Ulrich Kobl, also had two maids.⁷

Farmers like Hans Gasser and Ulrich Kobl were not subservient to an immediate overlord, and thus ranked among the better-off peasant families of the predominantly rural population of South Tirol. The situation was quite different for Anna Gasser's brother, who lived in Gufidaun, which was under the jurisdiction of the Bishop of Brixen: there peasant farmers were not so free.⁸

The sources do not reveal the degree to which Hans and Anna Gasser were affected by peasant grievances. We do know that Hans felt the grievances keenly enough to become a leader of the peasants in this region. Perhaps Anna participated for the sake of her children, to ensure a better future for them and to make sure the family retained its property. Unlike our society today, in which church and state operate separately, in sixteenth-century society the religious, social, and political lives of people were intricately connected; religious resistance was viewed as political and civil disobedience. Thus, Anabaptists were arrested for both heresy and insurrection. This was the case for both women and men, as the story of Anna Gasser will illustrate.

In the early years of the sixteenth century in various parts of Europe, the common people expressed their grievances against the authorities of church and state by armed revolt. The Reformation principles heralded by Martin Luther gave the common people a platform from which to voice their dissatisfaction. The Meran articles, which represented the grievances of the peasants from the Eisack and Etsch (Adige) river valleys of Tirol, express some of these views:

> They speak of the abuses in the social body which "hinder the Kingdom of God," a chief one of which is that men have forgotten to observe love to Christ and goodwill to the neighbour and that the land's resources have been used selfishly and not for the common good. The insurrection was a revelation of divine justice in order to bring back brotherly love and concern for the common good.⁹

The complaints of the peasants in the different regions were very specific to these areas. Where the Gassers lived, the peasants objected to being denied the right to fish in the pond behind the castle of their overlord, Lienhard von Völs. They also complained of having to remove snow from the steep roof of his castle.[10]

In Tirol as a whole, socio-economic problems and religio-political issues were intertwined, in part due to the unique political makeup of this Austrian territory. Unlike Ferdinand I's other territories, the burghers and peasants formed a distinct fourth order in Tirol and had direct representation to the territorial ruler. Moreover, the upper class (lower nobility) was smaller in Tirol than in the other Austrian territories, a fact that seriously weakened their influence. Thus, by tradition, the common people were stronger politically, which motivated them to actively seek redress of their grievances, and at times even to take initiative in calling the meeting of the Estates. This they did in May of 1525.[11] At the same time Archduke Ferdinand I, who became the ruler of Tirol in 1520, was determined to gain full control of local government. Since he faced a perennial threat of war with the Turks, he needed to control the Estates for financial purposes.[12] The religious issues of the Radical Reformation became the means by which the archduke sought to control local authorities and subjects. The proceedings against Anabaptist heretics, who were by that token considered to be insurrectionists, were one means by which to do this.[13]

In North Tirol, the first Lutheran preachers had been appointed in the mining region of Schwaz, and the first clashes between Ferdinand and his subjects took place there, in January 1525.[14] In the south the peasant farmers and artisans found a leader in Michael Gaismair, secretary to the bishop of Brixen. In May 1525 he led a small army across the mountains of Tirol, only to be defeated by the forces of the archduke. Gaismair was able to escape and fled to Italy where he remained until his death. But local peasant leaders like Hans Gasser were not so fortunate; they had to remain in Tirol, where their actions both past and present were carefully scrutinized by a government determined to root out political insurrection and punish anyone who had been involved with Gaismair. As far as the common people were concerned, their grievances remained. For some, resistance to church and state took a new direction after 1525, as peasant farmers and artisans, as well as government officials and members of the nobility, joined the fledgling Anabaptist movement. In the years immediately following the peasant revolt, Anabaptist membership increased noticeably. By 1527 the outlawed sect had established itself in the same geographic regions where the revolt had taken place.[15] Women participated as actively as men in the development of Anabaptism in Tirol, comprising nearly half the membership of the group between 1527 and 1529.[16]

In the early months of 1527, a number of persons in other regions of

Europe had been accused of belonging to the Anabaptist sect. They included the prominent leader Michael Sattler, who was arrested in a region of the Black Forest that also belonged to Austria and was administered from Innsbruck.

> On April 4, 1527, Ferdinand wrote from Olmütz about the "strange sect" which claims that there is another baptism beside that which was "instituted by Christ himself our Saviour according to the holy Gospel." "Such and similar actions lead only to rebellion, bloodshed and the extermination and destruction of all government and honourable estates even more than heretofore." He urges special watchfulness in Tirol in order to prevent it from entering.[17]

By August 20, 1527, the first general mandate of Ferdinand I "against all Protestants"[18] was issued, and again the new movement was "associated with revolt and the total destruction of the societal order."[19] However, Ferdinand and his advisers were out of touch with what was happening in his domain. By the time this decree was published, a local radical preacher by the name of Wölfl already had carried the message of reform to many places in North and South Tirol.[20]

The wandering preacher [Winkelprediger] named Wölfl, born in the Sarn Valley north of Bozen, had worked for seven years as a lowly herdsman. But feeling called of God, he began to preach and teach. Early in January 1527, he was arrested and interrogated three times in Brixen. His extensive testimony, the first of its kind in Tirol, gives ample evidence that religious and social discontent were still very much alive in this Austrian territory. He had been in contact with many people, including a woman named Landberger in North Tirol, who told him that "he should simply preach and let nothing stand in his way; if they expelled him from one place, he should move on to another place and preach."[21] Wölfl did just that and carried his radical evangelical critique from the regions of Innsbruck into South Tirol, where he was supported widely. In fact, he was invited by Anton von Wolkenstein to spend time at the residence of this noble family at Plankenstein, located in the village of Uttenheim in the very heart of the Puster Valley. Anton's wife Elisabeth (see her profile in this volume) and their two younger sons, Paul and Sigmund, all became Anabaptists.[22] Wölfl's statement that "if he would be drowned or executed, five other people would come and preach the word of God in his place" demonstrates not only the extent of this man's influence, but also the intensity of radical and Anabaptist dissent in the Tirol by January 1527.[23] The government's strategy of eliminating radical evangelical leaders in the hope of dissipating sectarian groups was already insufficient at this early date.

Wölfl's message found resonance not only among the upper classes but also among many commoners and their families. The most famous of his converts was Jacob Hutter (see the profile of his wife, Katharina in this volume).[24] In 1534, just two years before Jacob Hutter's execution, Wölfl himself died as an Anabaptist martyr in the city of Meran.[25] But in 1526 Wölfl had gathered other dissatisfied persons around him with his preaching and radical evangelical ideas.[26] By 1527 a network of believers, many of whom (including Hans and Anna Gasser) would later be arrested as Anabaptists, extended from Bozen to Klausen and Gufidaun and all along the Puster and its side valleys.[27]

Wölfl was not the only evangelical preacher active in South Tirol. The Gasser family was mentioned in the earliest references to Anabaptists in the court records for Sterzing, a town located south of the Brenner Pass, where discontent among the large mining population had erupted in revolt in 1525.[28] Several months before the names of Hans and Anna Gasser appear in the court records, the government had been discussing the activities of Anna's brother, whose given name we do not know–he is always referred to by his family name, Mairhofer. On December 23, 1527, soon after the first interrogations in North Tirol of key leaders, Leonard Schiemer and Hans Schlaffer, Ferdinand I issued a general mandate to the twenty-seven district rulers [*Landrichter*] and crown administrators [*Pfleger*] in both North and South Tirol out of concern about the expanding activities of Anabaptists. In this mandate the activities of three men were singled out; one of them was Anna's brother. It was stated that Mairhofer, a merchant from Klausen called Messerschmidt, and another man whose name still eluded the authorities, had recently conducted a meeting in Sterzing. A number of women and men had been persuaded to become Anabaptists at this meeting or "sinagog," as the government called Anabaptist conventicles. The three men had left secretly, but were expected to be preaching elsewhere. Thus, local authorities were instructed to diligently seek out, arrest, and interrogate (with the use of torture) instigators and principal leaders like Mairhofer. The government feared the clandestine nature of this sect and suspected that "these people were planning a new insurrection and rebellion under the guise of Anabaptism."[29] Because the activities of Mairhofer were considered a great threat, the government issued a wanted poster for him.[30] And because the father of Anna Gasser and her brother lived in Lüsen, the bishop of Brixen in particular was instructed to publish the mandate in his bishopric.[31]

Bishop Georg carried out the orders of the archduke and on the last day of December 1527, the Innsbruck government sent him approval for the arrest of two Anabaptists from Klausen, namely Ulrich Müllner and the wife of Gilg Bader.[32] From the orders given Bishop Georg to capture Mairhofer and any other Anabaptists, we know that Anna's brother remained free. Both Müllner and Gilg Bader were staunch supporters of Wölfl and members of the Anabaptist group in Klausen; both had been cited along with Messerschmidt several times in Wölfl's testimony. Anna's brother had conducted meetings in the home of Ulrich Müllner in Klausen after he left Sterzing.[33] The sources do not reveal why Gilg Bader escaped arrest while his wife did not. We do know, however, that Wölfl received hospitality and lodging in the Bader home in addition to preaching there. On one such occasion he had described the cross of Christ to be "nothing more than a heavy stick as one would throw to a dog or use as fuel to heat an oven."[34]

Other women besides Gilg Bader's wife were involved in the radical and anticlerical happenings in Klausen. Wölfl had related in his testimony how Gilg Bader, the proprietor of a bathhouse, and Messerschmidt (with the aid of Messerschmidt's wife who knew how to write) had composed a threatening letter to the local priest, Herr Steffan, who had warned Wölfl to leave Klausen. They attached it to the church door and stated that they would beat the priests if they interfered with Wölfl. Messerschmidt, who travelled in relation to his work, had brought from Augsburg a book that was read in many places in the Puster Valley; he also had allowed Wölfl to preach in front of his store in Klausen.[35] Perhaps Gilg Bader's wife was present along with Messerschmidt's wife when the threatening letter was composed. In any case, she would have been fully aware of the incident as would have Hans and Anna Gasser.

Approximately a year after Wölfl's interrogation, on February 13, 1528, news of the arrest of a number of Anabaptists who had participated in the Peasants' War reached Ferdinand I, sent by officials from the two districts, Wangen and Altenburg, bordering on the Ritten.[36] Hans and Anna were in this group of prisoners. As a peasant leader and former confidant of Gaismair, who had been implicated with Ulrich Kobl "in an alleged plot to assassinate one of Ferdinand's administrators," Hans Gasser was a prime suspect.[37] However, we know that the names of *both* Hans and Anna appeared "several times in the lists of prominent Gaismair supporters during the events around Brixen in May and June 1525."[38] The government viewed their heretical activities as a continuation of the political, religious, and social insurrection in which they clearly had been involved in 1525. No doubt many women participated in the peasant revolt in Tirol as they did in other parts of Europe, but only in a few cases can this be documented. The fact that we have this information for Anna Gasser makes her story quite unusual.[39]

We do not know when, where, or by whom the Gassers had been baptized. However, a report six days later clarified the reason for their arrest. Earlier in February, Baron [*Freiherr*] Lienhard von Völs, the governor [*Hauptmann*] of this region, had arrested both Hans and Anna for having allowed Anna's brother to conduct a "sinagogue and meeting" in their home. It was hoped that their interrogation would now reveal to the authorities hidden activities in which the Anabaptists were engaged.⁴⁰ Clearly the archduke was continuing the search for Peasants' War participants and perceived Hans as well as Anna to be political rebels. The knowledge that Anna's brother had left Sterzing and was now preaching in the region of the Ritten indicated that the Anabaptist movement was expanding.

The communique of February 19 instructing Lienhard von Völs how to deal with the Gassers also advised him to investigate and curtail the work of two other Anabaptist leaders, namely Ulrich Kobl from Ritten (like Hans Gasser, a former confidant of Gaismair) who had escaped to Bern, Switzerland, and George Blaurock, who had proselytized in Tirol when he and his wife Els were exiled from Switzerland.⁴¹ When Kobl fled to Bern in February his wife, Margret, probably remained in Tirol because she was pregnant. At her first arrest in May 1528 she was near the end of her pregnancy [*hoch schwanger*]. Special instructions were given to keep her in prison until she had given birth and at that time to put her on trial if she still persisted in her Anabaptist faith. Later we learn that Margaret recanted. The Kobl family was in the same congregation as Hans and Anna, as will be seen shortly.⁴²

At first Hans and Anna benefited from the leniency of local authorities who were chided for not dealing with Anabaptists like the Gassers severely enough, especially considering the intense proceedings being conducted against Anabaptists in Bozen and Rattenberg at that time.⁴³ The Gassers were given the benefit of the doubt and released after their first arrest. For the next five months no reference is made to them in the court records. Fewer arrests of Anabaptists took place in midsummer, but near the end of the season, as the authorities again sought them out, Hans, Anna, and members of their family and household were implicated further in the testimonies of other Anabaptists.⁴⁴

The escape of Ulrich Kobl from prison precipitated the arrest of his wife, Margret, at the end of August 1528. This was Margret's second time in prison and as a *relapsi* (one who had rejoined the Anabaptists) she was treated more severely. Accordingly, she furnished the names of several Anabaptist families and their servants from the district of Wangen. The list included the Gassers' maid Lucia, the Gassers' sons, and other servants as well as Sigmund Sackmann, his wife, Stoffl Mair from Eggen, and his wife and brother.⁴⁵ If the prisoners admitted to being Anabaptist, the judge [*Gerichtsherr*] of Wangen was to put them on trial.

The degree to which maids and servants were intricately involved in the Anabaptist movement must not be underestimated. Margret Kobl's maid Els had brought some things to Ulrich Kobl's prison cell which had helped him escape. Although Anna Gasser's maid Lucia testified to the authorities, she remained in prison and was soon joined by her employers. Anna's second maid, a young woman named Agatha, was arrested in the following year (March 1529) along with the Gassers' son, Thomas.[46] However, Agatha's imprisonment was not lengthy; she was released due to her tender age.[47]

By November 28, 1528, Hans and Anna Gasser were in prison once more, this time arrested by Jakob von Fuchs, the crown administrator [*Pfleger*] of Altenburg. The testimony of Wilhelm Schuster of Deutschnofen brings to light some of Hans and Anna's activities. Schuster, who had provided food and drink to the fleeing Ulrich Kobl and those with him, stated that Hans Gasser had sheltered Anabaptists, including himself.[48] The arrest of Anna as well as Hans demonstrates that both husband and wife were held accountable for these actions.

The Innsbruck government was now less inclined to be lenient and took measures to ensure that their instructions to local officials would be carried out. Jakob von Fuchs was praised for his arrest of Anabaptists, including Hans and Anna Gasser; two other men, Benedict Sackmann and Stoffl Mair from Eggen were also arrested and interrogated under torture. It is not clear whether, as with Hans and Anna, the wives of these men were imprisoned as well. The authorities from Altenburg and Bozen were now to choose two witnesses [*Geschwörene*] for the interrogation. The purpose of the interrogation was, above all, to determine who else belonged to the Anabaptist sect.[49] A month later the prisoners from the Ritten testified again and were then moved to Bozen so that Jacob Hupher from the neighbouring district could interrogate them further and carry out the punishments that the mandates decreed. The officials in Innsbruck felt the rule of Georg von Firmian in Wangen lacked order and that he could not be trusted to carry out the wishes of the central government.[50]

Early in January 1529, Jacob Hupher dealt with the seven prisoners: Hans and Anna Gasser, their maid Lucia, Benedict and Anna Sackmann, and Stoffl Mair and his wife.[51] They were faulted for not having reported to the authorities within the period of grace that had been extended by the government to all Anabaptists of the territory in 1528.[52] In fact, they had become involved with the Anabaptist movement after the time of grace had expired. For these things they deserved severe punishment. But considering their remorse [*Reue*] and their circumstances, namely that they had been led astray, they would be pardoned under certain conditions.

The government's statement that they had been led astray could mean the prisoners were using this as an excuse to escape punishment. It could also mean the government viewed these prisoners as naïve. Four of the prisoners were female; naïvete was taken for granted for all persons of the lower classes, particularly if they were female.[53] It could also be that the government was willing to give these Anabaptists the benefit of the doubt.

The conditions of the pardon were as follows. First, all the prisoners were to receive corporal punishment administered at the pillory. For the women in the group, the beatings were to be more modest. This gave some consideration to the two women in the group who were pregnant, namely Anna Gasser and the wife of Stoffl Mair (referred to as the Mairin). Pregnant women were usually released from prison until they had given birth, but because the crimes of Anna Gasser and the Mairin were of such a serious nature, they were not to be released until they had been punished publicly.[54] Second, all of the prisoners were to do penance [*Busse*] and pay a sum of money as a guarantee that they would not rejoin the Anabaptists [*Burgschaft*]. Third, they were to give a written promise confirmed with an oath [*Urfehde*] to leave the territory of Tirol and ". . . never come back as long as they live."[55] If the prisoners refused the terms of repentance, all but the two pregnant women, Anna Gasser and the Mairin, would be put on trial. Anna's husband received the most severe punishment of all; his execution was decreed.

The terms of the pardon were certainly harsh. But for some reason, by February 13, 1529 (a month and a half later), Jacob Hupher had not carried out any of the punishments. Moreover, he gave the prisoners permission to attend a dance, possibly just prior to Lent, which was usually ushered in by festivities. In any case, Archduke Ferdinand's government was greatly amazed that such a thing had been allowed, considering his earlier instructions. Ferdinand expressed displeasure about this news and about the fact that Jacob Hupher was eager to gain the release of the prisoners.[56] For Hans Gasser the clemency did not last. By March 9, 1529, he had been executed on the pretext that he had broken the oath by which he had promised to have nothing more to do with Anabaptism. Hans had given shelter to his brother, a fugitive from prison, had warned him and given him food; such a serious crime could not be tolerated. Since Anna, like her husband, had been in prison previously, she now remained a prisoner despite the fact that she was pregnant. Once more we see that she was also held accountable for the actions that had taken place in their home, even though she was spared execution. The Mairin also remained in prison to await further action from the court following the birth of her child.[57]

Almost a month and a half later, on April 23, 1529, the orders came to release Anna Gasser from prison and grant her a second pardon. It is at this time that we learn about Anna's unique experience. She had suffered a miscarriage while in prison. Either because they felt somewhat responsible for Anna's tragedy or because they wanted to absolve themselves of any responsibility for the event, the Innsbruck government now pointedly asked Jacob Hupher, the judge in Bozen, why Anna Gasser had been kept in prison for such a long time after her miscarriage. The other prisoners had all been pardoned and released in mid-March.[58] Moreover, they wanted to know whether torture had been used when she gave her testimony to the judge and sworn witnesses. Unfortunately, these questions remain unanswered in the records available to us. We only know that, unlike most pregnant women who were released until they had given birth, Anna Gasser had had to remain in prison and there lost her child.[59]

Even less information is available for the Mairin regarding when or where she had her child. We do know, however, that early in July 1529, the request of Stoffl Mair and Benedict Sackmann for the freedom to come and go as they chose in and around Bozen [*Handel und Wandel*], was granted to them, but not to their wives. Moreover, the judge was advised to make sure that Anna Sackmann and the Mairin fulfilled the conditions of their pardon.[60] This is the last we hear about these two families, but Anna Gasser's story continues.

Later that year, in October, the court discussed the welfare of Anna Gasser's living children. The property and goods of arrested Anabaptists were confiscated routinely by the government. In cases where Anabaptist prisoners managed to escape and did not return, their property was inventoried and sold, with the income going to the government. This was especially significant when Anabaptist parents left behind children who needed financial support. In some cases family members, or other persons responsible for the children, then requested possession of the property or the income from it. Questions relating to the Gasser property had been raised by the *Pfleger* of Ritten soon after Hans's execution.[61] His wife's continued imprisonment may have delayed dealing with these matters. However, when Anna Gasser was pardoned, the court had to take action, and a guardian was duly appointed for her children. The appointment of a guardian could indicate that some of her children were still dependent.[62] On the other hand, in property matters, which were under the jurisdiction of the civil law, a woman was not allowed to speak for herself or her children. However, when arrested for heresy, a woman did not need a guardian to speak for her because accusations involving heretical activities came under criminal law and required every person to speak on his or her own behalf.[63]

The sources do not reveal how the court ruled in regard to Anna's children. However, this same report discussed Anna's request to leave the district in which she lived, something that had been denied her when she was first pardoned. The government reasoned that giving such permission would only tempt her to leave permanently, and therefore denied the request.[64] Their suspicions were indeed correct. Anna took matters into her own hands and in three months was gone, leaving her home and children behind.[65] There was nothing new in her choice; she had disregarded government instructions before in order to obey a higher authority and make her faith in God a priority. For Anna Gasser, living without her children became a matter of course.[66]

Anna Gasser's story illustrates that some Tirolean women and men continued their socio-economic, political, and religious protest by joining the outlawed Anabaptist movement. Anna held radical political and religious views and was not afraid to act on them, either in the Peasants' War or the outlawed Anabaptist movement. Although she chose to resist government authority, her participation was not as intense as that of her husband or she, too, would have been executed. However, as the wife of a peasant leader and Anabaptist, and the sister of an Anabaptist preacher, she made choices with severe consequences. She endured the shame of a public beating at a time when she was already pregnant. Like many other Anabaptists, on her first release from prison she rejoined the movement. At her second arrest, her continued imprisonment speaks for the danger she still posed to the government, even after her husband had been executed. Not only did she become a widow due to Anabaptism, she eventually lost all her children, including one who had not yet been born. Despite these losses, Anna Gasser survived persecution and probably lived out her life among the Anabaptists in Moravia. The pivotal role that women like Anna had in their families, households, and congregations was essential to the establishment of Anabaptism in the Tirol. Without their participation the movement could not have survived.

Notes

1 Geographically, the Brenner Pass is the dividing line between North and South Tirol. This profile is based on the published court records edited and summarized in TA, Ost.II. It is likely that more details of Anna Gasser's story will come to light when these court records are utilized more fully, using the handwritten accounts themselves. Extensive use has been made of a data base compiled by the author, which was used for "Faith and Action: The Role of Women in the Anabaptist Movement of the Tirol, 1527-29" (unpublished cognate essay, Master of Arts, History, University of Waterloo, 1990).
2 The districts [*Gerichte*] of Ritten and Wangen were located approximately 10 kilometres northeast of Bozen, on the eastern slopes [*Abdachung*] of the Sarn Valley. References to the Gassers and those associated with them are made in terms of their being "on the Ritten," indicating they lived on the mountain slopes.
3 The average age of marriage in early modern Europe was 15 to 18 for women and 25 for men. See Edith Ennen, *Frauen im Mittelalter* (Munich: C. H. Beck, 1985), 229. Men who were apprenticed travelled to places further away. See Lyndal Roper, "'Going to Church and Street': Weddings in Reformation Augsburg," *Past and Present* 106 (February, 1985).
4 The term "common people" refers to men and women of the lower social orders. See also, Lyndal Roper, "'The Common Man', 'The Common Good', 'Common Women': Gender and Meaning in the German Reformation Commune," *Social History* 12 (January, 1987).
5 Edith Ennen describes aspects of the domestic economy [*Binnenwirtschaft*] in *Frauen im Mittelalter*, 88.
6 Regarding the arrest and testimony of Thomas, see TA, Ost.II, p. 203. Barbara was arrested in May 1533 and interrogated in Brixen. She stated she was not an Anabaptist, and had left home to live in Sterzing because of her father's heresy. Now she was on her way to visit her relatives. Just recently on Palm Sunday, she had attended mass [*der*

hochwurdigen sacrament] and gone to confession. At her release she would attend church faithfully. The information about Barbara Gasser is in TA, Ost.III, document 129, pp. 116-17.

7 Margret Kobl and Anna Gasser are the only two women among the 268 mentioned in connection with Anabaptism in Tirol between 1527 and 1529 who each had two maids. In the court records, the maids are always referred to in reference to the wife and not the male head of the household, that is, as Anna Gasser's maid, the Margret Kobl's maid.

8 Regarding the brother in Gufidaun, see TA. Ost.II, p. 39. When Ulrich and Margret Kobl fled, their property was inventoried and sold by the government for 1300 florin (gulden). TA, Ost.II, p. 222. One thousand gulden were "the equivalent of twenty times the yearly salary of a carpenter." Stephen B. Boyd, *Pilgram Marpeck, His Life and Social Theology* (Durham, NC: Duke University Press, 1992), 6. Besides freeholders like Gasser and Kobl, there were *landesfürstliche Bauern and Freistiftbauern* in the Tirol. Freeholders, who had a looser relationship to their overlord, were on the whole more confident people whereas ordinary farmers suffered from the increase in rents [*Abgaben*] during the first half of the sixteenth century, a time when Tirol was overpopulated. Rudolf Palme, "Zur Täuferbewegung in Tirol, Soziale Schichtung, geographische Verbreitung und Verfolgung," *Mennonitische Geschichtsblätter* 42/43 (1986/87): 50-51.

9 Günther Franz, ed., *Quellen zur Geschichte des Bauernkrieges* (Darmstadt: R. Oldenbourg, 1963), 272, cited in Walter Klaassen, *Michael Gaismair, Revolutionary and Reformer* (Leiden: E. J. Brill, 1978), 32-33.

10 Walter Klaassen related to me that he visited the former castle of Leonard of Völs while doing research on peasant grievances. He noticed that the roof of the castle was indeed steep and he could immediately understand why the peasants of that region would have complained, considering the risks involved in such a task. The district of Völs, whose feudal overseer were the Lords of Völs, was located on the eastern side of the Eisack River. See TA, Ost.II, p. 80.

11 Klaassen, *Michael Gaismair*, 32.

12 The Turks are specifically mentioned in the mandates in November 1527 and April 1528. See TA, Ost.I, p. 8; p. 116.

13 Another means by which the Archduke sought to solidify his central government was through the office of the *Pfleger*, an official who reported directly to him and held political and judicial authority at the local level. He was head of the local government, that is, chief administrator for the crown. The majority of the communications between Tirol and Innsbruck in regard to the treatment of Anabaptist prisoners are addressed to the *Pfleger*. See Gerald Strauss, *Law, Resistance, and the State, The Opposition to Roman Law in Reformation Germany* (Princeton, NJ: Princeton University Press, 1986), 254, 268.

14 Peter Blickle, *The Revolution of 1525, The German Peasants' War from a New Perspective*, trans. Thomas A. Brady, Jr. and H. C. Erik Midelfort (Baltimore, MD: The Johns Hopkins University Press, 1981), 120. See also, Werner O. Packull, "The Beginning of Anabaptism in Southern Tyrol" in *Sixteenth Century Journal* 22 (1991): 718-20.

15 Walter Klaassen, *Michael Gaismair*, 108. Regarding the first Anabaptists in the Tirol in 1526, see n.20 below. By the time Hans and Anna were arrested for the first time in 1528, the prominent South German Anabaptist leader Pilgram Marpeck had already been deprived of his job as a judge in Rattenberg and with his wife had become an Anabaptist exile in Strasbourg. Also by this time, the noblewomen Helena von Freyberg and Elisabeth von Wolkenstein had established Anabaptist centres in Münichau and

Uttenheim respectively.
16 Hecht, "Faith and Action," 33.
17 *Tiroler Landesregierungsarchiv, Von der Königlichen Majestät II*, 35v-36 cited in Walter Klaassen, *Michael Gaismair*, 108.
18 The mandates were "laws of the Holy Roman Empire which gave instructions to the higher officials." "Mandates," ME, III, 446-47.
19 Walter Klaassen, *Michael Gaismair*, 108.
20 In the testimony of Hans Hut, who died in Augsburg in 1527, we have a report from Kaspar Färber, a native of Tirol. He told Hut at Augsburg in May of 1526 that "several brothers in the Inn Valley had been baptized and were leading a Christian life." C. Meyer, "Zur Geschichte der Widertäufer in Oberschwaben," *Zeitschrift des historischen Vereins für Schwaben und Neuberg I*, 1874, 245, cited in Klaassen, *Michael Gaismair*, 107. It was the report from Färber "which moved Hut to request baptism from Denck." Werner O. Packull, *Mysticism and the Early South German-Austrian Anabaptist Movement, 1525-1531* (Scottdale PA.: Herald Press, 1977), 64. From the testimony of Ursula Binder, who was with her husband doing mission work when arrested, we know that Hans Hut's influence reached as far as Salzburg because the Binders had been sent out by Hut. See TA, Ost.II, p. 26. Leonard Schiemer, imprisoned and executed in Tirol, was also Hut's disciple. The prominent Swiss leader Jörg Blaurock was proselytizing in regions just west of Tirol in May 1525 and April 1526. In the spring of 1527, he brought Anabaptism into Southern Tirol "during his first missionary journey down the Adige Valley." Packull, "The Beginning of Anabaptism in Southern Tyrol," 722. Despite these outside influences from the north and the east, local radical preachers, like Wölfl and Anna's brother, native to Tirol, were very significant. See Klaassen, *Michael Gaismair*, 107-8. (Wölfl's lengthy testimony provides a wealth of information about the early development of the Anabaptist movement in Tirol, but he does not mention the end times, a theme prevalent in the followers of Hans Hut.)
21 See Matthias Schmelzer, "Jakob Huters Wirken im Lichte von Bekenntnissen gefangener Täufer," *Der Schlern, Monatszeitschrift Für Südtiroler Landeskunde* 63, (November 1989): 618. The appendix contains Wölfl's testimony, 615-18.
22 The numerous places frequented by Wölfl and the people who supported him, including commoners, women, government officials, members of the clergy, and members of the nobility, are discussed by Schmelzer, "Jakob Huters Wirken," 596-99.
23 Schmelzer, "Jakob Huter's Wirken," 598.
24 In 1535 when Jacob Huter and his wife Katharina were captured, the government questioned Caspar Huter about the events of 1526. Caspar Huter related that in 1526 when Jacob was apprenticing as a hatmaker with him in Stegen, Jacob had heard the *Winkelprediger* preach in Pflaurentz near St. Lorenz and immediately became Wölfl's follower. Jacob then purchased a New Testament at the market in Bozen and proceeded to read from it and preach to Caspar and his household. But his employer would not tolerate such activities and Jacob Hutter soon left. TA, Ost.III, document 378, p. 309; p. 311; p. 314.
25 TA, Ost.III, p. 263.
26 TA, Ost.III, p. 262. Wölfl said the Mother of God had appeared to him in a vision, although he also stated that she was not a mediator to God. He also made reference to St. Leonard. At the same time he had eaten meat on Fridays and Saturdays with Messerschmidt in Klausen. Wölfl is referred to as a precursor [*Vorbote*] of Anabaptism in Tirol. See Schmelzer, "Jakob Huter's Wirken", 596, 599, 616.

27 Packull calls the group to which Hans and Anna belonged "a radical evangelical-sacramentist party" See his article, "The Beginning of Anabaptism in Southern Tyrol," 722.
28 Peter Blickle, *Die Revolution von 1525* (Munich: R. Oldenbourg, 1983), 189. Also: Blickle, *The Revolution of 1525*, 120.
29 TA, Ost.II, p. 39.
30 Regarding the wanted poster see: Eduard Widmoser, "Das Tiroler Täufertum im Tiroler Unterland" (Dissertation, Leopold Franzens Universität, Innsbruck, 1948), 57.
31 TA, Ost.II, p. 40.
32 TA, Ost.II, p. 42.
33 Karl Kuppelweiser, "Die Wiedertäufer im Eisacktal" (Dissertation, Leopold Franzens Universität, Innsbruck, 1949), 55.
34 Schmelzer, "Jakob Huters Wirken," 617.
35 Ibid., 616.
36 TA, Ost. II, document 74, pp. 78-9.
37 Packull, "The Beginning of Anabaptism in Southern Tyrol," 722-23.
38 This source, *Von der Königlichen Majestät II*, 145v. is given in Klaassen, *Michael Gaismair*, 110.
39 Margret Kobl's mother, the *Gallpüchlerin*, who later became a leader among the Anabaptists (see n.42 below) was also accused during the Peasants' War. In June 1526 she was found guilty of "sinful talk" [*freventlich Reden*] and was to be arrested as well as have her house searched for letters. See Marion Kobelt-Groch, *Aufsässige Töchter Gottes: Frauen im Bauernkrieg und in den Täuferbewegungen* (Frankfurt, Germany and New York, NY: Campus Verlag, 1993), 191, n. 14. Regarding the participation of women in the peasant revolts in other parts of Europe see Marion Kobelt-Groch, "Von 'armen frowen' und 'bösen wibern' - Frauen im Bauernkrieg zwischen Anpassung und Auflehnung," ARG 79 (1988).
40 This report is dated February 19, 1528. TA, Ost.II, document 79, pp. 80-81.
41 In regard to Blaurock, see n.20 above. Blaurock was arrested in Tirol in August and executed in September 1529. TA, Ost.II, document 389, p. 274; p. 286. The single reference to his wife Els in the Austrian records tells us that she was exiled from Switzerland too. TA, Ost.II, p. 81.
42 On January 29, 1528, Ferdinand's government sent orders to Jacob Hupher to arrest Jörg (likely Blaurock) and Adam and Kobl. This could be an indication that Kobl, Margret's husband, was associating with Blaurock at this time. Margret's mother, the Gallpüchlerin, was also named in this report, probably because the government was already familiar with her unlawful actions during the peasant revolt. See TA, Ost.II, p. 66. and n.39 above. A report of February 2, 1528, states that the Gallpüchlerin was pardoned and swore an oath. However, she continued her Anabaptist involvements and was subsequently included with a list of other Anabaptist leaders in the regions around Bozen. See TA, Ost.II, p. 70; p. 81; p. 183; p. 185. See Claus-Peter Clasen, "The Anabaptist Leaders: Their Number and Background, Switzerland, Austria, South and Central Germany, 1525-1618," MQR, 49 (April 1975): 144. Regarding Margret Kobl's first arrest see TA, Ost.II, p. 134; p. 136. Another daughter of the Gallpüchlerin was also an Anabaptist. See TA, Ost.II, p. 81.
43 TA, Ost.II, pp. 91-2.
44 The number of arrests reached its peak in both 1528 and 1529 during the month of May. This reflects the practice of transhumance practised by alpine farmers. See Fig.1 and Fig.2, which show the pattern of arrests graphically in Hecht, "Faith and Action," 32ff.

45 TA, Ost.II, documents 208 and 209, pp. 164-65. Sigmund Sackmann and his wife, who were part of this group, are only referred to once. Later, Benedict Sackmann and his wife, Anna, were included with the Gassers and Stoffl Mairs. Like her husband, Margret Kobl was able to escape prison a second time. See TA, Ost.II, p. 164; p. 176; p. 221.
46 Regarding Els, see TA, Ost.II, p. 164. Regarding Lucia, see TA, Ost.II, p. 203. Approximately 50 (20 percent) of the total number of women who were Anabaptists in Tirol between 1527 and 1529 were single and many of these were maids in Anabaptist households. Likely the majority of them were between 15 and 25 years of age. Many were employed in the homes of neighbours, friends, or relatives. If they were far from home and family they may been more open to the influences of Anabaptism, especially if their employers joined the movement. Merry E. Wiesner tells us that "Most women who worked outside their own homes worked as domestic servants. Service was a stage in life for many women, until they had reached the age they could marry and had earned a small dowry. It was also a permanent 'career' for many, who worked their way up in a large household from goosegirl to children's maid to serving maid to cook, or who more likely remained with a family as its single servant for twenty, thirty, or forty years. They rarely received much more than room and board as their wages." *Working Women in Renaissance Germany* (New Brunswick, NJ: Rutgers University Press, 1986), 83.
47 In discussions of Agatha's case, reference was made to her youth and naïvete which is why she was pardoned. She and the two young boys who were prisoners were to be punished as an example to prevent other young people from becoming involved in the Anabaptist movement. The number of young people involved in the movement was of concern to the government. TA, Ost.II, p. 203; p. 213.
48 TA, Ost.II, p. 178; p. 180.
49 TA, Ost.II, p. 180.
50 TA, Ost.II, p. 184. From subsequent entries we know that two of the wives from this group of prisoners, Anna Gasser and the wife of Stoffl Mair (referred to as the Mairin), were pregnant. They were to remain where they were until they had given birth.
51 TA, Ost.II, document 252, pp. 188-89.
52 During the winter season, people were more isolated, and in some of the mountain villages where conventicles were held they had not heard of the laws against Anabaptists. A mandate in February 1528 addressed this problem and extended the 'period of grace' to April 1528, during which time Anabaptists could report themselves to the government and receive a pardon. TA, Ost.II, p. 88.
53 "Roman law stressed women's alleged physical and mental weakness, . . . and held women, along with peasants and the simple-minded, as not fully responsible for their own actions." Merry E. Wiesner, "Frail, Weak, and Helpless: Women's Legal Position in Theory and Reality," in Jerome Friedman, ed., *Regnum, Religio et Ratio: Essays presented to Robert M. Kingdon* (Kirksville, MO: Sixteenth Century Publishers, 1987), 162.
54 In reference to the corporal punishment, the instructions were: "doch in demselben gegen inen, den weibern, etwas beschaidenheit zu halten," TA, Ost.II, p. 189. A ruling on the treatment of pregnant women was issued from Vienna by Ferdinand I on December 13, 1527. See TA, Ost.I, document 30, p. 54.
55 TA, Ost.II, p. 189.
56 TA, Ost.II, p. 194.
57 TA, Ost.II, p. 197; p. 217.
58 Benedict and Anna Sackmann, Stoffl Mair, and Anna's maid Lucia were pardoned in mid-March. TA, Ost.II, p. 200.
59 See TA, Ost.II, document 317, p. 221, regarding Anna Gasser.

60 TA, Ost.II, document 368, p. 258.
61 TA, Ost.II, document 277, pp. 199-200.
62 TA, Ost.II, p. 292.
63 Sixteenth-century lawmakers as a rule "did not make gender distinctions in criminal procedure . . . and both sexes were required to confess in capital crimes, which led to judicial torture." Wiesner, "Frail, Weak, and Helpless," 161-63.
64 TA, Ost.II, p. 292.
65 The date of this report is January 12, 1530. TA, Ost.II, p. 325.
66 From the experiences of Katherine Zell, the childless wife of a Protestant Reformer in Strasbourg who took up writing as her occupation, we know that for sixteenth-century women to be without children was viewed negatively. In discussing how sixteenth-century women challenged the division between private and public activity, Wiesner notes that Katharina Zell wrote in "Eine Brief an die Genze Bürgerschaft der Stadt Strassburg": "I have never mounted the pulpit, but I have done more than any minister in visiting those in misery. Is this disturbing the peace of the Church?" See Roland Bainton, *Women of the Reformation in Germany and Italy* (Minneapolis, MD: Augsburg Publishing House, 1971), 72, cited in Merry E. Wiesner, "Women's Defense of Their Public Role," in Mary Beth Rose, ed., *Women in the Middle Ages and the Renaissance, Literary and Historical Perspectives* (Syracuse, NY: Syracuse University Press, 1986), 21.

ANABAPTIST WOMEN IN TIROL WHO RECANTED

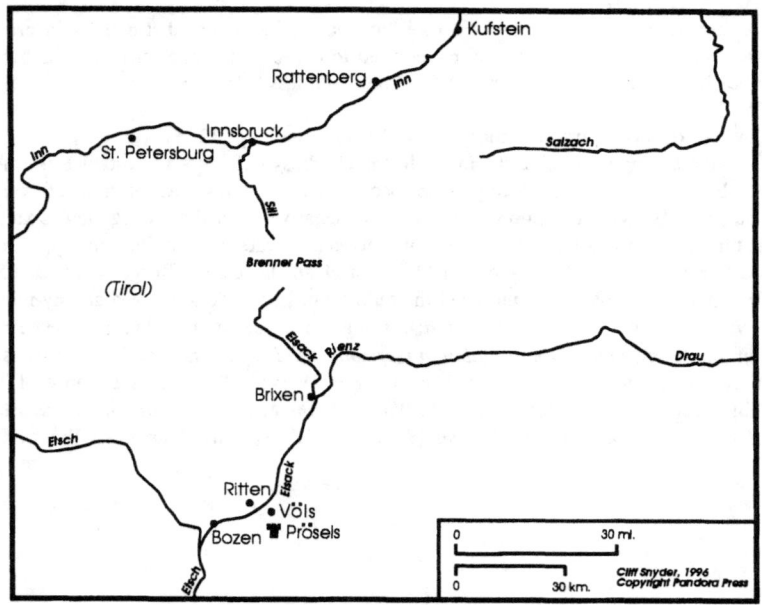

There were some women in the Anabaptist movement for whom recantation and pardon were alternatives to execution and death. In the Tirol of 1527, when a person was arrested for the first time, he or she was given the choice of recanting or renouncing adherence to the outlawed sect of Anabaptism, thereby negating their baptism as an adult and promising to have nothing more to do with the movement. The opportunity to recant, which the government gave arrested Anabaptists, was possible if the only crime they had committed was the rebaptism itself. In some cases pardons were granted to women at the initiative of the government, while at other times women were pardoned only after they had recanted.

The court records for the Austrian territory of Tirol reveal fifty cases between 1527 and 1529 where the recantations and pardons of Anabaptist women were discussed. A study of these cases demonstrates the efforts of the authorities to bring about conformity, first by means of elaborate public rituals. This worked in some cases, but not in all. Recanting Anabaptists were using the same approach as had their fourteenth-century predecessors in heresy, who had remarkable success in concealing their presence by practising "occasional conformity." To avoid detection, they went through the motions of complying with established ritual and recanting when they were arrested.[1]

Undoubtedly there were many different reasons why women recanted when they were first arrested, although information is sparse regarding their motivations. In some cases individuals decided to recant in order to save their lives, not wanting to abandon their families; in other cases recantation simply bought time, but did not indicate conformity. We know this by the number of cases where persons were arrested a second time. Within the Anabaptist community recantation did not preclude reinstatement. Women from all levels of society recanted. Whether they were from the upper classes, like Elizabeth von Wolkenstein or Helena von Freyberg, or from among the commoners, each had her own reason for doing so.

The procedures for recantation were outlined in a mandate of the Archbishop of Salzburg as early as November 1527. The usual recantation procedure included a public recantation [*Widerruf*], an oath [*Urfehde*], repentance as prescribed by the parish priest [*ires pharrer's Buss*], and payment of court costs [*Bezahlung der Atzung und Gerichtskosten*]. Moreover, each person, whether male or female, was required to make an individual public statements to prove a change of mind and a rejection of what the government viewed as sectarian belief. A directive sent out by Archduke Ferdinand, ruler of the Austrian territory of Tirol, on February 1, 1528, instructed local officials to make sure that each person would speak his or her own recantation.[2] In other words, a husband, father, or other male guardian could not recant on behalf of a woman. Just as in the question of rebaptism, a woman had to undertake this action herself. Even if a woman had been influenced by other members of her family or household, the government insisted that the actual recantation had to be spoken by her. It was similar in the matter of pardons. All individuals, male or female, had to appear in person and prove themselves ready to accept their punishment.

A recantation was usually carried out on three consecutive Sundays in the church in front of the congregation. Only then could a person be reinstated in the established church. The swearing of an oath to the secular authorities was to ensure that the person would take no further action against the government. But since the women had committed a criminal offence, they were required to swear an oath in the same manner as the men. This may have been somewhat unusual for them.[3] In most cases prison costs had to be paid before the prisoner could be released. When pardons were granted, they often included recantation and punishment, depending on the severity of the crime. For some women a request [*Bittschrift*] for their release from prison was submitted on their behalf by family members and friends.

In some cases only certain members of the family were involved in the Anabaptist movement. At other times entire households were affected by Anabaptist ideas and many of the persons involved were women. As with the fourteenth-century Cathar heretics of Mountaillou in Southern France, an individual "infected with dogmatic deviation" soon spread the disease to other members of his or her household.[4] In the city of Bozen in the Tirol, for example, the women in the household of the painter Bartlme Dill, as well as the wife and maid of Sebastian Ess's household and Sigmund Treibenreif's maid were imprisoned as Anabaptists in 1528. In the end all chose to recant.[5]

The seven women from the Dill and Ess households all escaped punishment, but this was not the case for all women who recanted. The types of punishments meted out to women who recanted or were pardoned usually indicate the extent to which they had been involved in the movement after their rebaptism. Martha Weltzenberger of St. Petersberg was sentenced to imprisonment for eight to fourteen days with little food, for which she had to pay, in addition to the recantation in the church, the oath, and the penance required by her priest. Such corrective measures were not prescribed for Lienhard Spitzhamer of Rattenberg and the maid from his household who were tried at the same time, and who both chose to recant. The additional punishment meted out to Martha Weltzenberger indicates that she had been more involved in the Anabaptist movement than were her fellow prisoners.[6] There were other cases where recanting women were kept in prison on a starvation diet. A group of fourteen prisoners arrested May 23, 1528, also from St. Petersberg, included eight women: three wives, two mothers, the daughter of one of the mothers, a single woman, and an older woman referred to as a caregiver [*die alt Phlegerin*]. All fourteen prisoners, including the women, were to be kept in prison and thereafter to give an oath and if they were able, to pay court costs.[7]

A number of the women who recanted were pregnant. The severity of their treatment and punishment again reflects the varying degree to which each of them was involved in the Anabaptist movement. When a woman stated at her arrest that she was pregnant, her punishment was usually postponed until after she had given birth. Instructions issued by the government in Vienna on December 13, 1527, told the local officials to allow pregnant and nursing mothers who requested recantation to go home if they promised to return when summoned by the court. However, this did not mean that pregnant women were spared imprisonment, punishment, or the same sentences as Anabaptist men. In the government mandates, corporal punishment was the mildest form of correction and was dispensed in a number of cases where Anabaptist women were pregnant and willing to recant.

Anna Gasser, whose story is told elsewhere in this book, was in prison several times. In January 1529, she was with a group of Anabaptists imprisoned in Bozen who were to be beaten in public at the town pillory. The four women in the group, of whom two, Anna and another woman, were pregnant, were to be punished more moderately.[8] In April 1529, after her husband had been executed, Anna Gasser was finally released from prison, but by then she had experienced a miscarriage.[9]

Corporal punishment also was included in the treatment of Anna Krätlerin who lived on the hillside of Stäbis in the district of Bregenz, and the wife of Lienhard Fundnetscher from Völs. Both women were pregnant and wished to recant. In the case of the former, she was allowed to delay the public beating until after the child was born. Like Anna Gasser, her husband had been executed earlier as an Anabaptist.[10]

Waldburga Ameiser, another Anabaptist woman who was pregnant and chose to recant, was imprisoned for four months in 1529. When she was finally released in September, her mobility was severely restricted.[11] The court record states:

> The housewives of Jörg Ameiser, Cristoff Gschäl and Lienhart Vischer are to be pardoned under the usual conditions. They are to submit a written statement and oath that has been confirmed by citizens, that they will not leave the district for one year and the county of Tirol for as long as they live.[12]

As this reference indicates, two other women were given this same sentence. This fact establishes, first, that pregnant women were given similar punishments to women who were not in this condition, and second, that women were very mobile and accustomed to being able to move about.

Some women who recanted were punished with limitations on where they could live and work. For Anna Sackmann of Bozen and the wife of Stoffl Mair from the neighbouring community of Ritten, who received such punishment, it meant curtailment of their activities. A directive of July 1529 allowed the husbands, but not the wives, to resume their daily affairs in Bozen.[13] In this particular case, the different treatment of husbands and wives may indicate that the women had been more involved than their husbands in the Anabaptist movement. Such constraints on the activities of Anabaptist women were intended to restrict these women, to the private sphere of their own households, probably to prevent their proselytizing.

The case of Elizabeth Wolfram illustrates the way in which a recantation could take place. Elizabeth was a younger woman; she and her brother were the only members of their family who had joined the Anabaptist movement. She gave her oath at the castle of Prösels, which was located near the town of Völs on a hillside called the Schlern. But her recantation took place at mass in the church of Völs. It consisted of her kneeling and holding a burning candle and publicly recanting after the blessing on three consecutive Sundays. Because of her participation in Anabaptism, Elizabeth was to forfeit "life, limb and goods." However, because her brother submitted a request [Bitte] for her pardon, and because her friends and the officials from the county of Völs interceded for her, she was pardoned and her punishment reduced to public penance. The burning candle that Elizabeth Wolfram was required to hold at her recantation symbolized her submission to the established church she had tried to leave by becoming an Anabaptist.[14]

In the three years between 1527 and 1529, one notices a change on the part of the government, in that officials were less and less inclined to allow persons to recant or to give them pardons as time went on. Accordingly, the number of women who fled or who were executed increased. A directive sent from Innsbruck to the local officials at Kufstein, concerning two Anabaptist women who had been arrested in April 1529, illustrates this point. The government stated that:

> Whereas up until now and from day to day, we have found, that virtually all who are pardoned rejoin the Anabaptist and Lutheran sect and then the directives of the royal mandates of our gracious lord are not observed, so in the name of the king, it is our command to you that you treat each of the two women according to the royal mandate and let the due process of law take its course.[15]

The "due process of law" meant the death sentence. By the end of April 1529, when this order was issued, the government of Archduke Ferdinand was no longer willing to give women who joined the Anabaptist movement the benefit of the doubt, as the order to execute these two women shows. Because of the large number of "relapsed" Anabaptists, recantation no longer was granted as readily as it had been earlier. A short time later, Ferdinand I issued a statement himself in regard to the decisions made at the recent Imperial Diet of Speyer. Addressing his officials, he said: "You all know what the effects of Anabaptism have been up until now. Therefore it is of great necessity that throughout our territories we search diligently and watch carefully, especially in the mountain regions."[16]

The actions of those women who endured the shame and embarrassment of recantation as well as the punishments that sometimes, as a dissimulation method, accompanied it, demonstrate the extent to which many women were actively involved and deeply committed to the Anabaptist movement of the Tirol in its early stages. Sixteenth-century women were accustomed to having very little to do with the institutional church and had very little influence in official religious matters.[17] Thus, for Anabaptist women, particularly those living in the predominantly rural environment of Tirol, to undertake a public action such as recantation from the church pulpit, with all their friends and neighbours in attendance, was highly significant. These women had joined the Anabaptist movement in search of an outlet for their religious faith, yet for reasons of their own agreed to go through the humiliation of a public renunciation.

The record makes clear, however, that the efforts of the authorities to humiliate and awe Anabaptist women through elaborate recantations did not always work. Therefore the severity of punishment and the number of executions increased over the three-year period. Many Anabaptist women were tenacious and rejoined the Anabaptists after their recantation or pardon.

For persons who had relapsed, the government was not inclined to show mercy when they were arrested a second time: the death sentence was inevitable for them.

The Recantation of Lamprecht Penntz and His Wife: A Case in Point
Lamprecht Penntz was a baker by trade. He and his wife were both named in a directive from the government of Ferdinand I to the district governor [*Landrichter*] of Hertenberg in June 1528. By this time the case of Lamprecht Penntz had already been discussed once. A report in mid-May had informed the governor of Hertenberg that Hans Velcklehner's sister, a fleeing Anabaptist woman, had been to see her brother in Telfs and had also met with Lamprecht.[18] Perhaps after this meeting the baker went home and persuaded his wife to join the Anabaptists, too. The sources are not clear on this. We do know, however, that by June both Lamprecht and his wife were in prison in the district of Hertenberg because they were Anabaptists.

The directive of June 1528 discussed a request for the pardon of all Anabaptist men and women imprisoned in Hertenberg. This request had been made to the central government by the inhabitants of three villages in the district, namely Telfs, Oberhofen, and Pfaffenhofen, as well as by all the prisoners' relatives. The government's response was quite explicit. The prisoners could not be excused from the mandate that had been sent out at the end of May.[19] Moreover, two married couples, Hans and Barbara Velcklehner and Lamprecht Penntz and his wife, were singled out and mentioned specifically.

One week later, Lamprecht Penntz and his wife had the possibility of leaving prison. It seems that Hans and Barbara Velcklehner had escaped prison, but the Penntz couple had remained behind. Because of this and the fact that a request had already been submitted on their behalf, orders were given for their release, providing they pay for the expense of their upkeep in prison and do penance.[20]

It was not until October of the same year that the government of Innsbruck sent out the exact procedure for the penance and recantation of Lamprecht Penntz and his wife. As was usually the case, it was to take place in the local church on three consecutive Sundays. They were to walk barefoot in procession with the parish priest around the church, kneel in front of the altar during the mass, and then read the outlined recantation [*Widerspruch*] publicly to everyone present. Only in this way could they be reinstated in the church. A translation of Ferdinand's instructions in the Penntz case is presented below.

Since there are no further references in the court records to the baker and his wife, we may assume that they complied and no longer associated with the Anabaptists.[21]

RECANTATION PROCEDURES

October 10, 1528, Innsbruck. –The government of Ferdinand I to Lamprecht Haun, Judge of Hertenberg. –Sends a directive to pardon Lamprecht Penntz and his wife. The wording of the recantation is enclosed.[22]

Faithful one! We have read your report regarding Lanndtprechten [Lamprecht] Penntzen and respond with the order that you ensure that they both be present on three consecutive Sundays in front of the high altar in their parish church before the observance of mass, in order to join the usual procession and walk barefoot in front of the priest around the church. Penntz is to bring up the rear and his wife is to carry a cross in her hands.[23] Following that they are to give a public recantation in the church as recorded on the enclosed papers. Then they are to remain in front of the altar on their knees for the duration of the mass and receive absolution from the priest after that. This is the mandate from his majesty, the 10th day of October, 1528.

1. I confess, that through damnable unchristian teaching and instruction, I fell away from the Christian baptism, and no longer adhered to it.

2. In addition, I confess that I did not believe in [*nichts gehalten*] the holy mass and the most worthy sacrament and did not believe that the bread and the wine truly contained the body and blood of Jesus Christ our Saviour.

3. I confess that I did not place my faith in [*nichts gehalten*] the mediation of Mary, the Mother of God and the saints or in many other articles of the Christian faith. I have erred and did not believe and have gone against the practice of the Christian Church and have instructed others in my erroneous faith.

All this I recant voluntarily and with proper understanding [*mit guetm vorwissen*]. I contradict all of (my previous belief) and praise God the almighty before those assembled in this church, promising to desist from such error, never again to associate with it, and also to believe all that which the united [*gmayn*] Christian church has established and ordained. I also want to attend confession with my priest and partake of the holy sacrament when he deems it appropriate.

Taken from the *Kopialbuch*, "Causi Domini" 1527-1529, Fol.304v., in the *Landesregierungsarchiv für Tirol*.

Notes

1. Richard Kieckhefer, *Repression of Heresy in Medieval Germany* (Pennsylvania: University of Pennsylvania Press, 1979), 53
2. TA, Ost.II, p. 68.
3. Women living in urban areas did not participate in civic ceremonies where the oath of citizenship was taken annually in the town square by heads of households. Lyndal Roper, "'The Common Man', 'The Common Good', 'Common Women': Gender and Meaning in the German Reformation Commune," *Social History* 12 (January, 1987), 19.
4. Emmanuel LeRoy Ladurie, *Mountaillou, The Promised Land of Error*, trans. Barbara Bray (New York: Vintage Books, 1978), 30.
5. TA, Ost.II, p. 80; p. 117; pp. 180-81.
6. TA, Ost.II, p. 99.
7. TA, Ost.II, p. 142.
8. TA, Ost.II, p. 189.
9. TA, Ost.II, p. 221.
10. TA, Ost.II, p. 144; p. 158; 182-83.
11. TA, Ost.II, p. 231; p. 235; p. 249; p. 254; p. 265.
12. TA, Ost.II, p. 283.
13. TA, Ost.II, p. 258.
14. TA, Ost.II, document 279, p. 201. A Protestant woman in sixteenth-century France, known in the records only as an honest widow of Tours, used Scripture in her discussion with priests and monks and told them she was a sinner, but didn't need candles to ask God to pardon her faults. Moreover, they themselves were the ones who walked in darkness. The widow of Tours made it clear to the priests and doctors of theology that they had no power over her soul. See Natalie Zemon Davis, "City Women and Religious Change," *Society and Culture in Early Modern France, Eight Essays* (Stanford, CA: Stanford University Press, 1975), 78, 79.
15. TA, Ost.II, p. 223.
16. TA, Ost.II, p. 229.
17. Leona Stucky Abbott, "Anabaptist Women of the Sixteenth Century" (unpublished masters thesis, Eden Theological Seminary, 1979), 44.
18. TA, Ost.II, document 150, p. 133.
19. TA, Ost.II, document 165, p. 142.
20. TA, Ost.II, document 174, p. 146.
21. TA, Ost.II, document 220, p. 173.
22. This is Mecenseffy's summary. What follows is a translation of the original document as printed in TA, Ost.II, p. 173.
23. The penance procedures sent out in November 1527 to crown administrators [*Pfleger*] by the Archbishop of Salzburg stipulated that penitent men and women were to wear plain clothing onto which a cross was sewn. See TA, Ost.II, document 18B, p. 18.

ELISABETH VON WOLKENSTEIN OF UTTENHEIM

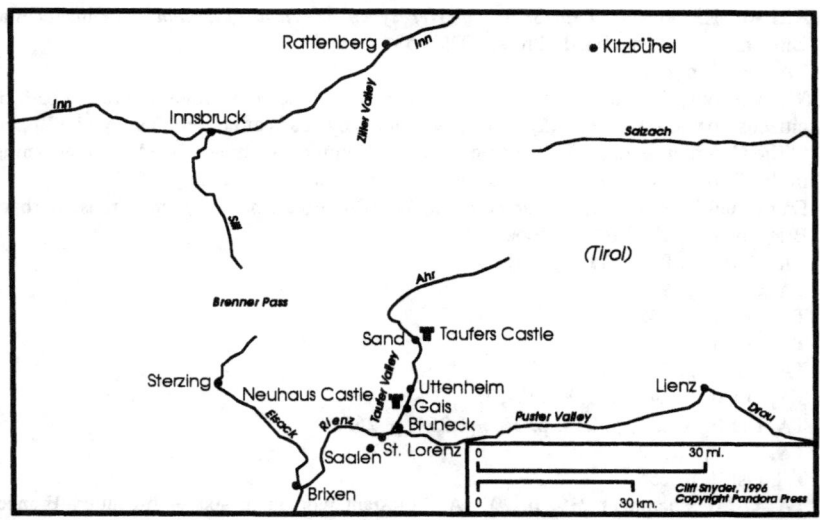

In the centre of the village of Uttenheim, near the church, stands the Plankenstein residence. Since 1563 it has been the property of the lords of Wolkenstein. It stands out from the newer buildings surrounding it because of its noble architectural lines, its beautiful window trellises, and the sundial on the south facade. To this day it is remembered by the local people as the residence of the Wolkensteins; it was here that Elisabeth von Wolkenstein and her family once lived.

Elisabeth von Wolkenstein's family

Elisabeth's family belonged to the nobility, but their origins are not known to us. However, we do know from the sources that she was the wife of Anton von Wolkenstein-Trostburg and is always referred to in the Anabaptist court records as Elisabeth von *Wolkenstein*. The Wolkensteins are a famous Tirolean noble family whose family tree reaches back into the second half of the thirteenth century. Among the ranks of the Lords or Barons [*Freiherr*] of Wolkenstein from the fifteenth century is the renowned poet and singer, Oswald von Wolkenstein (ca. 1376-1445.) The following excerpt from the Wolkenstein family tree provides a glimpse of where Elisabeth fits in the genealogical relationships of the von Wolkenstein family.[1]

Elisabeth von Wolkenstein of Uttenheim

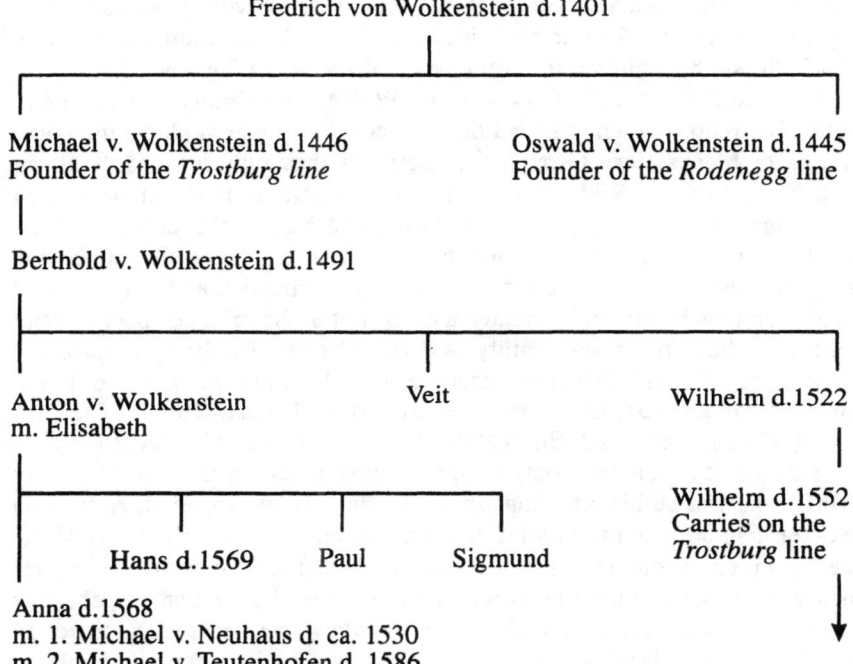

Elisabeth had one daughter, Anna, and three sons, Hans, Paul, and Sigmund from her marriage with Anton von Wolkenstein. Anna was first married to Michael von Neuhaus, a court judge [*Hofrichter*] of the bishopric of Brixen. After the death of her first husband in 1530,[2] she married Michael von Teutenhofen,[3] who was favourably disposed toward the Anabaptists. He gave them free access to his castle, Neuhaus, near Gais.[4]

Elisabeth's husband, Anton von Wolkenstein, crown administrator of the territorial district of Uttenheim, which Emperor Maximilian I (the territorial ruler of Tirol at the time) had leased to Melchior von Meckau, bishop of Brixen (1489-1509) in the year 1500. In 1520 Bishop Christof I von Schrofenstein (1509-21) dismissed Anton von Wolkenstein as crown administrator, for reasons unknown to us, and appointed Hans von Rost to this office.[5] It is possible that Anton Wolkenstein had already become involved with Reformation ideas by this early date, putting him at some distance from the bishop and causing the bishop to withdraw his trust in him.

Elisabeth Joins the Anabaptist Community of Faith

We know that by 1526 at the latest, Anton von Wolkenstein invited the wandering preacher, Wölfl, to his residence at Uttenheim in order to hear his preaching and biblical interpretations. Wölfl was from the Sarn Valley and was working here and there in the Puster Valley. Anton von Wolkenstein had a great interest in Reformation ideas, and he also introduced his wife Elisabeth and his children to the message of the new religious faith.

Wölfl spent eight days with the Wolkenstein family in Uttenheim. In his discussions he emphasized that one could no longer believe the pope, priests, or monks since through their sermons they only led people astray with false teaching.[6] Without a doubt Elisabeth and her husband, as well as their sons Paul and Sigmund, were influenced by Wölfl's critique of the dominant Christian teachings and his reform ideas. However, since the religious views of Wölfl were not yet clearly Anabaptist, and still included many Lutheran beliefs, they created a deep split in the faith perspectives and actions of the Wolkenstein family. As will be seen, Elisabeth accepted the Anabaptist faith and also encouraged her sons Paul and Sigmund to do the same. Her oldest son, Hans, remained true to the Roman Catholic Church.

On the other hand, Elisabeth's husband, Anton von Wolkenstein, was arrested in 1527 on the basis of information given to the authorities by Wölfl, who was at this time imprisoned. During his interrogation, Anton von Wolkenstein admitted to holding Lutheran beliefs, but on July 26, 1527, he recanted them in the presence of the governor and regents in Innsbruck. He also vowed that in future he would not admit either Lutheran preachers or teachers of other sects into his house or allow them to preach there. In addition, he promised to hand over all the Lutheran and sectarian books in his possession, keeping none back, to the Lower Captain [*Unterhauptmann*] of Bruneck, Jörg Botsch, and the parish priest of Taufers, Sigismund Zott (1525-44). Moreover, in future he would no longer purchase, send for, or accept any books that contained dissenting beliefs, but would read only the true Christian Bible.[7]

Jacob Hutter began his mission work in 1529, after the execution of the Anabaptist leaders Michael Kürschner and George Blaurock. When he began preaching, baptizing, and celebrating the Lord's Supper in the Taufer Valley, Elisabeth of Wolkenstein was among the first of his sisters in the faith. She remained with the community of faith led by Jacob Hutter when he made numerous trips through the region and came into the Taufer Valley on missionary journeys from Moravia to Tirol.

Elisabeth also met with Jacob Hutter when he was proselytizing in the Taufer Valley during the months of September 1531 to March 1532. She attended his meetings, baptisms, and celebrations of the Lord's Supper, held either in the Neuhaus Castle at Gais or in the forest behind the castle. Elisabeth herself invited the Anabaptists to her noble residence at Uttenheim. We do not know when Elisabeth herself was baptized, or who baptized her. However, according to the later testimonies of captured Anabaptists, she had not attended mass in the church on the specified holidays or taken part in either confession or the Lord's Supper for several years prior to 1532.

Moreover, she had forbidden her cook at Uttenheim to attend (Catholic) church services. Instead, Elisabeth herself read to her, from the Holy Bible and other books. In this way she proclaimed the teachings and beliefs of the Anabaptists to the small circle of those around her.[8]

In the meantime, Jacob Hutter left Moravia for the fourth time and travelled through Tirol on a missionary journey. Between the fall of 1532 and the summer of 1533, he won many followers, especially in the Puster Valley. At first his work was centred at St. Lorenz in the district of St. Michelsburg. When Hutter's presence became known to the local authorities, the Bishop of Brixen (Georg III of Austria), and the government of Innsbruck stepped up their efforts to locate him. Jacob Hutter retreated to the forests above St. George and the Neuhaus Castle at Gais, and the Taufer Valley. He had free access to the castle of Neuhaus. The administrator [*Hauspfleger*] of the castle was Erhard Zimmermann, a friend and supporter of the Anabaptists. He allowed them to use the castle because the lord of the castle, Michael von Teutenhofen (son-in-law of Elisabeth von Wolkenstein), who resided in Brixen, did not object to having the Anabaptists frequent his castle.[9]

Besides receiving protection at Neuhaus Castle, Jacob Hutter was sheltered by Elisabeth von Wolkenstein at Uttenheim. The Anabaptists met in her house for discussion, Bible readings, and celebrations of the Lord's Supper. Elisabeth also allowed her two younger sons, Paul and Sigmund, to participate in the Anabaptist meetings. The extent to which her husband, Anton, heard Jacob Hutter and participated in celebrations of the Lord's Supper cannot be determined from the sources. In any case, in his interrogation of 1534 Anton insisted that after his recantation of 1527 he had never met with Jacob Hutter.[10]

In addition to Jacob Hutter, the Anabaptist leader Hans Amon Tuchmacher from Bavaria, the treasurer [*Säckelmeister*] of the Anabaptists, Hans Mair Paulle and his wife, as well as Anabaptists baptized by Jacob Hutter, namely, Valthin Luckhner from Sand in Taufers and his wife, Paul Rumer, Veronika Grembs, and Anna Stainer (all three of whom were from St. George), and many others, visited Elisabeth. Her cook gave the authorities information about these visits and the religious discussions. However, it is not known what topics Elisabeth discussed with her brothers and sisters in the faith, since she always sent the cook away when the Anabaptists came into her home.[11]

Elisabeth was not only a believing Anabaptist, but also a benevolent helper to her religious believers; she lived her Anabaptist confession of faith in good works toward her neighbours. She provided food and lodging, as well as protection from persecution, to many of her religious brothers and sisters. When the wife of Hans Mair Paulle was in the last stages of her pregnancy and awaiting the arrival of her child, Elisabeth took her into her home so that she could give birth to her child in a secure environment. Two Anabaptist women, Veronika Grembs from St. George and the wife of Winkler from Saalen near St. Lorenz, took care of the new mother until she and her child were strong enough to leave the residence.[12]

For seven years Elisabeth von Wolkenstein lived quietly and unobserved according to her Anabaptist faith, and practised good works towards fellow believers. In this way she most certainly contributed to making the Anabaptist movement so strong and widespread in the Taufer Valley. For some time the government stood by, powerless to prevent the Anabaptist movement gaining strength. When they finally reacted, the resulting persecution was severe: they proceeded with arrest, torture, and execution. In this connection, the administrator of Neuhaus Castle, Erhard Zimmerman, was arrested on orders from the government of Innsbruck on December 20, 1533, by the proprietor and crown administrator of Taufers, Fridrich Fueger.[13] In his interrogation at the castle of Taufers, the prisoner named those whom he knew to be Anabaptists or who had some connection with the Anabaptists, among them, Elisabeth von Wolkenstein, her husband, Anton, and of course her two sons Paul and Sigmund. Fueger knew that these von Wolkensteins had not taken part either in confession or holy communion for several years.

Elisabeth's Arrest, Interrogation and Anabaptist Testimony
Erhard Zimmerman's declarations aroused the suspicion of the authorities that Elisabeth von Wolkenstein was an Anabaptist. They suspected that her husband, despite his recantation of July 26, 1527, had returned again to his Lutheran beliefs.[14] Erhard Zimmerman was, in fact, released after being questioned, but was secretly observed by spies of the Innsbruck government and the bishop of Brixen.[15]

On January 10, 1534, the Innsbruck officials instructed the crown administrator of Taufers, Fridrich Fueger, to collect information about the conduct of Elisabeth von Wolkenstein and her husband.[16] Accordingly, Fueger made inquiries to the parish priest in Taufers regarding the last time the two had been to confession and taken holy communion. Persons from the Taufer Valley who were already in prison on suspicion of being Anabaptists were also questioned about the von Wolkensteins. As a result the authorities discovered that the sect was very strong and widespread in the Taufer Valley, and that the residence of the Wolkensteins in Uttenheim and the castle of Neuhaus were the principal meeting places of the Anabaptists. As a result the administrator of the Neuhaus Castle, Erhard Zimmerman, was taken captive once more on January 28, 1534, and brought to the castle of Taufers.[17] In his interrogation, conducted under torture, Erhard Zimmerman substantiated to Judge Hans Egle that Elisabeth von Wolkenstein, her husband Anton, and their sons Paul and Sigmund, had not attended any

(Catholic) church services for several years and had not gone to confession or taken holy communion. He knew that Elisabeth frequently attended Anabaptist meetings and that Anabaptists received food, lodging, and protection in her home at Uttenheim.[18]

The government of Innsbruck now had enough indicators of the heretical behaviour of the Wolkenstein family. Thus, on January 28, 1534, they ordered the arrest of Elisabeth von Wolkenstein, her sons Paul and Sigmund, her husband Anton, and the family's cook. The arrest was to be carried out under the leadership of the vice marshal [*Untermarschall*] of Innsbruck, Erasmus Offenhauser.[19]

The vice marshal made his way with two single team wagons to Fridrich Fueger in Taufers who made several soldiers available to him. Following these secret preparations, Offenhauser and his men surprised Elisabeth von Wolkenstein, her son Paul, her husband Anton, and their cook in their noble residence at Uttenheim and took them captive. Elisabeth and her cook were brought to the Taufers castle. Her husband Anton and her son Paul were brought by Erasmus Offenhauser to Innsbruck, where the government imprisoned them in the tower called the *Kreuterturm*.[20] Anton later testified to being Lutheran, which he never entirely recanted.[21] Paul, only nineteen or twenty years of age, had in fact not been rebaptized, but testified that he adhered to the Anabaptist faith; he recanted and forswore, however, after several interrogations and further instruction.[22] His brother Sigmund, only seventeen years old, was still free at this time, but participated in Anabaptist meetings and celebrations of the Lord's Supper. He had been rebaptized, was arrested in May 1534, and remained imprisoned in Brixen until March 1536. Although he recanted Anabaptism during his interrogation before the judges, he resisted the demand to recant publicly. In order to be released from prison, he declared himself ready in 1536 to join the imperial army and to go to war; this was accepted, but he never returned from the wars.[23]

Elisabeth von Wolkenstein and her cook were interrogated at the beginning of February 1534 at the castle at Taufers. Torture may have been used, or perhaps only threatened, in the case of the cook, but no torture was used in Elisabeth's case, in respect of her noble birth.[24] Hans Egle, the judge of Taufers, presented the following questions, as formulated by the government, to the female prisoners:[25]

- Why have you not gone to confession and holy communion for the past several years?
- Why have you not gone to church like other good Christians?
- Have you been rebaptized? If so, by whom and when were you rebaptized? Who witnessed the rebaptism?
- Have your husband Anton and your son Paul also been rebaptized?
- What are your views concerning the seven sacraments: confirmation, the sacrament of the altar, the sacrament of penance, the anointing of the

sick, the ordination of priests, the sacrament of marriage, and infant baptism?
  - Do you know the names of Anabaptists and where are they staying?
  - Did you participate in Anabaptist meetings and celebrations of the Lord's Supper? Where did these take place?
  - Who brought you to the Anabaptist faith? Who persuaded you to join the sect?
  - Do you believe in the virginity of Mary? Do you believe that God the Father hears the prayers of believers through the intercession of Mary and the saints?
  -Do you choose to stay in Anabaptism or are you ready to leave the sect and repent?

Elisabeth's individual answers to these interrogation questions were duly recorded and on February 8, 1534, they were sent to Innsbruck; unfortunately, to date this report has not been found in the archives. According to a communication of the government of Innsbruck to the crown administrator of Taufers, Fridrich Fueger, on February 15, 1534, Elisabeth admitted that she had joined the Anabaptists and had been rebaptized. In addition, while questioning her the judge ascertained that Elisabeth's faith included some very grave errors. Moreover, she was determined not to change her mind and held firmly to her false convictions.[26]

After Elisabeth von Wolkenstein had testified in the Taufers Castle to being an Anabaptist, and her husband had testified in Innsbruck to being a Lutheran, the guilt of the married couple was clearly evident. As members of heretical movements, they no longer had any legal rights to their residence or property. On the basis of the imperial mandates, their stationary and movable goods were inventoried and confiscated. Four farmers in Uttenheim, Christoff Mairhofer, Hans Strigel, Thomas am Bach and Hans Kaltschmid, were appointed to manage them. Very soon, however, the government of Innsbruck recognized that farmers could not simply be given custody of property of the nobility. On February 14 they assigned the management of all the possessions to Hans von Wolkenstein, the eldest son, who had remained true to the Roman Catholic church.[27]

At the request of the Innsbruck government, on February 22 the bishop of Brixen sent two learned priests (Egidius Harrischer, parish priest from Brixen, and Wolfgang Steinmetz, parish priest from St Lorenz) to the Taufers Castle in order to instruct Elisabeth in the true Christian faith. Ulrich Geltinger, the crown administrator of Schöneck, was to represent the secular authority in the questioning and teaching process.[28]

The parish priest from Brixen, Egidius Harrischer, was not able to question Elisabeth. He died on March 2, 1534, immediately after his arrival in Taufers. So, in the presence of the crown administrator of Schöneck, Wolfgang Steinmetz, the parish priest of St. Lorenz, conducted the interrogation of the Lady, instructing her in the true Christian faith so that she would renounce her heresy. During this discussion, Elisabeth conceded many points of Anabaptist faith. However, she remained firm in her conviction that *confession* and *the sacrament of the altar*, as well as *infant baptism* were to be rejected. In these matters she wanted to keep the teachings of her Anabaptist brothers and sisters. However, she requested the judicial authorities to give her one year's time to think about these doctrinal issues before making a final decision. During this time she wanted to ask God for grace, to enlighten her regarding the genuine religious truth, and to lead her to the right faith.[29]

In the meantime, on March 22, 1534, her oldest son Hans and her son-in-law Michael von Teutenhofen made a request of the authorities to be allowed to speak with Elisabeth in prison, in order to convince her of her error. The government welcomed this effort by her close relatives and allowed her son and son-in-law to converse with Elisabeth in prison in the presence of the crown administrator of Taufers, Fridrich Fueger, the local judge, Hans Egle, and sworn witnesses, in addition to the beneficiary and cathedral priest in Brixen, Wolfgang Wiser, and the parish priest of Taufers, Sigismund Zott.[30]

We do not know what resulted from this meeting. It seems, however, that at first Elisabeth was not ready to give a full recantation. The government of Innsbruck found it necessary to send a report to King Ferdinand I concerning the capture and interrogation of Elisabeth von Wolkenstein and, at the same time, that of her husband, Anton, and son Paul. They sought direction on how to proceed against the prisoners.[31]

In his answer of April 15, 1534, the king ordered that Elisabeth be given a *third* hearing with "serious" interrogation. In other cases, "serious" questioning meant that torture was to be used during the interrogation. We do not know whether Elisabeth was tortured or only threatened with torture. Disturbed as he was by the events occurring in Münster in northern Germany, the king wanted detailed information from Elisabeth about her own activities as well as the goals and plans of the Anabaptist movement.

King Ferdinand I also was willing to have her son Hans and son-in-law, Michael von Teutenhofen, meet a second time for discussion with Elisabeth in prison, in case the judicial process alone did not bring the desired results. Either the crown administrator or the judge of Taufers, as well as the sworn witnesses, were also to be present.

The court met in mid-April 1534. However, this time the government of Innsbruck instructed that another official, Vice Marshal Erasmus Offenhauser, be in charge. The crown administrator and proprietor of the territory of Taufers, Fridrich Fueger, the judge of the territorial district of Taufers, Hans Egle, and the resident court secretary, Martin Stangl, also were present. The court officials presented the defendant with the following questions, which the government of Innsbruck had formulated previously:

- When were you baptized, who baptized you, and where is that person now?

- For what reason did you become involved with the devious sect of Anabaptism?

- What were you told by the leader who baptized you; who was baptized with you; what are the intentions and plans of the Anabaptists?

- In which places have you attended the meetings and celebrations of Lord's Supper of the Anabaptists? Did you make space available to them in your house for their meetings and give them shelter?

-Do you know the names of others who are in the movement?[32]

Following the interrogation, Erasmus Offenhauser and Fridrich Fueger had to report to the government of Innsbruck that neither the judicial process nor the discussion with close relatives, her son Hans and her son-in-law, Michael von Teutenhofen, had convinced Elisabeth von Wolkenstein of her guilt or persuaded her to recant fully. Thereupon, the government took a different approach to the problem and requested the bishop of Brixen to send a priest well-versed in theology to Elisabeth at the Taufers Castle, in order to instruct her in the true Christian faith and to bring her to a knowledge of her error.[33]

Elisabeth Gives a Christian Confession, Swears an Oath and Delivers a Public Recantation

As instructed by the government of Innsbruck, the court met on May 8, 1534, for the *fourth time.* Among those in attendance were two very learned theologians and members of the clergy: Albert Kraus, the suffragan bishop and priest of Brixen, and Wolfgang Wiser, appointed and beneficed preacher in the cathedral of Brixen. Also attending, as was usual, were Fridrich Fueger, Hans Egle, and Martin Stangl, district court secretary of Taufers. At this important hearing Elisabeth von Wolkenstein–perhaps under threat of torture–finally testified on all the points of which she was accused in deviating from official Christian teaching, and declared that she adhered to the true Christian faith. She said:

- I acknowledge that infant baptism is justified and good.

- I acknowledge that confirmation is a sacrament, as established by the Christian Church.

- I acknowledge the sacrament of penance and according to Christian order, I will attend confession as do other Christian people.

- I also acknowledge the sacrament of anointing the sick in the same manner as my ancestors did, and declare myself ready to receive it in the same way, as all believing Christian people want to receive it, when I am sick with a fatal disease.

- I believe, that in the Holy Mass, by the consecration of the priest, bread and wine are transformed into the body and blood of Christ, and that Christ is fully present in the sacrament of the altar in the form of body and blood. I will receive the sacrament of the altar at the prescribed times like

other believing Christians and no longer, as I did until now, as the symbol of body and blood of Jesus Christ in both kinds (bread and wine).
- I acknowledge marriage as a sacrament.
- I acknowledge ordination to the priesthood as a sacrament.
- I will attend church on the prescribed Holy Days, unless hindered by sickness or the weakness of old age, and there listen to the sermon and celebrate the Holy Mass.
- I believe in the virginity of Mary and acknowledge Mary and the saints as intercessors for the Christian. I believe that Mary and the saints intercede with God when Christians request this of them in prayer.
- I believe that the holy Christian Church did not err by instituting the sacraments and by proclaiming these doctrines.[34]

Elisabeth's words represented her full confession of the traditional Christian faith. The judicial process now required that she swear an oath and afterwards present a public recantation in her parish church. With her oath, Elisabeth was obliged to accept all the conditions required by the government in the mandate of May 12, 1534. She knew what awaited her if she broke her oath and rejoined the sect. The government made it very clear to her that if that were to happen she would be treated like any other person; she would not receive mercy from the government, but would be punished with death as laid down in the imperial mandates.[35] In order to regain her freedom, Elisabeth yielded to pressure from the authorities and repeated the following words to the judges, as they were outlined for her:[36]

- I will not take revenge on anyone, neither the government nor the others who put me in prison.
- I am prepared to recant publicly from the pulpit in front of the people in my parish church at Taufers, as is appropriate, on three successive Sundays during the Holy Mass.
- I am willing to accept and carry out the penance imposed on me by my parish priest.
- On three Sundays in succession I will follow the priest in the procession in the church holding a burning candle and, after the procession stand, for as long as the mass continues, in the anteroom (Atrium or Paradise) of the church holding the burning candle and doing penance.
- I promise that following the recantation and the oath I will have nothing more to do with the [Anabaptist] sect for the rest of my life.
- I promise that for the next year I will not leave the district of Uttenheim, to which I belong.
- I commit myself not to leave the princely territory of Tirol for the rest of my life.
- I am prepared to pay the costs for my imprisonment and court proceedings.

With these words Elisabeth swore the oath before the judges. Conscious of her noble status–perhaps also out of a feeling of inner resistance against having been forced to separate herself from her deeply felt Anabaptist convictions, which she had lived so intensely–she sought to be spared public humiliation and requested the government of Innsbruck to release her from recanting publicly in front of the people in the church. This is the only explanation for the explicit government orders sent to Fridrich Fueger on June 3, 1534, that everyone who recanted from the sect of Anabaptism had to render a public recantation. Therefore, even Elisabeth von Wolkenstein, despite her noble status, could not be excused from public recantation.[37]

But Elisabeth did not yet give up her struggle to avoid a public recantation. She claimed that she could not read. But the government knew from the testimonies of other captured Anabaptist prisoners that many times Elisabeth had taught others in small Anabaptist circles and had read from the Bible and other books. Thus the authorities were not disconcerted by her excuse. They outwitted the lady by instructing her to repeat what the priest would recite to her in the pulpit of the parish church of Taufers, in case she could not read herself.[38]

For the next several months her name disappears from the records. On October 9, 1534, there is a note that Elisabeth von Wolkenstein recanted in the parish church of Taufers.[39] She spoke the following words:

> I, Elisabeth, wife of Anton von Wolkenstein, confess that I erred when I became a member of the devious and seductive sect of the Anabaptists. Because I regret this from the bottom of my heart, I recant and forswear publicly, give my assent, and commit myself to live from this moment onward for my whole life, according to the principles of the true Christian church and in no way to deviate from it.[40]

Following that confession Elisabeth von Wolkenstein was pardoned. The government of Innsbruck allowed her to relocate to Brixen to live with her daughter, Anna, and son-in-law, Michael von Teutenhofen. Her husband, Anton, was already there. On June 6, 1534, Michael von Teutenhofen had received permission from the government for his father-in-law to settle in Brixen. By giving this permission, the government was making an exception.[41] Of course Elisabeth, like other repentant Anabaptists, had to swear that she would not depart for one year following her pardon from the territorial district in which she lived. For the government, Elisabeth's wish to give up her residence in Uttenheim was surely convenient, since in that way they could avoid the continuation of her support to Anabaptists and her receiving them into her home.

The events recounted above mark an important period in the life of a woman who sacrificed herself for the renewal of the Christian faith, convinced that only thus could she lead fellow men and women, and herself, into the Kingdom of God. Why she did not endure the battle to its obvious conclusion, that of a martyr's death, as did her teachers Wölfl from the Sarn Valley and Jacob Hutter, remains closed to us. The authorities of the state and the public representatives of the church in fact silenced Elisabeth of Wolkenstein with their cunning and their threats. Despite that, they could not erase the evidence of her work. The influence she radiated surely encouraged many others in the Taufer Valley to risk taking the path to renewal.

Notes

1 As with Helena von Freyberg, the prefix "von" denotes her noble status. The genealogical background of Elisabeth von Wolkenstein was determined from the Anabaptist court records [*Täuferakten*]. No mention of Elisabeth von Wolkenstein is made in the genealogy of Stephan von Mayrhofen, "Genealogien, Stammbäume mit Urkunden des Tiroler Adels," 7 Bde., Handschrift im Museum Ferdinandeum. In his Genealogien II, leb. No. 48 [*Stammtafel*], Mayrhofen gives 1522 as the year of Anton von Wolkenstein's death. He also names Margareth Egger von Kestlan as his wife. Since the Anabaptist court records indicate that Anton of Wolkenstein was still living in 1534 and that Elisabeth (whose noble origins are not named) was his wife, Mayrhofen's genealogical tables are in error on this point.

2 The exact year of Michael von Neuhaus's death cannot be determined. Various indicators in the sources point to 1530 as the likely date. Hofarchiv Brixen, Hofregistratur (hereafter HR) 1527-1530, Bd.11, Blatt (hereafter Bl.) 455v.-457v.; HR 1530-1533, Bd.12, pp. 36, 242, Bl.533, 551r.; Hofakt (HA) Fasz. 15904, 15848. I am grateful for the assistance I received at the Tiroler Landesarchiv, Innsbruck, the Museum Ferdinandeum, Innsbruck, the Hofarchiv, Brixen, and the Landesarchiv, Bozen.

3 Tiroler Landesarchiv (hereafter TLA), Innsbruck, Kopialbuch, *Causa Domini* (hereafter C.D.) 1532-1536, Bl.166r.-167r; published in TA, Ost.III, document 289, p. 243.

4 Hofarchiv Brixen, HA Fasz. 6428, published in TA, Ost.III, document 251, BI, pp. 215ff.

5 In Tirol the *Pfleger*, the chief administrator for the Crown, and held political and judicial authority at the local level. Erika Prast, "Die vier Pustertaler Herrschaften–St.Michelsburg, Schöneck, Uttenheim und Heunfels unter Brixener Pfandherrschaft 1500-1700," (Dissertation, Innsbruck, 1975), 320-22.

6 Hofarchiv Brixen, Hofratsprotokoll (hereafter HP), 1515-1530, Bd.1 pp. 759-66, published in Matthias Schmelzer, "Jakob Huters Wirken im Lichte von Bekenntnissen gefangener Täufer" in *Der Schlern, Monatszeitschrift für Südtiroler Landeskunde* 63, 11 (Nov. 1989): 615-18.

7 TLA Innsbruck, C.D. 1527-1529, Bl.35v.-36r., published in TA, Ost.II, document 6, pp. 4ff.

8 Hofarchiv Brixen, HA Fasz. 6428; published in part and summarized in TA, Ost.III, document 251 A-D, pp. 215ff.

9 Hofarchiv Brixen, HA Fasz. 6428; published in TA, Ost.III, document 251 A, BI, pp. 215f.

10 TLA Innsbruck, C.D. 1532-1536, Bl.179v.; summarized in TA, Ost.III, document 294, p. 248.

11 Hofarchiv Brixen, HA Fasz. 6428; published in TA, Ost.III, document 251, BII, pp. 219ff.

12 Ibid.

13 Hofarchiv Brixen, HA Fasz. 6427; summarized in TA, Ost.III, document 222, p. 195.
14 TLA Innsbruck, C.D. 1532-1536, Bl.142r.; summarized in TA, Ost.III, document 229B, p. 198.
15 TLA Innsbruck, C.D. 1532-1536, Bl.141v.-142r.; summarized in TA, Ost.III, document 229A, p. 197.
16 TLA Innsbruck, C.D. 1532-1536, Bl.142r.; summarized in TA, Ost.III, document 229B, p. 198.
17 TLA Innsbruck, C.D. 1532-1536, Bl.146r.; published in TA, Ost.III, document 238A, pp. 203ff.
18 Hofarchiv Brixen, HA Fasz. 6428; published in TA, Ost.III, document 251A, BI, pp. 215ff.
19 TLA Innsbruck, C.D. 1532-1536, Bl.147v.-148r.; published in TA, Ost.III, document 238C, p. 205.
20 TLA Innsbruck, C.D. 1532-1536, Bl.147v.-148r.; published in TA, Ost.III, document 238C, D, pp. 205ff.; TLA Innsbruck, "An der königlichen Majestät" 1532-1535, Bl.291v.-292r.; summarized in TA, Ost.III, document 268, p. 231.
21 Hofarchiv Brixen, HA Fasz. 6428; summarized in TA, Ost.III, document 294, p. 248.
22 Hofarchiv Brixen, HA Fasz. 6428; published in TA, Ost.III, document 332A, B pp. 267ff., and document 325 p. 264.
23 TLA Innsbruck, Hofregistratur, Abt.XIII., Pos.1, Fasz. 33; summarized in TA, Ost.III, document 395, pp. 320ff.
24 TLA Innsbruck, C.D. 1532-1536, Bl.147v.-148r.; published in TA, Ost.III, document 238C, p. 205.
25 TLA Innsbruck, C.D. 1532-1536, Bl.147v.-148r.; published in TA, Ost.III, document 238D, pp. 205ff.
26 TLA Innsbruck, C.D. 1532-1536, Bl.150v.-151v.; summarized in TA, Ost.III, document 251C, D, p. 220.
27 TLA Innsbruck, C.D. 1532-1536, Bl.149v.; summarized in TA, Ost.III, document 246, p. 213.
28 Hofarchiv Brixen, HR 1533-1534, Bd.13, 765-766; summarized in TA, Ost.III, document 253, p. 221.
29 Hofarchiv Brixen, HR 1533-1534, Bd.13, 783-785; summarized in TA, Ost.III, document 261, p. 224.
30 TLA Innsbruck, C.D. 1532-1536, Bl.159v.; summarized in TA, Ost.III, document 279, p. 238.
31 TLA Innsbruck, "An der königlichen Majestät" 1532-1535, Bl.291v.-292r.; summarized in TA, Ost.III, document 268, p. 231.
32 TLA Innsbruck, C.D. 1532-1536, Bl.166r.-167r.; summarized in TA, Ost.III, document 289A, B and the postscript, p. 243.
33 TLA Innsbruck, C.D. 1532-1536, Bl.180r.-180v.; summarized in TA, Ost.III, document 296, p. 249.
34 Hofarchiv Brixen, HA Fasz. 6428; summarized in TA, Ost.III, document 300, pp. 250ff.
35 TLA Innsbruck, C.D. 1532-1536, Bl.183r.; summarized in TA, Ost.III, document 305, p. 255.
36 TLA Innsbruck, C.D. 1532-1536, Bl.185r.v.; briefly summarized in TA, Ost.III, document 311, p. 258. The government noted also that Elisabeth had been giving support to Anabaptist leaders in her home. This would end if she went to live with her daughter and son-in-law. However, first she would have to recant publicly.
37 Ibid.
38 TLA Innsbruck, C.D. 1532-1536, Bl.183r., 185r.v.; summarized in TA, Ost.III, document 305, p. 255, and document 311, p. 258.

39 TLA Innsbruck, C.D. 1532-1536, Bl.206v.; the original document is in the Hofarchiv Brixen, HA Fasz. 6428; briefly summarized in TA, Ost.III, document 324, p. 264. In this summary the government of Innsbruck responded negatively to Sigmund Wolkenstein's request to forgo a public recantation. They said Helena von Freyberg was going to do this and his mother Elisabeth already had. Elisabeth was not as fortunate as Helena von Freyberg, who was finally allowed to deliver her recantation in private to an official at Innsbruck.
40 TLA Innsbruck, C.D. 1532-1536, Bl.183r.; published in TA, Ost.III, document 305, p. 255.
41 Hofarchiv Brixen, HA Fasz. 6428; summarized in TA, Ost.III, document 294, p. 248.

KATHARINA PURST HUTTER OF STERZING

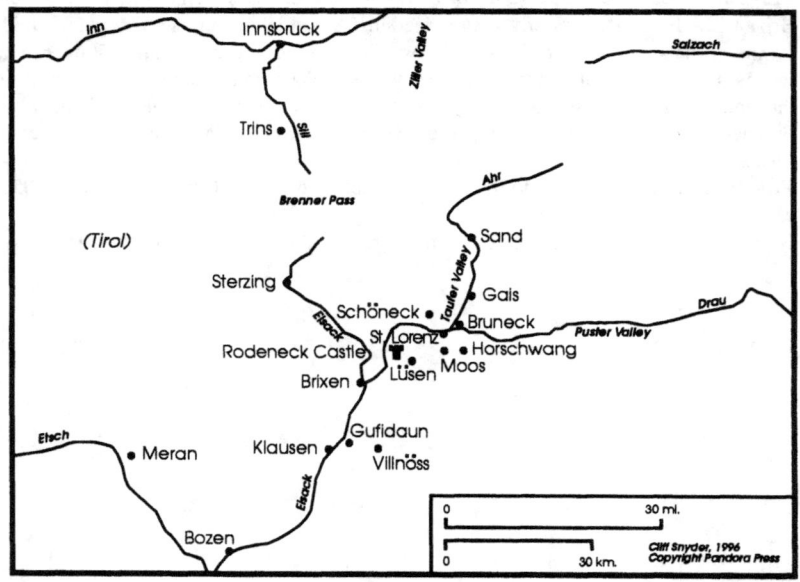

The best-known Anabaptist leader of the Tirol was Jacob Hutter. In 1529 he succeeded George Blaurock, who was executed in Gufidaun in that year. Our interest here, however, is not in Jacob, but in his wife Katharina, about whom little has been written to date. Her life was characterized by an enthusiasm for the true Gospel, and like many other Anabaptists, she suffered a martyr's death. Katharina Hutter's life also reveals the conditions under which Anabaptists had to live during the early years of the movement in the Tirol, the problems and restrictions they faced, and the fear of being discovered and imprisoned that pervaded their days.

The house where Katharina was born was most likely located near Sterzing, in South Tirol. We know little about her parents except that her family name was Purst.[1] The sources relate that in 1532 Katharina worked as a maid in the household of Paul Gall and his wife, Justina, whose birthname was Rumlerin. It was in Trins, close to Sterzing, that Katharina became acquainted with the Anabaptists. Many Anabaptist brothers and sisters found refuge, lodging, and shelter in the Gall household. These people, who zealously accepted the teachings concerning genuine discipleship, and who tried to live according to these teachings, must have impressed the young maid. She participated in the nocturnal meetings at which often as many as thirty people were in attendance. Many of the Anabaptists hid in the forests. Hillside huts on the surrounding slopes provided them shelter. Katharina and Justina Gall, individually or together, often brought food to the people in the forests, always in the fear of being caught and made to testify regarding their actions and convictions.[2]

Jacob Hutter, who was chosen as a servant of the Gospel by the Anabaptist conventicles of the Puster Valley in the Tirol, also came to visit the home of the Galls. Probably there was particular attention paid to him since he was the principal leader of the group. Katharina and Jacob were approximately twenty to thirty years old when they met. In the court proceedings that took place later, Katharina stated (in the words of the court scribe) that she had been "persuaded and convinced to join the Anabaptist sect" in the Gall household. It was there, following a confession of her faith, that she was baptized by Jacob Hutter, her future husband.[3]

In an effort to eradicate the movement in the Tirol, the Bishop of Brixen delegated individuals to hunt down Anabaptists. Unfortunately, these "Anabaptist hunters" had information about the secret meetings being held, and this led to misfortune for the Gall couple and Katharina. It appears that Katharina was arrested along with all the other members of the Gall household in 1533. At first they were imprisoned in Sterzing, but later the prisoners, Katharina included, were transferred to the tower of the castle at Rodeneck.[4] After lengthy interrogation and detailed questioning concerning the members, principal leaders, and local leaders of the Anabaptists, the places where they met, and above all, concerning their beliefs, Katharina and the Gall couple recanted. By this time Jacob Hutter had left the Tirol on his fourth trip to Moravia. We do not know if the desire to see him again played a role in Katharina's recantation, but she undertook the humbling procedure of recanting on three consecutive Sundays in the local church. Publicly, in front of all those in attendance, she disavowed her Anabaptist faith and performed the penance required of her by the parish priest. Katharina and the Gall couple were pardoned and set free on the basis that they had seen the error of their ways. The subsequent flight of Justina Gall and Katharina Purst to Moravia demonstrates that their recantation was the result of coercion, and lacked inner conviction. In Moravia they could be united with their brothers and sisters in the faith; they could find refuge in the Anabaptist community and live out their faith undisturbed. However, Paul Gall did not succeed in making this journey, for he was captured and put on trial for breaking his oath. On June 25, 1533, he was executed in Rodeneck.[5]

There was a prolonged and interesting epilogue concerning the Gall family, as discussions continued concerning inheritance. The handsome sum of 2,500 gulden as well as a house at the gate in Brixen rightfully belonged to Justina Gall and her children. But since Justina had again "fallen into Anabaptism," she and her children were denied their inheritance. The bishop of Brixen confiscated all the assets, but Paul Gall's brother registered a complaint against this action and succeeded in obtaining the inheritance of the Anabaptist family for himself.[6]

It is not certain whether Katharina spent the next two years in

Moravia, but it is likely that she did. We hear about her again in 1535. In that year she married Jacob Hutter at the Pentecost celebration in a Moravian Anabaptist community. The young couple were married by one of the leaders of that community Hans Tuchmacher (Amon), who came from the Puster Valley originally.

In the meantime, persecution broke out also in Moravia, the "promised land" of the Anabaptists. The dissolution of the Anabaptist kingdom in Münster, with all its negative consequences for Anabaptists everywhere, also affected the communities in Moravia. The local Lord, Kuno of Kaunitz, under pressure from Archduke Ferdinand, withdrew his protection of the Anabaptists, and the communities began to scatter. The *Hutterian Chronicle* relates: "So therefore Jacob Hutter took his bundle on his back. His assistants did the same, and the brothers and sisters and all their children went in pairs, following their shepherd Jacob."[7] It was a forced expulsion. Families had to leave their homes and survive in open fields; all had to fend for themselves. Jacob Hutter wrote several letters to the local lord and lamented the situation: "We are living in the wilderness on the barren pasture, under the clear sky. We don't know where we should go. Our houses and properties are still unsold." Jacob Hutter himself was in danger of being captured. In order to protect him, the Anabaptists decided that he and his wife should return to the Tirol. Thus it was that Jacob and Katharina made their way back to their homeland.[8]

It may have been several weeks before they neared the Puster Valley, where Jacob Hutter had been born in the hamlet of Moos, near Bruneck.[9] They journeyed over the mountains to Sand in Taufers, accompanied by a schoolmaster named Hieronymus who had been baptized by Hutter. There they knew of like-minded people and hoped to find food and lodging. By July 25, 1535, St. Jacob's Day, Hutter was again conducting baptisms in the Puster Valley. But it soon became evident that Jacob Hutter could no longer travel unrecognized through this country. Persons had been assigned by the government specifically to be on the lookout for him. This became evident after a meeting of Anabaptists in Taufers. The arrest of one of the brothers after the worship service was a serious warning for Hutter. Thus, the three wanderers did not remain in Taufers, but rather travelled to Elln, near St. Lorenz and Bruneck, in the hope of finding protection and lodging. There they asked a brother in the faith, Waldner, to take them in. However, he refused them entry. He had recently "left the Anabaptist teaching" and wanted nothing more to do with the movement. Katharina reacted with sharp words. She said: "Waldner is a destructive person and a useless Christian,"[10] meaning that he had forfeited his life as a Christian and as a respectable human being. The Hutters then turned towards Hörschwang where they were welcomed by a brother in the faith by the name of Ober. Disregarding the danger, Hutter preached in Hörschwang and its environs.

He baptized Ober and his entire household in the same manner as is recorded in the book of Acts concerning Lydia (Acts 16). The Ober household included his wife, their daughter Dorothea, two male servants, and a couple who worked there, Wolf and Els.

From Hörschwang the Hutters went to Lüsen. Here, near the top of the mountain, there existed at that time a small Anabaptist congregation. The Hutters and Hieronymus stayed with a woman named Prader who, along with her son Melchior, had joined the Anabaptists despite the fact that her husband was totally against the sect. At one point there was a secret Anabaptist meeting in the forest near Lüsen, following which the group returned to Hörschwang. As a result of the activities of Hutter, the people of that region and the government authorities were again made aware of the Anabaptists. The small group stood in danger and could no longer remain in Hörschwang. But where were they to go? All over the Tirol there were "hunters" appointed to seek them out. Finally they prepared to leave during the night for Klausen on the Eisack River, accompanied by a young woman named Anna Stainer. They crossed the bridge near a guardhouse on the hillside in the dark of night in order to reach Klausen. Their path led them through the whole village and across the Eisack River for a second time in order to reach the house of Stainer, the sexton. Jacob Hutter did not want to remain there, and preferred to go on, but he did not know where to turn. He suggested going to Villnöss, a place he had known in earlier times and where he had friends. He said he wanted to go to Jörg Müller. But Katharina had heard no good reports about this man. She said: "He has fallen away and therefore is a dangerous person"; however, his wife and a woman surnamed Niclauer were her dear sisters in the faith, although Niclauer himself was not to be trusted. It was difficult to distinguish between friend and foe. Clearly, Katharina had learned to trust several women and thought she could depend on them. Jacob Hutter said they would go "wherever God would lead them."[11]

The journey to Klausen was the last one the Hutters took together. They were arrested on November 30, 1535, on St. Andrew's Day, in the Stainer house. The sexton's wife, Anna, and a niece of the same name, were captured at the same time. In her testimony the sexton's wife stated:

> Around midnight there was a knock at the door. I did not want to open it since shortly before that some drunk people had been making a ruckus in the street. But the knock was repeated and a woman asked for entrance. When I unlocked the door, two women and a man stood outside and pleaded with me to let them warm themselves by the fire. Only when they came into the light did I notice that they were Anabaptists (Anabaptists did not carry weapons). Out of mercy I allowed them to warm themselves by the

fire but made it clear that they were to be on their way again shortly. I did not give them anything to eat or drink. When the three left the house they fell into the hands of the authorities from Klausen who arrested them.[12]

All the prisoners were held captive in the castle of Branzoll above Klausen.[13] Jacob Hutter, as "instigator and leader" of the Anabaptist communities, was later brought to Innsbruck. He endured terrible tortures and finally was burned at the stake in early February 1536.[14] At first Katharina was imprisoned at Branzoll, along with the two women from the Stainer household. Then all three women were taken to the castle at Gufidaun, and their cases were given over to the judge there. Since the authorities believed the older Anna Stainer when she said that she was not an Anabaptist, she was released following a public recantation and payment for the costs of her imprisonment.[15] Katharina and the younger Anna Stainer underwent many interrogations. Probably under threat of punishment or torture, Katharina gave the names of leaders and members of the movement, emphasizing that the key leaders were all in Moravia. For every Anabaptist interrogation there was a standard list of questions regarding their faith. Included were questions asking when the prisoners had last been to confession and taken the sacraments, what they believed about Mary the Mother of God, and their views on infant baptism. This time Katharina made no secret of her convictions. She gave no consideration to the possibility of recanting in order to be pardoned. She stated that she "had only contempt for both the mass and the sacrament which monks or priests elevated above their heads. Also, the church building was nothing but a pile of stones and meant nothing to her." This was her clear testimony. She referred to infant baptism as "a bath in dirty water" [*Sudelwäsche*]; the sacrament was an "abomination and stench before God."[16] Her drastic expressions show, on the one hand, how Anabaptists customarily described the established church, but on the other hand, these expressions were a self-confident deprecation of the established church, as Katharina had experienced it in the bishopric of Brixen. When asked about her husband, who obviously had been accused of wanting to get rich, she said: "What my husband and brother in the faith receives as payment, he shares with the poor widows, young children and other needy brothers and sisters."[17] The interrogators did not understand that the money had been given to Hutter for the Anabaptist congregations and that he administered their common treasury.

Although Katharina Hutter had recanted once already in 1533, she continued attending meetings and had even travelled to the "promised land" of Moravia to become part of the Anabaptist movement again; she was what the government called a *relapsi*.[18] This fact alone would have been enough for the judges to issue a death sentence. Why she got another chance is difficult to understand. In any case, orders were given to the religious authorities to try to persuade her to recant. A "respected and knowledgeable" priest from Brixen was to be sent to her and Anna Stainer for this purpose.[19] Also, "knowledgeable" women were to speak with Katharina and try to make her see the error of her ways. Katharina remained steadfast; she would not deny her faith again. Because her stubbornness made such an impression on the judges, she was not sent to work in the bishop's residence in Brixen[20] for fear that she would lead others astray into the Anabaptist "sect." However, there obviously were people interested in her welfare. Possibly she had advocates not only among the Anabaptists, but also among the officials of the bishop. In fact, she succeeded in escaping from her imprisonment in the castle of Gufidaun. This surely could not have happened without outside help. One source reports that Katharina was pregnant at the time.[21] The earliest the child could have been born would have been February or March of 1536. But we have no information about a birth taking place. In spite of this, it is possible that pregnancy was the reason for Katharina's leaving prison. In any case, the sources are silent about the end of her imprisonment. They simply state: "Katharina Hutter escaped from the prison at Gufidaun shortly after April 28, 1536."[22] Where she went following her imprisonment is not known. For just under two years she was able to live unhindered, a freedom limited by the fear of being discovered. In 1538 Katharina Hutter was arrested again in the village of Schöneck near Bruneck, and since she was one who had rejoined the Anabaptist movement or "back slid" a second time, she was executed immediately.[23]

Katharina Hutter was granted only a short life. At the time of her death she was probably just over thirty years old. The desperate times did not allow her to establish a permanent household, to have children, or to see them grow up. The few short months of her marriage were marked by deprivation, unsettled circumstances, and anxiety. She and her husband never did have a secure place to live. They found themselves fleeing constantly, especially when the Anabaptists in Moravia were expelled from their homes; they were plagued constantly by the fear of falling into the hands of their persecutors. They never knew exactly who they could trust. But Katharina carefully sought out the people with whom she wanted to stay; she was informed about the people living in the mountains and valleys around Brixen and was aware of their thinking. Through her personal contacts she may have had closer connections with the small Anabaptist groups than did her husband.

The spiritual upheavals during the years of the Reformation affected Katharina and Jacob Hutter in the same manner. They wished to serve God and to contribute what they could so that the undistorted word of God would be made known. The Anabaptist communities were places where brothers and sisters could live together. As brothers and sisters they supported one another and strengthened each other in the faith. This new point of view was given expression when Katharina referred to Jacob Hutter as her married "brother and husband." In God's sight he was first of all her brother, and secondarily he was her husband. When she was imprisoned for a second time, another recantation was out of the question for Katharina. She demonstrated strength and remained firm in her convictions. She could not turn back from the path she had chosen. Thus, she also proved her faithfulness to her husband who had preceded her in death. Both of their lives had come to an end all too quickly. For us there remains the memory of two people who in all their suffering displayed a remarkable strength of faith.

Testimony of Katharina Hutter, Given before December 3, 1535, at Klausen.[24]

Katharina, legitimate daughter of Lorentzen Pursst testified:

Approximately three years ago she was working in Trins for Paul Gall. Gall, Paul Rumer and others, some of whom have been executed and some of whom have left for Moravia, persuaded and encouraged her to come to [meetings of] the Anabaptist sect. There Jacob Hutter, a minister and leader, who is now her married brother and husband, baptized her. Following that they left for Moravia, and there, around the time of this past Pentecost, she married Jacob Hutter in proper fashion. Hans Tuchmacher, her brother as well as an Anabaptist leader, married them.

And on this past St. Jacob's Day, she and this same man, her married brother and husband and another one of her brothers in the faith, a man named Jerome, a schoolmaster, who also was baptized by Jacob Hutter, together came up from Moravia, over the Taurien mountains to Taufers, where they sojourned for a time in the forests. They went to a man named Waldner on the mountainside above Elln. However, he had fallen away from the Anabaptists and had become a destructive [zernichter] person.

From there they went to Hörschwang on another mountain to a man named Ober who was one of their beloved brothers, and also his wife and their daughter, named Dorothea, as well as two male servants, both named Martin, and a young fellow named Wolf, and his wife named Els, all of whom Jacob Hutter converted and baptized. Hutter also baptized the aforementioned Waldner at Elln, but he had become a useless Christian again, and had left the Anabaptists.

After that they visited a man named Prader and one named Braun several times in Lüsen, but Prader is not of their opinion and faith as they are, although his wife and son, named Melchior, are. They stayed often in Prader's house, along with the aforementioned Jerome, who also was with them on these occasions. And Hutter, her husband, baptized many people in the forests of Lüsen.

Approximately fourteen days ago Hutter baptized around seven or eight people in Trins and Sterzing in the cellar of a cartwright's house which is named The hard worker or The Haggler. The man was not home at the time and is not an Anabaptist. She does not know them, and thinks that they may have been miners.

From there, she and Hutter along with Anna, Stainer's daughter, went again to Hörschwang to a man named Ober and stayed with him for a time. After that (when they realized that they were being watched), they went through the forests under cover of darkness and along the streets of Klausen, crossed the bridge at the guard hut and went through the town of Klausen and over the bridge to the sexton's house, arriving there around midnight. They wanted to leave again right away but did not know where to turn. Her husband and brother, Jacob Hutter, told her that he wanted to go to Villnöss to a man named Niclauer or back to Jörg Müller in Villnöss or wherever God would lead them.

The wife of Niclauer was her dear sister, but not her husband. Like Jörg Müller and his wife in Villnöss, Niclauer had been baptized by Hutter the previous fall, but Müllner had become useless [i.e., had since left the Anabaptists].

Moreover, she could see no use for either the mass or the sacrament of the altar, which monks or priests lift above their heads, nor for the church building, which was nothing but a "walled pile of stones" [*gemaurten steinerhauffen*], or for the baptism of infants, which was nothing more than a bath in dirty water [*ain sudlwesch*]; and the sacrament was nothing more than an abomination and a stench before God. All this was from the devil.

Niclas Niderhofer from the district of Schonegg and a young woman by the name of Ulian, who worked as a maid at Khyens, and another person whom she did not know, were baptized on St. Jacob's Day by her accused husband, Hutter. They had found protection and lodging several times with these people at Hörschwang.

With whatever means or money available to him, her married brother and husband, Jacob Hutter, provided for the poor widows, poor young children and other poor brothers and sisters who were in need. As far as she knew none of the leaders or her brothers were now in Tirol, rather they were all in Moravia at this time.

Notes

1 Testimony of Katharina Hutter, December 12, 1535. See TA, Ost.III, p. 300.
2 Proceedings regarding the Anabaptists Paul Gall and his wife Justina Rumlerin between 1532 and 1536. TA, Ost.III, p. 48, p. 52-53, p. 97, pp. 115-16, p. 125, p. 138, p. 164, pp. 168-69, p. 300, p. 315.
3 Testimony of Katharina Hutter. TA, Ost.III, p. 300.

4 Proceedings of Paul Gall and his wife, Justina Rumlerin. See n. 2 above.
5 TA, Ost.III, p. 138.
6 TA, Ost.III, p. 403; p. 447.
7 *The Chronicle of the Hutterian Brethren, vol. I* (Rifton, NY: Plough Publishing House, 1987), 135.
8 Rudolf Wolkan, ed., *Das grosse Geschichtsbuch der Hutterischen Brüder* (Cayley, AB: Macmillan Colony, 1982), 109, 111-12.
9 "Jakob Hutter," ME, II, 851.
10 Testimony of Katharina Hutter, December 3, 1535. TA, Ost.III, p. 300.
11 Testimony of Katharina Hutter. TA, Ost.III, p. 301.
12 Translated from TA, Ost.III, p. 302.
13 See the testimony of Anna Stainer, November 30, 1535, in TA, Ost.III, document 365A, pp. 292ff.
14 "Jakob Hutter," ME, II, 853.
15 Instructions of the Innsbruck government to councillors of the bishop of Brixen. TA, Ost.III, document 371, pp. 308-09, and document 372.
16 Testimony of Katharina Hutter, December 3, 1535. TA, Ost.III, p. 301.
17 Ibid.
18 Directive of the Innsbruck government to the crown administrator [*Pfleger*] of Rodeneck. TA, Ost.III, document 389, p. 319.
19 Directive of the government of Innsbruck to the councillors of the bishop of Brixen. TA, Ost.III, p. 319, p. 323.
20 Directive of the councillors of the bishop of Brixen to the crown administrator [*Pfleger*] of St. Michelsburg. TA, Ost.III, p. 321. I assume that the person being discussed is Katharina Hutter since the other women who are named, the Lasacherin and the daughter of the day labourer, would not have been given so much attention. The birth place of Jakob Hutter, Moos near Bruneck, belonged to the district of Michelsburg.
21 "Jakob Huter," *Mennonitisches Lexikon*, II, p. 377.
22 TA, Ost.III, p. 323.
23 According to Werner O. Packull, Katharina Hutter was imprisoned at least four and possibly five times: at Sterzing (?) in 1532, at Rodeneck in 1533, at Bozen in 1533, at Klausen (Branzoll) and Gufidaun in 1535-36, at Schöneck in 1538. See his book *Hutterite Beginnings: Communitarian Experiments during the Reformation* (Baltimore, MD: Johns Hopkins University Press, 1995).
24 Testimony of Katharina Hutter, December 3, 1535, while imprisoned in Branzoll in Klausen. TA, Ost.III, pp. 300-1.

WIVES, FEMALE LEADERS, AND TWO FEMALE MARTYRS FROM HALL

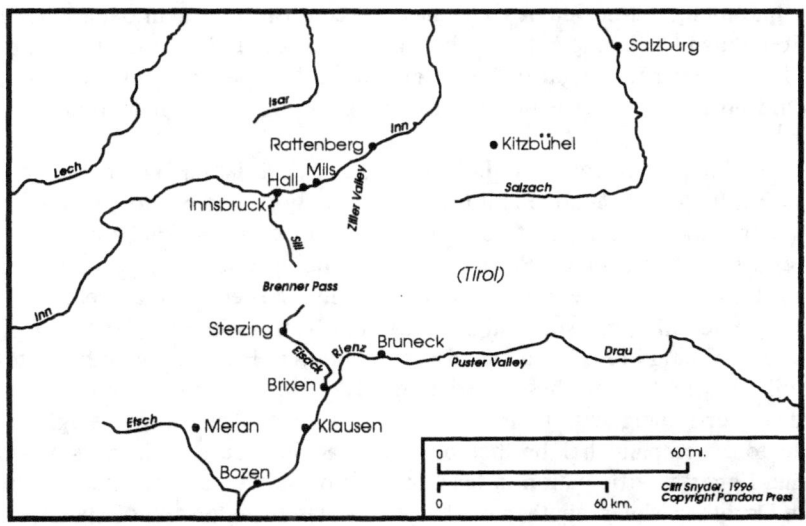

In the regions around the city of Hall, the Anabaptist movement grew dynamically between 1526 and 1529. To combat this growth the authorities stepped up the persecution of Anabaptists by executing key leaders like Leonard Schiemer and Hans Schlaffer, as well as women and men from the ranks of the "commoners."[1] However, the government's hope that the elimination of certain leaders would weaken and subdue the Anabaptist movement was not realized. By 1528 Anabaptism had established itself firmly at the grass roots level in the Austrian teritory of Tirol. Peter Egger the baker was among the local leaders working in and around the city of Hall. The first mention of him in the court records was made in April of 1528, just two months after the execution of Hans Schlaffer. It was reported that Peter, his "one-eyed sister," and another man had been preaching and baptizing in places west of Innsbruck and Hall. Peter had left his wife and his many children behind in order to teach and proselytize; his sister participated in this itinerant ministry.[2]

Although Peter Egger had fled from Hall, he left by choice. By September 1528, Peter Egger's wife Cristina was forced to leave Hall as well; she was exiled from her home because of her Anabaptist involvements. The multiple applications submitted on her behalf for a pardon that would allow her to return confirm that, despite her participation in the Anabaptist movement, Cristina had the strong support of others. The number of children she had to care for also favoured granting her a pardon. Thus, in February 1529 the government allowed her to come back under certain conditions. She was required to retract her faith publicly on three consecutive Sundays during mass and to perform whatever penance the local priest required of her. Third, she had to sign an affidavit [*Urfehde*] and confirm it with an oath, agreeing to relinquish her membership in the Anabaptist sect and to remain in the city of Hall. The affidavit also was a guarantee for the government that she would not take further action against the government for their treatment of her.[3]

Not until August of the same year was Cristina Egger mentioned again in the court records, and then only briefly in relation to her husband. After the arrests of August 1529 at a secret meeting of Anabaptists in the forests near Mils, where Peter Egger was hiding out, the local authorities were told to guard the Egger house carefully, suspecting that Peter would come to see his wife some night under cover of darkness.[4] Cristina Egger chose to remain in Hall and care for their children. But other members of the family did not hold to these restrictions. There is mention of both a son and a daughter fleeing with their father.[5] Peter's sister Anna, being single, was able to accompany her brother on his preaching tours. It is possible that Anna Egger's participation in teaching and proselytizing influenced women like Dorothea Maler, another Anabaptist woman from the city of Hall, to join the movement.

Dorothea Maler was part of the group of twenty Anabaptists arrested on August 15, 1529, the day in the church calendar when the assumption of the Virgin Mary [*Frauentag*] was celebrated. Peter Egger, the leader through whom Dorothea had joined Anabaptism, was one of the suspects related to this group, but he managed to avoid arrest. The majority of the prisoners chose to recant, but Dorothea Maler and Anna Ochsentreiber, whom Dorothea had brought into the movement, remained steadfast and later paid for their faithfulness with their lives.[6]

The execution of two women from the group arrested on August 15 was commemorated in a Hutterite hymn entitled: "A Song about (or by) Anna Malerin and Ursula Ochsentreiberin, Who Were Drowned at Hall in the Inn Valley."[7] A translation of this hymn follows. However, in comparing the Anabaptist court records for Tirol and the narration of these events in the Hutterian chronicle and the martyrology, there was an evident mix-up of their names.[8] The family name Ochsentreiber in all likelihood referred to Anna's husband's occupation as herder of the village cattle. Among the 268 women named in the court records of Tirol between 1527 and 1529, this is the only occurrence of the name.[9] The uniqueness of this name, its juxtaposition with the family name of Maler in both the *Chronicle of the Hutterian Brethren* and the *Martyrs' Mirror*, the fact that a hymn was written to commemorate the death of the two women, and the close similarity between the events recorded in Anabaptist sources and the court records lead to the conclusion that Anna Maler and Ursula Ochsentreiber, and Dorothea Maler and Anna Ochsentreiber refer to the same women. Their Christian names were incorrectly recorded in one or the other of our sources.

It could be that the Anabaptists from Hall had purposely chosen to meet on the festival day of August 15, when many people would be engaged in religious activities and less attention would be paid to them. In any case, court officials set about trying to get as much information as possible from the twenty or more prisoners they had managed to arrest in the forests of Mils. In the reports of the first interrogation, only the names of the male leaders, Peter Egger and Hans Amon, were mentioned. It was known that Peter Egger had associated with Hans Amon, the cloth weaver [*Tuchscherer*] who also was active around Hall at this time.[10] Amon later would take over the leadership of Jacob Hutter's followers who practised communal living in the more tolerant atmosphere of Moravia.

By the end of August, the authorities had interrogated two unnamed women about the meeting that had taken place in the forests of Mils near Hall. In their first testimony the women had tried to play down the significance of the gathering, a fact the authorities found hard to believe, since it had taken place in such a "suspicious and secret place."[11] The women also had been reticent about giving the names of those attending and so they were to be questioned a second time on the assumption that they could at least name the people who had been sitting next to them. If they still refused to give the names of fellow believers, the officials were to use torture during the questioning. The authorities were determined to find out what had gone on at the meeting, whether these two women had been baptized, who their leader was, who had brought them to the meeting, and if these Anabaptists would be meeting again. Their goal was to eradicate the "devious sect" of Anabaptism. Because there are no further references to these two women we do not know if they actually were questioned again. Perhaps they were the women to whom Dorothea Maler was related, referred to in the reports about Dorothea. The absence of additional names in the report of Dorothea Maler's interrogation does not allow us to say for certain.

Little more than a week later, on September 7, 1529, it was reported that Dorothea Maler and the two women with whom she was imprisoned in Hall, Anna Ochsentreiber and Katharina Praun, had testified before a jury of sworn witnesses. Dorothea in particular had talked about her meeting in the forests of Mils with several men, including a man named Scherer, Peter Egger the baker, and a man whose name she did not know, but who wore a beige-coloured [*leybfarben, leberfarben*] coat. Moreover, Dorothea stated that Peter Egger wanted to depart for the Ziller Valley to the south,[12] over the next mountain range. The authorities had already heard that Peter Egger was taking part of the group southward. Dorothea now confirmed this information, which made the government more determined than ever to spare no effort in removing Peter Egger as Anabaptist leader.[13]

The information concerning Anabaptism in the Ziller Valley was not encouraging to the government. In May and June of 1529 they already had been told about a woman in the Ziller Valley (they did not have her name) who had in her possession a book with names of eight hundred Anabaptists who had been baptized.[14] It was reported that in Schwaz, which had a population of twelve hundred, there were eight hundred Anabaptists.[15] Thus, there was a strong network of local Anabaptist leaders in the regions south of Innsbruck and Hall, and now Peter Egger was going there too; the network was broadening out. The Ziller Valley was a safer place for the Anabaptists since it was governed by the Archbishop of Salzburg and the rulers of Tirol had less authority there. Dorothea's information about Peter Egger's whereabouts was therefore very significant for the government. However, a second report, also dated September 7, 1529, informs us about the details of Dorothea's own experience and her intricate involvements with both Anabaptist leaders and female members of the movement.

While all three women, Dorothea Maler as well as Anna Ochsentreiber and Katharina Praun, had given testimonies, Dorothea's case was different in that she was a *relapsi*. In other words, she had been arrested once before and had recanted to obtain release. Leniency was not something Dorothea Maler could hope for. After swearing to leave the Anabaptist movement and being freed by the government, Dorothea had allowed two women to persuade her to become involved again. Then Dorothea and these women had met with the fleeing Scherer, his son, Peter Egger, and a third man who wore a beige-coloured coat. Several women from the village of Wattens and other places in the forests of Mils (Muls) had also been there. For these actions the government was no longer willing to accept that she was innocent. They now said: "it could be surmised and was altogether thinkable that, she was not that simple-minded." She had talked to the women from Wattens and knew some of them as well, despite having claimed otherwise in her first testimony. Any excuse she had made of not knowing these women would no longer be acceptable. Therefore, the judge of Hall was instructed to question her again in the presence of the same witnesses who had listened to her before. Furthermore, if she did not cooperate, the questioning should include torture, "as befitting a woman." The interrogators were to find out the names of her husband and of the other women, what she had heard from these women and from the leaders with whom she had met, and what she had intended to do. In particular, they were to ask her if she was not sorry to have recanted her Anabaptist faith. Regardless of her answers, she, Anna Ochsentreiber, and Katharina Praun were to be guarded carefully in the prison of Hall until further instructions were given by the government at Innsbruck.[16]

We do not have a record of Dorothea's own words, but from a subsequent report about her second interrogation we know that she remained firm in her Anabaptist faith. Seven days later, on September 14, 1529, the judge at Hall was instructed to set a date for her trial. Whatever would be decided at that time was to be carried out immediately.[17] If recantation had spared her once, Dorothea did not consider it an option again and she was now willing to die a martyr's death. Katharina Praun chose to recant and was given a pardon a month later, on October 16, 1529,[18] but there are no further references to Anna Ochsentreiber in the government (court) records. Nevertheless, her name appears together with Dorothea/Anna Maler's in all the records kept by the Anabaptists themselves. It is virtually certain that she shared a martyr's death with Dorothea.

Dorothea/Anna and Ursula/Anna were not the first or the last women to become Anabaptist martyrs during the early years of the movement in this region; they were but two of forty-nine women executed in the Tirol between 1527 and 1529.[19] This number represents 40 percent of the total number of all persons executed in Tirol during these years and is a higher percentage than the proportion of women named in the *Martyrs' Mirror*, in which 33 percent of all martyrs are women. The execution of Anabaptist women in the Tirol began in 1528, just as it did for Anabaptist men. The number of women who died as martyrs doubled between 1528 and 1529. Thus, by the fall of 1529, the authorities did not hesitate to carry out executions as quickly as possible, as the case of Dorothea Maler and Anna Ochsentreiber confirms. The persecution reached its peak in the Tirol between 1530 and 1534, with the result that the number of Anabaptists leaving Tirol for Moravia increased substantially. Much later the Anabaptist-Hutterites who lived in Moravia began to record their history and the hymns that commemorated their persecution.

We do not know when the hymn honouring Dorothea/Anna and Ursula/Anna and their martyrdom was written. However, a second report, bearing the same date as that ordering the trial of Dorothea Maler (September 14, 1529), was sent to the mayor and town council of Hall. It reveals that hymns had a significant and consequential role for Anabaptists themselves as well as for members of the population who heard their singing. The report as summarized by the editor of the Tirolean court records reads:

> The Mayor should prevent the Anabaptist prisoners from being kept together as a group [*zusammengelegt*], for then they sing hymns as is the practice in their sect. This causes trouble among the common people who hear them, and gives strength to the prisoners to persist in their heretical belief. There should be enough prisons in Hall to keep the prisoners in solitary confinement.[20]

If either or both Dorothea and Anna had composed the hymn that follows, perhaps it was already being sung at this time.[21] In any case, it is notable that the stories of these two women were deemed worthy of being committed to memory so that we could read about them to this day.

A Song about (by?) Anna Malerin and Ursula Ochsentreiberin, Who Were Drowned at Hall in the Inn Valley[22]

1. On the day of our Lady, Christ brought together his little lambs. He congregated them quickly in Mils in the green woods.

2. But the wolf came running and scattered the lambs in the valley. They ran very quickly and loudly cried out to God.

3. Then the shepherd came and clearly proclaimed the Word of God to them. He taught them well. May God ever and in all eternity reward him.

4. Now would you like to know what happened? With God's spirit the Holy Gospel was clearly proclaimed, how Christ fed his disciples on the mountain.

5. Now we wish to utter complaints to God in heaven that they wish to banish the word of God from the whole world. We will never buy the word of God for money.

6. And because we will never buy it for money we must leave wife and children. Mark this well. We will not give the priests any money.

7. The Gospel now is clear as day, and causes great grievance and anguish to the monks and priests. [It says that] they should never be great lords.

8. And God will not put up with it any longer; the truth is taken into the whole world. The [monks and priests] do not think this is good. They shear the sheep and suck the lifeblood out of them.

9. And since they never can succeed they make up many lies, [such as] the baptism which Jesus commanded his dear disciples (to practise) is wrong.

10. Now take note of what we have written: infant baptism was instituted for money. That is why they shed much innocent blood.

Amen

Notes

1 Leonard Schiemer was executed January 14, 1528, just two days after giving the authorities a long list of persons, including 28 women, whom he had baptized in Tirol and Bavaria. The execution of Hans Schlaffer followed shortly thereafter on February 4, 1528. Exactly two months later, on April 4, orders were given for the execution of two women and one man, Apolonia Niedermair, Hans Schneider, and his wife, Eva. They were the first commoners to be put to death. The many reprimands from the central government indicate that the local authorities had delayed repeatedly in dealing with these prisoners. See TA, Ost.II, p. 66, pp. 69-70, p. 76, p. 80, p. 90, p. 97, p. 117.
2 TA, Ost.II, p. 119. Claus-Peter Clasen includes Anna Egger on the list of leaders in Tirol. See his article, "The Anabaptist Leaders: Their Numbers and Background, Switzerland, Austria, South and Central Germany 1525-1618," in MQR, 49 (April 1975): 144.
3 TA, Ost.II, p. 170, p. 192.
4 TA, Ost.II, p. 274.
5 TA, Ost.II, p. 282, p. 484.
6 TA, Ost.II, document 403, pp. 284-85; document 404, pp. 285-86; document 409, p. 288.
7 The hymn is recorded in Rudolf Wolkan, *Die Lieder der Wiedertäufer, Ein Beitrag zur deutschen und niederländischen Litteratur-und Kirchengeschichte* (Nieuwkoop: B. De Graaf, 1965), 16-17.
8 See *The Chronicle of the Hutterian Brethren*, vol. I (New York: Plough Publishing House, 1987), 73; see *Martyrs' Mirror*, 437.
9 See the names of Anabaptist women listed in Linda Huebert Hecht, "Faith and Action: The Role of Women in the Anabaptist Movement of the Tirol, 1527-1529," (unpublished cognate essay, Master of Arts, History, University of Waterloo, 1990), 126-30.
10 Hans Amon is called the "Tuchscherer von Hall." Although he came from Bavaria, he is associated here with the city of Hall where he was active in the Anabaptist movement at the time. TA, Ost.II, p. 276.
11 TA, Ost.II, document 395, pp. 280-81; especially p. 281.
12 The records state that Peter Egger was the son of the man named "Scherer" who lived near a trench ("im Graben"), perhaps near the town wall. Since Hans Amon was referred to earlier as the "Tuchscherer" or weaver of cloth, the possibility exists that Hans Amon was Peter Egger's father. This would mean that Hans Amon was much older than our present information indicates. TA, Ost.II, document 403, pp. 284-85, especially p. 285.
13 TA, Ost.II, document 396, pp. 281-82.
14 The first reference to this woman and the book she had in her possession was reported May 26, 1529. See TA, Ost.II, p. 239. In the second reference to this woman, dated June 5, 1529, Mecenseffy summarizes the directive of the central government at Innsbruck to Cristan Noel, the local official [*Pfleger, Berg und Landrichter*] of Schwaz, as follows: "The earlier instructions to him are repeated, to search for the woman, who is supposed to be a leader [*Vorsteherin*] and is supposed to have baptized 800 people. He is to make inquiries of Leonhard Lackner's widow and Georg Obermayr as to where she is at the present time." TA, Ost.II, p. 249.
15 Mecenseffy's summary for a report dated May 29, 1529, is as follows: "The judge is to use torture in questioning Anabaptists imprisoned in Rattenberg, regarding who belonged to the sect in Schwaz, where the membership was reported to be 800. Their names and occupations were to be recorded." TA, Ost.II, p. 243. The population figure for Schwaz as 1200 is given in the article by Johann Loserth and Robert Freidmann, "Tirol," ME, IV, 725.

16 TA, Ost.II, document 404, pp. 285-86. The quotations are from p. 285.
17 TA, Ost.II, document 409, p. 288.
18 TA, Ost.II, document 419, p. 293.
19 Hecht, "Faith and Action," 43.
20 TA, Ost.II, document 410, p. 288.
21 Helen Martens has suggested that the word "von" in the title, which means either "about" or "by," could indicate that the women composed the hymn. The subject matter of the hymn, namely the experience of the two women, and the grievances of fellow Anabaptists, also points in this direction. On the other hand, the reference to leaving wife and children could indicate a male author.
22 Translation of "Ein Lied von Anna Malerin und Ursula Ochsentreiber in 1529" in *Die Lieder der Hutterischen Brüder* (Cayley, AB: Macmillan Colony, 1974), 46. Also found in Wolkan, Die *Lieder der Wiedertäufer*, 16ff., and the Pressburg Codex 236, 24.

URSULA HELLRIGEL OF THE ÖTZ VALLEY AND ANNELEIN OF FREIBURG

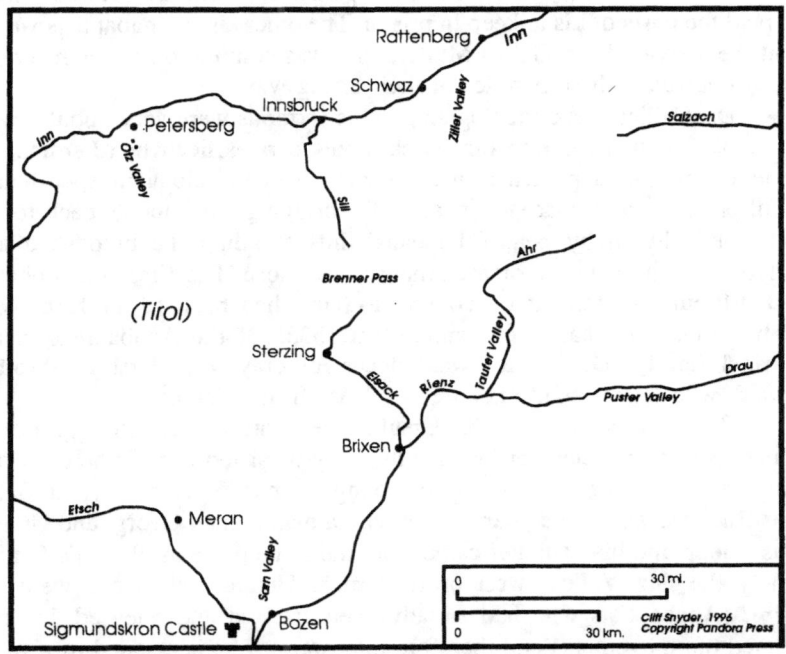

The persecution of Anabaptists in Tirol reached its peak in the mid 1530s. During this time many of the pursued believers left their homes in the Austrian territory and escaped to Moravia to make a new life for themselves where the rulers were more tolerant. If the fleeing Anabaptists safely reached Rattenberg on the Inn River and were not caught on the boats travelling eastward, they were relatively sure of reaching what some called "the promised land." It was one thing that whole families made their way to Moravia, but quite another that even young people sought to leave their homeland for the sake of their faith. Ursula Hellrigel was one such person. She languished in the prisons of Tirol five years before finally being allowed to join the Anabaptists in their new home. The government responded to Ursula's staunch adherence in her Anabaptist belief with severe punishment, then with repeated postponement, and seemingly forgot about her. However, the persistence of family members and others seeking her release finally brought results. Ursula's story is unusual in itself, but the fact that she wrote a hymn makes this young woman all the more significant.

In May 1538 the seventeen-year-old Ursula Hellrigel, daughter of a peasant farmer, was one of ten Anabaptist prisoners held at the St. Petersberg castle in the upper Inn Valley. One of the prisoners, a former priest, was an Anabaptist leader and therefore was transferred to the prison in Brixen.

Another member of the group, a youth of nineteen years, planned to recant and would be released after he had done penance, sworn the oath [*Urfehde*] and paid the costs of his upkeep in prison. The other eight Anabaptists would await the arrival of Dr. Gallus Müller, who was coming to St. Petersberg in order to persuade these heretics of their erring ways.[1]

Dr. Müller was a theologian and his sermons were very popular with the people. He had come to Innsbruck three years earlier when Ferdinand I appointed him as a preacher in his court. With his eloquent speech and skilful persuasion, he had a reputation for bringing Anabaptists back to the established church by peaceful means, thus avoiding the bloodshed and martyrdom that so many of the Anabaptists chose. His first and probably most difficult assignment on coming to Tirol had been to try to convert Jacob Hutter, who had been captured in 1535. Of the Anabaptists in the Hellrigel family, Dr. Müller was successful only with Ursula's brother Oswald, who later sought his sister's release from prison.[2]

By mid-October 1538, Ursula was part of another group of Anabaptists in St. Petersberg who stubbornly persisted in their heresy. This group included Anastasia Ruepp, a young woman of eighteen, her father Hans Ruepp, a sixty-five-year-old woman, a man named Georg, and Ursula. Hans Ruepp and his daughter came from the same place as Ursula's family, namely the Ötz Valley, west of Innsbruck. Ursula and Georg were not *relapsi* (Anabaptists who had already been arrested and released, but had rejoined the movement) and therefore they were to be persuaded to give up their Anabaptist beliefs. But the efforts of Dr. Müller failed, and so the government used other means. For six and a half months the prisoners were kept on a meagre diet, all to no avail. In light of these unusual circumstances, the local authorities now asked the king for advice on what to do next. In particular, they wanted to know if the imprisonment of the two young women [*Dirnen*], Ursula and Anastasia, should be prolonged. The idea of enclosing the prisoners behind brick walls was not a good one since the inhabitants in these valleys were simple and naïve [*einfältig*], and did not shy away from punishment or even death.[3] Little did the officials know just how persistent young women such as Ursula could be, and little did Ursula know just how long her imprisonment would last. The king sent his response in early November. He instructed the authorities in St. Petersberg to do everything in their power to persuade the five tenacious Anabaptists to recant in order to save their souls.[4]

Eleven months later, in September 1539, special mention was made of Ursula's case. She had been in prison for almost a year at this point because of repeated postponements of her case. This had resulted in undue costs and so the judge was instructed to draw on her inheritance to pay for these expenses.[5] Upon investigating the matter, the crown administrator [*Pfleger*] discovered that the family property had been given to her married brothers and sisters. Thus the judge was to request 30 florin and 56 kreuter from the family to pay the expense of keeping Ursula in prison. This amount was equal approximately to two-thirds the annual salary of a carpenter of that time.

Ursula was still in prison fifteen months later. Early in 1541, Ferdinand's government informed Wilhelm von Liechtenstein, who governed the regions bordering the Adige River, that Ursula Hellrigel would be sent first to the castle at Haselburg south of Bozen and then be transferred to Sigmundskron, which lay at the confluence of the Eisack and Adige Rivers. Here she was to be kept on a minimal diet and given minimal clothing. Since Liechtenstein was the chief ruler it would be his job to take charge of transferring the prisoner and the costs would be covered by the district of Bozen. Later the central government decreed that 10 florin should be paid by the treasury of Tirol to cover the costs of Ursula's imprisonment.[6]

Again, more than a year passed before any further attention was paid to Ursula's case. In December 1542 she was moved to Innsbruck and imprisoned there with a group of Anabaptists. The court records do not reveal why she had been moved.[7] However, here she was to remain until further notice. The *Chronicle* records that Ursula was in prison at Innsbruck with an Anabaptist named Jörg Liebich, who had come back to Tirol from Moravia, and that she was tied to his feet when he was racked. Neither of them recanted, but both endured long imprisonments before being released.[8]

Finally, ten months later, on October 9, 1543, Ferdinand's government advised the local authorities to release Ursula Hellrigel. Her physical health may have been the primary concern for her pardon. But her tender age and the fact that others had spoken on her behalf were also taken into account. Moreover, Ursula had to agree to leave the territory of Tirol and never return to her homeland on penalty of losing her life. As before, her relatives were to pay for the expense of her imprisonment.[9]

One might have expected that Ursula would gladly have adhered to these restrictions in order to gain release from prison. She did agree to leave her home, but she refused to swear that she would never return. Surprisingly, the authorities gave in to her objection and agreed to release Ursula merely on the basis of her promise to leave. However, they stipulated that if in fact she did return, she would be treated like anyone else.[10] Perhaps Ursula was encouraged to negotiate the terms of her release by the fact that those supporting her were doing the same. Her guardian, Peter Müller, her brother, Klaus Hellrigel, and other relatives requested that the government waive payment of her expenses. To this the government responded negatively, since Ursula possessed property. In the end, her guardian agreed to pay the required 50 florin and the government's view remained unchanged. They would not allow her to return safely to Tirol.[11]

Ursula did in fact leave Tirol and spent the rest of her life among the

Hutterite Anabaptists in Moravia. The hymn she wrote, which is translated here,[12] provides some clues as to what sustained her during her five-year imprisonment. She was not the only member of her family who composed hymns; Zacharias Hellrigel (1580-1630) wrote five hymns.[13] Probably because of her hymn, Ursula's story is one of the few women's stories included in the history later written by the Hutterites in Moravia.[14]

Annelein of Freiburg

A few words must be said about the song that follows. Although there is general agreement among scholars that the hymn was in fact written by Ursula Hellrigel, since it was copied into Hutterite codices under her name, the hymn itself was published and printed only in the *Ausbund*, the Swiss Brethren hymnal, where it appears as hymn number 36. The *Ausbund* attributes the hymn not to Ursula, but to Annelein of Freiburg, about whom very little is known.[15] The *Martyrs' Mirror*, published in the Netherlands in 1660, borrowed the text of the *Ausbund* hymn, and rendered it into prose. It is clear that T. van Braght was convinced that the hymn was written by Annelein of Freiburg, who had been martyred in 1529. Oddly enough, Ursula Hellrigel also came to be included in the *Martyrs' Mirror*, but only as part of the story of the imprisonment and temptation of Jörg Liebich, (see the group profile of women in the Hutterite *Chronicle*). Ursula's hymn writing apparently was not known to van Braght. However, he did know that Ursula lived out her days with the Hutterites in Moravia, and did not suffer a martyr's death, but rather "obtained release, and unharmed in her faith and conscience, returned to the church and there fell asleep in the Lord."[16]

The *Martyrs' Mirror* contains information about Annelein of Freiburg (apparently from Freiburg in Breisgau, in southwestern Germany) which is duplicated nowhere else. This information is virtually all that is known about her.

> This Anna of Freiburg was zealous in the fear of the Lord and as she believed in Christ, and was baptized upon faith in Him, and thus sought to arise with Christ, and walk in newness of life, the adversary could not endure it; therefore Anna was envied, accused and apprehended by his ministers, and after steadfastly suffering many torments, sentenced to death, and drowned in the water, and afterwards burned with fire. This happened at Freiburg, in the year 1529. When she was about to die, she spoke the following prayer to God, and left these admonitions to all descendants.

After this introduction, the *Martyrs' Mirror* prints the prayer/song, which closely matches the *Ausbund* hymn in language as well as content, after which the *Martyrs' Mirror* then adds the following postscript, with reference to Annelein of Freiburg: "Thereupon she voluntarily submitted to death, and was drowned in the water, as mentioned above."[17]

It is no longer possible to unravel how Ursula's hymn came to be attributed to Annelein in the *Ausbund*, or why it was preserved only in the Swiss Brethren hymn tradition, and not in the Hutterite hymn tradition. Still, the hymn/prayer was associated with an Anabaptist woman prisoner of faith in both traditions. It is written in the first person throughout, and is a prayerful testament of faith. It deserves a place in this collection.

Anabaptist hymns generally were written to the tunes of popular and well-known songs. In the place of musical notation, the song is prefaced by the identification of the particular tune to which it was meant to be sung.

Ausbund

The 36th Song

Another Song of Annelein of Freiburg, Who was Drowned and then Burned, 1529.

To the tune of "In You I Have Hoped, Lord."

1. Everlasting Father in heaven,
   I call on you so ardently,
   Do not let me turn from you.
   Keep me in your truth
   Until my final end.

2. O God, guard my heart and mouth,
   Lord watch over me at all times,
   Let nothing separate me from you,
   Be it affliction, anxiety, or need,
   Keep me pure in joy.

3. My everlasting Lord and Father,
   Show and teach me,
   Poor unworthy child that I am,
   That I heed your path and way.
   In this lies my desire.

4. To walk through your power into death,
   Through sorrow, torture, fear and want.

>
> Sustain me in this,
> O God, so that I nevermore
> Be separated from your love.

5. Many travel along this road,
   The cup of suffering lies there,
   And also many untrue teachings
   Which try to turn us away
   From Christ our Lord.

6. To you I raise up my soul, Lord,
   I depend on you in misfortune.
   Do not let me come to harm,
   That my enemy not stand over me
   On this earth.

7. They have imprisoned me.
   I wait, O God, with all my heart,
   With very great longing,
   When finally you will awake
   And set your prisoners free.

8. O God, Father, make us like
   The five virgins of your kingdom,
   Who were prudently careful
   To wait for the bridegroom,
   With his chosen flock.

9. Eternal king of heaven,
   Feed us and quench our thirst
   In a spiritual way
   With your food of truth
   Which never perishes

10. If you withhold your food from us
    Everything is lost and useless.
    Without you we bring forth nothing.
    Through grace we trust in you,
    It will not fail us.

11. I do not doubt God's power.
    His judgements all are true.
    He will not abandon anyone

Who stands firm in the faith,
And stays on the true paths.

12. Be comforted you Christians and rejoice,
    Through Jesus Christ forevermore,
    Who gives us love and faith.
    God comforts us through his holy word,
    On that we should rely.

13. I entrust myself to God and his church.
    May he be my protector today,
    For the sake of his name.
    May this come to pass, Father mine,
    Through Jesus Christ, Amen.

Notes

1 TA Ost.III, document 491, p. 377.
2 This information is from the article by Johann Loserth, "Gallus Müller," ME, III, 769. See also Johann Loserth, "Ursula Hellrigel," ME, II, 695, where Loserth states: "Though she was not versed in the Scriptures, she clung to her faith because her coreligionists lived less frivolously than the world. Her mother, an Anabaptist, had died in prison."
3 TA, Ost.III, document 523B, p. 396.
4 TA, Ost.III, document 523C, p. 396.
5 TA, Ost.III, document 567B, p. 417.
6 TA, Ost.III, document 655, pp. 474-75.
7 In the Hutterite account, the editors state that from the Petersberg tower Ursula was "transferred to Liebich's prison in Vellenburg Castle, and finally to the *Kräuterturm* at Innsbruck." See *The Chronicle of the Hutterian Brethren*, vol.I (Rifton, NY: Plough Publishing House, 1987), 232, n.1.
8 TA, Ost.III, p. 500, p. 695; *Martyrs' Mirror*, 466-67; Josef Beck, *Die Geschichts-Bücher Der Wiedertäufer in Österreich-Ungarn* (Nieuwkoop: B. De Graaf, 1967; Reprint, Vienna, 1883), 157-59. See also the profile on women in *The Chronicle of the Hutterian Brethren*, n. 49.
9 TA, Ost.III, document 741C, p. 518. In regard to her health problems, the editor includes a phrase from the original court record: "umb weiplichen geschlechts blödigkhait willen."
10 TA, Ost.III, document 741C, p. 519.
11 TA, Ost.III, document 746A and B, p. 522.
12 See Rudolf Wolkan, *Die Lieder der Wiedertäufer, Ein Beitrag zur deutschen und niederländischen Litteratur-und Kirchengeschichte* (Nieuwkoop: B. De Graaf, 1965), 178; *The Chronicle of the Hutterian Brethren*, 232, n.2.
13 "Ursula Hellrigel," 695.
14 See ME, II, 695, regarding Zacharias Hellrigel. Additional references to Ursula in the *Chronicle* are: 190n., 191n.
15 In the ME, I, 123, Christian Neff states that the *Ausbund* hymn attributed to Anna of Freiburg was not written by her: "manuscripts of the Hutterian Brethren make it clear that the author was Ursula Helriglin." See also *Chronicle* references in note 12, above.
16 *Martyrs' Mirror*, 466-67.
17 *Martyrs' Mirror*, 434-35.

WOMEN IN *THE CHRONICLE* OF *THE HUTTERIAN BRETHREN*

In 1620 a very good looking young sister named Susanna, the daughter of Hans Ausgeben (storekeeper) who had been murdered [. . . was taken to the Polish camp Krems.] Sister Susanna to her great distress and agony of heart had to stay even longer among the ungodly soldiers, who wreaked their lust on her. Finally God sent help [. . . and] her great longing was realized and on November 5 she returned to the church community . . . with tremendous joy and thankfulness we received all those who had been released. After the severe trials they had suffered we counted it a great mercy of God. . . .[1]

Susanna's story reveals a fragment of women's historical experience within an early Hutterite community. The loss of her father at the hands of an army of the centralizing state, and the danger and distress of imprisonment because of Anabaptist belief, were common potential experiences to any member of the Hutterite faith. Her story shows too, though, that a woman's experience of imprisonment differed from that of her brothers in the faith because she was susceptible to sexual assault. It was seemingly a unique feature of the Hutterites of early modern Europe to welcome back women like Susanna–and there were many–who had survived rape as a trial of faith, rather than casting them from the shelter of the community as unclean creatures. As much as Susanna's story reveals, it also obscures. Because of the nature of the source, one can do no more than guess at Susanna's response to her imprisonment and multiple rapes. Was her faith in fact tested and strengthened, or was Susanna never again able to function intellectually and emotionally? Was she in fact welcomed back to her community as fully as were male victims of imprisonment and torture? Guessing answers is not understanding history. The questions are raised to illustrate the difficulty of reconstructing the fullness of women's lives from isolated fragments recorded by male chroniclers. Only rarely is one able to glimpse a woman at work in the fields, the sewing room, or missionizing beyond the settlement, and never does she emerge as much more than a shadowy image, usually unnamed. But if one is patient and compiles all the glimpses and fragments found of Hutterian women, it is possible to begin a collective biography of their lives within their communities.

The Hutterian Brethren, or more simply, the Hutterites, were one of three main streams of Anabaptism that arose early in the sixteenth century, the other two being the Swiss Brethren (later called Mennonites) and Dutch Mennonites. The persecution of these "re-baptizers" by the Holy Roman Emperor Charles V and his successors saw many Anabaptist refugees migrate from South Germany, Switzerland, and Austria to the relative tolerance of Moravia. It was here between 1525 and 1530 that, following division from other Anabaptists, a community of shared goods was conceived and established under the leadership of Jacob Hutter, from whom the Hutterites take their name.[2] The idea of communal property was part of the larger theological concept of *Gelassenheit*, which meant self-denial and complete submission of the individual will to God, and, for the Hutterites in particular, submission to the community. Other distinguishing features of the Hutterian Brethren included their adherence to pacifism, non-involvement in functions of the state, and separation from secular society.

Between the years 1529 and 1621, approximately one hundred Hutterite communities, or *bruderhofs*, were established in Moravia, with a total population of between twenty and thirty thousand. The latter decades of the sixteenth century have commonly been called a "golden period" for the Hutterites. Their phenomenal growth and relatively unhindered development was attributable to the protection of Moravian nobles who tolerated the communistic way of life of the Hutterian communities (a system generally feared in Europe as a potential threat to the structure of economics and politics) in return for the labour they provided on noble estates. Hutterites benefitted from the Moravian nobles' assertion of independence from the central government in Vienna, and in 1564, and during the reign of Maximilian II, the toleration was endorsed in Vienna.

It was during this era that the social structure and organization of the Hutterian communities was solidified. Originally, the practice of communally held property was established by Anabaptist followers as a means of overcoming the material hardships of enforced travel. Gradually, educated Hutterites developed a theology that emphasized not only the discipleship of Jesus, personal suffering, and the need to discipline the will of the body to that of the spirit, but also the sharing of goods. Jacob Hutter, in 1533, defined the community of goods as a crucial aspect of salvation and the concept became doctrinally necessary for discipleship and salvation.

It was during the "golden period" of stability and prosperity that the Hutterites began a characteristic concern with documenting their history and beliefs. Probably the most history-minded of the Anabaptists, the Hutterites accumulated over the centuries a wealth of writings about themselves. Central to this archival tradition, and one of the earliest writings, is *Das grosse Geschichtsbuch der Hutterischen Brüder*, which in its 1987 English translation is titled *The Chronicle of the Hutterian Brethren*. This eight-hundred-page chronicle of early Hutterian history was penned by various members of the community, beginning in the late 1560s. Covering the period 1517 to 1665, the *Chronicle* has several predominant elements: lists of the appointments and deaths of Hutterian leaders; theological treatises and orders of discipline for the community written by leaders; details of community establishment and migrations; accounts of imprisonment and martyrdom of Hutterian members; and records of various disputes within the community.

Though the roles of women and men are not examined in any direct way in the *Chronicle*, it is nevertheless a useful source in the historical interpretation of how gender roles were conceived and practised in the Hutterite communities. In particular, the *Chronicle* is a difficult source for the historian of women to interpret. It reveals women's past only in a fragmented and incidental manner. That past, moreover, is not seen from a "woman's angle of vision," as Margaret Conrad has said,[3] but is filtered through male perspectives. Even so, a partial reconstruction of some social and economic aspects of the lives of Hutterite women is possible from the fragments retrieved from the *Chronicle*, and a hazy outline of the mosaic of their history can be initiated.

Hutterites thought of their community in natural, organic terms and as subject to the order perceived in nature. The social hierarchy of the *bruderhofs* was intended to mirror the natural order ordained by God. The concept extended to the role of women in Hutterite society. Both men and women obeyed the Lord. Both men and women obeyed the elders. Women, though, obeyed their husbands, too. Peter Riedemann, a Hutterite leader imprisoned for the faith in Marburg in 1540, defined the ideal position of women in Hutterite society in his *Confession of Faith*.

> We say first, that since woman was taken from man and not man from woman, man hath lordship but woman weakness, humility and submission, therefore she should be under the yoke of man and obedient to him, even as the woman was commanded by God when He said to her: 'the man shall be thy Lord'. Now since this is so she should heed her husband, inquire of him, ask him and do all things with and naught without his counsel. For where she doeth this not, she forsaketh the place in the order in which she hath been set by God, encroacheth upon the Lordship of the man and forsaketh the command of her Creator as well as the submission that she promised her husband in the union of marriage: to honour him as a wife her husband.[4]

While men and women were equally free to choose to follow Christ, receive adult baptism, and possibly suffer imprisonment and death for their beliefs, within the earthly realms of family and community Hutterites were no less patriarchal than the rest of early modern society.

While Hutterite women may have been "peers in the faith," to use Lucille Marr's phrase,[5] they were for the most part subordinate in the social order: in other words experience did not reflect theological equality. There is of course the question of whether earthly subordination of women to men can co-exist with equality of the sexes in God's eyes. Is this so, or is it more likely that the social order in fact reflected a theological understanding of how women and men were viewed in the celestial realm as well?

There was, in any case, a rigid prescriptive role for women in Hutterite society, gender roles being defined in terms of a literal reading of the New Testament and a theological need to mirror God's perceived ordering of society. It is important to remember that cultural attitudes significantly affected the choices Hutterite women were able to make and to a large extent prefigured the shapes of their lives, but there is no point "judging" the past by late-twentieth-century ideals of equality. Real historical understanding means looking beyond the Hutterian ideal of women's role to ask questions about what defined and gave meaning to the lives of Hutterite women. We have no access yet to their thoughts, but by reconstructing women's activities within Hutterite society as far as the source will allow, we can begin to see how their productive and reproductive work, their faith, and their sheer strength in the face of persecution shaped the history of the women of the Radical Reformation.

Women appear in the *Chronicle* in seven distinct designations: as workers; as missionaries; as martyrs to the faith; as wives; as widows; as sexual temptresses; and as survivors of rape.

Women as Workers

Within the Hutterite church community, particularly during times of stability and growth, social and economic organization was highly structured and roles for both women and men were well-defined. The concern for order, which was obvious in the spiritual outlook of the Hutterites, was also evident in the hierarchical nature of leadership within the community. Women were not eligible for positions of spiritual or economic leadership, nor did they have a voice in filling those roles, as women were not allowed to vote or speak at community meetings.

The work roles of both Hutterite men and women provided the substantive daily reality in which faith, family, and community relationships were practised. The belief that communal life best realized discipleship in the temporal world had practical implications for Hutterite work patterns, which were highly ordered. Within the *bruderhof*, members were divided into work departments according to their skills, under the direction of "work distributors." The Hutterites were known for their abilities in many trades and indeed, many of the men named in the *Chronicle* are identified by trade. They included carpenters, millers, cobblers, bakers, masons, clockmakers, barber-surgeons, weavers, vinedressers, and coppersmiths.

The references to women's work, by contrast, are noticeably sparse. The labour of women within the community was presumably of a domestic nature and likely performed according to a structured regimen similar to that of the men. In 1572 one member wrote to "dear sisters in the spinning room at Klein Niemtschitz in Moravia."[6] Similarly, letters carry greetings to "your

Lora, with her faithful daughters in the weaving room. . . . All my love to those in the kitchen, Margret with her dear sisters," and "Maria, and the others in the sewing room."[7] In a 1663 listing of men and women killed by Turkish and Tartar invaders, specific women are referred to by their occupation. Included are: "Marie, the school seamstress; Marie, the cook; Katharina, the children's nurse; Katharina, the weaver; Katharina, the herdsmaid."[8] Later, the chronicler recorded the death of "Katharina the sister in charge of the women's bath house," who died near the camp in Branc.[9] Other brief references mention sisters working in the laundry, sisters making baskets,[10] and a 1605 incident mentions "strong young sisters" working at the harvest.[11] While it is unclear from the *Chronicle* what women's agricultural labour actually entailed, it is obvious that a rigid gendered division of labour existed. According to a sixteenth-century observer:

> Nowhere did I see men and women together but everywhere each sex was performing its own work apart from the others. I found rooms in which there were only nursing mothers, who, [were] without the supervision of men. . . . The duty of caring for the nursing mothers and children was committed to the nursing mothers alone. Elsewhere I saw over a hundred women with distaffs. One was a washerwoman, another a bed-maker, a third a stable-maid, a fourth a dish-washer, a fifth a linen maid, and so all the others had a particular work to do. And just as the duties were systematically assigned to the women, so each one of the men. . . .[12]

Like the men, women on occasion worked outside the community as housekeepers and wet-nurses on nearby estates. In 1607 Christoph Andreas Fischer criticized the tendency of noblewomen to prefer Hutterite women-servants:

> The children will get nothing but poison and contempt for the Christian faith. Already the children of these nobles have Anabaptist stomachs, for they have sucked these things from their nurses and have grown up under their influence.[13]

Other sources indicate that Hutterite women were known for their midwifery and other health care skills; the *Chronicle*, however, makes scant reference to this aspect of their work.[14]

Hutterite women also performed roles as teachers of young children. Within Hutterite communities, small children were removed from the direct care of their parents at about age two when they were given into the care of the "little school," supervised by a schoolmother and her female assistants.

At age five or six children would move into the "big school," where they came under the tutelage of the male schoolmaster who also received assistance from sisters.[15] The role that women of the community held in the care, education, and discipline of young children was obviously an important one. Women would have been expected to be well-versed in the Bible and principles of church order to enable them to pass the traditions and beliefs on to children. A description of one *bruderhof* says: "Their children were brought up communally, entrusted to God-fearing sisters, who conscientiously took care of them and led them to the Lord through Christian discipline."[16] Hutterian leader Peter Riedemann stated that women appointed as caregivers were recognized to be "competent and diligent" and were charged to "lay the word of God's testimony in [the children's] mouths and teach them to speak with or from the same, tell them of prayer and such things as children can understand."[17] Yet it was the male schoolmaster who bore the ultimate responsibility and carried the primary authority over the children of all ages. According to Hutterian leader Peter Walpot's 1568 address on school discipline, the sisters were only to act under the schoolmaster's supervision since "women are women and the weaker vessel" and might not be able to maintain proper discipline among the children.[18]

The overall lack of attention given in the *Chronicle* to the duties of women in the operation of the community suggests that their domestic labour was taken for granted more and held in less esteem than the oft-mentioned crafts and trades performed by the men. At least this seems true in the creation of a public historical record like the *Chronicle*. At any rate, it is evident that within the communal focus and collective performance of their work, Hutterites adhered to a traditional gender division of trades and agricultural labour, as well as nurturing roles.

Missionaries
If the roles of women and men were well-defined within the *bruderhof*, it may be that outside the community there was more latitude in overcoming the limitations of gender. An important role within the Hutterian community, particularly during the "golden age" of the late sixteenth century, was that of missionary. Although there is no specific mention in the *Chronicle* of women being appointed as missionaries, in instances where women were arrested and imprisoned for their religious beliefs, it is likely that capture occurred while they were away from the community on such missionary journeys.

For instance, in 1539 Leonhard Lanzenstiel was appointed as a "servant of the gospel" and sent as a missionary to the Tirol. The account of his return concludes with the following: "But Leonhard's wife, Apollonia, was arrested and taken to Brixen. Because she held steadfastly to faith in Christ and refused to recant, she was drowned."[19] The fact that the town of

Brixen is in southern Tirol suggests that Apollonia had in fact accompanied her husband on his missionary journey and had quite likely been giving public testimony to her faith as well. The couple may have separated to carry out their mission since it is unusual that she was captured and martyred while Leonhard was able to return home.

Further substantiating the speculation that women also acted as missionaries is the criticism directed against the Hutterites that their servants (preachers) "took [the sisters] on journeys around the country." In reply, "The servants answered that they did this only so that the people they met would rejoice with the church in the grace of God."[20] It would seem that the presence of women was an advantage in the missionary effort.

Missionary work, even if not officially sanctioned, may have given women the opportunity to escape from the narrow range of activities that was theirs within the *bruderhof*. By giving testimony of their faith and bringing people to the church in the unofficial capacity of travelling believers, they could in a sense assume the roles of preacher and teacher that were forbidden to them within their own community.

Martyrs

Apollonia Lanzenstiel was not the only Hutterite woman to be martyred for her faith. As a heretical sect, the Hutterites were frequently subject to arrest, torture, and execution for holding Anabaptist beliefs. Martyrdom could be the fate of either men or women, although the *Chronicle* provides more detailed accounts of male martyrs than women. Women who were imprisoned and suffering torture or impending death are described as possessing "manly" courage, as if such an attribute were uncharacteristic of the female sex. The *Chronicle* describes the drowning of Anna Maler and Ursula Ochsentreiber in 1529 as follows: "They armed their womanly hearts with such manly courage in God that everyone was astonished at their steadfastness."[21] The following is the story of Christine Brünner of Bregenz:

> [She] had prepared to travel to the community where her daughter was. She was about to leave her house when the constable and the executioner's assistant arrested her unexpectedly. They took her to Egg, a village about two miles from the town of Bregenz. There she was severely racked six times to make her abandon her good resolve and betray those who had sheltered the brothers and shown them kindness. This she refused to do. She armed her woman's heart with manful determination and held faithfully and firmly to the truth God had shown her, even though she had not been baptized by water and had never seen the church community of the Lord with her own eyes.[22]

And in 1558, following the capture and imprisonment of twelve men and women, the *Chronicle* says: "Even the sisters were cheerful and sang, which terrified other people."[23] Through faith and martyrdom, these women transcended the limitations of their temporal and inferior feminine nature as understood by their communities, and became equal with men in heaven.

That women were not martyred only as appendages of their husbands is evident in the fact that few instances are recounted in which a husband and wife are arrested and executed together. In 1529 the *Chronicle* relates the story of four men and four women arrested together, although none seemed to be married to one another. In this case, the four women are named: "Christine Töllinger from Penon (a widow), Barbara from Tiers, Agatha Kampner from Breitenberg, and her sister Elizabeth."[24] In this account, the testimonies of all eight are provided and show little difference in their command of scripture and Anabaptist principle. The testimonies of the four women are, in fact, quite detailed in describing their convictions about infant baptism, the observance of mass and feast days of the church, and the role of the priesthood. All of the prisoners were eventually executed. It is clear that in most cases of capture and imprisonment, women were acting on their own and not through their husbands. To be martyred, while a tragic fate indeed, provided a woman with the chance to behave and express herself in ways not normally permitted or recognized within her community.

Wives

Like other Protestants, the Hutterites rejected clerical celibacy and raised marriage to a position of sacred importance as part of God's will.[25] They stressed the necessity of companionability in marriage, but more important than romantic or sexual companionability was that of religious or spiritual partnership. Marriage was considered to be a union of man and woman ordained by God, through the intercession of the elders, and not a romantic relationship entered into by human choice. According to one historian of the Hutterites, emotional attachment in marriage was in fact discouraged, and romance and courtship before marriage was considered to be "the product of an individualistic and secular civilization."[26] As a result, Hutterites adopted the unique marital custom whereby the elders of the community chose spouses for young people who were prepared to get married. Two Hutterite men, in seeking to establish a community near the city of Elbing in Prussia in 1604, described the ritual to the city council as follows:

> If a bachelor or widower among them wished to marry, he could not just pick whom he wanted but must turn to the elders. They would go to the sisters and ask among the widows and unmarried women if any wished to get married. They did not mention names

or put pressure on the sisters, who they felt should rather remain unmarried. If a sister responded and was suggested to the brother and if he accepted her gladly, the two would be married; but there was no compulsion. There was no courting among them; but if this should ever happen, the elders would decide, according to the situation, whether the two involved might be married.[27]

If this was the normal pattern for matching, it would seem that the man had the upper hand of choice, first in approaching the elders when he was ready for marriage, and second, in accepting or rejecting the woman suggested to him. The woman, for her part, took little initiative in the process. The marriage ceremony took place almost immediately following the matching ritual in order that no opportunity be given for romantic courtship.[28] The ceremony itself was also a religious service, rather than a wedding celebration. This is illustrated in a *Chronicle* entry of 1581.

> We had to leave Wostitz, where we had lived for eleven years, because Count Franz von Thurn at Purschitz ordered us off his estates. It all started because our brothers and sisters at Wostitz, who owed him service as his tenants, refused to help at a wedding banquet he gave, to which many noblemen were invited. The housekeeper, who was one of our sisters, refused to go and prepare the hens and geese or have anything to do with it. We have to refuse such service because it goes against our faith. It would burden our consciences to assist at weddings and banquets where there is no thought of God, only indulgence in lusts of the flesh, luxurious living, ostentation, and excessive eating and drinking. What God has created is abused. . . . Not that we despise marriage but we cannot tolerate the sinful conduct that accompanies these occasions.[29]

As might be expected, the practice of arranged marriage was not without its problems. Frequently cited is the 1578 account of a non-Anabaptist who visited his Hutterite sister at her home community. Describing the process of matching spouses, he reports: "My sister Sara was not eager to take her husband, but could say nothing against it . . . they are not coerced, but they may not do anything against the leaders."[30] There seemed to be little recourse for the young woman who did not favour the partner chosen for her. Historian Robert Friedmann observes that strict marital matching began to decline in the seventeenth century as the disciplines of the common life began to deteriorate and as young people asked to be told beforehand with whom they would be matched.[31]

Hutterite marriages (whether arranged or not) were not necessarily unhappy or unloving unions, however. In 1536 Hieronymus Kräls wrote to his wife from prison:

> My own dear wife, my most beloved Traindel . . . I am sending you a Christian song. . . I am sending it out of heartfelt love . . . I thank God for you; I thank my heavenly Father who in His grace gave you to me and united us through His faithful servants. . . . Greet all the saints for me, and where I have wronged you, forgive me, for Christ's sake.[32]

Similarly, in 1538 Hans Wucherer wrote with affection to his "dearly beloved wife," calling her to be faithful after he is put to death. In his counsel to her, he invokes the typical virtues of the pious Christian woman: "Serve [God] day and night in holiness and righteousness, in gentleness and humility, in kindness and patience, in love, faith, self-control, and wisdom. . . . Be quiet and chaste, leading a godly life in Christ, as befits a devout widow. . . ."[33] There is no encouragement in Wucherer's letter to this woman to remarry, quite the contrary, and, judging from the numerous references in the *Chronicle* to "widows and orphans," it would seem that there were many women of this status within the Hutterite communities. The references further suggest that widows were by and large dependent on the community for support and protection.

While the institution of marriage itself was not denigrated in Hutterian writings, the union between a woman and a man was clearly secondary to the divine union of an individual believer with God: "the bond with God counts a thousand times more than the bond of marriage and our promise to God must be kept above all else."[34]

Vorsteher Peter Riedemann in fact defined marriage between woman and man as the "last and lowest" of the three grades of marriage, the first being that of God with the soul or spirit and the second that of the spirit with the body.[35] The understanding that religious allegiance took precedence over a marriage commitment led the Hutterites to accept separation between believers and unbelievers. Should one partner in a marriage choose to join the church community while the other did not, the believing individual was allowed to leave the unbelieving spouse. This principle, explicated at length in a 1547 statement on the five articles of faith, caused significant controversy between the Hutterites and the world.[36] Preferable to separation, however, was "willing consent" on the part of the unbelieving partner to live with his or her spouse without being a hindrance to the new faith or to the upbringing of their children in the way of God. Such unions were allowed

> provided that the unbelieving husband is content to have his believing wife . . . live with him according to her faith–that he

allows her to listen to the Word of God, to remain among the faithful, to reject the world and whatever is against her conscience, to teach her children the way of God and not the way of the world . . . , and whatever else her faith requires. If, then, the unbelieving husband is happy with this and does not mislead or oppose his wife, she should remain with him.[37]

In such a situation a suitable place would be found for wife and husband in the "neighbourhood of the church community." As well, a wife was not expected to follow her expelled husband and leave the *bruderhof*.

Some historians have suggested that the practice of separation was empowering for women in that it gave them under certain circumstances divine sanction to exit an unsatisfactory marriage.[38] Certainly in theory the practice seems to have been equally applicable to women and men. If understood quite literally, it could also be interpreted as subverting the hierarchy that existed in the family. A 1545 outline of Hutterian articles of faith declares that "whether husband or wife, the believer is the head," and further, "if a believing wife is pressed by her unbelieving husband to do anything against her conscience, she owes obedience to God rather than to her husband. . . ."[39] In cases where both partners were believers, the biblical decrees concerning wifely obedience and submission as described in Riedemann's *Confession of Faith* (cited earlier) may have overridden a woman's autonomy. If a woman gained autonomy in the rare situation where she chose to leave an unbelieving spouse, by far the larger part of her marital relationship was shaped by expectations of obedience and submission. At the same time, one aspect of marital separation that may have undermined a woman's position was the fact that a believer was not permitted to remarry after separating from an unbelieving spouse. This would likely have created problems for women who were left with no particular marital status–neither married, widowed, nor single.[40]

It is extremely difficult to know with any certainty how often marital separation occurred over questions of religious belief. The expectation, based on a literal reading of scripture, that wives were to submit to and obey their husbands suggests that wives were more likely pressured to follow their husbands into communal life than vice versa. Men may in fact have resisted joining the Hutterites if it meant following a woman's initiative, quite possibly a sign of weakness. When it came to making a major life decision such as joining the Hutterites, there may have been much potential for discord, as is suggested in the following example. In 1533 Georg Fasser gave up his possessions to the church and "as head of the family, ordered his wife and children to submit willingly to the Lord and his people by doing the same." His unnamed wife, however, had kept hidden some money which "belonged to her and the children," an action for which she was admonished and disciplined by the community.[41] This incident raises an important question regarding the freedom that women had in joining the Hutterite community as well as the difficulties they might have faced if left without the economic supports provided by a family unit.

It was the duty of a husband to guide his wife's spirituality. The following anecdote reveals that sixteenth-century men were not above testing the effectiveness of their guidance.

> When Hans Král returned home to the community, he did not make himself known, but went into the house where beggars were received and asked for alms. His own wife was in the kitchen. She put some soup in front of him, but she did not give him a spoon, (expecting him to have his own). When he asked for a spoon his wife said to him 'Do I have to give my spoon to every fool?' . . . It is said that his wife was disciplined for the way she spoke to him: even if she did not recognise her husband, it was wrong to call anybody a fool, even an unbeliever.[42]

Clearly Král took his position as spiritual head within the family seriously, postponing a greeting to his wife after a long absence in order to test the *bruderhof*'s attitude toward beggars. Král practised the Hutterian doctrine that community claimed primary devotion after God, the family of procreation only secondary devotion.

Within marriage, motherhood, much more than fatherhood, was emphasized by the chroniclers of the Hutterites, in part as an element of the suffering that was ordained as the lot of the brethren. For example, with reference to a raid by Turks, Tartars, or Hungarians in 1605, the *Chronicle* records: "Most terrible of all was the way they ruthlessly carried off innocent little babies, thrown on the horses' backs with feet bound together and heads hanging down. Many mothers had to witness that."[43] Many fathers did as well, but Hutterite men were not characterized by a "fatherhood" identity; it did not grant them a new spectrum of suffering, at least openly, as it did women. If the role of women expanded and improved in status within the family as a result of Reformation theology, as some scholars have argued,[44] the role of motherhood increasingly became the main definition of women's identity and circumscribed alternate roles.

Widows

For women who lost their husbands through death, the communal nature of Hutterite society provided a certain guarantee against loss of shelter or sustenance. At the same time, the portrayal of widows–of which there seem to have been many–in the *Chronicle* emphasizes their weakness and dependency on the community. Widows were identified as among the non-productive members of the community in a 1596 letter.

> It happens that out of ten people in the community, scarcely one is able to earn anything, however little. This is true especially of those who have come recently and are not used to this country. . . . We also have many weak and needy people, to say nothing of the old, the many helpless little children, the widows and the orphans. The healthy brothers and sisters have to care for these and do the daily chores as well, without earning a penny.[45]

Obviously the fact that widows remained fully supported within the *bruderhof* was a positive one. Yet, on a second level of interpretation, the tone or phrasing of Hutterite statements about widows raises questions regarding the value placed upon women's work in general. It is obvious from the *Chronicle* that many of those widowed were young and healthy. Their children were placed in the care of the nursery and the school. Why, then, are references made to the "many widows . . . who cannot earn their own bread?"[46] Such a reference seems odd, given the multiplicity of women's work roles, both in actual production and in community service. The phrasing does emphasize the perception that women without husbands were economically dependant and does not, in fact, mirror the reality of widows' economic participation. Perhaps because Hutterites perceived women's work as an adjunct to primary male production, a widow's economic role was further devalued because she lacked a producing partner. Neither speculation can be resolved with the given source. But certainly, within the context of European agricultural society, a Hutterite widow had greater assurance of physical support than many women on the "outside."

Sexual Temptresses
The story of Jörg Liebich's imprisonment for the faith reveals that Hutterites, despite their theoretical elevation of marriage as spiritually desirable, did not escape an association of the feminine with the carnal, evident in the thought of the ancient Greeks and central to medieval Roman Catholicism.[47] A direct association of women with (carnal) evil is clear in the chronicler's description of Liebich's spiritual trials in prison.

> This dear brother had to endure a great deal from the devil, who tempted him in visible form, particularly during the first year. He came to him in the guise of a young woman who tried to embrace him. When Jörg knelt and prayed, the devil in woman's form lay down on his bed, and he had a very hard time to drive him away or roll him off.[48]

Jörg's psychological torment, (as this scene is interpreted by the modern reader as opposed to the chronicler who clearly believed in the physical presence of the devil) was acutely associated with images of women's sexuality: it was an entity to be feared as threatening to male spirituality. A real woman also tempted Liebich in the Vellenburg Castle prison.

> Over and above this, to fill up the measure of his temptations and omit nothing, the ungodly brood of Satan put a sister next to Liebich in the prison, chained her to his feet, and left them together for a long time. She too was imprisoned for her faith, a beautiful young woman named Ursula Hellrigel. It is easy to imagine what the devil and his brood would have liked to see, but the two feared God and did not give way to temptation.[49]

Perhaps a more positive view of women's sexuality is evident in the latter passage. Despite the heavy emphasis upon Jörg's perspective (she, not he, appears as the dominant agent of sexual temptation and was seen as such by the prison keepers and by the chronicler), Ursula too, it appears, was tempted: her sexuality is acknowledged and her self-control is made explicit. The chronicler implicitly reveals the contrast between pre-modern attitudes to women as biologically sexual beings, albeit strongly associated with danger, evil, and theological fear, and those of the modern period, which emphasized women's passivity and asexuality.

Survivors of Rape

A striking portrayal of women in the *Chronicle* is as survivors of rape. By the mid-seventeenth century, as Hutterian communities were increasingly subject to persecution and attack, especially from Turkish forces, women frequently became subject to rape. Repeated references occur to soldiers who "turned on the sisters and neither respected nor spared their womanhood," who "violated several sisters," or who "horribly mistreated some sisters, even one who had given birth only two hours before."[50] Explicit use of the term rape is made in many cases. The community at Stiegnitz was plundered and "a sister in the advanced stages of pregnancy was raped."[51] At Pribitz "four sisters were raped by the enemy."[52] "At Damborschitz they stripped many brothers and raped ten sisters. After completely stripping a young seamstress, they raped her until she lay as though dead."[53] The "greatest heartache" in attacks on seventeen communities in 1619 "was that forty men and women were cruelly murdered and that many God-fearing sisters, both married and unmarried, were raped."[54] A 1620 entry recorded that "more than one sister has been raped by many soldiers. They would gag a sister, and one after the other would wreak their lust on her."[55] The chronicler saw this as sufficient reason to withhold the ransom demanded in exchange for Hutterite prisoners, because paying it would mean "rewarding those who had so horribly mistreated our people."

In 1605 the Hutterite community at Pribitz had agreed to pay the ransoms demanded by "Turks or Hungarians" for their imprisoned sisters: "they might value one sister at a hundred talers, another at two hundred, another at as much as two hundred ducats, according to how young or good-looking they were." These women were among twenty-three "strong, young sisters" who travelled to Tscheikowitz for the harvest. "The enemy surprised the sisters from Pruschanek who were harvesting in the Tscheikowitz fields. They ruthlessly carried off almost all of them, and several were cruelly mistreated."[56] In Landshut,

> three sisters were raped. One of them had a baby at her breast, and she lifted her hands in desperate entreaty to spare her baby, but nothing deterred them; they tore the baby from her breast, flung it aside and violated her.[57]

"A sister's terror" is sympathetically chronicled in 1621:

> A dreadful thing happened. A sister from Tscheikowitz who had been in the hands of the Walloons there had fled and was in the mill at Ungarisch Ostra, when she heard that the imperial army was advancing. . . . Overwhelmed with fear and despair, she cast her little baby into the March River. She was on the point of leaping in herself to escape from falling again into the hands of these sodomites, but she was held back and admonished for her lack of faith.[58]

Discussing the beginnings of the Thirty Years' War, the *Chronicle* noted in 1622:

> It is impossible to record all the inhuman savagery vented on us and other people during this ungodly, cursed war raged by Spaniards, Walloons, Poles, and the German imperial troops, and how many honourable and faithful older sisters, expectant mothers, mothers of newborn babies, desperately ill sisters, unmarried sisters and little girls eight and nine years old, even young boys (which is completely contrary to nature) were shamelessly raped in public.[59]

Indeed, "many God-fearing people wished they might die rather than see the great misery of our poor little flocks or hear the shameful violation of our women and girls."[60]

It is this community response to rape that marks its treatment in the *Chronicle*. Although the graphic evidence of rape (the chronicler even recording that people could hear it happening) is in itself valuable as an aspect of the universal history of women, the Hutterite context contained an arguably unique characteristic. The *Chronicle* indicates that survivors of rape were accepted into Hutterite society and resumed their community roles after the attacks.

> Two sisters who had been taken captive by the Turks returned to the church. They were Traudel Ochsenfuhrmann, a married sister, and Sarah Nähter, a single sister. . . . They had been in captivity at Ofen (Buda) for two and a half years, during which they endured brutal treatment and abuse against their will. They came back to the church with unharmed consciences. Praise and thanks be to God Almighty in all eternity for freeing them from this Mohammedan bondage and keeping them firm in faith.[61]

Similarly:

> Sister Susanna, to her great distress and agony of heart had to stay even longer among the ungodly soldiers, who wreaked their lust on her. Finally God sent help, and she was released. . . . and on November 5 she returned to the church community. So, in the end all the captured sisters returned to the church. . . . With tremendous joy and thankfulness we received all those who had been released.[62]

In contrast, Susan Karant-Nunn indicates that Lutheran women and girls in Zwickau were treated brutally after surviving rape, and were shunned by or formally excluded from their communities. She cites the example of a nine-year-old girl who was raped and then put outside the city walls with enough wool for a skirt and half a florin "lest [she] have a corrupting effect" upon the godly society.[63]

It is possible to suggest that the Hutterites, particularly because of their doctrine of non-resistance, viewed rape as analogous to martyrdom and torture: it was a gender-specific means of suffering for the faith. In this view the Hutterites appear to be compassionate and inclusive toward women in their recognition of the particular risks borne by non-conformist women within a hostile European society. Furthermore, to the extent that sixteenth-century rape law was constructed around the protection of male property–that is, the protection of wives and daughters, but also the protection of lines of inheritance–it is possible that rape held different meaning for a society that eschewed private property altogether.[64]

The expectation that a communal social order based on submission to God might have an equalizing effect on gender does not seem to be borne out in the sixteenth and seventeenth century Hutterian communities. The sharing of material property was in fact accompanied by a structured hierarchy of status within the social order as well as stratification based on sex. Within the community women and men were differentiated by their access to religious authority, by their separation in economic roles, and by the relative valuation of their productive contribution to the life of the *bruderhof*. As workers, Hutterite women followed the traditional gendered division of labour of pre-industrial society, with the qualification that they produced for the whole community, not within the family for family survival. Women's work was crucial to communal social survival, and to argue, as did Riedemann, that women played a supportive or secondary economic role, understates and undervalues the nature of their participation. While the marriage customs of the Hutterites limited the freedom of both partners to a certain extent, for a woman whose personal status was more closely tied to her marital status, both the matching of spouses and the separation of spouses created unique problems. Widows within Hutterite society did have the benefit of material support, but it appears that their status within the community may have declined through the loss of a husband and their work was completely undervalued. Although images of women's sexuality in the *Chronicle* played upon common early modern associations, the treatment of survivors of rape stands out as unique. Raped women were received back into the community with rejoicing, thus raising questions about the relationship between doctrines of nonresistance and private property to the perceptions of violent crimes against women. It was in fact outside of the social, religious, and economic order of the community itself that Hutterite women may have found the greatest autonomy and freedom of activity. As travelling missionaries, women were released to speak in a manner unacceptable within their own community and in common purpose with male believers. When they allowed themselves to be martyred for their faith, they rose to a level of significance that was otherwise unattainable. To the extent that courage and perseverance were traits unexpected in a female, women martyrs may have in fact surpassed the honour given to men. Thus, Hutterian women and men became peers in the faith only at the point at which women were removed from the community structure and thus from the authority of their male peers.

Notes

1 *The Chronicle of the Hutterian Brethren*, vol. 1 (Rifton, NY: Plough Publishing House, 1987), 651-52. Hereafter referred to simply as the *Chronicle*.

2 Two standard works on Hutterian history are John A. Hostetler, *Hutterite Society* (Baltimore: Johns Hopkins University Press, 1974) and Leonard Gross, *The Golden Years of the Hutterites: The Witness and Thought of the Communal Moravian Anabaptists during the Walpot Era, 1565-1578* (Scottdale, PA: Herald Press, 1980). The Hostetler book is also a sociological study of contemporary Hutterite society. A history

that is confessional in its approach is John Horsch, *The Hutterian Brethren, 1528-1931: A Story of Martyrdom and Loyalty* (Cayley, AB: Macmillan Colony, 1985). Historical studies of Hutterite women are almost non-existent. One recent essay is Wes Harrison, "The Role of Women in Anabaptist Thought and Practice: The Hutterite Experience of the Sixteenth and Seventeenth Centuries," *Sixteenth Century Journal* 23, 1 (1992): 49-69.

3 Margaret Conrad, "Sundays Always Make Me Think of Home: Time and Place in Women's History," in Veronica Strong-Boag and Anita Clair Fellman, eds., *Rethinking Canada: The Promise of Women's History* (Toronto: Copp Clark Pittman, 1986), 69.

4 Peter Riedemann, *Account of Our Religion, Doctrine and Faith* (Rifton, NY: Plough Publishing House, 1970), 98. Originally published 1545.

5 M. Lucille Marr, "Anabaptist Women of the North: Peers in the Faith, Subordinates in Marriage," MQR, 61 (October 1987): 347-62.

6 *Chronicle*, 461.

7 *Chronicle*, 371.

8 *Chronicle*, 781.

9 *Chronicle*, 784.

10 *Chronicle*, 537, 544.

11 *Chronicle*, 583-84.

12 The observations of a Roman Catholic traveller among the Hutterites in the mid-seventeenth century, published in novel form: *Der Abenteuerliche Simplicissimus*, by Hans Jakob Christoph Grimmelschausen, cited in Horsch, 67.

13 Cited in Hostetler, *Hutterite Society*, 56.

14 Historian Mary Ault Harada notes that Hutterite midwives were utilized by many non-Hutterites. See "Family Values and Child Care During the Reformation Era: A Comparative Study of Hutterites and Some Other German Protestants" (PhD thesis, Boston University, 1968), 129.

15 *Chronicle*, 405, 562. Also Riedemann, 130-31.

16 *Chronicle*, 155.

17 Riedemann, 130.

18 "The Address Which Peter Walpot, Together with Other [Elders] Delivered to the Schoolmasters at Nemschitz, November 15, 1568," in John Hostetler et al., *Selected Hutterian Documents in Translation* (Philadelphia: Communal Studies Center, 1975), 7.

19 *Chronicle*, 186-87.

20 *Chronicle*, 199.

21 *Chronicle*, 73.

22 *Chronicle*, 631.

23 *Chronicle*, 354.

24 *Chronicle*, 69-73.

25 The history of Hutterite women as mothers and wives generally confirms the historiographical pattern established by Susan Karant-Nunn with reference to the Lutheran women of Zwickau, and that of Miriam Chrisman pertaining to Strasbourg. Each argues that the Reformation placed marriage and, therefore, women within it, upon a morally acceptable and even desirable footing. As such, the dominant pre-Reformation association of women as evil temptresses and as essentially carnal beings was somewhat downplayed in favour of an ideal of partnership within the family. See Karant-Nunn, "Continuity and Change: Some Effects of the Reformation on the Women of Zwickau," in *Sixteenth Century Journal* 12 (1982): 17-42; Miriam Chrisman, "Women and the Reformation in Strasbourg," in *Archive for Reformation History* 63 (1972): 143-67.

26 Robert Friedmann, "Hutterite Marriage Practices," in Harold S. Bender, ed., *Hutterite Studies* (Goshen: Mennonite Historical Society, 1961), 81. Friedmann says that the mixing of the sexes generally was not encouraged and thus women and men even ate separately at community meals.
27 *Chronicle*, 562, footnote.
28 Friedmann, 124.
29 *Chronicle*, 485.
30 "Report of Stephan Gerlach on His Visit to the Hutterites, September 22-23, 1578," cited in Joyce L. Irwin, *Womanhood in Radical Protestantism, 1525-1675* (New York: Edwin Mellen Press, 1979), 130-32.
31 Friedmann, 124.
32 *Chronicle*, 149, footnote. See also, Jörg Wenger.
33 *Chronicle*, 175, footnote.
34 *Chronicle*, 292.
35 Riedemann, 98
36 See *Chronicle*, 286-93. The practice of marital separation incited accusations against the Hutterites that they were "kidnappers and divorcers because at times a believer would join the church and leave his unbelieving partner, if she was unwilling to follow him." *Chronicle*, 244.
37 *Chronicle*, 291.
38 See, for instance, Claus-Peter Clasen, *Anabaptism: A Social History, 1525-1618* (Ithaca: Cornell University Press, 1972); Marion Kobelt-Groch, "Why Did Petronella Leave Her Husband? Reflections on Marital Avoidance Among the Halberstadt Anabaptists," MQR, 62 (January 1988): 26-41.
39 *Chronicle*, 236.
40 Merry E. Wiesner demonstrates the centrality of marital status to a woman's life in the sixteenth century in her essay, "Nuns, Wives, and Mothers: Women and the Reformation in Germany" in Sherrin Marshall, ed., *Women in Reformation and Counter-Reformation Europe: Public and Private Worlds* (Bloomington, IN: Indiana University Press, 1989), 8-28.
41 *Chronicle*, 110.
42 *Chronicle*, 493.
43 *Chronicle*, 582.
44 R.W. Scribner, *The German Reformation* (Atlantic Highlands, NJ: Humanities Press International, 1986), 59; Steven Ozment, *When Fathers Ruled: Family Life in Reformation Europe* (Cambridge, MA: Harvard University Press, 1983), 99; Julia O'Faolain and Laura Martines, eds., *Not in God's Image* (New York: Harper Colophon Books, 1973), 194.
45 *Chronicle*, 532.
46 *Chronicle*, 568.
47 See Natalie Zemon Davis, *Society and Culture in Early Modern France* (Stanford, CT: Stanford University Press, 1975), 88-89, regarding Greek attitudes toward women's "hysteric animal (the womb)," which meant she could rarely restrain herself from cuckolding her husband.
48 *Chronicle*, 231.
49 *Chronicle*, 232.
50 *Chronicle*, 94, 667, 576.
51 *Chronicle*, 636.
52 *Chronicle*, 638.
53 *Chronicle*, 663.

54 *Chronicle*, 641.
55 *Chronicle*, 652.
56 *Chronicle*, 584.
57 *Chronicle*, 637.
58 *Chronicle*, 657.
59 *Chronicle*, 667-68.
60 *Chronicle*, 642.
61 *Chronicle*, 710.
62 *Chronicle*, 652.
63 Karant-Nunn, "Continuity and Change," 32.
64 See London Feminist History Group, *The Sexual Dynamics of History* (London: Pluto Press, 1983), 41.

WOMEN IN THE HUTTERITE SONG BOOK
(*DIE LIEDER DER HUTTERISCHEN BRÜDER*)[1]

The Role of Song in the Hutterite Tradition
Singing has been an integral part of the life of all Hutterites throughout their entire history. This has been so in part because they live in isolation from the rest of the world and have shunned almost all recreational activities, and in part because they take seriously the biblical injunction to "make melody" to the Lord.[2] The old *Chronicle* lists those activities that traditionally have not been allowed:

> There was no playing [*Spielen*], no dancing and card playing, no carousing nor drinking. There was no singing of shameful songs of which the world is full, but Christian and spiritual songs and songs of the Bible.[3]

The importance of singing in the lives of the Hutterites, and the significance they still attach to this activity cannot be overestimated.[4] In addition to providing enjoyment and a means of self-expression, many of the songs provide the drama that the Hutterites do not enjoy in the theatre: the drama of the many spellbinding stories in the Bible, or the songs about their own martyrs and courageous missionaries. Every Hutterite knows these songs and can sing a great many from memory.

Besides being an important means of recreation, singing was and remains an important part of Hutterite worship services. This may be attributed in large part to the fact that the important Hutterite theologian, Peter Riedemann (d. 1556), based his theological view of music on the writings of Balthasar Hubmaier rather than on those of Conrad Grebel. Grebel, an erstwhile disciple of Zwingli, echoed his former master's sentiments regarding the use of music in worship, probably the Latin chant, when he wrote:

> The worship service in general must be simple in all its details, and liturgical singing should be omitted in order that the spirit of the worshipper may be concentrated in true devotion upon the Word of God.[5]

Grebel's letter to Thomas Müntzer (1524), in which he chides him for writing a German mass, illustrates the former's hermeneutics. In contrast to Luther's dictum, "If it is not clearly forbidden in Scripture, you may do it," Grebel's was, "If it is not expressly commanded in Scripture, you may not do it."

> Whatever we are not taught by clear passages or examples must be regarded as forbidden, just as if it were written "This do not; sing

not". . . . We must not follow our notions, we must add nothing to the Word and take nothing from it.

Nowhere, he reiterated, can any teaching about singing in church be found in the New Testament. From the letters of Paul to the Ephesians and Colossians, Grebel concluded that the apostle forbade singing, but encouraged Christians to sing only in their hearts, that it is the word of God that "profits" believers, not the song.[6]

Balthasar Hubmaier (d. 1528), on the other hand, expressed satisfaction that singing was being retained in worship services, but he regarded as inefficacious music which was not sung with the proper spiritual attitude or in a tongue unfamilar to singers and/or congregation:

> With singing and reading in the churches I am well contented (but not as they have hitherto been conducted) when it is with the Spirit and from the heart, and with the understanding of the words and edification of the Church as Paul teaches us. But otherwise God rejects it and will have none of our Baal cries.[7]

Nowhere in Anabaptist or Hutterite theology is music given the divine dimensions that Luther accorded it. Instead, the great Hutterite bishop Peter Riedemann, like St. Augustine, saw danger in enjoying the music for itself:

> To sing spiritual songs is good and pleasing to God if we sing in the right way, that is, attentively, in fear of God, and as inspired by the Spirit of Christ. . . . Where this is not the case, and one sings for carnal pleasure (aus Fleisches Lust) for the sweet sound or for some such reason, he that does so sins greatly against God, for he uses his Word, which was given for his salvation . . . as leading to the lust of the flesh and to sing. . . . It is a worldly song, for it is not sung in the Spirit. He, however, who sings in the Spirit considers diligently every word . . . why it has been used and how it may serve to his betterment.[8]

These words regarding singing are still the final authority for the Hutterites.

When the Hutterites adopted their present opposition to musical instruments is not entirely clear. The song text of an early Anabaptist hymn in *Die Lieder der Hutterischen Brüder* suggests that the earliest Anabaptists considered the playing of instruments an appropriate means of praising God.[9] Although Conrad Grebel opposed all music in church, neither Hubmaier nor Riedemann expressly voiced opposition to the use of musical instruments. But already before the middle of the sixteenth century, Hutterites were so opposed. Wolfgang (Wolf) Sailer, the most prolific

Hutterite songwriter, unequivocally opposed the use of instruments in one of his hymns.[10] In another Hutterite song, Paul Glock expressed the belief that instruments, like rich, beautiful clothes and other ornaments, separate people from God.[11] However, the Hutterites probably shunned musical instruments simply because their use was not taught by precept or example in the New Testament. The numerous examples of the use of instruments, even commands to use them to praise God which are found in the Old Testament, have not been translated into precepts by Hutterites.[12]

Today, as in former centuries, formal worship is observed in the Hutterite colonies not only twice on Sundays but also every evening before supper for approximately half an hour; the hymns are central.[13] The order of worship is very simple: three or four verses of a hymn, a sermon, prayer, and two additional verses of the same or another hymn.[14] At no time in their history has this worship service had anything added to or subtracted from it. As the singing in the colonies is not accompanied and there is no director, one person starts singing and then the others join in. It is not uncommon for a woman to begin songs. Almost the whole period from the Saturday evening worship service to the Sunday evening worship service, except for the time spent in resting and eating, is spent in formal and informal worship. After the half-hour service on Saturday evening, the Hutterites sing hymns informally, have religious discussions and retell the stories of Hutterite history. The Sunday morning service, comprising unaccompanied singing of the old Anabaptist/Hutterite songs and a strictly biblical sermon, is approximately one-and-one-half hours in length; the Sunday evening service approximately three-quarters of an hour. In addition, the unbaptized members of the community attend Sunday school in the afternoon. Part of this time is spent in reciting the hymns that the young people had memorized during the week.

Singing also is a most important part of the annual Hutterite fall wedding festivities. This celebration is not limited to the one day, but may include up to four evenings prior to that day. On these evenings singing is the main activity, lasting from three to four hours (the other activities include eating, drinking, and conversation). The repertoire of "wedding songs" comprises gospel songs and hymns, many of which are not in any of the three song books, but hand copied or sung from memory. On Sunday morning the couple exchange vows during part of the time regularly allotted to the morning worship service. This is followed by a wedding meal and singing. Then after a period of rest and/or socialization, the evening meal is taken and the final wedding song sung.

Hymns also have played, and continue to play, a central role in the education of children; Hutterites regard the inculcation of faith and values as one of the primary functions of music.[15] Many of their songs contain teachings peculiar to the Hutterites: the teaching of concepts, for instance, such as *Gelassenheit* and community of goods.[16] Since obedience (to the Scriptures and Hutterite authority) is considered a moral virtue of greatest importance in the Hutterite communities, it is not surprising that they are fond of one particular song that deals with this subject. Hutterites refer to this song as *Ein schöner Spiegel*. Its introduction is as follows:

> It is good to have a mirror which will show us how to be obedient to our elders and guard against misfortune and help us to live uprightly before God, so that we may experience joy and blessings.

It continues with the enumeration of those children mentioned in the Bible and the Apocrypha who were obedient: Joseph, Samuel, David and Tobias; and then of those who were disobedient and disrespectful, such as Assa, Ham, Esau, Miriam, Korah, Absalom, and those naughty boys who taunted Elisha because of his baldness. The song concludes by citing the tragedy that ensues when children are disrespectful and disobedient.[17] From the sixteenth to the eighteenth centuries a thorough knowledge of Hutterite songs (and articles of faith) was considered important as preparation for the eventuality of imprisonment and questioning by authorities.[18]

Women and the Songs of *Die Lieder der Hutterischen Brüder*

In view of the central educational role played by songs and hymns in the Hutterite tradition, one may well ask: What role do women play in those hymns? How are women portrayed? What ideals were traditionally communicated to Hutterite women through their hymnody?

The songs in *Die Lieder der Hutterischen Brüder* were written by men; all but twenty-one of 347 were written in the sixteenth century. They include devotional, historical, biblical, and clearly didactic songs. Those not as clearly didactic usually end with moralizing, sometimes comprising one verse and sometimes numerous verses. Some were written from prison as letter-songs to family members or the whole community; some are in the form of prayers; others are highly polemical.[19] One contains a confession of sinfulness and a plea for mercy.[20] Despite the fact that all the authors of the songs in LHBr were men, it includes numerous songs about women. Six are devoted exclusively to the stories of female biblical persons. Although another song is referred to as the (apocryphal) story of Tobias, the other protagonist in that story is Sara, the daughter of Raguel; in fact, it is the longest song in LHBr, comprising over one thousand lines. The subject of five other songs about women are canticles: those of Hanna, Debora, and Mary, the mother of Jesus. Biblical women are mentioned in twenty-five additional songs. The apocryphal Susanna is the subject in six songs, more than any other woman in LHBr.

Several songs in LHBr make reference to Anabaptist/Hutterite women, but only one divulges the name of an Anabaptist woman. This is particularly striking in contrast to the many songs that tell stories of individual male Anabaptist/Hutterites, many of which are stories of martyrdom. In several songs about groups of Anabaptists who were apprehended and tried, men are named, but the women are simply referred to as "sisters."[21]

One of the numerous biblical songs that found resonance among the Hutterites is by the Hutterite Wastel Wardimer. In the song beginning *Nun hört was ich euch singen will*, he celebrates the godliness of numerous women of the Bible and the Apocrypha. Most are from the Old Testament; Sara, Rebekka, the midwives in Egypt, Debora, Ruth, Naomi, the unnamed daughter of Jephtha, Hannah, Sara the daughter of Raguel, Susanna, Esther, Judith, the unnamed mother of the Maccabees, and Assanath; the only women from the New Testament are Elizabeth and Mary.[22] The author does not mention the fact that Sara laughed when the divine visitor said she would have a child at a very old age, but merely states that she had faith. Rebekka is praised for loving the son whom God loved; the Egyptian midwives for fearing God and not killing Hebrew infants at birth despite the Pharoah's commands; Miriam for leading the women in a song of thanksgiving and praise to God; Debora (an Israelite judge) for prophesying that Sisera would fall to a woman, then leading an army of 900 (*sic*) warriors to defeat Sisera, and thereafter praising God in song; Ruth for leaving her people, the Moabites, after the death of her husband, to go with her mother-in-law; Jephtha's daughter for willingly going to her death because of the vow her father had made; Hanna for giving up the son she had promised to God and composing a canticle; Sara, Raguel's daughter, for ceaselessly praying for a husband after she had lost seven; Susanna for not allowing herself to be seduced although it could cost her life; Esther for risking her life for her people; Judith for decapitating the Babylonian general Holofernes while he was lying in his bed; the mother of the Maccabees for encouraging her sons to be faithful although it might cost them their lives; and Assanath the Egyptian woman who did not know God's law but was pure. He praises the woman who washed Jesus' feet and then dried them with her hair (the author names her Mary although Luke left her unnamed). Like all Hutterites, Wardimer sermonizes at the end of the song:

> Consider carefully the womanly virtues,
> How women should live in the sight of God.
> Peter says they shall be subservient
> And be a good example for unbelievers.
> Their ornaments shall not be beautifully groomed hair or much gold
> But a gentle quiet spirit. v. 22

For they who trust in God, as Sara did,
Will be highly regarded by God . . . v. 23

Those who believe in Christ will suffer much tribulation
Women will lose children, house and husband.
But if they faithfully confess their faith
They will receive a crown that will not wither. v. 26

Unlike Wardimer, who has only words of praise for the biblical women he cites, an anonymous author in *Ein schöner Spiegel* metes out both praise and blame; in his song, Miriam is criticized for not being respectful towards her brother Moses, and as a result she contracts leprosy.[23] The song *Susanna war in Ängsten schwer*, by Anthonius Erfordter, is actually a song about four women.[24] In it, Susanna and Judith are praised as women who feared and loved God, and Bathsheba and Jezebel are reviled. Bathsheba is depicted as caring "not a whit about her honour and being 'false' towards her devout husband." But in not one of the numerous songs in LHBr in which David is one of the subjects is there is a negative word about him. He is held up as a hero and a devout man in every instance.[25]

It is surprising to note that entire songs devoted to the stories of Esther and Susanna are included in LHBr. Why are the songs about these particular individual women? The lessons to be learned from these two stories, according to their authors, are about trusting God. Why not entire songs about Hannah, Jephtha's daughter, Miriam, Sara, Ruth, Debora, or Mary Magdalene, who also had faith? Is it because numerous ingredients of high drama are present in the stories of both Queen Esther and Susanna; that there is conflict between the clearly good and the clearly evil in both; that danger, suspense, and intrigue are present in both to a higher degree than in the stories of some of the other women of the Bible?

Both female characters, Esther and Susanna, are extremely beautiful women. Both are very courageous. Esther risked her life to save her people, knowing that she could face a death sentence for appearing before her husband, the king, without being summoned. Susanna chose to remain chaste although her would-be seducers threatened to falsely accuse her if she did not submit to their advances, and she knew that if she were found guilty of adultery she would be stoned to death. In addition, Esther's character evokes sympathy because she had risen from being a Jewish orphan to becoming the queen of a very powerful Persian king. The villain in the story of Esther is the highest court official and the second most powerful man in court, who published orders that all Jews be eliminated because the Jewish palace gatekeeper refused to bow down to him. The two villains in the story of Susanna are lecherous judges who had become obsessed by the beautiful wife of a well-to-do man. The setting is exotic in both stories: the story of

Esther takes place in the royal palace. A major part of the story of Susanna takes place in a lush garden. The ending in both stories is a happy one for the heroines. Esther is successful in saving her Jewish people, and in addition is rewarded with great wealth. Already on her way to the execution site after having been condemned to death for adultery, Susanna is saved at the very last moment. All three villains are punished with death. Ironically, Haman is hanged on the very scaffold that he had built especially for the Jewish gatekeeper, and again ironically, the lecherous judges are stoned to death.

The plots of both stories seem somewhat contrived (in fact, it is not known if the stories are true or true in part), but both surely are popular because they have all the elements of riveting drama. But the story of Susanna has the added element of eroticism. Enjoying her garden, Susanna, the wife of Joakim, wishes time alone and sends away her maid and goes to the garden house. Two judges who had long been in love with her come to the garden house and seek Susanna's sexual favours. When she will not submit to their advances, the judges threaten that they will accuse her of adultery. Still Susanna will not submit. In court the men accuse her of adultery with a young man who, they said, had escaped before they had been able to apprehend him. She is found guilty and condemned to death by stoning. But as she is being led to the execution site, the youthful Daniel tells the court to ask the judges under which tree they had found the amorous pair. Their testimonies are at variance and the righteous and chaste Susanna is saved.[26]

Susanna is held up as an example of a virtuous woman in four additional songs in LHBr. She is one of fifteen God-fearing women in Wastel Wardimer's *Nun hört was ich euch singen will*; she also receives mention in two songs by Raiffer, *Freut euch ihr Frommen Gottes schon*, which primarily shows how God rewards good men of the Bible and punishes wicked men, and *Gott sein Gnad' und Barmherzigkeit*. Raiffer wrote the latter song in prison in Aachen as encouragement for his fellow prisoners. To the six women who were imprisoned there at the same time, he wrote in verses nine and ten, that they should keep in mind the godly women of the Bible and Apocrypha who had remained steadfast in their faith in God.[27]

More surprising than the inclusion of these particular stories in LHBr is the fact that the Hutterites still sing both songs about Susanna. They are printed anonymously in the hymnal: the thirty-nine verse *Zu Babel war ein Bürger* and the thirty-four verse *Von wunderlichen Dingen*.[28] The biblical Queen Esther is the subject of two songs in LHBr; the fifty-four verse *Nun merkt ihr Frommen* was written by Wolfgang Sailer; the other, *Zu Zeiten ist gesessen zu Susan in dem Schloss*, comprising eighty-four verses, is printed anonymously. An important part of the story of Esther for Hutterite theology is that of Vashti, the Persian king's first wife. He gave a banquet "for all his princes and servants, the army chiefs of Persia and Medea and the nobles and governors of the provinces."[29] The feast lasted 180 days, followed by a seven-day feast for all the people of his capital city. After long nights of partying, the king sent for his queen to show off her great beauty. But she refused to come, and one of the guests, an important minister, fearing that her display of independence might cause other wives to follow her example, urged the king to depose Vashti, adding, "there will be contempt and wrath in plenty."[30] The king consulted his legal experts, stripped Vashti of her title and issued a decree that "every man be lord in his own house."[31] It was then that the king sent for the most beautiful women in his land and chose Esther to be his queen.

Every bit as surprising, perhaps more so, than the inclusion of the numerous songs about Esther and Susanna in LHBr, is the inclusion of the story of the biblical Judith. Whereas Esther and Susanna are victims, Judith is the perpetrator of a horrific murder of a man lying in bed in a drunken stupor! Not only did Judith cut off Holofernes' head; this very beautiful widow first enticed the guards to allow her to enter the enemy compound by saying (untruthfully) that she would inform the enemy when the Jews sinned, as that was the only time that they could be defeated. Why should Judith be cited as an example when, for some Hutterites, for instance, David is not to be emulated as a player of musical instruments because he was responsible for the shedding of innocent blood? Yet this song of sixty-seven verses was written by a Hutterite, Christl Schmidt, to a sixteenth-century melody that the Hutterites still sing today.[32] The song ends with the statement that when they honour him, God has always aided and assisted his people in tribulation and struggles, as He helped Judith, and that was the reason why Judith uttered a song of praise to the majesty of the Lord. The author even presents Judith as a metaphor for the bride of Christ, and advises the singers to look up to her as an example of virtue, decorum, modesty, and trust in God, so that they can overcome the enemy as she did.

Another of the several songs in LHBr, the inclusion of which is surprising, begins *Zu singen will ich heben an*. Its beginning is similar to many other songs in LHBr, but its continuation is not. Was the author of the apocryphal Esdras, on which this song is based, a misogynist or cynic?[33] Or is he merely voicing the age old dichotomy—men's simultaneous fear of and love for, and/or irresistible attraction to, women? In the song, three men debate the question of what or who is strongest in this world. The first argues that it is wine, the second that it is the king; the third, Zerubbabel, a descendant of David,[34] argues that it is women. These are his arguments: All humankind is born of and raised by women, women tend the vineyards, and life could not continue without them. The man (who does not know God) fritters away his life, foolishly gathers silver and gold, often lives a wild life, but regards all as nothing compared to the love of a wife, and leaves father and everything and clings to the woman until death parts them. Many go out of their minds because of women. Zerubbabel then gives an account of a great and very powerful king whom he knew personally: a woman struck him, took the crown off his head, and robbed him of his honour. Wine has no power in comparison; the king and all men and women [Menschenkinder] are unrighteous–but especially women, it seems.

> The whole host of women is unrighteous,
> So too, all their endeavors [Werk] forever,
> Nothing good can be found in them.[35]

It is striking that the author of the song does not revile women in his commentary on the story, but states that sin makes all humankind irrational [toll], causes them to lord it over and mislead others; perhaps also to rob and steal and murder. It is not surprising that he then adds that no one is more powerful than God, and Truth can be found only in God. All of humankind, on the other hand, is full of deception and craftiness and seeks the things of this world. However, God loves those who shun evil, reveals His will to them, grants them wisdom and honour, and gives them the gift of His love.

In two songs in LHBr, Rebekka of the Old Testament is treated as a symbol of the church. In the lengthy song about her becoming the bride of Isaac, she is depicted as chaste, pious, beautiful (of course), and as not having known a man. Arriving in Negeb she puts on her veil before entering Isaac's tent. In the "sermon" comprising three verses at the end of the song, the author Braitmichel points out that God chose a chaste young woman; so must Christ's messengers, the church, be the pure bride of Christ.[36] For Riedemann the moral of the story is slightly different. Just as Rebekka, after receiving the message [Botschaft] from Isaac immediately goes with the messenger to meet her bridegroom, so must the church quickly go to meet its bridegroom, Christ. In his song in praise of virtuous biblical women, Wastel Wardimer briefly comments on the story of Isaac blessing Jacob, and Rebekka's involvement. He points out that she loved the son whom God loved, but does not mention that in that story she also was involved in deception.[37] In the song by Nikolaus Herman (but printed anonymously in LHBr) in which a Sunamite widow is mentioned, he tells the biblical story of this woman, including the fact that she believed the prophet, but he does not sermonize.[38]

Many songs in LHBr, anonymous or by Hutterites, contain theology or teachings regarding women that Hutterites have always emphasized. In the song devoted exclusively to the story of Esther, the theme is obedience and its opposite. The anonymous author devotes a full eight of eighty-four verses[39] to the account of Vashti's disobedience, the minister's counsel to the king to depose her and let it be known throughout the kingdom that all women must fear (or be subservient to [*fürchten*]) their husbands, and the king's proclamation to that effect. But the author not only tells the long story, he devotes two verses to reminding women, especially, that Vashti was "cast from the kingdom" because of her disobedience. From this example women should learn to honour their husbands and to be subservient. No mention is made of Esther's act of disobedience in appearing before the king without a summons. In his song, Sailer urges believers to "learn virtue" from Esther, follow her example, live uprightly; as a result the King will reward them with riches, they will reign with Him forever, and there will be no more fear or tribulation.[40]

The story of Mary the mother of Jesus also serves Hutterite theologians/songwriters well. In two songs about her, Wolfgang Sailer holds up Mary as a model, although not exclusively for women. All believers are to do as Mary did, be willing to abandon reason [*Legt weg Vernunft und Sinne*],[41] and [*Nicht fassen mag's die Vernunft*],[42] give up their will [*So wird gedämpfet Vernunft und eigener Will*],[43] and do the Lord's bidding, as Mary did. If they wish to have Christ and God's word conceived in their hearts they must free themselves of vain things.[44] And they must ask God as Mary did.[45] (The Hutterites sing another sixteenth-century song about Mary, not in LHBr, *Es wollt Gott Jäger jagen*, to the melody of a folk song *Es wollt gut Jäger jagen*. Mary is described as the *Vielreine [a virgin]* who is prepared to do the will of God).[46]

Nowhere in the numerous songs in which Eve is mentioned in LHBr is she treated harshly. But Sailer's phrase about Eve's transgressions is unique in this volume of songs. His treatment of the story is much like that of the Bible, but in one song, after stating that Eve disregarded God's commands he adds that she *caused the man to do her will*.[47] Otherwise Sailer regards all humankind as having followed in the footsteps of Adam, not Eve.[48] And nothing is revealed in another song in LHBr about the questionable past life of the woman at the well in Samaria who meets Jesus. The importance of the story for the author apparently is the fact that she believed Jesus was the Messiah. In the one verse about her,[49] she is only quoted as saying to the people, "Come and see if this man who told me about my past is not the Messiah."

Songs about Anabaptist/Hutterite Women in LHBr
It is not perfectly clear whom the Hutterite Jörg Wenger is addressing in his song beginning *Andl mein Lieb*, which he wrote from prison in Brixen, but it seems to be the only song in which a man expresses tenderness to a woman. He begins the second verse with more terms of endearment, *Treindl o liebste Schwester mein*. As Hutterites refer to their wives as *eheliche Schwester* [wedded sister], it is probably correct to assume that Treindel was his wife, since his words reveal that she is the one dearest to his heart. Andl

and Jörgl (without the "dear" before his name), his small children are addressed in the third verse. Wenger commends Andl's devout heart [*Gemüt*] to God and wishes for her that she will remain patient when the Lord disciplines her. He reminds Treindl that it is by grace that they are children of God, and hopes for her that she will have no regrets about (the loss of) worldly things. Finally he encourages her to cry out to God in times of suffering.

Only one Anabaptist woman is named within a song in LHBr.[50] She is identified there only as the poor widow Christina, but is named in the superscription as Christina Brünnerin. (The full name of the man, Jost Wilhelm, is cited in the same song.) The story of Jost's imprisonment, questioning, and death comprises nine verses in the song, but Christina's story comprises only two. There is no way of telling whether little else was known about Christina, whether the writer did not try to gather more information, or whether Christina's inquisition was similar to Jost's and did not warrant repeating.

The fate of only ten female Anabaptist martyrs is revealed in songs in LHBr or in their superscriptions: one beheaded, one burned, and eight drowned. Dozens of male Anabaptists/Hutterites, however, are named, and numerous entire songs are devoted to the accounts of the imprisonment, torture, and death of individual male martyrs. But this is not totally surprising as the authorities targeted preachers and missionaries, who were almost exclusively male, for capture and execution.

It must again be emphasized that only one Anabaptist woman's name appears in a song in LHBr, (and only her first name at that). But there are songs in LHBr in which female martyrs are not mentioned at all, or merely referred to as "several" or "some" women or included under "persons." For instance, the first superscription for the song about Anabaptist martyrs at Alzey in December 1529, *Herr Gott in deinem Reiche*,[51] informs the reader that it is a song about the brethren who suffered death at Alzey on the Rhine; the second, that "the following is another lovely song about some [*etlich*] Christian heroes who were put on trial [*gerichtet*] in Alzey in 1529." But in the song itself we are informed that the "Christian heroes" comprised nine men [*Brüder*] and several [*etlich*] women [*Schwestern*], that all were imprisoned because of their faith and greatly mocked and scorned; but that they put their fate into the hands of God. Four entire verses are devoted to the imperial mandate: All Anabaptists, male and female, of the age of accountabilty are not to be spared but to be brought to trial, and if they do not recant, to endure death by fire, water, sword, or in any other manner. The song continues with the statements that all remained true to their faith; that they joyfully sang in prison, and that the nine brethren were beheaded and "the sisters" were drowned.

This song also includes the only account in LHBr of an Anabaptist woman who took on the role of pastoral ministry. We are told that she came to comfort and encourage the Anabaptist prisoners in Alzey in 1529. And as in virtually every case in LHBr, this woman remains a nameless martyr. Her story forms four of the forty-one verses:

> v. 26
> I must tell you something else,
> Take note of it in the community.
> When the above named heroes
> Were still imprisoned,
> A sister came to the prison;
> She comforted them greatly
> (She encouraged them) to remain faithful and glorify God
> As so many other believers (*Frommen*) had done before them.
> v. 27
> And to regard this short period of suffering
> (As nothing compared) to the everlasting joy
> Which would be their reward.
> They should remain truly steadfast
> (In their faith) that God is on His throne in heaven,
> He would richly bless [*ergötzen tun*] them
> On account of such suffering.
> v. 28
> When (the authorities) discovered
> That their devout sister
> Had admonished them to remain steadfast,
> They brought this devout little lamb
> To trial in short order.
> And pronounced the sentence
> That she should be burned.
> v. 29
> And that was quickly accomplished
> Without mercy and justice,
> (They) ended her life by means of fire,
> And now she is counted among
> The devout heroes of God;
> With brief words I had to
> Quickly tell you
> (In order) to honour the just little lamb.
> v. 30
> And thus they all remained steadfast
> (in their faith) in God.
> And now no one can rob them
> Of their good names.[52]

In another case the reader is informed that there are five songs by or about the Hutterite Martin Maler who, with six other Anabaptist prisoners, (one of them a miller's boy), was beheaded in Schwäbisch Gmünd.[53] The superscription for the third song (the second of two songs in LHBr beginning *Wer Christo hier will folgen nach*)[54] reads only: "Another song about the seven brethren." In this song three of the brethren are named: Maler, Wolf Esslinger, and Bamberger; at the end a boy [*Knab*] is mentioned but not named. In Martin Maler's song of eighteen verses about these brethren,[55] almost half are about the young lad and his refusal to recant even though a nobleman offered to save him. None of the seven brethren are named in this song. In a third,[56] only Martin Maler is named; verses 22-29 incl. are about the testimony of the sixteen-year-old miller's boy before his death.[57] It would appear that the hearts of the total populace were so touched by the heroism of the young lad that no Anabaptists or Hutterites made a note of the fact that one of the martyrs was a woman. She is not mentioned in the Hutterite *Chronicle* or in LHBr.[58]

The superscription for the song beginning *Nun wollt ihr hören singen* by Hutterite Hans Gurtzham in LHBr[59] informs the reader only that it deals with "three Christian persons who were condemned [*gericht*] for [*um*] God's truth," but it names the martyr Hans Staudach. The song tells of the three (Gurtzham and two others) being arrested and imprisoned in Vienna for their faith, of their joy at meeting four other Anabaptist/Hutterite prisoners, including Staudach, and of the subsequent trial and heroic witness and death by the sword of the four other prisoners. Two of the "three Christian persons," besides Gurtzham, were Michel Matschidel and his wife, but the latter two are not named in the song or the superscription. Although the reader is informed that Gurtzham was secretly drowned in Vienna in 1550, there is no account in LHBr of the fate of either the preacher Michel Matschidel or his wife.

Yet another song, *Nun wollen wir aber singen*[60] is about nine brethren and three "sisters" who were captured and brought to trial in Bruck an der Muer in Styria (Austria) in 1528 (so we are informed in the superscription). The prisoners wrote the beginning of the song and referred to themselves only as "twelve evangelical persons." The person(s) who completed the song described their fate: the men made a ring and knelt down to pray, then joyfully got up to meet their death, but before they were beheaded, told the *Freimann* that they hoped that God would forgive him and be merciful to them. Then we are told their further fate: the nine (men) were beheaded, and because they could not be swayed, [*von Gott wolltens nicht wanken*], the three *Fräulein*, (not called "sisters" in this case) smilingly went to their deaths by drowning [*Das jüngst lachet das Wasser an*], and all the men and women were buried in a deep grave.

At a later date and in another territory, in Aachen in 1558, twelve

Hutterites, six men and six women, were taken captive (the men are named, but not the women).[61] The fate of the six unnamed women is summed up in two short verses in the song–they had to endure imprisonment for a "long time," and despite many efforts by Roman Catholic clergy to persuade them to recant, they remained steadfast. Subsequently they were flogged, just as their Lord had been, Raiffer reminded the reader, and released. They were the few fortunate ones who were able to return to the Hutterite community.[62] This same song is unique in that they are included in its acrostic: HANSL HAINRICH MATHIAS TILMAN HANS WERNER SAMBT UNSERN LIBEN SCHWESTERN Täten Euch Zu Wissen Wie Es Uns Geht In Dem Hören (Little Hans, Heinrich, Mathias, Tilman, Hans, Werner and our dear sisters inform you as to how we are faring in the Lord).[63] A fair number of songs in LHBr were written by several authors, but unfortunately, no indication is given that the female prisoners participated in the writing of this song.

In another song Raiffer noted that both men and women came to witness the hanging and burning of the Hutterites.[64] Both Adam and Raiffer also noted that at least some of the women who were taken prisoner were mothers of very young children, and that they commended their children to God as they were being taken away to their place of incarceration.[65] It was not uncommon for Anabaptist/Hutterite prisoners to sing loudly so that the other prisoners could hear them and be encouraged. It is not unlikely that it was for this purpose that the preacher Raiffer wrote the song *Gott sein Gnad und Barmherzigkeit*.[66] First he encouraged all the "pure children of God" to put their trust in God and in Christ the mediator that they will provide preachers; he admonished them to be united in love and faith; he assured them God would not forsake them in any circumstances. Then he addressed the brethren specifically, admonishing them to be steadfast; and in the ninth verse he encouraged the women [*Schwestern*] to recall the devout women of the Bible and Apocrypha–Sarah, Miriam, Debora, Esther, Judith, Susanna, and the mother of the Macabees,[67] six of whom had remained steadfast in times of tribulation and/or danger, and all of whom lived honourable lives and were manly (!) in spirit. It also is interesting to note that a more than cursory examination of the songs in LHBr draws one to the conclusion that Raiffer's song is one of a very few in which the author prays for his enemies.[68]

Conclusions

An initial reading of the texts of many of the songs in LHBr gives cause for surprise and wonder. Most of the songs in LHBr were written in the sixteenth century, all of whose known authors were men. Yet it contains a considerable number of songs celebrating the characters, lives, and/or deeds of women, and what women! and what lives! What, for instance, did the

Anabaptists/Hutterites have in common with the conniving killer Judith? Why songs about women not found in the regular Bible, but in the Apocrypha? And why more about Susanna than about any other woman, including Mary, the mother of Jesus? What purpose did these songs serve?

Upon more reflection, however, the surprise and wonder abates as it becomes clear that the songs have served multiple purposes. One deduces that, on the most obvious level, they have served as entertainment. This has been important because throughout their history Hutterites have read virtually no books other than the Bible and their own songs and history. (In America the children, however, have read prescribed books in school). They have not attended dances or dramatic performances. In the sixteenth century they did not go to the marketplace to hear the newest scandals or horror stories (today they do not watch television or listen to radios nor do they attend live dramatic performances or movie theatres). The stories about Esther, Judith, and Susanna make for good drama and are good entertainment, especially because all three have good outcomes. Then there is also the love story about Sara in LHBr. Seven times she gets married and seven times the husband dies before the marriage is consummated. Will the eighth be able to avoid the curse and live happily ever after with his Sara? Again, good entertainment, laden with suspense. But is this also, perhaps, a lesson to the many Anabaptist/Hutterite women who lost their husbands?

Some of the same stories also correspond to the lives of sixteenth-century Anabaptists and Hutterites. For two centuries their preachers, missionaries, and sometimes the women among them were taken captive, tortured and put to death; in the sixteenth century, Hutterites never knew when the next hordes would come to plunder, pillage, steal, and rape in their communities. One can hardly imagine that in their communities the Hutterites would sing the latest song about their latest martyr. But they would be able to sing, perhaps, the stories about those women whose lives were in danger and who trusted God for deliverance from their enemies, and thus experience catharsis.

Why some of the other story-songs of women (and men) of the Bible? One need only recall that it was in the sixteenth century that, for the first time in many centuries, the Bible could be obtained easily and read in the vernacular. It has been well documented that the early Anabaptists and Hutterites had a very high view of this book, and what better way to learn the biblical stories than through song? Their education consisted primarily of learning the three Rs and a trade; thus the children read the songs, then wrote them out (in Gothic script as they still do), recited them, and finally sang them. In this context it bears mentioning that Hutterites had universal education in the sixteenth century when a large part of the rest of the world remained illiterate.

No doubt many of the songs in LHBr became a part of the Hutterite repertoire because their characters were meant to be models, and occasionally anti-models, for their young people. The women in numerous biblical songs had faith, they praised God, they trusted God to save them in moments of danger, they asked for help in overcoming the enemy, and they risked their lives in order to save their people or to remain chaste. (Debora led an army, but in that regard [as a leader, and of men, moreover] she has not served as a model for Hutterite women.) And why the grisly story about Judith? Was it because both the song and the Bible indicate that she was devout and prayed for God's help before she decapitated Holofernes; and that although she partied alone with the lustful general, she was not defiled? Or did it find resonance with sixteenth-century Anabaptists/Hutterites because they could cleanse themselves of their own murderous feelings against the enemy as they read or sang the song? And will Hutterite women secretly have relished the thought, as the song says, that it is a great shame for a man to be killed by a woman?

Why so many songs about Susanna and only one about Judith? Both were devout and called upon God for aid, and both were pronounced chaste. But it is easy to see that Judith was not as worthy a model as Susanna. Not only is Judith's deed not one that Anabaptist and Hutterites could teach their young people to emulate; Judith also arrayed herself in her costliest, most beautiful raiments and jewellery in order to find favour with men!

Some of the stories of biblical heroines in LHBr serve as models, specifically for young women for example, of sexual purity, particularly those about Mary, the mother of Jesus, Rebekka, and Susanna; but particularly those about Susanna. Because stories that include chaste young men are rare, one gets the distinct impression that the onus is on the young Hutterite women to see to it that their young men remain pure.

Some of the songs, and in particular those about Esther and Susanna, served well in inculcating faith in their young poeple. Both women were in danger of losing their lives, both prayed (in the biblical account Esther does not pray although in the song in LHBr, Esther fasts and prays and asks other to do the same), and God delivered them. The lesson in faith is a simple but important one for sixteenth-century youth: have faith, pray, and God will deliver you from danger and death.

In the song by the Bohemian Lutheran pastor, Nikolaus Herman,[69] the Shunammite widow is described as having faith: not faith in God, but in the words of the prophet. Herman simply states that she believed and when she did what Elisha had commanded her to do, the oil flowed almost ceaselessly and she was able to pay her debts. Is this meant to give Hutterites the impression that believing is the most important lesson in the story, and that they should believe (accept the authority of) their preachers?

The many songs in LHBr about obedience, *Gelassenheit*, giving up one's will, walking the narrow way, and communal life make it clear that they are key tenets to be taught to Hutterites of both genders. But those whose subject is obedience are often meant as a lesson specifically for girls and women. Witness the excessively great number in which women have been enjoined to be obedient to their husbands. One Hutterite author also put words into the mouth of God. After reminding women that God had spoken to the woman in the garden of Eden and had told her that because she had broken His commandment she would bear children with great pain, he quoted the biblical words: "Your husband shall rule over you" [*So beherrsch dich dein Mann*], and added "You must bow down to him" (or be subservient- [*Dich vor ihm bücken*]).[70]

The many songs about Anabaptist and Hutterite martyrs and other heroes in LHBr comprise both story and exhortation to trust God in all of life's difficulties. A considerable number include, in dialogue form, an account of lengthy interrogations and the replies of the (male) prisoners. In these songs the men boldly proclaim their faith (and sometimes let the inquisitors know how little regard they have for both judges and clergy). It is regrettable that no song includes accounts of such interrogation and the responses of women. They must also have been interrogated, as several songs, including the only one about the female who came to minister to prisoners, give evidence that they were tried and that they remained steadfast.

It is also regrettable that the Anabaptist/Hutterite men who wrote songs did not learn from the Bible that it is acceptable for women as well as men to be named. And again one must say that it is regrettable that they were not sensitive to the fact that they had the same double standard as the rest of society: that they condemned the woman for having an adulterous affair, but not the man. One would also like to know if sixteenth-century Hutterite women wrote songs, and if they did, why none seems, to have been retained.

In spite of the way that Anabaptist and Hutterite women are treated in LHBr, one must concede that women are generally not treated unsympathetically in this book of songs. The prime example of this is Eve, who has been regarded by many throughout history as a symbol of the Great Temptress. But the Hutterites generally just recounted the story as it is found in the Bible; the leader, Hans Amon, simply states that Eve and Adam were led astray by lies and ruses.[71] Some Hutterites, Christof Scheffman, for example, even gave equal status to men and women in their songs. In his fifty-seven-verse song, *O reicher Gott im Himmelsthron*[72] based on Eusebius' account of the persecution and/or martyrdom of biblical characters and early Christians (replete with the most grisly details), he devotes five verses to Hutterites [*wir*]. He mentions no names, but states that men and women and young unmarried adults of both genders did not prize life above commitment to their faith.[73] The teaching about women's subservience to men is, and has been throughout their history, regarded by Hutterite women as a scriptural injunction, and therefore not to be questioned.

Despite these negative aspects of some of the songs in LHBr, we owe a debt of gratitude to the authors of the songs in LHBr and to those who copied them for centuries and managed to retain them despite persecutions so severe that only thirty-five Hutterites were left in the middle of the eighteenth century. Many authors told their own stories or the stories of other men and women in a surprisingly dispassionate way, just as their chroniclers did for the most part. But the accounts in the songs in LHBr differ in one way from those of the Hutterite *Chronicle*. The latter tells not only the stories of heroes, but also of the failings of some of their people. The songs only celebrate the heroes; for instance, the song about Raiffer and those imprisoned with him tells of inquisitions and death, but does not mention the man who recanted.[74]

As was stated at the outset, the singing of historical, devotional, and biblical songs has been of utmost importance to Hutterites through the ages. But it has taken on special significance for women. They have never taken part in community government, nor have they attended meetings or voted, but singing is one activity in which they have been able to participate fully. Not only that, they can be song leaders, and in this way: in accordance with their ancient practice, and because they make use of no instruments (not even a pitch pipe), one Hutterite begins a song and waits for the others to join in. That person is often a woman. This brings to mind the song about the debate about power, and causes one to wonder if perhaps some Hutterite women may have taken (secret) delight in Zerubbabel's arguments.

Notes

1 *Die Lieder der Hutterischen Brüder* was first published in Alberta in 1914; its songs were taken from three manuscripts. The 1962 edition which is cited in this chapter was published in Cayley, Alberta by the Hutterian Brethren in Canada. It contains 347 songs written to some 130 borrowed melodies. Hereafter cited as LHBr.
2 By the term "world," the Hutterites mean all non-Hutterites, but they do make distinctions as to the degree of worldliness of different groups. In the seventeenth century, according to Grimmelshausen, only the children indulged in such recreational activities as going for walks after every meal for approximately one hour. During the walks, the children also prayed and sang. See Victor Peters, *All Things Common; The Hutterian Way of Life* (Minneapolis: University of Minnesota Press, 1965), 23.
3 John Horsch translated the word "Spielen" as "betting" in *The Hutterian Brethren* (Cayley, AB: Macmillan Colony, 1985), 22. The word also applies to the playing of musical instruments in their writings. Except for the word "playing," this translation is by John Horsch, ibid., 22.
4 L. E. Deets quoted a Hutterite woman as saying, "Singing is surely the nicest thing in the world" in *The Hutterites: A Study in Social Cohesion* (Gettysburg: Times and News Publishing Co., 1939), 40.

5 H. S. Bender, *Conrad Grebel, Founder of the Swiss Brethren*, (Goshen, IN: Mennonite Historical Society, 1942), 208. For Zwingli's comments, see *Huldreich Zwingli's Werke* (Zurich: Ausgabe durch Schuler und Schultess, 1927), vol. II, 788.
6 George H. Williams and Angel Mergal, eds., *Spiritual and Anabaptist Writers* (Philadelphia: Westminster Press, 1957), 75-79.
7 Rufus M. Jones, *Studies in Mystical Religion* (London: Macmillan and Co., 1909), 382.
8 LHBr, Preface.
9 "Let the trumpets, psaltery and harp sound
Whoever lives, shall sing and leap for joy before God
Be of good cheer in Him."
Die Posaunen lasset klingen
Psalter und Harfe gut,
Was Leben hat soll singen,
Jauchsen und vor Gott springen,
In ihm seid wohlgemut. LHBr, 51, vs 20b.
10 "Organs and cymbals, as you know, are (or induce) troubled spirits." Orgeln und Zimbeln, wie du weisst, Ist betrübter Geist. LHBr, 200, v. 2.
11 LHBr, 727, vs. 5-7.
12 Perhaps the reason is found in Paul Tschetter's diary written when he visited America: "The old Mennonites allow Musiken. When I came to Brenneman on Sunday morning he asked whether we enjoyed playing [*Spielen*]. We said No. He had a Farlefan in his home, and began to play it. When he had finished I told him the Apostle had said, 'Sing and play to the Lord in your hearts.' He replied, 'The good David played on a stringed instrument.' But I said, 'King David also was a warrior and caused much blood to flow.'" A.J.F. Zieglschmid, ed., *Klein Geschichtsbuch der Hutterischen Brüder* (Philadelphia: The Carl Schurz Memorial Foundation, 1947), 585. Seventeenth-century codices and LHBr all contain an anonymous verse in which instrumental music is described, among other things, as being worthless in the pursuit of blessedness. See the Preface to the LHBr.
13 The daily services were not neglected in times of great persecution or when only a few Hutterites were together. For instance, when a few Hutterites traversed the great plains of North America in their search for land at the end of the nineteenth century, P. Tschetter made numerous entries in his diary regarding singing and reading and prayer before and after meals, regardless of whether they were alone or with non-Hutterites.
14 No Hutterite preacher prepares his own sermons, but reads those written in the seventeenth century.
15 The curriculum of ca. 1765 is described thus: "(Memorizing) prayers, singing and writing." A.J.F. Zieglschmid, ed., *Die älteste Chronik der Hutterischen Brüder*, (Ithaca, NY: Cayuga Press, 1943), 306. Stephan Gerlach, later professor at Tübingen, who visited the Hutterites in 1573, wrote that the girls learned to pray, to read and write a little, and the boys learned reading and writing and a craft.
16 One such ordinance of the seventeenth century reads in part: "Youth are to be brought up in the fear of the Lord and diligently to read the epistles, hymns and confessions of the brotherhood and much more." Another, of 1654, reads thus: "Give the songs and epistles and accounts of faith of the brethren who have been put to death [*gerichtet*] to the youth or whoever can read, so that they can diligently read them, become familiar with and commit them to memory, so that everyone will have a better grounding in the articles of faith; so that if some of them later are confined to prison or otherwise are called upon to defend their faith, they know of the Lord what they should know." Zieglschmid, *Klein Geschichtsbuch*, 520.

17 LHBr, 323.
18 LHBr, 41, 593, 867.
19 The polemical songs in LHBr condemn not only the pope, but the Reformers and secular rulers. Some of these are found on 166, vs. 60-64, by Michel Kramer; *Gross Wunder tut mich zwingen*, 201, particularly vs. 3-15 by Wolfgang Sailer, 370, vs. 61 and 62.
20 LHBr, 313.
21 There were considerably more Anabaptist/Hutterite male martyrs, as the authorities were most interested in targeting *Sendboten* [missionaries] for capture, and most were men. However, some women also preached and others whose "offences" seem to be have been no more serious than listening to a sermon also lost their lives.
22 LHBr, 313.
23 LHBr, 324, v. 16.
24 Ibid., 113 ff.
25 In Witzstad's song, David is lauded for not harming Saul because Saul is the Lord's anointed (324, v. 6); in Blasius Schuster's song, David is depicted as the courageous God-fearing youth who defeated Goliath (376); in an anonymous song, as obedient to his father, very attractive, dearly beloved of God, fearless of and defiant towards Goliath (379). An unnamed author quotes David's fire-breathing condemnation of the godless who will go to hell and experience "lightning, hail, sulphur and fire" (328, v. 20). Raiffer recounts the numerous times that God saved David (555, v. 20). Other biblical male personages who transgressed the commandments of God are also not reviled in LHBr; there is no mention, for example, of Noah's drunkenness and lying with his daughters. Augustin Sailer states that God was merciful to Noah because Noah was devout (159, v. 53). An author identified only as B.S. cites Noah as being faithful [*treu*] (427, v. 3) and Raiffer praises him as a devout servant of God who was saved because he believed God (554, v. 15). Needless to say, men such as Ahab, Haman, Herod, Nebuchadnezzar, et al. and women such as Jezebel are depicted as villains, plain and simple.
26 Another suspense-filled song based on the legend of an early female Christian martyr, Pura, by a South German Anabaptist, Hans Büchel, although not included in LHBr, is found in the earliest Anabaptist songbook, *Ausbund*, and in several Hutterite codices (Hab.15 and S.n.11.999). According to this song, during the reign of Emperor Valerianius, Pura is condemned to a brothel for her faith. There a young male Christian overhears her prayers for deliverance, exchanges his clothes for hers, and enables her to escape. The first client at the brothel after this event, a member of the imperial court, is enraged when he finds the young man in the room where Pura was supposed to be domiciled. The young Christian man is condemned to be beheaded, but when Pura hears of this, she offers to die in his place; however, the young man will not consent to this sacrifice. The judge then condemns both to death by fire. According to the young man's testimony before they died side by side, Pura had baptized him and many others. (I am indebted to Ursula Lieseberg's *Studien zum Märtyrerlied der Täufer im 16. Jahrhundert* (Frankfurt am Main: Verlag Peter Lang, 1991), 139-44, for the above). One cannot discount the possibility that this song did not, as widespread acceptance among the Hutterites because of the statement that a woman baptized new Christians (and men at that).
27 LHBr, 568-69.
28 Ibid., 422, 396.
29 See the book of Esther in the Old Testament, 1:3.
30 Ibid., 1:18.
31 Ibid., 1:22; LHBr, 400, vs. 7-14.

32 Ibid., 407. The author is identified as Christof Schmidt by Adolf Mais, "Die Verbreitung der Liederhandschrift des Andreas Ehrenpreis," *Österreichisches Volksliedwerk* (1962): 66.
33 LHBr, 297, by a Hutterite, either Achtznit or Sailer, a song of 29 verses sung to Schiller's *Melodie*, the melody suggesting that the author was cognizant of Meistersinger craft. The song is based on 3 Esdras, 3 and 4.
34 Zerubbabel, who was born in the sixth century B.C., helped to rebuild Jerusalem and replace the worship vessels that had been desecrated by the Babylonians.
35 "Ungerecht ist ganz der Weiber Schar, Und alle ihr Werk immerdar, Nichts guts an ihn zu finden."
36 LHBr, 697, by Braitmichel, who died in 1573.
37 Ibid., 314.
38 Ibid., 337.
39 Ibid., 399, vs. 7-14.
40 Ibid., 263, vs. 52 and 53. It appears that a melody of one of these songs [*Estherweis*] may have been given as the tune for at least one other Anabaptist song; if so, Anabaptists and/or Hutterites must have sung this song at one time in their history. Lieseberg, *Studien*, 306.
41 LHBr, 214, v. 23.
42 Ibid., 199, v. 9.
43 Ibid., v. 12.
44 Ibid., vs. 8 and 14.
45 Ibid., v. 10.
46 *Gesangbüchlein*, 556. The subject of the secular song is that of a hunter whose game is young virgins to be ravished by his lord and then released.
47 LHBr, 271, v. 6.
48 Ibid., v. 14.
49 LHBr, 572, v. 9. The Hutterites still sing a song about the woman at the well in Samaria, John 7:37, *Es kam ein Fräulein mit dem Krug* by Benedikt Gletting, a Swiss, whose songs were published between 1560 and 1579.
50 Ibid., 817.
51 Ibid., 40.
52 LHBr, 43f., vs. 26-30 incl.
53 Ibid., 48.
54 Ibid., 52.
55 Ibid., 53.
56 Ibid., 55.
57 Lieseberg, *Studien*, 116, states that he was fifteen years old.
58 I am indebted to Lieseberg, *Studien*, 116, n. 231 for the information about this woman.
59 LHBr, 136.
60 Ibid., 25.
61 Ibid., 562, v. 70; 563 v. 88. Five of the men are named within the song: Heinrich Adam, Hans Beck, Hans Raiffer, Matthias Schmidt, Tilman Schneider.
62 Ibid., 563 vs. 89 and 90.
63 LHBr, 582. Acrostic is a very old poetic device by which first (occasionally last) letters or words of each stanza together form a word or a group of words. By studying the acrostic, sometimes the names of the writer or recipient, or both, can be identifed; sometimes the trade and/or the place of origin of the writer is also included.
64 Ibid., 559, v. 39.
65 Ibid., 583, v. 9; 615, v. 15.

66 Ibid., 567.
67 Ibid., 568, v. 9. These are eight of the same women whom W. Wardimer had named in his song before 1553.
68 LHBr, 558, v. 23.
69 LHBr, 337.
70 Ibid., 309, v. 15. In another song, 272, v. 12, it says: *"Dein Herr der Mann soll sein füran."*
71 Ibid., 119, v.4.
72 Ibid., 669.
73 Scheffmans's song, *O reicher Gott im Himmelsthron*, is of particular interest for several reasons: the Hutterites still sing it, and its melody appears to be the only, or perhaps one of a few, composed by Anabaptists or Hutterites. For more about Scheffman's songs, see Helen Martens "Hutterite Songs: The Origins and Aural Transmission of these Melodies from the Sixteenth Century," unpublished PhD dissertation, Columbia University, 1969; also Helen Martens, "Die Lieder der Hutterer und ihre Verbindung zum Meistersang im 16. Jahrhundert," in *Jahrbuch für Volksliedforschung*, 26 (1981): 31-43.
74 Ibid., 557.

III.

NORTH GERMAN/DUTCH ANABAPTIST WOMEN

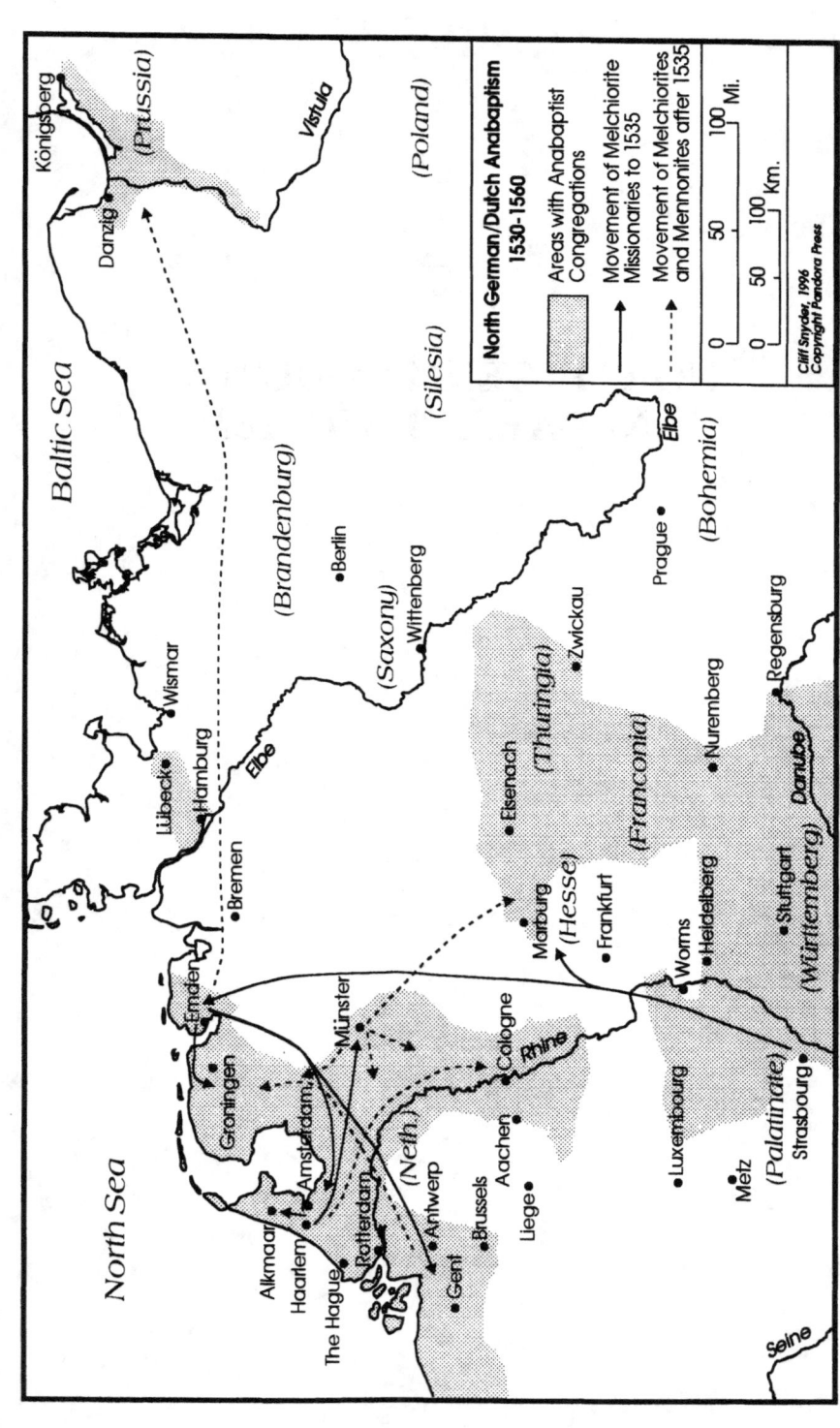

THE NORTH GERMAN/DUTCH ANABAPTIST CONTEXT

Melchiorite Anabaptist Origins
The beginnings of Anabaptism in North Germany and the Netherlands, unlike the Anabaptism of Switzerland or that of South Germany and Austria, can be traced to the overwhelming influence of one man, who stamped the northern movement with very discernible features.[1] That man was Melchior Hoffman, and his brand of Anabaptism proved to be both fruitful and unstable. The roles open to women differed widely in Melchiorite Anabaptism, depending upon the historical stage and the geographical region one happens to examine. In Hoffman's own founding community in Strasbourg, women played prominent ministerial roles; by contrast, toward the end of the brief reign of the "Anabaptist Kingdom" of Münster in 1535, women were required to be placed under the "lordship" of a man by the institution of polygamy. The general attitude of emphatic male lordship, if not the practice of polygamy, was continued by David Joris and his followers after Münster; a more literalistic mode of biblical submission of a woman to a man within a monogamous marriage was upheld resolutely by Menno Simons. The profiles that follow are drawn from all of these historical and ideological phases of the Melchiorite movement. Profiles of Melchiorite Anabaptist women of Strasbourg are included in this section even though, geographically speaking, Strasbourg is located in the south, not the north.

Melchior Hoffman and Strasbourg to 1533
Melchior Hoffman was a furrier by trade; he was literate, and a persuasive and powerful speaker.[2] By 1523 he was active as a Lutheran lay missionary in Livonia (1523-26). The work of the Holy Spirit was centrally important to Hoffman already in his early years as a Lutheran, and it appears that Karlstadt was more influential for him than was Luther.[3] Hoffman's attraction to apocalypticism was already evident in his early work: the Holy Spirit was being poured out on all people; the two witnesses of the Last Days (Elijah and Enoch) were already present in the world; but the Sword was to be used only against evildoers, and not in the church.[4] Hoffman's career as a Lutheran preacher was rocky and brief. His open break with the Lutheran reformers came in the matter of the Lord's Supper, in which Hoffman denied a real presence. By April 1529, Hoffman's break with the Lutheran stream was complete. Lutheran clergy now were added to the list of false prophets; henceforth Lutheranism was a "new Popery." Hoffman soon moved south to Strasbourg, where he came into contact with several varieties of Anabaptism and spiritualism. Present in the city were conventicles of Swiss Brethren, spiritualist followers of Hans Denck, followers of Pilgram Marpeck, the spiritualist Caspar Schwenckfeld, and a group of enthusiastic disciples of Hans Hut.[5]

Hoffman brought to Strasbourg his own overriding concern with the

Last Days and prophetic scripture and its interpretation, but he also appropriated elements from different theological streams, as they suited him. Beginning in 1530, he published several books of biblical prophecy in Strasbourg at the press owned by Margarethe Prüss, which got both him and the press into trouble (see the profile of Margarethe Prüss, in this text). We do not know who baptized him, but it is clear that he joined no existing group in Strasbourg. Rather, he formed his own.[6] His first Anabaptist writing, *The Ordinance of God* (1530), emphasized the same Anabaptist distinctives noted elsewhere in the movement: sinners are called to unite with Christ through repentance and water baptism; believers celebrate the Supper of unity (understood in a memorial sense); and believers submit to and practice discipline within the community of the covenant.[7] But to these common Anabaptist themes, Hoffman added a strong appreciation for the work of the Holy Spirit in contemporary believers, an extraordinary conviction that he was witnessing the Last Days, and an equally strong conviction that he had received from the Spirit the interpretive "Key of David" with which to unlock prophetic mysteries, both contemporary and scriptural.

The interest Hoffman expressed in prophetic scripture and the apocalypse, visible in the writings he published in Strasbourg in 1530, was paralleled by an equally strong interest in contemporary prophecy, an area of ministry open to women as well as men. Hoffman distinguished four possible roles for members of his congregations, namely as apostles, prophets, pastors, and regular members. It was in the second category that a place of leadership open to women was institutionalized in Hoffman's congregations.[8]

Except for a report of women apostles in northern Germany,[9] the office was usually limited to Melchiorite men; it was quite otherwise in the leadership category of prophets. Almost half of the seventeen or eighteen active prophets in Hoffman's community were women.[10] Lois Y. Barrett was able to find no explicit theological justification for the involvement of women in these positions, apart from Hoffman's citing of Joel 2:28-29 and Acts 2:17-18: "In the last days . . . I will pour out my Spirit upon all flesh, and your sons and your daughters shall prophesy . . ."[11] Given Hoffman's conviction that he was living in the last days, such scriptural justification undoubtedly was considered self-evident and not requiring further proof. Hoffman later would be responsible for publishing the dramatic visions of Ursula Jost, which dealt with the End Times–another Anabaptist writing also published by Margarethe Prüss's press in Strasbourg. These visions were destined to have a large impact in North Germany and Holland. Hoffman was convinced that God was speaking directly through such contemporary prophets[12]; we will profile in this book two of these Melchiorite prophets of Strasbourg, Ursula Jost and Barbara Rebstock.

By April of 1530 the authorities in Strasbourg had heard enough and decided to arrest Hoffman, but he managed to leave town one step ahead of them; he resurfaced in the north, in the city of Emden. He is said to have baptized three hundred people there.[13] Much as had Hans Hut earlier, Hoffman baptized persons who became zealous evangelists and baptizers of others; in both cases the expectation that Christ's return was imminent seems to have provided a special impetus for evangelism. The way for Anabaptism in the Low Lands had been prepared by the Sacramentarian movement, and Anabaptism very quickly became a mass movement of religious resistance.[14] From the Emden beginnings, Hoffman's version of Anabaptism spread into the Netherlands, where it had great success.[15] But in December 1531 disaster struck, when the Melchiorite apostle, Jan Volkerts Trijpmaker, was put to death along with nine others. Hoffman suspended baptism, and the Melchiorite movement in north Germany and the Netherlands went underground.[16] Melchior Hoffman remained at large, working both in Strasbourg and in the North, until May of 1533, when he allowed himself to be arrested in Strasbourg, sure that this event signalled a crucial turning point in the End Times scenario. He was to die in prison some ten years later.

The Melchiorite Anabaptist movement had taken strong root in the Netherlands, particularly in the cities of Amsterdam, Leeuwarden, and Groningen; the East Friesland region in the far north remained strongly Anabaptist from the start. The province of North Holland, directly north of Amsterdam, was soon evangelized (the cities of Alkmaar, Hoorn, and Enkhuisen), and Anabaptist conventicles and martyrs appeared in this region from 1534 on. The southern area, including Zeeland, Flanders and Brabant (with the city of Antwerp as an important Anabaptist centre), was reached later, beginning around 1534. And of course, outside the Netherlands proper, in nearby Westphalia, the city of Münster grew to become the Anabaptist focal point in the north in the years 1534 and 1535.[17]

Crusading Anabaptism in the Lowlands to 1536
Soon after Melchior Hoffman was imprisoned in Strasbourg in 1533, the Melchiorite baker from Haarlem, Jan Matthijs, began his prophetic activity in Amsterdam, initiating a second phase of Melchiorite development.[18] Led by dreams and visions, he reinstated baptism on the basis of his authority as the "Enoch" of the Last Days and claimed direct authority for many other actions as well.[19] Among those baptized by Matthijs and sent out as apostles was Jan van Leiden, later to be proclaimed "King of Münster and the world." Matthijs believed that he was the Enoch of the End Times, and came to believe that Münster, not Strasbourg, was the true New Jerusalem of the Last Days.[20] With Hoffman held increasingly incommunicado in the Strasbourg jail, Matthijs's interpretations came to be more and more accepted in the north.

Obbe Philips, who baptized both David Joris and Menno Simons, described another aspect of the revelatory events that took place in the north less than half a year after Hoffman's arrest in Strasbourg.

> There arose a baker of Haarlem named Jan Matthijs, who had an elderly wife whom he deserted, and he took with him a brewer's daughter who was a very pretty young slip of a girl and had great knowledge of the gospel. He enticed her away from her parents with sacred and beautiful words and told how God had shown great things to him, and she would be his wife. He carried her secretly with him to Amsterdam and brought her to a clandestine place.[21]

The brewer's daughter was Divara (see her profile). She would outlive Jan Matthijs to become the wife of Jan van Leiden; as such she became the "queen of Münster" and the leading wife among the sixteen wives Jan van Leiden eventually came to marry.

The baptism Matthijs and his apostles resumed was reminiscent of Hans Hut's mode of baptism. Hut, Hoffman, and Matthijs interpreted Anabaptist baptism in the apocalyptic sense of the TAU, following Revelation 7:3: a mark on the forehead of the 144,000 elect.[22] Matthijs's message had three central components: 1) This is the time of the working of the Spirit; 2) God is about to return and judge; and 3) those who are baptized will be spared.[23]

Parallel to events in the Netherlands were the reforming activities in the city of Münster in Westphalia. The leader of the reforming party there was Bernhard Rothmann.[24] By January of 1534 the reforming situation was exacerbated when Rothmann and other leading figures accepted rebaptism at the hands of two of Jan Matthijs's apostles.[25] By January of 1534 some 1,400 people had accepted rebaptism in the city, including nuns who had left their cloister and accepted baptism.[26] After elections for city councillors of February 23 fell to the Anabaptists, Jan Matthijs himself entered Münster, claiming prophetic authority; three days later the bishop began the military siege of Münster.[27] The Anabaptists were to hold the city for sixteen months.

The city soon was organized by the legislation of community of goods, with deacons appointed to care for the poor. Those who would not listen to the prophet Jan Matthijs were to be expelled from the city.[28] He preached with confidence that the second coming of Christ would take place, at the latest, by Easter 1534. On the fifth of April, Easter Day, citizens lined the city walls in expectation of viewing the spectacle of God destroying the heathen. In what was perhaps an act of desperation at the tardiness of divine intervention, Jan Matthijs finally sallied forth with a few companions, confident that God would come to their aid. He quickly was hacked to pieces, his head paraded on a lance by the besieging soldiers. Less than two months later, a young woman named Hille Feicken (profiled in this book), originally from Friesland, set out from Münster on an equally desperate mission: she felt called to assassinate the besieging bishop in a re-enactment of the story of the prophetess Judith and her royal victim Holofernes. She was discovered and executed before accomplishing her objective.

With the death of Jan Matthijs the way was clear for Jan van Leiden to assume power within the city. His credentials were not impressive: he was a tailor, a salesman, and an amateur actor, all of twenty-four years old, who had left a wife in Leiden. Nevertheless, he claimed that God had told him in a dream that he was to be Jan Matthijs's successor, and such was his personal charisma and ability that he managed to assume that role. In July of 1534 he married Divara and began instituting changes in the city's organization, primarily along Old Testament lines. By the end of that month he had instituted polygamy within the city (in which women now outnumbered men by more than two to one). In September of 1534 a prophet in the city proclaimed Jan to be "King over the New Israel and over the whole world."[29] King Jan now took on the role of the "new David," king of the righteous and castigator of the unrighteous.

As 1534 drew to a close, the great hope within the city of Münster lay with Anabaptist support outside the city. One such centre of support was the city of Deventer; the profile of Fenneke van Geelen provides a view of the Münsterite period from the Deventer perspective. By April 1535 the situation inside the city was desperate, for the massive support from outside had not materialized. The final taking of the city began June 25, 1535. It was made possible through the betrayal of the city by two of its citizens, and initiated a two-day bloodbath. The hundreds of dead eventually were buried by neighbouring peasants. Jan van Leiden was paraded around the countryside for show, and finally in January 1536 he, Bernhard Knipperdolling, and Bernd Krechting were publicly tortured for hours with red-hot tongs and eventually executed before the cathedral. Their remains were hung from the tower of St. Lambert's church in three iron cages. They had been preceded in death by Divara, who had been executed days before with little public fanfare.

The Melchiorite Movement after Münster: David Joris

After the fall of Münster, the Melchiorite movement in the north moved into a third phase of development. A small number of supporters of militant action (at first led by Jan van Batenburg) continued in existence, with ever-decreasing numbers. The first serious attempt to gather various Melchiorites together after the fall of Münster was undertaken by David Joris, who emerged as the most important Melchiorite leader in the north in 1536.[30] He, along with Menno Simons who would soon be his rival, had been one of the few Melchiorite leaders opposed to the crusading interpretation of Anabaptism during the height of excitement in 1535.[31] Joris maintained that the visible kingdom would come into being sometime in the future, as a result of God's action. Attempting to establish a visible kingdom by human agency in the here and now, as had been attempted by the Münsterites and was being continued by the Batenburgers, was a mistake. Joris emphasized instead the inner, spiritual life and the invisible, spiritual kingdom in what he was convinced were the days leading up to God's final action in history. He also became increasingly convinced of his own prophetic call as the "third David," a spiritual call that he and his followers were convinced gave a special authority to his visions, insights, and pronouncements.

Women who participated in Joris's movement are well represented in the following profiles. It appears that in spite of the fact that Joris emphasized male dominance (he continually advised men to let their "beards grow" in their relations with women), nevertheless his teaching exerted a strong power of attraction for women, not least women of the nobility.[32] The group profile of some of the women close to Joris provides some insight into that dynamic. The dramatic story of Anna Jansz, perhaps the best-known follower of David Joris because of her inclusion in the Mennonite martyrology, the *Martyrs' Mirror*, is also recounted below, as is the tragic story of the aristocratic martyrs, Maria and Ursula van Beckum, who were executed as Anabaptist heretics. Their Jorist convictions are probable, although not established beyond all doubt.

Joris's preeminence in post-Münsterite Anabaptism in the Low Lands up to ca. 1540 is undeniable. However, his failure in 1538 to convince the Strasbourg Melchiorites of his spiritual and prophetic authority marked the beginning of the end of his dream to unite actual and erstwhile Melchiorites under his mantle. Strasbourg had retained authority in the movement because of the continuing presence of Melchior Hoffman (albeit in jail) and the continuation of a strong Melchiorite community in that city. Central to the functioning of that community was the prophetic leadership of the prophetess Barbara Rebstock, and it was her intervention that was instrumental in the failure of Joris's bid for prophetic recognition. Rebuffed by the Strasbourg Melchiorites, Joris continued to "spiritualize" his message even further; eventually he was content to drop all external signs of Anabaptism, such as water baptism, a visible "separation from the world," and the celebration of the Lord's Supper. By 1544 he had disappeared from the Netherlands, reappearing in Basel under a pseudonym. He died there undetected by the authorities in 1556, although his movement continued in his absence into the next century.[33]

The Melchiorite Movement after Münster: Menno Simons
Joris's primary leadership rival in the Low Lands was Menno Simons, who became an Anabaptist after the collapse of Münster. Menno's unspectacular,

steady pastoral leadership in the decades following Münster eventually redefined the Melchiorite movement in the north, to the point that by the time of Menno's death in 1561, the Anabaptist communities he had organized (by 1561 commonly called "Mennist" or "Mennonite") far outnumbered other groups. Menno (b. 1496) had been ordained a priest in the Catholic church in 1524 at Utrecht, and served in the parish of Pingjum near Witmarsum. His path to reform began with doubts about the sacramental claims relating to the Lord's Supper. In January 1536, he suddenly left the priesthood and "sought out the pious," either in Leeuwarden or Groningen. He received baptism at the hands of Obbe Philips, and married Gertrude, who would accompany him until his death in 1561. They became parents to two daughters and one son.[34] He was ordained an elder sometime early in 1537, again by Obbe Philips, and began a tireless mission of reorganizing the scattered Melchiorites. By 1542 the authorities had put a price of 100 guilders on his head, but miraculously, in spite of constant travel and a life spent underground, Menno was never betrayed or apprehended.

In distinction to David Joris's prophetic claims and spiritualizing message, Menno emphasized the authority of the Bible and the establishment of a visible church of the righteous. In particular Menno criticized the "idolatrous duplicity" of the David Jorists, who sometimes conformed outwardly to local religious practices, while secretly practising Anabaptism. Menno's insistence on a "visible church" made avoiding detection a difficult task; the many hundreds of Mennonite martyrs in the Netherlands give witness to the high cost of maintaining this public witness. Approximately one-third of all Mennonite martyrs included in the *Martyrs' Mirror* were women.[35] The profiles of Elisabeth Dirks, Soetken van den Houte, and Anna Hendriks are three selected from that large number.

What roles were open to women in the later Mennonite communities? While the Strasbourg Melchiorites and David Joris disagreed about the gender limits of the prophetic office, Menno simply denied Melchior Hoffman's "prophetic office" to women and men alike. Not surprisingly, in light of the prophetic disasters that had occurred in the 1530s, Menno turned resolutely to Christ and the letter of scripture, to be interpreted by duly called preachers and teachers. In light of Swiss practice [*Schleitheim*], Hutterite practice, and early Melchiorite practice, how was leadership in the "community of saints" constituted in Menno's following? There was, first of all, no thought of either the Holy Spirit or congregations commissioning women to the office of preacher, teacher, or elder: the "pious preachers and teachers" were to be "men whom the Holy Ghost has ordained bishops and overseers in His church."[36] Menno taught the "biblical submission" of women to their husbands "in all reasonable things," but did not belabour the point; rather he wrote as though the matter were self-evident.[37] Lucille Marr has noted that "The conjugal relationship . . . took second place to the fellowship of believers. Women were encouraged to manage their households and to wait at home for their ministering and fugitive husbands." For example, Menno did not encourage the wife of Leenaert Bouwens to join her husband as an equal in his pastoral ministry.[38] This may represent a pragmatic stance on Menno's part, taken because of harsh persecution and a fear of upsetting the social order. In any case Menno, as Betti Erb has noted, "cannot be considered a champion of women."[39]

Menno's closing of the prophetic office to both women and men certainly eliminated a potential position of leadership for women such as had been exercised in the early Melchiorite movement by Ursula Jost, Barbara Rebstock, and others. Speaking generally, the progression away from the prophetic office to a more literal biblicism had the effect of restricting pastoral and leadership possibilities for women.[40] Nevertheless there is evidence that women continued to exercise informal leadership in the Mennonite setting, as they did also in the rest of the later Anabaptist movement. The case of Elisabeth Dirks, who appears to have functioned as such an informal leader, teacher, and possibly also deaconess, is well known to readers of the *Martyrs' Mirror* and is retold in her profile.[41] In some cases women were better educated than their husbands and were able to give them help in reading scripture.[42]

Women in the north also became notable hymn writers. In an era when essential doctrinal teachings were transmitted more by song than by prose, hymn writing was an extremely influential contribution. Soetjen Gerrits of Rotterdam, who was blind, composed an entire book of Anabaptist hymns that was published in Haarlem in 1592; the hymns of Vrou Gerrets of Medemblik also were published in a separate edition in 1607.[43] Both Soetjen Gerrits and Vrou Gerrits of Medemblik are profiled here. Numerous individual hymns composed by Dutch Anabaptist women also were sung, collected, and printed.[44] Finally, it was among the descendants of Menno that the office of "deaconess" was established; by 1632 the office was established well enough that the ninth article of the Dordrecht Confession, section 5, described the pastoral duties of women chosen to be deaconesses.[45]

Conclusion

There is no easy generalization about the role played by women in the North German/Dutch Anabaptist movement. The roles open to women were defined differently, depending upon the historical period and the leader in question. The North German/Dutch Anabaptist movement was characterized in its early Melchiorite stages by a strong prophetic strand and a corresponding emphasis on the Last Days, which Melchior Hoffman was sure he was witnessing. Hoffman himself opened the prophetic role for women, convinced that in the

Last Days, the spirit of God would be poured out upon women and men alike.

The prophetic movement that Jan Matthijs built in the Netherlands upon Melchiorite foundations appears to have moved progressively away from recognizing the prophetic potential of women; the position of women in Münster deteriorated to the point that all women were supposed to be under the "headship" of a man–a teaching that was institutionalized in polygamy. After the disasters of prophetic, End Times enthusiasm, the movement was recreated by the Obbenite faction, first by David Joris, and then in more permanent fashion by Menno Simons, in a decidedly non-apocalyptic mode. The establishment of Mennonite deaconesses early in the seventeenth century continued an earlier tradition of the involvement of North German/Dutch Anabaptist women in a variety of ministerial roles.

Notes

1 The following is drawn from C. Arnold Snyder *Anabaptist History and Theology: An Introduction* (Kitchener, ON: Pandora Press, 1995), chapters 10, 18 and 19.
2 "This Melchior was a very fiery and zealous man, a very smooth-tongued speaker who was celebrated for his great calling and commission . . ." Obbe Philips, "A Confession," in George H. Williams and Angel Mergal, eds., *Spiritual and Anabaptist Writers* (Philadelphia: Westminster Press, 1957), 208 (hereafter SAW).
3 Klaus Deppermann, *Melchior Hoffman: Soziale Unruhen und apokalyptische Visionen im Zeitalter der Reformation* (Göttingen: Vandenhoeck and Ruprecht, 1979), 45, 47, 49.
4 Ibid., 65-66.
5 Cornelius Krahn, *Dutch Anabaptism* (The Hague: Nijhoff, 1968), 87-89.
6 See the detailed analyses of Deppermann in *Hoffman*, passim; Krahn, *Dutch Anabaptism*, 89-91; 112-117.
7 Krahn, *Dutch Anabaptism*, 95; English translation of the Ordinance in Williams, SAW, 184-203. This writing has survived only in a Dutch language reprint of 1611; it was printed originally in East Frisia, in the local dialect, although the editor of the critical edition of the text, S. Cramer, argues on textual evidence that the original text was "thought in German." S. Cramer and F. Pijper, eds., *Bibliotheca Reformatoria Neerlandica*, vol. 5 ('s-Gravenhage: Nijhoff, 1909), 133-34.
8 In light of this, one might want to modify slightly Sprunger's statement that "Article IX [of the Dordrecht Confession] on officers in the church for the first time in Mennonite theology made a recognized place for women officers, the deaconesses." Keith L. Sprunger, "God's Powerful Army of the Weak: Anabaptist Women of the Radical Reformation," in Richard L. Greaves, ed., *Triumph over Silence: Women in Protestant History* (Westport, CN: Greenwood Press, 1985), 51.
9 See Ernst Crous, "Anabaptism in Schleiden-in-the-Eifel," MQR, 34 (July 1960): 189, who identifies Bernhartz Maria of Niederrollesbroich as one such woman "apostle."
10 See the profiles of Ursula Jost and Barbara Rebstock in this volume. Also, Lois Y. Barrett, "Wreath of Glory: Ursula Jost's Prophetic Visions in the Context of Reformation and Revolt in Southwestern Germany, 1524-1530," (PhD dissertation, The Union Institute, 1992), 202.
11 Ibid., 203.

12 Ibid., 89. Following his rejection by Bucer, Hoffman gathered together earlier followers of Denck, especially some "prophets." Among them were Katharina Seid, Andreas Klaiber, Lienhard Jost, Ursula Jost, Barbara Rebstock, and Hans Rebstock. The Rebstocks had been banned from Esslingen and had been influenced by Hut. Deppermann, *Hoffman*, 178-80. Translation of Ursula Jost's visions is found in Barrett, "Wreath."
13 Krahn, *Dutch Anabaptism*, 96.
14 Ibid., 118-19.
15 Ibid. Page 100 suggests that Hoffman also worked in the Netherlands with some success during 1531. For an opposing view, see Gary K. Waite, *David Joris and Dutch Anabaptism, 1524-1543* (Waterloo, ON: Wilfrid Laurier University Press, 1990), 40, n. 18.
16 Ibid., 285-87.
17 See Krahn, *Dutch Anabaptism*, 118-27.
18 On Matthijs, Rothmann, and events in Münster, see James Stayer, *Anabaptists and the Sword* (Lawrence, KS: Coronado Press, 1976), 227-80.
19 Stayer, *Sword*, 227-28.
20 Deppermann, *Hoffman*, 292-93.
21 Williams, SAW, 213-14.
22 Deppermann, *Hoffman*, 289.
23 Christoph Bornhäuser, *Leben und Lehre Menno Simons'* (Neukirchen-Vluyn: Neukirchener Verlag, 1973), 15.
24 See Willem J. De Bakker, "Bernhard Rothmann: Civic Reformer in Anabaptist Münster," in Irvin B. Horst, ed., *The Dutch Dissenters: A Critical Companion to Their History and Ideas* (Leiden: E.J. Brill, 1986), 105-16.
25 On Rothmann's theological development, see Martin Brecht, "Die Theologie Bernhard Rothmanns," *Jahrbuch für Westfälische Kirchengeschichte* 78 (1985): 49-82.
26 Gerd Dethlefs, "Das Wiedertäuferreich in Münster 1534/35," in Hans Galen, ed., *Die Wiedertäufer in Münster* (Münster: Aschendorff, 1986), 22.
27 Ibid., 24-25.
28 Ibid., 26.
29 Ibid., 30.
30 Stayer, *Sword*, 284, and more recently, Waite, *David Joris*, especially chapter 6.
31 Ibid., 267-68.
32 See also Gary Waite, "David Joris' Apology to Countess Anna of Oldenburg," MQR, 62 (April 1988): 140-58, and "The Post-Münster Melchiorite Debate on Marriage: David Joris' Response to Johannes Eisenburg, 1537," MQR, 63 (October 1989): 367-400.
33 Stayer, *Sword*, 298-302; Waite's account of these crucial years clearly maps not only the rise and fall of David Joris's leadership fortunes, but also the stresses and strains experienced by Dutch Anabaptism following the collapse of Münster.
34 Bornhäuser, *Leben und Lehre*, 30.
35 Analysis of women in the martyrology has been done by: Wayne Plenert, "The Martyrs' Mirror and Anabaptist Women," *Mennonite Life*, 30 No.2 (June 1975); John Klassen, "Women and the Family among Dutch Anabaptist Martyrs," MQR, 60 (October 1986). See also Leona Stucky Abbott, "Anabaptist Women of the Sixteenth Century," (masters thesis, Eden Theological Seminary, 1979). Jennifer H. Reed, "Dutch Anabaptist Female Martyrs and Their Responses to the Reformation," (masters thesis, University of South Florida, 1991); Jenifer Hiett Umble, "Women and Choice: An Examination of the *Martyrs' Mirror*," MQR, 64 (April 1990); Jenifer Hiett Umble, "Spiritual Companions: Women as Wives in the *Martyrs' Mirror*," *Mennonite Life*, 45 (September 1990).

36 Leonard Verduin, trans., *The Complete Writings of Menno Simons* (Scottdale, PA: Herald Press, 1956), 171 (hereafter CWMS).
37 In one of the few direct references, Menno says "Be obedient to your husbands in all reasonable things so that those who do not believe may be gained by your upright, pious conversation without the Word, as Peter says." CWMS, 383.
38 M. Lucille Marr, "Anabaptist Women of the North: Peers in the Faith, Subordinates in Marriage," MQR, 61 (October 1987): 347-62; citation on 355.
39 Betti Erb, "Reading the Source: Menno Simons on Women, Marriage, Children, and Family," CGR 8 (Fall, 1990): 302. Cf. CWMS, 113. Nevertheless, Menno was sympathetic and pastoral. See, for example, the story of "The Little Swan of Emden" as told by Harry Loewen in *No Permanent City, Stories from Mennonite History and Life* (Waterloo, ON: Herald Press, 1993), 24-26, which shows a different side of Menno Simons.
40 A. Jelsma, "De positie van de vrouw in de Radicale Reformatie," *Doopsgezinde Bijdragen*, nieuwe reeks 15 (1989): 25-36, esp. page 34.
41 See ME, II, 185; *Martyrs' Mirror*, 481-83; retold in Roland Bainton, *Women of the Reformation in Germany and Italy* (Minneapolis: Augsburg Publishing House, 1973), 145-49, and also in Sprunger, "God's Army of the Weak," 53-54.
42 "Claesken of Workum (1559) was better educated than her husband who could not read or write, and gave a much better account of her faith before execution. Her prosecutors accused her, because of her good education, of seducing her husband into Anabaptism. Claudine le Vettre's husband, himself a minister of the Word, praised her astonishing knowledge of Scripture. 'For whenever he could not find a passage, he would ask his wife Claudine, who would at once clearly indicate to him what he sought.'" Sprunger, "God's Army of the Weak," 59.
43 See ME, IV, 570; ME, II, 502. Also the survey of Dutch Anabaptist hymnody in Rosella Reimer Duerksen, "Anabaptist Hymnody of the Sixteenth Century," (D. Music dissertation, Union Theological Seminary, 1956), 50-64.
44 As, for instance, the poems of Judith Lubbertsdochter. See ME, III, 410. See Sprunger, "God's Army of the Weak," 56.
45 Deaconesses were to "visit, comfort, and take care of the poor, the weak, the afflicted, and the needy, as also to visit, comfort, and take care of widows and orphans; and further to assist in taking care of any matters in the church that properly come within their sphere, according to their best ability." Cited in ME, II, 22. See the entire article on "Deaconess," in ibid., 22-25.

MARGARETHE PRÜSS OF STRASBOURG[1]

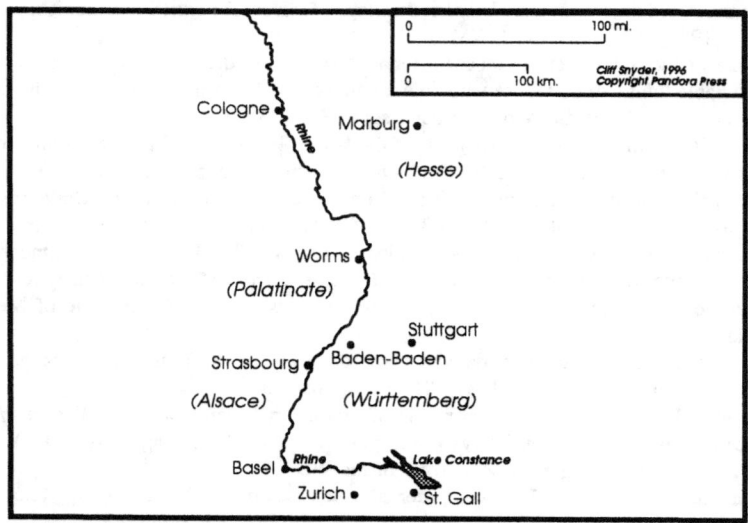

And being of the female sex did not turn me from the enterprise of publishing, nor the fact that it be more a manly office. . . . It is not new or unheard of for women to have such a trade, and one can find many of us who exercise not only the typographical art, but others more difficult and arduous, and who obtain thereby the highest of praise.
Jeanne Giunta, book publisher of Lyon, 1579.[2]

In sixteenth-century Strasbourg men were "printers" and women were "printers' wives." Being female, however, did not prevent Margarethe Prüss[3] from becoming involved in the enterprise of publishing which, as described by her contemporary Jeanne Giunta, a publisher in Lyon, was "more a manly office." Although there were several women in Strasbourg who practised the art of printing, officially women were not recognized as printers. In a world where only men were printers, Margarethe found a way to defy the norm. Margarethe's story then, is the story of a printer who, according to the society in which she lived, was not a printer. Furthermore, in a world where printing radical reforming literature was punishable by law, Margarethe published these documents anyway. Thanks in part to the art of printing, the radical ideas of the sixteenth-century reformers spread quickly throughout Alsace and far beyond. The printshop owned by Margarethe Prüss, *Zum Thiergarten* [At the Animal Garden], played a key role in making the writings of Anabaptist leaders widely available.

Unfortunately, as is the case for many of her female contemporaries, there is limited documentation on Margarethe (d. 1542). One can nevertheless glean significant information about her from the life stories of the men around her, including her father, her brother, and her three husbands. For example, it is well known that among those sympathetic to the early Anabaptist movement in Strasbourg were to be found members of Margarethe's family, the well-known printers named Prüss. But we do not know when or if any member of the family was baptized, although circumstantial evidence suggests that she was an Anabaptist. While Margarethe's third husband, Balthasar Beck, is referred to as an Anabaptist in several sources, no date of a believer's baptism has been found to confirm that he or Margarethe officially joined the movement.

The crux of Margarethe's story is that, as a sixteenth-century woman in Strasbourg, the only way for her to have a career as a printer was to marry a printer. Margarethe probably learned aspects of the printing business as a young girl assisting in her father's shop. But although she, along with her brother, inherited the family business when their father died, Margarethe could not carry on as a printer unless the man she married was also a printer. Guild rules prevented her carrying on as a single woman and a printer. Ironically, as the daughter of a master printer, Margarethe could confer both printing and citizenship rights on a husband or a son–rights that she herself could not hold. Cognizant of these restrictions, it would seem, Margarethe married a printer. When he died, she married another. And when her second husband also died, Margarethe Prüss married yet a third printer. A unique and important aspect of Margarethe's story is that not only did she marry one printer–she married three.

What is significant about each of her husbands is that they all took the risk of printing documents first of the evangelical, and then of the radical reforming stream. The Prüss press lost money more than once because of the censorship (which meant confiscation and destruction) of the radical materials that had been printed. As the common ownership link throughout the history of the Prüss press during the early years of the Reformation in Strasbourg, Margarethe clearly was aware of the ideological bent of the books being produced by her press. In fact, it appears that Margarethe's choice of husband/printers was coloured by her commitment to the continued printing of radical materials. This woman pragmatically contributed to the movement of the early Anabaptists, and radical reform generally, in the best way available to her in her context.

Unlike the men in her family, Margarethe probably did not go through an extensive formal apprenticeship (usually four years) in order to become a printer. We know that her brother Johann, and her first husband, Reinhardt Beck, had trained with Margarethe's father. It had not always been the case that women were barred from formal apprenticeship in the trades. During the thirteenth and fourteenth centuries, both girls and boys were allowed to apprentice, but gradually the ordinances of the guilds either specifically forbade girls to apprentice or merely neglected to mention them.

However, as the daughter of a master craftsman, and given her continuing active interest, Margarethe probably received informal training in her father's shop. It was common practice for the daughters of master craftsmen to work for their own families until they married, as opposed to doing domestic service for others. Young girls learned domestic skills by their mother's side, as well as often learning aspects of their father's trade. This proved financially advantageous for the family, since it could benefit from a few years of their daughter's unpaid labour. But training in a trade did not necessarily do the girl any good in the long run, since it was very unusual for a woman to marry a man in the same line of work as her father. And since formal entrance into most trades was barred to women by the sixteenth century, the informal family training received was often all for naught.[4]

If a woman wanted to continue in the career direction learned from her father, she had to follow a path much like Margarethe's: marry someone in that trade. Even though a woman had not been formally apprenticed, if she had the skills and the interest, she could do almost anything in the shop that her husband did. If a craftsman husband died, women like Margarethe often carried on the family business for a short time as widows; but younger widows generally married again, as did Margarethe. Because most widows did not marry men in the same line of work as their first husbands, they had to shift to the career of their second husband. In what appears to have been a deliberate choice, Margarethe did not have to adapt herself to another career during her second or her third marriages.

Although atypical, Margarethe's story is not unique. Mie Roybet, a woman in sixteenth-century Lyon, also married three printers and was imprisoned for printing religious documents not approved by the authorities. Another sixteenth-century woman from Lyon, Antoinette Peronet, also outlived two husbands and married a third, all of them connected to the publishing business, namely a printer, a bookseller, and a publisher, respectively.[5]

Whether married or widowed, however, printers' wives generally had neither the status of citizenship, the right to membership or a vote in the guilds, or the right to become a craftmaster. In order to have the "right to exercise a trade," a shop owner had to have citizenship and guild membership. While there is evidence of an unusual case where the unmarried daughter of a Strasbourg printer actually purchased citizenship in 1525 and joined the guild like other printers, there is no evidence that this woman, Walpurga Wähninger, ever printed any books in her own name. Rather, she probably worked as a proofreader or corrector. The important element of Walpurga's story is that this woman wanted to be publicly recorded as a member of the guild, even though as a woman she could have no voting rights. The guild system was a system developed by men with male interests in mind. And as a general rule, men wished to exclude women from working in their trades, even in those cases where women could afford the price of citizenship and guild membership.[6]

In practice, marriage to a craftmaster/printer often meant that the wife was as much a "printer" as was her husband. Judging from sixteenth-century practice, Margarethe's duties likely included responsibility for collecting debts and keeping the books. In fact, in the recorded inventories, many of the debts owed to craftsmen are listed as being owed to the craftsman's wife. It was often the wife's job to handle shop purchases and distribute salaries and food to the journeymen. In the unpaid role of an accounts administrator, the wife was responsible for large amounts of money. And although her role within society was that of a "printer's wife," not as a printer herself, her status should not be minimized. For a woman to identify herself as "the wife of the printer" was not merely an indication of her marital status; it also was her occupational title.[7] A woman like Margarethe knew that her role in the family business was as important as her husband's. Her particular skills and tasks were recognized and her pride at being the wife of a printer, rather than the wife of a day labourer, who had no permanent job, came not only from her husband's profession, but also from her own.

Participation by the wife in the printshop was often economically essential. Since the success of the family business was the goal of both the husband and the wife, they co-operated in production. They not only worked together, they also were customarily named as co-vendor or co-purchaser and jointly owned their business property. Such joint ownership was unique to the guildsfolk; prospective husbands and wives among the rich merchants and patricians clearly reserved their separate inheritances and specified dowry. In the world of the crafts people, material expression was given to the gospel dictum that husband and wife were one flesh.[8] This certainly was the case with Margarethe and her three husbands, for in sixteenth-century court records from Alsace, Margarethe was identified as the owner of the printshop.[9] While the guilds placed firm restrictions on women, they did acknowledge the importance of the master's wife. In fact, they required every master craftsman to be married. The guilds recognized that it was up to the wife to feed and clothe her family–in Margarethe's case this meant eight children and her husband–and the employees, including apprentices, journeymen, and domestic servants.[10] In addition, if her husband was away, the wife ran the shop and supervised the workers.

Although Margarethe was the master printer's wife and had a great deal of responsibility, within the shop there were nevertheless clear distinctions between what she was allowed to do, as a woman, and what the men around her could do. These distinctions were often based on the belief that there were certain things which it was not "proper" for women to do. In addition, many falsely believed that husbands never let their wives in on trade secrets. Sixteenth-century popular belief that menstruating women posed dangers for both technical and natural processes also often prohibited the wife from being in the shop at certain times of the month.[11]

In contrast to the men in the business, Margarethe's work and status in the shop changed, not according to her own training or ability, but according to her relationship to the man in charge. As a daughter, she assisted without pay. As a wife, she was in partnership with her husband. Finally, as a widow, she was in charge of the business of her former husband–but with restricted legal rights–until she was able to marry again.

The social status of printers steadily increased during the fifteenth and sixteenth centuries. Printers traditionally had been referred to as artisans and craftsmen, but sixteenth-century documents refer to printing as "an art." Printing was recognized as distinct because it produced a uniquely valuable product able to influence human thought.[12] The masters of this new technology immediately were granted special respect and assigned to the *Steltz*–one of the most prestigious of the twenty guilds in Strasbourg.

Johann Prüss, Sr. (1447-1510), Margarethe's father, had begun printing in Strasbourg in 1480, during the final phase of a long, slow period of growth when a total of less than forty books were produced each year in the city.[13] He soon rivalled one of the city's best printers, Henri Knoblochtzer, in the art of illustration. Prüss was originally from Württemberg and did not actually acquire his right of citizenship in Strasbourg until about 1490, when he was over forty years of age. According to the tax registry of 1503, Johann Prüss, Sr. had a bookshop window at the front of his printshop, for which he paid an annual tax of eight shillings. In addition, he also had a small shop among those next to the cathedral.[14] By 1504, Prüss had established himself in his printshop and soon became well known for his magnificent missals and breviaries.

Margarethe's father died in 1510, just as the Strasbourg printing industry was entering a boom period that lasted almost twenty years. During this time, the city's production doubled from forty to about eighty books a year. One cause for the boom seems to have been the Reformation–the Reformation debates monopolized the presses in the 1520s. This publication boom was followed by an erratic decline from 1529 to 1544, with a sharp depression from 1546-56. Gradually book production in Strasbourg returned to a stable level of around fifty books per year.[15]

Although Johann Prüss, Sr. died on November 16, 1510, the last work to have been printed in his shop, a Strasbourg breviary, did not appear until March 1, 1511. The project was probably finished under the guidance of his son, Johann, who theoretically carried on the family shop alone for a while, although no doubt Margarethe was present and helping out. Margarethe's first husband, Reinhardt Beck, her father's typographer, soon joined the Prüss family business. But already in the first year of this new partnership, Johann, Jr. moved his part of the business to a new printshop on Ste-Hélène Street. It is quite possible that a conflict precipitated this separation, but there is no documentation that clarifies the question.[16] Upon his marriage to Margarethe in 1511, Reinhardt Beck took over the shop and Johann, Jr. found a new location. Perhaps there was not enough business at the one press to allow both Johann and Reinhardt to make a living, but one still wonders why it was Johann, and not Reinhardt, who left to begin another press. Perhaps Margarethe's role was the deciding factor.

Unfortunately, Margarethe's brother's new business never matched the volume of printing of his father's shop, nor did he achieve the same reputation. Nevertheless, in spite of a number of financial embarrassments, Johann, Jr. managed to make an arrangement with his creditors, allowing him to continue to print in Strasbourg until at least 1551. During the Reformation he printed a few of Martin Luther's treatises and some of Karlstadt's writings; he also had the honour of being one of the first, if not the first, in Strasbourg to print works in French.[17]

Women like Margarethe played a key role in ensuring that established businesses were carried on. A crucial link in the process was the inheritance of a press by a daughter, who then passed it on to her husband through marriage. In fact, a printer's marriage to another printer's widow or daughter was as important as inheritance from father to son, since property was transferred through daughters as often as through sons. There were seven instances in Strasbourg during the late fifteenth and sixteenth centuries that a press passed from the husband/owner to the widow, and then to the second husband, who took over as director of the press. During the same period, six printers' daughters married printers, resulting in the passing on of four shops to the sons-in-law. Three of these transfers took place through Margarethe.[18]

Margarethe's first husband, Reinhardt Beck, originally from Cologne, purchased his Strasbourg citizenship on May 17, 1511, and would have been assigned immediately to the *Steltz* guild. The Strasbourg magistrate assigned new citizen printers to the guild in order to control the new industry and to assimilate the new printers into the city's political system.[19] Since it was necessary for Reinhardt to buy his citizenship, obviously he was not yet married to Margarethe; the right to citizenship would have been bestowed upon him automatically, free of charge, immediately following their marriage. Reinhardt and Margarethe were married sometime later in 1511.[20]

As a citizen, a man had the right to vote in his guild for the representative from that guild to the city's senate. His status of citizenship gave him the protection of the city and the right to exercise a trade. Once purchased, these rights of citizenship automatically passed on to all legitimate children. (Many men and women within the city walls were not citizens, but rather *Inwohner*, or inhabitants with no rights or privileges.) Through his marriage to Margarethe, Reinhardt Beck achieved social advancement, as was also the case for Margarethe's second and third husbands. Indeed, marriage was the most important route for social and material advancement for both males and females. At the time of their marriage, both sons and daughters were in a position to inherit a share of property from their parents, allowing them to set up their own businesses.[21]

With his marriage to Margarethe, Reinhardt gained part ownership in the inherited Prüss printshop. When Margarethe's brother left, Reinhardt became the sole proprietor of the business and remained so until his death in 1522. For a brief period of time, soon after their wedding, Margarethe and Reinhardt moved their business to Baden. Their stay in Baden may have been the result of the outbreak of the plague in Strasbourg in the winter of 1511. But already by March 18, 1512, they had returned to Strasbourg, according to the publication date and place found in a book which Reinhardt printed.[22]

A significant shift in the productions of the *Zum Thiergarten* printshop occurred as early as 1519, when Reinhardt Beck deserted the Catholic repertoire of Margarethe's father in favour of evangelical works. Margarethe's role in this shift is unclear, although her influence must not be discounted, particularly in view of the ideological bent of the subsequent husbands she chose to marry. At any rate, Margarethe and Reinhardt took the risk of printing reformation documents quite early on, when they printed Lutheran treatises, including at least one by Martin Luther. From their printshop also came numerous missals, treatises by humanist authors, the works of classical writers, grammar texts, and dictionaries. Most of the material was in Latin, although some documents also were in vernacular German, and thus available to the general population.[23]

When Reinhardt Beck died early in 1522, Margarethe transferred the printshop to a house she owned on the *Marché de Bois* [Wood Market] in Strasbourg. There she founded another printshop, *am Holzmarkt* [At the Wood Market], which she operated alone until she hired Wolffgang Forter to help. Forter later married Margarethe's daughter, Ursula. Through this marriage, Forter also obtained his right of citizenship. According to the citizenship document, "Wolffgang Forter the printer received the right of citizenship from Margarethe Reinhardt Beck, because of his wife (Ursula), the deceased printer's daughter."[24] Once again the irony is apparent: Margarethe (named here in conjunction with her deceased husband), herself not a citizen, could pass on rights of citizenship to a man indirectly through her daughter, Ursula.

With the death of Reinhardt in 1522, Margarethe's status changed immediately. The death of a master craftsman most directly affected his wife's status, since the guild's most common restrictions affected the widows of their members. A crucial restriction was how long a wife could continue to operate her husband's shop. In the mid-fifteenth century, a widow generally was limited to one or two years. Later, this was further restricted to as little as two months. And in some cases, a widow was only allowed to finish work that her husband had begun. Sometimes a widow could only continue if she had a son who would eventually inherit the business.[25] While we do know that Margarethe and Reinhardt did have two sons, no mention is made of either of them taking over the printshop at this time.

Despite guild restrictions, city governments usually were more willing to allow a widow to continue the family business. Governments, however, did not base their choice on the widow's wishes, but on their own interests: if a widow continued the business it meant that the family could be self-supporting and would not need financial assistance from the government. Providing financial assistance could become a tremendous burden, especially when 10 to 15 percent of the shops were run by widows at any one time.[26]

Her status as a widow brought Margarethe close to financial independence and "full social maturity."[27] However, it had to be a temporary condition. One guild restriction was particularly hard on widows: all workshops were required to employ at least one journeyman. This often proved a great financial drain for widows, so much so that many could not afford to continue operating their husbands' shops. As a result, the right to continue operating a workshop, even temporarily, was only a theoretical privilege for most widows. The guilds had their own reasons for placing such restrictions on widows; they wanted to ensure that the widow remarried. In fact, the primary reason why a guild would even allow a widow to continue the operation of her husband's shop for any length of time was only to protect the workshop until the widow was able to remarry and transfer her guild and citizenship rights to a new husband. And in some cases, depending on her age, the guilds crassly classified a widow not with the status "widow," but as "future wife."[28]

Some guild members had difficulty allowing widows to continue their husband's business for any length of time. Among the guilds there were those who feared that if a widow was given "master status" in a trade organization with a limited number of places for masters, it could further curtail the opportunities for young men wanting to enter the guild. This argument was the catalyst for the many other arguments articulated against widows. Some argued, for example, that a widow should not run a shop because her sexuality was no longer under the patriarchal bond of a man. Gossip about widows and fear of their "untamed sexuality" was common. There is the case of one woman who remarried because of "the evil talk" she had to endure as a widow.[29]

Any or all of these factors would have contributed to Margarethe's decision to remarry. By 1524, within two years of her first husband's death,

Margarethe was no longer a widow. Her second husband, Johannes Schwann of Marburg, took over the printshop on the date of their marriage.

In 1509 Johannes Schwann had entered the order of the Franciscans at Marburg and from there was sent to the monastery in Basel. However, he left the monastery in 1522 and went to Wittenberg. In a letter dated February 27, 1523, addressed to his father Daniel Schwann of Marburg, Johannes gave his reasons–supported with biblical references–why he could no longer remain a Franciscan. In this letter he attacked the pope and the Roman Catholic understanding of salvation, stating instead that faith alone could save. While faith alone might save, it did not earn a living. And so it was that Johannes Schwann made his way to Strasbourg, where he learned the trade of printing–he may have apprenticed in the Prüss shop, although there is no evidence concerning the matter.[30]

The guilds made it very attractive for a man in Johannes Schwann's position to marry a widow like Margarethe. The guild entrance fees were often reduced or even eliminated in such cases. The guilds also lessened the length of time required of a man like Johannes to work as a journeyman before becoming a master. And of course, upon his marriage, Johannes received a house and a fully equipped shop with apprentices and journeymen.[31]

It is unclear whether it was through her second husband that Margarethe was influenced in a radical and Anabaptist direction. It is more likely that as a literate woman and for a time the sole proprietor of a print shop, she was well aware of the reforming ideas in circulation in the city.[32] She probably was sympathetic to radical reform prior to her second marriage; in fact her decision to marry Johannes Schwann was probably dictated in part by his own agreement with her theological convictions. At any rate, under the direction of Schwann, the Prüss press printed not only some of Luther's writing, but also writings by Andreas Karlstadt and Clement Ziegler, the radical Strasbourg gardener and lay preacher. Ziegler had appeared before the magistrates several times requesting permission to publish his religious treatises; his requests were denied. The document that the Prüss press printed on June 2, 1524, was a short summary of biblical references to idolatry and where such idolatry might be found in the religious practices of the day.[33] Given that the city was in tumult at this time concerning the practice of the mass and the veneration of religious "images" (the prime targets for charges of "idolatry"), the decision to publish this tract was a deliberate political action in favour of radical reform. The city records state that the book was "printed in Strasbourg by Johannes Schwann . . . [who] had taken over the printery from his wife Margarethe Prüss, of whom he was the second husband."[34]

The Strasbourg court records also refer to the Prüss printing of a second book by Ziegler. The second document concerned the virginity of

Mary and her first-born child, Christ. Reception of the document in Catholic regions was made easier because of the two woodcut prints of Mary with the child that adorned the document. From a copy of this booklet in the Dresden State Library, it has been determined that the printshop responsible for its publication "was that of Johannes Schwann, or in particular, of his wife, Margarethe Prüss." The printing date, determined by the document's content and tone, was either early in the year or in the summer of 1524.[35]

Margarethe's second marriage lasted only two years, for Johannes Schwann died in 1526. Because she once again assumed ownership of the printshop, Margarethe had no lack of suitors. By May 27, 1527, she had remarried. Her third husband, the printer Balthasar Beck (d. 1551), was from Kirchheim an der Eck, an Alsatian village situated on the small river Eckenbach. Beck probably learned the printing trade in his native village, where the brother of the Strasbourg printer Johann Grüninger had a printery.[36] With her marriage to Balthasar Beck, Margarethe once again passed on citizenship rights and guild rights, as well as the ownership of her printshop, for the third and last time.

Her third husband was even more markedly radical than had been Johannes Schwann. It was commonly repeated that Balthasar Beck was an Anabaptist, although there is no surviving documentation that proves the allegation. But it is undeniable that Balthasar Beck was favourably disposed to Anabaptism. When a certain Anabaptist, named Cornelius of Middelburg in Zeeland, was interrogated on November 27 and December 3, 1533, he specifically mentioned Balthasar Beck as one of his contacts. Cornelius stated that he had come to Strasbourg to visit his imprisoned Anabaptist colleague Melchior Hoffman, and declared that he had not gone to the home of any Anabaptist, except to the home of the printer Balthasar Beck.[37]

From the Prüss-Beck press now came the works of Anabaptist and Radical Reformation leaders. Beginning in 1529, the Beck press published a series of writings by the progenitor of North German/Dutch Anabaptism, Melchior Hoffman. The first was a dialogue concerning the disputation held in Holstein on the subject of the sacrament of the Supper; it was followed in the same year by a booklet concerned with prophecy in scripture and the trials "of these last times." In 1530 the Beck press published yet another Hoffman work entitled "Prophecy or prediction from the true, holy, divine scripture," which was followed by Hoffman's lengthy "Exposition of the divine Revelation of John." Later in 1530, Melchior Hoffman edited the visions of the prophetess Ursula Jost (see her profile in this volume), which the Beck press published as well. This book of visions and revelations had a great influence in the Netherlands. The last book by Hoffman to be published by the Beck press was Hoffman's figurative analysis of the "lights" of the Old Testament, also published in 1530.[38] Thus, in the space of only two years, the Beck press published six controversial and radical books written by Melchior Hoffman, some of which exerted a significant influence on the Anabaptist movement of the Low Countries.

Those who dared to print the writings of the Radical Reformers and Anabaptists often took great business risks. The Prüss printing business lost money when, in 1530, Melchior Hoffman's book of prophecies from the holy scriptures and his edition of Ursula Jost's visions were censored, confiscated, and the remaining copies destroyed. In April 1530 a warrant was issued for Balthasar Beck's arrest because of his printing of Hoffman's works. There was no trial, however, since Hoffman managed to escape and fled the country. Although the remaining stock of these banned books was destroyed, many copies had been shipped out and exerted their influence elsewhere. The printing of Sebastian Franck's *Chronicle* by the Prüss-Beck press on September 5, 1531, also proved to be a significant financial loss when it, too, was censored. Once again Balthasar Beck was ordered to appear before the censors for printing this unorthodox and encyclopedic "church history" by Franck. As before, while the magistrate ordered that all copies be destroyed, a good number must have been salvaged, for many are still in existence.[39] Margarethe's family involvement with the Radical Reformation movement was not only tied to printing; in 1542 her daughter Margarethe married Sebastian Franck.

There also is speculation that a pamphlet entitled "A brotherly warning to master Mathis" may have been printed by Margarethe herself. This pamphlet appeared in Strasbourg either late in 1522 or early in 1523. It has been determined that the author's name, Steffan von Büllheyen, was probably a pseudonym. From the evidence in the text, whoever wrote it, whether man or woman, was intimately familiar with the events and the life of Strasbourg. The pamphlet's structure is a dialogue between a father, attached to the Roman Catholic church, and his son, who is taken by the "new ideas" of the Reformers. Not unlike most pamphlets of the time, this one is partisan, glorifying an "evangelical" and reprimanding his enemy. While this pamphlet is not a theological text, popularized theological themes appear throughout. Furthermore, it gives precise information about the Matthias Zell affair that had occurred in the latter months of 1522. The pamphlet sheds light on one strand of public opinion about that turn of events.[40]

Matthias Zell, the parish priest of Saint-Laurent of the cathedral in Strasbourg, had preached since 1521 in what was considered a "lutheran" manner. At the end of 1522, he was cited to appear before the episcopal vicar. His case lasted until March 1523, when public opinion in favour of these "new ideas" swung the decision in Zell's favour. Although the case was, strictly speaking, theological and political, it was widely discussed by the general public, even (or perhaps especially) in the pubs.[41]

The pamphlet in question appeared in two editions in 1522-23.

Edition A was printed by Jean Knobloch, the elder. Edition B, containing fewer typographical errors, was printed by an unknown Strasbourg printer at about the same time. Some sources name Johannes Schwann as the printer, while others insist that Johann Prüss, Jr. printed it. Although a precise date of the pamphlet's printing cannot be determined, it probably appeared soon after the events themselves took place. In light of the fact that Schwann did not begin printing in Strasbourg until 1524, after his marriage to Margarethe, one can eliminate his name from the list of possibilities. Based on the assumption, then, that the pamphlet was printed in 1523, its publication can only be attributed to Johann Prüss, Jr. or to Margarethe. By 1522-23 Johann Prüss, Jr. had already left the family printshop to start his own printing business. While it is possible that he may have printed this pamphlet in his new shop, it is just as possible that Margarethe printed it herself after the death of her first husband.

In spite of the obstacles, it is altogether possible that Margarethe oversaw the printing of a few books on her own. We know that other sixteenth-century women definitely did write and publish; Margarethe, who owned her own printshop, certainly had the opportunity to do likewise. In Strasbourg the remarkable Katharina Zell, wife of Matthias Zell, wrote tracts and republished all the songs of Michael Weisse's 1531 evangelical songbook from Bohemia. This was the largest German hymnal published in the first half of the sixteenth century; it contained 157 songs to 112 melodies. Katharina, aware of this wonderful, popular hymnal, made its songs accessible to all by publishing them in four small booklets between 1534 and 1536.[42]

Another woman, the wife of the printer Hans Hergott from Nuremberg, is known to have published Anabaptist hymns. Like Margarethe, Kunigunde Hergott survived the death of her radical printer husband (d. 1527) and carried on his printing business. It has been determined that in 1529 Kunigunde anonymously published a hymn, *"Freut euch, freut euch zu dieser Zeit,"* written by the Anabaptist Balthasar Hubmaier. Kunigunde also published the first copy of another Anabaptist hymn called *"Kumpt her zur mir spricht Gottes Sohn."* This song, written by the Anabaptist songwriter Georg Grünwald in 1530, the year of his death, was later published in other songbooks.[43]

While the printing activity of the successors of Johann Prüss, Sr. continued for a period of forty-one years after his death until 1551, the content of the books printed by his successors differed greatly from that of his own publications. Whereas the father of the Prüss family had printed religious books in the Roman Catholic tradition, his successors made Reformation polemic available to German-speaking readers in western Europe. Although the risks of censorship were well understood, printers like Margarethe willingly undertook those risks. The spread of reforming ideas depended in part on print for the diffusion of those ideas. Sympathetic people in positions of influence, such as Margarethe Prüss who owned and controlled a press, were key to the furthering of the radical theology of the Reformation.

As the possessor of the inheritance rights to the Prüss family printing business, Margarethe played a pivotal role. She passed on that business to three husbands in succession, and eventually to her children, who are named as heirs in the official document of her death, dated May 23, 1542. Margarethe willed her property to all of her eight children: seven from her marriage to Reinhardt Beck (Ursula, Sebastian, Onuphre, Margarethe, Anne, Juliane, and Reinhardt, Jr.) and one from her marriage to Johannes Schwann (Elisabeth). Although it was clearly written in the will that Margarethe wished for all of her children to receive an equal share of the inheritance, apparently Elisabeth was refused her part of the house on the *Marché de Bois*. As a result Elisabeth became estranged from the family. It was not until September 22, 1546, that reconciliation was achieved. Another child, Juliane, was a nun in the St. Nicholas convent for several years. Juliane, too, was refused her part of the inheritance. We do not know if she received what was due to her, or whether there was a continuing conflict between her and the rest of the family. Margarethe's son Reinhardt is the only one of whom we know further details: he became a printer in Basel.

Key to Margarethe's story was her decision to marry printers that enabled her to continue in this line of work and to retain some measure of control of the Prüss family printing business. She utilized the best means available to her as a woman of her time. Margarethe exercised control over the materials published in her printshop through her choice of husbands. The printers whom she married either were Anabaptist sympathizers or Anabaptists themselves. While we do not know with certainty that Margarethe herself accepted rebaptism, her strong religious convictions are evident in the material published in her printshop. The evidence is indirect, but persuasive: with each husband, the materials printed at Margarethe's shop became more radical.[44] As a printshop owner and a woman, Margarethe overcame the limits of the role assigned to women by sixteenth-century culture and as a result, made a significant contribution to the early Anabaptist movement far beyond the city of Strasbourg.

Notes

1 Dedicated to the memory of my Grandfather, John L. Gascho, for whom Anabaptist history was part of his personal story. The author acknowledges the Centre for Renaissance and Reformation Studies at the University of Victoria College, University of Toronto, for providing access to their archives.

2   Cited in Natalie Zemon Davis, "Women in the crafts in sixteenth-century Lyon," *Feminist Studies* 8 (Spring 1982): 47.
3   There are various spellings of Margarethe Prüss in the records: Marguerete/ Margarete/Margarite/Margareth Pruess/Preuss Beck.
4   See Zemon Davis, "Women in the Crafts."
5   Ibid., 57-58, 66.
6   Miriam Usher Chrisman, *Lay Culture, Learned Culture: Books and Social Change in Strasbourg, 1480-1599* (New Haven: Yale University Press, 1982), 23. In general the sixteenth century was marked by a trend to exclude women from the crafts. See Merry E. Wiesner, *Working Women in Renaissance Germany* (New Brunswick, NJ: Rutgers University Press, 1986), 2.
7   Ibid., 195. The printing trade was not unique. "For a woman to become a baker, she had to marry a baker." Merry E. Wiesner, "Nuns, Wives, and Mothers: Women and the Reformation in Germany," in Sherrin Marshall, ed., *Women in Reformation and Counter-Reformation Europe* (Bloomington: Indiana University Press, 1989), 23.
8   Lyndal Roper, *The Holy Household: Women and Morals in Reformation Augsburg* (Oxford: Clarendon Press, 1989), 11, 40.
9   TA, Elsass, I, p. 588.
10 Merry E. Wiesner, "Women's Work in the Changing City Economy, 1500-1650," in Marilyn J. Boxer and Jean H. Quataert, eds., *Connecting Spheres: Women in the Western World, 1500 to the Present* (New York: Oxford University Press, 1987), 66.
11 Zemon Davis, "Women in the Crafts," 55.
12 Chrisman, *Lay Culture*, 3.
13 Ibid.
14 Francois Ritter, *Histoire de l'Imprimerie Alsacienne aux XVe et XVIe Siecles* (Strasbourg: F.-X. Le Roux, 1955), 63.
15 Chrisman, *Lay Culture*, 3.
16 In contrast to Ritter's telling of this story, Chrisman interprets these particular events as involving a possible conflict: "Margarette ... married her father's typographer, Reinhardt Beck, who took over the shop in 1512, forcing Johann II to find a new location." Chrisman, *Lay Culture*, 16.
17 Ritter, *Histoire*, 218.
18 Chrisman, *Lay Culture*, 325 n. 93; 22 ff.
19 Chrisman, *Lay Culture*, 15.
20 Ritter, *Histoire*, 220-21.
21 Roper, *The Holy Household*, 32.
22 Ritter, *Histoire*, 223.
23 Ibid., 222-24.
24 Ibid., 224.
25 Wiesner, *Working Women*, 157.
26 Wiesner, "Women's work," 66.
27 Roper, *The Holy Household*, 143.
28 Ibid., 53.
29 The case of the widow of Hans Jaeger of Augsburg, cited in ibid., 53.
30 Ritter speculates that this is a possibility, although he offers no evidence to substantiate it. Ritter, *Histoire*, 225.
31 Wiesner, *Working Women*, 162.
32 Miriam Chrisman suggests that Margarethe held radical views prior to her second marriage. Miriam U. Chrisman, "Women and the Reformation in Strasbourg, 1490-1530," in ARG 63 (1972), 159.

33 For an overview of the contents, see Krebs and Rott, *Elsass*, I, pp. 8-10.
34 Ibid., 10.
35 Ibid., 10-11.
36 Ritter, *Histoire*, 226.
37 Ibid., 230.
38 See Klaus Deppermann, *Melchior Hoffman* (Gottingen: Vandenhoeck and Ruprecht, 1979), 346-47 for a listing of these works (numbers 8-13).
39 Ritter, *Histoire*, 230-31.
40 See "Ein bruderliche warnung an meister Mathis . . ." in Marc Lienhard, *Un Temps, une Ville, une Réforme: La Réformation à Strasbourg* (Hampshire: Variorum, 1990), 42ff.
41 Ibid., 38.
42 Helen Martens, "Hutterite Songs: The Origins and Aural Transmission of their Melodies from the Sixteenth Century," (PhD dissertation, Columbia University, 1969), 184-85.
43 Noted in Martens, "Hutterite Songs," 173, n. 1; 177.
44 "Since the Spiritualist-Anabaptist direction was maintained from one husband to the next and since Margarette provided the element of continuity, it is impossible to believe that she was not a strong factor in determining the ideological commitment of the press." See Chrisman, *Lay Culture*, 22-23.

URSULA JOST AND BARBARA REBSTOCK OF STRASBOURG

Ursula Jost and Barbara Rebstock were two of the most influential Anabaptist women in Strasbourg; down the Rhine into the Low Countries. Both were prophets, and Barbara also was counted as an "elder of Israel" in one of the Anabaptist congregations in Strasbourg. Both had a deep impact on Melchior Hoffman, the catalyst for Anabaptism in the Netherlands and Friesland. The leadership that both women exerted was directly related to their prophetic vocations.

Ursula Jost

In the year 1530, sometime before April 23, a forty-page booklet appeared in Strasbourg. It was entitled *Prophetic Visions and Revelations of the Workings of God in These Last Days, Which Were Revealed Through the Holy Spirit from 1524 until 1530 to a Lover of God, Seventy-seven of Which Are Recorded Here in This Booklet.*[1] No publisher was mentioned in the provocative little book. On its cover–surrounded by drawings of Christ coming again in glory and judgement, the end-time messengers Enoch and Elijah, and an emperor bowing to the whore of Babylon who was riding on a seven-headed dragon (Revelation 17)–appeared the name of Melchior Hoffman, a well-travelled preacher of reformation. Yet it was clear that only the foreword and the afterword were his writing. The narrator of the visions, the *gottes liebhaberin* ["lover of God," feminine], was not named. There is, however, little doubt as to the author of the booklet of visions: an Anabaptist woman named Ursula, wife of Lienhard Jost, a Strasbourg butcher who also saw visions and whose visions also were edited by Hoffman and printed later that year.[2]

Within the book itself are only a few clues to the author's identity. In her own introduction to the visions, the author mentions that her husband had recently been released from custody and that her husband had experienced visions before she did.[3] This description of her husband fits the situation of Lienhard Jost, mentioned by Martin Bucer in 1533.[4] Melchior Hoffman's afterword confirmed that the author's husband also had a prophetic gift and that his book would appear soon.[5] Lienhard's visions were published in 1530 and reprinted again in 1532.

The first official mention of *Prophetische gesicht* was on April 23, 1530, when the Strasbourg city council denied the request of Melchior Hoffman for a designated building in which Anabaptists could meet for worship. The council noted that this was the same Hoffman who had maligned the emperor in his interpretation of the twelfth chapter of Revelation and the same Hoffman who had published the visions of a woman. The council decided to ask for the arrest of Hoffman, who was an author and the printer of the book in question.[6] Shortly after April 30, the printers Balthasar Beck (Margaretha Prüss's husband) and Christian Egenolff were arrested and questioned. They claimed to know nothing about Melchior Hoffman nor "his woman." But the reference is valuable, because in it the city council secretary mentioned the (abbreviated) name of the book.[7]

The first known mention of Ursula's name, however, came in the introduction to a publication by Hoffman in 1532.[8] In it Hoffman reprinted the twenty-second vision of *Prophetische gesicht* (there called the twenty-sixth vision) and attributed it to "the prophetess Ursula, the wife of the prophet Lienhard Jost of Strasbourg."[9] This reprinting of the vision also was referred to in the proceedings of the Strasbourg synod of 1533 as the "vision of Ursela, prophetess of Strasbourg, 1525."[10] The proceedings also mentioned that Melchior Hoffman valued highly the "prophet Lienhard Jost and Ursula the prophetess," and felt that not a letter should be taken away from their prophecies.[11] Also from 1533 is a record of a request from the Dutch Anabaptist Cornelius Polderman to visit Melchior Hoffman; in this request Polderman mentioned the popularity of the writings of "Linhart Josten and his wife" in the Low Countries.[12] A vision of Ursula's, in addition to those reported in *Prophetische gesicht*, was among fourteen Anabaptist writings that the city council of Speyer sent to the Strasbourg city council in 1537.[13] The Speyer council wanted to warn Strasbourg of the possible civil ill effects of the writings, such as the vision of Lienhard Jost that prophesied an uprising in Strasbourg and the reestablishment of the Roman Catholic teaching of the emperor and pope in the city.[14]

No comprehensive biography of Ursula Jost can be written. We know only a few facts about her life and the life of her family. Her husband, Lienhard Jost, who was also a visionary, was a butcher by trade[15] and came from Illkirch, a village immediately south of Strasbourg. Ursula and Lienhard lived in the Krutenau,[16] a neighbourhood on the southeast edge of the city near the Butcher's Gate, where the nearest parish church was St. Stephen's. In 1524, the year of Ursula's first recorded visions, she and Lienhard were already married and Lienhard had just been released from imprisonment in a hospital.[17] After 1530, the year Ursula's visions were published, there are no more unambiguous records concerning her. By 1537, records of a woman called Agnes appear among Anabaptists in Strasbourg, and by 1539 the records say that Agnes is Lienhard Jost's second wife.[18] Thus it is likely that Ursula died sometime between 1530 and 1539.[19] She and Lienhard had at least one child, Elisabeth (Elsa), who by 1543 was old enough to have been recently married.[20] Lienhard was still alive as late as 1549.[21] If one figures the average marriage age at twenty for women of the time, Ursula could have been born sometime shortly before 1500 and might have been in her thirties at the time of her visions.

Why should a booklet of "prophetic visions and revelations" cause such a stir? In the religious and political turmoil of the early sixteenth century, the Free Imperial City of Strasbourg was a meeting place for many people and ideas. It was a geographical crossroads; its series of causeways and pontoon bridges constructed across the marshy Rhine in 1388 constituted Europe's last bridge over the river before the sea. So, it was an important centre for commerce; through Strasbourg, goods were moved from eastern Europe to France, from Upper Germany and the Swiss Confederation to lands down the Rhine.[22]

Strasbourg was a political and religious crossroads as well, in large part as a result of the relatively tolerant policy of the city of Strasbourg. Few religious dissenters were executed, even though that was the official policy of the Holy Roman Empire after the second Diet of Speyer in 1529. Few were tortured or had their property confiscated, as happened regularly elsewhere in the Empire. Some dissenters were imprisoned. Most simply were expelled from the city and its territory. The priority for the Strasbourg council was "civic peace and unity." Even the official clergy, whose sympathies were with a Zwinglian reformation rather than with a Lutheran, were told not to stir up controversy and were to write only "mild" rebuttals to suspected heresy.[23] As a consequence, religious dissenters of all sorts found refuge in Strasbourg. There they also found printers; between 1522 and 1534 Strasbourg became the centre in Europe where dissenting writings were exchanged.[24]

The case of the influential Margarethe Prüss, a Strasbourg printer, can be mentioned here (see her profile in this volume). Her father had been a printer, and during two intervals of widowhood she directed the family shop by herself. Her third husband was Balthasar Beck, the printer of Ursula's *Prophetische Gesicht*. Anabaptist preachers came to Strasbourg to meet Beck and Prüss and arrange for publication of their work. The Prüss/Beck shop printed the treatises of Hans Bünderlin, Caspar Schwenckfeld, and Melchior Hoffman, as well as Sebastian Franck's controversial *Chronica*.[25]

The Peasants' War of 1525 surrounded Strasbourg, but stayed away from the city itself. The magistrates of the city made the political compromises necessary to keep most of the Strasbourg citizens out of the war. In the aftermath of the peasants' defeat, the lines of division became much sharper between the reformers who were willing to collaborate with the civil authorities and those who were not. The religious groups who met outside the church walls met with disapproval from the so-called magisterial reformers.

Among the Anabaptist leaders in Strasbourg in 1529 was a Swabian furrier named Melchior Hoffman. Until repudiated by Martin Luther, he travelled in Livonia, Sweden, Estonia, Denmark, and East Friesland, preaching a Lutheran gospel highly coloured with biblical interpretations predicting the imminence of the end times. Sometime shortly after coming to Strasbourg, Hoffman came into contact with the circle of religious dissenters of which the prophets Lienhard Jost and his wife Ursula were a part, and Hoffman turned toward Anabaptism. After having his commentary on Revelation as well as the books of Lienhard's and Ursula's visions printed in Strasbourg, Hoffman travelled to the Low Countries to introduce his form of Anabaptism there.

The Anabaptist group around Hoffman was one of a probable three clusters of Anabaptists meeting in Strasbourg during the period 1525 to 1535. There were an estimated two thousand Anabaptists in Strasbourg in 1530, according to one contemporary report,[26] perhaps 10 percent of the population. Of the approximately 180 Anabaptists who appear in the extant city records between 1526 and 1537, 113 can be assigned to one of these three groups on the basis of their place of meeting, the person who baptized them, or other Anabaptists whom they named as associates. Of these 113, fifty-one were probably connected with the Hoffman group, which was made up largely of people native to the Strasbourg area (in contrast to the Anabaptist group made up mostly of Swiss refugees).[27]

This Melchiorite Anabaptist cluster was quite open to prophecy. A summary of a 1537 document from Speyer lists seventeen Anabaptist prophets for whom the Strasbourg city council should watch out (although three of them were not actually from Strasbourg).[28] The remaining fourteen persons were probably residents of Strasbourg and connected with the Hoffman group: Melchior Hoffman, Johann Pommacher (or Eisenburg), Heinrich the shoemaker and his wife, Valentin Dufft the goldsmith, Wilhelm Blum the miller (whether Wilhelm, Sr. or Jr. is not clear), Agnes (within two years Lienhard Jost's second wife), Barbara Rebstock (Kropf), Margret, Lienhard Jost and his wife (referring to Ursula), Elsa (perhaps their daughter Elisabeth), Apollonia, and Joseph Lorenz.[29] Also listed earlier in the document were Gertrud, Joseph Lorenz's wife, Valentin Nessel, Adam, perhaps Adam Schegel or Hans Adam, and Johann von Miltenberg.[30]

Of the visions of Margret, Elsa, Apollonia, Heinrich's wife, and Joseph Lorenz, nothing is known. Gertrud was said to have heard the alarm bell in the cathedral beginning to sound.[31] Adam said the Lord had shown him that "we still have 700 brethren at Strasbourg."[32] Heinrich the shoemaker saw himself as Enoch (to Melchior Hoffman's Elijah), one of two witnesses of Revelation 11:3; Valentin Dufft and Wilhelm Blum evidently also saw themselves in this role.[33] Agnes had a vision that Melchior Hoffman was named Daniel. Furthermore, she saw a face with open jaws and two tongues, which was identified as that of Luther. Johann von Miltenberg saw how Strasbourg would be besieged by three armies.[34] Valentin Nessel prophesied that war would break out in 1537.[35] Of Melchior's prophecies, the document has only fragments:

> Here Melchior wrote that the Lord had shown him how he would lie in prison for three and a half years and how, after that, he

would build a beautiful city and he himself would be just as beautiful. He saw how the *pater noster* [the Lord's Prayer] and the mass were heard again in church in Strasbourg. He saw how Bucer had a false Bible in the disputation against Melchior. Great slaughter at Münster.[36]

Likewise, the reports of Lienhard Jost's visions are fragmentary. Among the "many strange dreams and visions" were a vision of fire falling from heaven, followed by a new earth; a vision that Melchior would not be released before the Carthusian monastery burned; a vision that the pope's and the emperor's teachings would take over Strasbourg again and there would be an uprising and great bloodshed between the authorities and their subjects; how the preachers said that Melchior's eyes would be put out; how Lienhard ate a sumptuous meal with Johann [Eisenburg?] which the heavenly Father had prepared for him; how a group of "brethren in the temple at Strasbourg had seen the Lord when Lienhard had prayed for them and was heard."[37] A book of Lienhard's visions was printed in 1530 and reprinted in 1532,[38] but no copy of the book is known to be in existence. A publication by Hoffman, as well as a book of Lienhard's seven prophecies reviewed at the 1533 Strasbourg synod, reported Lienhard's prophecy that, in this age, Strasbourg was the spiritual Jerusalem, just as Rome was the spiritual Babylon. The Strasbourg walls would reach into all the world, and Strasbourg would be the centre for apostolic mission.[39]

A description of one of Ursula's visions that does not appear in *Prophetische gesicht* was also among the documents sent from Speyer in 1537:

> She saw how Dr. Hedio was thrown down from the pulpit, and the people were walking up to their ankles in blood. After that came a person with a red rose and ran into the cathedral. The horse was crazy, and on it sat a man in armor who acted as if he would murder us and the Bernese [the Swiss Anabaptists].[40]

In *Prophetische gesicht*, Ursula's seventy-seven visions are primarily apocalyptic in character. The excerpts printed below show the symbolic nature of the visions and their connection with biblical and late medieval images of the wrath of God and God's future victory over evil. Ursula's visions helped readers cope with crises by putting them in the context of God's ultimate plan for the present age. The crises of the period of her visions, 1524 to 1530, were unmistakable: the burden of the land tithe on the peasants, the Peasants' War, the overturning of the power of the Roman Catholic Church in many cities, the persecution of religious dissenters. Some of these crises Ursula's visions put in the context of God's judgement and wrath. In other cases, the visions called for patience and endurance until the time when God would save the chosen people. The visions of *Prophetische gesicht* gave meaning to history. They asserted that God was in control of history. In the end, the winners would not be the bishops or the cavalry of the nobility or evil forces; those who would be saved and given the crown of life would be those who had become as children, who had followed the narrow path.

Barbara Rebstock

In the Speyer document there were also brief reports of the visions of the prophet Barbara Rebstock, from Fellbach near Stuttgart. She and her husband Hans (or Kropfhans) Rebstock, a weaver, had come to Strasbourg from Esslingen. The Anabaptist congregation there had been influenced by Hans Hut and his apocalyptic preaching. Barbara had been baptized, however, by someone named Schütz Enderlin.[41] In March 1530 she went back to Esslingen after receiving a stipend for helping care for refugees at the Strasbourg poor house, the former Franciscan monastery, of which sometime Anabaptist Lucas Hackfurt was in charge.[42] But Barbara was back in Strasbourg by 1534. One of her visions confirmed the dream of the "Italian prophet"[43] that, if the people of Strasbourg did not reform, the city would become a village.[44] An earlier report (1534) from another Anabaptist who was being questioned by the authorities told of Barbara's vision of great snow and water.[45] Melchiorites from the Netherlands travelled to Strasbourg to see Barbara because they had heard of her visions and her miracles.[46] Most of what little other information we have about Barbara's visions comes from Obbe Philips. He reported in his *Confession* (writing about 1560 as a disillusioned Melchiorite) that Barbara had prophesied through a vision that Melchior Hoffman was Elijah.

> She saw a white swan swimming in a beautiful river or watercourse, which swan had sung beautifully and wonderfully. And that, she interpreted to apply to Melchior as the true Elijah. She had also seen a vision of many death heads on the walls around Strasbourg. When she wondered whether Melchior's head was among them, and she tried to see, she became aware of Melchior's head, and as she gazed upon it the head laughed and looked at her in a friendly way. Thereafter she saw that all the other heads came alive, one after the other, and they all began to laugh. . . .
>
> She also saw a vision that occurred in this manner. She saw in the vision a great drawing room or beautiful salon, grand and stately, and full of brethren and sisters all sitting properly around the room

in a row. And there stood a youth in the middle with a white garment draped about him. And he had in his hand a golden chalice full of a strong drink and he went along the row from one to the other offering each the chalice, but no one could touch the drink, so strong was it. At last he came to one brother named Cornelius Polterman, who was Melchior's disciple. He took the chalice from the youth's hand and drank from it before all. This fantasy was interpreted to mean that Cornelius Polterman would be Enoch.[47]

Barbara's prophetic role appeared to be not only proclaiming symbolic visions, but also counselling right behaviour. According to Claus Frey at his trial, it was she, along with Melchior Hoffman and Valentin Dufft, who insisted that Frey give up his second (common-law, "spiritual") wife.[48]

It appears that, within the Anabaptist group of which Ursula and Barbara were a part, visions were common. Lienhard was a leader among the visionaries, praying with others that they also could "see the Lord." There were at least eighteen prophets in the group, of whom eight were women.

The Role of Women among the Strasbourg Melchiorites

The relatively large role for women among the Melchiorites in Strasbourg was focussed on women as prophets. Nowhere do we have a concise and complete rationale of this role for Anabaptist women in Strasbourg. However, they probably would have agreed with Katharina Schütz, wife of parish pastor Matthis Zell but a sympathizer with various radicals, when she wrote of a role for women in the church based on Elizabeth's receiving the Holy Spirit (Luke 1:41), women prophesying and receiving the Spirit in the day of the Lord (Joel 2:28-29; Acts 2:17-18), and there being no difference between men and women in Christ (Galatians 3:28).[49]

Melchior Hoffman also quoted Joel 2:28-29 (Acts 2:17-18) about sons and daughters prophesying. "Such a time is now at hand as was in the time of the apostles, when God is pouring out his Holy Spirit on all flesh, and the sons and daughters prophesy," he wrote in the foreword to his commentary on Revelation.[50] Hoffman saw women's prophesying as connected with the new thing that God was beginning to do in history. He wrote in his foreword to Ursula Jost's prophetic visions that, just as God had given revelations in the past through the prophets, and also through Jesus Christ, and through the Apostle John and, indeed, to all God's servants, so now the divine counsel is being revealed through this woman who is a lover of God. Hoffman went on to quote Isaiah 42:9, "I have declared to you a new thing and will let you hear it before it springs forth." When a new thing was coming to pass, it should be no surprise that God gave prophetic visions to a woman who, through these prophecies, was authorized to teach others about the power of God.[51]

Not all Anabaptists, even those who approved of prophecy and had Melchiorite connections, were as supportive of women's prophecy as was Hoffman. The Dutch Anabaptist leader David Joris came to Strasbourg in 1538 to meet with the "elders of Israel" there in an attempt to become the recognized leader of the Melchiorites, now that Melchior Hoffman was in prison. Among the "elders of Israel" present at the meeting were the prophets Lienhard Jost and Barbara Rebstock. David Joris had evidently sent them letters previously, trying to convince them of the superiority of present revelations to past revelations in Scripture, or as he phrased it, the "spirit" instead of the "letter." In response to Joris's letters, Barbara Rebstock had told the other Melchiorites that such ideas were false and devilish. Her position, and the position of Melchior Hoffman and others in Strasbourg, was that dreams, visions, and prophecies were valuable as an addition to Scriptural revelation, but not as a replacement for it.

On the first day of the debate, Joris was trying to show his own spiritual superiority and kept asking the Strasbourg elders:

> "Do you now know well the fear of the Lord, humility, meekness, longsuffering, friendliness, mercy, chastity, truth, simplicity, and innocence? Then I will be silent. Do you have them all? Give me an answer now."

> After they all had been silent for a long time, Barbara spoke up, breaking in out of order: [she] hindered the answer which they were now supposed to give. But she began and spoke in this way . . . :

> "May I also speak a word? For my spirit impels me."

> Ian P[ont]: "Yes, since the Spirit impels you, why should you not speak?"

> Barbara spoke: "May it proceed as the Lord has acted with me. I think that some who are here want to pluck the fruits from our tree before they are ripe. Therefore the Lord warns us that no one speak further, for he will have to answer for it."

> D[avid]: "Do you say this through the Lord?"

> Barba[ra]: "I was compelled to do so. . . . For we have been under the fear of the Lord for over ten years: do you believe that we are godless?"

> D[avid]: "Now I say that you have not spoken from the Lord but from the Devil. For you have interrupted our discussion and have disturbed the Spirit [by hindering the answer]. For here, good has not spoken to good, on account of those who sit next to her."
>
> Ian [Pont]: At this, Ian Pont spoke again: "Her heart is such that it is necessary to speak of this matter. Therefore she is not in need of such [rebuke]."
>
> D[avid] spoke to the brothers and stood up: "I say to you, that you are not small nor poor, but your understanding is veiled, so that you do not see. I would like to let you know how you might serve God more. But the will of Satan has its way [here]. For he comes to disturb the Spirit, to plug the ears of the oppressed by the serpent's deception. And now I say to you further: Since you have believed her, then I will cease to speak to you any longer. And I, as a servant of the Lord, warn you all, proclaiming to you the day of the Lord, that you beware, for he is near, and I will be free of you. For I was ready to instruct you and also to correct you, as the Lord has given me ability, so that you will not be surprised on that day. . . . Behold, I warn you that you not let yourselves be misled. Men, regard yourselves above the women; then you will not be deceived. Understand that rightly."
>
> Ian P[ont]: D[avid], you speak too hastily and judge too hastily, for you perhaps do not understand her speaking.[52] For she admonishes us all, that we should watch where we are going.
>
> The conversation remained stuck here, and the morning continued without anyone sitting down.[53]

David Joris was so upset that a woman's prophecy had thwarted his aims that he later wrote in the margins of the minutes:

> Consider the sense of it. They asked if I would like to have a report of this. Had they not spoken, I would have filled her mouth with silence; her hand which opposed me in the truth I would have placed against her mouth. But they regarded her spirit to such an extent that she hindered their response.[54]

Although David Joris could not tolerate such a role for women, the men in Barbara Rebstock's own congregation in Strasbourg were willing to defend this role on her behalf because she was "under the fear of the Lord." Her spiritual competence gave her a leadership role. Although Ursula was probably dead by the time of the Joris debate, her prophecy had set a precedent for Barbara's.

In the first part of the sixteenth century, as in the late Middle Ages, women were sometimes seen as spiritual authorities because of their visionary and prophetic experiences. They based their claim to authority not on office, but on experience, an extraordinary vocation. Such experience often took the form of prophetic visions.

According to Elizabeth Alvilda Petroff, visions were a socially sanctioned activity that freed a woman from conventional female roles by identifying her as a genuine religious figure. They brought her to the attention of others, giving her a public language she could use to teach and learn. Her visions gave her the strength to grow internally and to change the world, to preach, and to attack injustice and greed, even within the church. Through visions, she could be an exemplar to other women, and out of her own experience she could lead them to fuller self-development.[55]

This visionary tradition was often apocalyptic because women's prophecy was seen as a certain sign that the new order was beginning. Preaching by women (and lay men) was a sign of the End, as promised in the Bible. German almanacs of the time claimed that this prophecy had been fulfilled and, thus, the last days were at hand.[56] Even if the old order had given men authority over women, in the new order women shared in the outpouring of the Holy Spirit through dreams and visions.

Such was the context of Ursula Jost and Barbara Rebstock, early Anabaptist prophets and, in the case of Barbara, an "elder of Israel."

Prophetic Visions and Revelations of the Workings of God in These Last Days . . .

Ursula Jost

After my husband and spouse was released from custody and was let go, he and I together prayed earnestly and diligently to God, the almighty merciful Father, that he would let me also see the wondrous deeds of his hand. God's grace and kindness granted this to us, and these visions written down here all appeared to me. I saw all these visions and wonders in the glory of the Lord, which always unfolded itself before me.[57] And in it I received knowledge of the meaning of these visions of divine wonders. After that it always came together again and went away and disappeared. The course of these revelations, visions, and stories began, as one counts after the birth of Christ Jesus, our Lord:

1524 years.

The first vision

And I saw first that the glory of the Lord came upon me and unfolded and showed itself in such bright splendor[58] that I could not recognize the shape because of the brightness of the glory of the Lord. After that, this same splendor of the Lord became a beautiful wreath above me.[59]

The second vision

At night on St. Michael's Day[60] in the year 1524 mentioned above, I saw appearing by my bed a shape as if it were a gleam of light, and I was alarmed that it might be an appearance of an apparition[61] or of a ghost and on that account was in great fear and dread.[62]

The third vision

Then I saw further,[63] that is, over my bed, that the glory of the Lord came upon me and appeared over me in the form of a cloud, as if this cloud filled the whole room. And this cloud divided and separated or opened up. In it I saw a large inexpressible brightness like the shining of the sun. And in the brightness of this glory I saw a form as if it were a lattice, and in the openings of this lattice appeared stars, which were bright as burning lights. And the inside of the lattice became visible, and I saw a figure like God the Father himself. He extended his almighty right hand, and I saw in his left hand a likeness of a globe. Then the glory of the Lord spoke to me and said, "If I pull back my hand, what will become of all you upon the whole earth? All of you together will become nothing."[64]

The twenty-ninth vision.

Then it happened in the week after St. Matthias's Day[65] in that year that the glory of the Lord came upon me and unfolded. Then I saw in the sky many guns, large and small.[66] Between them I saw a path adorned with brightness and with many colors. And it was extremely narrow. And I also saw clouds, which were entirely the color of blood.

The thirtieth vision.

Then I saw that a stream of boiling hot water was flowing through the whole earth. And I saw that the people had burned their feet in the fiercely hot water and, because of this, had been made to fall down.

The thirty-first vision.

On the Sunday after mid-Lent, 1525,[67] I saw in the glory of the Lord that water and fire fell down from heaven.

The thirty-second vision.

On the following Wednesday[68] the glory of the Lord surrounded me and unfolded. And I saw that it had again rained down from heaven water, fire, brimstone, and pitch.

Then I saw that the people raised their hands and heads to God. Then the glory of the Lord closed, and thus closed, it came upon me. Then my heart spoke with wonder, "Oh, almighty God! What is this, and what might it mean? Give me knowledge of your secret judgment." Then the glory of the Lord opened again and spoke to me, "Then you will see the judgment and wrath of God, of which it is written in the Scripture."

After this wonder, I saw people lying down who were burned from this fire, brimstone, and pitch. And I saw the same mixture moving around and around across the whole earth.

The thirty-third vision.

Then I saw on the next evening that there stood a large well-decorated hall, and in it were many handsome young men with many and all kinds of stringed instruments.

The thirty-fourth vision.

On the Friday before Palm Sunday[69] in 1525, the glory of the Lord again approached me and unfolded. In it I saw a pretty green tree, which had many thousands of green branches. And I saw that out of the tree sprang a fountain.

Then I saw two men coming who were well-dressed. They picked up a pretty green piece of sod[70] from the ground. And I saw that, with it, they struck the fountain and stopped it up.

Then I saw that the water of this fountain rose and flowed out to the branches a thousandfold.

And then I saw that there came a great host of people who were from the common folk. They drank the drops which ran off the branches, and they were all satisfied. And I saw that they had raised their hands and their heads to God the eternal Father, and to him gave the highest praise and thanks.[71]

Notes

1 *Prophetische gesicht und Offenbarung/ der götlichen würckung zu diser letsten zeit/ die vom xxiiij. jar biß in dz xxx. einer gottes liebhaberin durch den heiligen geist geoffenbart seind/ welcher hie in disem büchlin lxxvij verzeichnet seindt.*
2 No copy of Lienhard Jost's book is extant. But it is referred to in Obbe Philips's confession, translated and reprinted in George H. Williams and Angel M. Mergal, eds., *Spiritual and Anabaptist Writers* (Philadelphia: Westminster, 1957), 211-13.
3 *Prophetische gesicht*, A ij vo.
4 Martin Bucer, *Handlung inn dem offentlichen gesprech zu Straßburg iungst im Synodo gehalten gegen Melchior Hoffman* . . . (1533).
5 *Prophetische gesicht*, C vij vo.
6 TA, *Elsass*, I, document 211, pp. 261-62.
7 TA, *Elsass*, I, document 212, p. 262.
8 *Von der wahren hochprächtlichen einigen maijestat Gottes und von der wahrhaftigen menschwerdung des ewigen worts und sohns des Allerhögsten*, published in Strasbourg or Hagenau. See TA, *Elsass*, I, document 298, pp. 411ff.
9 Printed in Friedrich Otto zur Linden, *Melchior Hofmann, ein Prophet der Wiedertäufer* (Haarlem: Erven F. Bohn, 1885), 435-37.
10 TA, *Elsass*, II, document 444, p. 184.
11 TA, *Elsass*, II, document 444, p. 186.
12 TA, *Elsass*, II document 461, p. 213.
13 TA, *Elsass*, III, document 799, p. 112, gives the content of this vision.
14 The content of Lienhard's vision is summarized in the message from Speyer.
15 TA, *Elsass*, II, document 665, p. 453; it is doubtful that he is the same person as the "stiff-necked" Anabaptist from Grafenstaden (near Illkirch) who was a shoemaker, mentioned in ibid., document 680, p. 468.
16 TA, *Elsass*, II, document 363, p. 15.
17 *Prophetische gesicht*, A ij vo.
18 TA, *Elsass*, III, document 799, pp. 113, 115; document 907, p. 317.
19 It is extremely unlikely that Ursula and Lienhard divorced or otherwise separated. There is no further mention of Ursula. Moreover, Lienhard remained a member in good standing in the Hoffmanite Anabaptist group, in contrast to Claus Frey, who took a second wife although his first wife was still living, and was expelled from the Anabaptist congregation. On Claus Frey and the action of the Anabaptist congregation concerning him, see TA, *Elsass*, II, document 361, pp. 11-12; document 362, p. 13.
20 TA, *Elsass*, IV, document 1294, p. 36. The record says that Elisabeth was Lienhard's daughter, not Agnes's daughter, as Klaus Deppermann says in *Melchior Hoffman: Social Unrest and Apocalyptic Visions in the Age of Reformation*, translated by Malcolm Wren (Edinburgh: T and T Clark, 1987), 206. Originally published as *Melchior Hoffman: Soziale Unruhen und apokalyptische Visionen im Zeitalter der Reformation* (Göttingen: Vandenhoeck and Ruprecht, 1979). Page references will be to the English edition.
21 TA, *Elsass*, IV, document 1676, p. 297.
22 Miriam Usher Chrisman, *Lay Culture, Learned Culture: Books and Social Change in Strasbourg, 1480-1599* (New Haven: Yale University Press, 1982), xiv; Chrisman, *Strasbourg and the Reform: A Study in the Process of Change* (New Haven: Yale University Press, 1967), 4.
23 Lorna Jane Abray, *The People's Reformation: Magistrates, Clergy, and Commons in Strasbourg, 1520-1598* (Ithaca, NY: Cornell University Press, 1985), 35, 109.
24 Deppermann, *Melchior Hoffman*, 165-66.

25 Chrisman, *Lay Culture*, 22-23, 30, 36.
26 TA, *Elsass*, I, document 224d, p. 277, (October 22-23, 1530).
27 Lois Y. Barrett, "Wreath of Glory; Ursula's Prophetic Visions in the Context of Reformation and Revolt in Southwestern Germany, 1524-1530," (PhD dissertation, The Union Institute, 1992), 190, 213-19.
28 TA, *Elsass*, III, document 799, p. 115 (December 23, 1537).
29 TA, *Elsass*, II, document 799, p. 115.
30 TA, *Elsass*, III, document 799, pp. 109-15.
31 TA, *Elsass*, III, p. 112.
32 TA, *Elsass*, III, p. 115.
33 TA, *Elsass*, III, p. 114.
34 TA, *Elsass*, III, p. 113.
35 Ibid.
36 TA, *Elsass*, III, p. 114.
37 TA, *Elsass*, III, pp. 110-11.
38 TA, *Elsass*, I, document 343, p. 561.
39 TA, *Elsass*, II, document 444, pp. 184-86, (October 23-29, 1533).
40 TA, *Elsass*, III, p. 112.
41 TA, *Elsass*, II, document 540, p. 304, (April 18, 1534).
42 TA, *Elsass*, IV, document 207bb, p. 420.
43 Venturinus, an itinerant preacher who visited Strasbourg in February, 1529, perhaps a Spiritual Franciscan.
44 TA, *Elsass*, III, p. 111.
45 TA, *Elsass*, II, document 540, p. 304.
46 TA, *Elsass*, II, document 540, p. 300 (April, 1534).
47 Williams, *Spiritual and Anabaptist Writers*, 212.
48 TA, *Elsass*, II, document 362, p. 13.
49 Miriam Usher Chrisman, "Women of the Reformation in Strasbourg," in ARG, 63 (1972): 153.
50 Melchior Hoffman, *Außlegung verheimlichen Offenbarung Joannis* (Strasbourg: Balthasar Beck, 1530), A iij vo.
51 *Prophetische gesicht*, A i vo, A ij.
52 David Joris's first language was Dutch; Barbara Rebstock's was High German.
53 From the minutes of the meeting, published as *Was Dauid Gerg zu Straßburg mitt Melcher Hoffman vnd andern gehandlet...*, reprinted in TA, *Elsass*, III, document 836, pp. 179-80; translation from the Dutch with assistance from Gary K. Waite. For a translation of the full transcription of the "Strasbourg Disputation," see Gary K. Waite, ed. and trans., *The Anabaptist Writings of David Joris, 1535-1543* (Scottdale, PA: Herald Press, 1994), 183-245.
54 TA, *Elsass*, III, p. 179.
55 Elizabeth Alvilda Petroff, *Medieval Women's Visionary Literature* (New York: Oxford University Press, 1986), 6.
56 Paul A. Russell, *Lay Theology in the Reformation: Popular Pamphleteers in Southwest Germany* (Cambridge: Cambridge University Press, 1986), 217.
57 I have chosen to use the English neuter pronoun to refer to the "glory of the Lord," since it normally appeared to Ursula as a cloud that opened to reveal visions and then closed again.
58 *Glast* = *Glanz* in modern High German.

59 *Krantz.* In earlier times, crowns for royalty or victors were wreaths made of laurel, parsley, olive branches, or oak leaves, after the Roman custom. It is not clear whether the glory became a wreath made of leaves and branches, or whether the glory, which is like a cloud, simply became circular, shaped like a wreath. The wreath is often a symbol of sovereignty, honour, glory, or victory, particularly the victory of the Christian martyrs. See Arnold Wittick, *Symbols, Signs and Their Meaning* (Newton, MA: Charles T. Branford Co., 1960), 167-68.
60 Friday, September 29. Days of the week, saints' days, and other holy days for the years 1524-1530 are taken from H. Grotefend, ed., *Taschenbuch der Zeitrechnung des deutschen Mittelalters und der Neuzeit*, 4th ed. (Hanover and Leipzig: Hansche, 1915).
61 *Ein gespenst eines bedrueckniss; gespenst* here has the more abstract sense of "appearance" or "deceptive illusion."
62 Those reporting mystical experiences of the presence of God typically mention fear as an initial emotion. Cf. Matthew 28:1-10; Luke 1:29-30; 2:9-10; 9:34.
63 The third vision is evidently a continuation of the second vision, occurring the same night.
64 Cf. Exodus 3:20; Deuteronomy 11:2; Isaiah 5:25; 14:26-27; Jeremiah 6:12; Ezekiel 6:14. In the Old Testament, the outstretched hand of God signifies God's acting for salvation or vengeance. So drawing the hand back means God's ceasing to act in saving ways.
65 St. Matthias's Day is February 24. The week after, in the year 1525, would have been February 26 to March 4.
66 Guns = büchsen. Large and small, meaning cannons and handheld guns. Or, büchsen could also mean any kind of cylinders.
67 In 1525, Lätare was March 26. Mitfasten, or mid-Lent, could refer to that day or to the whole week before Lätare. The date of the vision thus could be March 26 or April 2. See Grotefend, *Taschenbuch*, 81.
68 March 29 or April 5. See the previous note.
69 April 7.
70 Wasen = Rasen. See Alfred Götze, *Frühneuhochdeutsches Glossar*, 6th ed. (Berlin: Verlag Walter de Gruyter and Co., 1960), 223.
71 *Prophetische gesicht*, A viii vo-B ii.

HILLE FEICKEN OF SNEEK

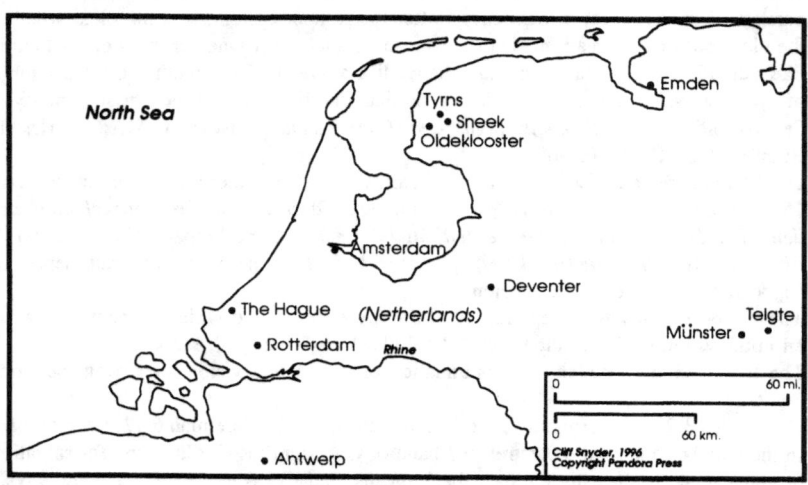

One of the most disturbing chapters of the history of the city of Münster began in February 1534 when the Anabaptists came to power.[1] A month earlier, in January 1534, the persons sent out by the Netherlands prophet Jan Matthijs had carried out the first adult baptisms in the city. In doing so they carried forward the process of reform that had begun some years earlier with anticlerical activities that gradually had led to the introduction of the Reformation. The groundwork had already been laid for the Anabaptists. Their rule lasted sixteen months, taking shape under the charismatic leadership of Jan Matthijs and ending wretchedly under the regency of King Jan van Leiden. When the starving "New Jerusalem" fell on June 24, 1535, after a long siege,[2] not only were countless people buried, but their hopes as well. The city had once attracted believers from near and far like a magnet. Here they had imagined themselves to be safe from apocalyptic threats and nearer to God than ever before. Everything seemed destined to turn out well in Münster. The so-called godless were not desired here. They were summarily driven out.[3] Monastery and church were relieved of excessive decoration, and the community of goods established new biblically based standards for brotherly and sisterly togetherness.

The Anabaptist woman Hille Feicken[4] was part of the community of god-fearing people who wanted to begin a new life in the chosen city of Münster. Our history books would probably have disregarded her completely and we would not even know the name of this Frisian woman who was described as beautiful, had she not dared to risk the extraordinary. When Hille Feicken went forth on June 16, 1534, to free the besieged Münster from prince-bishop Franz of Waldeck, she had lived in the city for only a few months. She found in Judith of the Old Testament a role model, another woman who had once dared to attempt a magnificent rescue and had completed it successfully with God's help. The events that were said to have taken place two thousand years ago in Israel and were so inspiring to Hille Feicken can be told in a few words. The city of Bethulia, despite being destined for destruction after a long Assyrian siege, was rescued in the end. Judith, the humble, deeply devout widow of Manasseh, succeeded in her heroic action. In the most desperate moment, she left the city, accompanied by her maid, and made her way to the camp of the feared king Holofernes, who soon came to trust the beautiful stranger. After a festive banquet the moment came. Judith pleaded for God's presence, reached for a sword and beheaded the drunken commander. She returned home, bringing the head of the defeated enemy with her. While the Assyrians fled for their lives, Judith was celebrated as the liberator. All of Bethulia now lay at her feet.

This story attracted attention. From earliest times, not only scholars but also artists and literary critics have taken great interest in the charming Judith and her act, and have tried to understand her story. Whether she was revered as a saint and lifted to the highest Heaven or condemned as a cunning seductress, Judith became an object of male fantasy. On the other hand, women discovered still other, very different, sides to her story. The liberator of Bethulia became an example for those united as "sisters," vividly reminding those of her sex of what god-fearing women were capable. The medieval woman Christine de Pisan[5] kept the memory of the strong, magnanimous Judith alive in her writings; the baroque artist Artemisia Gentileschi did the same in her paintings.[6] In our own time, the winner of the 1992 Nobel Peace Prize Rigobertá Menchú, also applauded the god-fearing heroine, declaring Judith to be her prototype.[7] Judith could be admired and praised as an example of female strength, but perhaps no woman ever came as close to the biblical heroine as the Anabaptist Hille Feicken, who is remembered in history as the Judith of Münster.

We do not know much about her, but the two testimonies she gave following the failure of her plans[8] and what the chroniclers report about her[9] are enough to give us a picture of this very determined person. When Hille arrived in Münster, probably at the end of February or the beginning of March 1534, she could not yet foresee what awaited her. Perhaps she had known the story of Judith for some time, but the idea of repeating such a bloody deed was unimaginable. After all, the siege had only just begun and was not yet in any way threatening in nature. No one in Münster spoke of the need to free the city. If there was anything that already bound Hille to Judith, it was her deep trust in God, which controlled her completely and which had motivated her to come to the chosen city. As had many others, Hille came to Münster not out of curiosity or material need but rather for reasons of faith. She was a committed Anabaptist who, in her home town of Sneek in Friesland, had already received baptism based on her faith,[10] thereby sealing her covenant with God. This act of baptism, undertaken by an Anabaptist leader unknown to us, had certainly been a decisive event. It was a step which, according to Anabaptist criteria, marked a resolute end to her former life in a world known to be depraved. The sources are silent about who introduced her to the Anabaptist life and faith. Since there were plenty of Anabaptists in and around Sneek, she could have encountered them inadvertently or could have attended one of their meetings because she was interested. In any case, there is nothing to indicate that Hille came to her Anabaptist identity through relatives or friends, which was so often the case in Anabaptist circles. Despite the fact that her father worked as a day labourer for so-called "devout people"[11] who may have had links to the Anabaptists, it doesn't appear that he was one of them or that he would have gone to Münster with his daughter.

This was not the case with her husband, Psalmus. At her interrogation, Hille made clear that she had him to thank for all her knowledge.[12] This statement leads us to conclude that not only did she have an important primary relationship with Psalmus, but more than that, he was actually the key person in her life as an Anabaptist. However, Psalmus also presents us with insoluble puzzles. Thus, early on, there was already doubt that this man with the unique sounding name had ever existed. Hille was charged with lying and with simply inventing her marriage to Psalmus. It is impossible to determine the truth on the basis of the sources available to us.[13] But, since Hille's statements otherwise ring true, it is doubtful that Psalmus existed only as her fantasy. The solution could lie elsewhere. Several factors indicate that the name "Psalmus" was given to him by the Anabaptists, which has resulted in the total loss of this man's original identity. Assuming that Hille spoke the truth, there was a Frisian who sat in the Council of Twelve who could have been her husband: Peter Simons. He came from Tyrns near Sneek, and was already known as an Anabaptist when he left for Münster in February 1534. This prominent Frisian, who was likely killed in March or the beginning of April 1535 at the storming of the Oldeklooster,[14] could well have been not only the brother of the later famous Menno Simons, but also the heretofore unknown husband of Hille Feicken. The few surviving sources point in that direction.

Why Hille did not go to Münster together with Psalmus, but only followed him three weeks later, cannot be fully explained. Reasons of security could have played a role. Perhaps, rather than leaving too quickly, they chose to test the situation in the chosen city first. Psalmus could have been on the road gathering information. On the other hand, there were attempts to have the brothers come to Münster first with the valuables. The sisters were to deal with whatever was left and then follow. Like other women, Hille took this course of action. In her testimony she stated that she had given what she owned to the poor.[15] If Psalmus had been important to the process by which she became an Anabaptist, he appears to have become meaningless to his wife in Münster itself. At least she no longer mentions him in relation to her life or her later attempt to liberate the city.

We do not know what form Hille's arrival in Münster took, or if she was satisfied with life there. Indeed, her basic attitude would have made her integration there easier, but even so, doubts could have arisen. Perhaps the encounter with Psalmus was a disappointment. If he really was part of the Council of Twelve, then he certainly would have identified completely with the official views of the leadership. Part of the strongly patriarchal organization of the city was that the women were simply to obey the men. But precisely in this matter, Hille could have had problems, since she did not feel responsible to any earthly authority, but to God alone. She soon became acquainted with one of the leading Anabaptist men. The last of her money, perhaps a tenpenny piece, was taken from her by Bernt Knipperdolling when she arrived in the city,[16] and in this manner she got her first impression of the ideal of Anabaptist community of goods. Presumably it was in his house that she received, from the hand of the future king Jan van Leiden, those round metal coins [*Marke*], which, like all the brothers and sisters, she constantly carried with her. "The Word becomes" or "became flesh" were the words impressed on them. Hille stated that this "sign" was taken from her only later, in the bishop's headquarters in Telgte.[17] As with all of the other Frisians who had come to Münster, she was lodged in the monastery of Niesinck, which the nuns had been forced to vacate on February 27 and 28.

During her interrogations Hille was quite critical; she expressed disapproval of a number of things in Münster. In her eyes the city was by no means an island of the blessed; instead, conduct was in many respects very earthly. Perhaps the negative depiction can be blamed on the conditions of the interrogation. But until the very end, Hille never gave the impression that she was an unstable person, easily made insecure and prone to opportunistic statements. How great her dissatisfaction actually was, and against whom and which institutions her critique was directed specifically, can only be surmised. Hille answered only those questions that were put to her and her answers were brief for the most part. It seems she was displeased with the manner in which the believers treated one another, particularly the way leading personalities related to the "simple" brothers and sisters. Although Hille had given everything away to the poor in Sneek, she appears to have had doubts about how the community of goods worked out in practice in Münster, and saw the dispersal of goods, rather, as something she was compelled to do.[18] There was little evidence of love of one's neighbour or of friendly instruction; it seemed to her that God's word had been lost somewhere enroute. But that was not all; there was more. Hille believed she had recognized that there was in Münster no governmental authority.[19] In the final analysis, her judgement on the conditions of government could mean that Hille did not accept any of the influential Münsterite Anabaptist leaders as legitimate authorities. Whether it was Knipperdolling, Jan van Leiden, Jan Matthijs, or even Bernhard Rothmann, in the eyes of this woman it seems they were all nothing more than ordinary brothers in the faith who carried out the duties of ruling for the good of the community. But their "service of the neighbour" was perceived by Hille to be more negative than positive.

Naturally, Hille would not have found everything in Münster to be unjust or disappointing. It would be wrong to focus only on her critical comments. After all, there was also a solidarity with the Anabaptist community, whose members sought to establish a new life here in Münster and who later fought desperately for their existence against threats from the outside. God had led Hille to this place and at some point made her aware that she, like the biblical Judith, should rescue her people from their deep distress. The sources do not disclose when or in what circumstances she received this commission from God. Hille only declared that she felt inner restlessness and was moved deeply. In particular, her soul was troubled.[20] Evidently, after God had visited her, she could no longer rest for even a minute. She had to become Judith because God wanted it that way. But could she really be sure that it was actually God, and not the devil, who had given her this task. A woman from Holland in whom Hille had confided advised her to test herself, and later in her testimony doubts came to her again. Nevertheless, she quickly swept them away. No, for her there was no other choice; if she were not to anger God, she had to carry out Judith's feat once more.

The circumstances had forced Hille to cling to her conviction that she was inspired. The enemy was at the walls of the city. The believers were encircled in a closed city, alternatively in high spirits and in fearful anticipation, all the while depending solely on God's help. This set of circumstances was as significant for the success of the Judith metamorphosis as the deep fear of God that gave Hille courage and authenticity. Hille informed her interrogators on what it was like to be a member of the holy community and, along with the other citizens of Münster, to experience the time of siege all too personally. As a woman she was in no way removed from all of the defensive activities. Thus, in answering the questions regarding her activities in Münster, Hille stated that, like the other women both older and younger, she had worked at the ramparts of the city.[21] She had worked along with the others in securing and defending the city. These very important tasks were required equally of both brothers and sisters, even if there were gender-specific differences in how they were carried out. Whereas the men were armed and defended the city against the enemy in battle, the women were responsible for the lime and the boiling tar on the walls. They also wove wreaths and soaked them in boiling tar, to further hinder the advancing foe.[22]

In this situation, which she experienced as unbearable due to the prevailing threat and, at the same time, the deep hope, Judith was awakened to new life. Unfortunately, the sources give us no information as to when and where Hille came in contact with her biblical example for the first time. The call that she received some time later was one thing; the requisite basic knowledge of the biblical heroine another. Perhaps she had heard the story in a public sermon or even discovered it herself in the Bible, though we do not even know if Hille could read. The encounter with the biblical story that had such important consequences for her could have taken place after the death of Jan Matthijs. Totally obedient to the will of God, Matthijs and several others had advanced out of the city at the beginning of April 1534, and, after an unsuccessful engagement, had been killed and cut into pieces by the enemy.[23] This enormously painful but also very dangerous incident caused insecurity in the entire holy community, and threw them into a state of crisis even more than Hille's later unsuccessful attempt to liberate the city. However, a catastrophe was avoided. The tactful manoeuvering of Jan van Leiden, who later became king, quieted the outraged souls. In the end, the death of Jan Matthijs could be explained: had he trusted in God's strength and not his own, and like Judith had asked the people to fast and pray. Perhaps this speech, presumably given by van Leiden after the death of Jan Matthijs, was Hille's first encounter with the biblical Judith.[24] However, a brief reference of that kind to the virtuous heroine would probably not have been enough to awaken Hille to new life.

Presumably, Hille had known about Judith for some time and, to go a step further, perhaps it was Hille who had inspired Jan Matthijs, whose pitiable end at the gates of Münster bore a certain parallel to Hille's own fate. Allegedly, he knew of Hille's inspiration; it is entirely possible that the matter pleased him. Led and protected by God, and completely successful, Judith promised the perfect solution for the "New Jerusalem," which was in such deep distress. But there was one problem: the biblical heroine was a woman who, added to everything else, cast shame on the entire world of men. It is known that women who acted independently were not much favoured in Münster, but perhaps the story could be rewritten in a way that it fit into the male-dominated milieu. Suddenly the unclearly motivated yet bold failure of the prophet appears in a completely different light. Jan Matthijs could have appropriated Hille's inspiration for himself and adapted it according to his own discretion. As a male it was not possible for him to assume the role of the biblical heroine himself, but it was possible that he appropriated her way of thinking, her spirit, and her success. Unfortunately we can find no statement to suggest how influential Hille was. The evidence only shows that she was in contact with the leading figures and moved in the circles of those who set the tone for the city. Perhaps she had simply come to the point where she chose to make her request known. She could also have supported Jan Matthijs morally and personally, edging him closer to acting as he did. The decisive factor is that, under his rule, Hille could not act on her own convictions. Only after his unexpected death did Hille's great hour draw near, but some time elapsed before she could carry out her action.

No one sent her. The frequently offered view that Hille merely served as a tool for someone else has no basis.[25] Rather, she held tenaciously to her intention and sought to realize her plans despite the death of Jan Matthijs. Her aim was not to imitate the biblical heroine in every detail, but to refashion the material of the story freely as it applied to the actual conditions in which she found herself. It would have to suffice that the action and the heroine coincided in the broadest sense with the biblical events. Most important of all was that the goal of liberating the besieged city would be achieved anew. The consequent deviations between Hille and the biblical Judith must be accepted as unimportant. For example, unlike Judith, Hille was not a rich widow. Nor did she have a maid who could have followed her into the camp of the enemy. Whereas Judith left Bethulia in the early morning, Hille supposedly went in the full light of day and, in addition, with much less adornment than her biblical model who wore rings, as well as bracelets and earrings.

These differences would not have affected how Hille carried out her actions. The consent of male leaders, on the other hand, was another matter. It is known that the biblical Judith had no problems leaving the city. Usia, ruler of Judah, and the elders trusted her and let her go forth. Hille could only dream of such good will. While her biblical example could dedicate herself undisturbed to her God-given task, Hille first had to overcome barriers in the form of Jan Matthijs or Jan van Leiden, which mercilessly had been placed between her and her Lord and threatened the whole undertaking. If Hille had wanted to identify completely and totally with Judith, she quickly would have been forced to give up her plans, since hindrances of this kind did not fit the idealistic plan of action in the biblical story. Hille, however, did not face unilateral resistance. It seemed that in Knipperdolling she had found a spokesman who, more than many others, was prepared to support her and also provide her with the things she needed. He gave her money and presumably also the three rings[26] that were taken from her after she was captured. But why exactly did Knipperdolling show interest in Hille's commission, when Jan van Leiden considered it to be mere fantasy? Since Knipperdolling was hardly less hostile to women than other leading figures, it was not due to a recognition of the equality of the sisters. For him, too, they were only second-class saints. It is more likely that he considered Hille to be a kind of "spiritual comrade" who could be of value to him in his struggle for power. Perhaps we can best understand the relationship between the two as a partnership of convenience. Both profited from one another.

Hille used Knipperdolling as an advocate, while he saw in her the saintly woman who fought for God and who could help him to finally achieve his long-awaited goal of a spiritual kingdom.

A further critical departure in Hille's actions from the biblical events is apparent. Allegedly, the prince-bishop was to die in a totally different manner than Holofernes. Every "genuine" Judith, who holds herself in some esteem, must kill the enemy with a sword, as happened in the biblical story. In Münster, however, everything was different, for supposedly Hille had planned to kill Franz of Waldeck by means of a poisoned shirt.[27] It was an incredible story that could have contributed in no small way to making Hille Feicken a figure in Westphalian legend. But in reality, the mysterious piece of clothing probably did not exist. Otherwise there would likely have been references to such an instrument of murder during the interrogation. However, not a word was said on this subject. Not even Knipperdolling knew about it. Evidently Hille had not disclosed to him how she wanted to carry out the task, saying only she would rely on God's help. She would simply go forth and trust in God, who would certainly reveal to her at the right time how the prince-bishop, Franz of Waldeck, was to be murdered. This nonspecific planning referred to by Knipperdolling seems believable enough and is better suited to the deeply religious Hille than the treacherous "attack by means of poison." Where the story about the poisoned shirt originated can no longer be established, although the idea was not an impossible one. In other circumstances, someone could certainly have been put to death successfully with an article of clothing prepared for that purpose, be it with gloves, wigs, shirts, or the like. Traditionally it was a well-known and feared method of murdering someone, and played a role in folklore and stories.

If Hille had actually succeeded in murdering Franz von Waldeck, perhaps all of Münster would have lain at her feet as all the inhabitants of Bethulia had once long ago for the godly Judith. For only a short time, a few hours, at most a few days, did the fate of the still young Münsterite Anabaptist kingdom rest in the hands of this woman who had been in the city only a few months. On the sixteenth of June 1534, Hille started out. She did not go far. Three foot soldiers took the dressed up stranger into custody. What had begun so enthusiastically, ended wretchedly. In contrast to her biblical prototype, the Münsterite Judith was not successful in fulfilling her mission. It seems that betrayal was involved. The respected Münsterite citizen Hermann Ramert, who had distanced himself from the Anabaptists, is said to have betrayed Hille's plans.[28] What he disclosed about the plan of attack was so startling that the prince-bishop pardoned the deserter and promised protection to any of his family who still remained in the city when the conquest should take place. Ramert was able to rescue himself, but for Hille there was no pardon. On June 26, at first without torture but one day later with it, she confessed to the monstrous plan: she had gone out of the city as Judith, in order to make the bishop into a second Holofernes. Her plans had failed and here, finally, we see that the unhappy ending to the whole undertaking no longer resembles the story of the biblical heroine as it did so closely up to this point. This is true of the external event, but inwardly Hille Feicken totally remained a Judith to the point of death. Self-assured and full of trust in God, feeling very devout, she is reported to have said that the executioner would have no power over her. Once more, she deluded herself.

Notes

1 Regarding the rule of the Anabaptists in Münster, see Ralf Klötzer, *Die Täuferherrschaft von Münster, Stadtreformation und Welterneuerung* (Münster: Aschendorff, 1992) which contains a review of the literature and detailed bibliography; Karl-Heinz Kirchhoff, *Die Täufer in Münster 1534/35, Untersuchung zum Umfang und zur Sozialstruktur der Bewegung* (Münster: Aschendorff, 1973); Karl-Heinz Kirchoff, in Franz Petri, ed. "Das Phänomen des Täuferreiches zu Münster 1534/35," in *Der Raum Westfalen, Bd.VI, Fortschritte der Forschung und Schlussbilanz* 1 (Münster: Aschendorff, 1989), 277-422.
2 In this regard see Karl-Heinz Kirchhoff, "Die Belagerung und Eroberung Münsters 1534/35, Militärische Massnahmen und politische Verhandlungen des Fürstbischofs Franz von Waldeck," in *Westfälische Zeitschrift*, 112 (1962): 77-170.
3 Ernst Laubach, "Jan Mathys und die Austreibung der Taufunwilligen aus Münster Ende Februar 1534," in *Westfälische Forschungen* 36 (1986): 147-58.
4 Hille Feicken belongs among some of the most interesting female figures in Anabaptist Münster. In the past she has been misinterpreted often, slandered, or even forgotten completely and has been rediscovered only recently in academic research. See Marion Kobelt-Groch, "Als Judith auszog, den Fürstbischof zu töten, Hille Feicken und die Frauen im Täuferreich zu Münster," in *Aufsässige Töchter Gottes, Frauen im Bauernkrieg und in den Täuferbewegungen* (Frankfurt, and New York: Campus Verlag, 1993), 64-146.
5 Christine de Pizan, *Das Buch von der Stadt der Frauen* (Munich: Deutscher Taschenbuch Verlag, 1990), 174ff.
6 Regarding the theme of Judith in the work of Artemisia Gentileschi, see Mary D. Garrad, *Artemisia Gentileschi, The Image of the Female Hero in Italian Baroque Art* (Princeton, NJ: Princeton University Press, 1989).
7 Elisabeth Burgus, *Rigoberta Menchú, Leben in Guatemala* (Bornheim-Merten: Lamuv Verlag, 1993), 132.
8 Joseph Niesert, ed., *Münsterische Urkundensammlung*, vol 1 Urkunden zur Geschichte der Münsterischen Wiedertäufer (Coesfeld: Bernard Wittneven, 1826), 40-46.
9 See "Meister Heinrich Gresbeck's Bericht von der Wiedertaufe in Münster" in Carl A. Cornelius, ed., *Berichte der Augenzeugen über das Münsterische Wiedertäuferreich* (Münster: Theissing'schen Buchhandlung, 1853: photo reprint, Münster: Aschendorff, 1983), 44ff.; *Geschichte der Wiedertäufer zu Münster in Westfalen*, Hermann von Kerssenbroick, (Münster: Aschendorff, 1881), 529-34 in particular.
10 J. Niesert, ed., *Münsterische Urkundensammlung*, 45; Albert F. Mellink, *De Wederdopers in de Noordelijke Nederlanden 1531-1544* (Groningen: J.B. Wolters, 1953), 42.
11 J. Niesert, ed., *Münsterische Urkundensammlung*, 40.

12 Ibid., 41.
13 Regarding "Psalmus" see Kobelt-Groch, *Aufsässige Töchter Gottes*, 92-100.
14 James M. Stayer, "Oldeklooster and Menno," in *Sixteenth Century Journal*, 9 (1978): 56ff.
15 J. Niesert, ed., *Münsterische Urkundensammlung*, 45.
16 J. Niesert, ed., *Münsterische Urkundensammlung*, 42; Regarding community of goods, see James M. Stayer, *The German Peasants' War and Anabaptist Community of Goods* (Montreal: McGill-Queen's University Press, 1991), 123-38.
17 J. Niesert, ed., *Münsterische Urkundensammlung*, 42.
18 Ibid., 43.
19 Ibid.
20 Ibid., 44.
21 Ibid., 42.
22 von Kerssenbruick, *Geschichte der Wiedertäufer zu Münster*, 490ff.
23 "Meister Heinrich Gresbeck's Bericht," 38ff.
24 von Kerssenbruick, *Geschichte der Wiedertäufer*, 501.
25 One version is found, among other places, in "Meister Heinrich Gresbeck's Bericht," 45, and in "Ketter-Bichtbok" (Der Munsterischen ketter bichtbook, 1534) in Robert Stupperich, ed., *Schriften von katholischer Seite gegen die Täufer*, (Münster: Aschendorff, 1980), 166.
26 J. Niesert, ed., *Münsterische Urkundensammlung*, 44, 46. See also the testimony of Knipperdolling from January 20, 1536: ". . . und Knipperdollingk gab ir mit xii gulden und ii gulden ringe." *Berichte der Augenzeugen über das münsterische Wiedertäuferreich*, 404.
27 von Kerssenbruick, *Geschichte der Wiedertäufer*, 531.
28 Ibid., 532.

DIVARA OF HAARLEM

Life and death decisions often have been based on gender. When the city of Münster fell on June 24, 1535, after a long siege, the great slaughter began. It was primarily the men who died. The conquerors made short work of the approximately eight hundred remaining Anabaptists capable of bearing arms. Only a few escaped. The women were treated with more leniency. Those who were pregnant or had just given birth retained the special protection they had been given from the outset. In addition, many Anabaptist women who behaved prudently or were able to prove their innocence could hope for mercy.[1] In contrast to their brothers in the faith, the sisters were often considered to be followers who had accepted Anabaptist ideas, but had not expressed them openly. Their antagonists never doubted that a few male leaders were responsible for the events of Münster. They had driven the "common people" to derangement and had abused them for their own satanic plans.

    This male-centred view very likely contributed to the fact that the hostile victors gave relatively minor attention to the most prominent woman of the Anabaptist kingdom of Münster.[2] Divara, the royal spouse of Jan van Leiden, was taken prisoner and executed a few days later. Not even the record of an interrogation or a confession has survived, but then perhaps such testimonies never existed. A chronicler reported that on July 7, Divara, the most notable of van Leiden's queens, Knipperdolling's wife, his mother-in-law, and two other Anabaptist women who stubbornly stuck to their convictions, were executed.[3] That is all that is known about the end of Divara, allegedly a beautiful woman. A number of things suggest that she may have remained true to her Anabaptist convictions. Jan van Leiden, who apparently did not know that his wife had already been put to death, is said to have expressed the wish that she should be persuaded to relent from her convictions. He himself regretted much of what had transpired under his regency, although he did not abandon his Anabaptist principles. Divara had been dead for several months when Jan van Leiden suffered a death of unspeakable agony together with Krechting and Knipperdolling on January 22, 1536. One after the other the three comrades were bound to a stake and tortured with glowing tongs. Their corpses were immediately placed in iron cages and hung in public view from the tower of St. Lambert's church.[4] The queen was spared all that.

    Her quiet end stands in extreme contrast to the brilliant and glittering life she had as the royal spouse at the side of Jan van Leiden. Divara was not his only wife, but was the actual first lady of the state, the true queen. The other fifteen wives had to subject themselves to her unconditionally. Usually identified by critical observers and opponents of these events derisively as playmates, mistresses, or concubines, these fifteen were secondary spouses who lived in the shadow of the privileged Divara. She was said to be of medium height, quite obese, and, at an age of over twenty years, somewhat older than the other wives.[5] Divara, who came from Haarlem in the Netherlands, had first arrived in the chosen city as the wife of the prophet Jan Matthijs, who was killed just outside the gates of Münster in April 1534. In his confession of January 20, 1536, Jan van Leiden denied that he had been attracted to the wife of Matthijs while her husband was still alive.[6] However, this protestation does not sound credible. The wife of the prophet had aroused his attention for some time. The die had been cast in the house of Knipperdolling. Allegedly Jan van Leiden had a revelation there in which he saw Matthijs pierced by a spear, after which he received the commission to marry Divara.[7] And that is what happened. In July, a few weeks after the death of Matthijs, she became his wife. After Jan van Leiden had raised himself to the position of spiritual and worldly monarch over the commonwealth of Münster and the whole earth, Divara became the queen of the Münster Anabaptists. She apparently believed that this was an honour awarded her not so much by divine providence as by the generosity of her husband when the prophet Johann Dusentschuer proclaimed him king on August 31, 1534.[8] There had been no reference to a queen. Once more God seemed to have forgotten the women or, as had happened so often, had put their fates solely into the hands of men.

Unfortunately the sources do not reveal what Divara felt for her husband, who was a man portrayed by his contemporaries in the darkest hues. Did she freely consent to the marriage or did she consider it a forced measure that she could hardly refuse? Perhaps she did not even know that Jan van Leiden had come to Münster as a married man, but without his wife whom he had left behind in Leiden.[9] Divara must have known from the beginning that she was not her new husband's only wife. Jan van Leiden took other wives in addition to Divara; it was his right to do so. The law providing for polygamy passed in July 1534 not only allowed, but actually commanded, men to take several wives.[10] The rationale for this measure was certainly not only to increase the divine community, but also to solidify it internally. By this measure, the more numerous women were subordinated to the male will and integrated into the system. No sister, young or old, was to be allowed to take personal responsibility for the shape of her life in Anabaptist Münster. This departure from monogamy, while allowed only to the men and biblically legitimated, was not to everyone's taste, as events were soon to show. Uncontrollable excesses and marital conflicts soon generated scepticism about the new order and conjured up resistance to it from both men and women.

Divara was evidently more successful than other Anabaptist women in reaching a modus vivendi with the other wives. There is no indication that there were ever scenes of conflict or jealousy. We do not know, of course, what actually happened behind closed doors. What is certain is that Divara was in no position to object to the further marriages of her matrimonially enthused husband on the basis of her pregnancy, since the purpose of marriage was fulfilled by generating a child. One chronicler reports that Jan Matthijs was the father of the little girl born to Divara, and not Jan van Leiden. There was great rejoicing at the birth.[11] The king, it appears, was not perturbed to be only a stepfather. The very thought that the holy community had grown by one soul was reason enough for celebration.

Although Divara had perhaps married a man she did not love, and had to tolerate other wives besides herself, it would be a mistake to regard her simply as the object of male caprice. Divara, too, may have pursued her own advantage. She did, after all, belong to the elite of the Münster Anabaptist society as the wife of the prophet Jan Matthijs after their arrival in Münster. It was a position that she was able to secure through her marriage to Jan van Leiden and to enhance as a representative royal figure. This does not imply that Divara had power or even influence. As the wife of Jan Matthijs, she had remained in her husband's shadow. To outside observers at least, she appears simply to have been a kind of phantom attending her famous husband. There is no hint that she influenced his decisions or shared them. She kept in the background with quiet modesty; that was the way it had to be. Divara's silence conformed completely to the ideal wifely deportment that Jan Matthijs expected from his sisters in the faith. They had to subordinate themselves and acknowledge the husband as lord. Whether Divara agreed with all the regulations and the leadership style of Münster's elite is another matter. Unfortunately the sources reveal nothing about Divara's character, her thoughts, or feelings. The brutal way in which Matthijs appeared to treat people could certainly have deterred her. Perhaps she even empathized with all the men, women, and children, so-called godless people, who were driven out of the city into the bitter cold on February 27, 1534.[12] Fear may have shut her mouth and compelled her to conform totally. Many an obstinate Anabaptist woman who dared to criticize or to oppose her husband went to prison or was executed; even prominent women were not spared the most severe punishments. Elisabeth Wandscherer is a case in point. As one of the wives of the king, she had dared to resist. She had betrayed him and her faith, Jan van Leiden explained months later.[13] Apparently Elisabeth was fed up with Anabaptist life and her royal spouse and wanted out. But it never came to that. A chronicler reports that Jan van Leiden himself took the executioner's sword and struck off the head of his insubordinate wife in the presence of the assembled people. No one, including the other wives, seems to have objected. After the deed was done the surviving royal wives sang "To God on high be glory,"[14] and perhaps Divara, too, joined in.

Compared to Elisabeth Wandscherer, Divara was an accommodating wife. Nowhere in the sources is it suggested that she either resisted or voiced criticism. If she was pale and unpretentious at the side of Jan Matthijs, as queen of Münster she changes into a splendidly adorned royal figurehead without any real power. She appears to have submitted to her royal spouse like a puppet. Beauty and wealth dismissed any inclination to doubt. She lacked for nothing. For several months she had the privilege of living like a queen. Surrounded by unlimited wealth, dressed and adorned with costly clothing and jewellery, she was the king's equal in her luxurious lifestyle.[15] Like him, she had her own retinue. According to the so-called Court Ordinance of Jan van Leiden, the queen and the other wives had a total of eleven servants, among them a steward, a chef, a cook, two attendants, and one lackey.[16] In comparison to the retinue of the king, which consisted of over one hundred persons, Divara's was very modest and exclusively provided to deal with the private needs of the ladies. It included no political office.

The living quarters also reflected the status of the royal household. The king had declared one of the most attractive buildings in the cathedral square as his residence. His wives were accommodated in an adjoining house, which was connected by a door to the royal palace.[17] Added to all the clothing, jewellery, and pomp that the royal family enjoyed in their earthly paradise was a generous allotment of food. There were those who went hungry in the besieged city. Efforts were made to alleviate the distress, but it was a losing battle. Divara and the other wives of the king were better off than many a despairing Anabaptist woman who could see no way of saving her starving children. Softened leather, cow dung, cats, mice, grass, whitewash scratched off the walls, and much more is reported to have been food for the starving brothers and sisters in the extreme affliction of the siege.[18] Whether the royal pantries were full to the last we cannot say. If one is to believe the black-and-white interpretation of the chronicler, the king and his court lived in luxury[19] while the people were afflicted with misery, illness, and want. In fact, not even Jan van Leiden got off scot-free. As the situation became more and more hopeless and many were leaving the city in despair, he declared that he would give up all of his wives except Divara.[20] The new matrimonial order had shattered. The royal ladies as well as all the extra wives in the Anabaptist kingdom were granted freedom to leave their husbands and the doomed "New Jerusalem."

Many of the brothers, however, would not give up their first wives. Divara, too, remained. It cannot be established now whether she was coerced or whether she did so out of devotion. It is possible that Divara also considered fleeing. Probably she saw that flight would not improve her situation. Many ordinary Anabaptist women who fell into the hands of the surrounding military were treated generously; Divara could not hope for any mercy. The queen could not escape accountability since she too had become guilty. Even if at first sight it does not appear to be so, by virtue of being a grandiose figurehead Divara was a pillar of the Anabaptist system. For this important reason, Jan van Leiden could not dispense with Divara. He needed her to stabilize what he claimed was his divinely legitimated kingship, which could easily begin to totter. Considerations of political advantage may well have played a role when he first took to wife the young widow of Jan Matthijs. In Divara the future king not only secured for himself a reputedly beautiful woman; with her he also managed to inherit some of the lustre of the prophet. As the first wife of the king, Divara later strengthened his position by representing the many women of Münster, and giving them a sense that they shared directly in the rule of the kingdom. This is important, since the four thousand women–there were many more of them than there were men–could easily have created unrest. It was for good reason that the dominant Anabaptist leaders were concerned from the beginning to control the sisters and to fit them into the male hierarchy. It was Divara, in her dominant position, who was able to pacify the women without endangering the dominance of the men. In their frequent public appearances, the royal pair demonstrated repeatedly the ideal relationship and matrimonial harmony between the brothers and sisters. Jan van Leiden set the tone; Divara obeyed. Whether they appeared in the cathedral square on horseback or on a palace balcony, it was always the king who spoke and acted; Divara remained silent. It seems that in her public appearances she never spoke or made any decisions. It was her duty to support the might and dignity of the king to his advantage. We may assume Divara enjoyed the glittering role she was allowed to play in this male drama. She was not made to feel that she was completely dependent or merely the means to an end. On the contrary, it was very important for Jan van Leiden to pay homage to his beautiful wife before the people without in the least subjecting himself to her.

An example was the unusual Lord's Supper celebration which took place on October 13 on the cathedral square and called the queen to new duties. The whole population was present and seated at long tables, the men sitting with their wives. Side by side with Divara, the king walked up and down the rows of the faithful, speaking words of admonition and encouragement. After all had eaten, the Lord's Supper was celebrated. The king, the queen, and Knipperdolling broke small round wafers and gave them to the brothers and sisters with the wine.[21] Most unusual for a woman, Divara had performed a sacramental act heretofore reserved for men alone and had overstepped the boundaries of orthodox church practice. It was certainly a significant departure from tradition although it should not be overrated. What happened not only fits totally with the Anabaptist understanding in which traditionally valid norms and usages had been reduced to absurdity and lost their value, but also with the authoritarian leadership style of Jan van Leiden. Divara could participate actively in the communion rite only because he wanted it that way.

Jan van Leiden did even more to lend the first lady in the kingdom the image of a figure who demanded respect. When the names of the gates and streets were changed, he provided that henceforth there would be not only a King's Gate and a King Street, but also the female counterpart, namely, a Queen's gate [*Königinnentor*] and a Queen Street [*Könniginnenstrasse*].[22] As a sign of her importance, Divara was allowed to wear a crown just like her husband, and to have her own retinue and hold court. All of this points toward certain rights and authority which, on closer examination, prove to be an illusion. There is nothing to indicate that Divara conducted government affairs or held audiences as would take place in a genuine court, though she was allowed to take charge of a smaller circle of servants and perhaps also of the other wives who were subordinate to her. But here too we may presume that her influence was not great, circumscribed by the narrow boundaries set by Jan van Leiden. Not only did he decide with which woman he would spend the night, he also set himself up as the judge over life and death, as in the case of Elisabeth Wandscherer.

Apparently then, Jan van Leiden ruled his wives just as he ruled the people, with extreme harshness. None was his equal, not even Divara. Even if in official public appearances she was the only one he tolerated at his side, she always remained subject to him. Only once did she go ahead of him. She preceded him in death.

Notes

1 Karl-Heinz Kirchhoff, "Die Belagerung und Eroberung Münsters 1534/35, Militärische Massnahmen und politische Verhandlungen des Fürstbischofs Franz von Waldeck," in *Westfälische Zeitschrift* 112 (1962): 141-44.

2 In contrast to Hille Feicken, the "Judith of Münster," the queen of Jan van Leiden was never forgotten. Divara has been an important figure all along, who at least was recognized and often received widespread attention, not the least of which is the opera by José Saramago and Azio Corghi, "Divara - Wasser und Blut," composed for the 1200-year celebration of the city of Münster, published in Gernot Wojmarowicz, ed. *Musikalische Bekenntnisse. Dokumente und Reflexion zu einer Konzert-und Opernreihe des Symphonieorchesters und der Städtischen Bühnen Münster* (Münster: Aschendorf, 1995), 73-102; 103-108. See a discussion of the opera by Ralf Klötzer see *Mennonitische Geschichtsblätter* 51 (1994): 171ff.

3 *Geschichte der Wiedertäufer zu Münster in Westfalen*, (Münster: Aschendorff, 1771: photo reprint 1929), 197.

4 Regarding these executions, see "Anton Corvinus, hessischer Prediger, an Georg Spalatin, über die Hinrichtung Jan van Leidens, Bernd Knipperdollings und Bernd Krechtings, Januar 1536," in Richard van Dülmen, ed., *Das Täuferreich zu Münster 1534-1535, Berichte und Dokumente* (Munich: Deutscher Taschenbuch Verlag, 1974), 281ff.

5 See von Kerssenbroick, *Geschichte der Wiedertäufer zu Münster*, 59ff. where a contemporary portrait of the queen is given. It is reproduced in *Die Wiedertäufer in Münster, Stadtmuseum Münster, Katalog der Eröffnungsausstellung vom 1 Oktober 1982 bis 7 Februar 1983* (Münster: Aschendorff, 1983), 191.

6 See "Testimony of Jan van Leiden, Jan. 1536," in Carl A. Cornelius, ed., *Berichte der Augenzeugen über das Münsterische Wiedertäuferreich* (Münster: Theissing'schen Buchhandlung, 1853; photo reprint, Aschendorff, 1983), 401.
7 Ibid.
8 von Kerssenbroick, *Geschichte der Wiedertäufer*, 47ff.
9 See "Testimony of Jan van Leiden, July 25, 1535," in C. Cornelius, ed. *Berichte der Augenzeugen*, 370.
10 Regarding the new order on marriage, see Ralf Klötzer, *Die Täuferherrschaft von Münster, Stadtreformation und Welterneuerung* (Münster: Aschendorff, 1992), especially 97-102 and 115; Matthias Hennig, "Askese und Ausschweifung, Zum Verständnis der Vielweiberei im Täuferreich zu Münster 1534/35," *Mennonitische Geschichtsblätter*, 40 (1983): 25-45; James M. Stayer, "Vielweiberei als 'innerweltliche Askese,' Neue Eheauffassungen in der Reformationszeit," *Mennonitische Geschichtsblätter*, 37 (1980): 24-41 and Auke J. Jelsma, "De Konig en de Vrouwen, Münster 1534-1535," *Gereformeerd Theologisch Tijdschrift*, 75 (1975): 82-107.
11 See "Meister Heinrich Gresbeck's Bericht von der Wiedertaufe in Münster," in Cornelius, *Berichte der Augenzeugen*, 157.
12 Ernst Laubach, "Jan Mathys und die Austreibung der Taufunwilligen aus Münster Ende Februar 1534," *Westfälische Forschungen*, 36 (1986), 147-58.
13 Joseph Niesert, ed., *Münsterische Urkundensammlung*, Urkunden zur Geschichte der Münsterischen Wiedertäufer (Coesfeld: Bernard Wittneven, 1826), 181.
14 von Kerssenbroick, *Geschichte der Wiedertäufer*, 176ff.
15 See "Meister Heinrich Gresbeck's Bericht," 89ff., 109, 137.
16 "Des Münsterischen Königs Jan van Leiden Hofordnung (1534/35)," in Richard van Dülmen, ed., *Das Täuferreich zu Münster 1534-1535, Berichte und Dokumente*, 158.
17 von Kerssenbroick, *Geschichte der Wiedertäufer*, 60.
18 See "Meister Heinrich Gresbeck's Bericht," 188ff.; see also, Karl-Heinz Kirchhoff, "Berichte über das münsterische Täuferreich 1534/35 in einer Hamburger Chronik," *Westfälische Zeitschrift* 131/132 (1981/82): 194.
19 See the report concerning the misery in the city in von Kerssenbroick, *Geschichte der Wiedertäufer*, 157-61.
20 See "Meister Heinrich Gresbeck's Bericht," 190ff.
21 Ibid., 110ff.
22 Ibid., 154ff.

FENNEKE VAN GEELEN OF DEVENTER

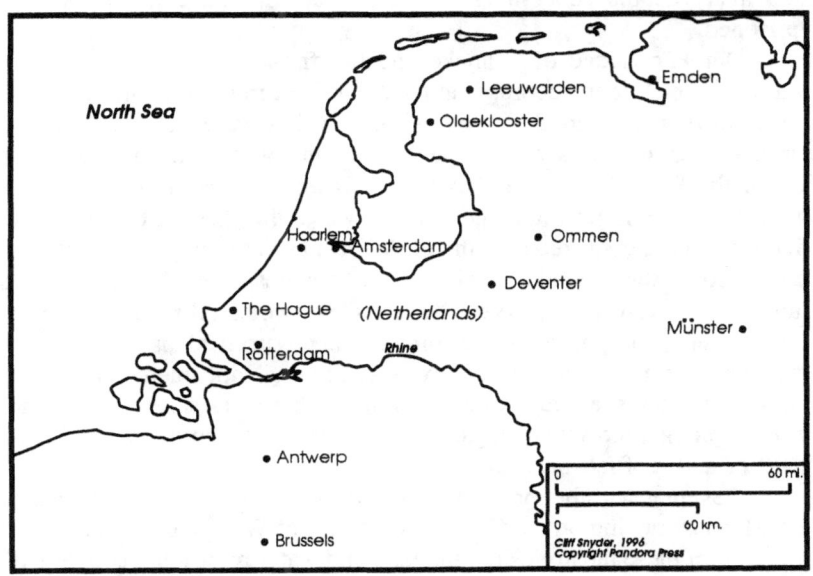

On April, 17, 1535, in Deventer (at the time the largest city in the northeastern Netherlands), a woman was killed on account of her faith. For the first time, the city government had arrested an Anabaptist woman. As commonly was done in the Netherlands at that time with heretic women sentenced to death, she was bound in a sack, cast into the river before the city, and drowned. With this execution of Fenneke van Geelen came the end of the first persecution of the Anabaptist community [*doperse gemeente*] in the city.[1] The dissenters must have practised their faith quietly, or at the very least given the city government no further offence, for there is little further notice concerning them. We come across only a single later reference in the city archives. The calm endured until 1571,[2] seven years before the city would side with the prince of Orange and the Reformation was officially established. Then a second wave of persecution broke out anew, with accusations, arrests, and finally executions within the small Anabaptist fellowship in the city.

It is possible to bring these first martyrs to life on the basis of the small number of court records[3] that have survived from the first period of 1535, in which Fenneke was named. Of the second group of martyrs from 1571 we possess an impressive personal witness. One of the prisoners, Ydse Gaukes, wrote three letters from prison in the Noordenberg tower to his associates in the faith. Thieleman van Braght later included them in his *Martyrs' Mirror* as a testimony to Ydse's undaunted faith, and as a support and example for his remaining co-religionists.[4] These personal documents relate many details concerning the faith, state of mind, and lives of the imprisoned.

Our knowledge of Fenneke and her friends of 1535 comes solely from the official court records that have survived in the city archive. These records have preserved their confessions, which were drafted during the hearings, their sentences, and the punishment that was inflicted on them. The view of the Deventer Anabaptists from this time is, therefore, that of their persecutors, the inquisition and, in its wake, the city authorities. As is evident from the court records, the questions put to the imprisoned followed the protocol of the official inquisitors, and only those answers that served the course of justice were preserved. Nevertheless, we can discover much from them. Other, more personal, documents have survived as well, such as testaments and transfers of property; less personal documents, such as the city account books, are also extant. Using all these sources, it is possible to form an image, however vague, of the first Anabaptist community in Deventer and its first martyrs.

Deventer was the most important commercial city in the northeastern Netherlands, drawing on the German territories of Westphalia and the Lower Rhine. From these territories ran the land and water routes that converged on Deventer and the IJsel river, and then ran along the IJsel to the sea. Deventer formed part of the renowned Hanseatic League along with other IJsel cities. Five annual international markets attracted many merchants, who filled the city each year from March to mid-November with their presence and their business.

The city also was important in cultural respects. It was the cradle of the Modern Devotion, established by the Deventer native, Geert Grote.[5] In the late Middle Ages, its Latin School attracted hundreds of students from the northern Netherlands and neighbouring German lands. From 1479 to 1483 Erasmus had attended school there[6] and the literary community of the city had become familiar with his humanistic programme of thought. An independent and literate circle of learned citizens emerged who could follow the new developments in religious thought and practice. A stream of books and pamphlets rolled off the printing presses and were bought and read in the markets and inns. In Fenneke's time, Deventer was still an important printing centre and Luther's new ideas became known quickly. Even private translations of the New Testament,[7] published in the vernacular, appeared in the city. The citizens were accustomed to independence in government and were used to conducting their religious life in a self-reliant manner.

Around 1520 Luther's doctrine of the justification through faith alone caused a shock in Deventer, as it did elsewhere. The origin of the first Anabaptist community in Zurich, where baptism was solemnized on adults as a conscious testimony of their faith, was closely linked to the perceived need to acquaint oneself with the Bible, the foundation of the faith. The preaching of Melchior Hoffman concerning the approaching endtime, in which the Revelation of John played such an important role, gave the Anabaptist movement in the north a new direction.[8] His prediction that the endtime was near made a deep impression, in Deventer as elsewhere. Many received adult baptism at the hands of itinerant preachers as a sign of their entrance into the community of believers. This rebaptism and the common priesthood of the believers inevitably caused a profound conflict with the official church.

Far-reaching changes in governmental affairs took place at the same time. In 1528 Charles V was formally installed by the magistrates of the city as the new sovereign lord.[9] With this action Deventer promised to be faithful to the new prince. Charles, for his part, pledged to maintain uncurtailed the old rights and privileges of the city. On the surface everything seemed to be in order. However, all too quickly the imperial administration applied new pressure on the free imperial city. For the Catholic Habsburger, who sought to govern his lands in a centralizing fashion from his Brussels court, the Deventer magistrates had become a thorn in the side, because of the patience and boldness with which they governed their citizens, and because of their mild dealing with the feared heretics. The *lutherye*, as it was called in the placards, spread more and more. The events of 1534 and 1535 in Münster, where the Anabaptists, streaming in from all regions, had deposed the civic government and proclaimed the city to be the new Jerusalem–the place where they could witness the approaching endtime–were the direct motivation for the Brussels authorities to put a stop to the heretical movements. Thus in 1534 and 1535 the first large-scale persecution emerged in the Netherlands.

Deventer, too, was suspect of Anabaptist sympathies. On February 17, 1534, the militant *Stadholder* of Overijssel, Georg Schenk van Toutenburg, who was devoted to the cause of the Habsburg Emperor Charles V, informed his court at Brussels that messengers were on the way from Münster. The rulers in Brussels had designated Overijsel, the province to which Deventer belonged, as the first target for action. But as soon as they settled their affairs there, they turned particular attention toward heretical Deventer. As early as February 1534, Jan Matthijs of Haarlem stayed in the city for a time, while in transit to Münster. Some two months later, on April 29, the magistrates responded to the emperor's edicts with a number of expulsions.[10] Furthermore, the council and community swore a solemn oath to have no fellowship with *lutherye*, but to oppose it with force.

It is evident that toward the end of 1534 Deventer was regarded as a centre of Anabaptism. On December 17, 1534,[11] the magistrates received a letter from Schenk van Toutenburg, the *Stadholder*, with instructions to persecute the Anabaptists sharply and, furthermore, to insure that no help be sent from the city to the Münsterite heretics and rebels, who now had their backs against the wall as a result of the bishop's siege of his city. In this letter, Schenk reminded the city government of his petition to take care that its merchants not supply the Münsterites with wares or provisions.

A week later, on December 24, 1534, Schenk stated in his two letters to the city[12] that he had been informed that the fugitive Anabaptists from the IJsel towns had found shelter in the countryside, and enjoyed protection from the officials or *drosten*, all against his express command. Sometime around January 20, 1535, Schenk sent another letter,[13] now with information that the Anabaptists were planning to incite the people to rebellion, in order to relieve Münster. Two subsequent letters[14] from the governor [*Landvoogdes*] and from Schenk a few days later give us further details. That Brussels had every reason to be concerned, especially with respect to the attitude of the governing classes, would become all too clear later.

In besieged Münster, when the expected brothers did not arrive from the Netherlands in December 1534, Bernt Rothmann, the city's theologian, published *Concerning Vengeance*[15] in which he made an emotional summons to the covenanters to join the Münsterites in their fight against the godless. With a thousand copies of the book and a large sum of money, four men left the beleaguered city. One of them was the husband of Fenneke, Jan van Geelen, and around New Year, 1535, he brought the book into Amsterdam and travelled from there to Brabant. Meanwhile the inflammatory text also became known in Deventer. For the besieged Anabaptists in Münster, the city of Deventer had taken on even greater importance, particularly when the Münsterite "king" Jan van Leiden had a vision in which it was revealed that along with Münster and Strasbourg, Deventer, too, would be one of the elect cities of God. As a result, some fourteen days later, during a meeting of Anabaptist leaders in Sparendam among whom were a number of persons from Deventer, there was a discussion of how Deventer might be taken by means of an attack.

Although this was an alarming situation for the central authorities, it did not lead to immediate measures on the part of either Schenk or the city government. Did they not know of the plan, or did the danger not appear great to them? A message from Münster to the Deventer Anabaptists in the middle of January advised them not to become active, but for the present to remain calm, at least outwardly. Nevertheless the city government, because of the continuous rumours and pressure from the central authorities, was forced to arrest four Anabaptists later the same month.

On 25, or at the latest 27 of January, Willem Glasmaker, Johan Lubelei, Herman Schroer, and Johan van Winssem were apprehended.[16] According to the accusation, they had allowed themselves to be baptized in the house on the Waterstraat owned by the former burgomaster Johan van Winssem, the father of the last-named. With many others, they belonged to the group of Deventer citizenry that maintained close relations with nearby

Münster, which had been occupied roughly a year before by their co-religionists. In Münster, as they believed was quite clear from the Scriptures, God's presence and will would soon become manifest. Many had gone to the "new Zion" from Deventer, attracted by "God's kingdom on earth," or travelled there regularly. Among them were Hylle, the widow of burgomaster Lubbert van Renssen, the noble joffer ter Poirten, the master apothecary Joriën, and burgomaster Johan van Winssem himself, all of whom were members of the Deventer patriciate. Johan van Geelen, the husband of Fenneke van Geelen, was the most famous of these emigrés. It is striking–and this appears also in the court documents in which the later confessions of the arrested were recorded–that many members of distinguished families in the city belonged to the Anabaptists or were closely allied to them through family ties.

The Deventer magistracy could not escape passing the death sentence upon the four arrested men. On Saturday, February 6, 1535, the four men were brought to the central market place, the Brink, and executed there with the sword. Fearing a revolt, and wishing to keep sympathizers at a distance, a cordon of four to five hundred armed men was posted around the place of execution. The four condemned Anabaptists remained firmly obstinate in their convictions until the end, and when the mass was celebrated before their execution, they scornfully turned their backs on the holy sacrament. They also wanted nothing to do with confession of their sins to a priest. Schenk's harsh position was illustrated again shortly thereafter with new arrests and similar sentences. On February 17, two more Anabaptists, Jacob van Herwerden and Jellys Gallam, were executed.[17]

Who were these people for whom their new faith was so important that they preferred to give up their lives publicly, rather than abjure even with a mere pro forma word or signature? Although we never will be able to give a satisfactory answer, it is possible to say something further regarding their place in the urban community and the role that they played in it. In order to shed further light on this, we will look more closely at Fenneke's life and then trace what is known of her.

Fenneke, or Fenne van Gellen, Geel(en), Ghelen (there are differing spellings), was the wife of Jan or Johan van Geelen. Jan became a citizen of Deventer in 1525 for the customary fee of four stuivers. Herman van der Beeck stood surety for him. Herman was a respectable Deventer citizen of the lower nobility, who possessed a large house in the Roggestraat and a farmhouse on the other side of the street. Where Johan came from is not mentioned in the record. He probably came to know Fenne in Deventer and they were married there. A document dated February 10, 1534,[18] stated that they possessed two farms or rural properties in the parish of Ommen, perhaps the region from which Jan originally came. Fenne and Jan van Geelen had at the least two children, a boy and a girl, as is apparent from a later testament.

Shortly after the execution of the four men on the Brink, it appears that Fenne's life became irrevocably linked with that of her usually absent, and later self exiled, husband. In the beginning Jan could still move about unhindered in Deventer. On February 10, 1534, Ash Wednesday, he and Fenne had been able to look after their affairs personally in the presence of the magistrates, as the record from that date demonstrates. But after his activities became better known, and when he was promoted from being a messenger of Münster to being the financier of King Jan van Leiden, and finally one of the Münsterite leaders, Jan's position in Deventer became untenable. His extensive circle of connections, both within and outside the city, made it possible for him to remain undiscovered by the investigators of the court in Brussels.

We gain a vivid image of Jan's appearance thanks to a description distributed by the governess Maria of Hungary in order to aid in his arrest;[19] a copy also was sent to the Deventer magistracy. Jan van Geelen–"who has a wife," as was emphatically reported to the magistracy, "dwelling inside your city"–is described as a medium-sized, solid man with a pale face. He had no beard, but wore a black *paltrok* or overcoat, and black *hose*, a style of trousers that had three creases cut through above the knees to show the colourful and expensive material underneath. On his torso he wore a black *wambuis*, or jacket. On his head he wore a black cap, which was *doorstoken*, or interlaced with a black veil, and he was armed with a *roer*, or pistol. His sharp intelligence, intellectual resourcefulness, and restless, fanatical nature made him an important leader of the Anabaptists and a formidable opponent of the representatives of Charles V.

There may have been some in Deventer who would have been deterred by the executions of February 6, 1535, but certainly Fenne van Geelen was not one of them. Her house stood on the Lange Bisschopstraat, one of the most important streets of the city, on the route along which the four victims would have walked on their way from the Bisschopshof, where the session of the court was held, when they were led to the scaffold at the marketplace, the Brink. From her dwelling she would have seen her friends going by.

Fenne's name was not mentioned in the court records of this first group of martyrs. There is nothing to suggest that she had left the city or was detained there. Apparently not impressed by the executions, Fenne allowed herself to be baptized on February 9, three days later. This expressly forbidden rebaptism did not remain hidden from the city government, for about a week later the servants of the court arrested Jacob van Herwerden and forced him to confess, a confession that would become fatal for Fenne.[20] Jacob van Herwerden was a co-worker of Jan van Geelen, and during the questioning he admitted to having brought a letter from Jan to

Fenne. In this, as he further confessed, Jan had requested–had insisted, in fact–that she let herself be baptized, "*of hie wolde sie nyet kennen voir syn wyff*" [or he would no longer regard her as his wife]. On top of this, as proof of her good will, she was to send him twenty guilders, although he did not need it. Following receipt of this letter, Fenne had allowed herself to be baptized by Jacob, together with her servant, a tailor.

In a letter from the Deventer magistracy to their Amsterdam colleagues and dated February 17, 1535,[21] we read that Jacob van Herwerden, who was executed almost immediately, alleged that Münster could maintain the defence of the city no longer than Pentecost. Furthermore, Jacob's confession confirmed that a new revolt was being prepared by Jan van Geelen against Deventer.

According to Jan van Leiden's visions, Deventer's Anabaptists, led by Jan van Geelen, would yet surprise the city, even though the attack attempted earlier had been foiled by treachery. Because of that treachery, the signal for the first attack on the city, a white weathercock on a house above the Brink, could not be used and the attack was cancelled. The letter Jacob van Herwerden had handed over to Fenne undoubtedly had spoken of the new plan of attack. Jan would have written that their intention was to keep themselves ready, hidden in some houses, and that the agreed-upon place for this plot was *een sunderlynge plaitze achter den Bruederen*, that is, a small square behind the Franciscan Brothers' church. The gentlemen of the council would have to pay close attention, certainly during the mid-Lent market, when the Anabaptists would have an opportunity to lodge easily in the city posing as foreign merchants. But ultimately the second assault upon the city did not take place either.

It remains a mystery why Fenne was arrested so late, only on Saturday, April 17, 1535, and executed by drowning, two months later than the main group of martyrs. In her confession,[22] which is preserved among the court records, she admitted to having been baptized by Jacob van Herwerden on Shrove Tuesday, February 9, 1535. Her confession and the earlier confession by Jacob therefore agreed. Nothing is known about the exact procedure of her execution and the precise place in the river where she was drowned. From similar condemnations, we know that a woman–drowning was a female punishment–was bound in a sack, the sack weighted with stones, and then was thrown into the water; or alternatively, a millstone was tied to a woman's neck and then she was cast into the water.

It appears unlikely that the severe position taken by the city towards Fenne was prompted simply by her rebaptism. Most likely her husband's active role in the Anabaptist storming of the Cistercian abbey of Oldeklooster in Friesland on March 28, 1535, determined her sentence.

Schenk, who for once declared pleasure over the forceful intervention of the city in the punishment of the heretics, nevertheless found himself opposed by the civic leaders when it came to the confiscation of Fenne's possessions. They did not allow the central rulers from Brussels to seize her goods, but said that these should fall to the city. They would thereby be in a position to put into effect Fenne's last testament[23] and to follow the stated desires concerning her movable goods and household effects. This appears indeed to have been a posthumous honour when we interpret carefully her preserved testament and the annotations that were added to it.

The reverse side of the document says: *Testamentum Fenneke van gele hir gedrenckt um die wederdoepe* [Testament of Fenneke van Gele, drowned here because of rebaptism]. City secretary Verheyden had written on a loose page next to it: *soe veer die eirsame Raidt will benedigen* [as far as the honourable council will permit].

Fenne's first concern, as is evident from this testament, went out to her still young children. "I desire of the honourable lords of Deventer that they send this to my children," a wish she further underlined with "according to God's will." Her son Jacob received the tablewares–eight dishes, eight mugs, three fine vegetable dishes–three pairs of candlesticks, three pairs of bed linens, three of the best hand cloths, the best table linens, three pairs of pillows, the bedtick with two more pillows and six new chair cushions. Next he received her newest robe, her black robe and both of his father's robes. For him also were his mother's best waistband with a camel hair garment that was kept in her wardrobe. Also bequeathed to her son were "my large trunk," the chest in which Fenne, as was common then, kept her clothing, and the wardrobe, her bed, and best bolster with a blue cover.

To her daughter Fenne gave her *tersoer*, the sideboard, and her two rings, her red robe and her purple skirt. Also her worsted cloak with the two camel hair sleeves and six chair cushions. The further household goods she must have divided among others whom we do not know. Others were not forgotten. Thus joffer ter Loe received Fenneke's silver *ruiker*, a holder for a small ball of scent, and her sister received small silver shovels embossed with roses. To her niece Egbert, a daughter of her sister, she bequeathed her best *kovele*, her cape with the blue camel hair guard-braces, hanging shoulder straps to protect the sleeves, and two camel hair sleeves. Finally, also for Egbert, there were two kerchiefs.

Fenne's elderly mother, who obviously lived with her, caused her some worry. By means of her testament Fenne attempted, at least for the initial time after her death, to ensure shelter for her mother. In her testament she requested urgently that her mother be allowed to live in her house for another year, and thereafter when the house, according to her understanding, would be lived in by others, that her mother be granted the *achterkamer*–the back part of the house–for the rest of her life. Beyond this her mother received the warm fur coat which Fenne herself wore, and the right to use the remaining eating utensils. Furthermore, 2 guilders, which lay in her buffet, were for her mother.

At the end of her testament Fenne summarized debts owed her and debts that she owed. The city builder still owed her 5 pounds, on which he had already paid back 9 brabant stuivers. Also, Reinier Kistemaker still had to pay her 21 brabant stuivers, and Johan Timmerman owed her 3 philipsgulden. She herself still owed "the woman of Coesfelt" 31 brabant stuivers and she also was in debt to a certain Albert van Delden. To what extent the testament was executed, we do not know. In any case, the city first settled overdue taxes, as well as two years' hearth tax for four hearths.

Fenne's death must have made a deep impression in the city, not least upon the members of the magistracy, of whom a fair number had family members who had been involved with Anabaptism, or still were. Later payments to Fenne's children indicate that the city authorities felt themselves responsible for them and were willing to spend money for their upbringing. Little Jacob was boarded with Hendrik van Holten, who had written Fenne's testament on the day of her execution. From the Chamber accounts [*kameraarsrekeningen*][24] of 1536 and 1537, it appears that Hendrik had received a monthly amount for the four months that he had boarded the youth and renumeration from what Fenne had left behind in cash. Thereafter, the youth received training from the city in order that he learn a trade, for which a fixed sum of money was paid. Moreover, in 1546 Jacob received a final payment of 6 gold gulden. Apparently he now was grown and could provide for his own needs. Around the same time Fenne's daughter, who in the meantime had married a certain Jan van Laer, received 10 gold gulden from the aldermen and council, apparently as a final payment.

What can we conclude, albeit with some reservations, from Fenne's testament? What is striking is Fenne's cool-headedness only hours before her death. Her testament shows that she had a clear understanding of her business position, her husband having long ago become a fugitive. With her testament she availed herself of what was perhaps her last chance to care for both her children and her mother, and she took the opportunity to give her family and friends a last token of her affection. Also striking in this testament is her unexpressed trust that the managers of her dwelling would respect her wishes. Fenne must have known well those who had condemned her to death and would have known that they might nevertheless be depended upon in the execution of her last will. The precisely described allocation of her mentioned possessions also confirms her trust in the authorities.

From the nature of her goods and the fact that she possessed a house on one of the most important streets of Deventer, we may gather that she was prosperous. Her social position, too, must have been considerable; she provided something of silver, after first caring for her direct family, to a noblewoman (a *joffer*), a friend or a family member. The indebtedness of three Deventer residents to her, among whom was the city carpenter, could point to a substantial amount of trade that she conducted in her house on the Lange Bisschopstraat. The data concerning Fenne van Geelen uncovered so far in the Deventer archives tell us no more. Perhaps more will come to be known about her after a more complete and systematic investigation of all the city records from the period.

With the conclusion of the restoration of the Great or Lebuinus church in 1992, a mural painting was placed inside this Reformed church of Deventer. Fenne was portrayed as a detail in this mural. Her image was included there in order to maintain the memory of all the forgottten martyrs of Anabaptism who, well before the coming of the official Reformation, were called upon to die for their faith.

Notes

1 For a history of the Mennonite (*Doopsgezinde*) church of Deventer based on the sources, see B. Rademaker-Helfferich, *Een wit vaantje op de Brink. De geschiedenis van de Doopsgezinde gemeente te Deventer* (Deventer: Arko Boeken, 1988), available from the Doopsgezinde Gemeente Deventer, Brink 89, 7411 BX Deventer, The Netherlands. The rich archives–the oldest diaconal book dates from 1637–of the Mennonite church of Deventer (hereafter cited as ADG) are on permanent loan to the Gemeentelijke Archiefdienst Deventer (Deventer Municipal Archives; hereafter cited as GAD).

2 During the uprising of the Low Countries against Spain, from the second of July 1569 on, Deventer had to billet a Spanish garrison under colonel Mondragon, who immediately began to interfere in the city's administration and instigated a fight against heresy, all against the will of the magistracy. The persecution of 1571 should be seen in light of these events.

3 The court protocols and other archival materials having to do with the Anabaptists in particular and the Reformation in general during the period from 1522 to 1587 are found in the Deventer city archives (GAD). The majority were published, with historical explanations, by J. de Hullu in seven publications, as reported in the bibliography of Rademaker-Helfferich, *Wit vaantje*, 188. For the court records from 1535, see J. de Hullu, *Bescheiden betreffende de Hervorming in Overijssel: Deventer 1522-1546* (Deventer Boek-en Steendrukkerij, 1899).

4 The three letters were printed with the title "Twelve Christians at Deventer, Ydse Gaukes [. . .] 1571," in T.J. van Braght, *Het bloedigh tooneel der doopsgezinde en weereloose Christenen, die om het getuygenisse Jesu [. . .] geleden hebben en gedoodt zijn* (Amsterdam: Hieronymus Sweerts,... [et al.] 1685; reprinted Dieren: Vereenigde Doopsgezinde Germeente te Haarlem, 1984, with introduction by S.L Verheus and T. Alberda-van der Zijpp) II, pp. 552-60.

5 See C.C. de Bruin, E. Persoons, and A.G. Weiler, eds., *Geert Grote en de Moderne Devotie* (Zutphen: Walburg Pers, 1984).

6 See A.C.F. Koch, *The year of Erasmus' birth, and other contributions to the chronology of his life* (Utrecht: Heantjens, Dekkert and Gumbert, 1969).

7 Such as the New Testament published in Deventer, October 5, 1532 (NK 2468). NK is the usual citation abbreviation for W. Nijhoff and M.E. Kronenberg, *Nederlandsche bibliographie van 1500-1540* (1919-1961). This translation from Luther bears a great resemblance to NK 2459 (1525).

8 See Klaus Deppermann, *Melchior Hoffman. Soziale Unruhen und apokalyptische Visionen im Zeitalter der Reformation* (Göttingen: Vandenhoeck and Ruprecht, 1979).
9 For a chronology of events in Deventer, see Rademaker-Helfferich, *Wit vaantje*, passim. In addition, A.F. Mellink, *De wederdopers in de Noordelijke Nederlanden 1531-1544* (Groningen: J.B. Wolters 1954; photo reprint with introduction, Leeuwarden: Gerben Dykstra, 1981).
10 De Hullu, *Bescheiden*, 169-70.
11 Ibid., 173-74.
12 Ibid., 174-75.
13 Ibid., 183-84.
14 Ibid., 184-87.
15 Bernhard Rothmann, in R. Stupperich, ed., *Die Schriften Bernhard Rothmann*, (Münster: Aschendorff, 1970).
16 De Hullu, *Bescheiden*, 191-201.
17 Ibid., 201-02; 209-12.
18 GAD, *Renunciatieboek*, 1524-1549 (RA 55, q, p. 141 sub 5 and p. 142, sub 1). According to the confession of an unnamed Anabaptist, Jan actually was born in the little village of Geel in the bishopric of Utrecht. Further archival work should clarify this question.
19 De Hullu, *Bescheiden*, 212. Also Mellink, *Wederdopers*, 71, n. 4.
20 De Hullu, *Bescheiden*, 210-11.
21 Ibid., 216-18.
22 Ibid., 218-19.
23 For the notes concerning the execution, see the *Register van Criminele Sententies* (Register of Criminal Sentences), GAD, RA 2. For Fenne's testament, GAD, RA 50.
24 GAD, *Cameraarsrekeningen*, 1536-37.

WOMEN SUPPORTERS OF DAVID JORIS

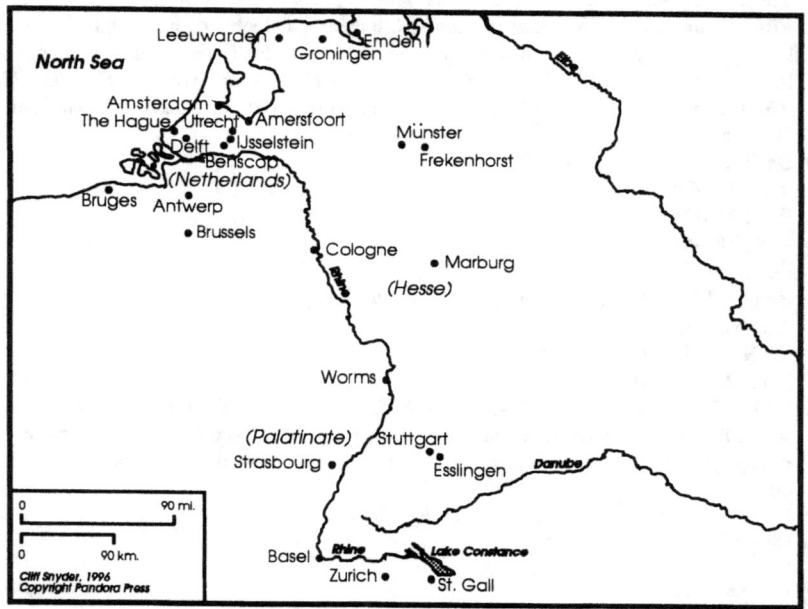

In his writings the Dutch Anabaptist leader David Joris (c. 1501-1556) expressed a rather negative evaluation of the role of women in the church.[1] One might therefore expect that women played a negligible role in his religious mission or among his Anabaptist following. Such is not the case. Women from all social estates were actively engaged in Joris's branch of Anabaptism, providing critical support and constant encouragement for the religious fugitive. Some of them, such as Anna Jansz, helped Joris develop his ideas and sense of mission.

Maritje Jans de Gortersdochter and Dirkgen Willem

The women who had the greatest contact with Joris obviously were those within his family, especially his wife and mother. Unfortunately not very much is known about them. Most of what little information we do have is from a biography of Joris written by a close associate (or perhaps himself).[2] We do know that his mother was Maritje Jans de Gortersdochter, who had married Joris de Koman or Joris van Amersfoort, a lesser merchant from Amersfoort who seems also to have been a member of one of the popular chambers of rhetoric, drama societies that performed plays in most of the cities of the Low Countries.[3] David's mother had been forced to leave her home city of Delft, Holland, for a time "because of the disagreement and great injustice of the world, having fled from her parents or friends like a runaway into this strange land."[4] It appears that the young couple moved to

Bruges, Flanders, where they had their first-born son (David's baptismal name was John, and he was later called Johan van Brugge or John of Bruges). They named him David because his father was performing the part of King David in a play. After having set up a shop, possibly after returning to Delft, Joris, Sr., and several of David's siblings died of the plague. David was therefore raised by his widowed mother, and their relationship seems to have been particularly close. This might help explain David's sensitivity and early interest in religious devotion. When David was apprenticed to a wealthy merchant after his father's death, he did not find this vocation to his liking, preferring to pursue his greater interest in art. So he left "on the pretext of his mother's business," and worked in his father's shop for his mother until he found a master glasspainter with whom to complete his apprenticeship.[5]

Contrary to the views of later polemicists who attempted to discredit Joris by writing that his parents came from low estate, David's mother seems to have been from a fairly prosperous bourgeois family in Delft. Several incidents from Joris's generally reliable biography confirm this. In fact, there was a possibility that David "would have been brought into the chancellery of the court [probably the Court of Holland in The Hague] by one of his mother's friends."[6] It appears that it was Maritje's social and family connections in the city of Delft that were largely responsible for her son's ability to escape serious punishment. According to the biography, when David was arrested in 1528 for spreading anticlerical tracts, he was released from prison without recantation (although he was first tortured and banished from the city), apparently because "some of his relatives had made a letter of obligation or guarantee, speaking on his behalf."[7]

Maritje not only helped to steer Delft's upper classes away from serious prosecution of her son, she also supported and housed his wife and family when David was on the run or in hiding. Shortly after completing his journeyman's tour to France and England in 1524, David married Dirkgen Willem, about whose past little is known. Like David's mother, Dirkgen was extremely important to David's life and intellectual development, although, once again, we must rely on male voices for our information about her.

It is known that Dirkgen and David had a large family. Ten children are identified in the sources and at least eight of these were born prior to the family's move to Antwerp in 1539.[8] Dirkgen, then, must have been a remarkably strong and resourceful woman, for not only did she have to care for their young family on the many occasions when David was on the run, she also travelled frequently with her husband. Of course she was ably assisted by her mother-in-law until the latter's execution in 1539. Even with such help, the emotional stress and physical hardship involved in being the spouse of a notorious heretic must have been considerable. For religious fugitives hiding from the law, pregnancy and childbirth presented special problems; simply finding a place to give birth could be difficult. Fortunately for Dirkgen, it appears that relative safety could be found in Maritje's home. After hiding in Gorkum on the Waert during the winter of 1535-36, David and Dirkgen were forced to leave their temporary sanctuary so that Dirkgen "could make her childbed" in Maritje's home in Delft, where she "lived in freedom" (Dirkgen gave birth to David, Jr. in early February 1536).[9] Later that year David rejoined Dirkgen and their children at his mother's home even though, according to the biographer, he did not "want to burden anyone, yes, not even his own mother."[10]

At times Dirkgen was forced to travel with her husband as well as with an infant too young to be left with David's mother. This occurred, for example, when the couple sought refuge in Strasbourg in the spring of 1535, at the height of Anabaptist persecution in the empire. The biographer recounts that

> it was then that he was forced to roam freely upon the earth, and it is known to everyone the kind of edicts and mandates which were issued against these people. Furthermore this same man was very anxious, and had to run sometimes here, other times there. He was hidden by some for money, by some because of old acquaintance, and by others because of friendship. He had to leave behind wife and child. Then, when it was Easter [March 28, 1535], he was forced to leave by necessity and hardship and went away secretly at great expense. But this was dangerous because he had his wife and infant son (named Joris) with him, which caused him anxiety and danger everywhere.[11]

One can easily imagine the kind of distress that Maritje and Dirkgen felt at being left to care for themselves and the children with the knowledge that the authorities could arrest them at any moment. The biographer remarks that the separation "happened lamentably so often, that God in heaven, yes even a heart of stone, would have pitied them."[12]

Providing financially for the family occupied both parents. As was typical for artisan families, it appears that Dirkgen took care of the retailing part of David's glasspainting business. At one point the biographer notes that David "had gained many valuable jobs through his wife, from those who took particular pleasure in his craft."[13] When her husband was unable to work because of illness or flight, Dirkgen turned to her own resourcefulness; to finance the trip to Strasbourg in 1535, she sold some of her clothes and jewelry.[14] In 1537, Delft's sheriff reported that when Joris was banned again from Delft in 1535, he had left behind considerable property. Dirkgen managed to reach an agreement with the sheriff de Heuter so that only a relatively small portion would be handed over to the magistracy.[15]

However, there were times when neither of them could work and, like most artisan families, they had to rely on relief. According to the biographer, such times of hardship "hit his wife harder than him," presumably because she was most active in the care of the children.[16] When Joris returned to Holland after the expiry of his banishment in 1531, he was unable to find much work. Then he became so ill he could not work for nearly two months; at the same time Dirkgen was in child-bed. The couple was forced to count on subsistence support from fellow religious dissenters.[17]

According to the limited sources, it appears that Dirkgen shared her husband's religious views, at least to a certain degree. The anonymous biographer, for example, recounts that both of them practised "public confession of sins" and the expulsion of the sinful flesh (the devil):

> It is nearly impossible to believe how David Joris was at this time inspired once or twice . . . to make free and fearless confessions in order to tread under his feet or to cast away his shame which he had held unjustly against the Lord for so long. This also happened with his wife. For they drove out and bound Belial, the devil and Satan (which had brought them such evil), according to the Scriptures.[18]

That Maritje, too, believed very strongly in her son's spiritual calling is evident from two stories drawn from the biography. First, Maritje seems to have assisted her son's developing conception of his mission. The biographer recounts the following vision that Maritje had of her son, proclaiming that all people must follow the path taken by David:

> This was shown to his mother (just before the Spirit of truth illumined him [i.e., in his visions of December 1536]) through a vision in the night. In this vision she saw him sitting on a horse with his eyes bound shut, a hat upon his head, a cloak placed on his body, and shoes and spurs. He has forgotten what he held in his hand, (he believes that it was a gun or a bow) and at his side was a sword. Some ran alongside his charger, although he rode very quickly. All people were troubled or in an uproar about him. These runners desired to lead the horse by hand along another path. But if they struck down David Joris, then everyone would go his own way, as is very well known. And everyone cried, "this is the way to journey." But David spurred on the horse and desired to go straight ahead. But there was no visible road ahead, nor could anyone find a way to travel, for it was full of thorns and thistles, growing very deserted and wild, and no path was seen nor perceived. But he rode alone straight ahead. The runners (I believe

indeed) left him and shouted after him from every side very derisively, harmfully and abusively, saying that he had run astray and become lost. But he did not listen to their cries, but instead followed after his soul (though as a blind man). He, however, did not know at all the kind of road which was ahead of him, except by experience. And see, after they had cried out after him, screaming and opposing him with these and other comments, and after throwing things at him, they finally stood still. They watched him for a long time, until it was finally revealed to them that all of them must go the same way if they did not want to be lost. His mother, however, kept this in her heart and said nothing of it to anyone, until she deemed the time was right in the development of doctrine. She then revealed it to David just as she had seen it, with these and further details.[19]

Anna Jansz, then, was not the only woman in David's circle to encourage his sense of calling. Unfortunately we will never know what other words of encouragement and advice Maritje gave to her son. If this story is at all reflective of her belief concerning David and his mission, we can conclude that he owed much for his religious zeal to her.

The second example is the story of Maritje's execution on February 21, 1539. In spite of her social connections, Maritje was imprisoned in the wake of the arrest and execution of several Davidites in Delft who were suspected of plotting the overthrow of the city. While the rumours were false, several of the over two dozen Davidites arrested were former militant Batenburgers, so the Delft citizens' concerns over an attempted coup were understandable. Under the circumstances, Delft's authorities had to at least make a show of a thorough investigation. Maritje was therefore arrested on a charge of rebaptism. According to the account of her execution from the city's *Criminal Book* [*Crimineelboek*]:

> Today the 21 February anno 1538 [old style] Maritje Jan de Gorters daughter, widow of Joris de Koman and mother of David Joris, was executed with the sword because she was rebaptized. Also, because the same [Maritje] was very penitent, she was therefore executed in the Celebroeders cloister and there buried.[20]

Adding further details to this sketchy account is Joris's biographer:

> Finally they imprisoned David's mother, took her houses and inheritance, also her and his belongings, things which he still needed. His own children helped carry these possessions and place them on the wagon. . . . These same possessions were sold on the

public market for the profit of the sheriffs. This is what one of his daughters told another who sat nearby, that it was just like what happens in the houses where someone has died, where everyone argues over the possessions. These possessions were worth more than other goods, because they were this person's belongings. Finally, before she was executed, even the houses were sold as well. At first she was very feeble and trembled in the face of her execution, but after this she was given some time to reflect on the kind of death she wanted. She was given three choices: drowning, blood-letting, or execution by the sword. Her prison was in a cloister, in a room where she was allowed to be cared for by a friend or niece, a Magdalene sister. Here she sat and reflected upon her life, how she had not yet walked piously enough. Finally she chose to be put to death by the sword, and regarded herself to be blessed in this by God's grace, because it would occur for His sake. When midday arrived, the same day that she made her decision, one or two from the court were sent with the executioner into the room and asked her "what kind of death?" She had decided on the sword, but the executioner had nothing with him except a sharp dagger, because they thought she would want to bleed to death, which was the easiest death. Behold, while she was sitting on a chair, he cut off her head together with some of her fingers, because her hands were held high and folded together. After this they attended to her and lamented her life and buried her body behind the altar in the church. This was very respectable, because she was one of the upper class of the city. And it happened in this way with the man's mother, because she had confessed and professed before the council that he, David, was as good and true in his teaching as the prophets and apostles, and with other words she had professed this with a steadfast heart. But it was not certain that she, who had friends, really had to die for this reason, if she had not opposed the sheriff so vigorously. For her human nature overcame her when she heard that all her belongings, house, and farm would be taken away from her and sold while she still lived. She therefore spoke somewhat foolishly. One was not sure of her state of mind when she said, "if you take my possessions, then take also my blood." At this he spoke, "this will indeed happen." He remained obstinate, because she had disgraced him before the magistrates, asking him what right he had to her possessions. For they were not to go to him, but only to her son's and daughter's children, but not to him or to his; he should be careful what he did.[21]

According to the records, Maritje was buried in the Cellebroeders cloister, which was a tertiary order that tended the sick and buried the dead for the city. Having a choice of manner of execution and being buried in a church confirms Maritje's above-average social status. That she had family members in the sisters of Magdalene, another tertiary order associated with the Franciscans, also supports this conclusion.

David's wife, Dirkgen, barely escaped capture during this round-up of suspects. Sadly, however, in her flight she was forced to leave behind several of their children:

> When the wife of David Joris had been forced to flee, she had left behind her small children who had stayed in the house of David's mother. She had been able to take along with her only a nursing infant (named Gideon). But then the mother of her husband David was also imprisoned (as described above) and all her belongings, what was left of them, including the house and farm, were taken away. This had been predicted before and written by the Prophet Micah, not to mention described in the gospel. The children were forced to go running about and begging in the streets. Then they were taken to the sheriff, and boarded here and there, wherever it pleased him. He forbade anyone to touch them, neither friend nor relative, for he placed all of them in different locations from each other, one here, another there.[22]

The somewhat different response of the parents to the distress of their children may reflect some variation in the level of affective attachment. According to the biographer, "Father and mother could only hear about and observe all of this. There were good hearts who desired to rescue and release them, but their father David said that they should keep still and let it be, they must suffer with the father." Then, when one young associate, Jan Jansz van den Berch, offered to rescue the children, "their father, David, would not hear of it, even though the mother would have agreed to it if it would not be too perilous. They therefore desired that he not attempt it, and David, with many fine reasons, forbade it earnestly, saying he would wait until God provided." Even so, the youth attempted to deliver one of the young daughters who had recognized him and cried out to him "O Johan, where is my mother? O, where will I find her?" Offering to help her return to her mother, Jansz was caught on the way to Amsterdam. The daughter was eventually released to a cloister. When news of this reached Dirkgen, she asked for help from one of their relatives, a Magdalene sister, who managed to return the girl to her mother. Jansz, however, was tortured and executed.[23]

In June 1539, Dirkgen and sixteen other Davidites were arrested in Utrecht. When she was captured, Dirkgen had to "abandon her daughter, who carried their small infant. The child with the infant departed from her imprisoned mother and being in a strange city she was in bitter sadness, as one can imagine." After a terrifying journey the child finally arrived in Delft.

All but two of those arrested in Utrecht were executed on June 11, although Elsken, the first wife of Jorien Ketel, was drowned the following month, on July 18. Those who were spared were a Jan Hermensz, who was released after he successfully maintained his innocence through a session of torture on June 22, and Dirkgen, who, for reasons now unclear, was released on June 18. The description of her sentence from Utrecht's "Daily Council Book" (*Raads-dagelijksch boek*) provides little rationale for the decision: "on 18 June Dirkgen, the wife of David Joris of Delft, was found innocent, acquitted and released."[24] Clearly the authorities knew the identity of Dirkgen's husband. Yet they found her innocent and released her a week after her associates were beheaded or drowned. Even the longer description of her interrogation yields few clues to the puzzle of her release:

> Also Dirkgen, David Joris' wife of Delft, who was apprehended by the sheriff of the imperial majesty on account of the city of Utrecht, because she was found with some belonging to the sects of Anabaptism, some of whom were executed here by the sword and the others by water; whereupon being informed by the aforementioned sheriff, the court and others at diverse times and places well and sharply examined the aforementioned Dirkgen. But they could not discover that she was baptized, nor that she had joined the sect of Anabaptism, nor that she was favourably disposed toward this same sect, for which reason she had been brought to justice before the mayors and aldermen of this city. The mayors and aldermen, after considerable deliberation with the council, having well considered and taken into account the information provided by the sheriff against her and the confession of the aforementioned Dirkgen, inform the sheriff of the imperial majesty and duke of Brabant, count of Holland and lord of the land of Utrecht, concerning the court's decision, that the aforementioned Dirkgen shall be absolved and released from prison.[25]

Perhaps the authorities were holding her to tempt her husband to give himself up to them in exchange for her? If so, why release her so soon? It may be possible that the authorities were planning to follow her after her release in the hopes that she would lead them to her husband. If so, the plot obviously failed. The brief description of her interrogation and sentence suggests that the Utrecht authorities did not regard Dirkgen as a willing supporter of her husband's heresy. As the spouse of a heretic, she was not automatically implicated in her husband's crimes. It is possible that she had never been rebaptized. Although she was "severely examined," it seems that

Dirkgen was not formally tortured, suggesting that her unfortunate compatriots had also vouched for her innocence, presumably out of devotion to her and David. They may also have instructed her to deny any serious involvement in their movement so that she, at least, might be saved.

The biographer provides much more detail concerning her interrogation, presumably as she later described it. In this source we learn a great deal about Dirkgen's views of her husband, although there is no court record corroborating her statements:

> They interrogated her intensely about her husband, wanting her to tell them where he was. She told them that she did not know, and this was true. The pious heroes who were with her counselled her as best they could so that she would be soon released to join her children, but such could not occur. For the prosecutor or advocate of The Hague [Reynier Brunt, prosecutor-general of the Court at the Hague] together with Jan Sondersyl [The sheriff of Utrecht], were so bitter and envious of her, that they shamefully accused her and the brothers who had been executed at Delft and Haarlem of desiring to attack the cities. Jan Sondersyl said that he still had their confessions with him. The woman asked permission from the good magistrates and the mayor of Utrecht if she could speak freely and respond to this and she gave her confession about this. She was so enraged and angry about the crude, proud lies which they had told behind David's back, shaming him publicly. She insisted that he prove it or be called an evil and false witness. David had proven himself to be excellent and had spoken to the brothers only about virtue, honour, faithfulness and piety, which she had seen of them. They desired to execute her swiftly because she had associated, travelled, eaten and drank with these people, even living and hoping with them. She furthermore told them that she did not need to know what sort of people her husband led. She would not be guilty of condemning or bringing about the death of her husband (if she desired to be an honourable woman) because she knew far better than anyone else, that he feared the Lord and loved the truth of Christ, seeking to do good to everyone. He just could not conceal the blessedness which he had received from God. For she could testify only a little about the matter and of what kind of result had come to him. She would say much good if it was not already common knowledge. She was therefore willing to die.[26]

Fortunately for her, she did not have to. The biographer claims that when both the suffragan bishop and Reynier Brunt died in the same year, Utrecht's magistrates refused to proceed with executions for heresy without imperial or ecclesiastical pressure. Yet Brunt did not die until October 15; unless he fell ill in June and was forced to leave the proceedings in the hands of local officials, it seems unlikely that his death had much to do with Dirkgen's release. Evidently the biographer sought to depict Dirkgen in as "heroic" a role as possible. On the basis of the limited evidence, it seems most likely that Dirkgen was able to present herself as a devoted wife who had maintained some distance from her husband's heresy. It appears that the Utrecht magistrates were convinced.

After her apparently miraculous release from prison, Dirkgen returned to Delft where she eventually was able to gather together the scattered children. Not surprisingly, she immediately demanded of her husband that he find a secure haven for her and their family. David eventually joined them, until his presence in the city became known to the authorities (possibly one of the conditions for Dirkgen's release was to remain separated from her husband). David, too, did not want to leave his wife, even if it meant capture. Unfortunately, when Dirkgen was able to spend time with her husband, she was forced to be separated from her children. She then returned to them, not able to tolerate being away from her offspring. When David in a fit of pique demanded she return to him, Dirkgen responded "that she had been advised not to travel until he had obtained a safe place, then she would come again to him as a good wife should for her husband."[27] At this time efforts to find a permanent refuge were intensified, and in the summer of 1539 the family moved to relative safety in Antwerp.

After this relocation, Dirkgen and David's home life stabilized. Unfortunately there is no source comparable to the anonymous biography to take up the story of Dirkgen after 1539. We do know that Dirkgen and the family moved with David into a manor outside of Antwerp and then, together with the noble van Berchem family, moved to Basel in 1544. There they resided in comfort, following the lifestyle of their noble patrons.

Another glimpse of Dirkgen's possible influence on Joris is seen in a series of three missives sent by Joris in November 1543 to "his household" in Antwerp. The first two of these letters (in the unpublished "Hydeckel" volume of early correspondence) were sharp in tone, warning those of his house, "both young and old" that he had seen that morning "Satan ruling inside my house." While this and the next letter do not explain the precise problem that Joris is addressing, he advises them to listen more carefully to his teaching, to guard themselves against lies, and to mourn over their sin. The third letter, however, is much more conciliatory, it seems on account of "Dir.," presumably Dirkgen. His apologetic tone was perhaps a result of Dirkgen's intervention.[28] In this letter, moreover, Joris denies that he is an archheretic and a bringer of discord. It seems, then, that while absent from the manor, Joris had heard that someone had arrived at his household attempting to convince his family and noble patrons that he was nothing but a schismatic. Presumably Dirkgen then allayed his fears.

We cannot know how often Dirkgen was forced to act as conciliator; her role in maintaining peace within the Joris group may have been considerable. It may be no coincidence that the unity of the Basel Davidites began to unravel after Dirkgen fell ill in the summer of 1555 and seems to have remained precarious until her death in August 1556. In any event, when a neighbour came to her asking if the rumours were true that her husband was the notorious heretic, fear of disclosure hastened her demise. She died on August 22. She was followed three days later by her ill and distraught husband.[29] Like David's mother, Dirkgen appears to have played a critical, if little acknowledged, role in the life and career of David Joris. While her thoughts and aspirations are now lost to us, it is clear that she was not only a devoted mother, but a strong and determined individual.

Noblewomen and Joris
David Joris owed a great deal to the support that he received from other women. The volumes of his correspondence contain a large number of missives to such female supporters. While little is known of the general rank-and-file women followers (even Anna Jansz was from a prosperous family), we do know a little more about the several noblewomen who supported, tacitly or openly, David's circle of Anabaptists.[30]

In general, it appears that aristocratic women were frequently much more tolerant of, and perhaps more interested in, religious dissenters than were their male colleagues. For example, the lady of IJselstein, countess of Buren and Leerdam, seems to have been quite tolerant of religious radicals, perhaps because of a personal connection with the groups around David Joris. One of Joris's key lieutenants, Jorien Ketel (1511-44), as a youth had been a personal attendant to the countess. Although the countess did not possess any independent political power, as consort to Floris van Egmont and mother of the Maximiliaan Egmont, count of Buren, she could exert considerable sway over her family on many issues.[31]

Her son, in fact, showed considerable reluctance to prosecute the known Anabaptists in his jurisdiction. Reinforcing this trend was the fact that Maximiliaan's noble bailiff, Gysbrecht van Baeck also had personal contacts with radical reformers. In 1534 van Baeck had provided a residence for the radical Anabaptist preacher Hendrick Rol, who had earlier been made private chaplain at the IJselstein manor. Not surprisingly, the court of Holland soon complained about the lax posture taken by van Baeck and his superior toward religious dissent. In a letter to regent Mary of Hungary (February 17, 1534), members of the court noted that "it has come to their knowledge that at IJselstein and Benscop there are residing many persons, infected with the sect of Luther and other sects and the officer [bailiff] of the count of Buren is showing no diligence in capturing them."[32]

It comes as no shock, then, to hear that in 1544 van Baeck's wife, Elsa van Lostad, was jailed as a supporter of David Joris. The case provoked considerable debate among Overijsel officials. While *stadholder* Maximiliaan was forced to deal publicly with the issue, his approach was to allow the proceedings to become hopelessly stalled in questions of legal jurisdiction until Elsa was finally released in 1548. In many cases, pressure from imperial authorities overcame local reluctance to prosecute Anabaptists. It appears that in this case, however, *stadholder* Maximiliaan was powerful and cunning enough to frustrate even the regent and the Court of Holland. One can only speculate about the level of personal persuasion Maximiliaan's mother was able to bring to bear on her broader circle of aristocratic friends and family.

Another example of noble support for David Joris's Anabaptism confirms the central role played by noblewomen. Joris's anonymous biographer relates the story of Joris's visit in 1538 to the family of Gossen van Raesfelt, which resided at that time in Raesfelt, near Münster in Westphalia. Gossen was married to Jacoba van Hackfort, the daughter of the ruling Twenthe bailiff, Count Barent van Hackfort.[33] Based on a reading of Joris's correspondence, it appears that the essential point of contact and support between Joris and this noble family was Jacoba. Several letters from Joris to Jacoba and her household have survived, both in the published and unpublished (the "Hydeckel") volumes. In three of these letters, Joris encourages her and her household in the faith. Jacoba's wealth may be indicated by the following passage where, in response to her query, Joris discusses his attitude to worldly possessions:

> So know, my beloved, that such outward things do not gladden me. I would much prefer to live in the poorest habit, house and manor. But I cannot render advice to anyone except to live in godly attention according to my encouragement or to the opportunity of the Holy Spirit. For I do not find nor feel my kingdom [here], for it is not of this world. Therefore do not take joyful pride in these things, but use them as I do, with thanks to God who has willed it.[34]

He also advised this noblewoman to be generous toward the "pious people of God," although he affirmed that what was truly valuable was not the money itself, but her attitude in giving. She and her household were expected to do good to the people of God, "on account of the sake of righteousness, according to each one's ability. Not that you send me money, but to send it out of such a heart, that is more valuable. For if you sent me in goods nothing more than a favourable heart, that is love to me," and is "worth more to me, than if someone sent me a hundred thousand pounds of gold."[35]

In another letter from 1543, Joris exhorts Jacoba to regard the despising of the world as a testing from God. "Therefore do not be appalled with me but remain fast and unmovable in the time of offence and possess your soul with patience." She is told to "spit out" the flesh and the world, to keep herself piously, to trust and doubt not, then she "will not fall" but be eternally protected from destruction.[36]

Judging from a letter written on September 28, 1547, it seems that opposition to Jacoba's faith had increased. She apparently had written a letter of complaint to David. Based on his response, it seems that she was harbouring doubts about Joris's teaching, reflecting the serious opposition she was facing. In reply he told her that he would not pray that she be delivered from such tribulation, but that she learn to trust even more in God against her many opponents. He advised her to take comfort in her children, for whose believing hearts David is thankful. They owe their first instruction in the faith, he affirmed, to their mother's "word and teaching of the fear of the Lord in humility and obedience," and he hoped they would continue in the same. She should regard her current tribulation as the best "examination to purification."

Presumably part of Jacoba's difficulty was her relationship to her husband, now the Twenthe bailiff. One can easily imagine her conundrum, seeing that part of her husband's responsibilities included the prosecution of religious dissenters, including some of Joris's own followers. In spite of this, Joris tells her to

> maintain yourself piously, faithfully and friendly with your husband; be obedient to him in everything that is good or not against God. If he has wronged you exceedingly, you should patiently endure and be quiet without any noise or many words. Trust your God and expect him in your heart where you can hear him testify, inspiring and teaching you with understanding. Do not turn to foolishness; keep your heart pure and free of all that is perishable, vain and deceitful before the Lord your God who has chosen you as his temple and dwelling in Christ Jesus.[37]

Perhaps to counteract the sin of pride, common among the social elite, Joris reminded his noble supporter to avoid prideful "self-glory," and instead to "become always more poor of spirit."

How did this noblewoman's support of Joris's version of Anabaptism affect her relationship with her husband? Was she able to convert him? While Raesfelt's later career as the Twenthe bailiff indicates he was no friend of Anabaptists, he may have been more open-minded before receiving his office in 1539. However, it is possible that Jacoba played a part in her husband's decision to stop his persecuting activity after he had the van Beckum sisters executed in 1544 (see their profile in this volume). It appears that Raesvelt was pressured by the higher authorities, especially regent Mary of Hungary, to execute the sisters. In 1551, he arrested three more Anabaptists, but pleaded to the Overijsel *stadholder* that they were "poor, simple, and uneducated people who are now so pathetically misdirected by bad teachings. . . ."[38] He did not execute any peaceful Anabaptists after this date.

Part of the appeal of Joris's ideas for some members of the second estate may be found in Joris's elitist language and hints about deep, spiritual truths hidden to the masses. Clothed in obscure, mystical, and deep-sounding language, Joris's teaching could be understood only by the spiritually enlightened, or by a spiritual elite. Those who were accustomed to regarding themselves as members of a social elite may have been drawn naturally to Joris's approach.

Among the noble supporters of Joris was the Countess Agnes van Limburg-Styrum, abbess of the Westphalian convent at Freckenhorst. Several letters that Joris directed to her have survived. Agnes came from a pious and well-connected noble family; her father was Count Adolf van Limburg zu Styrum and all four of her sisters also had entered monasteries. Countess Agnes became abbess of the wealthy Freckenhorst cloister in the bishopric of Münster in 1527. Membership in this cloister was dominated by the daughters of noble families. Like most noble members of cloisters, these residents identified themselves more as noblewomen than as nuns, although it is evident that Countess Agnes took her religious mission seriously. She certainly accepted the call for religious reform, for immediately upon her election she began to reform the cloister in an evangelical fashion. By 1532 her monastery had separated from the Catholic Church. Among other things, the centuries-old veneration of the miraculous Freckenhorst Cross was ended.[39]

Soon Countess Agnes was associating with Anabaptists, and by the early 1540s, Joris was writing to her as a supporter, albeit an often hesitant one. According to the court testimony of Dirick Schomecker, a Batenburger who claimed to have joined Joris's side, this noblewoman had become a supporter of Joris, once "giving the Jorists fifty Taler" and hiring only Davidites as the foundation's servants (the cook and fisherman were specifically identified as Davidites).[40] Schomecker also remarked that when he had tried to marry the sister of Hinrick Reekers, a Davidite, he discovered she was now staying in the monastery. It is clear from Joris's correspondence and the surviving court records that Joris's followers in the area held their meetings within the monastery walls. Based on the Batenburger practice of luring young women into polygamous relationships, it seems that the convent also acted as a sanctuary for Anabaptist women seeking both spiritual enlightenment and an escape from male Batenburger acquaintances.

Joris's words to the abbess included both traditional religious platitudes and his more esoteric teaching. He thanks his noble patroness for her love and support and addresses her in the proper way as "your grace," affirming that he was her debtor and servant.[41] At the same time, Joris magnifies the spiritual authority of the "third David," and hence of himself.

The stream of divine wisdom flowing from the throne of God (depicted visually in Joris's *The Wonder Book*) is identified as the "fountain of grace in the house of David, a living, heavenly spirit," and as the promised David. While his reader may be "little upon the earth," Joris writes, she was to take hope in the coming new world and kingdom when the children of God would be restored to their rightful place of glory. Perhaps Joris sought to allay his noble supporter's fear of loss of social status by providing her with a new spiritual identity. He also sought to win her complete attention and devotion, advising her to "listen and believe no other voice, word, or doctrine, except that which I hear." For Joris was called to the "service and office of the Spirit" and

> though there are few who perceive the love of the truth . . . you should rejoice, oh my beloved, and be joyful in the hope of the righteous nature of the future time and new world, which will be revealed in us, and we in them.[42]

Joris furthermore stressed the elite nature of the message that Agnes and others had accepted from him. Several times Joris refers to the *"kentenisse Christi"* as a spiritual understanding of Christ mediated directly to him and his followers. He defined it as the

> word of the Spirit which has come to you so that you by it might see and love his most beautiful nature and be pulled away from all perishable desires of this evil world to the unending love of truth in the heavenly glory.[43]

By his sacrifice, Christ has forgiven all sins and "has called us into the kingdom of Zion, into the peace of his love." God's people have been elected by him from the beginning; they are the true children of God, who will reign with Christ, who do not seek their honour and glory in this world. Their opponents, Joris argued, are not filled with the "spiritual, Jewish, heavenly language, the divine, Hebrew tongue," with which one can receive the "divine understanding of the promised David and the true Mosaic arts."[44] The countess, then, could expect to become a member of Joris's spiritual elite.

Other elements of Joris's esoteric teaching also appear in his correspondence with countess Agnes. He insisted that the devil was not a corporeal being with independent power. Rather, the Christian's true enemy was her or his own evil desires.[45] He also spiritualized the rite of believer's baptism, depreciating "external water baptism" in favour of a spiritual baptism, although he always acknowledged that water baptism was valid if received with an earnest heart and confirmed with good works of faith.[46]

By the 1540s, Joris allowed his followers to practise what has been termed Nicodemism, conforming externally to the outward trappings of official orthodoxy while continuing secretly to cherish his more esoteric teachings. Perhaps Agnes von Limburg found this aspect of Joris's teaching particularly appealing, for while she clearly initiated several evangelical reforms, Freckenhorst also retained many of the distinctive elements of a medieval monastery. While not explicit here, Joris's reputation as a staunch advocate of religious toleration may also have been a factor in his gaining noble support. For those of the aristocracy who regarded themselves as too sophisticated to accept more separatist and literalist doctrines, Joris's spiritualistic interpretation of Anabaptist tenets provided a fruitful point of contact. But the struggle to win permanent support was difficult.

A letter dated 1551 indicates that the abbess had become disillusioned with Joris's teaching. He writes "it has come to me that your soul has no more pleasure in my writings." He then concludes: "but if you cannot overcome the fear in your heart . . . so I will allow it. I will nevertheless not forget your grace in my heart."[47] It appears that in the end, Joris lost the support of this influential noblewoman.

Undoubtedly the most important support that Joris received from the nobility came from a well-connected family from the region of Antwerp. Once again the central figure is a noblewoman, Anna van Etten, the lady of Schilde manor and widow of Jan van Berchem. Shortly after Joris and his family found refuge in Antwerp, they were invited to stay in the Schilde manor, presumably at Anna van Etten's invitation. Here Joris made the acquaintance of three of van Etten's children: Joachim, the older son at twenty-two, Reinier, and the younger daughter, Anneken. In 1532 Van Etten's older daughter, Wybrechte, had married Cornelis van Lier, lord of Berchem and hence she had become the lady of Berchem. Furthermore, Cornelis's sister, Anna van Lier, was a regular visitor to the manor. Joris's most important noble patrons in and around Antwerp were thus Anna van Etten and Anna van Lier, respectively mother-in-law and sister to the lord of Berchem. It may have been as a result of their personal sway that Cornelis van Lier also was won to Joris's side.[48]

Van Lier was a considerable ally. He was the ruling lord of Berchem, and as such had regained from the Antwerp magistrates the right of high justice in his domain. He and his mother-in-law, moreover, were quite wealthy, and according to the testimony of Ketel, it was van Lier who financed the publication of Joris's very expensive magnum opus, *The Wonder Book*. When the noble patrons fled with Joris to Basel in 1544, van Lier managed to rescue a portion of his property before confiscation by the emperor. He thus was able to support both his own and Joris's family in noble style after their arrival in Basel.

Interestingly, van Lier did not reside long in Basel, but moved to Strasbourg. He seems, however, to have continued supporting Joris, at least to a certain extent, and maintained correspondence with the rest of his family in Switzerland. The central figure of Joris's noble patronage in Basel was clearly Anna van Etten. Relations between her noble family and Joris's were solidified by the marriage of her son Joachim to Joris's young daughter Clara (she could not have been older than eighteen years).

Why did Anna van Etten accept Joris, a notorious heretic and one of the most wanted men in the empire, not only into her manor (presumably as an informal chaplain), but into her family? Unfortunately, we do not have adequate sources to respond to this query. Anna and the other women in her and Joris's household were asked this question by the Basel authorities after public disclosure of Joris's identity in 1559. Their responses were equivocal and tell us little about their experience in the prophet's family, in large measure because before his death Joris had advised them to be evasive in the face of questioning so as to save their lives. The Basel authorities, moreover, were not prepared to apply any serious pressure to any of the suspects in the Joris case, including the women.[49]

The women of the van Etten and Joris families therefore affirmed first that "they knew no other faith" than that taught in "all the general articles of our faith and doctrine" and such had been taught in the Joris home. Second, they replied that "they learned nothing else from their lord and father except always to live a God-fearing, pious and sincere life." Third, he had read to them from no other writings "except those written to teach children in piety and virtue." Fourth, he had warned them to remain with their known faith and not to "accept any other saviour except Christ Jesus the true son of God." Were these words then a denial of their father's faith? Hardly, for Joris frequently defended his teaching by affirming that it in no way went against approved confessions of faith or the Apostles' Creed. Unfortunately the confession of the Davidite women tells us little about their true beliefs.

When questioned on what she had known about Joris and why she had left her homeland to follow him to Basel, the elderly Countess Anna simply responded that

> she had never known or heard of the sect of the Davidites. That she had left her fatherland to travel here because she needed to hear the gospel which was not generally well taught in the Netherlands, nor was it allowed. When she now heard that this David Joris desired to go upland [i.e., to Basel], she was pleased and desired to travel with him. For this reason, therefore, she sold her goods to join him on the journey. Afterwards she married her son Joachim to his daughter. She had known that he was also called David Joris, but she knew nothing else of his previous life.

Nothing in this confession would have unduly upset Joris, who would have agreed that the gospel was not well taught in his homeland and that Anna would be best served to travel with him to Basel, where she would be able, under his tutelage, to learn it correctly. Obviously the countess and the other noblewomen in Joris's immediate circle would not have made such great sacrifices if they did not believe in his teaching.

The historical record makes it clear that a number of Joris's most important supporters were noblewomen. At least one, the Countess Agnes of Limburg, wielded a fair degree of authority in her own right. Others, such as the duchess of Buren, Elsa van Lostad, Jacoba van Raesfelt, Anna van Etten, and Anna van Lier may have exerted considerable influence on their sons or husbands on behalf of religious toleration or in persuading them to support Joris. Given the important role played by French noblewomen in the Huguenot movement, the fact that some noblewomen in the Netherlands would sponsor a religious dissenter such as Joris is not surprising. By doing so they could fulfil roles of leadership and patronage that were increasingly closed to them by male colleagues in more orthodox circles. With the Protestant rejection of the cloister, reform-minded noblewomen also may have joined unorthodox reform circles to fulfil their religious aspirations. Like so many of his male contemporaries, Joris depreciated the role of women in the church, but showed considerable deference to noblewomen. Their social standing and political influence may have overcome, at least to a certain extent, Joris's more typical misogynistic leanings.

Notes

1 Joris's early correspondence is found in the "Hydeckel," *Jorislade*, vol. 9, Sendbriefen, Manuscript and Rare Book Department, University of Basel. For his published correspondence, see David Joris, *Christlijcke Sendbrieuen* (N.p., N.d. [Delft, J. Vennecool, c.1600]); David Joris, *Het tweede Boeck der Christlijker Sendbrieuen*, (n.p., n.d. [Delft, J. Vennecool, c.1600]); and David Joris, *Het derde Boeck der Christelijcker Sendbrieuen* (N.p [Netherlands], 1611]). For Joris's printers, see Paul Valkema Blouw, "Printers to the 'arch-heretic' David Joris: Prolegomena to a bibliography of his works," in *Quærendo* 21 (1991): 163-209. For a list of Joris's "Hydeckel" correspondents, see Gary K. Waite, "Writing in the Heavenly Language: A Guide to the Works of David Joris," in *Renaissance and Reformation / Renaissance et Réforme*, n.s. 14 (Fall 1990, date of issue December 1991): 297-319.
2 A translation of the anonymous biography and several of Joris's early works may be found in Gary K. Waite, ed. and trans., *The Anabaptist Writings of David Joris, 1535-1543* (Scottdale, PA: Herald Press, 1993). Several of the tracts included in this volume present Joris's views on women and marriage. Unless otherwise indicated, all translations are mine.
3 See Gary K. Waite, *David Joris and Dutch Anabaptism, 1524-1543* (Waterloo, ON: Wilfrid Laurier University Press, 1990), 49; for Joris, Sr. as a rhetorician, see also Gary K. Waite, "Popular Drama and Radical Religion: The Chambers of Rhetoric and

Anabaptism in the Netherlands," MQR, 65 (1991): 227-55, esp. 245-46.
4   Waite, *Anabaptist Writings*, 34. For Joris's biography, see also Waite, *David Joris*.
5   Waite, *Anabaptist Writings*, 36-37; Waite, *David Joris*, 50-51.
6   Waite, *Anabaptist Writings*, 36.
7   Ibid., 39.
8   See esp. Paul Burckhardt, "David Joris und seine Gemeinde in Basel," *Basler Zeitschrift für Geschichte und Altertumskunde*, 48 (1949): 5-106, esp. 23.
9   Waite, *Anabaptist Writings*, 44.
10 Ibid., 53.
11 Ibid., 42.
12 Ibid., 50.
13 Ibid., 59.
14 Ibid., 60.
15 Samme Zijlstra, *Nicolaas Meyndertsz. van Blesdijk* (Assen, 1983), 13-14.
16 Waite, *Anabaptist Writings*, 64.
17 Ibid., 60.
18 Ibid., 76.
19 Ibid., 62-63.
20 "Gemeentelijke Archiefdienst Delft, Oud Rechterlijk Archief 36, "Het eerste Crimineelboek," fol. 179r. I am thankful to B. van der Wulp, adjunct gemeentearchivaris, for providing a photocopy of this source. It is also cited in D. van Bleyswijck, *Beschrijvinge der Stadt Delft* (Delft, 1667), 763; and Friedrich Nippold, "David Joris von Delft. Sein Leben, seine Lehre und seine Secte," in *Zeitschrift für historische Theologie* (1863-64), 1-166; 483-673, esp. 602.
21 Waite, *Anabaptist Writings*, 81-83.
22 Ibid., 83.
23 Ibid., 94-95.
24 A.M.C. van Asch van Wijck, ed., "Bescheiden betreffende het eerste tijdvak van de geschiedenis der hervorming in de stad en provincie Utrecht, 1524-1566," in *Berigten van het Historisch Genootschap te Utrecht* 4 (1851): 139.
25 N.G. Kist, "Dirkje. David Joris' huisvrouw," *Archief voor kerkelijke geschiedenissen* 8 (1848): 198-200.
26 Waite, *Anabaptist Writings*, 96-97.
27 Ibid., 99-100.
28 The three letters are found in the unpublished "Hydeckel," housed in the Rare Book and Manuscript Department of the University Library of Basel, 470^r-76^r.
29 See Roland H. Bainton, *David Joris. Wiedertäufer und Kämpfer für Toleranz im 16. Jahrhundert* (Leipzig: M. Heinius, 1937), 92-93.
30 On sixteenth-century Dutch noblewomen in general, see Sherrin Marshall, *The Dutch Gentry, 1500-1650* (New York: Greenwood Press, 1987); for Dutch women and religion, see Sherrin Marshall Wyntjes, "Women and Religious Choices in the Sixteenth Century Netherlands," *Archiv für Reformationsgeschichte*, 75 (1984): 276-89. For noblewomen's support of French religious dissent, see Nancy Lyman Roelker, "The Role of Noblewomen in the French Reformation," in *Archiv für Reformationsgeschichte*, 63 (1972): 168-95.
31 For a more detailed discussion of Joris's relationship with the nobility, see Gary K. Waite, "The Dutch Nobility and Anabaptism, 1535-1545," in *The Sixteenth Century Journal*, 23 (1992): 458-85. Fuller source citations can be found in this article.
32 Karl Rembert, *Die Wiedertäufer im Herzogtum Jülich* (Berlin, 1899), 316, 318.
33 Waite, *Anabaptist Writings*, 68; Waite, "Dutch Nobility," 466-68.

34 David Joris, *Het tweede Boeck der Christlijker Sendbrieuen*, (N.p., n.d. [Delft, J. Vennecool, c.1600]), part I, 70^v-71^r.
35 "Hydeckel," 406^{r-v}.
36 Ibid., 458^r-60^r.
37 David Joris, *Christlijcke Sendbrieuen* (N.p., n.d. [Delft, J. Vennecool, c.1600]), part I, 54^v-55^r.
38 Waite, "Dutch Nobility," 468, as well as the other sources listed there.
39 Waite, "Dutch Nobility," 479-82; Friedrich Brune, *Der Kampf um eine evangelische Kirche im Münsterland, 1520-1802* (Witten-Ruhr, 1953), 41.
40 Karl-Heinz Kirchhoff, "Die Täufer im Münsterland: Verbreitung und Verfolgung des Täufertums im Stift Münster 1533-1550," in *Westfälische Zeitschrift*, 113 (1963): 87. In Joris's published correspondence there is also a letter to Herman, cook at Freckenhorst, dated Oct. 21, 1549. In Joris, *Het tweede*, part I, 53^{r-v}.
41 "Hydeckel," 346^v-54^v.
42 Ibid., 173^v-80^r, esp. 179^{r-v}.
43 Ibid., 346^v-47^r.
44 Ibid., 174^r.
45 Ibid., 349^v; on Joris's view of the devil, see Gary K. Waite, "'Man is a Devil to Himself': David Joris and the Rise of a Sceptical Tradition towards the Devil in the Early Modern Netherlands, 1540-1600," forthcoming in *Nederlands Archief voor Kerkgeschiedenis / Dutch Review of Church History*, 75/1 (1995); and Gary K. Waite, "David Joris en de opkomst van de sceptische traditie jegens de duivel in de vroegmoderne Nederlanden," in Gerard Rooijakkers, Lène Dresen-Coenders, and Margreet Geerdes, eds., *Duivelsbeelden in de Nederlanden* (Baarn, 1994), 216-31 (chapter translated by Pieter Visser).
46 "Hydeckel," 293^{r-v}.
47 David Joris, *Het derde Boeck der Christelijcker Sendbrieuen* (N.p. [Netherlands], 1611]), part II, 4^v-7^v.
48 Waite, "Dutch Nobility," 472-74; Waite, *David Joris*, 163-92.
49 For their interrogation, see Bainton, *David Joris*, 212-14.

ANNA JANSZ OF ROTTERDAM

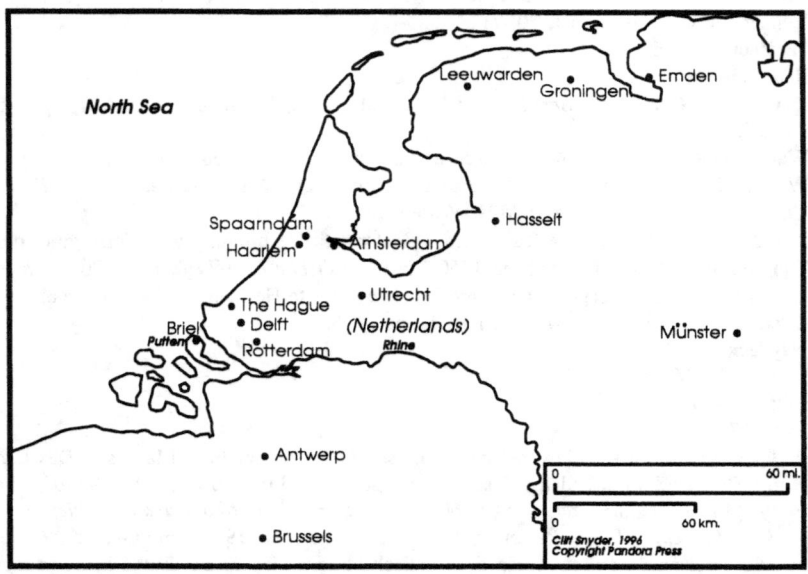

Anna Jansz has been immortalized as a model martyr in both the *Martyrs' Mirror*[1] and the *Ausbund*,[2] but modern scholars have had second thoughts. The Dutch Mennonite Karl Vos considered Anna somewhat "unbalanced, nervous, over-strung" and given to "fantastic expectations of the coming kingdom."[3] He insinuated that her relationship to David Joris was not purely spiritual and suggested that the authorities in Rotterdam, known for their leniency, executed Anna because she was considered a threat to society. More recently A.F. Mellink suggested that Anna found her way into the *Martyrs' Mirror* by mistake or "despite her revolutionary past." He declared her song, "I Can Hear the Trumpet Sounding," the "Marseillaise" of early Dutch Anabaptism.[4] Nevertheless, despite such opinions and some misgivings regarding the revolutionary "Trumpet Song," an "exception in Mennonite martyr literature," the image of Anna as the model martyr entered the *Mennonite Encyclopedia*. Her "Testament" has been described as "a glorious confession of faith and evidence of a faithful mother's love which deserves to be better known."[5] But is the Testament authentic? And what of Anna's relation to Joris, who has been considered an enigma in Anabaptist-Mennonite history?[6] What of Anna's role as a woman in the Anabaptist movement? Are there some lessons here about gender roles? The state of the sources makes some of these questions easier to answer than others.

Born on the island of Putten in 1509-10 and heiress to a small fortune, Anna Jansz came from the socially privileged. Her home stood on the merchant street of Briel,[7] a city strategically located between the provinces of Holland and Zeeland and within easy travelling distance of Rotterdam, Delft, and The Hague. Anabaptism came to this area late in 1533, represented by Gerrit Boekbinder and Jan Beukelz [Jan van Leiden], two missionaries commissioned by Jan Matthijs. Matthijs, soon to be master of Münster, had ordered the resumption of baptism after its temporary suspension by Melchior Hoffman. The growing movement fed on apocalyptic excitement. Its members saw in Hoffman and Matthijs the two witnesses of Revelation 11:3, the endtime Elijah and Enoch.

Although not among the original converts in Briel,[8] Anna and her husband, Arent Jansz, soon joined the growing movement. Anna was only twenty-three or twenty-four years of age and her baptizer, Meynaart van Emden, could not have been much older when he baptized her. Contemporary sources identify Meynaart as a "young fellow," a weaver with a limp,[9] whom modern scholarship has somewhat euphemistically described as an "early bishop" of Dutch Anabaptism.[10] As best as can be determined, Anna's baptism occurred in February or March of 1534,[11] because Meynaart was active in nearby The Hague during March and a few weeks later in Amsterdam. He broke out of the Amsterdam prison in May.[12] In June a number of his converts, including Anna's husband, fled from Briel.[13]

But what of Anna's conversion to Anabaptism? The lack of specific evidence does not permit conjectures as to personal motives and certainly none in terms of gender considerations. But the broader context proves suggestive. The movement, initiated by Hoffman but stalled because of his suspension of baptism, received new impetus from Jan Matthijs's resumption of leadership in late 1533 and soon fell under the spell of events unravelling in Münster. On February 23, 1534, elections brought the Anabaptists to power in Münster. The expulsion of the "godless" followed, while an invitation went out for "all believing covenanters in Christ" to flee "Babylon" and join the "New Jerusalem." The response was impressive; thousands heeded the call. They came from Gelderland, Brabant, Zeeland, Utrecht, South and North Holland—by boat, by foot, or with horse and cart—men, women, and children, rich and poor.[14] Five ships of "covenanters" were intercepted at Haarlem and six in Amsterdam. Twenty-seven ships and more than three thousand persons were blocked before they reached Bergklooster near Hasselt in Overijssel, which was designated as a gathering point by Matthijs. From there a "prophet" was to lead the trek to Münster. Noon on March 14, 1534, had been chosen as the beginning of the great exodus.[15]

Seen in the above context, Anna's baptism by Meynaart during February or March of 1534 must have meant more than a commitment to a holy life of discipleship. It took place in the long shadow of events in Münster, in an atmosphere charged with apocalyptic expectations. Anna's baptizer, Meynaart, clearly belonged to the pro-Münster faction. Mellink, the most knowledgeable Dutch scholar, described him as an "outspoken revolutionary" who one year later, in May 1535, prepared the "great attack" on Amsterdam.[16] Earlier, during December 1534, another pro-Münster radical, Jan van Geelen (see the profile of Fenneke van Geelen), had arrived with copies of Bernhard Rothmann's *Of Vengeance* (*Van der Wrake*). Meynaart was present at a meeting of leaders at Spaarndam, where van Geelen's message, that the time of grace was past and that the "saints" would be delivered before Easter 1535, had been discussed. Subsequently Meynaart informed the Anabaptists in Amsterdam that the time of vengeance had come. He warned against long absences from the city lest they find the city gates closed upon their return. Yes, according to the apocalyptic scenario the "Lord's banner was to be erected" in Amsterdam, "the sound of the trumpet to be heard."[17]

Anna's song, "I Can Hear the Trumpet Sounding," sung to the tune "I Want to Travel East," vibrates with the apocalyptic excitement of the period 1534 to 1536. Its inclusion in a collection of songs by David Joris that date from July 1529 to December 1536 substantiates the early origin of Anna's "Trumpet Song."[18] Together with her Testament, the "Trumpet Song" appeared in print along with an open letter from Joris during 1539.[19] All this and more suggest that Anna and Joris were more than casual acquaintances. In fact, a curious episode in Joris's life, as described by his anonymous biographer,[20] may explain the origin of that acquaintanceship.

Joris had found refuge with a woman whose husband had been absent for almost two years in England. It so happened that Joris, attracted by her "great piety" and "spiritual virtues," fell in love with this woman.[21] She in turn admired him for his understanding and wisdom in the Holy Spirit. Fleshly temptations were suppressed by earnest prayer and the concentration of their affection on "the source and object of all true love." This idyllic situation appears to have been rudely interrupted sometime in 1536, when the husband returned unexpectedly for a visit. Since reports of uncouth behaviour abroad had preceded him, his wife refused to see him, fleeing the house instead and leaving a frightened Joris to deal with the angry husband. A few days later the frustrated husband returned to England, spreading rumours "among the brethren" that his wife had become insubordinate and unfaithful. Shortly thereafter, two or three brethren arrived from England in an apparent bid to mediate the husband-wife feud. After several days of discussions and much prayer, it was decided–against Joris's wishes–that the visitors would accompany Joris back to his home and wife in Delft. The young hostess was presumably encouraged to follow her husband to England. The facts of the case clearly fit Anna Jansz, who returned from England with a fifteen-month-old son in November 1538 in order to consult with Joris. Evidence suggests that she had corresponded with Joris from England.[22] Curiously, our sources tell us nothing about the fate of her husband and the father of her child, but it is possible that he had fallen victim to the persecution unleashed by Thomas Cromwell in early October of that year.[23]

That Joris retained contact with brethren in England is documented by his pastoral epistle written in early 1537.[24] A few weeks before drafting this epistle, Joris had received an encouraging letter from a female supporter which, according to his own recollection, addressed the "office which he held and should hold."[25] Scholarly consensus considers Anna the author of that letter.[26] Given the contacts between Anna and Joris, it should be no surprise to find his influence in Anna's "Trumpet Song."[27] The 1539 edition of this song came off the press of Dirk van Borne, who published a number of works by Joris. The publication of Joris's letter with Anna's Testament[28] and "Trumpet Song" in one pamphlet by van Borne suggests that she was considered of Joris's party.[29] However, the "Trumpet Song" seems definitely of an earlier vintage. A comparison of its content with Rothmann's *Of Vengeance* illustrates why the authorities considered the song seditious. Rothmann had urged the brethren to rally without delay to the "banner of divine righteousness," citing a contemporary proverb that "those who miss the fight will receive no spoils." He alluded to the seventh trumpet of the Apocalypse with the recommendation that a captain be chosen in order to "raise the standard" and blow the trumpet. Ploughshares were to be beaten into swords, pickaxes into spears; God's people would be "liberated" from the "captivity of Babylon" and would rejoice in the punishment of the wicked. A new song would be heard in Zion as the saints with two-edged swords in their hands "would execute vengeance upon the heathen and punishment upon the people; bind their kings with chains, and their nobles with fetters of iron." The apostolic witness was to be laid aside for the armour of David.[30]

Anna's "Trumpet Song" follows a similar theme and abounds with apocalyptic allusions. Her leitmotif appears to be vengeance.[31] Like Rothmann she rejoiced in the coming "double" punishment of the godless. But instead of reaching for the sword, those ready to see God's vengeance were encouraged to reach for a "harp" and "sing a new song." Like Rothmann, Anna associated the "seal of God on the forehead" mentioned in Revelation 9:4 with the "sign of Thau" described in Ezekiel 9:4, suggesting that she too considered baptism as the apocalyptic sealing of the 144,000 elect.[32] The elect were the "male child" born to the woman in the wilderness persecuted by the "great dragon" [Rev.12]. The chosen were encouraged "not to fear his feathers nor his claws" but to lift their heads in anticipation of their inheritance.[33] Christ their king was coming to slay the godless. The last four verses paint a particularly graphic picture of evil proliferating, weeds covering the field of the approaching harvest time. The sickle is about to be "thrust into the earth." The summer is over, the sound of the seventh trumpet is in the air; the "great vine press of the wrath of

God" is ready to be trodden [Rev. 14:19-20]; yet some still despise the time of grace and heed not the warning. The outpouring of the seventh bowl would bring the punishment of Babylon to be followed by the "marriage feast." "Messengers were calling everywhere," the faithful were encouraged to lift up their heads and to put on their wedding garments, to "take the road in haste, lest they be punished along with Babylon." The last three verses open the scene on the great apocalyptic supper of the King of kings [Rev. 19:17-21].

> Verse 11: At Borsa and Edom, so the author has read
> The Lord is preparing a feast
> From the flesh of kings and princes.
> Come all you birds,
> Gather quickly.
> I will feed you the flesh of princes.
> As they have done, so shall be done to them.
> You servants of the Lord, be of good cheer.
> Wash your feet in the blood of the godless.[34]
> This shall be the reward for those who robbed us.
>
> Verse 12: Be pleased therefore, rejoice and be glad.[35]
> Play a new song on your harps;
> Delight in our God
> All you who foresee vengeance.
> The Lord comes to pay
> And to revenge all our blood.
> His wrath is beginning to descend.
> We are awaiting the last bowl [Rev. 16:17:21].
>
> Verse 13: Oh bride, go to meet your Lord and King.
> Arise, Jerusalem, prepare yourself.
> Receive all your children alike.
> You shall spread out your tents.
> Receive your crown, receive your kingdom.
> Your King comes to deliver.
> He brings his reward before him.
> You shall rejoice in it.
> We shall see his glory in these times.
> Rejoice, Zion, with pure Jerusalem.

This, then, was the message of the "Trumpet Song" credited to Anna. Of the sources attributed to her, it must be considered the oldest, and bears little resemblance to the "Martyr Song" attributed to her, which, as noted below, was written posthumously and was based on her Testament.

Turning to Anna's martyrdom it is clear that she returned from England sometime in November 1538. With her was her fifteen-month-old son Isaiah and a female companion.[36] Curiously, a fellow traveller recognized the two women as Anabaptists because of their singing and notified the authorities. Was it the "Trumpet Song" that betrayed her? The reaction of the authorities in Rotterdam could suggest so. Interrogations revealed further that Anna had returned from England in order to consult with Joris.[37] On January 23, 1539, she and her companion were sentenced to death by drowning, a sentence carried out the following day. Anna's last ordeal belongs to the most moving scenes in martyr literature. On her way to the execution with her son on her arm the distraught mother offered her fortune to any of the spectators willing to adopt her son. A local baker responded, promising to raise the child as his own. According to a postscript in the *Martyrs' Mirror* the baker kept his pledge and was rewarded with divine favour. He was able to add two breweries to his possessions and his adopted son Isaiah rose to become mayor of Rotterdam.[38] The man who had betrayed Anna met a very different fate. He drowned when a bridge collapsed as he crossed to witness Anna's execution. His descendants lived in abject poverty.

In his capacity as mayor, Isaiah must have been in a position to access the court records of his mother's trial. Her letter to Joris copied in Isaiah's own hand apparently survived into the next century.[39] Presumably Isaiah also cherished his mother's last testament;[40] after all, it was addressed to him. A comparison of this Testament with the "Trumpet Song" reveals unmistakable similarities, but also differences. While it abounds with allusions to the Apocalypse and refers to the sign of Thau, the tone of the Testament seems subdued. The accent has shifted from vengeance to patient suffering. The Thau has become a metaphor for the martyr's crown and "the cup of bitterness." The cross had been the way of all true followers of the Lamb. It was to be the experience of those under the altar [Rev. 6:9-11] whose number was still being completed and who raised their voices imploringly: "When wilt thou avenge the blood that has been shed?"

Deeply moving is Anna's spiritual advice to her son Isaiah: seek the kingdom of Christ among the persecuted, the poor, the down-trodden, the despised.

> But where you hear of a poor, simple, cast-off little flock [Luke 12:32], which is despised and rejected by the world, associate with them; for where you hear of the cross, there is Christ; from there do not depart. Flee the shadow of this world; become united with God; keep his commandments; observe all his words to do them; write them upon the table of your heart; bind them upon your forehead.

> Deal the bread with an open, warm heart to the hungry; clothe the naked, and suffer not to have anything twofold; for there are always some who lack (Matt. 26:11). Whatever the Lord grants you from the sweat of your brow above what you need, give to those of whom you know that they love the Lord [Gen. 3:19; Ps. 112:9]; and suffer nothing to remain in your possession until the morrow, and the Lord shall bless the work of your hands and give you his blessing for an inheritance.[41]

Only hearts of stone would fail to be moved by these lines or fail to appreciate their Christ-like spirit. Here beats not only the heart of a mother's last farewell but also the pulse of a chastened Anabaptist movement, the faithful remnant, the "despised little flock," sorely oppressed.

One further document already mentioned deserves attention here. It is the "Martyr's Song." This song appeared first alongside Anna's Testament in a 1570 edition of *Het Offer des Heeren*, a forerunner of the *Martyrs' Mirror*.[42] Claiming Anna as its author, the song proves to be a poetic version of her Testament. Only the introductory and the last verses expand the content. The rest, twelve of the fourteen verses, repeat the substance of the Testament.[43] The purpose of the song was community edification. It remains, nevertheless, historically valuable because it provides a window into the shaping of the martyr tradition that provided subsequent generations with a sense of history and identity. Of special interest is the evidence that when this song crossed the cultural borders into German, it led to an expansion of the original from fourteen verses to twenty-two. It was in this expanded form that the song appeared in the *Ausbund* of 1583.[44] Obviously in translation the song is once more removed from its original source. The sign of Thau has become the Tauf [baptism]. Even the date of Anna's martyrdom has been skewed;[45] all these are indicators that historical accuracy had become less important than the lesson to be conveyed. As the martyrology matured into the mainstay of tradition, original apocalyptic impulses faded from the collective memory or were transmuted into the timeless plea of a persecuted minority: "How long, oh Lord, how long?" The "Trumpet Song" was left behind to be recovered only by historians.

It may be concluded that Anna Jansz's spiritual sojourn, beginning as a convert to an apocalyptically inspired movement and ending as a model martyr four years later, seems symbolic of a broader collective transmutation in which David Joris, her spiritual mentor, appears to have played a prominent, if brief, role. Anna died well before Joris took his peculiar spiritual high road. Her inclusion in the *Martyrs' Mirror* was therefore not a mistake but entirely justified. Revolutionary and peaceful Anabaptists, Jorists, and *Doopgezinde*, initially co-existed in the same movement and as in the case of Joris, for a time at least, in one and the same person.

Subsequent efforts by representatives of the pacifist branch to disown their revolutionary or spiritualist cousins are now more difficult to accept at face value. Joris has assumed a significant if transitional role in the story of post-Münster Anabaptism.[46] However to agree with Vos that Anna belonged to Joris's camp does not mean agreement with his characterization of her as "unbalanced" and "overstrung." Instead, what emerges from the sources is an all too human heroine longing and hoping for the kingdom of justice and peace.

Anna's Letter to David Joris, 1536 or 1538

May the Lord who inhabits eternity–whose eyes are upon all things, whose throne is untouchable, whose glory is unfathomable, whom the host of angels serve with trembling (Oh how much more do we), who is mighty in wind and in fire, whose word is true and whose speech sure, whose orders are mighty and whose shape [*Gestalt*] is terrible, whose presence dries out the valleys and from whose anger the mountains flee, whose future appearance we await with longing–increase and fulfil in you what he has begun to His praise. I thank my Father and glorify my Saviour for the gift of His grace [manifest] in your wisdom, which comes from above through an exalted spirit and the wonderful counsel of God to the honour and glory of His most holy name and the cleansing and purification of His people. Blessed are you in the Lord, my brother. May your hands not cease nor tire to continue as you have begun to work in the enterprise of the Lord. Be the winnow in the hand of the Lord; prepare an acceptable people onto the Lord so that He can come speedily to His temple. Everything that is stained is an abomination to Him, as is written: "Cursed is the man who offers an unclean offering to the Lord." Therefore, oh you mighty leader of Israel, beloved of the Lord, look diligently after the Lord's vineyard. Prune its saplings and do away with what hinders its growth or with what may displease the Lord. The Lord will increase your strength and give you even more wisdom; for He takes delight in you. He has made you a watchman in His house, a shepherd for His flock. You are the most godly among those whose names are written. You are the noblest among the three to satisfy the king's pleasure. As you have testified with your blood through the earnest love to your God through whom you have obtained many gifts and the good will of the king, as is manifest daily. As the rain refreshes the earth and the dew the flowers of the field and makes their scent sweet to man, so do your warnings, teachings and instructions bring also refreshment and nourishment, even though the reader(s) may be of little understanding. They show them the way to the perfect wisdom of God in which they grow into a perfect man in Christ Jesus our Lord. Oh, how much beauty and goodness you have for others. Those who are like this increase more and more in the virtues until they come to

God Himself and are seen openly with Him in Zion. After the same we also sigh with longing, that we may see and behold the end of our faith. Oh, I delight that the cross is revealed and that the conflict begins. I hope that the Lord will answer my prayer and deliver me from this earthly tabernacle of my dwelling so that I may put off the dress of mourning and that I may receive the glorious jewellery of triumph of my Lord and come to behold God. Well, I will await His coming patiently as others, but it is hardly possible that He tarries much longer. Apparently I am not yet acceptable and pure enough; for this reason I labour day and night to prove myself pure before the Lord my God, and to lift up my head clean before Him. He Himself touches the hair of my eyelids, as one who loves me, so that I do not rest and sleep in danger. Indeed, the consideration of His grace and kindness towards me increases my longing for Him beyond measure. Naturally I take great delight in His commandment. Life would please me well in order to teach Him to the others, to make Him known to man, who He is and how carefully one ought to live in order not to offend Him. But I have to leave it and close my mouth. Behold, I dwell at all times in the midst of my enemies. As He says, these houses are not free from the vexation and harassment of the enemy. This is the way with the upright, who walk in the vision of God with fear and trembling; for they recognize and confess the height of their calling. That calling is holy, and they must earnestly guard themselves from all uncleanliness. They will not suffer anything unclean and yet they are often intimidated. Apart from all this, my heart, soul and spirit is at the point where I await our king and redeemer. Therefore I will not cease to cleanse myself as you admonish in all your letters. Yes, truly, truly, He is beginning to approach. I am taking notice of the appearance; His coming shows itself very clearly. Therefore let us look to it that we prove ourselves clean in everything. Oh, you sanctified of the Lord, act manly. Permit not yourself to be dismayed. It is only a little while until He shall come in order to give evidence of His glory in us, as a judgement upon the world, to His and our glory. Amen.

AUSBUND
The 18th Hymn

**Another Martyr Song by a Woman
Who Took her Leave in Rotterdam
Together with her Son.**

To the tune of: "Come Here to Me, Says God's Son"

1. There usually is great joy
   When one begets small children
   From the Lord God,
   And instructs them in God's teaching
   About good customs, discipline, and honour,
   So that they honour their parents.

2. Annelein received permission
   To see her son in Rotterdam,
   As her death drew near.
   Isaiah hear my testament,
   My last will before my death
   Now comes from my mouth.

3. I am going on the path of the prophets,
   The martyrs' and apostles' way;
   There is none better.
   They all have drunk from the cup,
   Even as did Christ Himself,
   As I have heard it read.

4. All the priests of the King
   Travelled on this path alone.
   From the beginning they came
   To stand upon this road,
   As God's true sons and children.
   This I have truly understood.

5. These same children under the altar,
   Who are a great multitude,
   Are described in the Apocalypse:
   How they were killed and murdered
   And executed with the sword,
   Persecuted and banished.

6. They cried out to God: O Lord!
   Righteous and Truthful One,
   How long until you bring order to the earth
   Among people everywhere?
   And take revenge on only those
   Who with great insolence

7. Have shed blood everywhere,
   Murdering innocent people?
   Are you willing to punish them
   So they no longer cause dishonour,
   Driving your own out of the land,
   Continuing in their sin?

8. God gives to all [His children] a white robe,
   And consoles them with the answer:
   To them must still be added
   Those who will also be judged
   Until the number of the pious
   Is filled and completed.

9. The twenty-four great elders
   Come before God's throne
   And lay down their crowns,
   Honouring the Lamb of God,
   Together with all the heavenly hosts
   Who live under the sun.

10. All of the pious children of God
    Who received the baptism
    Sealed upon their brow
    Also came this way,
    Following the Lamb wherever it went,
    Serving [the Lamb] with desire.

11. Such people must enter this valley,
    And all drink from the bitter cup
    Until the number is fulfilled.
    Zion, the worthy bride of God,
    To whom the Lamb itself is betrothed,
    Who has calmed the wrath of God.

12. Therefore my dearly beloved son,
    May you wish to do my will,
    And follow my teaching.
    If you know a people who spurn every luxury
    And pleasure of this world,
    May you wish to join them.

13. They are despised and rejected
    By this wretched world.
    They must carry Christ's cross,
    And have no secure place
    Because they keep God's word.
    They often are hunted down.

14. God lives with such people,
    Who are mocked by the world.
    Keep company with them.
    They will show you the true way,
    Lead you away from the path of evil,
    Guide you away from hell.

15. Fear no one; set your life
    Completely on the pure teaching.
    Set aside your body and earthly goods.
    Christ bought you at a dear price,
    Delivered you from the eternal fire
    With His worthy blood.

16. May the Lord sanctify you, my son,
    Sanctify your conduct.
    May you live in the fear of God
    Wherever you are in this entire land.
    In all the work you may do,
    Do not resist God.

17. Share your bread with the hungry,
    Leave no person in need
    Who professes Christ.
    Also clothe the naked,
    Have pity on the sick.
    Do not distance yourself from them.

18. If you cannot always be with them,
    Show your good will.
    Comfort the imprisoned,
    Welcome guests cheerfully into your home,
    And don't let anyone drive them out.
    Then your reward will be greatest.

19. Both your hands should be ready
    To do the works of mercy,
    To give twofold offerings;
    This is spiritual and worldly work:
    To set the prisoners free, strengthen the weak;
    Then you will truly live.

20. For the rest of what God gives you
    You will be taught by the sweat of your brow
    By God and the prophets,
    To give always to God's people.
    May they be happy with you;
    Give to them what they ask of you.

21. Do not let falseness come from you,
    Then you may have good hope.
    God also will reward you
    In His Kingdom in the other world.
    He will bestow it twofold;
    There should be no doubt of this.

22. On the one thousand five hundredth
    And thirty-first year
    Annelein paid with her life,
    Which in virtue soft and mild
    Was for Christians a beautiful model,
    Given in death as well as in life.

Laus Deo

Notes

1 The fullest account of Anna's martyrdom, her Testament, brief excerpts from her trial, and a letter to David Joris are found in the second edition of Thielemann J. van Braght, *Het Bloedig Tooneel, Der Martelaers Spiegel Der Doops-gesinde*, II (2d. ed.; Amsterdam, 1685, reprint 1984; hereafter *Martelaers Spiegel*), 48-50, 143-45. The

English translation gives only the Testament under the name Anna of Rotterdam, *Martyrs' Mirror* (Scottdale, PA: Herald Press, 1950), 453-54. For a more detailed discussion, see Werner O. Packull, "Anna Jansz of Rotterdam: A Historical Investigation of an Early Anabaptist Heroine," in *Archive for Reformation History*, 78 (1987), 107-38.

2 *Ausbund* (13th ed.; Lancaster, 1981), 110-15, song number 18.

3 Karl Vos, "Anneken Jans," in *Rotterdamsch Jaarboekje*, II (1918), 17.

4 A.F. Mellink, *De Wederdopers in de Noordelijke Nederlanden, 1531-1544* (Groningen: J.B. Wolters, 1954), 225-26.

5 ME, I, 127.

6 S. Cramer, who examined Anna's Testament while preparing a reprint of *Het Offer des Herren* of 1570, failed to probe Anna's background. He resolved the discrepancy in tone between her Testament and the trumpet song by claiming the Testament to be genuine and the trumpet song to be Jorist. However, Cramer's supporting arguments proved somewhat circular. The Testament was genuine because it contains the admonition to give up one's life rather than the truth. This stance made Anna a true Anabaptist [*Doopsgezinde*] in contrast to Jorists who left "the brotherhood" precisely on that point. Cramer held that the collectors of martyr stories, who included Anna's Testament within twenty years of her death, must have been well informed "since they no doubt still knew persons who were related to her or knew her friends." Her inclusion in the *Martyrs' Mirror* was therefore no mistake. The trumpet song, on the other hand, appeared in a collection of Joris's works in the 1580s, attributed to an Anna N. (not Anneke). It must be considered the product of the Jorist circle. However, as Cramer himself realized, the circles of *Doopsgezinde* and Jorists overlapped at least until the 1550s. Many Jorists were among the early victims of persecution. Most significantly, Cramer failed to explain why the trumpet song together with a letter by Joris should appear with the first printing of Anna's Testament in 1539. In this earliest printing the trumpet song is clearly attributed to Anna Jansz. Admittedly, this leaves a problem with the initial N appearing with the name of Anna in a later edition. One possible explanation could be that the N appeared only later as a misprint. S. Cramer, ed., *Bibliotheca Reformatoria Neerlandica*, vol. II: *Het Offer des Heeren* (Gravenhage: Martinus Nijhoff, 1904), esp. 71 n.

7 Van Braght, *Martelaers Spiegel*, 144: "staende ten Briel in de Coppoen-straet."

8 See Jan van Leiden's Confession of July 25, 1535, in C.A. Cornelius, ed., *Berichte der Augenzeugen über das Münsterische Wiedertäuferreich*, (Münster: Theissing'schen Buchhandlung, 1853; photo reprint, Aschendorff, 1983), 370-71. The leader of the original group in Briel was the leather merchant and shoemaker, Cornelius Pietersz. He was executed in Amsterdam in the fall of 1534.

9 K.Vos considered him an unsavoury character, "Meyndert van Emden," *Nederlansch Archief voor Kerkgeschiedenis*, II (1914), 164-66. Several other early Dutch Anabaptist leaders, including Menno, were lame. Vos, "Anneken Jans," 17.

10 Irvin B. Horst, *The Radical Brethren, Anabaptism and the English Reformation to 1558* (Nieuwkoop: B.de Graaf, 1972), 54.

11 At her trial in December 1538, she stated that it had taken place four years earlier. Van Braght, *Martelaers Spiegel*, 144.

12 Mellink, *Wederdopers in de Nederlanden*, 119, 208.

13 Two other women from this community, besides Anna, suffered martyrdom: Oede Willems at Utrecht and Janneke Symons at Zierikzee. Vos, "Anneken Jans," 16.

14 Cornelius Krahn, *Dutch Anabaptism* (The Hague: Martinus Nijhoff, 1968), 145-47.

15 George H. Williams, *The Radical Reformation* (Philadelphia: Westminster Press, 1962), 368-70.

16 Mellink, *Wederdopers in de Nederlanden*, 76 ff, 377.

17 Ibid., 120; Krahn, *Dutch Anabaptism*, 149-50.
18 *Een Geesteliick Liedt-Boecken*, reproduced by Irvin Horst as *Mennonite Songbooks*, Dutch Series, I (N.p: n.d.).
19 The title of this publication reads: *Hier begint dat// Testament dat Annecken zeliger ge. Esaias harem Sone bestelt hefft/ den XXIIII. dach// January. Anno XXXIX..... Met: Eyn gedicht oft Liedeken doer die seluige*, listed by A. van der Linde, *Bibliografie* of Joris's works (Gravenhage, 1867). The *Bibliografie* is available on microfiche in "Mennonite and related sources up to 1600" (Zug, Switzerland: Inter Documentation Co. AG) (hereafter MFCL, ME), 400/1. Only one copy of the 1539 printing survived. Vos reproduced the title page and song in "Anneken Jans," 23-28.
20 "David Joris sonderbare Lebensbeschreibung aus einem Manuscript" in G. Arnold, *Unpartheyische Kirchen-und Ketzerhistorien* (4 vol.; Frankfurt, 1729; reprinted in 2 vols.: Hildesheim: Georg Olm, 1967), II, 702-37. English translation of Joris's biography in Gary K. Waite, ed., trans., *The Anabaptist Writings of David Joris, 1535-1543* (Scottdale, PA: Herald Press, 1993). The detailed knowledge of the anonymous biographer points to Joris himself as author or as the primary source.
21 "Joris sonderbare Lebensbeschreibung," in Arnold, *Kirchen-und Ketzerhistorien*, II, 712ff.
22 Friedrich Nippold, "David Joris von Delft. Sein Leben, seine Lehre und seine Sekte," *Zeitschrift für die historische Theologie*, 34, (1864): 56, n. 97.
23 Among the victims was the main mover behind the Bocholt Conference, Jan Matthijs of Middelburg, and his wife. Horst, *Radical Brethren*, 83-85, 88.
24 "Joris sonderbare Lebensbeschreibung," in Arnold, *Kirchen-und Ketzerhistorien*, II, 715.
25 David Joris, "Twistraedt tot straatburch" is printed in part as Appendix 36 in Roland Bainton, *David Joris. Wiedertäufer und Kämpfer für Toleranz im 16. Jahrhundert* (Leipzig: M. Heinius, 1937), 185-91, esp. 188: "wat ampt ic voeren, of voer zyn zoude." See Waite, *Anabaptist Writings*, for an English translation.
26 The sources describing the effects of this letter on Joris are Nikolaas Meyndertsz van Blesdijk, *Historia vitae, doctrinae ac rerum gestarum Davidis Georgii haeresiarche* (Deventer, 1642), esp. 18-19; Joris, "Twistraedt"; and the anonymous biography in Arnold, *Kirchen-und Ketzerhistorien*, II, 713.
27 This is a point made by Bainton, *Joris*, 18.
28 K. Vos, "Brief van David Joris, 1539," in *Doopsgezinde Bijdragen*, LIV (1917), 163-67. Karl Rembert reproduced the 1539 edition of the Testament in *Die Wiedertäufer im Herzogtum Jülich* (Berlin: Goertners Verlagsbuchhandlung, 1899), 609-14.
29 It is found in *Vadderhan, de Liedekes, gemaeckt wt/ den ouder ende niewen Testamente, 1556*, MFCL, ME 907. Philip Wackernagel reproduced a 1569 edition in *Lieder der niederländischen Reformierten* (Nieuwkoop: B.de Graaf, reprint 1965), #5, 82. This version lacks the scriptural references.
30 Bernhard Rothmann, "Eyne Restitution" in Robert Stupperich, ed., *Die Schriften Bernhard Rothmanns*, I (Münster: Aschendorffsche Verlagsbuchhandlung, 1970), 282; also "Eyn Gantz Troestlick Bericht van der Wrake," in ibid., 285-87, 290, 293-94, 296. Prof. Tom Yoder-Neufeld drew my attention to the fact that this reversal of the plowshare passage of Isaiah 2:4 occurs in Joel 3:10.
31 Curiously, the Hamburg edition used by Vos here reads: "Het wort u noch vergolden in uwen schoot." However, the 1556 edition reads: "wert dobbel betaelt in uwen schoot" (v. 9); this could permit the inference that the 1556 edition was based on the first edition found in Joris's little song book, now lost. Other passages reminiscent of Rothmann are, "Soo si deden soo wert haer ghedaen" (v. 11); Anna alluded to "Cain's murdering seed" (v. 9), while Rothmann had spoken of the "murdering weapon of the bloodthirsty Cain."

Rothmann, "Eyn Bericht van der Wrake," 294.
32 Werner O. Packull, "The Sign of Thau. The Changing Conception of the Seal of God's Elect in Early Anabaptist Thought," in MQR, 61 (1987): 363-74.
33 The 1556 edition exchanges vs. 6 and 5. The sequence given in the Joris and Wackernagel editions seems more logical.
34 The edition used by Vos read: "wascht u voeten in der godlosen bloede." The same rendering is found in the 1556 edition. The 1569 edition, reproduced by Wackernagel, read: "de Vogels werde versaet va hare bloede," while Joris's songbook printed in the 1580s changed the line to read, "wacht ghii u voeten to storten bloede." Thus the most revolutionary part of the song was with time made innocuous. This editing process indicates that both editors and printers understood the line to be the most radical. Vos, "Anneken Jans," 27; Wackernagel, *Lieder der Reformierten*, 83.
35 We here follow the verse order found in the Joris and Wackernagel editions. The 1556 edition exchanges v. 13 and v. 12.
36 Anna and her companion, Christina Michiel Barents, the wife of the physician Matthijs van den Donck, who had fled to England from Louvain, were travelling from Ijselmonds to Rotterdam by coach.
37 Van Braght, *Martelaers Spiegel*, 143: "is uyt Engeland weder herwaerts overkomende/ om tot Delftz eenige saken te verrichten/ of/ soo eenige meenen/ David Joris of siin geselschap to spreeken."
38 Vos found this explicable since the baker adopted, along with Isaiah, Anna's full purse, and presumably a claim to her property in Briel. "Anneken Jans," 18.
39 Van Braght, *Martelaers Spiegel*, 144.
40 I compared van Braght's second edition of 1685 to the 1562 edition and found no significant changes.
41 Williams found here not only "the last echoes of the original Melchiorite gospel," but also "an extraordinary specimen of the martyr theology akin to that of the South German Anabaptists." *The Radical Reformation*, 386.
42 This particular edition was republished in 1578 and 1595. Anna's song was inserted right after her Testament. I consulted the microfiche copies MFCL, ME 706/1, 707/1, and 711/1. Since the editions listed in note 88 do not contain Anna's song, further research is needed to see whether these editions were sponsored by different groups and traditions within Dutch Anabaptism. The article in the ME, IV, on the *Martyrs' Mirror* does not sufficiently distinguish between the various editions of its precursors.
43 Out of twenty-six references in the song's margin, seventeen are found in the margin of the 1562 edition of the Testament. Even though Cramer had placed the martyr song beside the Testament, he did not note the dependance of the song on the Testament. Nor did he note that the 1570 edition of *Het Offer des Herren*, which he reproduced, represented a different editorial tradition than the 1562-63 edition.
44 The 1583 edition is in MFCL, ME 521/2. Verses 6, 7, 8, 12, 14, 18, 19, and 21 in the *Ausbund* are new or have elaborated on the original Dutch text.
45 Although Joris's original editions of the Testament had given Anna's time of death accurately as January 1539, the last verse of the song in the *Ausbund* has the date noted incorrectly as 1531.
46 Gary K. Waite, *David Joris and Dutch Anabaptism. 1524-1543* (Waterloo, ON: Wilfrid Laurier University Press, 1990).

MARIA AND URSULA VAN BECKUM

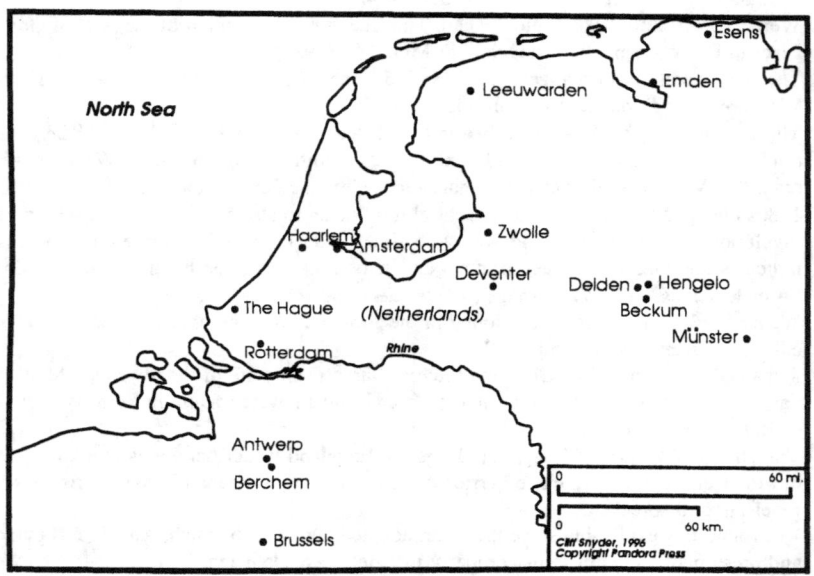

Anabaptism could be the sword of Christ that cut families apart. Sisters-in-law Maria and Ursula van Beckum were executed for their Anabaptist faith; their mothers bitterly opposed their Anabaptist persuasions and tried desperately to dissuade them. Jan, husband of Ursula and brother to Maria, kept his distance from both women, probably to avoid arrest and examination. He seems to have remained formally Catholic, the safest position for one who wished to retain land and noble rank.

One can only briefly recount the salient features of the arrest, interrogation, and death of Maria and Ursula because there is very little information about them in archival collections.[1]

We are not told anything about their conversion, baptism, and Christian calling. For us they emerge onto an Anabaptist stage only when Maria's mother learned of her daughter's Anabaptist persuasion and drove her from the family house and estate, likely at Beckum a few kilometres south of Hengelo in the province of Overijssel.[2] Perhaps the mother thought to shame the daughter into disavowing her new faith. Perhaps she was expressing her own humiliation and loss of honour as a noble lady of some regional prominence. We are not told anything of the family's wealth in land, nor where it ranked within the feudal hierarchy. Neither does Maria's father appear in our story.

Maria fled to Utrecht to the home of her brother, Jan, who seems to have taken her in without regret. Their mother unrelentingly sent a police officer searching for her. Gosen van Raesfelt, sheriff of Twenthe, heard about the refugee Anabaptist and put the governor on her trail. Van Raesfelt was a blood relative, next in line to this family's property, a family whose Anabaptist daughter was unmarried and whose son was childless. If he could have Maria and Ursula caught and removed, he might inherit the van Beckum property, even though he seems to have made no provision for eliminating Jan. His apparent plotting was the subject of gossip by other people of noble blood.[3] Early one morning the governor sent out a small posse, surrounded the house of Jan and Ursula, and seized Maria. Surprised and then terrified, she appealed suddenly to her sister-in-law, Ursula, to go with her to what would have been a chilling and unholy prison reception for a young woman. Ursula gained permission from her husband to accompany Maria, though up to this point the story gives us no hint that Ursula herself was a convert to the new faith. The hymn writers praised Ursula's gift of sisterly love, for good reason. As an Anabaptist, she faced certain death herself if she accompanied Maria to prison; had she remained at her home, she might have been able to escape.

Maria's mother was vengeful, and tried to force her daughter back into mother church. Ursula's mother and sister, also of noble rank, tried a gentler suasion. They came from their landed estates at Werdum by Esens in East Friesland,[4] today the northwestern corner of Germany, to talk her out of her error. They failed to dissuade Ursula, and the hymn record suggests Ursula's break with her mother was an angry one, her exchange of farewells with her sister more peaceful but still bittersweet.[5]

Maria and Ursula were taken back to Deventer, then to Delden. Interrogations followed, first by a Dominican prior from the monastery at Zwolle.[6] Since the thirteenth century the Dominicans had led in inquisitorial proceedings, dubbed by their monastic order rivals "the hounds of the Lord" [*domine canes*]. He failed miserably and turned nasty. The authorities sent for a distant theologian, called Burgundian in the records, probably from the court in Brussels.[7] He fared no better. The two would not be moved, and their examiners were amazed at both their pertinacity and theological skill. Sentencing them to death was inevitable. In 1529 Habsburg Holy Roman Emperor Charles V had issued a mandate commanding death for all Anabaptists. As King Charles I of Spain and overlord of the Netherlands, he was more earnestly Catholic than the papacy, a man too zealous to let heretics anywhere in his lands slip through his fingers to the peril of his own soul.

Surviving records tell us little about the content of the religious examination. The interrogators always asked about baptism—why had they been rebaptized? Both replied crisply that they had been baptized correctly—that is biblically—only once. Asked about the real presence of Christ in bread and wine, they denied it. That denial seemed always to surprise Catholic interrogators, although for several decades the Netherlands had been the locus of a sacramentarian movement that denied the real presence in the sacrament. The interrogators threatened death, both to shake the courage of their victims and also to speak realistic truth. The pair remained unmoved. One scribe laconically commented that the two were surprisingly articulate on issues about which they were expected to know little. That attitude provoked the author of the Lutheran hymn "Nun lasst vns frölich heben an" to comment extensively on the female as the weaker vessel, whose will God had to stiffen by special intervention,[8] a late medieval downgrading of women not shared by the Anabaptist hymnists. Maria and Ursula were formidable interlocutors for their presumably intellectually superior examiners.

On November 13, 1544, Maria and Ursula were executed by burning, a sign of Spanish influence; late medieval procedure against female criminals generally decreed death by drowning as more merciful. Maria did not blanch when chained to the stake, and scolded the executioner for cursing when he broke her chain. She exhorted the usual crowd of onlookers to think not of her end, but of their own. She prayed that God would forgive her persecutors. She died, apparently in peace, having made her good witness to the crowd.

Ursula was given the option of death by sword, but boldly chose burning also. Perhaps her married status gave her special privilege. Perhaps she was favoured to this slight degree because she was not the primary instigator of heresy in the family, only a follower. In our present state of research we cannot know the reason. Detecting what they thought to be some hesitation on her part, the attending clergy pressed her all the more to recant. She resisted. She remained steadfast in the face of burning faggots, with no break in spirit.

Maria and Ursula van Beckum rank among the few Anabaptist martyrs who attracted the attention of Protestant or Catholic authors. The Lutheran Ludwig Rabus[9] included an account of their interrogation and death, consisting primarily of two martyr hymns, probably composed by local friends of the pair, then translated into German for a wider public. Neither poem provides the detail found in several hymns written by Anabaptist friends. There is strong evidence that the regional nobility, still routinely Catholic, were much moved by the deaths of these two women. Some from among their number wrote at least one hymn to commemorate their courage.[10] A provincial prefect-administrator wrote about their executions. A poet and an artist, not Mennonite, published a broadside of this event, of which there is one extant copy in Zurich. Why did the deaths of these two Anabaptist women attract so much non-Anabaptist attention? Probably because most people of noble birth took the politically safe route and remained with the religion approved by whatever state they lived in. The van Beckum women were a striking exception.

But why did the Lutheran Ludwig Rabus include Anabaptist martyrs in his martyr book? Probably because these two women were of the nobility and were thought to be important people by the standards of their time. Perhaps Katharina Zell of Strasbourg had persuaded Rabus that he should be tolerant of religious dissidents who died for their faith.[11] At least it was an attempt. Rabus's stories muted the Anabaptist origin of Maria and Ursula; his description placed them only under suspicion of Anabaptism, with each vigorously asserting having been baptized rightly only once. That was a standard ploy of Anabaptists that normally fooled no one, nor was it designed to dissimulate. The Lutheran storytellers left the tale with that denial.

Some interpreters of the time detected a miracle in the executions of Maria and Ursula. A report circulated almost immediately that the bodies of both women were not consumed. Indeed, the next morning the bodies had been clothed, one poet reported, at the hands of pious Christian onlookers.[12] That could hardly be labeled a miracle. But the greening of the stake at which Maria had been burned, by the next day, was another matter. Eight years later an Anabaptist named Bartel, executed at Berchem by Antwerp, reported that the stake at which Maria had been burned burst into leaf the morning after the burning. Indeed, Bartel declared that the event shocked him into joining the group. Perhaps it was the final one in a series of persuasive events.[13] The Anabaptist elder Hendrik van Arnhem, to whom Bartel and his friend told the tale, remained skeptical.[14]

How are we to understand these accounts of what the sources call miraculous?

(1) This was an age expecting miracles and overly credulous, unlike our own age in both particulars. Most people lived in an atmosphere in which the divine, the world of spirit, easily and frequently penetrated and altered the world of nature. Indeed, in that age there was no natural science untouched by divine power.

(2) Executions were disliked by most onlookers, even though execution as public spectacle was highly popular. The crowd often berated executioners as the villains of the piece. And judicial officials who passed sentence and then observed the execution were accompanied by soldiers, in large part for their own protection. In this atmosphere of hostility to the regnant religion that flexed its political muscle too brazenly, people yearned for some expression of divine displeasure with the entire mess.

(3) Natural explanations can account for some aspects of these reported events. To consume a human body by fire requires an enormous amount of fuel–at that time essentially wood (or charcoal for a more intense heat), sometimes even peat, which provided only a low heat. We know from other burnings that the fires did not always consume the corpses.[15] Perhaps the governing officials required only that burning proceed until the victim

died. But by the same token, a stake only recently shaped from a tree trunk might have been only singed, depending on how loosely the victim was bound to it. (Sometimes hangmen tied their victims very loosely, to watch them jump.) In the case of the van Beckum women, there is no evidence that either victim was strangled prior to burning, a procedure frequently followed as being more humane.

We face another problem in interpreting this case. Some scholars think these women were followers of David Joris.[16] Others deny it, citing lack of evidence authenticating a Jorist position by these women, together with the observation that there was a general absence of Jorist followers in Overijssel.[17] But if they were Jorists, why did van Braght include them in his Mennonite martyr book? By 1544 there was enmity between the Mennists and Jorists. He did include tales of a few Jorists; and in the second edition of the *Martyrs' Mirror* in 1685, the editors inserted one or two additional Jorist stories.

Why did Mennonites come to include Jorists in their collection of heroines of the faith?[18]

(1) At the local level, Anabaptists of differing groups recognized much that they held in common, including the enmity of the state, and felt a genuine kinship. So the earliest of the Mennonite martyr books, *Het Offer des Heeren* of the first edition (1563), included Jorists.

(2) Rationalist influences among seventeenth-century Mennonites impelled them to practise a more tolerant attitude toward any Anabaptist "deviants" of an earlier time. Surely Mennonite minister Galenus Abrahamsz de Haan and his circle of friends would have included Jorists. For all his reputed conservatism, Van Braght had to have felt a similar compulsion.

The singular motif that fixed this tale in human memory until it was written down is the steadfast heroism of its principals. Most martyrs suffered through periods of utter agony. There are enough hints in this tale that Maria and Ursula were no exception. But both were gripped by a faith that bound them together, giving them courage when they needed it in trial and in witness at the stake. Later hymnists seized upon this steadfastness and its expression in sisterly love for special mention. Today the Amish sing only those stanzas that tell this moral lesson, in their *Ausbund* translation of an earlier Dutch hymn.[19]

Notes

1 The most credible detail comes from the hymns. The basic one, from which most other accounts derive, is "Droefheyt wil ick nv laten staen, En singen met verblijden," from the Dutch Anabaptist martyr book and hymnal *Het Offer des Heeren*, ten editions 1563-1599, 1570 edition in Samuel Cramer, ed., *Bibliotheca Reformatoria Neerlandica*, II

(The Hague: Nijhoff, 1904), 509-16. Someone translated it into German and added a significant amount of editorial comment, as "Trauren will ich stehen lassen," in the *Ausbund. Das ist: Etliche schöne Christliche Lieder, wie sie in dem Gefängnis zu Passau in dem Schloss von den Schweizer-Brüdern . . . gedichtet worden,* already in the 1583 first edition, No. 17 in the current editions. Other Anabaptist-Mennonite hymns on the van Beckums are "Ick heb droefhey vernomen," in *Veelderhande Liedekens,* 1559, but not subsequent editions; and "Ach Gott, ich mag wohl trawren," in *Ein schon Gesangbüchlein,* 1565-69. For still other hymns on the van Beckums, written by Christians not in the Anabaptist-Mennonite tradition, see nn. 7, 8, and 10 below.

2 The family estate was located at Beckum, perhaps 4 kilometres south of Delden and 6 kilometres southwest of Hengelo. Beckum exists as a place name today, but the family has long vanished. Our account does not tell us precisely where Maria lived with her mother.

3 Blaupot ten Cate, *Geschiedenis der Doopsgezinde in Zeeland, Utrecht en Gelderland* (Amsterdam: van Kampen, 1847), II, 15.

4 Cramer, BRN, II, 509, n. 1, for family name and genealogical data, together with place name.

5 "Droefheyt wil ick nv laten staen, En singen met verblijden," stanza 5; "Trauren will ich stehen lassen," *Ausbund,* No. 17, stanzas 9 and 10.

6 Identification by Cramer.

7 Hymns provide the basic account; ten Cate and especially Cramer give information on the Brussels connection. The Burgundian dukes had had overlordship over the Lowlands until 1477; the Lowlands portion of the inheritance went to the Hapsburgs, who ruled the region with an iron hand.

8 Printed in Ludwig Rabus, *Historien, der heiligen ausserwölten Gottes Zeügen, Bekennern, vnd Martyrern, so zum theyl . . . ersten Kirchen . . . zum theyl aber zu disen vnsern letzten zeytten . . . .* (Strassburg: B. Beck Erben, 1552-56; Dritte Theyl, 1555), fols. 180v.-184r.

9 Ibid.

10 "Ein New Lied, von zweien Jungkfrawen, vom Adell zu Delden, drey meil von Deventer verbranth, Jm Thone, Ein newes liedt wir heben an" (N.p., 1545). They were burned in mid-November 1544, so this hymn was published only shortly after the event. There were later printings in Nuremberg and Zurich. Cramer, BRN, II, 509, n. 1.

11 See Heinold Fast, ed., "Katharina Zell: Strassburg als Beispiel der Barmherzigkeit. Ein offenes Wort zur Duldung der Täufer," *Mennonitischer Geschichtsblätter,* 41 (1984): 30-33; she wrote to Rabus when he left Strasbourg for Ulm.

12 Rabus, "Nun lasst vns frölich heben an," fols. 182r-84r.

13 Fullest account in the *Martyrs' Mirror,* 500.

14 Karel Vos, "De Doopsgezinden te Antwerpen in de zestiende Eeuw," in *Bulletin de commission royale d'histoire de Belgique,* 84 (1920): 357.

15 For example, Leonhard Kayser, a Lutheran, burned in 1527.

16 For example, Ferdinand van der Haeghen, *Bibliographie des martyrologes protestant Néerlandais* (2 vols.; The Hague: Nijhoff, 1890), II, 658.

17 Cramer, BRN, II, 509, n. 1. Gary Waite, *David Joris and Dutch Anabaptism, 1524-1543* (Waterloo, ON: Wilfrid Laurier University Press, 1990), in this latest study of the Jorists and their leader, does not mention the van Beckums among the followers of Joris. He does count eight Jorists in Deventer, Overijssel, (page 147), far fewer than he finds in regions farther west and northwest. Still, in effect he does not declare on the issue.

18 We know of at least one other Anabaptist woman, Anna Jansz of Rotterdam, who was a Jorist (see her profile, in this volume). Samuel Cramer has a series of comments on van Braght's inclination to include Jorists. See [Samuel] Cramer, "Die

Geloofwaardigheid van van Braght," in *Doopsgezinde Bijdragen*, 39 (1899): 65-164, esp. 77-94.

19 *Ausbund*, No. 17, 94. The Indiana Amish sing at most stanza 29, which portrays Maria's witness to the spectators that they turn to God's grace, an evangelical appeal. Lancaster County and Holmes County Amish do not sing it. The best stanza for them would be 43, the last: praise God who gives strength from above at the Testing.

ELISABETH AND HADEWIJK OF FRIESLAND

The stories of Elisabeth and Hadewijk are intertwined and best told together. Both accounts appear in the *Martyrs' Mirror*[1] and, in part, in other literature.[2] That the stories are true is confirmed by Remmeltje Wubbers, who reported that she heard them frequently not only from her parents and others, but also from the woman who cared for Hadewijk during her last illness and to whom Hadewijk herself told the story.[3]

Elisabeth Dirks, called Lijsken or Lijsbeth in Dutch, was the daughter of nobility living in Friesland early in the sixteenth century. In order for her to receive a good education, her parents placed her, while she was still a child, in the convent Tienje near Leer in East Friesland, Germany. Here she learned the arts and other skills, including the reading of Dutch and Latin. After studying there some years she by chance came to possess a Latin New Testament or, as Hadewijk tells it, not by chance but through divine intervention.[4]

One day, when she was twelve years of age, she heard that a man had been executed in Leeuwarden because he rejected the mass as unbiblical, and that he had been baptized as an adult, though he had received infant baptism at birth.[5] This news troubled Elisabeth, as did the loose and carnal living of the nuns in the convent. As a result she began an intense study of her Latin New Testament. The more she studied the Scriptures the more she became discouraged about the goings on in the convent. When she tried to change her own lifestyle the suspicion of the nuns drew the attention of the Prior to her, until she was accused of harbouring heretical ideas and imprisoned, most likely on the convent premises.

After a year in prison, the nuns interceded on her behalf with the Prior and she was released, but kept under close supervision. While she had ample time for prayer, secret Bible study, and meditation, life in the convent did not improve. After enduring it for over ten years she decided she must leave, but how? Her parents would not understand if she asked them for help and her fate might be even worse if she returned home. Finally she decided to secretly ask the milkmaids for help. They were willing. One morning soon after, she walked out of the convent dressed as a milkmaid, carrying milk cans with her as was the custom. Where could she go now?

She first went to Leer. We do not know, though it seems possible, that someone had given her directions secretly. When she knocked on the door of a certain house, she was admitted and welcomed. It turned out that they were Anabaptists, though she may not have known what that meant. They cared for her and instructed her further in the faith, though they must have been delighted at her knowledge of the Bible. Yet fearing that she might be discovered in their small town close to the convent, they took her to the city of Leeuwarden, to the house of Hadewijk, also an Anabaptist.

Hadewijk's husband was gone, perhaps he was dead. We do not know. He had been a drummer in an army band. One day his unit was ordered to the market place to prevent possible rioting while a heretic was executed. The drummer himself was further ordered to beat his drums loudly to drown out any last words the heretic might say. The heretic was an Anabaptist and, as the drummer discovered, a good friend of his, though neither the drummer nor Hadewijk were Anabaptists at that time. He told Hadewijk that he would not go, but she told him not to cause trouble and to obey orders. So he went, but not before he drank enough liquor to dull his senses about what he would see.

At the market place the army kept order and the drummer beat his drums as ordered. But the liquor had loosened his tongue and he told the crowd that the martyr had been a very good man and that the clergy wanted him killed because of his piety. It were better, he said, to catch the many wicked men, even among the clergy, the adulterers and thieves, and to treat them that way. The crowd enjoyed his words; some laughed, some took them to heart, some said, "the drummer is drunk," while others said, "he's crazy." But that night, when he became sober, he remembered what he had said and knew he was in big trouble. He decided then and there to leave Leeuwarden immediately to save his life. He also decided to leave the Catholic Church. He begged Hadewijk to come with him, but she refused. She did not know where he had gone and never heard from him again.

In due time Hadewijk began to think more seriously about the martyr and her husband's words and actions. She found a meeting place of the Anabaptists, watched their conduct, and listened to their teaching. After a time she asked for and received baptism. It was to her in Leeuwarden that Elisabeth was brought by her friends from Leer, but soon they were both arrested. When those who arrested them came into the house, they found Elisabeth's Latin New Testament. And when they found her they said, "We have, we have the right man! We now have the teacher. Where is your husband, the teacher Menno Simons?" Then they took them to the prison, but locked them into separate cells.

The following day two monks in white robes ("*Witkovels*" i.e., of the Praemonstratensian Order) took Elisabeth to be interrogated before the city council. They asked her under oath whether she had a husband, and she replied,

"It is not permitted us to swear at all; our words shall be yes, yes, or no, no (Matt. 5:37): I have no husband."

The Lords: "We say that you are a teacher who has deceived many. We have been told this about you. We want to know who your friends are."

Elisabeth: "My God has commanded me to love my Lord and my God and to honour my parents. Therefore I will not tell you who my parents are (Exod. 20:12); what I suffer for the name of Christ is a reproach to my friends."

The Lords: "We will leave you alone concerning this, but we want to know which people you have taught."

Elisabeth: "Oh no, my lords, do leave me alone on this; but ask me about my faith, which I will so gladly tell you," (1 Peter 3:15).

The Lords: "We shall make you so afraid that you will tell us."

Elisabeth: "I hope by the grace of God that he will keep my tongue, that I shall not become a traitor and deliver my brother to death," (Ps. 39:2).

The Lords: "Which persons were present when you were baptized?"

Elisabeth: "Christ said, ask those who were there, or who heard it," (John 18:21).

The Lords: "Now we see that you are a teacher, for you make yourself equal with Christ."

Elisabeth: "No, my lords, that be far from me, for I do not consider myself higher than the rubbish which is swept out of the house of the Lord," (1 Cor. 4:13).

The Lords: "What then do you believe concerning God's house? Do you not hold our church to be the house of God?"

Elisabeth: "No, my lords, for it is written: You are the temple of the living God, even as God said, I will live in them, and walk among them," (2 Cor. 6:16; Lev. 26:9).

The Lords: "What do you believe concerning our mass?"

Elisabeth: "My lords, I think nothing of your mass, but I hold highly whatever agrees with the Word of God."

The Lords: "What do you believe concerning our high and holy sacraments?"

Elisabeth: "I have never in my life read of a holy sacrament in the Scriptures, but of the Lord's Supper," (Matt. 26:26).

The Lords: "Be quiet, for the devil is speaking through you."

Elisabeth: "Yes, my lords, for a disciple is not above the teacher," (Matt. 10:24).

The Lords: "You speak with a proud spirit."

Elisabeth: "No, my lords, I speak with free courage."

The Lords: "What did the Lord say when he gave the Supper to his disciples?"

Elisabeth: "What did he give them, flesh or bread?"

The Lords: "He gave them bread."

Elisabeth: "Did the Lord not remain seated there? Who then would have eaten of his flesh?

The Lords: "What do you believe concerning infant baptism, seeing that you have had yourself rebaptized?"

Elisabeth: "No, my lords, I have not been rebaptized. I have been baptized once upon my faith, for it is written that baptism belongs to believers," (Mark 16:15-16).

The Lords: "Are our children damned then, because they are baptized?"

Elisabeth: "No, my lords, that be far from me that I should judge children," (Matt. 7:1).

The Lords: "Do you not seek your salvation in baptism?"

Elisabeth: "No, my lords, all the water in the sea could not save me, for salvation is in Christ (Acts 4:12), and he has commanded me to love my Lord above everything, and my neighbour as myself," (Luke 10:27).

The Lords: "Do priests have the power to forgive sins?"

Elisabeth: "No, my lords, how should I believe that? I say Christ is the only priest through whom sins are forgiven," (Heb. 7:21).

The Lords: "You say that you believe everything which agrees with holy Scripture; do you then not believe the words of James?"

Elisabeth: "Yes, my lords, why should I not believe them?"

The Lords: "Does he not say, 'Go to the elder of the church, that he may anoint you and pray for you?" (James 5:14).

Elisabeth: "Yes, my lords, but are you then saying that you are of this church?"

The Lords: "The Holy Spirit has already saved you; you need neither confession nor sacrament."

Elisabeth: "No, my lords, I confess that I have overstepped the ordinance of the pope, which the Emperor has confirmed by decree. But show me any article in which I have transgressed against my Lord and my God, and I will cry woe is me, miserable sinner."[6]

This was the first interrogation. A second one followed later in the torture chamber. Since she would not confess voluntarily, thumbscrews were applied to her thumbs and forefingers until blood squirted out at her fingernails.

Elisabeth: "Oh, I cannot bear it any longer."

The Lords: "Confess, and we will relieve your pain." But she cried to the Lord her God:

Elisabeth: "Help me, oh Lord, your poor servant, for you are a helper in time of need," (Judith 9:3).

The Lords all said, "Confess, and we will relieve your pain, . . ." but she remained firm and the Lord took away her pain, so that she said: "Ask me, and I shall answer, for I no longer feel the pain in my flesh as I did before," (1 Cor. 10:13).

The Lords: "Will you still not confess?"

Elisabeth: "No, my lords." Then they applied screws to her shins, one on each. "Oh my lords, do not put me to shame; for no man has ever touched my bare body."

The Lords: "Miss Elisabeth, we shall not treat you dishonourably."

Then she fainted. And one said to the other, "Perhaps she is dead." But she awoke and said, "I am alive, and not dead."

Then they took off all the screws and pleaded with her.

Elisabeth: "Why do you talk to me with enticing words? That is the way to deal with children. . . ."

The Lords: "Will you take back all the words you said before?"

Elisabeth: "No, my lords, but I will seal them with my death," (Rev. 2:10).

The Lords: "We will no longer torture you. Will you voluntarily tell us who baptized you?"

Elisabeth: "Oh no, my lords, I have told you before that I will not confess this."[7]

In due time she was sentenced to be put into a sack and drowned. This was carried out May 27, 1549, at Leeuwarden. It is likely that she was the first known Anabaptist deaconess, an office that was officially recognized in the Dordrecht Confession of 1632, Article 9, which also states that they were to be ordained. It was a lifelong position.[8]

Meanwhile Elisabeth and Hadewijk had had no further contact with each other in prison, nor do we know the exact chronology of Hadewijk's further experiences. They had both been arrested on January 15, 1549.

One day Hadewijk was told that she would be examined in great detail about her faith the following day. This caused her great distress, since she could neither read nor write and felt totally unprepared and unfit for the ordeal. In her agony she prayed fervently to God for help and comfort. While she was praying she seemed to hear a voice saying, "Hadewijk." Since she saw no one she continued her agonized prayer for help until she heard the voice a second time calling "Hadewijk." But seeing no one she continued praying until she heard the same voice a third time, "Hadewijk, I tell you, leave." Then, seeing the door open, she put her bonnet on her head and went out the door. Not knowing where to go, she slipped into the nearby church.

No sooner was she in the church than she heard people whispering that an Anabaptist woman had escaped the prison and, since security was tight, sorcery was believed to be involved. She left the church, only to hear a street crier announce a 150 guilders reward for her capture. On impulse she made her way to the home of her former employers, whom she had served faithfully for many years, but they refused to take her in.

Not knowing where to turn, she suddenly found herself before the house of a priest where his servant, a "half-simple fellow" whom she knew well, was standing in the doorway. She begged him to hide her, which he did by taking her up into the attic. He brought her food and water, but when night came he made indecent advances to her. Her troubles seemed to be even greater now, and again she prayed to God for help, for the man was strong and passionate. Finally she told him that she was married, and his evil intentions would be adultery. Did he not know that adulterers and adulteresses had to burn in hell forever? Then he left her, saying, "This kind is too clever in the Scriptures; I can't compete with her."

The following morning he went to the market place where he knew he would find Hadewijk's brother-in-law selling buttermilk. He told him where Hadewijk was hidden, and they agreed that the brother-in-law would come to the back stairs of the priest's house in a boat when it was dark, and help her escape the city through the floodgate. The plan succeeded. She escaped to Emden, a safe city in East Friesland, Germany, where she found a home in the Mennonite [*Doopsgezinde*] minister's house. There she regularly attended the Anabaptist-Mennonite meetings, praising God for her marvellous delivery, and telling her and Elisabeth's story to all who would listen. And there, the chronicle reports, "she fell asleep in the Lord."

Notes

1 There is one account of Elisabeth in T. van Braght, *Martelaers Spiegel* (Amsterdam, 1685), and one of Elisabeth and Hadewijk, fol. 11:81-82 and fol. 11:156-58 respectively, from which this story is taken. The interrogation account is translated directly from this volume. The *Martyrs' Mirror*, 481-82, and 546-47 includes these accounts, as well.
2 *Het Offer Des Heeren* in *Bibliotheca Rerformatoria Neerlandica*, vol. 2, (Gravenhage: Nijhoff, 1904), 91-97, carries part of the story and a song about Elizabeth. The song is also found in the *Ausbund*, hymn no. 13, 70-77, 38 stanzas. See also Anna Brons, *Ursprung, Entwickelung und Schicksale der Taufgesinnten oder Mennoniten* (Norden, 1884), 109-113; S. Blaupot ten Cate, *Geschiedenis der Doopsgezinden in Friesland* (Leeuwarden, 1839), 73-75; Karel Vos, *Menno Simons, 1496-1561* (Leiden: E.J. Brill, 1914), 5, 250, 332ff; Rudolf Wolkan, *Die Lieder der Wiedertäufer* (Nieuwkoop: B. de Graff, 1965), 65; ME, II, 185.
3 *Martyrs' Mirror*, 547.
4 ten Cate believes the New Testament was given to her by the Prior of the convent. *Geschiedenis*, 74.
5 ten Cate believes this man to have been Sicke Freerks, also called Snijder [tailor], who was executed March 20, 1531, which would have made Elisabeth 30 years of age at her execution in 1549, but this remains conjecture. *Geschiedenis*, 74. It was Snijder's execution which, according to Menno Simons's own account, first caused him to think seriously about his faith. Menno left the priesthood in 1536, and later apparently worked extensively with Elisabeth, leading the authorities to believe that she was his wife. *Martyrs' Mirror*, 481. That Snijder was "rebaptized" is reported only in *Martyrs' Mirror*, 442, and by Menno. See Leonard Verduin, trans. and John C. Wenger, ed., *The Complete Writings of Menno Simons, c. 1496-1561* (Scottdale, PA: Herald Press, 1956), 668.
6 *Martyrs' Mirror*, 481-82; some changes to the translation.
7 Ibid., 482.
8 Irvin B. Horst, *Mennonite Confession of Faith* [Dordrecht] (Lancaster, 1988), 30.

SOETKEN VAN DEN HOUTE OF OUDENAARDE

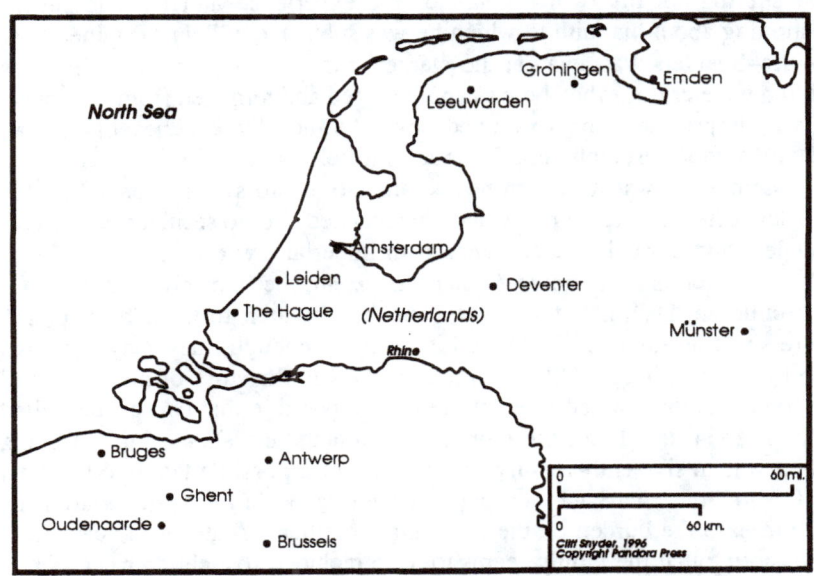

According to Soetken van den Houte, those who had professed and lived by God's truth had endured the brunt of persecution and martyrdom from the time of Abel: "they have been despised, scorned, persecuted and killed because they would not follow the wicked world with its false prophets."[1] The biblical past met this Flemish woman's present with a powerful concreteness: her life was a virtual microcosm of the Anabaptist experience of martyrdom in the sixteenth century. Soetken's husband was martyred; she herself was put to death for her religion; three other women with whom she was arrested were similarly executed; and she urged her own children to heed their example as participants in a tradition which she understood to be that of Christ and his apostles.

As with so many Anabaptists, little is known about Soetken's early life. She was forty years old when she was interrogated about her faith in Ghent in the summer of 1560, so she must have been born around 1520, just as the first Dutch translations of Luther's pamphlets were appearing in Antwerp. Sometime probably in the mid-1540s she married Gilein de Mueleneere. He may have belonged to the same family as Jeroen de Mueleneere, who in 1532 was punished for heresy in the thriving textile town of Oudenaarde, south of Ghent on the Schelde river.[2]

Gilein was both a textile worker and a schoolteacher who taught out of their home in Oudenaarde. On April 20, 1554, he was arrested by Nicolas de Hondt, the assistant and secretary to the tireless Flemish inquisitor, Pieter Titelmans.[3] De Hondt was aided by the lieutenant bailiff of Oudenaarde and three sheriffs. In his own account of the experience and the subsequent questioning about his faith to which he was subjected, Gilein explained how his wife–Soetken–was away at the market at the time of his arrest, how his children were crying when he was apprehended and removed from his house. He was imprisoned and examined several times by a series of Roman Catholic authorities, including Titelmans himself, but refused to concede that his religious views were erroneous and so to forswear them. For his persistence he was excommunicated, then handed over to secular magistrates, strangled, and burned in accordance with imperial law on July 19, 1554.

Soetken is best known for her *Testament*, the farewell address to her three children, David, Betken, and Tanneken, written to them from prison before she was executed in 1560. Interestingly enough, they may not have been her only children. Gilein expressly states in the story of his arrest and interrogations that he had five children.[4] It is possible that two of them died between 1554 and 1560, the mortality of infants and small children being what it was in sixteenth-century Europe. It is also possible that two were his from a previous marriage, and perhaps were taken in by relatives after his death to ease the burden on the now single mother. Whatever the case, it is worth noting that the family seems to have included five children, not three, in 1554.

Soetken's decision to leave her home was one made by many Anabaptists from towns throughout the Low Countries as they endeavoured to avoid detection and arrest by inquisitors and secular authorities. In her case, it entailed a trip from Oudenaarde to Ghent, about eighteen miles downstream on the Schelde. The men and women executed for their Anabaptist convictions in Ghent in the 1550s and '60s came from nearly thirty different communities in the Netherlands, including even northern towns like Deventer and Leiden.[5] Those from the north would normally pass through Antwerp, a city whose size and diversity helped provide anonymity sufficient to shelter the most Anabaptists of any town in the southern Netherlands.[6] In Soetken's case, the trip to Ghent involved only a short journey north to the town with the greatest concentration of Anabaptists in the province of Flanders. There she and her children (whether three or more) could hope to find support from others with similar spiritual inclinations. This must have been a concern for a woman who seems not to have remarried after her husband's death, and who would have faced the confiscation of Gilein's property after his execution. The fact that Soetken seems to have had a housemaid in Ghent suggests that she was not destitute.

Soetken herself had not yet been baptized; it was only after contact with Anabaptists in Ghent that she made this decisive commitment. No Anabaptist community seems to have existed in Oudenaarde in the early 1550s. Rather, she and her husband apparently belonged to a "sacramentarian" circle there,[7] a group whose views overlapped with Anabaptists in numerous ways. From the early 1530s through the 1550s, there was considerable fluidity between the two groups in the Netherlands.[8] This association with the sacramentarians in Oudenaarde explains Soetken's otherwise curious remark in her *Testament*, that her husband had confessed the truth about baptism and the incarnation of Christ "insofar as he could understand."[9] Writing in 1560 after her own rebaptism, Soetken understood Gilein to have been moving toward Anabaptism before his capture and execution prematurely interrupted his course. She may have witnessed his death. Even though he was not, strictly speaking, an Anabaptist martyr, Soetken told her children that he had laid down his life as an example to them, "this being the same way which the prophets, the apostles, and Christ himself have gone."[10]

Whatever effect her husband's death may have had on Soetken, it did not deter her from Anabaptist convictions in the long term. If anything, judging from her modest but precious literary legacy–the *Testament*, plus a shorter letter to her brother and sister (one of whom may have been an in-law)–the opposite was the case. She reminded her children in her *Testament* that from the time they had lost their father, her primary concern had been rearing them with a view to their salvation. This entailed Soetken's rebaptism, which occurred in Ghent in 1557.[11] Assuming she had arrived there shortly after Gilein's death, Soetken's decision was initially a good one if judged by the criterion of avoiding persecution: from February 1554 to March 1557 only one Anabaptist was executed in Ghent, the longest stretch of such calm in the city between 1550 and 1565.[12]

But 1557 was the worst year since the spring and summer of 1551, when no fewer than twelve men and women had been put to death for refusing to relinquish their Anabaptist views. The return of Titelmans in February 1557 yielded similar results, with nine executions of Anabaptists in March and April of the same year.[13] When Soetken made the commitment to receive baptism in this context, she surely was aware that her baptism by water and the Holy Spirit might well culminate in baptism by blood. It is even possible that the resolve of those put to death in the spring of 1557 triggered her decision to enter into full union with the community. Others who became Anabaptists were inspired by the martyrs' behaviour at their deaths to themselves join Anabaptist congregations.

Whatever Soetken's specific reasons for entering the community at this time, she seems to have become something of a leader for a conventicle of like-minded women in Ghent. Sometime prior to July 31, 1560, she was arrested there, along with three other women, for suspicion of heresy.[14] All three were unmarried and considerably younger than herself: Lijnken Claeys (twenty years old), Lijnken Pieters (twenty-five), and Martha Baert (twenty-one). It is Martha who seems to have been Soetken's housemaid; twice Soetken mentions her by name in the letter to her brother and sister, with another reference to "her maid Martha" at the outset of the song apparently written by Martha.[15] These three women had not yet made a full Anabaptist commitment, though they shared Soetken's views and thus expressed their desire to be rebaptized if given the opportunity. When they were interrogated on July 31 by Pieter Titelmans, the man who had questioned and excommunicated Soetken's husband, all four women openly expressed positions considered heretical by Catholic authorities. They gave common Anabaptist responses to standard questions posed by inquisitors in the sixteenth century: that the Catholic Church is not the true Christian church but the whore of Babylon, that the pope is an Antichrist, that the baptism of infants is without value, and that children who die without baptism are saved. Defending their positions with reference to Scripture, they also denied transubstantiation, maintained that confession of sins to a priest was unnecessary, repudiated the invocation of Mary and the other saints, rejected the existence of purgatory, and expressed their opposition to the swearing of oaths.

Inquisitorial officials, city magistrates, secular priests, and members of four different male religious orders from Ghent attempted to convince Soetken and her three companions that such notions were heretical errors which they should recant, after which they could return to communion with the Catholic Church. Martha Baert (and doubtless Soetken as well) saw the matter differently, integrating the experience of their attempts at persuasion into her song:

> The seducers torment me so much
> to draw me away from God's teaching
> I will not believe them
> for they seek to stupefy me.[16]

At least three separate attempts were made to dissuade them during the initial phase of their examinations, held in the city prison in Ghent, under the direction of Titelmans. Then Titelmans pronounced them excommunicated and handed them over to the civil magistrates.

If the magistrates had followed the letter of the imperial laws against heresy, most recently reaffirmed in Charles V's severe edict of 1550, they should have immediately condemned the women to death. But clearly they were not eager to execute Soetken and her companions, whose heterodoxy posed no obvious threat to civil tranquillity. On August 12 the magistrates appealed to the Dominicans, Augustinians, Carmelites, and Franciscans in Ghent, asking each to send representatives from their respective houses to try to persuade these women to recant, so that the mandated death sentence might be commuted to a lighter punishment. This was a common practice: secular magistrates with a frequently less than sophisticated grasp of doctrinal dispute and biblical exegesis often appealed to local clergy for help with heretics who held their ground. It is not difficult to imagine that for their part, beyond a concern to save these women from execution and damnation, the members of the respective orders saw this as a sort of competition and an opportunity for enhanced prestige, to succeed where Titelmans and his assistants had failed.

But within the next three weeks representatives of all four monastic orders would fail as well. Perhaps because of their traditional role as inquisitors since the thirteenth century, or perhaps because of the good relationship they enjoyed with Titelmans in Ghent, the Dominicans went first.[17] On August 14, Lambrecht Langheraert and Jan van den Heede reported to the magistrates that all four women remained persistent in their "mistakes and errors" and showed no signs of any conversion. Two Carmelites, Jan de Cuelenaere and Marcq Slesse, related the same thing to the magistrates after their attempt on August 22. They added that there seemed reason for hope in the cases of Martha and Lijnken Pieters, who appeared less set in their views than Soetken and Lijnken Claeys. On August 24, two Augustinian brothers likewise indicated their failure to change any of the four.

During the following week, acting on the report of the Carmelites, the magistrates moved Lijnken Pieters and Martha to separate cells in the castle of the counts of Flanders (the *Gravensteen*) in an attempt to weaken their resolve. On August 31 the final religious order, the Franciscans, sent their representatives, Philips van der Vaet and Lieven de Groote. Their efforts also proved fruitless; they reported that Soetken was the most resolute of them all. The inquisitors and learned men from four different religious orders had failed to persuade these women to change their minds. Still the magistrates kept trying, sending a team of city officials and a parish pastor on September 7. Lijnken Pieters began crying on this occasion and said she was willing to repudiate her views, but two days later retracted her promise, saying she had made it in a moment of weakness.

The authorities left Soetken and her three companions in prison for ten more weeks after this, hoping to diminish their resolve. City officials by themselves made an eleventh-hour effort to alter their disposition on November 18. Again the women expressed their determination, defended their views with reference to scriptural passages, and declared their preparedness to suffer death for them. It is not entirely clear, but it seems that Soetken's three children were by this time with her brother and sister in Bruges, having gone to them by way of Oudenaarde after her apprehension.[18] In the letter written to her brother and sister shortly before her death, Soetken gave eloquent testimony of the women's willingness to die: "we are so well-disposed to make our sacrifice that I am unable to express it. Indeed I could jump for joy when I think about that eternal good that is promised us as a possession, [and] for everyone who perseveres in all that the Lord has commanded of us."[19]

Readers familiar with Van Braght's *Martyrs' Mirror* will be acquainted with such statements in letters by other Anabaptists facing death. (Such resolve was not limited to Anabaptists, however, as many Protestant and Roman Catholic martyrs expressed the same ideas and demonstrated perserverance by their actions in the sixteenth century.) Soetken's own writings and past provide some clues for understanding the sources of this willingness to die in her case.

First, in the manner of a virtual flesh-and-blood concordance, she recounted in succession a host of Biblical promises about the rewards for those who endure persecution for Christ's sake. In her *Testament*, these rewards are the foundation supporting her repeated exhortations to her children about a number of Christian virtues. Italicizing the passages in the following quotation gives a sense of the ubiquity of biblical references in this section of her letter (and indeed, throughout it):

> See, my dearly beloved, choose rather to suffer uncomfortably with the children of God so that you might be rewarded with them, for to these will come all the beautiful promises, but they must endure much suffering, for *the kingdom of heaven suffers violence and the violent will enter it* [Mt 11:12]. It is also written, *with much tribulation must you enter into the kingdom of heaven* [Acts 14:22]. For David says, *we are led to death as sheep for the slaughter* [Ps 44:11]. And Paul says, *we who are alive are every day delivered over to death*. Further it is written, *you shall weep but the world shall rejoice; you shall be sorrowful, but your sorrow shall turn into joy* [Jn 16:20]. *You will have tribulation for a bit, but be comforted and be faithful unto death, and I shall give you the crown of life* [Rev 2:10]. *In the world you will have tribulation, but be comforted, I have overcome the world* [Jn 16:33].[20]

Presumably drawing these from memory, Soetken continues in this manner, knitting together biblical passages with the same theme for the benefit of her children as well as herself. Four months in prison certainly gave her ample opportunity to dwell on and pray about the passages she had read and discussed before with women like Martha and the two Lijnkens. Their power came from the fact that they were quite simply and literally believed to be *God's* promises. As Soetken wrote to her children, implying the incomparable importance of these verses, "who would not love such a Lord and Father, who has chosen us like he chose Israel and has given us his commandments and laws, that is, his Gospel, which teaches us to do his will and pleasure–and such has he made heirs of all the riches of heaven?"[21]

Secondly, Soetken's family members supported her during her imprisonment. The very first thing she does when writing to her brother and sister is to tell them that she has received two letters, adding "I thank you from the depths of my heart for all the friendship which you have always shown me and will continue to show me." Further on in the same letter she thanks her daughter, Betken, for a letter that had fortified her: "I am most joyful that the Lord spared me long enough to be joyful before my death because of your letter, through which you have strengthened me."[22] The prison walls in Ghent were porous enough for Soetken to know that her family members had kept her in mind and seem to have encouraged her behaviour, as did other Anabaptists with their own family members. (On the other hand, in her song Martha alludes to friends who urged her to capitulate to the demands of her interlocutors, so apparently the women did not enjoy unanimous support.) It is also safe to assume that Soetken experienced solidarity with the three younger women imprisoned with her, and to the extent that she was older and something of their leader, felt obliged to set an example for them.

Finally, the importance of Soetken's own contemporary models should not be underestimated. Her husband's martyrdom six years earlier had clearly remained with her, as she mentioned it and defended his witness at the end of her *Testament*. Moreover, she was in Ghent when nine Anabaptists were executed in 1557, another the following year, and nine again in 1559, the years immediately prior to her death. Shortly before her own apprehension, on June 27, 1560, Tanneken Gressy and Mynkin Souucs became the first Anabaptists to be secretly executed in Ghent.[23] Catholic authorities revealed their concern about possible public disturbance and admitted that public executions were buttressing rather than deterring Anabaptist co-believers.[24] Either their deaths would be rewarded with eternal salvation (in which case they had made a splendid trade-off), or they had died in vain. Clearly Soetken thought the former, and was strengthened by their deaths. She believed her own death would be similarly rewarded while a recantation would jeopardize her salvation, and so she stood firm time and again against the efforts of the "seducers" to dissuade her. The way in which these recent martyrs had met death reinforced, and was reinforced by, the biblical examples that also inspired her. "Your father and I have shown you the way, along with many others," she told her children. "Take an example from the prophets and apostles, indeed, Christ himself, who have gone this way—and where the head has preceded, there also the members must certainly follow."[25]

The *Testament* itself, with its veritable catalogue of Christian virtues supported by scriptural passages and Soetken's exhortation to her children to cling to and cultivate these virtues, is the clearest evidence of her care for her children. It is also apparent when she urges both David and her two daughters to read and write, skills both she and her husband, a schoolteacher, possessed.[26] One passage in Soetken's *Testament* is particularly worthy of attention for the way that it shows her love for her children confronting the demands of her faith.

> since your father was taken away from me, I have neither day nor night spared myself to raise you, and my prayer and concern were always for your salvation, and still now, being in chains, my greatest anxiety has always been that as a result of my prudence [*voorsicticheit*] I was unable to arrange things better for you. For when it was said to me that you had been led to Oudenaarde and from there to Bruges, that fell so heavily on me that I neither had nor have any greater sadness. But when I realized that my concern or provisioning could not help, and that for Christ's sake one must depart from all that one loves in this world, then I left all that up to the will of the Lord, still always hoping and praying that he will preserve you in his mercy, as he preserved Joseph, Moses and Daniel among godless men.[27]

Again it was scriptural promises and precedents that enabled Soetken to relativize even her love for her children in the light of salvation. She trusted that the same God who had protected his own in biblical times would watch over her son and two daughters as the Flemish winter of 1560 approached. Besides, their imminent separation was cushioned by the hope of familial reunion in heaven, where "we might see each other on the day of the resurrection with joy."[28] Soetken's faith enabled her to face martyrdom even at the expense of leaving her children because it encompassed the anticipation of seeing them in the future, when togetherness mattered most.

The magistrates' numerous efforts to convince the four women having failed, they sentenced Soetken, Martha, and Lijnken Pieters to death. On November 20, 1560, all three were beheaded inside the castle and their bodies thrown in a ditch outside the *Muidepoort*, one of Ghent's city gates.[29] For unknown reasons, Lijnken Claeys was spared at this time. She was executed on August 14, 1561, along with another Anabaptist woman, Tanneken Delmeere.[30] These two also were decapitated inside the castle–as with the other three women, plus the two from June 1560, an indication that magistrates feared a negative popular reaction to the public execution of heretics in Ghent at this time.

As with many other Anabaptist martyrs, some of these women's voices continued to speak to subsequent generations because Soetken's *Testament* and letter to her brother and sister, as well as Martha's song were preserved and published after her death. Several sixteenth-century editions were published in Dutch, and an undated German translation appeared as well. Beginning in 1586, the work was combined with a previous martyr-mother's farewell letter, that of Anna Jansz to her son Isaiah (see her profile in this volume). In the seventeenth century, several more editions appeared through at least 1679, and the *Testament* and letter entered the Dutch Mennonite martyrological collections that culminated in Van Braght's *Martyrs' Mirror* in 1660.[31]

In doing so, however, Martha's song ("O Godt ghy zijt myn Hulper fijn") was dropped, as virtually all the Dutch Mennonite songs by and about the martyrs were converted into prose between the last edition of *Het Offer des Heeren* (1599) and the Haarlem martyrology of 1615.[32] The tune for the song ("Wel hem de Godes vrede staet") seems to have been taken from a song written by Frans van Boelsweert with a very similar title ("Wel hem, de in Godes vreese staet"), which suggests that Martha knew this other Anabaptist martyr's song from memory.[33] (Frans had been executed as an Anabaptist in Leeuwarden in 1545.[34]) Her own song was reprinted in the 1583 Dutch Mennonite songbook, the *Second Songbook of Many Various Songs* [*Het Tweede Liedeboeck, van vele diversche Liedekens*],[35] but to the best of my knowledge has never before been translated into English. An English translation of the entire song follows, though without any attempt to retain Martha's rhythmic AABB rhyme scheme of the original Dutch. In some measure, this song condenses much of what we know about both Martha and Soetken as a female martyrs: their singular commitment to their faith, their defiance of those who sought to turn her from it, and their trust in God in the face of death.

Martha's Song (O Godt Ghy Zijt Mijn Hulper Fijn)

O God, you are my good helper
deliver me from the eternal pain
O Lord, preserve me in the presence
of the dragon with his multitudes.

O God, you are my refuge
from which all my meaning arises
O Lord, uphold me
In you stands my confidence.

My deliverer is God alone
Cleanse me from all sins
and truly forgive me
so that I might live eternally.

The flesh inflicts great suffering on me
What the Lord wants resists it

O Lord, remember mine
I'll deliver my body to you.

My sins are without number
O Lord, forgive me all of them
Behold my misery
and thaw it with your spirit.

The seducers torment me so much
to draw me away from God's teaching
I will not believe them
for they seek to stupefy me.

My friends also admonish me
that I should give up my faith
O no, I will retain that
up to death without any weakening.

Then all of them say in haste,
"Therefore you shall inherit
that eternal fire in the glow of hell,
you shall lose the kingdom of God."

Then I say to them with a calm spirit,
"This trial belongs to the Lord.
How dare you utter such things?
Indeed he will avenge evil."

Then they say "You vile beast,
never was there found
in Oudenaarde any so evil,
with such a wicked character."

When the wicked world strikes me
the Lord is my refuge
I hope that he will strengthen me
and powerfully work with me.

Ah, good brothers and sisters
let us always be mindful
of the Lord of Hosts
He will always preserve us.

I ask that all who hear this song
won't be terrified on your day
to accept the cross
God can help us persevere.

She who wrote this song
got into trouble with the blind leaders
They didn't take her prisoner;
she came by her own decison.

Notes

1. Soetken van den Houte, *Een Testament / gemaeckt by Soetken van den Houte / het welcke sy binnen Gendt in Vlaenderen metten Doodt beuesticht heeft / Anno M.D. en*[de] *.LX den xxvij.* [sic] *Novembris / Ende haeren kinderen Dauid / Betken ende Tanneken tot een Memorie ende voor het alder beste Goet heeft naghelaten.* . . . This edition is not among the editions catalogued in Ferdinand Vander Haeghen et al., *Bibliographie des martyrologes protestants néerlandais* [hereafter *BMPN*], vol. 1 (The Hague, 1890), 173-91, 656-59. However it is described in Marie-Thérèse Lenger, re-ed., *Bibliotheca Belgica*, vol. 3 (Brussels, 1964), 518. For Dirck Wylicx van Santen as the printer, see also Paul Valkema Blouw, "Nicolaes Biestkens van Diest, *in duplo*, 1558-83," in *Theatrum orbis librorum. Liber amicorum Presented to Nico Israel on the Occasion of His Seventieth Birthday*, ed. T. Croiset van Uchelen, K. van der Horst and G. Schilder (Utrecht, 1989), 321, 330 n. 70. I thank Mr. Valkema Blouw for the revised approximate date of publication as 1582 (the *Bibliotheca Belgica* gives c.1580). I have made my own translations throughout from Soetken's *Testament*, but for the sake of readers familiar with van Braght's *Martyrs' Mirror*, I have also given page references to Sohm's English translation (Scottdale, PA: Herald Press, 1950), 646-51, here at p. 648.
2. Johan Decavele, *De dageraad van de Reformatie in Vlaanderen (1520-1565)*, vol. 1 (Brussels: 1975), pp. 374-75, 460.
3. For the following account of Gilein's arrest, interrogations, and eventual execution, see Adriaen Cornelisz van Haemstede, *Historien Oft Gheschiedenissen der vromer Martelaren*, . . . (N.p., 1566), 346-73, and Decavele, *Dageraad*, vol. 1, 374-76. For Titelmans, see Decavele, ibid., 14-31; Johan van de Wiele, "De inquisitierechtbank van Pieter Titelmans in de zestiende eeuw in Vlaanderen," *Bijdragen en mededelingen betreffende de geschiedenis der Nederlanden* 97 (1982): 19-63; P. Beuzart, "Pierre Titelmans et l'Inquisition en Flandre (1554-1567)," in *Bulletin de la Société de l'Histoire du Protestantisme Français* 63 (1914): 224-42.
4. Gilein mentions his wife and "vijf cleyne kinderkens en[de] schaepkens"; Van Haemstede, *Historien* (1566), 348.
5. A. L. E. Verheyden, *Anabaptism in Flanders, 1530-1650. A Century of Struggle* (Scottdale, PA: Herald Press, 1961), 51.
6. Decavele, *Dageraad*, vol. 1, 436-37.
7. Decavele, *Dageraad*, vol. 1, 460.
8. See, e.g., A. F. Mellink, "The Beginnings of Dutch Anabaptism in the Light of Recent Research," in MQR, 62 (1988): 211-20, at 220.
9. Soetken, *Testament*, sig. [B7]; *Martyrs' Mirror*, 650. Cf. Decavele, *Dageraad*, vol. 1, 460 n. 141.

10 Soetken, *Testament*, sig. [B7r-v]; *Martyrs' Mirror*, 650. This makes all the more interesting the fact that Gilein ended up in the Reformed Protestant martyrological tradition (appearing not only in Van Haemstede, but also in the later editions of Jean Crespin's famous *Livre des Martyrs*, edited by Simon Goulart). I intend to explore this appropriation in a future article.
11 Decavele, *Dageraad*, vol. 1, 460.
12 A. L. E. Verheyden, *Het Gentsche martyrologium (1530-1595)* (Bruges: 1946), 12-31.
13 Verheyden, *Gentsche martyrologium*, 13-18, 23-24; Decavele, *Dageraad*, vol. 1, 445.
14 The information concerning Soetken and her companions' arrest and repeated interrogations is derived from J. B. Cannaert, *Bydragen tot de kennis van het oude strafrecht in Vlaenderen* (Ghent: 1835), 248-67, and Louis Antoine De Rycker, "Een proces voor ketterij, te Ghent. 1560-1561," in *Jaarboek van het Willems-fonds* (Ghent: 1878), 1-39.
15 Soetken, *Testament*, sigs [B8], C2, C4; *Martyrs' Mirror*, 650. At the outset of the song printed after Soetken's *Testment* and letter, we read: "Een schoen Geestelick Liedeken/ Ghemaeckt door die selue Urouwe Soetken vanden Houten Haer Maecht Martha," which I take to mean that Martha, the maid of the same woman, Soetken, wrote the song (Soetken, *Testament*, sig. C4). Perhaps they wrote it together and "ende" (which would have made the phrase clearer) was left out between "Houten" and "Haer."
16 Soetken, *Testament*, sig. C4v.
17 On the relationship between Titelmans and the Dominicans in Ghent, see Decavele, *Dageraad*, vol. 1, 17.
18 Soetken expressly says that she knew her children had been taken from Oudenaarde to Bruges (*Testament*, sig. B2v; *Martyrs' Mirror*, 648), and in the letter to her brother and sister she thanks them for the friendship she hopes they will continue to show her "in my three little lambs whom I'm leaving behind" (*aen mijn dry Schaepkens die ick achterlate*) (*Testament*, sig. [B7v]; *Martyrs' Mirror*, 650). This plus the fact that Soetken addresses her children directly later in this letter suggests that they were already in the care of her brother and sister.
19 Soetken, *Testament*, sig. [B8]; *Martyrs' Mirror*, 650.
20 Soetken, *Testament*, sigs [A8v]-B1; *Martyrs' Mirror*, 648.
21 Soetken, *Testament*, sig. B2; *Martyrs' Mirror*, 648.
22 Soetken, *Testament*, sigs [B7v], C2v; *Martyrs' Mirror*, 650, 651.
23 Verheyden, *Gentsche martyrologium*, 23-26.
24 Decavele, *Dageraad*, vol. 1, 452, 453.
25 Soetken, *Testament*, sig. C3; *Martyrs' Mirror*, 651.
26 Soetken, *Testament*, sigs "U"[=B]3r-v, B4v-B5, C3; *Martyrs' Mirror*, 649, 651.
27 Soetken, *Testament*, sig. B2r-v; *Martyrs' Mirror*, 648.
28 Soetken, *Testament*, sig. [B6]; *Martyrs' Mirror*, 649.
29 Verheyden, *Gentsche martyrologium*, 26-27.
30 Cannaert, *Strafrecht*, 267; De Rycker, "Proces," 22-24; Verheyden, *Gentsche martyrologium*, 27.
31 The various printed editions of Soetken's *Testament* are given in *BMPN*, vol. 1, 173-91, 656-59; for a brief overview of Dutch Mennonite martyrologies from *Het Offer des Heeren* (first ed. 1562-63) through the *Martyrs' Mirror*, see the ME, III, pp. 518-19.
32 For a brief account of this transformation, see W. J. Kühler, *Geschiedenis van de doopsgezinden in Nederland*, part 2, first half, 1600-1735 (Haarlem: Tjeenk Willink & Zoon, 1940), 99-101.
33 Franz's song has the same rhyme scheme as Martha's song and is reprinted in Philipp Wackernagel, *Lieder der niederländischen Reformierten aus der Zeit der Verfolgung im 16. Jahrhundert* (Frankfurt am Main: 1867; Nieuwkoop: 1965), no. 22, 97.

34 For the capital sentence passed against Frans Dammassoon [=van Boelsweert], see A. F. Mellink, ed., *Documenta Anabaptistica Neerlandica*, vol. 1, *Friesland en Groningen (1530-1550)* (Leiden: 1975), 74. Two years later, Jan Lambertszoon, another Anabaptist condemned in Leeuwarden, received and retained a song (probably the same one) by Van Boelsweert while in prison; ibid., 80.

35 ME, IV, 570; F. C. Wieder, *De schriftuurlijke liedekens. De liederen der nederlandsche hervormden tot op het jaar 1566* (The Hague: 1900), 163, 181, 197.

ANNA HENDRIKS OF AMSTERDAM

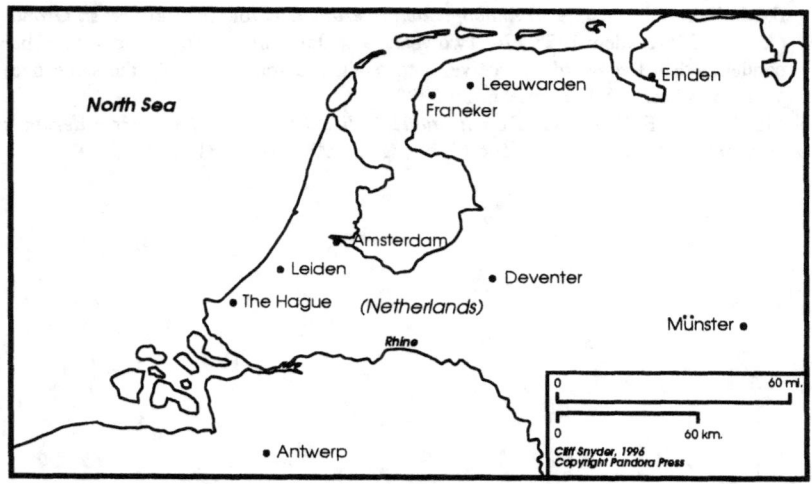

On November 10, 1571, Anna "Heyndrixs" or Hendriks (daughter of Hendrik), housewife from Franeker in Frisia, Netherlands, was executed in a barbarous manner.[1] The hangman tied her to a ladder, filled her mouth with gunpowder and cast her onto a bed of burning coals, probably charcoal. Why this excessive cruelty? Drowning was the standard form of execution for women in most of sixteenth-century Europe north of the Alps. What heinous crime had she committed to merit that punishment?

Anna, an Anabaptist sympathizer living in Amsterdam in the early 1550s, had fled to Franeker in Frisia; we are not told when she left. There she finally joined the Anabaptists around 1568, was baptized by a Jan van Giethoorn (Ophoorn in the court scribe's hand) in the house of one Heyndrick the tailor. She married Lambert Jansz, a smith, "in the secret Mennonist manner,"[2] and attended more Anabaptist meetings and communion services than she was willing to confess. Eventually she returned to Amsterdam for reasons no interrogator seems to have probed. There she was discovered by a next-door neighbour who, as an assistant sheriff, crusaded against Anabaptists and set about to uncover them. Apparently these two had known each other in her prior residence in Amsterdam, and he knew that she had converted to Anabaptism.[3]

Tried on October 3 by several city officials together with the sheriff, she doggedly held her religious ground and revealed as little about other Anabaptists as she could. Typically, sixteenth-century interrogators of Anabaptists grilled their victims to learn the names of other Anabaptists, especially leaders, together with the location of meeting places and their hosts. Her answers reveal standard Anabaptist practices: lay leaders moved from place to place and were replaced by new ones when they were caught–most of them had a short life expectancy; Anabaptist members from all walks of life fled to safer havens when pressures mounted in their home towns or villages; meetings of many worshippers took place on special occasions, such as the breaking of bread; meetings of five or six persons in private rooms were held to read and talk about the Word.

Anna's examiners had to be satisfied with a mere handful of Anabaptist names from her lips. She succeeded in suggesting only one or two for each of the meetings she reported, a grand total of only thirteen people, of whom three had died or been executed and one was geographically beyond reach.[4] It is possible that several of the nine who remained viable candidates for arrest were also out of bounds for her predators. Five of them were known to her only in Franeker and presumably were there still. Perhaps others of the nine had since passed on or been executed. She gave the names of two Anabaptists who lived on her own street, Sint Jannstraet, the same street where her detector lived. She might have assumed that he already knew them to be Anabaptists. To conceal while appearing to reveal required a certain cunning, something Anna seems to have mastered. No modern-day researcher can quite believe that she knew no more than thirteen Anabaptists.

In Franeker, Anna and her husband had used their house as a meeting place, but then abandoned that practice for reasons she did not reveal to her questioners. They invited small groups of Anabaptist friends to meet with them in their home to read the Word; sometimes Lambert did the reading. Hosting Anabaptist meetings was usually a punishable offense in its own right. Anna visited other meetings, large and small. In Franeker they sometimes were led at night to meeting places whose hosts they did not know; from other sources we know that the Franeker congregation was very large. In Amsterdam she visited a larger meeting in the home of boatman and lay leader Jan Querijnen near the Corsgen gate; he had been executed in 1569. She does not tell us whether she worshipped in his house before or after her Franeker residence. Her report of this meeting place appears to be an attempt to satisfy the urgings of her examiners while still revealing the name of only one host, since deceased. To satisfy her interrogators, she provided the name of the village where the leader of one meeting place just outside the city lived, namely in the village of Schreierstoren on the Ij River,[5] but she appeared not to know where they met. More frequent were gatherings of only a handful, apparently in various homes including her own. It is conceivable that she avoided larger conventicles because of fear of capture. Or perhaps she refused to mention others and her interrogators did not press her because they had enough evidence to incriminate her anyway.

Why did Anna return to Amsterdam from Franeker? The Spanish troops, under the fanatical persecutor the Duke of Alva, occupied Amsterdam and protected its citizens against the onslaughts of Anabaptist heretics much better than they were able to control the agricultural villages and market towns in Frisia. The surviving records do not tell us why she bearded the Spanish beast. Perhaps she fled because of dissensions in Franeker. In the 1560s Anabaptists in Franeker fell to wrangling with each other. In 1567 the large Anabaptist population there divided into several different groups, at first principally the Flemish versus the Frisians. That division excluded Leenaert Bouwens from service in Franeker, a minister who baptized hundreds of Anabaptists and who ultimately settled in that town. (Subsequent divisions, after the time of Anna and her husband, broke the Anabaptists of Franeker into at least four major groups.) These were not amicable separations. Each side condemned the other in savage terms.[6] Some Anabaptist peacemakers tried to bridge the gaps, sometimes with success. But we know of one Anabaptist peacemaker, Christiaen Jannsens Langedul, who was captured and then executed in 1567; he had called a meeting in Antwerp to settle disagreements among several Anabaptist parties there.[7] In any event, Anna and her husband were active Anabaptists during the early stages of Franeker splinterings, and perhaps they suffered from them and decided to flee. In her hearing, she reported nonattendance at Anabaptist communion services in Franeker because there was no one of their religious persuasion to administer the bread and wine. Such a report tallies with a known very low Flemish-party population together with a specific dispute about leadership of that group.

Why had Anna fled Amsterdam for Franeker earlier? Probably to seek some haven away from the heavier persecution by the Spanish in Amsterdam. Sixty years ago, a Dutch researcher decided that Anna had moved in Anabaptist circles as a sympathizer some twenty years earlier in Amsterdam. She associated, so that story ran, with at least two other young women, Aechgen Jacobdochter and Filistis Ericxdochter. Aechgen and Filistis were caught and tried, and subsequently renounced their interest in the movement; they had visited meetings both inside and outside Amsterdam, had consistently avoided the sacraments of the altar and of penance, and had associated with a cluster of Anabaptists. In their own hearings they repeatedly declared they had not wanted a second baptism. Still, they were sentenced to exile despite never having been baptized.[8] Anna escaped that police net and fled Amsterdam. Our 1938 researcher moved her all the way out to Franeker, in Frisia. The hearings of Aechgen and Filistis survive and tell us that they had a friend named Anna de Vlaster; that name appears as an alias for our Anna Hendriks in her 1571 hearing. Perhaps Anna de Vlaster did leave Amsterdam for Franeker in 1552, reverted to her patronymic Hendriks, and returned to Anabaptism in those relatively safer confines. We cannot know for certain, but it seems likely.

At both her arrest and her execution, Anna lashed out at a "Judas," a man whose personal name was Evert. "Thou Judas, I have not deserved to be murdered," she cried out as she was led to her bed of fire. She foretold God's vengeance upon him if he persisted in his anti-Anabaptist fury. He in turn vowed to catch as many Anabaptists as he could. This Judas was her detector, whom the official records name as assistant sheriff. But "Judas" does not indicate some police official in the straightforward, albeit cruel, pursuit of his duties catching Anabaptists and similar felons, but a former close associate of Anna's. Surely "Judas" has to have been someone who was once a member of that circle of earnest Anabaptist seekers. The records tell us that he "recognized" her, another clue of a prior sure acquaintance that hints at an Anabaptist connection on his part. Recanters from Anabaptism sometimes did turn informer. We have no evidence of any of them joining the police, but it could have happened. Anna's outrage at his betrayal was no ordinary cry for vengeance. Otherwise, her meek acceptance of certain death marked her demeanour throughout.[9]

Late in October Anna was tortured twice. Commonly the hangman routinely applied the thumbscrew to female suspects to confirm the accuracy of confession already made and to induce a fuller confession. For her second torture, the hangman likely would have suspended Anna's body with her arms tied behind her back, with or without weights. Normal judicial restraints in the treatment of females were rejected by the Spanish in their rage against heretics.

Unlike their Protestant equivalents, Anna's Catholic interrogators did not try to induce her to recant. They were looking for victims, not fresh converts. The eighteenth-century historian of Amsterdam, Jan Wagenaar, tells us that the late sixteenth-century Spanish garrison terrorized Amsterdam and checked a growing Dutch national sentiment toward greater political but also religious freedom.[10] Had Dutch nationals conducted Anna's trial and imposed a sentence, their Reformed leaders would have condemned but not killed her. We can explain the excessively cruel form of Anna's execution only as embattled Roman Catholics turning fanatical in order to regain people and territory lost to Protestants. A rabid zeal infused and provoked those Spanish, from King Philip through the Duke of Alva down to the common soldiers. Many Dutch people suffered from their excesses. In that same period from 1567 to 1575, those Spanish duplicated several dozen times the unconscionable form of execution of Anabaptist Anna Hendriks.

Why did the Spanish stuff Anna's mouth with gunpowder before they cast her on the fire? Probably to stop her speech, to prevent her making "a good witness" to her faith at the moment of execution, commonly the speech most favoured by the spectators. The author of the *Martyrs' Mirror* gives this explanation, one he likely got from the earlier hymn written to honour Anna. But why did she keep the gunpowder in her mouth; why not spit it out? Or, to prevent speech from victims, executioners applied a tongue screw, a device much surer than a mouth full of gunpowder. Gunpowder was commonly used to ensure quick death, as a "humane" gesture. But it was normally hung around the victim's neck, not stuffed into her mouth. The surviving records do not tell us with certainty why gunpowder was used in Anna's case.

Anna Hendriks was a staunch, steadfast servant of her Lord. Her interrogators thought her stubborn and obstinate. Her supporters composed and sang a hymn to honour her memory.[11]

Notes

1 The official record of Anna's Hearing, Oct. 3, 1571, was transcribed and published by A. F. Mellink in *Documenta Anabaptistica Neerlandica*, II (Leiden: Brill, 1980), 306-09. Tieleman J. van Braght discovered the official record of her sentence, and published it in *Het bloedig Tooneel, of Martelaers Spiegel der Doops-Gesinde* (Dordrecht: Jacobus Savry, 1660), II, 538 in the 1685 illustrated edition; translation in the *Martyrs' Mirror*, 874. Other accounts of Anna, in addition to that in the *Martyrs' Mirror*, are found in Greta Grosheide, *Bijdrage tot de Geschiedenis der Anabaptisten in Amsterdam* (Hilversum: J. Schipper Jr., 1938), 183-84; P. Sijbolts, "De Doopsgezinden te Middelburg in de 16de eeuw," in *Doopsgezinde Bijdragen*, 1908, 1-64; and N. v.d. Zijpp, "Anneken Hendriks," in ME, I, 126; John S. Oyer and Robert S. Kreider, *Mirror of the Martyrs* (Intercourse, PA: Good Books, 1990), 24-25. Early in this century, Dutch Mennonite minister Herman Bakels carried on an unedifying literary debate with a Dutch Catholic priest on the executions of Anabaptists. Like van Braght, he dug out the official hearing and sentence from the Amsterdam archives and reproduced them. He wrote briefly about Anna, but does not shed any light on the crucial or disputed issues. H[erman] Bakels, *Anneke's vuurdood* (Haarlem: H. Bakels, 1925).
2 So reports the Vonnis, printed by van Braght in *Martyrs' Mirror*.
3 Basic information on her and her peregrinations and visitations comes from Mellink's publication of the records of her hearing, in *Documenta Anabaptistica Neerlandica*, as cited in note 1. Unless I cite otherwise, data is from that source.
4 Here follow the names culled from her hearing: Franeker: three leaders or speakers, one deceased: Jan van Giethoorn, her baptizer; Gerrit Cornelis Boon, misnamed by her as Gerrit Heyndrixsz; he also had been executed earlier; Meus de bloockemaecker; five layfolk: Heyndrick, the tailor, and wife Machtelt; Aeltgen, maid, from Amsterdam but then in Franeker; Gryetgen, apple seller from Haarlem; Huybrecht Symonsz. Amsterdam: two leaders, one deceased: Jan Querijnen, leader, executed; Lyeven of Schreierstoren; three layfolk, one deceased (all lived on her street, Sint Jannstraet): Oloff the tailor, his first wife, deceased, Janneken; Anneken, bootlace maker.
5 Mellink supplies the present-day name of that village, named Schreyhouck by Anna.
6 For these affairs, see N. van der Zijpp, "Franeker," in ME, II, 370-72.
7 *Martyrs' Mirror*, 704; Oyer and Kreider, *Mirror of the Martyrs*, 42-43.
8 Mellink transcribed and published the hearings of Felistis Ericxdochter and Aechgen Jacobsdochter in *Documenta Anabaptistica Neerlandica*, II.
9 The Judas element comes from van Braght, who presumably found it in the hymn written about Anna. I do not find it in the official protocol of either the hearing or the sentence.

10 Jan Wagenaar, *Amsterdam in zyne Opkomst, Aanwas, Geschiedenissen, vooregten, Koophandel, Gebouwen, Kerkenstraat, Schoolen, Schutterye, Gilden en Regeering* . . . (Amsterdam: Yntema en Tieboel, 1760-[1794]), I, 321.
11 "Ick moet u nu gaen verclaren, Watter t'Amsterdam is geschiet," published in *Veelderhande Liedekens* of 1569.

SOETJEN GERRITS OF ROTTERDAM AND VROU GERRITS OF MEDEMBLIK

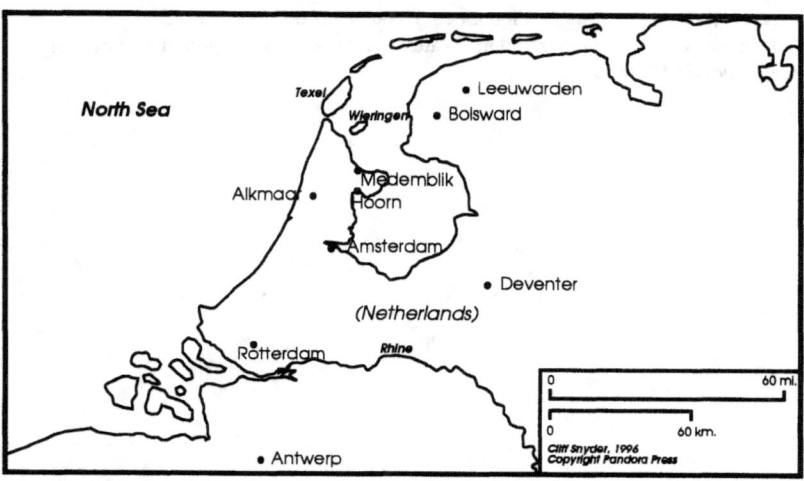

In or about 1559, a martyr's song, written by an unknown poet and commemorating six female martyrs who were executed at Antwerp, begins with "Babels Raets Mandamenten" [The Mandates of the Council of Babel]. Like most martyr songs, it deals with the martyrs' questioning, their torture, and execution. When describing the coarseness of the interrogators, the poet continues[1]:

> They harmed two maidens physically
> Those tyrants were hardly aware
> That each one of us is borne in pain
> Being procreated by women
> They haven't learned any reasonability
> From this experience through nature
> They almost totally neglect this matter
> That is why they became tyrants.

This sounds like an extraordinary early gender awareness by a sixtennth-century male Mennonite who cursed the Catholic persecutors for their cruel manifestation of masculine power. It is even more astonishing since this quote does not at all reflect the Aristotelian genealogical theory which was generally adopted in the early days of Anabaptism, especially by Melchior Hoffman and Menno Simons. Their views were closely connected with the incarnation of Christ, in which the virgin Mary, being a sinful human being, only passively provided her womb as a receptive field.

Three Comments on the Position of Mennonite Women

I have no intention of plunging into gender-related theories about Anabaptist/Mennonite women. However, I think it is fair simply to make some general comments emphasizing three aspects that serve as a framework for my analysis of the spiritual songs of Vrou Gerrits and Soetjen Gerrits, two female poets from the sixteenth- and early seventeenth-century Low Countries. In this matter I simply refer to studies of John Klassen, Keith Sprunger, M. Lucille Marr, Marion Kobelt-Groch, Sherrin Marshall, Auke Jelsma, and others.[2]

In the first place I think one can agree that the position of Mennonite women in general was very traditional: the woman was subject to the covenant of God. Especially in marriage, be it a companionate marriage or not,[3] the wife remained under the authority of her husband. She was supposed to be modest, meek, humble, and obedient, unadorned with gold and pearls and sober in her dress. This image, most literally derived from the Pauline creed, was common not only in the Protestant Netherlands, but particularly preached by biblicist leaders like Menno Simons and his spiritual descendants. Mennonite biblicism kept women from the more pronounced role that radical earlier and nonconformist Anabaptism had permitted them in many other fields of social and theological practice.[4] On the contrary, it would even lead to the stereotype of the prudish "Mennonite Sister" which would become an emblem of both honour and mockery in Dutch literature of the seventeenth century.[5]

However, most studies have dealt with Anabaptist/Mennonite women from the perspective of marriage and marital obligations. In my analysis I would like to emphasize the role of the unmarried women. There is reason to do so, since the single religious woman played a specific role in earlier Catholic society; women's convents, for instance, outnumbered male monasteries. Besides, in late medieval society there were a great number of single women because women commonly married at an older age. The Reformation did not change this pattern drastically.[6] So one may raise the question whether unmarried Mennonite women also had a different status, reflecting something of the life of single religious women in the pre-Reformation days, when many led privileged devout lives as nuns, *beguines*, or *klopjes* [holy maidens]. One example in Mennonitism is Elisabeth Dirks, who was well-educated in a convent near Leer in East Friesland, from which she finally fled. She preached Anabaptism until she was imprisoned in Leeuwarden in 1549, where she was mistaken for the wife of Menno Simons (see her profile in this volume).[7]

Second, one cannot deny the remarkable role many Anabaptist women played during the times of persecution and martyrdom. Although it appears that this position of equality to men ended as soon as the revolutionary zeal of Anabaptism faded away, and became a world-avoiding position in the second and third generation of Mennonitism, one must admit that Mennonite women still had a more egalitarian position compared to their Protestant sisters–despite the traditional biblistic marital concepts. One constant factor promoting this was, in my view, that Mennonite women enjoyed better conditions for gaining access to the modern medium of communication–the printed word of the Bible, in particular. In this respect both Anabaptist/Mennonite men and women were ahead of their non-Mennonite contemporaries. It is quite evident that in Anabaptism, unlike Lutheranism and Calvinism, an academically trained clergy was absent. This encouraged reading and learning by the self-educated, women included, of at least the New Testament. This phenomenon has hardly been recognized by Anabaptist gender historians, with the exception of my Dutch colleague Auke Jelsma.[8] There are numerous places in the surviving records where imprisoned female martyrs encouraged their children to read the Bible; just as numerous are the complaints of the persecutors about women knowing the Bible almost by heart. This aspect is reflected in the various martyrologies: whereas only 6.5 percent of martyrs are women in the Reformed or Calvinist martyrbooks of Jean Crespin and his Dutch counterpart Adriaen van Haemstede, at least 25 percent of the martyrs are women in the Mennonite *Het Offer des Heeren* and van Braght's *Martyrs' Mirror*.[9] Many of these women are known through the letters they sent from prison, a phenomenon that was unprecedented elsewhere.[10] Some of them also are known by hymns they wrote, like Anna Jansz, Soetken van den Houte's maid, Janneken van Aken (or van Houtte), and the previously mentioned Elisabeth Dirks.[11]

The third and final aspect I would like to emphasize is the use of feminine metaphors and imagery in Mennonite theological practice and thought. Keith Sprunger has pointed to this already, but I want to stress its relevance more strongly.[12] In Mennonite theology the holy church or the congregation is often depicted as the bride of Christ, the believers of the church as the new Eve, or the daughters of Israel; the heavenly ideal of Zion or the New Jerusalem is frequently expressed in female terms. In hymns, the allegorical use of the bride and bridegroom metaphors from the Song of Solomon also are frequently applied. Take, for instance, the hymn "Christus die ware Bruydegom goet" [Christ the very true Bridegroom], written by the influential Old Frisian Mennonite elder Pieter Jansz Twisck from Hoorn. Twisck describes the physical appearance of the bride–which is the congregation–in full detail, considering, for instance, the "breasts which are sweeter than wine" as representing the Old and the New Testaments.[13] All this non-masculine imagery–although most likely created by men–must have had some positive effect on the way Dutch Mennonites treated or regarded the women in their midst. The impact of the imagery calls for much deeper analysis of, and comparison with, this phenomenon in non-Mennonite Protestantism as well as within the Mennonite setting outside the

Netherlands.[14] Something of this high regard for women–albeit from the traditional male perspective–is reflected in a spiritual song entitled: "Van de eerbaer Vrouwen" [Concerning the Honourable Women], of which I cite the first two-and-a-half stanzas.[15]

> Since I have read
> That women are superior
> And praised as nowhere else
> So listen to my words.
> Therefore I too will
> Praise them, as you may hear
> In this merry song.
> Keep this in mind.
> A Woman who lives in virtue
> And in wisdom too
> Makes her husband joyful
> This is what Scripture teaches us
> She immediately cheers her man
> When he is in pain
> Through her sweet words
> He gains courage again.
> Women's wisdom
> Should be praised
> Since in our earthly place
> Women top everything. . .

The author then continues with reflections on several biblical examples like Debora, Susanna, Judith, Sara, Jahel, Mary, Elisabeth, etc.

Apart from those examples of virtuous women from the Bible, apart from the exemplary "manly courage" of the female martyrs, Dutch Mennonites of the late sixteenth and early seventeenth centuries–both men and women–had other female role models too, such as the two poets we turn to next.

Soetjen Gerrits and Vrou Gerrits

Very little is known about the lives of the remarkable Soetjen Gerrits from Rotterdam (born about 1540; died at Hoorn on December 26, 1572) and Vrou Gerrits from Medemblik (born ca. 1580; died at the age of twenty-five on September 6, 1605).[16] Soetjen Gerrits may be considered a second-generation Mennonite, who personally witnessed or heard described many imprisonments and executions of her persecuted brothers and sisters. In one song, for instance, she refers to the capture of martyrs in Delfshaven, near Rotterdam, in the years 1548-50.[17] In another she tells of the execution of five martyrs in Rotterdam in 1558.[18] She declares that these events caused much trouble for Mennonites in the Rotterdam area, after which many decided to leave the region. Most likely Soetjen Gerrits was among those who fled to safer places, most likely to Hoorn, a town north of Amsterdam, where she died some twenty years later.[19] The most astonishing thing about Soetjen is not the fact that she was gifted with poetic talents, but the circumstance of a sincere handicap: she was illiterate because of blindness. This is how the editor introduces her:

> What God wanted to establish through the humble and meek creatures who have trust and faith in him was shown in our days by the great miracle, demonstrating his mercy, of a woman who was blind and who could never read one single letter during her lifetime, nor distinguish *a* from *b*. Nevertheless God enlightened her with a gifted and miraculous intellect and gave her skill in his Holy Word and merciful Gospel, as you will immediately understand and notice from the following songs.[20]

This is amazing, particularly in light of the fact that her collected work, which was published in 1592 under the title *Een Nieu Gheestelijck Liedtboecxken* [A New Spiritual Hymn Booklet], comprised ninety-eight songs.[21] In practice it must have meant that she dictated her songs to some close friend or family member, a secretary, who was also in charge of her correspondence. How the lyrical process itself took place under these circumstances is another matter that will be taken up later. Her blindness may have caused her contemporaries to consider her particularly holy, which might account for the many requests she received to write songs from teachers and friends in mainly the western part of the Netherlands.[22] Although her collected work was published in 1592, twenty years after her death, it is clear that already during her lifetime her hymns were much appreciated. Some thirty-five hymns are to be found in various editions of the most popular contemporary hymnbooks, such as the *Veelderhande Liedekens*, which was printed as early as 1552 and used for both individual and congregational singing.[23] On the other hand, hymn writing by request soon became part of the Mennonite religious culture of the late sixteenth and seventeeth centuries, which in itself is again indicative of a high literacy standard: writing and reading meant not only access to intellectual and spiritual equality for both men and women, but was very soon to become a cultural achievement of literary exchange that could be enjoyed at large. This will become clear when we introduce the life and work of Vrou Gerrits.

Vrou Gerrits was a different kind of female role model, in particular for younger people. The relevance of her fifty-one hymns, is emphasized in an introduction in much the same way as with Soetjen Gerrits. Although the simple and meek of this world generally receive little esteem, the introduction reads, it is almighty God who enlightens them in divine matters. This is demonstrated by these songs of a young daughter who loved and lived according to the Holy Scriptures. At the end of the preface is a little biographical note that states:[24]

> This young daughter Vrou Gerrits followed the Holy Scriptures from her childhood onwards, so that she started to write Scriptural songs when she was thirteen years of age; she lived until she was twenty-five and then slept in the Lord, thus leaving behind a good example for the Youth.

At the end of her hymnbook, *Een Nieu Gheestelijck Liedtboecxken*, which was published two years after she died, there is a short note about how peacefully this weak woman found rest, in clear conscience, after a godfearing Christian life among pious people on the North Sea island of Texel.[25] Like Soetjen Gerrits, Vrou Gerrits had changed her domicile, which is also reflected in her hymns. However, in Vrou Gerrits's time the circumstances must have been quite different: she lived at a time when the Mennonites were settled and at ease, becoming socially accepted, assimilated, and economically prosperous. The atmosphere and historical background of her poetry is therefore quite different from that of Soetjen Gerrits. Vrou Gerrits also composed her songs mainly on request, primarily for close friends in and around her town of birth, Medemblik. Most requests came from women, or from religious gatherings of adolescents from neighbouring congregations. In those circles, too, young women played a prominent role.

Before entering the analysis of the form and contents of their hymns, I should emphasize the fact that at the time, a posthumous publication of collected hymns was unprecedented in Dutch Mennonite hymnody. Soetjen Gerrits and Vrou Gerrits, two memorable women, were in fact–after the period of martyrdom and its religious heroism–the very first subjects of a kind of "personality cult," which the Mennonites in general were very reluctant to take up. Again, I conclude that this was a manifestation of growing Mennonite cultural self-esteem as well as a high regard for women generally.

Some characteristics of their Hymns, in particular regarding the role of women

Before analyzing the contents, we may begin with some formal aspects of their hymn writing. Mennonite hymnologists conformed to the general practice of making new rhymed texts to already existing popular or religious melodies. This process of so-called *contrafacts* was promoted and practised by the literary institutions of those days, the chambers of rhetoric, which were to be found in each city. This generally applied method implied that both rhyme and rhythm were dictated by the adopted melodies.[26] Both Soetjen and Vrou Gerrits composed their hymns in this way. Soetjen used seventy-nine different melodies for her ninety-eight songs–a remarkable variety–of which some thirty-five were tunes of popular songs, most of them ballads and love songs. Vrou Gerrits used forty-three different melodies for her total of fifty-one hymns–only eight of them can be called secular tunes. This matches the shift from popular to religious melodies for spiritual hymn writing, which can be observed in the development of Mennonite hymnody during the sixteenth century. To sum up, as far as the formal aspect of their song writing is concerned, both women conformed to the general male-dominated Mennonite hymnological practice. However, one should keep in mind that the blind, illiterate Soetjen Gerrits must have been handicapped in fully applying the rhetoricians' conventions. Her great variety of melodies is an astonishing thing, which points to a remarkable auditive and mnemotechnical talent. On the other hand, since she was not able to see the visual effects of her compositions on paper, she was deprived of other typical and formal techniques utilized by rhetoricians.[27] One such technique, a favourite among Mennonites and very appropriate for the genre of songs-at-request, was the so-called acrostichon: poems that contained the letters forming the name of the person to whom the hymn was dedicated in the first capital letter of each stanza. Soetjen Gerrits was unable to apply this technique,[28] whereas eleven of Vrou Gerrits's hymns were typical acrostichons. The most elaborate is "Nu moet ick u o maghen / Een liet schencken eerbaer" [Now my dear maidens I must respectfully give you a gift of a song], which contains nine names of Vrou Gerrits's closest women friends from Medemblik–her own name included.[29] Apart from this, almost every one of Vrou Gerrits's songs bears the names or initials of the people for whom the song was intended.[30] There is a further striking difference: most of the recipients of Vrou Gerrits's hymns were girls and young women–at least 50 percent of her production–whereas Soetjen Gerrits wrote her songs for a less gender-specific audience: only some 19 percent were specifically intended for women.[31] The songs of the blind Soetjen Gerrits have another peculiarity: more then one-third of her songs start with a first line that reads "Ghenade ende vrede," [Mercy and peace], most of the time followed by some sort of greeting.[32] Soetjen wrote some songs-at-request for non-resident teachers who had been preaching in her area, or who had asked her by letter to send them a song. They all belonged to the Old Frisian Mennonite–branch and occupied high positions in the pastoral hierarchy.[33] Soetjen refers to her handicap only a few times, as, for instance, at the end of a song where she confesses that the contents of a letter had been burned in love, "Since I never could read on Earth."[34]

As far as the formal aspect of their poetry is concerned, one final remark should be made. These hymns reveal a prospering literary activity of communication by letter and through gatherings of young Mennonites, especially young women.[35] Both women refer to this phenomenon frequently, for instance by expressions of gratitude for a letter just received which will be replied to in return by a song. In the case of Vrou Gerrits, we know that she not only sent hymns but also letters; two of them are extant, both addressed to female friends. As with her songs, the contents are very admonishing and from a female perspective it is interesting to learn that she thought this medium to be most appropriate for women

> who are so powerless, yes so sick and weak of strength to help one another continuously with writing, admonishing and teaching.[36]

Now it is time to have a closer look at the contents of their songs, their message in general, and in particular the message for women who constituted the most substantial part of their audience. It will hardly be a surprise that the poetry of both women is very affirming of gender roles [*rolbevestigend*]. In this respect, the younger Vrou Gerrits is even rather dull. Time and again she makes admonitions about the virtuous life of a true Christian, about being a pious, God-fearing member of the church without spot or wrinkle–a prerogative especially of the orthodox Frisian Mennonites and about avoiding disharmony and living in peace. She warns the children to avoid gossip, mockery, foul play, street games, fleshly attractions and other evil things. In one of her very first hymns, which she wrote at the age of thirteen, her Mennonite sister-like ethics formed the main religious vocabulary.[37] In most hymns dedicated to her female friends, she points again and again to their specific female obligations: avoid the flesh and the world, live without sin, be chaste, sober, and modest. A song to one of her closest friends, Guiert Pieters, is typical. On the occasion of Guiert's forthcoming baptism ("now when you become a fertile twig of the vine"), she admonishes her friend to make herself clean and perfect inside since God's congregation must be spotless. Test yourself before you take this step, for your faith must create virtue, knowledge, modesty, meekness, godliness, and neighbourly love. Please examine yourself to see if you can meet those standards. In another song on the occasion of Guiert's marriage, she shows more personal concern: she regrets the fact that Guiert will not be around anymore. She remembers how they used to chat all night long and how they dreamed about their futures. She begs Guiert not to neglect their friendship and she prays to the Lord to make both of them fertile in their own ways. Love your husband and be submissive to him, she concludes, but please, my heartloving companion, never leave me completely.[38] More details could be given,[39] but I point to only one other aspect of her teachings: the frequently emphasized urge to read and sing, a message meant particularly for women, although once she also warns not to pretend religiousness by simple would-be reading. In that case they will be subject to mockery–a social aspect the world-shunning Mennonites, especially the Mennonite sisters, had to live with.[40]

Generally speaking, Soetjen Gerrits also dealt with the same ethical and religious topics, in a similar admonishing vocabulary, which is not surprising since most of the wording of spiritual, or scriptural, songs was derived directly from the Bible. In Soetjen's case, however, writing in what we call *de tale Kanaäns* [the language of Canaan], must have meant that she knew large parts of the Bible by heart.[41] In order to avoid repetition, I will look at some other characteristics of Soetjen's poetry. Her main concerns can be distinguished, as follows:

a. The first deals with the status of the newly born Christian who, after the healing process of rebirth, focuses on the spiritual benefits of the bride of Christ, or the inhabitants of Zion, or the New Jerusalem.[42] Closely linked with this theme is the congregation without spot or wrinkle, because the bride of the Lamb is immaculate. Since Christ chose his bride, he is watchful for her weaknesses–in that context she asks rhetorically: who would dare to put up a wife against her husband?[43]

b. Another theme is the suffering of the little flock in this world, particularly applied to the situation of martyrdom and persecution of her contemporaries. Rather touching is a song of comfort she sent to an anonymous brother who was in jail in Amsterdam. Again, one is astonished by her knowledge of the Bible. Since I have referred to this theme earlier in my introduction of Soetjen, I will leave this topic here.[44]

c. The next theme suits the main focus of this book–the respective roles and the relationship between man and wife. Since Soetjen is very outspoken about the position of the single woman, that aspect will be treated as a separate, fourth theme. Considering the position of man and wife, her starting point is religious equality, based on the Mennonite principle of the priesthood of all believers. She expresses this principle time and again in the equal vocation of both men and women, which implies for each gender, however, different relational and social obligations. So, for instance, in a song that she wrote for her second home town congregation of Hoorn, she says that husbands must love their wives and they are in charge of the domestic affairs; the wife should be as submissive as Sara, since management tasks are unworthy of a woman. (This might be considered a warning against the social phenomenon of docile husbands who were ridiculed for being dominated by their wives.[45]) Keep your house clean, be careful, gentle, and chaste; husbands must show you respect. Within the limits of the biblicistic marital concept, Soetjen promotes a type of companionship in marriage.[46] Equally traditional are her views about raising children, which is the responsibility of both parents. In one song, however, intended for young girls, she warns them not to follow a spiritually blinded father as their educational example: some of them even go crazy and are abusive–did Soetjen consider carnal men to be the weaker vessels?[47]

    d. To be honest, I do not think so, yet she cherished a particular feminine look at single women, which constitutes the fourth theme. She is explicit about this in at least six hymns, all intended for unmarried women. The most instructive is song nr. 63, a "Mercy and peace" hymn, which also refers to her personal situation. It deals with the chosen people of God who follow the footsteps of the Lamb. Leave the world, she exclaims, and follow your vocation. Women, especially, must be a light in the world–also a much-applied metaphor by the blind poet, emphasizing the brightness and clear sight once reborn and living in the spirit. Let there be no unchastity. Then comes the nucleus: the woman who marries does not sin, although many dangers will threaten her. Therefore, the best thing is to remain "uncoupled," single. This condition offers you the tranquility for prayer and devotion, unharmed by lust. I can witness for myself, she continues, that you should not underestimate this position: the divine cares and sorrows are manifold.[48] In another place she adds that being single, as in her case, offers the best opportunity to serve God and to stay holy in body and soul–this is what she calls her leisure. Besides, there is also the practical benefit: a one-member family does not cost much; its consumption pattern is very sober.[49] This particular esteem for the single religious woman is strongly reminiscent of the status of the Catholic *beguine* or "holy maiden," and has so far remained almost unnoticed in Mennonite historiography.[50] Only once does she suggest that being solitary might concern both men and women.[51] However, this vision–in my opinion a Catholic remnant–must have had some theological affinity with Dutch Mennonite orthodoxy as well, although it is nowhere explicitly expressed. Nevertheless, one might consider it to be a positive derivative from rather negatively formulated theories that were developed in defence of a much-questioned phenomenon of Mennonite orthodoxy–marital avoidance. Soetjen's Old Frisian Mennonites, in particular, held against all odds that the spiritual bond with Christ, called heavenly matrimony, exceeded all family ties and therefore legitimized a divorce for the sake of the spotless church.[52] This is confirmed by another song by Soetjen: "Christ is the Head and we are his body; we unworthy people are his Bride and wife, be aware of this: praise men or women who remain loyal to this marriage–this goes beyond the earthly marriage".[53] Besides, being a genuine biblicist Mennonite, Soetjen found immediate testimony of this in Paul's first letter to the Corinthians, chapter 7, from which we can trace many echoes in her hymns:

> But if you marry, you do not sin, and if a girl marries she does not sin. Yet those who marry will have worldly troubles, and I would

spare you that (verse 28).
But whoever is firmly established in his heart, being under no necessity but having his desire under control, and has determined this in his heart, to keep her as his betrothed, he will do well. So that he who marries his betrothed does well; and he who refrains from marriage will do better (verses 37-38).

Conclusion
In summary it may be said that without question the spiritual poetry of both Vrou and Soetjen Gerrits completely matches the traditional Mennonite concept of marriage and its implicit and explicit roles of women. At the same time, my evaluation of the position of Mennonite women in this generally male-dominated era remains positive, although their place in the religious and social scene was less pronounced, or at least different, than it was during the days of earlier radical Anabaptism and persecution. I would therefore like to modify Adela Torchia's provocative conclusion that only men built bridges and women eyed tomatoes. At least the activity of these two women shows self-conscious aspects of an admittedly mainly hidden culture of Mennonite everyday life. Nevertheless, those activities go beyond women's mostly unrecorded efforts to live a life of simple discipleship. Their contributions have not gone unnoticed in history's annals.[54] Some fragments of such female self-awareness and activity–though role conditioned, I admit once more–is reflected in the culture of literary exchange of letters and songs among Mennonite women. And a similar awareness is reflected by the lyrics of Soetjen Gerrits, who also mastered her physical and gender disadvantages–I doubt that she would ever have considered herself in those terms, but that may be our own twentieth-century-prejudiced handicap–by creating and promoting a specific, positive role as a single woman who was, above all, talented enough to comfort and admonish not only women, but also men. I refuse to qualify this as a simple peeling of tomatoes, but rather consider it building bridges between both sexes. The general appreciation of the work of these two women is confirmed by the reprints that were to follow: Soetjen Gerrits's hymnbook was reprinted in at least 1610, 1618, and 1632, whereas other editions of Vrou Gerrits's hymnbook appeared in 1609, 1621, and 1627.[55]

To counter my overall positive image, some critical mind might suggest that the publishers, the editors, and promoters of these hymnbooks in the first half of the seventeenth century, who were all men and mainly orthodox Frisian Mennonites, used (or should I say, abused) these female role models to oppress their sexual counterparts even more. To encourage this suspicion a bit more I give you some quotes from a hymnbook by Pieter Jansz Twisck, for decades the leader of the Old Frisians, and most likely one of the initiators in publishing both women's books. This may reveal a Mennonite macho view of some representatives of the other sex. In a song that begins with "Praise him, who has married a virtuous wife," he contrasts the Mennonite sister with a virago. The first is a pearl in a man's crown, but the other:

> Woe to him, who has a cross-grained wife full of vice, from whom the man shrinks in fear, because she leads a quarrelsome and evil life, who is wrathful, false and sour, unfriendly and mean. In that case it is preferable rather to live in a closet in a rough desert than with her in the same house. . . . Such a wife, poisoned with quarrel, discord and fighting is as tiresome as a dripping roof.[56]

I leave the suggestion completely to the reader's judgement–even dripping roofs give shelter, although Soetjen and Vrou Gerrits preferred to maintain and to promote their well-respected Mennonite-Madonna-like dryness.

Notes

1 *Offer des Heeren*, ed. S. Cramer, *Bibliotheca Reformatoria Neerlandica* (Gravenhage: Martinus Nijhoff, 1904), II, 581-86 (585):
Sy gingen twee Maechden pijnen
Luttel hadden de Tyrannen acht
Dat wy alle in smerte verschijnen
Door vrouwen voort worden gebracht
Van dees natuerlijck experiency
Hebben sy geen redelijckheyt geleert
Sy maken daer af cleyn mency
Dus zijn sy tyrannich verkeert.
2 Ineke van 't Spijker, "Mijn beminde huysvrouwe in de Heere.' Doperse vrouwen in de vroege Reformatie in de Nederlanden," in *Doopsgezinde Bijdragen* 11(1985): 99-108; Keith L. Sprunger, "God's Powerful Army of the Weak: Anabaptist Women of the Radical Reformation," in Richard L. Greaves, ed. *Triumph over Silence: Women in Protestant History* (Connecticut: Greenwood Press, 1985), 45-74; John Klassen, "Women and the Family among Dutch Anabaptist Martyrs," in MQR 60 (1986): 548-71; M. Lucille Marr, "Anabaptist Women of the North: Peers in the Faith, Subordinates in Marriage," in MQR 61 (1987): 347-62; Auke Jelsma, "De positie van de vrouw in de Radicale Reformatie," in *Doopsgezinde Bijdragen* 15 (1989): 25-36; Adela D. Torchia, "Purity and Perseverance: Menno Simons' Understanding of Practical Holiness and Early Anabaptist Women," in *Journal of Mennonite Studies* 12 (1994): 26-44. Marion Kobelt-Groch takes a different approach in dealing with Dutch Anabaptist women in *Aufsässige Töchter Gottes: Frauen im Bauernkrieg und in den Täuferbewegungen* (Frankfurt, Germany and New York: Campus Verlag, 1993).
3 Klassen, "Women and the Family," 559, 571; see the comments of Lucille Marr, "Anabaptist Women of the North," 348-53.
4 Lucille Marr, "Anabaptist Women of the North," 355-58; Jelsma, "Vrouwen in de Radicale Reformatie," 34; Sprunger, "God's Powerful Army," 57-58.

5 Piet Visser, "Aspects of social criticism and cultural assimilation: The Mennonite image in literature and self-criticism of literary Mennonites," in A. Hamilton, et al., eds., *From Martyr to Muppy: A historical introduction to cultural assimilation processes of a religious minority in the Netherlands: The Mennonites* (Amsterdam: Amsterdam University Press, 1994), 78-79.
6 Marshall, "Protestant, Catholic, and Jewish Women," 125; Jelsma, "Vrouwen in de Radicale Reformatie," 26; A. Agnes Sneller, "Reading Jacob Cats," in Els Kloek et al., eds., *Women of the Golden Age: An International Debate on Women in the Seventeenth Century Holland, England and Italy* (Hilversum: Verloren, 1994), 33-34, criticizes historians like Schama and Van Deursen for their limited perspective on women, considering them only in relation to men within the marital relationship: "The housewife as the female part of the married couple, the hussy as a slut" (on Schama); "Unmarried women do not form part of the author's conceptual system" (on Van Deursen). In Sneller's case those conceptual restrictions leave out independent women like Anna Maria van Schurman or Tesselschade Roemersdochter, both noted for their talents and influence in various domains of Dutch culture of the Golden Age. It should be noted that this observation is not limited only to feminist studies of the last two decades. Already in 1927 Johanna W. Naber dealt with the topic: *Vrouwenleven in Prae-Reformatietijd bezegeld door de marteldood van Wendelmoet Claesdochter* ('s-Gravenhage: Martinus Nijhoff, 1927).
7 Sprunger, "God's Powerful Army," 53-54; ME II, 185; see footnote 11 for more details.
8 Jelsma, "Vrouwen in de Radicale Reformatie," 27-28, 31-33; cf. Sprunger, "God's Powerful Army," 58-59, who points out this phenomenon, although in a far less pronounced way: "The educational level of the wife helped to determine her ability to participate in family and church." Jelsma, 27, tells a marvellous story demonstrating the great magic and power of control over the new medium by women, which at the same time was considered to be a great risk for the Counter Reformation forces. During the early Reformation period, a woman at Maastricht purchased some Protestant books on the street although she was illiterate. The bookseller took her home and taught her the art of reading within a few hours. When she came home her husband asked where she had been. She answered: "I have learned to read and now I know everything." The man was furious and warned the local priest. He made the woman confess and, so the story goes, after receiving absolution "she had completely lost knowledge of all letters."
9 Jelsma, ibid., 30.
10 Such as Maeyken Bosers (1564); Maeyken de Corte (1559); Maeyken Deynoots (1571); Lysken Dircks (1572); Janneken van Munstdorp (1573); Maeyken Wens (1573); Maeyken Wouters (1595). See their entries in ME for more details.
11 See, for Anneken Jans (1539), ME I, 126; Sprunger, "God's Powerful Army," 51; Gary K. Waite, *David Joris and Dutch Anabaptism 1524-1543* (Waterloo, ON: Wilfrid Laurier University Press, 1990), 68-70. For Soetken van den Houte: ME IV, 570; Janneken van Aken (or van Houtte): ME III, 87-88; Elisabeth Dirks: ME II, 185, in which Neff states that her song in *Sommige Stichtelycke Liedekens* (Hoorn, 1618) has not yet been identified, although it was listed by S. Blaupot ten Cate, *Geschiedenis der Doopsgezinden in Holland, Zeeland, Utrecht en Gelderland* (Amsterdam: P.N. van Kampen, 1847) II, 211. It is in fact to be found in the second appendix to Soetjen Gerrits's *Een geestelijck Liedt-boecxken, inhoudende veele stichtelijcke Liedekens,* (Hoorn: Zacharias Cornelisz; Amsterdam: Abraham Biestkens, 1618), extant in only one copy (University Library of Amsterdam, shelfmark Muz: 262) under the heading: "Hier volghen ses stichtelijcke Liedekens, by diversche persoonen ghemaeckt" [Here follow six edifying songs written by several persons], p. A1^r. It is the first hymn and begins

with: "De Heere die my heeft verkooren // Tot zijn Bruyt van der eeuwicheyt" [The Lord has elected me to be his eternal Bride]. It is rhymed to the popular melody of "Mijn Siele looft den Heere" (see F.C. Wieder, *Schriftuurlijke Liedekens. De Liederen der Nederlandsche Hervormden tot op het jaar 1566* ('s-Gravenhage: Martinus Nijhoff, 1900), nrs. 564 or 565. The introduction suggests that Elisabeth was its author: "Dit naevolghende Liedeken is van handt tot handt bewaert, en tot ons ghebracht, is wat herstelt, ende wort gheseyt eerst ghemaeckt te zijn, van Elizabeth die te Leeuwarden om't Woordt des Heeren verdroncken is, Anno 1549, de 27 Martij. Waer van ghy meucht lesen in de History der vromer Ghetuyghen Jesu Christi, ghedruckt Anno 1617 voor Zacharias Cornelisz in de Liesveltsche Bybel, tot Hoorn." [The following song passed from hand to hand and finally was brought to us; it has been corrected at some places and it is said that initially it was written by Elizabeth who was drowned at Leeuwarden for the sake of the Word of the Lord in the year 1549, March 27 (i.e., May 27). You may read about this in the (martyr book) *History der vromer Ghetuyghen Jesu Christi*, printed in the year 1617 for Zacharias Cornelisz (whose shop was named) in the Liesvelt Bible, at Hoorn]. The song is completely biographical and matches the story of Elisabeth's life which is to be found in van Braght's *Martyrs' Mirror*, 546-47. Cf. Cramer, *Het Offer des Heeren*, 91, footnote 1. Cramer did not know this song either. She must have written it after her escape from the convent near Leer in East Friesland and before her capture at Leeuwarden on January 15, 1549.

12 Sprunger, "God's Powerful Army," 67-68, referring to the Anabaptist "nuptial or bridal theology" as identified by G.H. Williams.

13 Pieter Jansz Twisck, *Kleyn-Liedt-Boecxken* (Hoorn: Zacharias Cornelisz, 1633), 66-68: "U borsten zijn lieflijcker dan wijn, / Oude ende Nieuwe Testament fijn." See for Twisck: ME IV, 757-59. The hymn had a suitable profane tune: "De schoone die my marteliseert" [The beauty-queen who torches me].

14 In early Dutch Mennonite hymnody, there is abundant proof of the general use of these metaphors. See, for instance, the many songs about New Jerusalem, Zion, or the daughters of Israel in a popular hymnbook like *Veelderhande Liedekens* (I quote from the 1559 edition). As an example I summarize the hymn "O Syon wtgelesen" [Oh elected Sion] (S6^v,; Wieder, *Schriftuurlijke Liedekens* nr. 759 and p. 23), in which the bride (the congregation) is summoned to cleanse herself, to put on the dress of justice, to adorn the body with the chain of piety, the ring of true faith and the gold of God's Word. The imagery of bride and bridegroom from the Song of Solomon is also generally applied. See, for more examples, Wieder nrs. 23, 83, 235, 280, 417, 633, 701, 704, 739, 758-61, etc. and his comments on pp. 49-52.

15 It is found in the 1638 edition of Soetjen Gerrits's *Geestelijck Liedt-boecxken*, in the first appendix with the separate title *Sommighe Stichtelijcke Liedekens, By diverse persoonen gemaeckt* (Hoorn: Zacharias Cornelisz; Haarlem: Thomas Fonteyn, 1632), nr. 38, pp. 122-24.

Naer dat ick hebbe ghelesen
Dat Vrouwen verheven zijn,
En boven al ghepresen,
Verstaet de woorden mijn.
Daerom moet ickse boven al
Prijsen soomen hooren sal,
Hier in dit vrolijck Liet,
So wie dit wel in siet.
 Een Vrouwe die in deuchden,
En oock in wijsheydt leeft,

Maeckt haren Man vol vreuchden,
So ons de Schrift uytgheeft:
Sy doet haren Man verblijden saen,
Als hem cont eenigh lijden aen,
Want door haer woorden soet,
So krijght hij eenen moet.
De wijsheydt van een Vrouwe,
Is wel te prijsen schoon,
Want in s'Werelts Landouwe,
So spannen sy de kroon:

16 The best information on Soetjen Gerrits is supplied by *Nieuw Nederlandsch Biographisch Woordenboek* (Leiden: A.W. Sijthoff's Uitgevers-maatschappij, 1924) VI, l. pp. 576-77; see ibid., l. p. 577 for Vrou Gerrits. For Soetjen's hymnbook see Bert Hofman, *Liedekens vol gheestich confoort. Een bijdrage tot de kennis van de zestiende-eeuwse Schriftuurlijke lyriek* (Hilversum: Verloren, 1993), 242-43 and W.A.P. Smit, *Dichters der Reformatie in de zestiende eeuw* (Groningen-Batavia: J.B. Wolters, 1939), 74-76. For Vrou Gerrits's hymnbook see Piet Visser, *Het lied dat nooit verstomde. Vier eeuwen doopsgezinde liedboekjes* (Den Ilp, 1988), 30. The information in ME, II, 502 is inaccurate. Van der Zijpp states that Vrou Gerrits "was erroneously considered the author of a small songbook, *Een nieu Gheestelijck Liedtboecxken*, of which there were three editions–1607, 1609, and 1621." In ME, IV, 570, van der Zijpp notes: "under the heading of Soetken Gerrits, Karel Vos confused Vrou Gerrets van Medenblick with Soetken Gerrits of Rotterdam. The article "Gerrets, Vrou, van Medenblick" (ME II, 502) is therefore in error." Vos created this error in *Mennonitisches Lexikon* (Frankfurt am Main: Weierhof, 1937) II, 84.

17 *Geestelijck Liedt-boecxken* (hereafter: SG, GL), nr. 75, p. R7^r: "Hoort, ick sal u verclaren / Wat in Hollandt is gheschiet / In den voorleden Jaren / Achtentveertich tot vijftich toe, siet" [Listen to what I tell you about what happened in Holland in the former years of 48 to 50]. It deals with two brothers, Quirijn and Huigh Joris from Delfshaven, who were beheaded in Delft in 1550. Cf. ME II, 30 and 837 where it is said that nothing else of these martyrs is known, apart from a statement by the sheriff of Delft. This song contains more details.

18 SG, GL, nr. 19, p. E5^r: "Een nieuwe Liedt wilt hooren / Wat te Rotterdam is gheschiet." She must have written the song when she was elsewhere; see, for instance, the third stanza: "Ick was met mijner herten / Met haer nae den Gheest verblijt" [With my heart I rejoiced with them spiritually]. This was a remarkable event, since the execution of Jan Hendricksz from Utrecht and two other men and two women was not carried out: the crowd of spectators were so offended by the slow and horrible progress that they violently freed the victims. See ME III, 76. Although Soetjen gives thanks for the lives of the liberated victims she also disapproves of the violence that was used to set them free.

19 Some echo of this sudden departure is found in SG, GL hymn nr. 36, I3^v, in which she confesses not to be in the mood to sing so shortly after "ons groot ellenden," our great misery. She comforts the ones who stayed behind to persist in their faith.

20 SG, GL, p. A2^{r-v}: "wat hy [God] al door den kleynen ende ootmoedigen heeft wille uytrechten, die in hem betrouwen ende gelooven ... Alsoo heeft ... God oock nu in onsen tijden groot wonder gewrocht, ende zijn genade betoont door een Vrou-persoon, de welcke blint geweest is, ende haer leven noyt letter en konde lesen, ofte *a* van de *b* heeft konnen scheyden, nochtans heeftse God met hoogh ende wondelijck verstant verlicht, ende begaeft in zijn Heylighe woort ende ghenade-rijcke Euangelium, als ghy in alle

klaricheyt kont verstaen ende mercken aen dese navolghende Liedekens." The editor is known only by the initials I.C., which stand most likely for Jan Cornelisz from Alkmaar. He composed a hymnbook, *Een Nieu Schriftuerlijck Liedt-boecxken, 't welck noyt in druck en is gheweest, ghemaeckt uyt den Ouden ende Nieuwen Testamente: Met noch twee Christelijcke Sendtbrieven, gemaeckt door den selven Autheur, ghenaemt I.C. van Alckmaer* (Hoorn: Zacharias Cornelisz, 1615). Although his name Jan Cornelisz is nowhere to be found in full, it was most likely his, since two of his hymns were dedicated to his brother "Jacob Cornelisz. Koeckebacker tot Alckmaer" (73 and 129). Apart from "Jacob" the most obvious other *J* in Dutch would be "Jan." There is no accurate information about him (cf. ME I, 36); the only fact of life revealed in his hymnbook is the acrostic referring to his marriage with Vrou Jansdochter in 1592 (76).

21 This is stated in the introduction of the first edition of SL, *GL*, p. A2^r, although the book contains in fact 104 hymns: 102 numbered songs and two songs appended after the index. The second edition of 1618 corrected the contents to 98 songs. Left out are songs nr. 8, "Beminde laet u niet beroouen" (B6^r), nr. 11 "Crijchsluyden cloeck' van aerde" (C5^r), nr. 15 "Den Winter is vergangen" (D5^v), nr. 48 "Ghenade ende vrede" (L8^v) and nr. 71 "Ghy Memelijckers met namen" (R1^r); the two appended songs were considered not to be her compositions. One hymn was added in the 1618 edition: nr. 77 "Hoort, lieve vrienden, al ghemeyn" (246). All the noncanonical Soetjen songs were included in the appended hymnbook: *Stichtelijcke Liedekens, By diverse Persoonen gemaeckt* (Hoorn: Zacharias Cornelisz, 1618).

22 Smit, *Dichters der Reformatie*, 75: "Thus it is understandable that Zoetjen Gerrits gradually assumed an air of holiness and was considered to be a mother in Israel also outside her immediate circle. People appreciated her opinion and advice; they accepted her admonitions as spoken in the name of God" [Zo wordt het verklaarbaar, dat Zoetjen Gerrits langzamerhand in een geur van heiligheid kwam te staan en ook buiten haar onmiddellijke kring beschouwd werd als een moeder in Israel. Men stelde prijs op haar oordeel en haar raad, men aanvaardde haar vermaningen als uitgesproken in de naam van God].

23 Hofman, *Liedekens vol gheestich confoort*, 243, footnote 316, lists 35 hymns in various editions of the *Veelderhande Liedekens*: 6 in VL 1556, 2 in *Veelderhande Gheestelijcke Liedekens* (1558), 10 in VL 1559, 19 in VL 66 [I counted 14], 11 in *Nieu Liedenboeck* (1562), 1 in VL 1569, 1 in VL 1582 and 3 in NL 1583. Some of these hymnbooks were not typically Mennonite, but in use by the Dutch Reformed. Hofman considers the period 1559-1562 to be her most productive years. In his listing of the contents of the *Veelderhande Liedekens* (1559), 345, Bijlage III, he omits Soetjen's hymn "Aenhoort een Liedt ghy Adams saet" (p. A7^v), which already was printed in the earlier 1556 edition. It also is found in *Gheestelijcke Liedekens* (1563), 12^r and *Schriftuerlicke Liedekens* (1580), 17^v, which also has "O Mensch aenhoort, des Heeren woort" (cf. Hofman resp. 358, nr. 13; [365, nr. 13, and 360, nr. 232). I reproduce Hofman's 1993 findings presuming that the 6 hymns of Soetjen Gerrits in *Veelderhande Liedekens* 1556 already were present in the recently discovered *Veelderhande schriftuerlijcke Liedekens* edition of 1552-54. See E. Hofman, "De Antwerpse drukker Frans Fraet en de verhouding tussen de vroegste gereformeerde en doopsgezinde liedboeken," in *Doopsgezinde Bijdragen* 20 (1994), 79.

24 Vrou Gerrits, *Nieu Gheestelijck Liedtboecxken* (Enkhuizen: Jaspar Tournay, 1607) (hereafter VG, *GL*), A3^v: "Dese jonghe Dochter Vrou Gerrits, heeft haer van jonghs op in de heylighe Schrift gheoeffent, alsoo dat sy begon Schriftuerlijcke Liedekens te dichten, doen sy derthien Jaer oudt was, ende heeft gheleeft tot vijfentwintich Jaer toe, ende is inden Heer ontslapen, ende heeft die Jeucht een goet exempel nagelaten."

25 Ibid, 193: "Een cort verhael, hoe dat het eynde, van Vrou Gerrets dochter gheweest is, ghelijck als sy van jongs op, Godt ghevreest heeft, ende in sijn gheboden ghewandelt, nae haer swackheydt, ende in liefde ende vrede met den Godtvruchtighen verkeert, ende heeft na Syrachs woort eenen goeden naem achterghelaten, end' is met een vrolijck gemoet, ende een geruste consciency, ende met een verlanghen, inden Heer ontslapen op Tessel, den 6. September, Anno 1605." [A short story about the end of Vrou Gerrits's daughter, who from her early days on feared God and walked in his commandments despite her weakness, and who had been lovingly and peacefully in the company of godfearing people; she left behind, as Syrach says, a good name, and died with a joyful mind and a conscience at ease and in great desire for the Lord on [the island of] Texel, on September 6, 1605.]

26 A good survey is offered by Louis P. Grijp, "A Different flavour in a psalm-minded setting: Dutch Mennonite hymns from the sixteenth and seventeenth centuries," in A. Hamilton, et al, eds., *From Martyr to Muppy: A Historical Introduction to Cultural Assimilation Processes of a Religious Minority in the Netherlands: The Mennonites* (Amsterdam: Amsterdam University Press, 1994), 110-23, esp. 114-16 and 123 for more literature.

27 Visser, *Het lied dat nooit verstomde*, 18-19.

28 The first edition of SG, GL has only one acrostichon, p. B6^r, nr. 6, revealing the name of "Bertraet van Sebenberghen," but this one was left out in the later 1618 and 1632 editions. One other technique, the use of a great variety of rhyme, even twice in one line, was applied once, in song nr. 82, p. T2^v : "Ick heb bedacht, een Liedt volbracht / Adams geslacht, is boos, dit acht" [I invented a song, Adam's descendants are angry, watch out], but this was in fact dictated by the original secular text of the melody she used: "Bedrijft jolijt, in's Weerelts tijdt" [Enjoy yourself during life on earth]. This song also has a "Prince," a formal dedication in the final stanza, originally intended to salute the prince, the chairman, of the Chamber of Rhetoric. Another "Prince" is to be found in song nr. 91, p. V8^r, "O Christen Broeders jent" [My sweet Fellow Christians]. Yet another rhetorician's technique was the so-called "stokregel": a final repeating line of each stanza, functioning like a refrain. Soetken used it for songs nr. 61, 68, 81, 95 and 99, but again this was most likely matrixed by the contrafact melody–in her case something that she knew by memory.

29 Acrostichons in VG, GL are to be found on p. 1, Aen Goertgen Allersdochter, p. 10, Aen Siberich Cornelisdochter, p. 19, Aelidt Heydrings Dochter, p. 69, Gwiert Pieters; p. 78, Geert Vechtersdochter; p. 104, Jan Volkertsoon; p. 120, Maretgen Ians Ende Anna I Dochters; p. 124, Martghe Iant[=s]dochter vvt (most likely unfinished, since the 'vvt' [= from] suggests to be followed by the name of a town, most likely Alkmaar); p. 125, Maritgen Dirccsdochter; p. 126, Maritgen Feeddesdochter; p. 130, Neel Cornelis, Triin Feddes, Mari Reiners, Triin Jansdochter, Mari Heindricks, Aerjan Kempesdochter, Vrou Gerrits, Guiert Pieters, Maritgen Feddes, dochters int ghemeyn.

30 At least 35 different full names and initials can be detected in or above her songs, all living in nearby towns and villages, the great majority of whom are women: at Amsterdam (Jan Folckertsz and his wife), Alkmaar (Anna Jans, Goortgen Allers, Maertgen Jans), Hoorn (Dieuwer Ariaens, Jan Pietersz Twisck, Marritgen Dircksdochter and some five women identified only by their initials), Medemblik (Aef Symons, Aerjan Kempesdochter, Allet Symons, Guiert Pieters, Jan Jansz, Mari Heindricks, Mari Reiners, Nel Cornelis, Trijn Feddes, Trijn Jans); the island of Wieringen (Aellet Heyndricks, Griet Cornelis); without residence: Geert Vechtersdochter, Heyndrick Dircksz and Siberich Cornelisdochter.

31 This phenomenon is easy to detect since most hymns generally have some kind of dedication, or greeting, in the first stanza, like: "Broeders ende Susters" [Brothers and Sisters], "Ghy Christen alle" [All you Christians], or "mijn lieve Suster in de Heer" [My dear Sister in the Lord]. The dedications of both women fall into five distinguishing categories, which can be specified as follows. Soetjen dedicated 17 percent of her hymns to both Brothers and Sisters–Vrou 10 percent; Soetjen 23 percent to Brothers only–Vrou 19 percent; Soetjen 18 percent to Sisters only–Vrou 50 percent; Soetjen 9 percent to the youth–Vrou 15 percent; Soetjen 33 percent without any specification–Vrou only 6 percent.

32 Hofman, *Liedekens vol gheestich confoort*, 243; 38 hymns have this type of incipit, for instance: "Ghenade ende vrede / Wensch ick Gods kinderen nu" [Mercy and peace I wish for you, God's children], or "Ghenade, vrede, wensch ick u / Mijn Suster, in den Heere" [Mercy, peace I wish to you my sister in the Lord]. A second favourite beginning (11 times) is "Een liedt wil ick beginnen" [I will start a song] or something similar, a type which is more often found in 16th century hymnbooks.

33 Soetjen composed songs for Jan Willemsz at Hoorn, song nr. 13, p. D1^r: "Den Broeder die my sandt / Een brief, wensch ick veel gracy" [To the Brother who sent me a letter, I wish him much grace]; to Thijs Gerritszoon and his wife, an elder also at Hoorn, nr. 42, p. K6^r, and nr. 100, p. Y7^r (his name was added to both songs in the 1618 and 1632 editions); and to Huyte Rijnnicx, an elder at Bolsward in Friesland, nr 70, p. Q7^r.

34 SG, *GL*, nr. 100, p. Y7^r, and likewise in hymn nr. 13, p. D1^r, for the Hoorn preacher Jan Willemsz at the end of which she states: "Weet dat ick noyt en las" [Be aware that I have never ever read]. In another song there is a reference to her physical blindness, hymn nr. 97, p. Y1^v in the line that she had "*heard* reading about Isaac."

35 This was a general practice, in particular in the first half of the seventeenth century. Several hymnbooks from different denominations contain abundant proof of this kind of send-me-a-song practice, for instance the *Groote Liede-Boeck* (1604) of the High German Mennonite elder Leenaert Clock from Haarlem, containing no less than 398 acrostichons; or the Waterlander Mennonite *Ryper Liedtboecxken* (1624-37), which also has several references to meetings of adolescents from various congregations. Visser, *Het Lied dat nooit verstomde*, 29 and 31; see also Piet Visser, *Broeders in de geest. De doopsgezinde bijdragen van Dierick en Jan Philipsz Schabaelje tot de Nederlandse stichtelijke literatuur in de zeventiende eeuw* (Deventer: Sub Rosa, 1988), I, 229-30.

36 One such letter is appended to her hymns, VG, *GL*, p. 180, intended for "haer Maets tot Medemblick," her friends at Medemblik: "die so crachteloos ja so cranck ende swack van vermeughen zijn, om malcanderen stadich met schrijven, met vermanen, ende met onderwijsinghe te dienen." The copy of the Mennonite Library in Amsterdam, shelf mark OK 65-310, has another letter in manuscript to some unknown female friends which is very instructive for the way those young women communicated. Hoewever, also in this case any personal confidence is almost completely absent: "I send you this humble poem and simple song trusting that you will receive it in gratitude; I also hope to receive something better in return in order, living far apart, not to completely forget one and other, but by means of letters inform each other every now and then how we are feeling both spiritually and physically." [vL dit sempel gedicht ende slechte lijedeken te senden vertrouwende dat het in danck sal ontfanghen worden ende verhoope oock voor dit wat beters van v te verwachten . . . op dat hoewel wij veer verscheijden woonen malcanderen niet gans en verghetten maer duer schrijuen somtijts eens laten weten hoe het met ons naden gheest ende vleijs al staet].

37 VG, *GL*, p. 55: "Een sterck gheloove crachtich / Wensch ick tot allen tijt" [A strong, pertinent faith is what I wish forever]. Her age is given in the last stanza.

38 Ibid., the first hymn on p. 69: "Ghy hebt voor u ghenomen / Na des Schrifts regel claer" [You have decided (to live) according the rule of Scripture]; the second one at p. 26: "Deur goede conversacy / Die wy hebben gehadt" [Since we had good conversation]; the book contains four more hymns dedicated to Guiert Pieters from Medemblik: pp. 74, 130, 147, and 159.

39 For instance the various references to quarrels among members of the congregation, so typical for the time [p. 60, "Satan is everywhere, even I am quarrelsome"]; pp. 89, and 141 in which she regrets that four friends are reluctant to enter membership now that the congregation is in disagreement.

40 Ibid., 130: read and sing, keep gathering and study the Bible; p. 120 which has the warning against societal critique. This refers to the criticism of Mennonite hypocrisy which was rather evident in Dutch culture. See Visser, "Aspects of social criticism," 76-78.

41 See, for instance, SG, *GL* nr. 78, p. S4^r: "Hoort vrienden, tot des Heeren lof" [Listen friends, in praise of the Lord], which admonishes about singing to the Lord and the attitude of humility. The text is loaded with Bible quotations such as James 5:13, Ephes. 5:19 and Colos. 3:19. This also points to another phenomenon of Mennonite hymnody: the Bible annotations which are to be found in the margins of almost every Mennonite hymnbook: Grijp, "A different flavor in a psalm-minded setting," 111-12. Soetjen, of course, was unable to add those annotations herself-therefore the editor has done the job which is specified in a post scriptum (p. Aa4^r). See also Hofman, *Liederen vol gheestich conforrt*, 285-303, esp. 299, where the post scriptum is cited.

42 See for instance SG, *GL* song nrs. 2, 12, 14, 16, 18, 48, 77, and 101.

43 SG, *GL* nr. 80, p. S7^v, stanza 8: "Een heerlijcke onbevleckte Ghemeent / Is de Bruydt des Lams verkoren" [A lovely immaculate congregation is the chosen bride of the Lamb]; nr. 53, p. M8^v, stanza 4 and 7: "Want Christus ons gekocht heeft, hoort, / Ghebaert al met zijn Gheest end' Woort / Tot zijne Bruydt . . . Of yemandt een mans vrou wou raen / Al teghens hem, waer't wel ghedaen?" [Christ has bought us, listen, gave birth to us with his Spirit and his Word, being his bride. . . . Whoever dares to advise a husband's spouse to act against him—would that make sense?]. Hymns dealing with hot items like banning and shunning are nrs. 66, 67, 76 and 89. In nr. 89 (p. V4^r) she is rather cynical about abusing the Bible for the sake of forcing splits.

44 See SG, *GL* nrs. 3, 5, 9, 10, 20, 27 (the song to the Amsterdam martyr), 40, 44, 45, 94 and 96.

45 At least in the early seventeenth century it became a humorous theme which is to be found in several literary products, like the poems of the famous Calvinist poet Cats and the playwright Bredero's *Farce of the Miller*. See Sneller, "Images of Seventeenth-century Women," 32-33 and Giesela van Oostveen, "It takes all sorts to make a world. Sex and gender in Bredero's *Farce of the Miller*," in Els Kloek et al., eds., *Women of the Golden Age. An International Debate on Women in the Seventeenth-century Holland, England and Italy* (Hilversum, Verloren, 1994), 55-64.

46 SG, *GL* nr. 35, I1^v; see also nrs. 58, 62 and 64 in which she comforts a woman who will set sail with her husband: as long as you cling to the Law of God you do not need to worry at all—without danger you may live "dry" for a whole year, i.e., without attending church services.

47 SG, *GL* nr. 97, p. Y1^v: 'Ontfanckt een nieu Liedeken soet / Maechdekens jonck van Jaren' [Receive a new sweet song, girls of young age], stanza 12:
Een Vader die noch is verblint,
Die leydt zijn kindt ter Hellen,
De sommighe zijn haest gram ghesint,

Dat sy haer wreet aenstellen,
En gaen nae dat verdoemen toe,
Hoe wel gheschiet haer, soo ick bevroe,
Die hier op worden ghevoedt in't goe.

A Father who is blinded
Directs his child to Hell
Some are even so ill-tempered
That they act brutally
Ending up in damnation
I think, how lucky are they
Who are being well-educated.

48 SG, *GL* nr. 63, P1ᵥ, stanza 11 and 12:
Sy en sondighen niet, die trouwen,
Wie dat in den Heer' vergaert,
Haer naeckt wel veel benouwen
Die den Echten staet aenvaert,
Het is beter onghepaert,
Soo haer Paulus verclaert,
Die hy gheerne hadde ghespaert.
 Niet dat sy in wellusten
Souden zijn levendich doot,
Maer wesen alleen in rusten,
Om te bidden, met minst aenstoot,
Godtlijcke sorghe groot
Comt haer toe, dat weet ick bloot,
Och lichtveerdicheyt, is mynen noot.

[Those who marry live not in sin,
Who join together in the Lord.
Yet, much anxiety surrounds those
Who accept matrimony.
It is better to be single
As Paul explains:
Those he would have liked to be saved.
Not that they should live in lust,
Being buried alive,
But peaceful, all by themselves,
In prayer, with no offence at all.
Great care for God
Is their task, I know that for sure,
Since thoughtlessness is my sorrow.

49 SG, *GL* respectively nrs. 72, p. R3ʳ and nr. 46, p. L4ᵛ; see, for more examples, song nrs. 38, 39 and 43.
50 Visser, *Broeders in de Geest* I, 262-63, refers to the phenomenon in a song by Jan Philipsz Schabaelje in which the unmarried state is promoted in a similar way, although in this circle of spiritualistic mysticism such views were primarily conceived as a mystical union with the heavenly Bridegroom. In Schabaelje's case his former fiancee, Judith Lubberts, even converted to Catholicism, spending the rest of her life in celibacy as a *klopje*, a "holy maiden"; ibid., pp. 76-77.

51 SG, *GL* nr. 46, p. L4ᵛ, stanza 5: "Wie nu alleen can blyven, / T'zy Mannen ofte Wyven, / Om den dienst des Heeren, Paulus raet daer wel toe." [Whoever wants to remain single in order to serve the Lord, be they men or women, should follow Paul's advice].

52 See, for instance, Menno's statement in his letter to Leenaert Bouwen's wife that the vocation of the church prevails over matrimony. Lucille Marr, "Anabaptist Women of the North," 354, and further for Dirk Philips's views, 355-56: "To them marriage was a spiritual ordinance rather than a carnal union," 356; "it is no surprise that Menno never esteemed marriage as preferable to celibacy," 357. Still the writings of Menno and Dirk are devoid of references to celibacy. See also Sprunger, "God's Powerful Army," 62-63, who refers to Michael Sattler's (?) treatise *On Divorce*, dealing with divorce and mixed marriages: "one should forsake rather than the fleshly than the spiritual, and not enslave one's conscience with the marriage bond, by honouring more the fleshly than the spiritual." Menno's position in *A Thorough Instruction and Account of Excommunication* is also quite clear: "The heavenly marriage between Christ and our souls must be maintained firmly and unbroken and . . . we may therefore not yield or deviate in the slightest to father or mother or husband or wife in any disobedience to His Word" ME III, 486.

53 SG, *GL* nr. 37, p. I4ᵛ, stanza 5:
Hy is het Hooft, ende wy het lijf,
Wy menschen onweerdich zijn Bruyt en wijf,
Verstaet dit recht,
Wel hem die hier getrouwe in blijft
In dese Echt.
Die boven de aertsche Echt heeft cracht.

54 Torchia, "Purity and Perseverance," 40-41: "While men have gone off to fight wars, build bridges, write books . . . women have often remained home doing things like eyeing the tomatoes. . . . The wars and the books and the bridges are recorded in history's annals. The gardens, mended coats and shoveled snow are not." Soetjen's story was recorded by the same Pieter Jansz Twisck in his *Chroniick Van den Ondergangh der Tyrannen, Ende de Jaerlijcksche geschiedenissen in Weereltijcke ende Kerckelijcke saecken. II. Deel* (Hoorn: Isaac Willemsz, 1620), 1280.

55 Of Soetjen Gerrits's hymnbook (1592) copies can only be located of the editions of 1618 (Hoorn: Zacharias Cornelisz.) and 1632 (the same publisher). Martin Schagen, *Naamlyst van Doopsgezinde Schrijveren en Schriften* (Amsterdam, 1744), 40, lists an edition of 1610, published by Abraham Migoen at Rotterdam, which now is probably lost, whereas D.F. Scheurleer, *Nederlandsche Liedboeken. Lijst der in Nederland tot het jaar 1800 uitgegeven liedboeken* (Utrecht: Hes-publishers, 1977), 26, lists an edition printed at Alkmaar in 1619, which is most likely a ghost: it is probably confused with a 1609 edition of Vrou Gerrits's hymnbook (see below).
Vrou Gerrits's hymnbook (1607) was reprinted in 1609 (Alkmaar: Jacob de Meester; Hoorn: Zacharias Cornelisz), in 1621 (Hoorn: Zacharias Cornelisz; Amsterdam, Abraham Biestkens) and in 1627 (Amsterdam: Jacob Aertsz Colom). Again, Schagen, *Naamlyst*, 40, lists another edition without a name, place, or year of publication. The information of Hans J. Hillerbrand, *Anabaptist Bibliography 1520-1630* (St. Louis: Center for Reformation Research, 1991), nrs. 5567A-F, is inaccurate since Soetjen Gerrits's hymnbooks are listed under the heading of Vrou Gerrits (cf. 5567, 5567C and 5567F).

56 Twisck, *Kleyn-Liedt-Boecxken*, pp. 87-91: "Weldien die een echtelijcke / En deuchtsame vrouwe heeft":
Maer wee hem daer beneven
Die een vrou is ghegheven
Ondeuchdelijck en stuer,

Waer voor den man moet beven,
Kijfachtigh quaedt van leven,
Toornigh, verkeert en suer,
Onvriendelijck en luer,
Tis beter suyver, puer,
Te woonen in een kluys,
In een woestijne guer,
Dan met haer in een huys.
. . .
Maer een vrou vol crakelen,
Oneenicheyt en schelen,
Wort by een druypent dack
Gheleecken . . .

APPENDIX

REVIEW OF THE LITERATURE ON WOMEN IN THE REFORMATION AND RADICAL REFORMATION[1]

The portrayal of early modern European women as cultivated and emancipated persons stems from Jacob Burckhardt's classic book on the Italian Renaissance written in 1860.[2] A similar approach was taken in two other nineteenth-century works on religious women, written to document the lives of important and saintly women. The Rev. James Anderson described the positive effects for women of the Protestant Reformation, which freed them from the control of priests at confession and rescued them from the celibate life so that they could "enjoy all the comforts of life, and occupy [their] fitting position as wife and mother."[3] Walter Walsch wrote about women martyrs because he could not convince a woman to take on this task, and because Anderson had neglected the topic. He illustrated that women were equal to men by virtue of their martyrdom.[4]

In the twentieth century, Roland Bainton continued the trend toward hagiography. His biographical sketches of saintly women, many of whom were from well-to-do and ruling families or married to Protestant reformers, expressed the idea that the Protestant Reformation brought women religious equality with men.[5] This optimistic view was supported by Miriam Chrisman,[6] Jane Douglass,[7] Elise Boulding,[8] Sherrin Wyntjes,[9] and Stephen Ozment.[10] Not all historians studying the Reformation of the sixteenth century, however, have affirmed Bainton's view. In her research on religious change in France, Natalie Zemon Davis disagreed with the view that women had achieved equality through Protestant reforms. She concluded that "women suffered for their powerlessness in both Catholic and Protestant lands."[11] Moreover, in her study of women in various radical Protestant groups, Joyce Irwin contended that the religious status of women essentially did not change until the Quaker movement of the seventeenth century.[12]

The debate on whether the Protestant Reformation brought any positive change to the lives of women was carried forward in the 1980s by specialized studies on various themes. Ian MacLean, analyzing various religious and philosophical texts, concluded that the negative ideas about women did not change in the sixteenth century.[13] In a detailed study of marriage law in the sixteenth century, Thomas Max Safly supported the opinion that continuity far outweighed change in the status of women in marriage.[14] Lorna Abray mentioned some negative effects of the reforms for women in her regional study of the Protestant Reformation in Strasbourg.[15] The research of Susan Karant-Nunn on women in Central Germany further confirmed the theme of continuity in the lives of women before and after the Protestant Reformation.[16]

This challenge and revision of the optimistic view that religious changes of the sixteenth century gave women equal status with men is also evident in the literature pertaining to Anabaptist women of the Radical Reformation. As in the debates concerning the Protestant Reformation, Roland Bainton suggested that women in the Anabaptist movement attained full religious equality with men, while Joyce Irwin and Claus-Peter Clasen challenged this assumption. However, none of these scholars systematically analyzed the Anabaptist court records [*Täuferakten*], one of the richest printed sources on Anabaptists, with a specific focus on women. The following survey of literature will show that the study of women's involvement in the Anabaptist movement has just begun.

One of the oldest and most widely used sources about women in the Anabaptist movement is the *Martyrs' Mirror*, which dates back to the seventeenth century.[17] The accounts of the martyrs are given in the historical context of Christian martyrs from the first century onward and are meant to edify the reader. In total, 270 of the 930 martyrs, or 30 percent,[18] were female–a high proportion in comparison to Calvinist female martyrs. But the idealization of the martyr accounts is reminiscent of Bainton's hagiographic biographies of Protestant women.[19] Research based only on the cases of women who were executed does not tell the whole story; it neither provides evidence about the total number of women involved in Anabaptism in a given area nor does it shed light on the role of those women who were not executed. Furthermore, as Werner Packull has pointed out in his case study of Anna Jansz, the martyrology is not always a reliable source for historical research.[20]

Nevertheless, one of the major themes relating to Anabaptist women has been their role as martyrs. Wayne Plenert analyzed the letters of Anabaptist women in order to emphasize their steadfastness in the faith.[21] A lengthier, more theological treatment of the subject was undertaken by Leona Stucky Abbott. She demonstrated how Anabaptist women transcended the societal restrictions of their time, but she referred to the martyr stories as "inadequate sources."[22] *The Martyrs' Mirror* also was used more extensively by Jenifer Hiett Umble, who categorized Anabaptist female martyrs on the basis of the passive and active choices they made.[23] John Klassen used the martyrology to illustrate the supportive relationships between husbands and wives.[24]

The martyrology was ranked high by Harold S. Bender, who gave new direction to Anabaptist studies in the 1940s. He assumed, as Roland Bainton had, that men and women had religious equality in the Anabaptist movement. Bender applied the earlier hypothesis of Max Weber to Anabaptist women, namely that women have always been more involved in the early stages of religious movements.[25] George Williams, in his monumental book *The Radical Reformation*, similarly based his view on Weber who had stated that:

The Anabaptist insistence on the covenantal principle of the freedom of conscience for all adult believers and thereby the extension of the priesthood of the Christophorous laity to women constituted a major breach in patriarchalism and a momentous step in the Western emancipation of women.[26]

Writing in the same time period, Wolfgang Schäufele described Anabaptist women as fully emancipated by virtue of their role in the missionary activities of Anabaptism.[27] But in Schäufele's view this full equality was restricted, as Anabaptist women could not preach, baptize, or participate in choosing leaders.[28] Neither Bender, Williams, nor Schäufele adequately supported or researched their conclusions about the role of women in Anabaptism.

One of the challenges to Bainton's assumptions and the optimistic views on the religious equality of women in the Anabaptist movement came from Joyce Irwin.[29] She claimed to have found no evidence for the equality of Anabaptist women, as Wyntjes and Boulding had suggested.[30] Choosing to focus on prescriptive sources, Irwin discussed the role of Anabaptist women mainly as presented in the writings of a few of the male leaders. Since these statements were made at a later stage of the Anabaptist movement, when it was no longer deemed necessary for women to participate in the same manner as they had earlier, they do not tell the whole story. The limited references to Anabaptist women's own experiences in Irwin's collection of sources are insufficient to clarify the discrepancy between theory and practice.[31]

The work of historian Claus-Peter Clasen is also a critique of Bainton's view of Anabaptist women. In his discussion of Anabaptist membership in the southern German-speaking lands, Clasen contended that Anabaptism did not offer women a role in religion that was different from their role in secular society.[32] While he clearly differentiated between the different time periods, and used 1529 as a cut-off point for the early phase of the Anabaptist movement in the South German and Austrian regions, Clasen did not clarify why there were a greater number of women participating in Anabaptism in the earlier period. Despite the fact that his numerous lists of Anabaptist members include many names of Anabaptist women, Clasen insisted that women did not make a significant contribution to the movement.[33] Clasen "combed more archival records than any scholar of his generation,"[34] and stated that "We are better informed about the outlawed Anabaptist sect than any other religious movement of the sixteenth century,"[35] but he neglected to discuss the contributions of women to the Anabaptist movement.

The analytical approach of Miriam Chrisman was a departure from Roland Bainton's hagiographic descriptions. She focussed on one location,

Strasbourg, and studied the activities of Protestant and Anabaptist women in greater detail. Her conclusion, that "Reaction to the Reform was an individual matter," distinctly expresses the most crucial aspect of Anabaptist belief, namely, that adult baptism was based on personal decision.[36] Natalie Davis commented that the Anabaptist movement was less professional, bookish, and hierarchical and in it "women were allowed to prophesy or speak in tongues along with men." Her work provided another indication that much more could be said on the subject of women in Anabaptism.[37] The detailed survey by Keith Sprunger on Anabaptist women suggests that we must look at the participation of lay persons rather than concentrate on key leaders in order to understand the role of women.[38] Sprunger made questions relating to the role of women central, and indicated how complex the study of Anabaptist women is, although some of his conclusions (for example regarding the leadership roles of women) need further study. In her recent book on Reformation Augsburg, Lyndal Roper ascribes a co-leader role to the wives of Anabaptists.[39]

More recent research by Lucille Marr and Betti Erb on the attitudes of Menno Simons toward women and family have both challenged and affirmed the optimistic views about the equality of Anabaptist women;[40] the contradictory interpretations of Bainton and Irwin remain with us. We cannot forget that the prescriptions of both Simons and Philips for expected female behaviour were written during a later phase of Anabaptist development when, as Max Weber's hypothesis suggests, the early openness to women's participation no longer applied.

Several newer studies have given more attention to the early years of Anabaptism and have used the descriptive court records [*Täuferakten*] to document what women actually said and did. An analysis of three years of court records from Tirol demonstrates that women did claim and achieve some degree of religious equality with men as they assumed the roles of believer, martyr, lay missioner, and lay leader.[41] The detailed biography of the noblewoman Helena von Freyberg, a leader in southern Germany and Austria,[42] indicates that lengthier sketches can be written for some Anabaptist women. It also amplifies what Sprunger said about the self-appointed and lay leadership exercised by Anabaptist women. Lois Barrett has examined the evidence on Ursula Jost of sixteenth-century Strasbourg. Ursula's prophecies were published and widely read in her time (see her profile in this volume). Barrett's translation of these visions into English furthers our knowledge of contributions by individual Anabaptist women.[43]

The recently published book by Marion Kobelt-Groch (*Rebellious Daughters of God: Women in the Peasants' War and Anabaptist Movements*) focusses on radical and Anabaptist women in northern, central, and southern Germany, as well the Austrian territories. Kobelt-Groch mentions the participation of many radical and Anabaptist women, but devotes more attention to a few, such as Hille Feicken, the Judith of Münster (see her profile in this volume) and Petronella from central Germany, who left her husband. The author's use of Peasants' War documents in addition to Anabaptist court records gives us the most comprehensive study of radical and Anabaptist women to date. The book includes a chapter on women's participation in the sixteenth-century peasant revolts that preceded and influenced the Anabaptist movement.[44] In accordance with her goal not to idealize female Anabaptist martyrs, Kobelt-Groch made the lives of Anabaptist women more important than their deaths, but the breadth of time and place covered limited the number of women's stories that could be included. Kobelt-Groch concludes that the priesthood of all believers was a reality for Anabaptist women only in the beginning years, when women were leaders along with men.

In conclusion, the newer research on women prophets, women leaders, and the ordinary women in the various Anabaptist movements represents a departure from the use of traditional sources such as the *Martyrs' Mirror*. Although the historiographical debate about the effects of both the Protestant and the Radical Reformation continues, the majority of historians agree that continuity outweighed change in the matter of the religious equality of sixteenth-century women. Chrisman has summarized this view in regard to women in Strasbourg.

> The Reformation did not make any fundamental change in the position of women in urban society–their role continued to be within the family and household. The significant change was the overthrow of the celibate ethic. As long as celibacy was regarded as the preferable state, women, by inference, occupied not only a secondary position but could easily be seen as an evil force, the temptation which threatened every man's salvation.[45]

A comment made by Kobelt-Groch in her book deserves mention here. In the short run and in the context of everyday life, women in the radical and Anabaptist movements experienced some successes as they participated in attempts to bring change to sixteenth-century life. Despite the fact that these successes may be viewed as unequal to those of men, there is a danger in focussing only on the long run, the continuity of history, and the larger cycles of historical change. Then, says Kobelt-Groch, "the small successes of women will become invisible once more and we will revert back to the view that in the past women made no contribution at all."[46]

It is the task of researchers on Anabaptist women to utilize the court records more extensively. The case study approach could be used both for individual Anabaptist women as well as for the regions in which Anabaptism was prominent. Such an approach would enlighten us on the participation of

Appendix 411

women at all levels of the Anabaptist movement. The research on sixteenth-century Anabaptist women has changed greatly since Dorothy Yoder Nyce asked questions about Anabaptist foremothers in 1980, one year after Joyce Irwin published her negative response to Roland Bainton's positive views on the religious equality of Anabaptist women.[47] The studies of Anabaptist women done since then have extended our horizon. We must, however, continue developing "new ways of seeing" in order to make Anabaptist women visible.[48]

Notes

1. This review of the literature has been updated and is taken from: Linda Huebert Hecht, "Faith and Action: The Role of Women in the Anabaptist Movement of the Tirol, 1527-1529" (unpublished cognate essay, Master of Arts, History, University of Waterloo, 1990), 5-11.
2. Hannelore Sachs, *The Renaissance Woman*, trans. Marianne Herzfeld (New York: McGraw-Hill, 1971), 7.
3. Rev. James Anderson, *Ladies of the Reformation, Memoirs of Distinguished Female Characters, Belonging to the Period of the Reformation in the Sixteenth Century* (London: Blackie and Son, 1855), ix.
4. For ten years Walter Walsch tried in vain to convince some woman to write this book. His motivation for writing the book is summed up as follows: "The memory of the just is blessed, and ought not to be forgotten. Men have suffered much for Reformation principles; but I venture to submit that the following pages prove that women have not been one whit behind their brethren in what they have endured for the love of Jesus and His sacred truth." *Women Martyrs of the Reformation* (London: The Religious Tract Society, 1867 [reprint, 1990]), v-vi. Walsch included the Anabaptist female martyr Elisabeth of Leeuarden in his book.
5. See Roland Bainton, *Women of the Reformation in Germany and Italy* (Minneapolis: Augsburg Publishing House, 1971); *Women of the Reformation in France and England* (Minneapolis: Augsburg Publishing House, 1973); *Women of the Reformation from Spain to Scandinavia* (Minneapolis: Augsburg Publishing House, 1977); *What Christianity Says About Sex, Love and Marriage* (New York: Association Press, 1957), 94. For a different biographical perspective of three of Bainton's German female protagonists, namely Katharina Zell, Wibrandis Rosenblatt, and Argula of Grumbach, see Maria Heinsius, *Das Unüberwindliche Wort, Frauen der Reformationszeit* (Munich: Chr. Kaiser Verlag, 1951), 12-36; 68-95; 134-159.
6. Miriam U. Chrisman, "Women and the Reformation in Strasbourg 1490-1530," in *Archive for Reformation History*, 63 (1972): 143-168.
7. Jane Dempsey Douglass, "Women and the Continental Reformation," in Rosemary Ruether, ed., *Religion and Sexism, Images of Women in the Jewish and Christian Traditions* (New York: Simon and Schuster, 1974), 292-318.
8. Elise Boulding, *The Underside of History: A View of Women through Time* (Colorado: Westview Press, 1976), 546-48.
9. Sherrin Marshall Wyntjes, "Women in the Reformation Era," in Renate Bridenthal and Claudia Koonz, eds., *Becoming Visible. Women in European History* (Boston: Houghton Mifflin, 1977), 165-191. Sherrin Marshall Wyntjes, "Women and Religious Choices in the Sixteenth Century," in *Archive for Reformation History*, 75 (1984): 276-89.

10 Stephen E. Ozment, *When Fathers Ruled, Family Life in Reformation Europe* (Cambridge, MA: Harvard University Press, 1983), 99. Ozment describes how women were liberated from monastic life to become wives and mothers. He reveals a patriarchal system to which Protestant reform brought a new emphasis on love in family relationships. His argument is weak, however, due to his use of texts of advice for households, namely, the Hausvater books, which are prescriptions and not actual descriptions of behaviour.
11 Natalie Zemon Davis, "City Women and Religious Change," in *Society and Culture in Early Modern France, Eight Essays* (Stanford, CA: Stanford University Press, 1975), 94.
12 Joyce L. Irwin, *Womanhood in Radical Protestantism 1525-1675* (New York: Edwin Mellen Press, 1979), xvii.
13 Ian MacLean, *The Renaissance Notion of Woman: A Study in the Fortunes of Scholasticism and Medical Science in European Intellectual Life* (Cambridge: Cambridge University Press, 1980), 1.
14 Thomas Max Safly, *Let No Man Put Asunder, The Control of Marriage in the German Southwest: A Comparative Study, 1550-1600* (Kirksville, MO: Sixteenth Century Journal Publishers, Northeast Missouri State University, 1984), 38.
15 "Despite the emphasis on reciprocal duties, the reformed household was not an egalitarian household. The pious home had to have a head and that head had to be the husband and father. This insistence on masculine control reflected both the normal sixteenth-century view that all social groups, including the family, had natural leaders established by God, and the enduring conviction that women were simultaneously weak and dangerous." Lorna J. Abray, *The People's Reformation, Magistrates, Clergy, and Commons in Strasbourg, 1500-1598* (Ithaca, NY: Cornell University Press, 1985), 217, 218-20.
16 Susan C. Karant-Nunn, "Continuity and Change: Some Effects of the Reformation on the Women of Zwickau," in *The Sixteenth Century Journal*, 13 (Summer, 1982): 16-42. Women did, however, speak publicly, justifying their actions on the basis of inspiration by the Holy Spirit. This has been discussed by Merry E. Wiesner, "Women's Defense of Their Public Role," in Mary Beth Rose ed. *Women in the Middle Ages and Renaissance, Literary and Historical Perspectives* (Syracuse: Syracuse University Press, 1986), 1-27.
17 Thieleman J. van Braght, *The Bloody Theater or Martyrs' Mirror of the Defenseless Christians Who Baptized Only Upon Confession of Faith, and Who Suffered and Died for the Testimony of Jesus, Their Savior, from the Time of Christ to the Year A.D. 1660*, trans. Joseph F. Sohm (Scottdale PA: Herald Press, 1950). The 1660 edition was republished in 1886 and 1950. The martyrology has been the only source available on Anabaptist women in the English language.
18 These figures are taken from Wayne Plenert, "The Martyrs' Mirror and Anabaptist Women," in *Mennonite Life*, 30 (June, 1975): 13-18.
19 Differences in content in the various editions of the martyrology are confusing. For example, one edition refers to Elisabeth Dirks of Holland as a teacher, another as a man. Furthermore, Bainton assumed that she was the wife of Menno Simons, a fact other research has proved incorrect. Bainton, "Women of the Anabaptists," in *Women in the Reformation in Germany*, 145-50. See the profile of Elisabeth Dirks in this volume.
20 "Our study resurrects the question as to the reliability of the *Martyrs' Mirror* as a historical source. Obviously, the ideal image presented there of Anna as a purely religious martyr in the tradition of nonresistance is not entirely accurate; . . . Only further detailed research will determine the number of 'misplaced martyrs' in the *Mirror*." Werner O. Packull, "Anna Jansz of Rotterdam, A Historical Investigation of

an Early Anabaptist Heroine," in *Archive for Reformation History*, 78 (1987): 147. See also the profile of Anna Jansz in this volume.
21 Plenert, "The Martyrs' Mirror and Anabaptist Women."
22 Leona Stucky Abbott, "Anabaptist Women of the Sixteenth Century," (masters thesis, Eden Theological Seminary, 1979), 34.
23 Jenifer Hiett Umble, "Women and Choice: An Examination of the Martyrs' Mirror," in MQR, 64 (1990): 135-145; Jenifer Hiett Umble, "Spiritual Companions: Women as Wives in the *Martyrs' Mirror*," in *Mennonite Life*, 45 (September 1990): 32-35.
24 John Klassen, "Women and the Family among Dutch Anabaptist Martyrs," in MQR, 60 (October 1986): 548-571. Jennifer H. Reed found support for Klassen's view in her research using the *Martyrs' Mirror*: "Dutch Anabaptist Female Martyrs and their responses to the Reformation," (masters thesis, University of South Florida, 1991).
25 "In the early Anabaptist movement women played an important role. . . . Later, after the creative period of Anabaptism was past, the settled communities and congregations reverted more to the typical patriarchal attitude of European culture." Harold S. Bender, "Women, Status of: Anabaptism," in ME, IV, 972. Max Weber hypothesized that the equality granted to women among the disprivileged classes rarely continues "beyond the first stage of a religious community's formation, . . . as routinization and regimentation of community relationships set in, a reaction takes place. . . ." *The Sociology of Religion*, trans. Ephraim Fischoff (Boston: Beacon Press, 1922), 104, 105.
26 This quotation is from the classic book by Max Weber, *Die Protestantische Ethik und der 'Geist' des Kapitalismus, Gesammelte Aufsaetze*, I (Tübingen 1922), 171, cited in George Huntston Williams, *The Radical Reformation* (Philadelphia: Westminster Press, 1962), 507.
27 "The woman in Anabaptism emerges as a fully emancipated person in religious matters and as the independent bearer of Christian convictions." Wolfgang Schäufele, "The Missionary Vision and Activity of the Anabaptist Laity," in MQR 36 (April 1962): 108. This idea is confirmed by Littell: "the Anabaptists were among the first to make the (Great) Commission binding upon all church members" in Franklin Hamlin Littell, *The Origins of Sectarian Protestantism, A Study of the Anabaptist View of the Church* (New York: Macmillan, 1964), 112.
28 Wolfgang Schäufele, *Das Missionarische Bewusstsein und Wirken der Täufer, Dargestellt nach oberdeutschen Quellen* (Lemgo: Neukirchener Verlag des Erziehungsvereins, 1966), 298.
29 Bainton discusses Anabaptist women in *Women of the Reformation in Germany*, 145-58. Irwin, *Womanhood in Radical Protestantism*, xii-xvii.
30 Wyntjes described the doctrine of baptism or rebaptism as an "equalizing covenant" and the Anabaptist priesthood as including both men and women. "Women in the Reformation Era," 175. Boulding stated that Anabaptists "practised complete equality of women and men in every respect, including preaching." *Underside*, 548. Unfortunately she did not substantiate her claim with primary sources.
31 The passage from Johannes Kessler, telling the story of Margaret Hottinger, excludes some important parts. See her profile in this book. Joyce Irwin, *Womanhood in Radical Protestantism*, 203ff. A recent article on Hutterite women of the sixteenth and seventeenth centuries follows the lead of Joyce Irwin in concentrating on prescriptive literature. The focus is on "Peter Riedemann's *Confession of Faith*, Hutterite letters, various church ordinances, and a sermon or treatise dealing with 'evil women'." See Wes Harrison, "The Role of Women in Anabaptist Thought and Practice: The Hutterite Experience of the Sixteenth and Seventeenth Centuries," in *The Sixteenth Century Journal* 23 (Spring 1992): 49-69, esp. 53.

32 Clasen's book has been described by James Stayer as "the major research achievement of twentieth-century Anabaptist studies" Stephen Ozment, ed., *Reformation Europe: A Guide to Research* (St. Louis, MO: Center for Reformation Research, 1982), 143. Clasen stated that "the sect showed no inclination to grant women a greater role than they customarily had in sixteenth-century society." Claus-Peter Clasen, *Anabaptism: A Social History, 1525-1618* (Ithaca, NY: Cornell University Press, 1972), 207.

33 Claus-Peter Clasen, *The Anabaptists in South and Central Germany, Switzerland, and Austria, Their Names, Occupations, Places of Residence and Dates of Conversion: 1525-1618* (Scottdale, PA: MQR, 1978). See also, Claus-Peter Clasen, "The Anabaptist Leaders: Their Numbers and Background, Switzerland, Austria, South and Central Germany 1525-1618," in MQR 49 (April 1975): 122-164. Historians studying other persecuted religious groups would disagree. For example, Shahar says of the Waldensians: "Such a group needs the support of all its members, and this precipitates the collapse not only of class divisions but also of divisions between the sexes." Shulamith Shahar, *The Fourth Estate: A History of Women in the Middle Ages*, trans. Chaya Galai (New York: Methuen, 1983), 258. The same idea is expressed by Keith Thomas, "Women in the Civil War Sects," in *Past and Present*, 13 (1958): 42-62.

34 This remark was made by the editor who introduced his article. Claus-Peter Clasen, "Executions of Anabaptists, 1525-1618, A Research Report," in MQR 47 (April 1973): 82; 115-152.

35 Claus-Peter Clasen, "The Sociology of Swabian Anabaptism," in *Church History*, 32 (1963): 150.

36 Her analysis of Anabaptist women in Strasbourg, although it was based on the court records, was little more than an introduction to the topic. She discussed only Anabaptist women, including two prophetesses. Chrisman, "Women and the Reformation in Strasbourg," 158-62, 166.

37 Davis, "City Women," 84.

38 Keith L. Sprunger, "God's Powerful Army of the Weak: Anabaptist Women of the Radical Reformation," in Richard L. Greaves, ed., *Triumph Over Silence, Women in Protestant History* (Connecticut: Greenwood Press, 1985), 45-74. Sprunger is implementing the methods that Scribner describes for Reformation history in general, namely, that the new history asks how religious ideas and doctrine were interpreted and put into practice by the people. Robert W. Scribner, review article: "Interpreting Religion in Early Modern Europe," in *European Studies Review*, 13 (1983): 90.

39 "As many of the male Anabaptists became involved with missionary work or were exiled from the town, the local movement came increasingly to depend on the women who remained, often the wives of the male Anabaptists. By holding meetings in their houses, they kept the congregations together and themselves became crucial figures in the movement's cohesion–a doubly important role in a Church so fragmented and clandestine. Conversions often followed household rather than guild lines, in striking contrast to the patterns of the spread of the early Reformation. Whether through force of circumstance or by design, women occupied a pivotal place in unorthodox religious sects that they never attained in mainstream evangelicalism." Lyndal Roper, *The Holy Household, Women and Morals, in Reformation Augsburg* (Oxford: Clarendon Press, 1989), 253-54.

40 Marr discussed the writings of Menno Simons and Dirk Philips on marriage and concluded that "women's role changed only minimally with the Reformation, even among the Radicals." M. Lucille Marr, "Anabaptist Women of the North: Peers in the Faith, Subordinates in Marriage," in MQR, 61 (October 1987): 347. The article by Betti Erb, "Reading the Source: Menno Simons on Women, Marriage, Children, and Family,"

in *The Conrad Grebel Review* 8 (Fall 1990): 301-19 presents the views of Menno Simons in a more positive light. See also Adela D. Torchia, "Purity and Perseverance: Menno Simons' Understanding of Practical Holiness and Early Anabaptist Women," in *Journal of Mennonite Studies* 12 (1994): 26-44.

41 Huebert Hecht, "Faith and Action," 11. See also, Linda Huebert Hecht, "Women and Religious Change: The Significance of Anabaptist Women in the Tirol, 1527-29," in *Studies in Religion, A Canadian Journal* 21 (1992): 57-66.

42 Linda Huebert Hecht, "An Extraordinary Lay Leader: The Life and Work of Helene of Freyberg, Sixteenth-Century Noblewoman and Anabaptist from the Tirol," in MQR 66 (July 1992): 312-341.

43 See Bainton, *Women of the Reformation in Germany*, 145 and Sprunger, "God's Powerful Army," 53. Lois Y. Barrett, "Wreath of glory: Ursula Jost's prophetic visions in the context of Reformation and revolt in southwestern Germany, 1524-1530," (PhD dissertation, The Union Institute, 1992); also "Women's History/Women's Theology: Theological and Methodological Issues in the Writing of the History of Anabaptist/Mennonite Women," CGR, 10 (Winter 1992): 1-16.

44 Marion Kobelt-Groch, *Aufsässige Töchter Gottes: Frauen im Bauernkrieg und in den Täuferbewegungen* (Frankfurt and New York: Campus Verlag, 1993). See also her articles: "Why did Petronella leave her husband? Reflections on marital avoidance among the Halberstadt Anabaptists," in MQR 62 (January 1988): 26-41; "Von 'armen frowen' und 'boesen wibern'–Frauen im Bauernkrieg zwischen Anpassung und Auflehnung," in *Archive for Reformation History*, 79 (1988): 103-137; "Frauen in Ketten," in *Mennonitische Geschichtsblätter* 47/48 (1990/91): 49-70. "Frauen gegen Geistliche," in *Mennonitische Geschichtsblätter* 49 (1992): 21-31.

45 Chrisman, "Women and the Reformation in Strasbourg," 166.

46 Linda Huebert Hecht, review of Marion Kobelt-Groch, *Aufsässige Töchter Gottes: Frauen im Bauernkrieg und in den Täuferbewegungen* (Frankfurt and New York: Campus Verlag, 1993) in MQR, 69 (January 1995), 107. See also: Kobelt-Groch, *Aufsässige Töchter Gottes*, 30.

47 Dorothy Yoder Nyce, "Are Anabaptists Motherless?" in D. Yoder Nyce, ed., *Which Way Women?* (Akron, PA: Mennonite Central Committee, Peace Section, 1980), 122-129.

48 See Joan Kelly-Gadol, "The Social Relations of the Sexes: Methodological Implications of Women's History," in *Signs*, 1 (1976): 810, and Merry E. Wiesner, "Beyond Women and the Family: Towards a Gender Analysis of the Reformation," in *The Sixteenth Century Journal*, 18 (Fall 1987): 311-321. See the Introduction to this volume, note 2.

INDEX

Aachen, 228, 234
Aarau, 22, 25-30
Aargau region, 20, 27
Adam (Schlegel or Hans Adam), 276
Adige (Etsch) River, 141, 197
adultery, 238. *See also* Susanna
Aken, Janneken van, 386
Alkmaar, 249
alms, 82, 85, 87, 88-91, 93, 97-99, 182, 213, 214, 278, 279. *See also* economics, mutual aid
Alsace, 3, 22, 108
Altenburg, 145, 147
Alzey, 232-33
Ameiser, Waldburga, 159; Jörg, 159
Amersfoort, 316
Amish Church, 2
Amsterdam, 249, 308, 311, 322, 337, 338, 381, 382
Anabaptism: beginnings, 1-4, 19-24, 71-81, 247-57; lay nature of, 7, 10, 54, 249; meaning of the word, 1; Moravian, 75-77, 202-43; as renewal, 19-20, 174; stages of development, 9-10, 20, 44, 46, 50, 385-86, 394; theology and practice of, 2-6, 378-79; underground, 82, 89, 92-93, 99-100. *See also* radicality, Melchiorite Anabaptism, Swiss Anabaptism, Austrian Anabaptism, diversity
Annelein of Freiburg, 198-201
anticlericalism, 2, 25-26, 34-35, 44, 46, 145, 182, 185, 192, 238, 266, 288, 360, 362, 368
antisacramentalism, 2, 25-26, 32, 45-46, 94, 353-54, 359, 361, 368, 380
Antwerp, 249, 317, 325, 331, 355, 365, 366, 367, 380
apocalypticism, 71, 73-74, 78, 96, 106-110, 247-57, 273, 276, 278-79, 280-82, 288-304, 307-11, 337-51; the New Jerusalem, 249, 251, 288, 293, 301, 307, 309, 337, 386, 392; third David, 252. *See also* visions, Jan Matthijs, Münster, Münsterite Kingdom
Apollonia, prophetess in Strasbourg, 276
Appenzell, 19,
Arnhem, Hendrik van, 355
Aschau, 125, 130
Äschlberger, Peter, 127
Augsburg, 20, 71-75, 82-105, 106-10, 111-23, 127-35, 145
Ausbund see hymns, Anabaptist: of the Swiss Brethren
Ausgeben, Hans, 202; Susanna, 202, 217
Austria, 5, 26, 72, 73, 143, 202. *See also* Tirol
Austrian Anabaptism, 71, 73-75, 78, 124-202
authority: of the Bible, 253; of the congregation, 51, 131-35; direct from God, 20, 34-35, 66, 131, 280, 291-92; of interpretation, 36; of prophecy, 250, 252, 279-80; of women, 49, 51, 132, 135. *See also* priesthood of all believers, discipline

Baden, 42, 264
Bader, Augustin 74, 86, 87, 90, 106-10; Sabina 74, 106-10
Bader, Gilg, 144-45; wife of, 144
Baeck, Gysbrecht van, 326-27
Baert, Martha, 366, 367-75
Bainton, Roland, 8
Bamberg, 72
Bamberger, Hutterite martyr, 234
ban *see* discipline: church
banishment *see* exile
baptism: believers', 5, 117, 198, 355, 361; by the Spirit 5, 33, 330, 367; by water, 4, 5, 8, 73, 114, 248, 367; by blood (martyrdom), 367; directly by God, 32-33; in Zurich, 4, 19, 306
baptism of adults, 1, 5, 9, 10, 26, 29, 32-35, 39, 40, 43, 47, 71, 124,

Index 417

180, 181, 184, 185, 189-90, 192, 208, 248, 249, 250, 259, 278, 288, 289-90, 308, 310-11, 320, 323, 337, 352, 353, 355, 359, 360, 366-67, 378, 380
baptism of infants, 3, 5, 19, 47-48, 66, 72, 82, 83, 107, 172, 182, 192, 209, 359, 361, 368
baptism as apocalyptic sign, 73, 106, 250, 307, 339, 341, 342
Baptist Church, 2
Baretswil, 54
Bartel, Anabaptist martyr, 355
Barbara from Tiers, 209
Barrett, Lois Y., 248
Basel, 20, 25, 33-36, 252, 270, 325, 326, 331-33
Batenburg, Jan van, 251
Batenburgers, 252, 320, 329
Bavaria, 92, 124, 125, 127, 167
Beck, Balthasar, 259, 267-68, 273, 275
Beck, Reinhardt, 259, 263-65, 270
Beckum in Overijssel, 352
Beckum, van: Jan, 352-53; Maria, 252, 352-58; Ursula, 252, 352-58
Beeck, Herman van der, 309
Bender, Harold, 9, 10
Benscop, 326
Berch, Jan Jansz van den, 322
Berchem, Jan van, 325, 331-33. *See also* Etten
Berchem, 331, 355
Berchtold, Balthas, 89
Bern, 20, 23, 26, 32, 146, 277; court of appeal in, 25
Beutelsbach 64-66
Bible, 2, 4, 19, 27, 28, 45, 46, 47, 51, 56, 66, 83, 93, 115, 166-67, 192, 201, 207, 209, 212, 222-23, 231, 279, 293, 306, 359, 389; and Apocrypha, 225-31, 235-39; biblical knowledge of women, 368-70, 386, 392; imagery, 386; interpretation by the uneducated, 3, 6; New Testament, 34, 45, 223, 224, 226, 231, 237, 306, 359, 360,
386; Old Testament, 226, 230, 251, 267, 288-89, 322, 365, 386; parables, 116, 135, 200; passages from the, 5, 26, 29, 49, 65, 120, 132, 248, 250, 273, 276, 279, 291, 339, 340, 341-42, 360-62, 370, 371; in the vernacular, 6-7, 236, 306; women in the Bible, 387. *See also* literalism (biblical)
Bibra, 72
Bichel, Hans, 120-21
Biel, 20, 32-37
Binder, Ursula, 76
Black Forest, 19, 20, 143
Blaichner, Martin, 118
Blaubeuren, 108
Blaurer, Ambrosius, 127
Blaurock, George, 44, 47, 75, 146, 166, 178
Blum the miller (Sr. or Jr.), 276
Boekbinder, Gerrit, 337
Boelsweert, Frans van, 373
bookshops, 33-35, 262
Borne, Dirk van, 339
Bosch, Sigmund, 118
Botsch, Jörg, 166
Boumgartner, Elsy, 44
Bouwens: Leenaert, 380; wife of, 254
Bozen, 127, 140, 144, 146-48, 157, 158, 159, 197
Brabant, 249, 337
Braght, Thieleman J. van, 305, 356, 370, 373, 386
Branzoll, castle of, 182
Braun, a man named, 184
Breitenberg, 209
Bregenz, 158, 208
Bremgarten, 28
Brenner Pass, 144
Brethren in Christ Church, 2
Briel, 336, 337
Brixen, 58, 61, 143, 167, 169, 170, 171, 174, 195, 207, 231; bishops of, 141, 142, 144, 165, 167, 170, 172, 179, 183
bruderhofs see Hutterites
Bruges, 317, 369, 372

Bruneck, 166, 180
Brünner, Christine, 208, 232
Brussels, 307, 308, 310, 312, 353
Bucer, Martin, 59, 108-109, 273, 277
Buch, village of, 49
Bülach, 39, 41
Büllheyen, Steffan von, 268
Bullinger, Heinrich, 46
Bünderlin, Hans, 74, 275
Buman (Guldin), Frena, 49, 50
Buren and Leerdam, countess of (lady of IJselstein), 326
Buren, count of (Maximiliaan Egmont), 326; mother of, 326

calling: from God, 8, 20-21, 41, 44, 50, 75; of male pastors, 21; to men and women equally, 8, 10; prophetic, 252; spiritual, 76, 319, 327
Capito, Wolfgang: aid to Sabina Bader, 108-109; wives of, 109
chambers of rhetoric, 316-17, 389-90
children of Anabaptists, 1, 6, 34, 41-42, 61, 62, 65, 90, 91, 106-109, 141, 149, 179, 180, 187-88, 212, 214, 232, 235, 253, 261, 263-64, 268, 270, 309, 312, 313, 317-18, 322-25, 338, 341, 365-72, 386; becoming as, 19, 278; obedience of, 225
Chiemsee, 125
Christ, 2-5, 11, 28, 32, 33, 34, 43, 45, 49-51, 53, 62, 131, 133-35, 141, 143, 145, 162, 172, 192, 198, 200-201, 204, 207, 211, 223, 227, 231, 234, 235, 253, 279, 282, 324, 328, 330, 332, 337, 339, 341-42, 343, 345, 347, 360-63, 365, 367, 370, 371, 372; bride of, 229, 230, 340, 386, 392, 393; the Head, 393; incarnation of, 384; second coming of, 250, 273
Christology, 113-22
Chur, 20, 61
Church of the Brethren, 2
church authorities: *see* Lutheran Church, Reformed Church, Roman Catholic Church
church and state, 141-42, 203, 365, 367-69
citizens, 26, 29, 58, 129, 306, 307, 308, 309; rights of, 259-67
civil authorities, 54, 65, 111, 126, 142, 144, 147, 165-74, 171, 187, 192, 227, 234, 273-74, 275, 298, 307-309, 311, 321-24, 326-28, 352-53, 365-69, 378-81; in Deventer, 308-309; hunting down Anabaptists, 168, 179, 181, 185; influence of wives, 328-29; lenient to women at defeat of Münster, 298; obedience to, 83; sympathetic to Anabaptists, 90, 146-47, 326-27, 336; tactics of, 127-28, 195-97, 318; tensions between central and local rulers, 148, 308, 311-12, 368, 381
Clasen, Claus-Peter, 9, 83
Claeys, Lijnken, 367-72
Coburg, 72, 73
Cologne, 263
common people (commoners): 3, 6, 7, 26, 36, 37, 54, 141-42, 144, 187, 191, 192, 298. *See also* peasants, laws
communication: 6-8, 23, 27-29; and Bible, 386; oral/aural, 7-8, 28, 35, 268; role of Anabaptist women in, 7, 85, 86, 94
community of goods *see* economics
conformity *see* recantation, Nicodemism
congregationalism, separated, 20, 74, 203,
Conrad, Margaret, 204
Constance, 20, 127
Cuelenaere, Jan de, 369

Dachser, Jakob, 82, 83, 96, 99
Dällikon, 38, 40, 42
Damborschitz, 215
deacons, 87, 89-90, 93, 95, 97, 250
deaconesses, 87, 255, 363; in

Index

Dortrecht Confession, 254, 363
death: natural, 30, 62, 66, 111, 132, 249, 252, 259, 262, 264, 267, 274, 326, 364, 389; beliefs regarding, 116-17; and burial, 30, 66, 320-22; and grieving, 120; and resurrection, 120, 200, 372. *See also* martyrdom
Debora, a judge, in Hutterite songs, 225, 226, 227, 235, 237
Delden, 353
Delden, Albert van, 313
Delfshaven, 387
Delft, 316-26, 337, 338
Delmeere, Tanneken, 372
Denck, Hans, 71, 72, 74, 75, 82, 247
Denmark, 275
Deutschnofen, 147
Deventer, 251, 305-15, 353, 366
devil *see* Satan
Dill, Bartlme, women in the household of, 158
Dirks, Elisabeth, 253, 254, 359-64, 385, 386; hymn of, 396 n.11
discipleship, 4, 8, 10, 11, 178, 203, 205, 337
discipline: church (ban), 5, 20; from God, 133-35, 232; in the Hutterite community, 203, 207, 210, 212-13; lacking in the Lutheran church, 64, 66; in Melchior Hoffman, 248; women's function in, 21, 51; *See also* authority
Divara, Queen of Münster, 250, 251, 298-304
diversity: of Anabaptists of Friesland, 380; of Anabaptist origins (polygenesis), 2; of Anabaptist spiritualists, 247; of Anabaptists in Strasbourg, 276; of belief among Anabaptists, 84, 96
divorce, 41
Dorfbrunner, Leonhard, 88, 90, 92, 96
Dorothea, the furrier's wife, 48
Doucher, Hans Adolf, 85-86, 93; Susanna, 84, 85-86, 88, 89, 92, 95-96, 98

dress, 21, 224, 237, 294, 301, 310, 312, 385
Dusentschuer, Johann, 299
Dufft, Valentin, 276, 279
Dutch Anabaptism *see* Melchiorite Anabaptism

economics, 3, 5, 6, 10; income of a carpenter, 59; taxes paid, 313; community of goods, 5-6, 74, 89, 93, 99, 107, 202-21, 224-25, 250, 288, 290-91; feudal lords and peasants, 111, 125, 141-42; support from nobility, 126, 327; in Hutterite communities, 212-14, 218; income of a civil servant, 126; properties and goods, 27, 29-30, 55, 58-62, 83, 92, 95, 107-108, 124-28, 132, 170, 179, 196-97, 217, 258, 261, 263-64, 270, 309, 312-13, 320-21, 336, 341, 366; tithe, 25, 35, 277; usury, 73. *See also* alms, mutual aid
education, 6, 124; for girls, 259-60, 359; use of songs for, 224-25, 236, 254, 391-94; Latin School, 306; universal among the Hutterites, 236
egalitarianism, 2, 3, 6, 8-12, 22, 46, 48, 50-51, 392; choices for women and men, 4, 8-10, 12, 47, 51, 59, 157, 187-88, 205, 259-60, 265, 270, 375; defense of Münster, 292-93; in the faith, 8, 9, 11, 77, 204, 218, 279, 388; in Hutterite songs, 238; and religious zeal, 385-87, 389, 394-95; and martyrdom, 22, 209; *See also* gender
Egenolff, Christian, 273
Egg, 208
Eggen, 146
Egger: Anna, 187-88; Cristina, 187-88; daughter, 188; Peter, 187-90; son, 188; Scherer, 189-90
Egle, Hans, 168-69, 171-72

Egmont *see* Buren
Eisack River, 141, 181, 197
Elbing, 209
Ellen (Elln), 180, 184
Emden, 249, 364
Emden, Meynaart van, 337, 338
Enderlin, Schütz, 278
England, 317, 338-39, 341
Enkhuisen, 249
Entfelder, Christian, 74
Eppan, 127
Erasmus, 84, 306
Erb, Betti, 254
Ericxdochter, Filistis, 380
Erlangen, 72
Eschamertor, 35
Esens, 353
Ess, Sebastian, wife and maid of, 158
Esslingen, 64, 278
Esslinger, Wolf, 234
Estonia, 275
Etsch River, 141, 197
Etten, van: Anna, 331-33; Anneken, 331; Joachim, 331-32; Reinier, 331; Wybrechte (lady of Berchem), 331
Eusebius, 238
evangelization: done by women, 9-11, 20, 21, 23, 33-35, 48, 64-66, 76, 77, 82-105, 126-27, 130, 167-68, 174-75, 183, 187-88, 190, 191, 354-55; informal, 7, 44; by martyrs, 381-82; in occupational networks, 91-93, 184; by Swiss Anabaptists, 64, 66; by wives of Hutterite missionaries, 207-208, 218. *See also* family
Eve, 11, 231, 238; daughters of Israel, 386; new Eve, 386
Evert (Judas), betrayer of Anna Hendriks, 379-80
exile (banishment), 22, 26, 27, 29-30, 33, 36, 46, 51, 58-63, 65, 72, 83, 85, 86, 88, 89-90, 91, 92, 94, 95, 97, 106-109, 127-29, 132, 187, 197, 212, 317-19, 380

faith: alone, 3, 266, 306; its meaning for Anabaptists, 1-5, 9-12, 19, 32-34, 36, 59, 62, 65-66, 195, 198-201, 202-18, 305, 306, 309, 328, 330, 332, 336, 343-48, 356, 360-63, 368-75, 391; practice of, 22; and works, 3. *See also* spirituality, piety
families: Anabaptist influences within, 19, 23, 38, 41-42, 43, 58-62, 111-16, 120, 125-26, 140, 144-45, 150, 158-59, 161, 165-75, 181, 184, 188, 195-97, 309, 317, 326-33, 341, 345-48, 352-53, 356, 367, 372; care for the elderly in, 312, 313; the Hottinger clan, 43-47; importance of 43; noble, 124-25; orphans, 6, 211, 214, 341, 373; and recantation, 157-59, 161; support of when in prison, 195-97, 371. *See also* networks
Fanwiler, Winbrat, 47, 49, 50
Fasser, Georg, 212
Feicken, Hille, 251, 288-97; Psalmus, 290-91. *See also* Simons, Menno: Peter
Felix, Hans, 60
Fellbach, 278
Ferdinand I *see* Tirol
Fieger, Hans, daughter of, 125
Fischer, Christoph Andreas, 206
Fisher, Hans, 42
Flanders, 249, 317, 365-77, 380
forgiveness, 131, 135, 211. *See also* authority
Forter, Wolffgang, 264
France, 275, 317,
Franck, Sebastian, 268, 275
Franconia, 72, 73
Franeker, 378-80
Frankenhausen, 71, 72
Frauenberg, Elizabeth von, 125
Freckenhorst, Westphalian convent, 329-31
freedom of the will *see* yieldedness
Freiburg in Breisgau, 198, 199
Freistadt, 72

Frey, Claus, 279
Freyberg, von: Christoph Georg, 125, 130; Georg Ludwig, 115, 130; Hanns Sigmund, 125; Helena, 75, 77, 78, 114-16, 124-13 9; Michael, 115; Onophrius, 125-26 129; Pankratz, 125, 130; parents of Helena, 124, 128; servants of Helena, 125-26; sons of Helena, 127, 129; Wilhelm, 125
Friedmann, Robert, 210
Friesland, 249, 251, 273, 275, 288-91, 353, 359, 360, 364, 378-83
Frisian Mennonites, 386, 390, 391, 393, 394
Frölich, Dorothea (Zieglerin), 86-87
Fry, wife of Konrad, 38; wife of Jakob, 38; wife of Felix, 38
Fuchs, Jakob von, 147
Fueger, Fridrich, 168-74
Fundnetscher, Lienhard, wife of, 159

Gais, 165-67
Gaismair, Michael, 142, 145
Gall: Justina Rumler, 178-79; Paul, 178-79, 184; brother of Paul, 179
Gallam, Jellys, 309
Gasser: Anna Mairhofer, 75 76, 140-55; Barbara, 141; Hans, 140-55; maid, Agatha, 141, 146-47; maid, Lucia, 141, 146-48; servants (male), 141, 146; sons of, 146; Thomas, 141, 146
Gaukes, Ydse, 305
Geelen, Fenneke (Fenne) van: 251, 305-15, 338; daughter of, 312, 313; husband of, Jan (Johan), 308-11, 338; mother of, 312, 313; niece of (Egbert), 312; servant of, 311; sister of, 312; son of, Jacob, 312, 313
Gelderland, 337
Geltinger, Ulrich, 170
gender, 85, 336, 337, 343, 354; in martyrdom, 202, 381; and Dutch Mennonite women, 384-405; in Hutterite communities, 204-207, 218, 232. *See also* egalitarianism, God: children of, sexuality
Gentileschi, Artemisia, 289
Germany, 3, 5, 72, 75, 76, 202, 247-57, 275, 353, 359
Gerrits, Soetjen, 254, 384-405
Gerrits, Vrou, 254, 384-405
Gertrude, prophetess in Strasbourg, 276
Ghent, 365-77
Girfalck, Thomas, 35
Giunta, Jeanne, 258
Glasmaker, Willem, 308
Glattfelden, 42
Gletzli, Regula, 48
God: 192, 202, 203, 204, 205, 208, 210, 217, 222-38, 281, 282, 318, 321, 322, 324, 327, 328, 330, 332, 340, 341, 347, 354, 360-63, 373-75, 385, 388, 389; children of, 121, 133-35, 199, 232, 330, 332, 330, 346, 370; judgement, wrath of, 277, 284, 338, 339-40, 344; as Lord and as Father, 121-22, 133-35, 170, 199-201, 282, 283, 284, 343, 345, 370; obedience to, 212; will of, 56, 131-35, 209, 211, 213, 370, 372
Göggingen, 86, 94, 98
Gortersdochter, Maritje, Jans de, 316-22
Gospel *see* Bible
grace, 2, 3, 117, 118, 120, 122, 131-35, 208, 211, 232, 282, 321
grass-roots reform, 2, 7, 8, 126, 187
Grebel, Conrad, 19, 44, 46, 47, 222-23
greetings: of Anabaptists, 100, 139 n.31; in letters, 120
Grembs, Veronika, 167-68
Greuel, Hans, 87, 96
Gressy, Tanneken, 371
Groningen, 249, 253
Gross: Jakob, 26, 28, 29, 83, 87, 88, 94-95, 96, 97, 99, 106; Veronica (Albrecht), 88, 94-95, 96, 97
Grossman, Hans, 38
Grote, Geert, 306

Groote, Lieven de, 369
Grüningen, 26
Grüninger, Johann, 26
Grünwald, Georg, 269
Gschäl, Cristoff, 159
Gufidaun, 140, 141, 144, 178, 182, 183
guilds: grocers, 92; printers, 259-67; in Strasbourg, 262
Guldi, Niklaus, 26

Haan, Galenus Abrahamnsz de, 356
Haarlem, 249, 250, 254, 298, 299, 307, 337
Habsburg monarchy, 107, 307, 353. *See also* Tirol
Hackfort, van: Count Barent, 327; Jacoba, 327-29
Hackfurt, Lucas, 278
Hadewijk: 359-64; husband of, 359-60
Haemstede, Adriaen van, 386
Hafner, Laux, 89
Haggler, the: house of the cartwright, 185
Hague, The, 317, 337
Haina, 72
Hall in Tirol, 58, 187-94
Hallau, 20
Halle in Thuringia, 73
handicaps: cross-eyedness, 187; a simple fellow, 363; blindness, 254, 388, 390, 393
Hanseatic League, 306
Harrischer, Egidius, 170
Haselburg, 197
Hasselt, 337
Hatmaker, son of, 35
Hätzer, Ludwig, 82
Haun, Lamprecht, 162
Hecht, Linda Huebert, 10, 75-76
Hedio, Dr., 277
Heede, Jan van, 369
Hegenmiller, Elisabeth (Els), 88, 91-92
Heinrich the shoemaker, 276; wife of, 276
Heisses, Gertraut, 86

Hellrigel: Klaus, 197; Oswald, 196; Ursula, 195-201, 214-15; Zacharias, 198
Hellwart, Georg, 64; Margaret, 21, 64-67
Hendriks, Anna, 253, 378-83
Hengelo, 352
heresy, 82, 156, 157
Hergott: Hans, 269; Kunigunde, 269
Hermensz, Jan, 323
Hertenberg, 161-62
Herwerden, Jacob van, 309, 310-11
Hess, Merni, 57
Hesse, 22, 73
Heyndrick, 378
Hieronymus, 180, 181, 184
Hirslanden, 47
Hirzel, 55, 56
Hoffman, Melchior, 247-57, 267-68, 273-80, 307, 337, 384
Hohenaschau, 125, 127
Holiness movement, women in the, 132
Holland, 249, 316, 337. *See also* Netherlands, Overijssel
Holofernes *see* Judith
Holy Days: assumption of the Virgin Mary, 188-89, 192; St. Andrew's Day, 181; St. Jacob's Day, 180, 184, 185
Holy Roman Empire: Charles V, 202, 273, 307, 310, 353, 368; Diet of Speyer, 275, 276; Maximilian I, 165, 203; and Anabaptism, 1, 353
Holy Spirit, 2-5, 8-11, 19-21, 34-36, 49-52, 74, 78, 119, 122, 131-35, 192, 223, 247-49, 251-54, 327, 338, 362; impelled a woman to speak, 280-81; inner/outer, spirit/letter, 4, 11, 51, 72, 114, 252, 253, 280; in the Last Days, 248, 255, 279; *See also* spiritualism
Holten, Hendrik van, 313
Hondt, Nicolas de, 365
Honigler, Konrad, 58
Hoorn, 249, 386, 387, 388, 392

Index 423

Hopfgarten in Tirol, 58, 59, 61
Horgen, 22, 54-56
Horgenberg, 55, 56
Hörschwang, 180, 181, 184, 185
Hottinger: Elsbeth, 47; Felix, 43, 51; Jakob the younger, 43, 48; Jakob the elder, 43-45, 51-52; Klaus, 43, 45, 46; Margret, 19, 22, 43-53; sons of Jakob, 47; Wishans, wife of, 44
Houte, van den: Soetken, 253, 365-77, 386; children of, 366, 371
Huber, Conrad, 85; Felicitas, 85, 97
Hubmaier, Balthasar, 5, 19, 20, 26, 82, 222-23, 269
Hug, Bartli, 38
Huguenot movement, 333
humanism, 84, 306
humour, 5, 46, 66
Hungary, Maria (Mary) of, 310, 326
Hupher, Jacob, 147-48
Hut: Hans, 71-78, 82-83, 95, 96, 99, 106, 109, 247, 249, 250, 278; wife of, 72-73
Hutter: Jacob, 75, 76, 78, 144, 166-67, 175, 178-86, 196, 203; Katharina Purst, 75, 144, 178-86
Hutterites, 2, 6, 253; communities in Moravia (*bruderhofs*), 76-77, 222-43; *Hutterite Chronicle*, 75, 77, 180, 188, 202-21; leaders of, 178-86, 189, 204, 207, 211, 218; martyrs, 233-35, 238; women, 202-43
Hutterite songwriters: Adam, 235; Braitmichel, 230; Anthonius Erfordter, 227; Paul Glock, 224; Hans Gurtzham, 234; Raiffer, 228, 235, 239; Wolfgang (Wolf) Sailer, 223, 228, 231; Christof Scheffman, 238; Christl Schmidt, 229; Wastel Wardimer, 226, 227, 228, 230; Jörg Wenger, 231
hymns, Anabaptist: and Anabaptist women, 188-89, 191-92, 232-35, 381, 384; Dutch, 387-94; Hutterite, in *Die Lieder der Hutterischen Brüder*, 222-43; melodies of, 199, 389-90; of the Swiss Brethren, in the *Ausbund*, 75, 119, 121-22, 198-201, 336, 342, 345-48, 356; written by women, 8, 11, 119, 121-22, 254, 192, 195, 199-201, 336-51, 368, 371, 372-75, 386, 384-405; written by men, 198, 223-39, 269, 338.
hymnbooks, 119, 269, 373
hymnsinging: 391-92 in prison, 191, 209, 232, 235; in secret, 100; of Soetjen Gerrits hymns, 388; while travelling, 341; *See also* meetings of Anabaptists: singing at
hymns, Lutheran: 119, 354; by Nikolaus Herman, 230, 237; martyr hymns by Ludwig Rabus, 354-55
hymns, Roman Catholic: by nobility on van Beckum sisters, 354

iconoclasm, 2, 25, 34, 46
Ij River, 379
IJsel: river, 306; towns, 308
IJselstein, 326
Illanz, 60-62c
Illkirch, 274
Imhoff, Barblen, 27, 29
imprisonment, 7, 8, 12, 21, 27, 29, 33-34, 36, 38, 40, 46-49, 51, 55-57, 83, 84, 86, 93-97, 106-108, 126, 129, 140, 145-50, 157-59, 161, 166, 169-74, 179, 182-85, 188-91, 195-201, 204, 207-209, 228, 231-35, 274, 276, 280, 282, 295-96, 320-21, 323-25, 337, 341, 353-54, 359-64, 365-77, 392; rape during captivity, 202, 217; interrogation questions, 169-72, 182, 189
individualism, 1, 4, 5, 8, 44, 209
Inn: River, 58, 125, 195; Valley, 188, 192, 195
Innsbruck, 58, 127-28, 143, 144, 147, 182, 187, 190, 196, 197;

government at, 166-74, 190;
Kreuterturm in, 169
Irwin, Joyce, 9

Jacob, Herr, 35
Jacobdochter, Aechgen, 380
Jansz: Anna, 252, 320, 336-51, 373, 386; Arent, 337, 338-39; Isaiah, 341, 373
Jansz, Lambert, 378, 379
Jelsma, Auke, 385, 386
Jerome *see* Hieronymus
Jerusalem, the New *see* apocalypticism
Joriën, the master apothecary, 309
Joris: Clara, 332; David, 247, 250, 251-52, 253, 254, 255, 280-82, 316-35, 336-51, 356; de Koman (Joris van Amersfoort), 316-17, 320. *See also* Maritje, Jans de Gortersdochter, Dirkgen Willem
Jost, Agnes, 274, 276; Elisabeth (Elsa), 274; Lienhard, 273-77, 279-80; Ursula: 248, 254, 267-68, 273-78, 279, 282-84; author of *Prophetische Gesicht*, 273, 279
Jost, Wilhelm, 232
Judith, in the Bible: in Hutterite songs, 226, 227, 229, 235, 236, 237; as model (Hille Feicken), 251, 288-89, 292-96
Justingen, 130

Kaiserstuhl, 42
Kalden, 111
Kallenberg, Hans, 27-29
Kaltschmid, Hans, 170
Kampner: Agatha, 209; Elizabeth, 209
Karant-Nunn, Susan, 217
Karlstadt, Andreas, 2, 3, 5, 71, 72, 247, 263, 266
Kaunitz, Lord Kuno of, 180
Kautz, Jakob 74
Keller, Michael, 129
Kemmerer, Anstadt 73
Kernn, Regula, 39, 40
Kessler, Johannes, 48-50

Ketel, Jorien, 326, 331; wife of, 323
Kicklinger, seamstress in Augsburg, 88
Kienast, 47
kings and queens: Anabaptist, 107-108, 251, 288, 291-94, 298-304; biblical, 226, 227-29, 230-31, 235, 236, 237
Kirchheim an der Eck, 267
Kitzbühel, 58, 59, 61, 124, 125, 127, 128
Klachtharen, 57
Klassen, John, 385
Klausen, 144-45, 181-82, 184-85
Klein, Gertrude, 66
Klein Niemtschitz, 205
Knipperdolling, Bernhard: 251, 291-92, 294-95, 298, 299, 302 mother-in-law of, 298; wife of, 298
Knobloch, Jean, the elder, 269
Knoblochtzer, Henri, 262
Knöll, Els, 90
Kobl: maid, Els, 141, 146; Margret, 141, 146; Ulrich, 141, 145-47
Kobelt-Groch, Marion, 385
Königsberg in Franconia 72
Krafter, Honester, 95
Krål, Hans, 213;
Kråls, Hieronymus, 211; Traindel, 211
Krätlerin, Anna, 158-59
Kratz Turm, prison, 55
Kraus, Albert, 172
Krechting, Bernd, 251
Kreler: Laux, 87, 89, 90-91, 95; wife of, 89, 90-91, 95
Krems, 202
Krutenau, 274
Kufstein, 160
Kunstbuch, 120-21, 131
Kürschner, Michael, 166

Laer, Jan van, 313
Landberger, woman in Tirol, 143
Landertz, Caspar, two sons of, 57
Landshut, 216
Langedul, Christiaen Jannsens, 380

Index　　　　　　　　　　　　　　　　　　　　　　　　　　　　　　　　425

Langenmantel, Eitelhans, 82, 94, 95, 98
Langeweile, 28, 29
Langheraert, Lambrecht, 369
Lanzenstiel, Apollonia, 207-208; Leonhard, 207-208
Laubenberg, von: Anna, 112; Caspar, 112
Laufen, 72
Lauterwein: Hans, 89, 90; wife of, 90
laws (of the sixteenth century): assumed commoners and women to be naïve, 147, 190, 196; position of women under, 149, 157, 323; on rape, 217
leadership: baptizers, 26, 33, 40, 66, 76, 78, 85, 87, 88, 92, 95, 96, 99, 106, 179-81, 184-85, 187-88, 247, 249, 250, 278, 309, 310-11, 326, 337, 378, 380; elders, 11, 59, 61-62, 107, 118, 204, 209-10, 253, 355; duties, 50; female, 8-12, 20, 21, 36, 49-51, 76-78, 85-99, 112-20, 126-35, 165-75, 187-91, 224, 233, 239, 248, 253-54, 280-82, 360-61, 363, 367, 370-71, 385, 388-89; in Hutterite communities, 205; lay, 7, 8, 10, 32-37, 76, 77, 126, 131, 187-90, 192, 280-82, 332, 378-79; male, 9, 21, 25-26, 38, 46, 48, 51, 61-62, 77, 82-105, 124, 126, 128, 130, 140, 143-46, 150, 166-67, 178-86, 187-90, 192, 195, 232, 234, 247-57, 266; purse-keepers, 89, 167, 182, 185. *See also* evangelism, prophets
Leer, 359-60
Leeuwarden, 249, 253, 359-60, 363, 373
Leiden, Jan van, 249-51, 283, 292-94, 298-304, 308, 310, 311, 337
Leiden, 366
letters and correspondence: and Anabaptist women, 8, 34, 58-61, 107-109, 111-19, 120-21, 126, 130; of David Joris, 325-33, 338, 343-44; and hymns of Gerrits poets, 386, 388, 390-91, 394; to Hutterite women, 205-206, 211; of Jacob Hutter, 180; of Soeten van den Houte and her daughter, 367, 369-71, 372-73;
Leupold, Hans, 84, 86-88, 90, 96
Liebich, Jörg, 197-98
Liechtenstein, Wilhelm von, 197; Lords of, 20
Lier, van: Anna, 331; Cornelis (lord of Berchem), 331
Limburg-Styrum, van: Count Adolf, 329; Countess Agnes van (abbess), 329-31
Linck, Martin, 47
Linck, Agnes, 20, 32-37
Linz, 72
literacy among Anabaptists, 3, 6-7, 34, 36, 45, 247, 363, 386; of women, 106, 109, 131, 145, 167, 174, 254, 266, 359, 359, 371-72, 386, 388, 391-92
literalism (biblical), 11, 19, 51, 74, 205, 212, 247, 253-54, 370, 385, 386, 392, 393. *See also* Holy Spirit: spirit/letter
Livonia, 247, 275
Lochman, Elsy, 44
Lochman, Regula, 44
Loe, ter, (noblewoman), 312, 313
Lord's Supper, 3, 5, 27-30, 32, 34, 39, 45, 50, 64, 66, 91, 93, 114, 166-67, 169, 170, 172, 247, 248, 252, 253, 302, 361
Lorenz, Doctor, 44-46
Lorenz, Joseph, 276; wife of, 276
Loserth, Johann, 128
Lostad, Elsa van, 326-27
love, Christian: 66, 131-35, 360; a gift from God, 201; of the neighbour, 141, 291-92, 362
Lubelei, Johan, 308
Lucerne, 25
Luckhner: Valthin, 167; wife of, 167
Lüsen, 140, 144, 181, 184, 185
Luther, Martin, 1, 2, 3, 71, 125, 141,

222-23, 247, 263, 264, 266, 275, 276, 306, 365
Lutheran church: attendance at, 64-66; in Augsburg, 106; church court, 64-67; clergy, 65, 82, 142, 166, 247, 275
Lutheranism, 125, 166-67, 169, 170, 247, 307
Lyon, 258, 260

maids *see* occupations and employment
Mair: Stoffl, 146-49; wife (Mairin), 146-49, 159; brother, 146
Mair, Simprecht, 91
Mairhofer, 140, 144-46, 150
Mairhofer, Christoff, 170
Maler, Dorothea/Anna, 75, 188-92, 208
Maler, Martin, 234
manliness: of women printers, 258. *See also* martyrdom
Mantz: Anna, 48; Felix, 19, 43, 44, 47; mother of Felix, 19, 43
Marburg, 266
Margret, prophetess in Strasbourg, 276
Marr, Lucille, 204, 253-54, 385
marriage: 140, 183, 204, 184, 364, 392; heavenly, 393; Hutterite, 209-13, 224, 231-32; influence of a spouse, 290-91, 325-26; leaving a non-Anabaptist spouse, 8, 11, 22, 40-42, 77, 127- 28, 132, 212-13, 250; leaving wife and children, 187-88, 192, 325; marital status, 212, 218; monogamous, 247, 253-54; polygamous, 299-300; secretive, 378; traditional, companionate, 385, 386, 387, 392, 394. *See also* patriarchy
marriage court: in Zurich, 40, 41
Marpeck: Anna, 77; Heinrich, 124; Pilgram, 58-60, 74, 77-78, 111-20, 124-27, 130-31, 135, 247; circle of, 59, 75, 77-78, 111-21, 130, 131

Marshall, Sherrin, 385
Martyrs' Synod, 106
martyrdom, 4, 8, 10, 12, 22, 23, 46, 51-52, 76, 144, 148, 160, 175, 178, 179, 183, 191, 196, 209, 232-35, 238-39, 249, 250-51, 252, 253, 254, 296, 298, 299, 303, 310, 317, 320-22, 323, 328-29, 355, 359, 360, 365, 367, 370-71, 372, 373, 378-83, 384, 387-88; beheading, 53, 108, 232, 234, 300, 309, 320-21, 323, 372; burned at the stake, 182, 232, 233, 354, 366; burned following drowning, 198, 323, 341; drowning, 35, 40, 53, 188, 192, 198-99, 207, 232, 234, 305, 311, 363, 371, 378; barbarous execution, 378, 381-82; government concern, 371, 372; manly courage of women in, 208, 218, 235, 387
martyrologies: of Jean Crespin, 386; of Haarlem, 373; of Adriaen van Haemstede, 386; *Het Offer des Heeren*, 342, 356, 373, 386; *Martyrs' Mirror*, 9, 188, 198, 252, 254, 305, 336, 340-42, 345-48, 356, 359, 370, 373, 381, 386; female martyrs in, 253, 386
Mary, the Mother of God, 162, 170, 173, 182, 226, 231 236, 237, 266-67, 384
Matschidel, Michel, 234; wife of, 234
Matthijs, Jan, 249-51, 255, 288, 292-94, 299, 300, 302, 307, 337
Mecenseffy, Grete, 128
Medemblik, 254, 384, 387, 389, 390
meetings of Anabaptists: confessing sins at, 49; hosted and convened by women, 48, 85-94, 97-100, 126-27, 129; location of, 26-27, 38, 41-42, 48, 49, 54, 64, 85-86, 92, 100, 126, 127, 129, 144-45, 166, 168, 172, 188-90, 275, 308, 360, 378-79, 380; nature of, 83, 92-93, 100, 166-67, 178-79, 180, 181, 329, 378-79; reading at, 28,

45, 379; singing at, 28; women provided food for, 178-79
Melchiorite Anabaptism 2, 74, 78, 247-57, 336; debate with David Joris, 280-82; members in Strasbourg, 276; in the Netherlands (Davidites), 316-35; role of Anna Jansz in, 336-51; role of women in Strasbourg, 279-82;
Melk, 72
Mellink, A. F., 336, 337-38
Menchú, Rigoberta, 289
Mennonite: origin of the word, 253
Mennonite Brethren Church, 2
Mennonite Church, 2
Mennonite Encyclopedia, 336
Meran: city of, 144; articles, 141
Messerschmidt, husband 144-45; wife of, 145
Meyer, Gabriel, 29
Miller, Laux, 88, 90, 95; wife of, 90, 95
miller's boy, a Hutterite martyr, 234
Mils (Muls), 188-90, 192
Miltenberg, Johann von, 276
miracles, 355, 363, 388
Mirandola, Pico della, 84
models, women as, 1, 225-39, 387-89
Modern Devotion, 306
monastic institutions and individuals, 34, 111-12, 113, 250, 266, 277, 278, 290, 311, 322, 329-31, 337, 353, 359, 360, 385, 393
Moos, 180
Moravia, 5, 20, 22, 23, 36, 62, 66, 107, 125, 130, 167-8, 179-80, 182, 185, 189; emigration to, 60, 150, 184, 197-98; Hutterite communities in, 76-77, 78, 202-43; persecution in, 180, 183; religious freedom in, 51, 195, 203
mothers, 213; and childcare *see* children; living in exile, 108-109; single, 6, 366;
Mountaillou, 157
Mueleneere, de: Gilein, 365-67, 371; Jeroen, 365

Mühlhausen, 72
Müller, Annthoni, 118
Müller, Dr. Gallus, 196
Müller, Jörg, 181, 185
Müller, Magdalena, 49, 50
Müller, Peter, 197
Müllner, Ulrich, 144-45
Münichau, 124-28; Lords of, 124
Münster, 129, 171, 180, 247, 249-53, 255, 327, 337-38; prince-bishop Franz of Waldeck, 288, 295-96; siege of, 249-51, 288-304, 307-11, 337-38
Münsterite Kingdom, 249-51, 288-304, 309, 310, 337. *See also* apocalypticism
Müntzer, Thomas, 3, 71-74, 222
Mürglen, Barbara, 49, 50
mutual aid: common treasury, 89, 167, 182, 185; gifts of money, 86, 89, 90, 94, 95; good works, 168; providing food, 167, 178. *See also* alms, economics
mysticism, 20, 72-74, 78, 131-35, 211. *See also* Holy Spirit

Nähter, Sarah, 217
Nessel, Valentin, 276
Nespitzer, Jörg, 84, 86-90, 96
Netherlands, 5, 247-57, 267, 273, 274, 276, 278, 288, 299, 305-15, 316-58, 366, 367, 378. *See also* Holland
networks: kinship, friendship and leadership, 76, 91, 92, 190. *See also* family
Neuhaus Castle, 165-68
Neuhaus, Michael von, 165
Nicholsburg, Moravia, 20, 72
Niclauer, 181, 185; wife of, 181, 185
Nicodemism, 331-32
Niderhofer, 185
Niessmüller, Maria, 65, 66
non-resistance *see* pacifism
Noordenberg tower, 305
Nuremberg, 20, 71, 72, 82, 107, 111, 269

oath, 21, 26, 33, 35-36, 41, 46-48, 55, 66, 83, 87, 90, 93, 95, 133-34, 148, 157-59, 172-74, 188, 197, 360

Oberhofen, 161

Ober, 180, 181, 184, 185; daughter of, Dorothea, 181, 184; employees of, Wolf and Els, 181, 184; two servants of (both named Martin), 181, 184; wife of, 181, 184

occupations and employment: amateur actor, 251; baker, 161, 187, 189, 205, 249, 250, 341; barber-surgeon, 205; bathhouse proprietor, 145; bookbinder, 35, 71, 72; bookseller, 71, 72, 260; brewer, 250; butcher, 94, 274; carpenter, 205; cartwright, 185; chief justice, 124; city secretary 26; civil servant, 58-60, 111; clockmaker, 60, 205; cobbler, 205; cook, 167, 169, 301; coppersmith, 205; crown administrator [*Pfleger*] see Tirol; day labourer, 290; diplomat, 87; domestic labour (Hutterite), 202, 205-207, 210, 215; drummer, 359-60; farmer, 43, 88, 140-41, 170, 195; farm employees, 181, 184; furrier, 26, 87, 247, 275; glassmaker, 92; glasspainter, 317-18; goldsmith, 90, 276; grocers, 88, 91-93, 98; hatmaker 26; herdsman, 143, 188; lacemaker, 85; lackey, 301; lawyer, 59; locksmith, 60; maids, 94, 98, 125-26, 141, 145-47, 158, 178, 185, 359, 366, 367; mason, 205; mayor, 308-309, 341; merchant, 145, 308, 316-17; miller, 108, 205, 276; mine owner, 125; miners, 144, 185; mining engineer, 58, 60; mining judge, 124; painter, 158; physicians, 112; printer, 82, 258-72; publisher, 260, 339; salesman, 251; saltseller, 46; seamstresses, 88, 94, 108-109, 206, 215; servants,

male, 141, 146, 181, 184, 301, 329, 363; sexton, 72, 181, 185; schoolteachers, 35, 61, 180, 184, 207, 365; sculptor, 85, 93; shoemaker, 46, 88-89, 276; shopkeeper, 112, 202; smith, 378; soap-maker, 59; spinners and weavers, 28, 49, 89, 90, 97, 109, 189, 205, 278, 337; steward, 301; tailor, 108, 130, 251, 311, 378; tanner, 61; textile worker, 365; vinedresser, 205

Ochsenfuhrmann, Traudel, 217

Ochsentreiber, Ursula/Anna, 75, 188-92, 208

Ofen (Buda), 217

Offenhauser, Erasmus, 169, 171, 172

Olmütz, 143

Orange, prince of, 305

Ostheim, 72

Othmar, Silvan, 82

Ott, Dorothea, 98

Ötz Valley, 195, 196

Oudenaarde, 365-77

Overijssel, 307, 327, 328, 337, 352, 356

pacifism, 21, 26, 66, 203, 217, 247, 343

Palatinate, 22

pamphlets, 6, 82, 317; printed, published by women, 268-69

Pappenheim, Marschalk von: Elisabeth, 112; Joachim, 111; Magdalena, 74, 77, 78, 111-18, 130; Sophia (Bubenhofen), 75, 111, 119-21; Walpurga, 75, 77, 111, 117-19, 121-22; Wilhelm, 112

pardon, 127, 147-49, 156-63, 174, 179, 182, 187, 191

Partzner, Jacob, 126, 128

Passau, 72

patriarchy, 9, 11, 51; among the Hutterites, 76-77, 204-205, 225-39; in the Münsterite Kingdom, 291, 293-94, 298-304;

women's subservience to men, 209-13, 229, 230-31, 238, 252, 253-54, 281, 328, 385, 391, 392
Paulle, Hans Mair, 167; wife of, 167-68
Paul, Apostle, 11, 29, 51, 223, 385, 393-94
peasants, 3, 4, 6, 7, 8, 19, 35, 45, 54, 141-42. *See also* common people, social status
Peasants' War, 3, 4, 20, 26, 35, 71, 72, 74, 140-42, 145-46, 275, 277; women in the, 145, 153 n.39, 149-50
Penntz, Lamprecht, recantation of husband and wife, 161-62
Penon, 209
Peronet, Antoinette, 260
Peter, Apostle, 65
Petroff, Elizabeth Alvilda, 282
Penthelin, Sebald, 91
Peutinger, Konrad, 84-95
Pfaffenhofen, 161
Pfeffer, Margaret, 34
Pfeiffer, Magdalena, 35
Pfistermeyer, Hans, 25, 26
Philips, Obbe, 250, 253, 255, 278
Pieters, Guiert, 391
Pieters, Lijnken, 367-72
piety: lay, 56, 360, 388
Pingjum, 253
Pisan, Christine de, 289
Plankenstein, 164
Polderman, Cornelius (of Middelburg), 267, 274, 279
polygamy: in Münster, 247, 250, 251, 255, 298-304; among the Batenburgers, 329; of Claus Frey, 279
polygenesis *see* diversity
Pommacher, Johann, 276
Poirten, ter, a noble, 309
Prader: husband, 181, 184; wife, 181, 184; Melchior, their son, 181, 184
Praun, Katharina, 189-90
prayers of Anabaptists, 226, 234, 235, 237, 354, 359, 362, 363, 370, 372; of confession, 133-35; in hymns, 121-22, 199-201, 225; for deliverance, 214
pregnancy and childbirth: 86, 146, 149, 167-68, 183, 317-18; and rape, 215, 216; Hutterite nursing mothers, wet nurses, and midwives, 206; miscarriage, 140, 148-49, 158; in Münster, 300; pregnancy and punishment, 158-59; and recantation, 158-59; childless women, 64
Pribitz, 215, 216
priesthood of all believers, 2, 3, 6, 45, 307. *See also* authority
printing and publishing, 248, 258-72, 306, 339. *See also* occupations and employment: printer
printshops: *am Holzmarkt*, 264; *Zum Thiergarten*, 258
properties and goods *see* economics
prophecy: among Melchiorite Anabaptist groups, 247-57; and women, 10, 11, 279-82; in the Hut tradition, 74, 76, 78; denied by Menno Simons, 253-54
prophets: female, 20, 44, 49-50, 248, 252, 273-87; male, 107-108, 247-52, 273-82. *See also* leadership
Prösels, 159
proselytization *see* evangelization
Protestant church: clergy, 83, 129
Pruschanek, 216
Prüss: Johann, Sr., 259, 262, 269; Johann, Jr., 259, 262-63, 269; Margarethe, 248, 258-72, 273, 275; children of, 270; Margarethe, daughter of Margarethe Prüss, 268, 270; Ursula, 264, 270
Prussia, 209
punishment of Anabaptists: all women to be punished the same, 48; branded on both cheeks, 85, 86; chaining women to the floor, 21, 65; clothed minimally, 197; corporal, 40, 85, 90, 91, 95, 140,

147-48, 150, 158-59; costs of imprisonment, 35, 40, 57, 157-58, 161, 173, 182, 196, 197; fines, 26, 27, 28, 30, 44, 46, 148; house arrest, 159, 174, 188; meagre diet, 48, 158, 196, 197; noblewomen punished, 129, 174; as penance, 159, 162, 173; severity of, 84, 158-59, 298; tongue cut out, 94. *See also* exile, imprisonment, torture
Purschitz, 210
Puster Valley, 166, 167, 180
Putten, 336

Querijnen, Jan, 379

Rabus, Ludwig, 353-54
radicality, 1-10, 111-17. *See also* egalitarianism
Raesfelt, van: Gossen, 327, 352-53; Jacoba, 327-29
Raesfelt in Westphalia, 327
Ramert, Hermann, 295
rape, 202, 215-18
Rassler, Paul, 126
Rat, Hanns, 126
Rattenberg, 58, 59, 125, 146, 158, 195
Ravensburg, 51
rearrested Anabaptists (relapsi), 55, 146-47, 157, 160-61, 182-83, 190-91, 196
rebirth (regeneration), 3, 4-5, 114, 392
Rebstock, Barbara (Kropf), 248, 252, 254, 273, 276, 278-82; Hans (or Kropfhans), 278
recantation, 36, 39, 40, 42, 48, 57, 75, 93, 97, 106-107, 126, 132, 146, 156-63, 169-74, 179, 182-84, 182, 188, 190-91, 196, 380; appeal against, 127-28, 371; had to be read, 161, 174; penance required in, 148, 157-59, 161-62, 172-74, 179, 188, 196; recanters became informers, 378, 381; refusal of, 47, 55-56, 85, 94, 197, 207, 234.

See also pardon
recreation: Hutterites, 222, 236
Reekers, Hinrick, sister of, 329
Reformed church: alienation from, 34-35, 39; critique of, 32-36, 56; educated theologian in, 45
Reformers: Protestant, 108-109, 127, 130-31, 268; radical, 131, 266,
refugees, Anabaptist, 20, 22, 23, 26, 59, 71, 72, 75, 76; giving shelter to, 28, 85-93, 97-99, 108, 126, 129, 147-48, 161, 167-69, 178, 180-85, 208, 388
Renssen, Hylle van, widow of Lubbert, 309
repentance: call to, 22; doctrine of, 4, 19, 50, 117; lacking in the state church, 56
Reublin, Wilhelm, 26, 94, 96
Rhegius, Urbanus, 82-83
Rhine River, 20, 25, 42, 232, 273, 275
Riedemann, Peter, 77, 204, 207, 211, 218, 222, 223, 230
Rieper, Johannes, 58, 61; Margaret, 58
Rinck, Melchior, 71
Ringmacher, Peter, 90
Ritten, 140-41, 145-47, 149, 159
Rodeneck, 179
Rol, Hendrick, 326
Roman Catholic church (of the sixteenth century), 1, 26, 32, 393; attempts to dissuade Anabaptist prisoners, 35, 170-72, 183, 196, 235, 353-54, 368-69; bishops *see* Brixen, Salzburg; critique of, 166, 266; doctrine and practice in, 169-70, 172-73; prince-bishop of Münster, 250-51, 292, 298; priests of the, 2, 3, 25, 28, 29, 46, 145, 157-58, 161, 162, 166, 168, 170-74, 179, 182, 183, 185, 188, 192, 253, 363; reinstatement in the church *see* recantation. *See also* monastic institutions and individuals, Peutinger, Titelmans, Tirol
Rost, Hans von, 165

Index

Rosenau, 129
Rotenstein, Jakob, 90; wife of, 90
Roth, Friedrich, 87
Rothmann, Bernhard, 250, 292, 308, 338, 339
Rotterdam, 254, 336, 337, 341, 345, 384, 387-88
Roybet, Mie, 260
Rudolf the bookbinder in Basel, 35
Ruepp, Anastasia, 196; Hans, 196
Rumer, Paul, 167, 184

St. Gall, 6, 19, 21, 26, 47-51, 60, 75, 108
St. George, 167-68
St. Lambert's Church, 251, 298
St. Lorenz, 167-68, 180
St. Michelsburg, 167
St. Petersberg, 158, 195-96; Georg, older woman, in prison at, 196
Sackmann: Sigmund, 146; wife of, 146; his brother, 146
Sackmann, Benedict, 147-49; Anna, 147-49, 159
sacraments: absolution, 162; abstinence from mass, 166, 169; Anabaptist belief regarding them, 2-3; last rites, 28, 30; recantation during mass, 159, 161-62, 173-74. *See also* Roman Catholic church: doctrine and practice, Lord's Supper, antisacramentalism
sacramentarianism, 5, 249, 353, 366-67
saints, 162, 170, 173; as idolatrous, 34; St. Augustine, 223; St. Ratha, 85-86; St. Urs, 34. *See also* Mary, the Mother of God
Salminger, Anna (Haller), 91, 94, 95, 97, 99; Sigmund, 82, 83, 91, 94, 95, 97, 99
salvation: Anabaptist understanding of, 2-4, 56, 71, 121-22, 371; of children, 368; in spiritualist debates, 113-14, 116-20. *See also* sin
Salzburg, 61, 72, 76, 88, 125, 190;

Archbishop of, 157, 190
Sarn Valley, 143, 165
Satan, 47, 118, 119, 121, 131-32, 214-15, 281, 319, 330, 361
Sattler, Michael, 19, 47, 143
Schachner, Georg, 87
Schaffhausen, 20
Scharnschlager: Anna, 22, 58-63; Leupold, 58-63, 118; Ursula, 58-62
Schäufele, Wolfgang, 9
Schelde river, 365-66
Schiemer, Leonard 74, 144, 187
Schlaffer, Hans 74, 144, 187
Schleiffer: Anna, 91; Barbara, 90-92, 94, 97; Claus, 87, 90-91; Gall, 91; Jörg, 91; Ursula, 91
Schleitheim, The Brotherly Union of, 20, 50, 253; and prophecy, 51
Schlern, hillside of, 159
Schmidt, Anna 77
Schneider, Hans Jacob, 118, 120, 130; Kunigunda, 77
Schnider, Appollonia, 39, 40
Schomecker, Dirick, 329
Schöneck (Schonegg), 170, 183, 185
Schorndorf, 64
Schreierstoren, 379
Schroer, Herman, 308
Schuster, Wilhelm, 147
Schwäbisch Gmünd, 234
Schwann, Daniel, 266; Johannes, 266-67, 269, 270
Schwarz, Adelheit, 22, 38-42. *See also* Spilman
Schwaz, population of, 190
Schwenckfeld, Caspar (von Ossig), 74, 112-19, 130, 247, 275
Scribner, Robert, 6
Scriptures *see* Bible
scripture alone, 2, 3, 6, 45
Seiler, Heini, 26
Senger: Rudolf, 26-29; wife of, 27-30; wife's sister and her husband, 28; Hans, 27, 28
separation from the world *see* congregationalism

sexuality: Aristotelian theory of conception, 384; indecent advances, 363; menstruation, 262; pre-modern perceptions of, 214-15; sexual assault *see* rape; sexual favours, 108, 228; sodomy, 216; temptresses, 214-15; untamed in widows, 265; the weaker sex, 77, 204, 207, 213, 354, 389, 391

shame and Anabaptist women, 132-34, 160, 237, 293, 321, 324, 362

sickness and disease, 28-30, 90, 112, 197, 216, 317; medicinal recipes for swelling, 60

Sidler, Annli, 39, 40

Sigmundskron, castle at, 197

Sigwein, Magdalena, 124; Ulrich, 124

Silesia, 75

Simons, Menno: his wife Gertrude, 253, 385; Peter, possibly his brother, husband of Hille Feicken, 290; use of his *Foundation of Christian Doctrine*, 66, 250, 251, 252-54, 255, 290, 360, 384, 385

sin, 116-18, 121-22, 131-35, 223, 230

singing *see* hymn singing

single women, Anabaptist, 158, 187-88; a positive view of, 393, 394; two women poets, 384-405; who were raped, 216, 217. *See also* monastic institutions and individuals, occupations and employment: maids

Slecker, Hanns, 55

Slesse, Marcq, 369

Sneek, 288-90

social status and Anabaptism, 7, 34, 88, 90, 111, 112, 141, 144, 157, 325, 326-33, 352, 354, 379; in Augsburg, 95; in Deventer, 309, 313; in Münster, 300-301; noblewomen, 111-23, 124-39, 164-77; patricians, 82, 113, 309; poor, 1, 6, 90, 109; upper classes, 6, 8, 58-59, 78, 111-23, 124-39, 164-77, 316-22, 336, 352-58;

Solothurn, 32-35

sources for Anabaptist research, 306, 312-13; biography, 318-24; chronicles, 48, 202; court records (*Täuferakten*), 8, 9, 10, 11, 38, 43, 45, 46, 47, 187, 188, 191, 305-306, 309; Criminal Book, 320. *See also* martyrologies, testimonies

South German/Austrian Anabaptism, 2, 9, 71-81, 247

Souucs, Mynkin, 371

Sparendam, 308

Spanish rulers in the Netherlands, 379, 381; Duke of Alva, 379, 381; King Philip

Speyer, 160, 274, 275, 276, 278

Spilman, Balthasar, 38, 40-41; his wife Adelheit *see* Schwarz; their daughter Barbara, 38; Elsa, 38

spiritualism: Caspar Schwenckfeld, 112-19; David Joris, 251-53, 327-31; of nobility and noblewomen, 252; radical, 130; in Strasbourg, 247

spirituality: of Anabaptist women, 113-22, 131-35, 327-29, 359-63, 388-94; of Hille Feicken, 289, 292, 296; of Hutterite women, 213; male spirituality, 215

Spitzendrat, 89, 90

Spitzhamer, Lienhard, 158; maid of, 158

Sprunger, Keith, 386

Stäbis, 158

Staffelstein, 73

Stainer, Anna (a young woman), 167, 181-83, 185

Stainer: the sexton, 181, 185; Anna, his wife, 181-82

Stainmair, glassmaker, servant of, 92

Stangl, Martin, 171, 172

state church *see* Reformed church, Lutheran church, Roman Catholic church, Protestant church, church and state

Staudach, Hans, 234

Steffan, Herr, 145

Steffan, Heini, 26
Steger: Hans, 59, 60; Regina 59, 61; Veronica, 61
Steinmetz, Wolfgang, 170
Stendiswil, 55
Sterzing, 144-46, 178, 179, 185
Steyr, 72
Stiegnitz, 215
Stierpaur: Crispin, 87; Scolastica, 87-88, 92, 95, 96
Strasbourg, 20, 75, 78, 107, 108, 125, 127, 247-49, 250, 252, 253, 258-72, 273-87, 331
Streicher: Helena, 74, 112-16; Agathe, 112; son of Helena, 112
Strigel, Hans, 170
Styria (Austria): Bruck an der Muer, 234
suffering, 28, 55, 74, 116, 133, 392; explained by Soetken, 370; of Hutterite women, 200-204, 208, 213, 217, 227, 232; of leaders, 40, 182; in women's martyr hymns, 341, 373-75
Susanna, from the Apocrypha, 225, 226, 227-28, 229, 235-38
Suter, Hans, 55, 56
Stuttgart, 64, 278
Swabia 19, 20, 111
Sweden, 275
Swiss Anabaptism (Swiss Brethren), 2, 9, 11, 19-24, 247; charismatic nature of, 50; distinctness of, 21; in Hesse 22; in remote areas, 54, 71; in Strasbourg, 247
Switzerland, 5, 19, 22, 25, 75, 107, 108, 146, 202, 247, 275, 332

Tartars, 206, 213
Taufers (Sand in), 166-74, 180, 184; castle, 168-74; valley, 166-68, 175
Tauler, John, 71
Taurien mountains, 184
Teck, Ulrich, 47
Telfs, 161
Telgte, 291
testimonies, translations of (unabridged), 56-57, 132-35, 162, 184-85; excerpts of verbatim statements, 32, 47-48, 169-70, 171-74, 181-82, 320, 323, 360-63
Teutenhofen, Michael von, 165, 167, 171-72, 174
Texel, 389
Theiller, Elsbeth, 22, 54-57
theology: debated by women, 32-34, 65-66, 111-20, 129-30, 131, 167, 353, 360-63, 364; feminine imagery, 233, 386, 392, 393. *See also* God, Christ, Eve, spiritualism
Thomas am Bach, 170
Thuringia, 73, 75
Thurn, Count Franz von, 210
Tirol, 3, 20, 58, 73, 74, 75-77, 114, 124-201; crown administrator [*Pfleger*], 124, 144, 147, 149, 165, 168, 170, 171, 174, 175 n.5, 196; Anabaptism in, 187; Ferdinand I, 124, 126, 127, 142-45, 148, 157, 160, 161, 162, 171, 180, 196-97; persecution in, 59, 61, 76, 146, 160, 191. *See also* Brixen
Titelmans, Pieter, 365-69
tithe *see* economics
Töllinger, Christine, 209
Torchia, Adela, 394
torture: in Anabaptist interrogations, 12, 22, 23, 39, 51, 59, 76, 83, 84, 87, 88, 90, 91, 93, 99, 108, 147, 148, 168, 172, 182, 189, 190, 251, 295-96, 298, 317, 322, 323, 324, 381, 384; for nobility, 169, 171; as public display, 251; the rack, 73, 84, 197, 208; thumbscrews, 40, 84, 88, 93, 362-63
Toutenburg, Georg Schenk van, 307-309, 311
transgressions, of Anabaptist women, 120; 131-35
travel of Anabaptist women, 108-109, 207-208, 317-18, 332-33, 341
Treibenreif, Sigmund, maid of, 158
Trins, 178, 184, 185
Trijpmaker, Jan Volkerts, 249

Tscheikowitz, 216
Tuchmacher, Hans Amon, 167, 180, 189, 238
Turkish forces, 107, 206, 213; raped Hutterite women, 215-17
Twisck, Pieter Jansz, 386, 394-95
Tyrns, 290

Ulian, maid at Khyens, 185
Ulm, 20, 75, 107, 111-13
Ulrich Zwingli, 1, 5
Ungarisch Ostra, 216
Unholtz, Jacob, 44
Urspring, 111
Üsöllring, Rudolf, 57
usury *see* economics
Utrecht, 253, 322-24, 337, 352
Uttenheim, village, of, 143, 164-77
Uttenreuth, 72

Vaet, Philips vander, 369
Velcklehner: Barbara, 161; Hans, 161; sister of Hans, 161
Vienna, 72, 203, 234
Villnöss, 181, 185
virtues: of biblical women, 229, 230, 231, 387; Christian, 370, 371-72; of the Christian woman, 211, 226, 385, 387, 391
Vischer, Gall, 85, 87, 89, 96
Vischer, Lienhart, 159
visions, 4, 74, 107, 248, 249, 251, 252, 277; apocalyptic, 277; of David Joris's mother, 319; of Jan van Leiden, 308, 311; and miracles, 278; in Strasbourg, 273-79; of Ursula Jost, 282-84
Vlaster, Anna de, 380. *See also* Anna Hendriks
Vogel, Agnes, 88
Völs, Lienhard von, 142, 145-46
Völs, town of, 159
Vos, Karl, 336, 343

Wädiswil, 57
Wagenaar, Jan, 381
Wähninger, Walpurga, 260

Waldhauser, Thomas, 85, 96
Waldner, 180, 184
Waldshut, 19, 20, 25, 26, 94
Walpot, Peter, 207
Wandscherer, Elisabeth, 300, 303
Wangen, 140, 145-47
war, 213, 215-17; at Kappel, 54; men go to war, 125, 169; of the Radical Ladies [*Damenkrieg*], 111-17, 130; Thirty Years' War, 54, 216. *See also* Peasants' War, Münster: siege
Wartburg, 2
Wasserberg, 40
Waert, Gorkum on the, 318
Watt, 22, 38, 41, 42
Weber, Max 10
Wegman, Martin, 92
Weiningen, 38
Weisse, Michael, 119, 269
Weisshaupt, Regina, 92
Wellenberg, prison, 47
Weltzenberger, Martha, 158
Wenger, Treindl, 231
Werdum, 353
Werner, Valtin, 118, 135
Westermair, Veit, 88
Westphalia, 249, 250, 295, 327, 329-31
Widerker, Anna, 48
Widholz, Andreas, 92
widows, 6, 86, 87, 90, 95, 109, 112, 125, 130, 150, 185, 209, 211, 213-14, 232, 260, 262-67, 269, 317, 320, 331, 366; in the Bible, 229, 230, 236, 237
widowers, 209
Wiedenmann: Katharina, 88-90, 95, 97; Simprecht, 87, 88-90, 95; maid of, 98
Wiener, Annli, 39; Margaret, 39
Wiesner, Merry, 131
wife beating, 21
Willem, Dirkgen, 316-26
Williams, George H., 8, 112
Winckler, Konrad, 40, 51
Winkler from Saalen, wife of, 168
Winssem, van: Johan, father, 308-309;

Johan, son, 308
Wirt, Lienhardt, 49
Wiser, Wolfgang, 171, 172
Wisinger, Maxentia, 85, 89
Witmarsum, 253
Wittenberg, 2, 72, 266
Wolfart, Bonifacius, 129
Wolfgang of Heilbronn, 29
Wolfram, Elizabeth, 159
Wolkenstein, von: Anna, 165, 174; Anton, (Trostburg), 128, 143, 164-69, 171, 174; Elisabeth, 75, 128, 143, 164-77; family tree, 165; Hans, 165-66, 170-72; Lords of, 164-65; Oswald, 164; Paul, 143, 165-69, 171; Sigmund, 128, 143, 165-69
Wölfl, 143-45, 165-66, 175
women, Anabaptist: groups of, 38-40, 44, 48, 88, 97, 367, 370, 371; as intermediaries, 130, 325-26; persevering, 66, 170-75, 183, 195, 197, 218, 298, 354, 369-70, 378; and silence, 175, 298, 302, 378, 381-82; speaking, 33, 44, 49, 149, 174, 254, 280-82, 353-55, 359; writing, 117-19, 129-35, 312-13, 336-51, 366, 338-39, 342, 366, 370-72, 390. *See also* testimonies, letters and correspondence, hymns, Anabaptist: written by women
worship: opposition to instruments in, 222-23; female songleaders in, 224, 239; Hutterite mode of, 222-25; views of Balthasar Hubmaier on, 222-23
Wostitz, 210
Wubbers, Remmeltje, 359
Wucherer, Hans, 211
Würzburg, 72
Württemberg, 20, 22, 109, 262

yieldedness (*Gelassenheit*), 77, 131, 135, 203; and freedom of the will, 4; Hutterite teaching on, 224-25, 237

young people, 147, 159, 169, 181-83, 185, 195-201, 214-15, 237, 238, 388-89, 390. *See also* occupations and employment: maids

Zeeland, 249, 267, 337
Zelestin, Anabaptist woman from Bavaria, 92
Zell, Katharina Schütz, 269, 279, 355; Matthias, 268-69, 279
Zender, Agnes, 25-31; Marquart, 29
Ziegler, Clement, 266
Zieglerin, Dorothea *see* Frölich
Ziller Valley, 189-90
Zimmermann, Erhard, 167-68
Zofingen, 25
Zollikon, 19, 20, 26, 43, 44, 54; wife of overseer, 44; woman in, 44
Zott, Sigismund, 166, 171
Zurich, 3, 4, 6, 19, 20, 23, 32, 43-49, 51, 54, 55, 61, 306, 354
Zwickau, 217
Zwingli, Ulrich, 1, 3, 5, 19, 46, 275
Zwolle, 353

Contributors to
Profiles of Anabaptist Women

Lois Y. Barrett - Executive Secretary of Missions, General Conference Mennonite Church, Wichita, Kansas.
    Author of:
        Ursula Jost and Barbara Rebstock of Strasbourg

Marlene Epp - Instructor, University of Waterloo
    Co-author, with H. Julia Roberts, of:
        Women in the *Chronicle* of the Hutterian Brethren

Cornelius J. Dyck - Prof. Emeritus, Associated Mennonite Biblical Seminaries, Elkhart, Indiana.
    Author of:
        Elisabeth and Hadewijk of Friesland

Brad Gregory - Assistant Professor of History, Stanford University.
    Author of:
        Soetken van den Houte of Oudenaarde

Linda A. Huebert Hecht - Independent Scholar, Waterloo, Ontario.
    Author of:
        Helena von Freyberg of Münichau
        Anna Gasser of Lüsen
        Anabaptist Women in Tirol who Recanted
        Wives, Female Leaders and Two Female Martyrs from Hall
        Appendix: Review of the Literature on Women in the
            Reformation and Radical Reformation
    Co-author, with C. Arnold Snyder, of:
        Ursula Hellrigel of the Ötz Valley and Annelein of Freiberg
    Translator of:
        Elisabeth von Wolkenstein of Uttenheim
        Katharina Purst Hutter of Sterzing
        Hille Feicken of Sneek
    Compiler of Index

Pamela Klassen - PhD Candidate, Department of Religion, Drew University, Madison, New Jersey.
    Translator of:
        Ausbund song 75, by Walpurga von Pappenheim
        Ausbund song 36, Annelein of Freiburg
        Ausbund song 18, Another Martyr Song by a Woman (Anna Jansz) Who Took Leave in Rotterdam

Contributors

Walter Klaassen - Prof. Emeritus, Conrad Grebel College, University of Waterloo.
>Author of:
>>Anna Scharnschlager of Hopfgarten Tirol
>>Margaret Hellwart of Beutelsbach
>>Sabina Bader of Augsburg
>
>Translator of:
>>Divara of Haarlem

Marion Kobelt-Groch - Dr. phil., lecturer, University of Hamburg, Germany.
>Author of:
>>Hille Feicken of Sneek
>>Divara of Haarlem

Elfriede Lichdi - Independent Scholar, Heilbronn, Germany.
>Author of:
>>Katharina Purst Hutter of Sterzing

Helen Martens - Prof. Emeritus, Conrad Grebel College, University of Waterloo.
>Author of:
>>Women in the Hutterite Song Book [*Die Lieder der Hutterischen Brüder*]
>
>Translator of:
>>A Song about Anna Malerin and Ursula Ochsentreiberin

Cheryl Nafziger-Leis - Ph.D. Candidate, Center for the Study of Religion, University of Toronto.
>Author of:
>>Margarethe Prüss of Strasbourg

John Oyer - Prof. Emeritus, Goshen College, Goshen, Indiana.
>Author of:
>>Anabaptist Women Leaders in Augsburg
>>Maria and Ursula van Beckum
>>Anna Hendriks of Amsterdam

Werner Packull - Prof. of History, Conrad Grebel College, University of Waterloo.
>Author of:
>>Anna Jansz of Rotterdam

Bonny Rademaker-Helfferich - Independent Scholar, Deventer, Netherlands.
Author of:
Fenneke van Geelen of Deventer

H. Julia Roberts - Ph.D. Candidate, Dept. of History, University of Toronto.
Co-author, with Marlene Epp, of:
Women in the *Chronicle* of the Hutterian Brethren

Matthias Schmelzer - Dr. phil., Lecturer, Realgymnasium, Brunneck, Italy.
Author of:
Elisabeth von Wolkenstein of Uttenheim

C. Arnold Snyder - Associate Prof. of History, Conrad Grebel College, University of Waterloo.
Author of:
Introduction
The Swiss Anabaptist Context
Agnes Zender of Aarau
Agnes Linck from Biel
Adelheit Schwartz of Watt
Margret Hottinger of Zollikon
Elsbeth Theiller of Horgen
The South German/Austrian Anabaptist Context
Magdalena, Walpurga, and Sophia Marschalk von Pappenheim
The North German/Dutch Anabaptist Context
Co-author, with Linda Huebert Hecht, of:
Ursula Hellrigel of the Ötz Valley and Annelein of Freiberg

Piet Visser - Director of Mennonite Archives at University Library, University of Amsterdam.
Author of:
Soetjen Gerrits and Vrou Gerrits

Gary Waite - Associate Prof. of History, University of New Brunswick.
Author of:
Women Supporters of David Joris
Translator of:
Fenneke van Geelen of Deventer
Soetjen Gerrits and Vrou Gerrits

Series Published by Wilfrid Laurier University Press for the Canadian Corporation for Studies in Religion / Corporation Canadienne des Sciences Religieuses

Editions SR

1. *La langue de Ya'udi : description et classement de l'ancien parler de Zencircli dans le cadre des langues sémitiques du nord-ouest*
   Paul-Eugène Dion, O.P.
   1974 / viii + 511 p. / OUT OF PRINT
2. *The Conception of Punishment in Early Indian Literature*
   Terence P. Day
   1982 / iv + 328 pp. / OUT OF PRINT
3. *Traditions in Contact and Change: Selected Proceedings of the XIVth Congress of the International Association for the History of Religions*
   Edited by Peter Slater and Donald Wiebe with Maurice Boutin and Harold Coward
   1983 / x + 758 pp. / OUT OF PRINT
4. *Le messianisme de Louis Riel*
   Gilles Martel
   1984 / xviii + 483 p.
5. *Mythologies and Philosophies of Salvation in the Theistic Traditions of India*
   Klaus K. Klostermaier
   1984 / xvi + 549 pp. / OUT OF PRINT
6. *Averroes' Doctrine of Immortality: A Matter of Controversy*
   Ovey N. Mohammed
   1984 / vi + 202 pp. / OUT OF PRINT
7. *L'étude des religions dans les écoles : l'expérience américaine, anglaise et canadienne*
   Fernand Ouellet
   1985 / xvi + 666 p.
8. *Of God and Maxim Guns: Presbyterianism in Nigeria, 1846-1966*
   Geoffrey Johnston
   1988 / iv + 322 pp.
9. *A Victorian Missionary and Canadian Indian Policy: Cultural Synthesis vs Cultural Replacement*
   David A. Nock
   1988 / x + 194 pp. / OUT OF PRINT
10. *Prometheus Rebound: The Irony of Atheism*
    Joseph C. McLelland
    1988 / xvi + 366 pp.
11. *Competition in Religious Life*
    Jay Newman
    1989 / viii + 237 pp.
12. *The Huguenots and French Opinion, 1685-1787: The Enlightenment Debate on Toleration*
    Geoffrey Adams
    1991 / xiv + 335 pp.
13. *Religion in History: The Word, the Idea, the Reality / La religion dans l'histoire : le mot, l'idée, la réalité*
    Edited by/Sous la direction de Michel Despland and/et Gérard Vallée
    1992 / x + 252 pp.
14. *Sharing Without Reckoning: Imperfect Right and the Norms of Reciprocity*
    Millard Schumaker
    1992 / xiv + 112 pp.

15. *Love and the Soul: Psychological Interpretations of the Eros and Psyche Myth*
    James Gollnick
    1992 / viii + 174 pp.
16. *The Promise of Critical Theology: Essays in Honour of Charles Davis*
    Edited by Marc P. Lalonde
    1995 / xii + 146 pp.
17. *The Five Aggregates: Understanding Theravāda Psychology and Soteriology*
    Mathieu Boisvert
    1995 / xii + 166 pp.
18. *Mysticism and Vocation*
    James R. Horne
    1996 / vi + 110 pp.
19. *Memory and Hope: Strands of Canadian Baptist History*
    Edited by David T. Priestley
    1996 / viii + 211 pp.

Comparative Ethics Series /
Collection d'Éthique Comparée

1. *Muslim Ethics and Modernity: A Comparative Study of the Ethical Thought of Sayyid Ahmad Khan and Mawlana Mawdudi*
   Sheila McDonough
   1984 / x + 130 pp. / OUT OF PRINT
2. *Methodist Education in Peru: Social Gospel, Politics, and American Ideological and Economic Penetration, 1888-1930*
   Rosa del Carmen Bruno-Jofré
   1988 / xiv + 223 pp.
3. *Prophets, Pastors and Public Choices: Canadian Churches and the Mackenzie Valley Pipeline Debate*
   Roger Hutchinson
   1992 / xiv + 142 pp. / OUT OF PRINT

Dissertations SR

1. *The Social Setting of the Ministry as Reflected in the Writings of Hermas, Clement and Ignatius*
   Harry O. Maier
   1991 / viii + 230 pp. / OUT OF PRINT
2. *Literature as Pulpit: The Christian Social Activism of Nellie L. McClung*
   Randi R. Warne
   1993 / viii + 236 pp.

Studies in Christianity and Judaism /
Études sur le christianisme et le judaïsme

1. *A Study in Anti-Gnostic Polemics: Irenaeus, Hippolytus, and Epiphanius*
   Gérard Vallée
   1981 / xii + 114 pp. / OUT OF PRINT
2. *Anti-Judaism in Early Christianity*
   Vol. 1, *Paul and the Gospels*, edited by Peter Richardson with David Granskou
   1986 / x + 232 pp.
   Vol. 2, *Separation and Polemic*
   Edited by Stephen G. Wilson
   1986 / xii + 185 pp.
3. *Society, the Sacred, and Scripture in Ancient Judaism: A Sociology of Knowledge*
   Jack N. Lightstone
   1988 / xiv + 126 pp.

4. *Law in Religious Communities in the Roman Period: The Debate Over* **Torah** *and* **Nomos** *in Post-Biblical Judaism and Early Christianity*
   Peter Richardson and Stephen Westerholm with A. I. Baumgarten, Michael Pettem and Cecilia Wassén
   1991 / x + 164 pp.
5. *Dangerous Food: 1 Corinthians 8-10 in Its Context*
   Peter D. Gooch
   1993 / xviii + 178 pp.
6. *The Rhetoric of the Babylonian Talmud, Its Social Meaning and Context*
   Jack N. Lightstone
   1994 / xiv + 317 pp.

The Study of Religion in Canada / Sciences Religieuses au Canada

1. *Religious Studies in Alberta: A State-of-the-Art Review*
   Ronald W. Neufeldt
   1983 / xiv + 145 pp.
2. *Les sciences religieuses au Québec depuis 1972*
   Louis Rousseau et Michel Despland
   1988 / 158 p.
3. *Religious Studies in Ontario: A State-of-the-Art Review*
   Harold Remus, William Closson James and Daniel Fraikin
   1992 / xviii + 422 pp.
4. *Religious Studies in Manitoba and Saskatchewan: A State-of-the-Art Review*
   John M. Badertscher, Gordon Harland and Roland E. Miller
   1993 / vi + 166 pp.
5. *The Study of Religion in British Columbia: A State-of-the-Art Review*
   Brian J. Fraser
   1995 / x + 127 pp.

Studies in Women and Religion / Études sur les femmes et la religion

1. *Femmes et religions**
   Sous la direction de Denise Veillette
   1995 / xviii + 466 p.
   * Only available from Les Presses de l'Université Laval
2. *The Work of Their Hands: Mennonite Women's Societies in Canada*
   Gloria Neufeld Redekop
   1996 / xvi + 172 pp.
3. *Profiles of Anabaptist Women: Sixteenth-Century Reforming Pioneers*
   Edited by C. Arnold Snyder and Linda A. Huebert Hecht
   1996 / xxii + 438 pp.

SR Supplements

1. *Footnotes to a Theology: The Karl Barth Colloquium of 1972*
   Edited and Introduced by Martin Rumscheidt
   1974 / viii + 151 pp. / OUT OF PRINT
2. *Martin Heidegger's Philosophy of Religion*
   John R. Williams
   1977 / x + 190 pp. / OUT OF PRINT
3. *Mystics and Scholars: The Calgary Conference on Mysticism 1976*
   Edited by Harold Coward and Terence Penelhum
   1977 / viii + 121 pp. / OUT OF PRINT

4. *God's Intention for Man: Essays in Christian Anthropology*
   William O. Fennell
   1977 / xii + 56 pp. / OUT OF PRINT
5. *"Language" in Indian Philosophy and Religion*
   Edited and Introduced by Harold G. Coward
   1978 / x + 98 pp. / OUT OF PRINT
6. *Beyond Mysticism*
   James R. Horne
   1978 / vi + 158 pp. / OUT OF PRINT
7. *The Religious Dimension of Socrates' Thought*
   James Beckman
   1979 / xii + 276 pp. / OUT OF PRINT
8. *Native Religious Traditions*
   Edited by Earle H. Waugh and K. Dad Prithipaul
   1979 / xii + 244 pp. / OUT OF PRINT
9. *Developments in Buddhist Thought: Canadian Contributions to Buddhist Studies*
   Edited by Roy C. Amore
   1979 / iv + 196 pp.
10. *The Bodhisattva Doctrine in Buddhism*
    Edited and Introduced by Leslie S. Kawamura
    1981 / xxii + 274 pp. / OUT OF PRINT
11. *Political Theology in the Canadian Context*
    Edited by Benjamin G. Smillie
    1982 / xii + 260 pp.
12. *Truth and Compassion: Essays on Judaism and Religion in Memory of Rabbi Dr. Solomon Frank*
    Edited by Howard Joseph, Jack N. Lightstone and Michael D. Oppenheim
    1983 / vi + 217 pp. / OUT OF PRINT
13. *Craving and Salvation: A Study in Buddhist Soteriology*
    Bruce Matthews
    1983 / xiv + 138 pp. / OUT OF PRINT
14. *The Moral Mystic*
    James R. Horne
    1983 / x + 134 pp.
15. *Ignatian Spirituality in a Secular Age*
    Edited by George P. Schner
    1984 / viii + 128 pp. / OUT OF PRINT
16. *Studies in the Book of Job*
    Edited by Walter E. Aufrecht
    1985 / xii + 76 pp.
17. *Christ and Modernity: Christian Self-Understanding in a Technological Age*
    David J. Hawkin
    1985 / x + 181 pp.
18. *Young Man Shinran: A Reappraisal of Shinran's Life*
    Takamichi Takahatake
    1987 / xvi + 228 pp. / OUT OF PRINT
19. *Modernity and Religion*
    Edited by William Nicholls
    1987 / vi + 191 pp.
20. *The Social Uplifters: Presbyterian Progressives and the Social Gospel in Canada, 1875-1915*
    Brian J. Fraser
    1988 / xvi + 212 pp. / OUT OF PRINT

Available from:

WILFRID LAURIER UNIVERSITY PRESS
Waterloo, Ontario, Canada   N2L 3C5

www.ingramcontent.com/pod-product-compliance
Lightning Source LLC
Chambersburg PA
CBHW051415290426
44109CB00016B/1311